Guide to
Networking Essentials,
Third Edition

Greg Tomsho

Ed Tittel and David Johnson

THOMSON

COURSE TECHNOLOGY

Australia • Canada • Mexico • Singapore • Spain • United Kingdom • United States

Guide to Networking Essentials, Third Edition

By Greg Tomsho, Ed Tittel and David Johnson

Senior Editor:
Will Pitkin

Product Manager:
Laura Hildebrand

Production Editor:
Danielle Power

Technical Reviewers:
Mike Feinour, Randy Weaver

Development Editor:
Jill Batistick

MQA Manager:
John Bosco

MQA Technical Lead:
Nicole Ashton

Associate Product Manager:
Tim Gleeson

Editorial Assistant:
Nick Lombardi

Marketing Manager:
Jason Sakos

Text Designer:
GEX Publishing Services

Compositor:
GEX Publishing Services

Cover Design:
Steve Deschene

For permission to use material from this text or product, contact us by
Tel (800) 730-2214
Fax (800) 730-2215
www.thomsonrights.com

Disclaimer
Course Technology reserves the right to revise this publication and make changes from time to time in its content without notice.

ISBN 0-619-13087-3

Contents

TABLE OF
Contents

CHAPTER TEN
Network Administration and Support 375

CHAPTER ELEVEN
Enterprise and Distributed Networks 421

Introduction

This book is intended to serve the needs of individuals and information systems professionals who are interested in learning more about networking technologies, but who may have little or no background in this subject matter. In the first edition of this book, the materials were originally designed to help individuals prepare for Microsoft Certification Exam #70-058, "Networking Essentials." They have been substantially revised and expanded for the second and third editions.

The third edition includes new coverage of Windows XP and .NET Server, hand-held and web-based computing environments, and thin-client computing, as well as coverage on firewalls and virus protection. In keeping with the latest trends in networking, this edition adds extensive new and updated coverage on network switches, VPNs, gigabit Ethernet, cable modem, and wireless networking, including the latest information on the 802.11 standards. In addition, this edition covers the latest NIC features, bus interfaces, and operating system features, including NetWare 6.0 and Red Hat Linux 7.3. These are just a sampling of the many additions and updates to this book, so read on and enjoy.

Where Should You Start?

This book is intended to be read in sequence, from beginning to end. Each chapter builds upon those that precede it, to provide a solid understanding of networking essentials. Readers are also encouraged to investigate the many pointers to online and printed sources of additional information that are cited throughout this book.

Features

To aid you in fully understanding networking concepts, there are many features in this book designed to improve its pedagogical value.

- *Chapter Objectives:* Each chapter in this book begins with a detailed list of the concepts to be mastered within that chapter. This list provides you with a quick reference to the contents of that chapter, as well as a useful study aid.

- *Illustrations and Tables:* Numerous illustrations of networking components aid you in the visualization of common networking setups, theories, and architectures. In addition, many tables provide details and comparisons using both practical and theoretical information. In some cases, we have chosen examples from desktop Microsoft operating systems to illustrate concepts or system facilities; in other cases we have chosen examples from Microsoft server operating systems for the same purposes. Where client-side functionality is important, we chose desktop operating systems for our examples; likewise we chose server operating systems where server-side functionality holds sway. Because most campus laboratories use Microsoft operating systems, we use their products for screen shots and Hands-on Projects for this book.

- *Chapter Summaries:* Each chapter's text is followed by a summary of the concepts it has introduced. These summaries provide a helpful way to recap and revisit the ideas covered in each chapter.

- *Key Terms:* Following the Chapter Summary, a list of new networking terms and their definitions encourages proper understanding of the chapter's key concepts and provides a useful reference.

- *Review Questions:* End-of-chapter assessment begins with a set of review questions that reinforce the ideas introduced in each chapter. These questions ensure that you have mastered the concepts.

- *Hands-on Projects:* Although it is important to understand the theory behind networking technology, nothing can improve upon real-world experience. With the exceptions of those chapters that are purely theoretical, each chapter provides a series of exercises aimed at providing students with hands-on implementation experience.

- *Case Projects:* Finally, each chapter closes with a section that proposes certain networking situations. You are asked to evaluate the situation and decide upon the course of action to be taken to remedy the problems described. This valuable tool will help you to sharpen decision-making and troubleshooting skills—important aspects of network administration.

Text and Graphic Conventions

Wherever appropriate, additional information and exercises have been added to this book to help you better understand what is being discussed in the chapter. Icons throughout the text alert you to additional materials. The icons used in this textbook are described below.

 Note icons present additional helpful material related to the subject being described.

 Tip icons highlight suggestions on ways to attack problems you may encounter in a real-world situation. As experienced network administrators, the authors have practical experience with how networks work in real business situations.

Hands-on Project icons precede each hands-on activity in this book.

 Case Project icons are located at the end of each chapter. They mark more involved, scenario-based projects. In this extensive case example, you are asked to independently implement what you have learned.

Endmatter

In addition to its core materials, this book includes several appendices.

- *Appendix A: Common Networking Standards and Specifications:* This appendix provides information about the standards-making process as it applies to networking, and coverage of the most important and influential network standards-making bodies both in the U.S. and worldwide.

- *Appendix B: Planning and Implementing Networks:* This appendix is an overview of the planning required prior to undertaking network design and installation, including user training requirements and post-sales technical support issues.

- *Appendix C: Network Troubleshooting Guide:* This appendix provides brief, cogent advice on how to recognize, isolate, and diagnose trouble on a network, be it related to media, hardware, or software.

- *Appendix D: Networking Resources, Online and Offline:* This appendix is a compilation of printed and online resources for understanding networking essentials.

- *Glossary:* This is a complete compendium of all of the acronyms and technical terms used in this book, with definitions.

Instructor Support

If you are using this book in an academic setting, materials are available to instructors to assist in teaching this course. All of the supplements available with this book are provided to the instructor on a single CD-ROM.

Electronic Instructor's Manual. The Instructor's Manual that accompanies this textbook includes:

- Additional instructional material to assist in class preparation, including suggestions for lecture topics, suggested lab activities, tips on setting up a lab for the hands-on assignments, and alternative lab setup ideas in situations where lab resources are limited.

- Solutions to all end-of-chapter materials, including the Review Questions, Hands-on Projects, Case and Optional Team Case assignments.

ExamView Pro 3.0. This textbook is accompanied by ExamView®, a powerful testing software package that allows instructors to create and administer printed, computer (LAN-based), and Internet exams. ExamView includes hundreds of questions that correspond to the topics covered in this text, enabling students to generate detailed study guides that include page references for further review. The computer-based and Internet testing components allow students to take exams at their computers, and also save the instructor time by grading each exam automatically.

PowerPoint presentations. This book comes with Microsoft PowerPoint slides for each chapter. These are included as a teaching aid for classroom presentation, to make available to students on the network for chapter review, or to be printed for classroom distribution. Instructors, please feel at liberty to add your own slides for additional topics you introduce to the class.

Coping with Change on the Web

Sooner or later, all the specifics we've shared with you about the Web-based resources we mention throughout the rest of this book will go stale or be replaced by newer information. In some cases, the URLs you find here may lead you to their replacements; in other cases, the URLs will lead nowhere, leaving you with the dreaded 404 error message, "File not found."

When that happens, please don't give up! There's always a way to find what you want on the Web, if you're willing to invest some time and energy. To begin with, most large or complex Web sites—and Microsoft's qualifies on both counts—offer a search engine. As long as you can get to the site itself, you can use this tool to help you find what you need.

The more particular or focused you can make a search request, the more likely it is that the results will include information you can use. For instance, you can search the string "network interface card" to produce a lot of data about the subject in general, but if you're looking specifically for, for example, a set of drivers for the 3COM 3C589 network interface card, you can get there more quickly if you use a search string such as **3C589 AND driver**.

Finally, don't be afraid to use general search tools such as *www.google.com*, *www.hotbot.com*, or *www.excite.com* to find related information. Although certain standards bodies may offer the most precise and specific information about their standards online, there are plenty of third-party sources of information, training, and assistance in this area that do not have to follow the party line like a standards group typically does. The bottom line is: if you can't find something where the book says it lives, start looking around. It's got to be around there, somewhere!

Contact the Author

I would like to hear from you. Please e-mail me with any problems, questions, suggestions, or corrections. I even accept compliments! This book has staying power so I would not be surprised to see a fourth edition in the future and your comments and suggestions are invaluable for shaping the content of the next edition. I can be contacted at *NetEss@tomsho.com*.

Visit our World Wide Web Site

Additional materials designed especially for you might be available for your course on the World Wide Web. Go to www.course.com and search for this book title periodically for more details.

ACKNOWLEDGMENTS

I would like to thank the team at Course Technology for this opportunity to improve and expand on an already excellent second edition of this book. This team includes but is not limited to Laura Hildebrand, Product Manager, Danielle Power, Production Editor, and the excellent work of the Copy Editors and Quality Assurance folks. Thanks also to Jill Batistick for her always-excellent developmental editing. I would also like to thank the reviewers, who guided me with excellent and helpful feedback on each chapter. A special thanks goes to my beautiful wife, Julie, and daughter, Camille, whose patience and support made this project successful.

1

INTRODUCTION TO NETWORKS AND NETWORKING CONCEPTS

After reading this chapter and completing the exercises, you will be able to:

♦ Understand basic networked communications and services

♦ Identify essential network components

♦ Describe the benefits of networking

♦ Understand and compare peer-to-peer and server-based networks

♦ Apply your knowledge when selecting an appropriate network type for small business use

♦ Suggest possible redesigns for a small but expanding network

Networks are vital to the business use of computers, especially for the applications and data that networks can deliver. If a single computer with standard **desktop software**—such as word processing, spreadsheets, and databases—can make anyone more productive, then interconnecting multiple computers on a network and bringing individuals and data together improves communications, fosters productivity, and creates opportunities for collaboration and the quick and easy exchange of information.

As a network administrator, you must understand the fundamental concepts involved in creating a network and in making any network do its job correctly. It's also important to understand what's involved in networked communications and which network models are appropriate in various business situations. This knowledge gives you a solid foundation for future network design, implementation, and troubleshooting tasks.

WHAT IS NETWORKING?

Networking involves connecting computers for the purpose of **sharing** information and resources. Even though the concept is basic, a great deal of technology is required to permit one computer to connect and communicate with another. In addition, there are many possible choices for physical connections and related software. In the following sections, you learn about the fundamental concepts that drive all networks. This helps you understand why networking is so important in the workplace.

Networking Fundamentals

The most elementary network consists of two computers that are connected to each other using some kind of wire or cable to transmit data from one machine to the other. No matter how many computers may be interlinked, or what kinds of connections may be in use, all networking derives from this basic description. In fact, when computers communicate, they most frequently do so in pairs—one machine sends information and the other receives that information. Even though this may seem elementary, the introduction of computer networks represents a significant advance from what any single computer can do alone.

The primary motivation for networking arises from a need for individuals to share data quickly and efficiently. PCs alone are valuable business tools, but without a network, PCs are isolated and can neither share data with other computers nor access network-attached **peripheral devices**, such as printers, scanners, and fax machines. In fact, such uses represent some of the primary benefits of networking.

Consider the following:

- Data sharing permits **groups** of **users** to exchange information routinely and to route data from one individual to another as workflow demands. Data sharing also usually means that master copies of data files reside someplace "special" on another computer elsewhere on the network and that users can access the master copy in order to do their work. When multiple users access the same file simultaneously, it's essential that their software be able to merge multiple updates to keep a single master copy consistent and correct.

- Because data sharing also permits messages, documents, and other files to circulate among users, it can also substantially improve human communication. Although no company installs a network simply to support **electronic mail (e-mail)**, e-mail remains the most popular networked application in most organizations, because it makes communication between individuals so easy and efficient.

- Peripheral **device sharing** lets groups of users take advantage of peripherals, such as printers, scanners, fax machines, and other devices attached directly to a network or to a generally available computer attached to a network. Companies thus can buy fewer peripherals but spend more on each one, so that better capabilities and higher levels of service become widely available. For many businesses, this capability alone justifies the costs and efforts involved in networking.

An old, well-known alternative to networking—passing a floppy disk from machine to machine—is often called a **sneakernet**. Sneakernet doesn't begin to approach the power and convenience of a real network; no group of standalone computers can rival the power and convenience of true networking. Any single computer that is not attached to a network is by definition a **standalone computer**. See Figure 1-1.

Figure 1-1   Standalone computer

If the computer in Figure 1-1 were connected to any number of other computers, as shown in Figure 1-2, then that computer could share its data with those other machines and obtain data from them. In addition, all machines involved could access the printer attached to the same network. In fact, this collection of equipment, plus the medium that links them together, is what represents a network. By extension, sharing resources on a network is called networking.

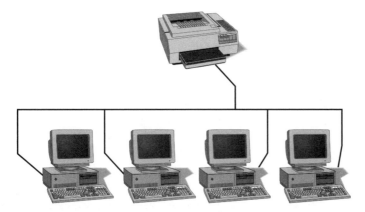

Figure 1-2   Simple network

Local and Wide Area Networks

Originally, networks used expensive and exotic technologies, and many of the earliest networks were entirely custom-built. These early networks seldom interconnected more than a dozen computers, nor were they likely to support more than one or two additional peripheral devices. The earliest networking technologies imposed severe restrictions on the number of interconnected machines and on the physical span of the networks involved.

One of the early implementations of **Ethernet**—still the most popular networking technology in use today—could support a maximum of only 30 users on a single network, with total span of just 607 feet. This works well in a small office environment with a limited number of connected machines, where the span from one end of the office space to the other—even allowing for characteristic twists and turns—falls within this limitation.

A small network, limited to a single collection of machines and one or more cables and other peripheral equipment, may be called a **local area network (LAN)**. LANs also form the basic building blocks for constructing larger networks, called internetworks. (An **internetwork** is a "network of networks" or a "networked collection of LANs.")

For larger organizations that occupy more than one floor in an office building or operate in multiple buildings in a campus environment, no single LAN can contain all the computers, cables, and other equipment necessary to bring the entire user community together. When the number of computers exceeds 100 and the distance to be spanned exceeds 1000 feet, an internetwork is a necessity.

Because of their limitations, early LANs were unable to meet the networking requirements of large organizations, especially those that operated in multiple locations. The benefits of networking were so great, though, that technology evolved to accommodate larger, geographically dispersed organizations.

As the scope of a network expands to encompass multiple groups of users (on LANs or on internetworks) in multiple locations, LANs can grow into **wide area networks (WANs)**. By definition, a WAN spans distances measured in miles and links two or more separate LANs. These LANs may be in locations just down the road from one another or at opposite ends of the planet.

Occasionally, you may encounter a network type called a **metropolitan area network (MAN)**. Essentially, MANs use WAN technologies to interconnect LANs within a specific geographic region, such as a county or a city. In most cases, however, a municipality or a communications carrier operates a MAN; individual organizations must sign up for service and establish a connection to use such a MAN. It's not uncommon to find large, complex networks involving all three of these network types: LANs for purely local access, MANs for regional or citywide access, and WANs for access to remote sites elsewhere in the country or around the world.

In large, complex environments, the number of users and devices on a network can grow into the thousands and beyond. The **Internet** is a WAN internetwork that includes hundreds of thousands to millions of machines and users worldwide.

Most businesses today use networks to store and share access to all kinds of data and applications. This is why networks are commonly regarded as critical business tools. Nearly all users in today's workplace use computers to connect to their company's networks.

A NETWORKING LEXICON

As you likely noticed by now, networking is a subject rich with specialized terminology and technology. Computer networks have spawned a language of their own, and half the challenge of becoming network literate lies in mastering this terminology. To make sense of the upcoming discussion of networking types, you must learn some new vocabulary.

Clients, Peers, and Servers

Fundamentally, any computer on a network plays one of two basic roles at any given moment: the computer acts either as a client or as a server. A **server** is a computer that shares its resources across the network, and a **client** is one that accesses shared resources.

Another way to understand this relationship is to visualize an information interchange best described as **request-response**. That is, a client *requests* information, and a server *responds* to such a request by providing the requested information (or by denying the request). Figure 1-3 depicts this relationship, called the **client/server relationship**.

Computer 1
client (user)

Computer 2
server

Figure 1-3   Client/server relationship

In some networking environments, certain computers take specialized roles and function more or less exclusively as servers, while ordinary users' machines tend to function more or less exclusively as clients. Such network environments are called **client/server** networks. Windows NT Server and Windows 2000 Server, for instance, represent operating systems designed for server use. Client/server networking makes it worthwhile to concentrate **central processing unit (CPU)** power and storage capacity in the servers because they represent shared resources.

In other networking environments, computers can function as either clients or servers, as circumstances dictate. For example, a computer may act as a server and provide resources to other machines, or it may request a resource from some other computer that acts as a client to that machine. Because all the machines on this type of network function at more or less the same level of capability, such machines are peers. By extension, this type of networking is **peer-to-peer**, because peers share and request resources from one another. Typical examples include Microsoft Windows 95 and Windows 98. Windows NT and Windows 2000 can also operate in peer-to-peer networking environments.

The Network Medium Carries Network Messages

To communicate successfully, computers must share access to a common **network medium**. For most networks, the medium takes the form of a physical cable that interconnects the machines that the medium services. However, many types of network media exist, including multiple types of metallic cable (twisted-pair and coaxial are the most common) and fiber-optic cable, as well as numerous forms of wireless media.

Whatever medium is involved in a network, its job is to carry the signals one computer sends to one or more other computers. To access any network, computers must attach to the network medium using some kind of physical interface; for PCs, this is usually a **network interface card (NIC)**, or **network adapter**. For large-scale networks, the probability is high that multiple media work together, or interoperate, across the total networking environment. This flexibility is what enables large, complex networks.

Any particular network medium imposes limitations on the number and type of devices attached to any single LAN and also dictates the maximum distance that any single LAN can span. At a minimum, the network medium also dictates the type of connector used to attach a NIC to a network.

Network Protocols

When connected to a network through a NIC or some other interface, a computer also must be able to use that connection. That is, for two computers on a network to communicate with one another successfully, they must share a common set of rules about how to communicate. At a minimum, such rules must include how to interpret signals, how to identify "oneself" and other computers on a network, how to initiate and end networked communications, and how to manage information exchange across the network medium. Such collections of agreed-upon rules are **network protocols**, or, more simply, **protocols**.

To communicate successfully, computers must not only share a common network medium, they must also have at least one protocol in common so that each can understand what the other is trying to communicate. For example, assume that a native Swahili speaker places a telephone call to a French speaker. Unless the two speakers have some language in common, it's unlikely they'll be able to communicate, even though they can establish a working connection (in the form of a telephone call). Likewise, computers must be able to communicate; this requires a common protocol. Network protocols invariably take names that represent arcane acronyms, including the following: **TCP/IP**, **NetBEUI**, and **IPX/SPX** or **NWLink**. In Chapter 6, you learn how to make sense of these strings of letters.

Network Software

Even though two computers might share a common medium and network protocol, they still might not be able to communicate with one another unless they can actually run programs that access the network. In other words, computers need network software to issue the requests and responses that let them take the roles of clients and servers.

In many network environments, computers invoke a layer of code, sometimes called a **network operating system (NOS)**, that controls which computers and users may access **network resources**. At the time of this writing, the most common network operating systems include the Microsoft family of operating systems, consisting of Windows .NET Server, Windows XP, Windows 2000, Windows NT, and Novell's NetWare. NOSs typically include both client and server components so that Windows .NET Server or NetWare 6.0 might represent the operating system used on a network server. Client software from either Microsoft, such as Windows XP Professional or Windows 2000 Professional, or Novell, which runs on client workstations, permits clients to access these servers.

At one layer above the NOS (or its client-side counterparts) resides a set of network applications that communicate across a network. Such applications range from specific network-oriented utilities or programs, such as e-mail and **Web browsers**, to extensions to file and print services that can access file systems or printers on a network and **locally attached** equivalents.

Network Services

Some experts argue that the real reason networks exist is to deliver services to users, where such services primarily reside on separate machines, or servers. The terms "services" or "network services" are about as generic as possible. Thus, you may hear that NOSs deliver file and print services, and that protocols deliver file-sharing, e-mail, and all kinds of other capabilities. In keeping with the client/server model for networking, network servers stand ready to deliver network services to those network users who request them.

In Chapter 6, you learn that network protocols not only define the kinds of messages and communications that computers can exchange with one another, but they also define the kinds of services that a network can deliver. There are those who argue that the real success of the Internet stems not from the common protocols it uses, but from the widely used and much-sought-after network services that those protocols support.

Here's a recap on the layered nature of networked communications: network applications use a NOS or client networking software to instruct a network protocol to access the network medium through the computer's interface; the medium can then address and exchange information with some other computer on a LAN or a WAN. Sometimes these information exchanges call on well-known services that network servers make available to network users. Each of these layers of software is essential for successful networked communications; each higher layer depends on the one beneath it to perform its specific tasks. In turn, each lower layer provides services to the layer above it to make its own contributions to the networking process.

Figure 1-4 depicts this relationship.

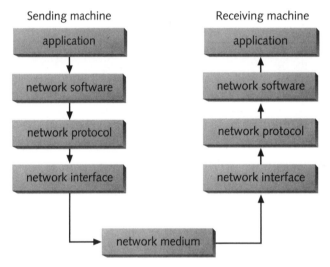

Figure 1-4   Layers of the networking process

NETWORK TYPES

Networks fall into two major types: peer-to-peer and **client/server** (sometimes also called **server-based**). Server-based networks are the most typical and represent the primary focus of the discussion here. It is essential to understand both types, especially as they compare and contrast with one another.

Peer-to-Peer Networking

As you learned, computers on a peer-to-peer network can take both a client and a server role. Because all computers on such a network are peers, these networks impose no centralized control over shared resources, such as files or printers. Any individual machine can share its resources with any other computer on the same network, however, and whenever its user chooses. The peer relationship also means that no single computer has any higher priority to access, or heightened responsibility to provide, shared resources on the network. See Figure 1-5 for an example of a typical peer-to-peer network.

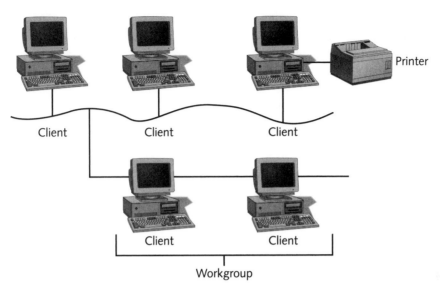

Figure 1-5 Typical peer-to-peer network

In a peer-to-peer network, every user must also act as a **network administrator**. That is, each individual user controls access to the resources that reside on his or her machine. Users may give everyone else unlimited access to their resources, or they may grant restricted (or no) access to other users on the network. Likewise, each individual user can decide whether other users can access resources simply by requesting them or whether other users must supply a password for access requests to succeed. (That is, users with the correct password can access such resources, but those who lack the proper password cannot.)

Because of this flexibility and individual discretion, institutionalized chaos is the norm for peer-to-peer networks, and **security** can be a major concern. On a peer-to-peer network, computers may be affiliated into loose federations called workgroups, but no network-wide security can be enforced. Those who know the right passwords can access the resources that those passwords guard, and those who do not cannot obtain them.

Although this system may work on small networks, it introduces the possibility that users may have to know, and remember, a different password for every shared resource on a network. As the number of users and resources grows, such networks can become unworkable—not because they don't operate properly, but because users can't cope with the complexity involved.

Likewise, most peer-to-peer networks consist of collections of typical end-user PCs, linked by a common network medium. Such machines are not designed to perform well as network servers. They can easily bog down under increasing loads, as more users try to access resources from any particular machine. The user whose machine is being accessed across the network also has to endure a reduction in performance while that machine is busy handling network information requests. For example, if a user's machine has a network-accessible printer attached, that machine slows down every time someone sends a job to that printer. This is fine for the other users, but may interrupt the user working at the machine attached to that printer.

On a peer-to-peer network, any computer can act as a server to share resources with other machines and as a client to access resources from other machines.

Another issue that impinges heavily on peer-to-peer networks is data organization. If every machine can be a server, how can users keep track of what information resides on which machine? If each of five users is responsible for a collection of documents, any one of them might have to search through files on all five machines to find a particular document. The decentralized nature of peer-to-peer networks makes locating resources increasingly difficult as the number of peers to check rises. Likewise, decentralization makes backup considerably more tricky: instead of backing up a single shared repository of data, each individual machine must be backed up to protect shared data.

Given these issues and complexities, peer-to-peer networks might not seem worth using. However, they offer some powerful inducements, particularly for smaller organizations (and networks, by extension). Peer-to-peer networks are the easiest and cheapest to install. Most peer-to-peer networks require only a suitable operating system (such as Windows 95 or Windows 98) on the machines, along with network interfaces and a common network medium. Once connected, users can immediately begin to share information and access devices. Even Windows 2000 and Windows XP support a special networking model, called the **workgroup model**, to permit groups of machines to work together as peers in the absence of a special-purpose server.

Peer-to-peer networks are uniquely well suited to small organizations, which tend to have small networks and small operating budgets. Peer-to-peer networks are also easy to use and require neither extensive staff training nor a dedicated cadre of network administrators. With no centralized control, the loss of any single machine means only the loss of access to the resources it contains; otherwise, a peer-to-peer network continues to function when one computer fails. For small businesses, peer-to-peer networks may represent a cheap, easy, and convenient way to take advantage of the increased productivity and communications that networks can provide.

Peer-to-Peer Networking Advantages

The following is a summary of the advantages of peer-to-peer networking:

- A peer-to-peer network is easy to install and configure.
- Individual machines do not depend on the presence of a dedicated server.
- Individual users control their own shared resources.
- Peer-to-peer networking is inexpensive to purchase and operate.

1

- Peer-to-peer networks need no additional equipment or software beyond a suitable operating system.

- No dedicated administrators are needed to run the network.

- A peer-to-peer network works best for networks with 10 or fewer users.

Peer-to-Peer Networking Disadvantages

The following is a summary of the disadvantages of peer-to-peer networking:

- Network security applies only to a single resource at a time.

- Users may be forced to use as many passwords as there are shared resources.

- Each machine must be backed up individually to protect all shared data.

- Every time a user accesses a shared resource, the user at the machine where the resource resides suffers reduced performance.

- There is no centralized organizational scheme to locate or control access to data.

- A peer-to-peer network does not usually work well with more than 10 users.

Server-Based Networks

Although it's proper to describe server-based networks as client/server, the server is so important to this type of network that NOS vendors such as Microsoft and Novell prefer to use the term that emphasizes this role. A server is best described as a machine whose only function is to respond to client requests. A server is seldom operated by someone sitting in front of it (and then usually only to install, configure, or otherwise manage its capabilities); thus, a server's substantive role on a network is to be continuously available to handle the many requests for its services that a community of clients can generate. See Figure 1-6 for an example of a typical server-based network.

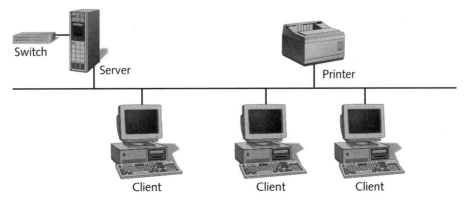

Figure 1-6   Typical server-based network

Server-based networks provide centralized control over network resources, primarily by instituting network security and control through the server's own configuration and setup. The computers used for servers usually incorporate faster CPUs, more memory, larger disk drives, and extra peripherals (such as tape drives and CD-ROM jukeboxes) when compared to end-user machines. Servers are manufactured to handle multiple requests for shared resources expeditiously. In most cases, servers are **dedicated servers** that handle network requests from their client communities. Because physical security—that is, access to the machine itself—is a key component of network security, it's also ideal to situate servers in special, controlled-access rooms separate from general office work areas.

Server-based networks also provide centralized verification of user accounts and passwords, so that one or more **specialized servers** act as sentries, guarding access to the network. Windows NT and Windows 2000, for example, use a **domain model** to manage named collections of users, groups, and machines and to control their access to network resources. Before users can access resources on the network, they must identify themselves to a domain controller, which is a server that checks **account names** and **passwords** against a database of such information that it maintains. This database is known as the **Active Directory** for Windows 2000 networks.

Only with valid account and password combinations can users access certain resources, and only network administrators can modify the security information in the domain controller's database. This approach supports not only centralized security, but also resource management with varying degrees of control, depending on the resources' importance, sensitivity, or location. In the Novell world, one or more NetWare servers provide similar controls over users and the resources they may access by using **Novell Directory Services (NDS)** to store and manage the same kind of security information that Windows domain controllers handle.

Server-based networks also typically require only a single logon to the network itself; users need not remember numerous passwords for individual resources. Likewise, network resources, such as files and printers, are more accessible because they are located on specific servers, not spread around individual users' machines across the network. Concentration of resources on a smaller number of servers also makes data resources easier to back up and maintain.

Unlike peer-to-peer networks, server-based networks are easier to scale. Peer-to-peer networks begin to lose their appeal as the population grows to 10 or more users; they bog down seriously when the network has more than 20 users. On the other hand, server-based networks can handle anywhere from a handful to thousands of users as networks grow to serve entire organizations or to keep pace with an organization's growth and expansion.

 Server-based networks rely on special-purpose computers called servers that provide centralized repositories for network resources and incorporate centralized security and **access controls**, which determine who can access what network resources.

Like peer-to-peer networks, server-based networks have some disadvantages. The most obvious is the additional overhead required to operate a server-based network. Server-based networks require one or more high-powered—and therefore expensive—computers to run special-purpose server software; this also adds to the cost of these networks. Such networks usually require at least part-time support from a knowledgeable person. Acquiring the necessary skills to manage a server-based network, or hiring a trained network administrator, adds significantly to the costs of operating such networks.

Server-based networks' centralization of resources and control has both negative and positive consequences. Although centralization simplifies access, coordinates control, and aggregates resources, it can also introduce a single point of failure on networks. Without an operational server, a server-based network is no network at all. On networks with more than one server, loss of any single server means loss of all resources associated with that server. In addition, if that lost server is the only source of access control information for a certain set of users, those users cannot access the network either.

Server-Based Networking Advantages

The following list summarizes the advantages of server-based networking:

- Centralized user accounts, security, and access controls simplify network administration.
- More powerful equipment means more efficient access to network resources.
- A single password for network logon delivers access to all resources.
- Server-based networking makes the most sense for networks with 10 or more users or any networks where resources are used heavily.

Server-Based Networking Disadvantages

The following list summarizes the disadvantages of server-based networking:

- At worst, server failure renders a network unusable; at the least, it results in loss of network resources.
- Complex, special-purpose server software requires allocation of expert staff, which increases expenses.
- Dedicated hardware and specialized software add to the cost of server-based networking.

Storage-Area Networks (SANs)

For the largest-scale networks—especially those with many thousands of users, or with particularly large collections of data to manage—a new type of network is coming into vogue. The **storage-area network (SAN)** uses high-speed network links between servers that may be located anywhere in an enterprise and centralized storage systems where data and applications reside. See Figure 1-7. The link that connects a server to a SAN storage device uses a high-speed network technology—such as Gigabit Ethernet—solely for the purpose of connecting servers to an extremely fast and highly reliable storage cluster located elsewhere on an organization's premises. Because the network link that connects SAN components is completely separate from the network that links clients and servers, this type of connection is a **sideband link** (because it occurs "off to the side").

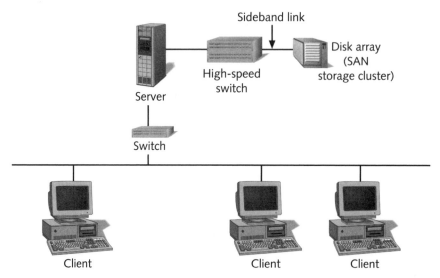

Figure 1-7   Typical storage-area network (SAN)

SANs provide centralized control over network storage, primarily by consolidating storage in a single locale at the site level. Such systems are considerably more expensive than conventional storage, but they offer considerable advantages as well:

- Use of high-speed network links makes access to SAN storage as fast as, if not faster than, conventional storage.

- Consolidation of all server storage permits all backups to occur in a single location and often involves large enough data collections that backups occur continuously in real time.

- Consolidation of all server storage permits organizations to buy the fastest, most reliable storage subsystems. Most of these systems include **hot-swappable** power supplies and disk drives that can be removed and replaced while the system stays operational, thus eliminating down time. Such capability is not always practical (or affordable) on a per-server basis.

- Consolidation of storage can add an extra level of security and access controls where needed, or they can behave "just like local storage," as far as servers are concerned.

1

- It's much easier to increase the storage capacity of a SAN storage system than it is to increase storage on a per-server basis, making it easier for organizations to keep up with rapidly growing storage needs.

Implementing a SAN means adding a second, high-speed network for SAN use to the servers that access any SAN storage devices. This includes an additional high-speed NIC for each such server, the cabling needed to link those servers to the SAN storage device (also known as a SAN storage cluster), and a high-speed switch to connect the network links from the servers to the storage cluster. The additional driver software required for the servers is easy to install and use. The storage cluster usually consists of a bank of high-speed, high-reliability disk arrays, with associated back-up subsystems, and a cache of replacement parts should any components fail. Many large organizations and companies are converting to this kind of storage networking because of the convenience, reliability, and control a SAN can deliver.

Personal Area Networks (PANs)

With all of the wireless devices we carry and our desire to be connected at all times, it is no wonder that a new networking technology that uses our own bodies as carriers for data signals is emerging. The **personal area network (PAN)** is a short-range networking technology that uses the body for transmitting signals. It is being developed to address the desire for connecting devices we frequently carry, including cell phones, pagers, **personal digital assistants (PDAs)**, and even watches.

A PAN can connect devices you wear or come in close contact with and has the ability to transmit to outside devices for a short range, typically within 10 meters or less, using a secure access method.

Devices in a PAN exchange information; for example, if you wanted to telephone Jim Goodfriend, you could speak "Call Jim Goodfriend" into a microphone worn on your body. Your cell phone would then contact your PDA to get the phone number from the address book and proceed to make the call.

Using a PAN, you could transfer information from a device you are carrying to a device another person is carrying through a gesture. For example, a handshake could transfer a business card from your PDA to the other person's PDA. Or, you could verify your identity to a computer or other device, such as an ATM, by a touch that would transmit your security information.

As of this writing there is no single standard for PANs, but Apple has developed a short-range networking technology, called Bluetooth, that is already in use, and the IEEE is creating a standard named P802.15—dubbed the wireless personal area network (WPAN).

 A PDA is a handheld computer used to perform personal organization tasks such as appointment and address book management.

Hybrid Networks

Modern Microsoft operating systems, including Windows NT, Windows XP, Windows .NET Server, and Windows 2000, straddle the boundary between peer-to-peer and server-based networks. That's because each of these operating systems can function as a peer in a peer-to-peer network and all three can act as clients on a server-based network. (Of these systems, only Windows NT Server, Windows 2000 Server, and Windows .NET Server represent true server operating systems.)

In fact, it's not unusual to find networks in which workstations function simultaneously as peers on peer-to-peer networks and as clients on server-based networks. Such **hybrid networks**, sometimes called **combination networks**, partake of the advantages and disadvantages of both peer-to-peer and server-based networks.

Server Hardware Requirements

Whether a machine functions as a server on a peer-to-peer network or as a server on a server-based network, handling service requests across a network invariably adds to a machine's processing load. The higher that load, the more important it is to purchase computers with additional power to handle demands for network resources. To get an idea of what's involved, review Table 1-1, which compares the minimum (and recommended) hardware requirements for Windows 98, Windows .NET Server, and Windows 2000 Server.

Table 1-1   Minimum (and recommended) requirements for Windows 98, Windows .NET Server, and Windows 2000 Server

Item	Windows 98	Windows 2000 Server	Windows .NET Server
RAM	4 (16+) MB	128 (256+) MB	128 (256+) MB
Disk type	IDE (EIDE)	EIDE (SCSI)	EIDE (SCSI)
Disk space	120 (1000) MB	1000 (2000) MB	1500 (3000+) MB
CPU types	80386+ (Pentium+)	Pentium (Pentium II+)	Pentium 133 (Pentium III+)
CPU count	1 (1)	1 (2 or 4)	1 (2 or 4)
NIC type	ISA (PCI)	PCI	PCI

Table 1-1 has several noteworthy implications. First, it's interesting to see how Microsoft's "bare minimum" values compare to the industry consensus on "recommended values." (These appear in parentheses for each entry.) Even though the bare minimum is not negligible, it doesn't approach the more-realistic values expressed in the recommended values. This is especially true for disk space, where the minimum provides room only for the operating system, and not much else. (Clearly, this is impractical on a workstation and doubly so on any server.)

The trend really worth noting is that the requirements jump appreciably when you compare the workstation operating system (Windows 98) to the two server operating systems (Windows .NET Server and Windows 2000 Server). Requirements automatically increase, and double in most cases. In fact, conventional wisdom holds that the best way to deploy a server is to stuff it with the fastest CPUs, as much **Random Access Memory (RAM)** and disk space as it can hold, and to install at least one of the fastest NICs available. That's why Windows 2000 Server and Windows .NET Server can handle up to 32 CPUs in a single system; it's also why special versions that can handle up to 64 or more processors are available for Windows 2000 and .NET Server.

Specialized Servers

Within the broad classification of machines that function as network servers, it's possible to assign a variety of specialty roles, depending on the services that such servers provide. On large networks, in particular, servers with specialized roles are often deployed. In Windows NT and Windows 2000 networks, such server types typically include application servers, communication servers, domain controllers/directory servers, fax servers, file and print servers, mail servers, and Web servers.

Application Servers

Application servers supply the server side of client/server applications, and often the data that goes along with them, to network clients. A database server, for instance, not only supplies query-processing and data-analysis facilities, but also acts as the repository for the huge amounts of data that often reside within a database.

Application servers differ from basic file and print servers in that they provide processing services as well as handle requests for file or print services. In file and print services, the client does its own file handling and print processing. Clients generally must run specialized client-side applications (or plug-ins to other applications) to enable them to communicate with an application server. For such applications, the client-side typically formulates requests and ships them to the application server, which handles all the background processing of the request and then delivers the results back to the client-side part. The client-side then formats and displays those results to the user. Microsoft **SQL Server** delivers complex client/server application support that runs on Windows NT Server and Windows 2000 Server; versions of Oracle with similar capabilities are available for Windows NT, Windows 2000, NetWare, and many flavors of UNIX, including Linux.

Communication Servers

Communication servers provide a mechanism for users outside a network to access that network's resources (inbound communications) and sometimes also permit users on that network to access resources outside the network's local scope (outbound communications). Often, installation of such servers on a network permits users who may be traveling or working at home to dial into the network via a modem. Windows 2000 Server includes a powerful communications server, called the **Remote Routing and Access Server (RRAS)**, that is skillful at handling dial-in network connections. Similar add-on products are available for NetWare and Linux as well, including products from companies such as Citrix.

Domain Controllers/Directory Servers

In general, directory services permit users to locate, store, and secure information about a network and the resources available from a network. Windows NT Server permits computers, users, groups, and resources to be combined into logical groups, called **domains**. Any user who belongs to a specific domain can obtain access to all resources and information that he or she has permission to use simply by logging on to the domain. The server that handles this logon service and that manages the collection of computers, users, and so on in a domain is a **domain controller** or **directory server**. Windows 2000 Server includes all the software needed to enable a network server to function as a domain controller and/or a directory server, as does NetWare 4.*x* (and newer versions); directory service add-ons for Linux are available from companies such as Netscape Communications Corp.

Fax Servers

Fax servers manage fax traffic for a network. They receive incoming faxes via telephone, distribute them to their recipients over the network, and collect outgoing faxes across the network before sending them via telephone. Such servers typically use one or more fax modem interfaces (often referred to simply as fax modems) to perform these tasks. As with most communication servers, Windows-, NetWare-, and Linux-based fax servers come from third parties instead of the platform vendors themselves.

File and Print Servers

File and print servers are the mainstay of the server world in that they provide basic networked file storage, retrieval services, and access to networked printers—functions that define the fundamental uses of most business networks. Such servers let users run applications locally but keep their data files on the server (and print those files when they want hard-copy output). Any Windows, NetWare, or Linux server can act as a file and print server.

Mail Servers

Mail servers handle e-mail messages on behalf of network users; this may involve simply acting as a clearinghouse for a local exchange of messages. However, mail servers also commonly provide "store-and-forward" services, in which the server holds incoming e-mail messages while waiting for users to access them. Likewise, the server can store outgoing messages until a connection to an appropriate external mail server is established and then forward the messages to their intended destinations. Microsoft **Exchange Server** represents sophisticated mail server software that runs on Windows NT and Windows 2000; likewise, numerous e-mail server programs for NetWare and Linux are also available.

1

Web Servers

As companies increasingly turn to software using the TCP/IP protocol (the one used on the Internet) to distribute information, no single service has gained popularity as quickly as the **World Wide Web (WWW)**. Windows .NET Server and Windows 2000 Server include a complete **Web server** (plus **File Transfer Protocol (FTP)** services as well) called **Internet Information Server (IIS)**. This is called **Internet Information Services (IIS)** in Windows 2000. NetWare includes a copy of a Netscape Web server as part of the distribution base for 4.*x* and 5.*x* versions; the excellent Apache Web server is available for free for Linux. Many organizational **intranets** (in-house TCP/IP-based networks) that use these operating systems also take advantage of these free Web server packages. In fact, Apache remains the most widely used Web server in the world (but the Microsoft IIS is also in the top five).

As networks grow larger and more complex, specialization of server roles is increasing. Windows NT and Windows 2000 are Microsoft's primary operating system software offerings designed to handle this broad range of needs. Likewise, NetWare and Linux are also built specifically to deliver such capabilities and services.

Web-Based Networks

The Internet and the WWW are becoming a part of our everyday lives. More and more, we rely on the services of the Web for communication, research, and even entertainment. With new developments in Internet communications and capabilities, this trend will only continue.

Most computers today are connected to the Internet, and the latest handheld devices, such as cell phones and PDAs, are getting connected through wireless communications.

Until recently, the Web was considered separate from our normal computing environment. We had to make a connection through a modem, run our Web browser to view Web pages, and start our e-mail program to check our e-mail. Today, by virtue of our always-connected environment due to cable modems and high-speed connections at work and at home, the Web has become an integral and seamless part of our computing experience. New technologies in the form of the Microsoft .NET initiative and Web-enabled devices promise to integrate the Web even further into our lives so that the Web *is* the network.

.NET Computing

The Microsoft .NET computing model uses the Web to not only deliver information, but also to deliver applications and to permit applications on different devices to communicate and share data. This allows a device with a wireless interface to the Web to download and run applications directly from the Web. It also permits a handheld computer to transfer information to and from a network server or other handheld computer using the Web as the network. This communication model allows information to be transferred from one place to another with unprecedented ease and convenience.

Web-Enabled Devices

We have talked about PANs. PANs allow devices within a person's personal space to communicate. Many of those same devices used in a PAN are Web-enabled devices that can gather and send information via the Internet.

Of course, there are other devices that are becoming Web-enabled. Automobiles can be equipped with a navigation system that not only tells you where you are, but also how to get where you are going. Need to know where the nearest gas station is? A Web-enabled navigation system can download and display a list of service stations in your proximity.

A host of devices are being created that can access the Web, thus shifting our networking paradigm from clients and servers to Web-enabled and not Web-enabled. The concept of client and server will still exist, but clients will become any Web-enabled device that needs information and servers will become any Web-enabled device that can provide that information.

SELECTING THE RIGHT TYPE OF NETWORK

Given the inherent limitations of peer-to-peer networking, there are several easy methods to decide what type of network is right for a given set of circumstances. It's appropriate to choose peer-to-peer networking exclusively *only* when all of the following conditions hold:

- The network includes no more than 10 users (preferably no more than five).
- All networked machines are close enough to fit within the span of a single LAN.
- Budget considerations are paramount.
- No specialized servers (for example, fax servers, communication servers, and application servers) are needed.

On the other hand, if a server-based network is already in use, adding groups that also use peer-to-peer capabilities is acceptable, as long as none of those groups exceeds 10 users.

A server-based network, by contrast, makes sense when one or more of the following conditions is true:

- More than 10 users must share network access.
- Centralized control, security, resource management, or backup is desirable.
- Users need access to specialized servers, or place heavy demands for network resources.
- An internetwork (more than one LAN) is in use, or WAN access is required.

There's a gray area here; for example, when a network has more than five but less than ten users, budget constraints often incline organizations toward peer-to-peer networking. However, if future growth is possible or specialized network servers sound appealing, it's best to start with a server-based network implementation.

1

CHAPTER SUMMARY

❏ This chapter discusses the basic elements of all networks. These include the presence of a networking medium (cabling) of some kind and the requirement that any computer that seeks to access a network must incorporate a physical interface (network adapter) to that medium.

❏ In addition to the hardware, computers must have a networking protocol in common to communicate, and they must include networking software that knows how to use the protocol to send and receive messages or other information across a network.

❏ Networks deliver services such as file sharing, printing, e-mail and other messaging services, and much more to their users.

❏ You learned about the four basic types of networks: peer-to-peer, in which any computer can function as either a client or a server as circumstances dictate; server-based, in which users act as clients of dedicated machines that take the server role; storage-area, in which network storage is centralized and data transfer occurs over high-speed links for faster access; and hybrid, which incorporates both peer-to-peer and server-based features.

❏ You were also introduced to a new network type called a personal area network (PAN), in which the network is limited to a small area around a person.

❏ Budget, number of users, types of applications or network services, and requirements for centralized administration and control are the major criteria you should apply to decide which type of network to deploy in any given situation.

❏ Not only do servers require specialized hardware and software, they also are capable of taking specific roles, acting as file and print servers, fax servers, e-mail servers, application servers, and so on.

KEY TERMS

Because this chapter begins an ongoing dialog on networking and introduces many terms, there is a large number of key terms to review. Familiarize yourself with these terms to ensure complete understanding of this material, which covers networking fundamentals for hardware, software, and services.

access control — A method to impose controls that permit or deny users access to network resources, usually based on a user's account or some group to which the user belongs.

account — The collection of information known about a user, including an account name, an associated password, and a set of access permissions for network resources.

account name — A string of letters, numbers, or other characters that identifies a particular user's account on a network.

Active Directory — The directory service environment for Microsoft Windows 2000 servers. Active Directory includes enough information about users, groups, organizational units, and other kinds of management domains and administrative information about a network to represent a complete digital model of the network.

application server — A specialized network server whose job is to provide access to a client/server application, and, sometimes, the data that belongs to that application as well.

client — A computer on a network that requests resources or services from some other computer.

client/server — A model for computing in which some computers (clients) request services and others (servers) respond to such requests for services.

client/server relationship — Applications may sometimes be divided across the network, so that a client-side component runs on the user's machine and supplies request and display services, while a server-side component runs on an application server and handles data processing or other intensive computation services on the user's behalf.

combination network — *See* hybrid network.

communication server — A specialized network server that provides access to resources on the network for users not directly attached to the network or that permits network users to access external resources not directly attached to the network.

central processing unit (CPU) — The collection of circuitry (a single chip on most PCs) that supplies the "brains" for most computers.

dedicated server — A network server that acts only as a server and is not intended for regular use as a client machine.

desktop software — Sometimes called *client software* or *productivity applications*, this type of software is what users run on their computers (which are usually on a desktop).

device sharing — A primary purpose for networking: permitting users to share access to devices of all kinds, including servers and peripherals such as printers or plotters.

directory server — A specialized server whose job is to respond to requests for specific resources, services, users, groups, and so on. This kind of server is more commonly called a *domain controller* in Windows NT Server and Windows 2000 networking environments.

domain — A uniquely named collection of user accounts and resources that share a common security database.

domain controller — On networks based on Windows NT Server or a Windows 2000 Server, a directory server that also provides access controls over users, accounts, groups, computers, and other network resources.

domain model — A network based on Windows NT Server or Windows 2000 Server whose security and access controls reside in a domain controller.

electronic mail (e-mail) — An abbreviation for electronic mail, a networked application that permits users to send text messages, with or without attachments of many kinds, to individual or multiple users, or to named groups of users.

Ethernet — A networking technology developed in the early 1970s and governed by the IEEE 802.3 specification. Ethernet remains the most popular type of networking technology in use today.

Exchange Server — A BackOffice component from Microsoft that acts as a sophisticated e-mail server.

fax server — A specialized network server that can send and receive faxes on behalf of the user community that it supports, receive incoming faxes from phone lines and direct them to users across the network, as well as accept outgoing faxes across the network and redirect them over a telephone line.

file and print server — The most common type of network server (not considered a specialized server). It provides file storage and retrieval services across the network and handles print jobs on behalf of its user community.

File Transfer Protocol (FTP) — A TCP/IP-based networked file transfer application with an associated protocol. It's widely used on the Internet to copy files from one machine on a network to another.

group — A named collection of user accounts, usually created for some specific purpose. For example, the Accounting group might be the only named entity permitted to use a bookkeeping application.

hot-swappable — Components such as power supplies or disk drives that can be removed and replaced without shutting off power to the computer, thus eliminating down time.

hybrid network — A network that incorporates both peer-to-peer and server-based capabilities.

Internet — The global collection of networked computers that began with technology and equipment funded by the U.S. Department of Defense in the 1970s. Today it links millions of computers worldwide.

Internet Information Server (IIS) — A Microsoft BackOffice component that acts as a Web server in the Windows NT Server environment.

Internet Information Services (IIS) — The Windows 2000 version of Internet Information Server.

internetwork — A network of networks, which consists of two or more physical networks. Unlike a WAN, an internetwork may reside in only a single location. Because it includes too many computers or spans too much distance, an internetwork cannot fit within the scope of a single LAN.

intranet — An in-house TCP/IP-based network, for use within a company.

IPX/SPX — An abbreviation for Internetwork Packet eXchange/Sequenced Packet eXchange, the set of protocols developed by Novell. Most commonly associated with NetWare, but Microsoft and other vendors' networks also support it.

local area network (LAN) — A collection of computers and other networked devices that fit within the scope of a single physical network and provide the building blocks for internetworks and WANs.

locally attached — Describes a device that's attached directly to a single computer, rather than a device that's available only over the network (which may be called network-attached or server-attached, depending on whether it has a built-in network interface or must be attached directly to a server).

mail server — A networked server that manages the flow of e-mail messages for network users.

metropolitan area network (MAN) — Uses WAN technologies to interconnect LANs within a specific geographic region, such as a county or a city. In most cases, however, a municipality or a communications carrier operates a MAN; individual organizations must sign up for service and establish connections to use a MAN.

NetBEUI — An abbreviation for NetBIOS Extended User Interface, the set of protocols developed by IBM in the 1970s and long used as the primary protocols on IBM and Microsoft networks. Today, NetBEUI is just one of many protocols supported by Windows NT and Windows 2000.

network adapter — *See* network interface card (NIC).

network administrator — An individual responsible for installing, configuring, and maintaining a network, usually a server-based network such as Windows 2000 Server or Novell NetWare.

network interface card (NIC) — A PC adapter board designed to permit a computer to be attached to some sort of network medium. The NIC handles the translation of digital information into electrical signals for outgoing network communications and translates incoming signals into their digital equivalent for delivery to the machine in which it's installed.

network medium — Usually refers to the cable (metallic or fiber-optic) that links computers on a network. Because wireless networking is possible, it can also describe the type of wireless communications used to permit computers to exchange data via some wireless transmission frequency.

network operating system (NOS) — A specialized collection of software that gives a computer the ability to communicate over a network and to take advantage of a broad range of networking services. Windows NT and Windows 2000 are network operating systems available in Workstation (called "Professional" in Windows 2000) and Server versions; Windows 95 and Windows 98 also include built-in network client and peer-to-peer capabilities.

network protocol — A set of rules for communicating across a network. To communicate successfully across a network, two computers must share a common protocol.

network resource — Any kind of device, information, or service available across a network. A network resource could be a set of files, an application or service of some kind, or a network-accessible peripheral device.

Novell Directory Services (NDS) — The centralized database of user, group, and resource information that permits one or more NetWare Servers to handle network logins and resource access requests, and to manage resource information for an entire network.

NWLink — An abbreviation for NetWare Link, a set of Microsoft-developed protocols that behaves exactly like Novell's IPX/SPX (but is named differently to avoid trade name infringement).

password — A string of letters, numbers, and other characters intended to be kept private (and hard to guess) and used to identify a particular user or to control access to protected resources.

peer-to-peer — A type of networking in which each computer can be a client to other computers and also act as a server.

peripheral device — Any hardware component on a computer that's not the CPU. In a networking context, it usually refers to some kind of device, such as a printer or a plotter, that users can share across the network.

personal area network (PAN) — A short-range networking technology that uses the body for transmitting signals used to connect handheld or wearable computing devices.

personal digital assistant (PDA) — A handheld computer used to perform personal organization tasks such as appointment and address book management.

protocol — *See* network protocol.

Random Acess Memory (RAM) — The memory cards or chips on a PC that provide working space for the CPU to use when running applications, providing network services, and so on. Where RAM on a server is concerned, more is usually better.

Remote Routing and Access Server (RRAS) — A software component bundled in Windows 2000 that combines RAS and Multi-Protocol Routing, in addition to packet filtering, demand dial routing, and support for Open Shortest Path First (OSPF).

request-response — A description of how the client/server relationship works by referring to how a request from a client leads to some kind of response from a server. (Usually, the response is the service or data requested, but sometimes it's an error message or a denial of service based on security.)

security — For networking, security generically is the set of access controls and permissions in place that determine if a server can grant a request for a service or resource from a client.

server — A computer whose job is to respond to requests for services or resources from clients elsewhere on a network.

server-based — A type or model of networking that requires the presence of a server, to provide services and resources and also to manage and control access to those services and resources.

sharing — One of the fundamental justifications for networking. In Microsoft's lexicon, this term refers to the way in which resources are made available to the network.

sideband link — A special-purpose network connection used only to ferry data for a specific purpose (usually, a separate high-speed network that interlinks storage-area network components), not to ferry general-purpose client/server network traffic. This terminology reflects such a link's use of a separate network that operates "off to the side," apart from regular network connections and traffic.

sneakernet — A metaphorical description of a non-networked data exchange method: someone, presumably wearing sneakers, copies files onto a floppy disk on one computer and then hand-carries the disk to another computer.

specialized server — Any of a number of special-function servers—an application server, a communications server, a directory server or domain controller, a fax server, an e-mail server, or a Web server, among others.

SQL Server — A Microsoft BackOffice component that provides a standard database management system (DBMS) for the Windows NT Server and Windows 2000 Server environments. SQL Server may be used as a standalone database server but is also required to support other BackOffice components, most notably Systems Management Server (SMS).

standalone computer — A computer that's not attached to a network.

storage-area network (SAN) — A specialized networking system that centralizes disk storage in a high-speed, high-capacity, high-reliability storage cluster. It uses high-speed sideband network connections so that users perceive no difference between a SAN and disk subsystems attached directly to a server.

TCP/IP — An abbreviation for Transmission Control Protocol/Internet Protocol, the set of protocols used on the Internet and embraced as a vital technology by Microsoft. At present, Windows 95, Windows 98, Windows NT, and Windows 2000 include outstanding support for TCP/IP.

user — An individual who uses a computer, either as a standalone or to access a network.

Web browser — The client-side software that's used to display content from the World Wide Web; also called a browser.

Web server — The combination of hardware and software that stores information that is accessible over the Internet via the World Wide Web (WWW).

wide area network (WAN) — An internetwork that connects multiple sites, where a third-party communications carrier, such as a public or private telephone company, carries network traffic from one location to another. Because WAN links can be expensive with charges based on bandwidth, few WAN links support the same bandwidth as that available on most LANs.

workgroup model — The Windows NT and Windows 2000 name for a peer-to-peer network that includes one or more Windows NT-based computers.

World Wide Web (WWW) — The TCP/IP-based collection of all Web servers on the Internet, which in the words of one of its originators, Tim Berners-Lee, comes as close to containing "the sum of human knowledge" as anything available on any network anywhere.

REVIEW QUESTIONS

1. What is the name for a network that connects two or more local area networks (LANs) together, sometimes across a large geographic area?

   a. metropolitan area network (MAN)

   b. wide area network (WAN)

   c. internetwork

   d. intranet

2. Which of the following operating systems support peer-to-peer networking? (Choose all that apply.)

   a. Windows XP Professional

   b. Windows 95

   c. Windows 98

   d. Windows 2000 Server

3. You work for a small company, where four users need network access. The budget is tight, so the network must be as inexpensive as possible. What type of network should you install?

   a. server-based network

   b. peer-to-peer network

   c. connector network

   d. CAVT network

4. The _____ is the cable or communications technology that computers must access to communicate across a network.

   a. medium

   b. protocol

   c. software

   d. connector

5. A _____ is needed to attach a computer to a network.

   a. transceiver

   b. network interface card (NIC)

   c. multistation attachment unit (MSAU)

   d. hub

6. Which of the following characteristics are associated with a peer-to-peer network? (Choose all that apply.)
   a. easy to install
   b. inexpensive
   c. user-managed resources
   d. centralized control
   e. one failed computer does not affect the network

7. A server computer shares resources for others to use. True or false?

8. A cable interconnects five computers and a printer in a single office so that users can share the printer. This configuration is an example of a _____.
   a. LAN
   b. MAN
   c. WAN
   d. all of the above

9. Six computers in Schenectady and two in Minneapolis share a set of documents and a common database. This configuration must be a _____.
   a. LAN
   b. MAN
   c. WAN

10. In the Flatiron Building, 140 computers all use Microsoft Office. This configuration must be a _____. (Choose the *best* answer.)
    a. LAN
    b. MAN
    c. WAN
    d. collection of standalone machines (no network)

11. At Clairfield Community College, 300 computers at the North and South campuses (two miles apart) interconnect to share files, printers, e-mail, and a database. This configuration must be a _____. (Choose the *best* answer.)
    a. LAN
    b. MAN
    c. WAN
    d. internetwork

12. A network that permits communication among devices such as cell phones and PDAs, but that has limited range is a _____.
    a. MAN
    b. PAN
    c. SAN
    d. WAN

1

13. Computers that can act as servers to other machines but can also request network resources should be called:

   a. nodes

   b. clients

   c. servers

   d. peers

14. Server-based networks may include any of the following server types. (Choose all that apply.)

   a. fax servers

   b. communications servers

   c. file and print servers

   d. application servers

15. Select the two major kinds of networks.

   a. client-based

   b. server-based

   c. peer-to-peer

   d. client-peer

16. Any two computers that communicate across a network must share a common language, called a _____.

   a. medium

   b. technology

   c. topology

   d. protocol

17. Of the assertions listed below, which are true disadvantages of peer-to-peer networking? (Choose all that apply.)

   a. A peer-to-peer network requires dedicated hardware and specialized software.

   b. Additional staff is needed to maintain a peer-to-peer network.

   c. Individual resources may each have their own unique passwords on a peer-to-peer network.

   d. There is no centralized security on a peer-to-peer network.

   e. none of the above

18. The primary reason to install a network is to _____ resources and services.

   a. share

   b. deliver

   c. create

   d. control

19. Some resources shared on a network typically include _____, such as printers, plotters, or tape drives.

    a. external devices

    b. internal devices

    c. peripheral devices

    d. applications

20. Networked applications such as e-mail permit users to communicate more effectively across a network. True or false?

21. On a peer-to-peer network, there is always at least one dedicated machine called a server. True or false?

22. On a peer-to-peer network, each user must act as _____ for his or her own machine.

    a. administrator

    b. controller

    c. gatekeeper

    d. facilitator

23. Peer-to-peer networks are not suitable if _____.

    a. tight security is required

    b. five users or fewer need network access

    c. budget is the primary consideration

    d. no one uses the network very heavily

    e. none of the above

24. The standard model for networks with 10 or more users is _____.

    a. peer-to-peer

    b. client-server

    c. server-based

    d. server-peer

25. A server does not ordinarily function as a client. True or false?

26. Servers that perform specific roles, such as fax servers, application servers, or communications servers, may best be described as _____.

    a. specialized servers

    b. custom servers

    c. file and print servers

    d. remote access servers

27. A network that combines peer-to-peer and server-based functionality is best described as a _____.

    a. custom network

    b. server-peer network

    c. peer-server network

    d. combination network

28. Of the following system components, which does a server require more of than a client? (Choose all that apply.)

    a. RAM

    b. disk space

    c. faster CPU

    d. more CPUs

    e. extra keyboard

29. Of the following operating systems, which does not function as a network server? (Choose all that apply.)

    a. Windows 95

    b. Windows 98

    c. Windows XP Professional

    d. Windows 2000 Server

    e. all of the above

30. Which of the following specialized servers is not included with Windows 2000 Server?

    a. Web server

    b. communications server

    c. fax server

    d. file and print server

    e. all of the above

31. Which of the following is the best expansion for the acronym SAN?

    a. special application network

    b. storage-area network

    c. server-area network

    d. super-available network

HANDS-ON PROJECTS

Numerous networking technologies, but especially those from IBM and Microsoft, have a long and rich association with a singularly enduring application programming interface (API) known as the Network Basic Input/Output System (NetBIOS). Originally developed by IBM in the 1970s and adapted for use on the first PCs in the early 1980s, NetBIOS remains a popular networking environment more than 20 years later.

Some observers say it's still around because no usable technology ever disappears entirely; others claim that because NetBIOS is so easy for developers to use, programmers will never let it die. Whatever the case, most Microsoft operating systems with networking capabilities support a series of NetBIOS-based networking capabilities, known as the NET commands, that can provide useful information about the network they can access. The projects that follow give you your first exposure to these powerful and useful, but cryptic, command-line utilities. As you revisit these commands throughout this book, more and more of their esoteric details should begin to make sense.

Project 1-1

In this project, you will explore the nuances of the NET HELP utility.

To use the NET HELP utility:

1. In a GUI operating system such as Windows 98, Windows XP, or Windows 2000, command-line utilities must be executed in a so-called DOS box. For Windows 98, follow this sequence of menu selections: **Start**, **Programs**, **MS-DOS Prompt**. For Windows 2000 and Windows XP, the sequence is: **Start**, **Programs**, **Accessories**, **Command Prompt**.

2. At the DOS prompt, type **NET HELP** (in either lowercase or uppercase) and press **Enter**. You should see something like the screen shown in Figure 1-8.

```
Command Prompt                                          _ 8 X

D:\>net help
The syntax of this command is:

NET HELP command
        -or-
NET command /HELP

    Commands available are:

    NET ACCOUNTS           NET HELP            NET SHARE
    NET COMPUTER           NET HELPMSG         NET START
    NET CONFIG             NET LOCALGROUP      NET STATISTICS
    NET CONFIG SERVER      NET NAME            NET STOP
    NET CONFIG WORKSTATION NET PAUSE           NET TIME
    NET CONTINUE           NET PRINT           NET USE
    NET FILE               NET SEND            NET USER
    NET GROUP              NET SESSION         NET VIEW

    NET HELP SERVICES lists the network services you can start.
    NET HELP SYNTAX explains how to read NET HELP syntax lines.
    NET HELP command : MORE displays Help one screen at a time.

D:\>_
```

Figure 1-8   NET HELP command

3. The command you're interested in is the View command. To obtain information about it, type **NET HELP VIEW** (in either lowercase or uppercase), and press **Enter**. You should see something like that shown in Figure 1-9. Read the screen.

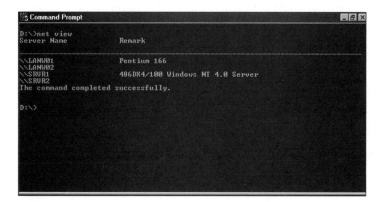

```
Command Prompt                                              _ 8 X
D:\>net help view
The syntax of this command is:

NET VIEW [\\computername | /DOMAIN[:domainname]]
NET VIEW /NETWORK:NW [\\computername]

NET VIEW displays a list of resources being shared on a computer. When used
without options, it displays a list of computers in the current domain or
network.

\\computername          Is a computer whose shared resources you want
                        to view.
/DOMAIN:domainname      Specifies the domain for which you want to
                        view the available computers. If domainname is
                        omitted, displays all domains in the local area
                        network.
/NETWORK:NW             Displays all available servers on a NetWare
                        network. If a computername is specified, the
                        resources available on that computer in
                        the NetWare network will be displayed.

D:\>_
```

Figure 1-9 NET HELP VIEW shows details of the NET VIEW command

4. The View command offers two levels of information. Type **NET VIEW** (in either lowercase or uppercase; hereafter, this reminder will not be given) on the command line, and press **Enter**. It shows you the names of the machines present on your network. Such a display appears in Figure 1-10. Notice that it lists the names of machines on the leftmost side, in a column labeled "Server Name" with optional "Remark" entries for two of the four machines listed. You should see something similar for your network, but with different machine names on the left and perhaps no remarks on the right.

Depending on your network setup, you may receive error or status messages such as "There are no entries in the list" or "Access denied." In this case, you will not be able to perform the projects that use the NET VIEW command.

```
Command Prompt                                              _ 8 X
D:\>net view
Server Name             Remark

\\LANW01                Pentium 166
\\LANW02
\\SRVR1                 486DX4/100 Windows NT 4.0 Server
\\SRVR2
The command completed successfully.

D:\>
```

Figure 1-10 NET VIEW command shows registered machines

The second type of listing that NET VIEW can provide appears when you append the name of a particular machine; for the example in Figure 1-11, the input read NET VIEW \\SRVR1 and produced the output shown. Pick a computer name from your network (a server name produces the most interesting results) and try using it with NET VIEW. It shows you the names of whatever network shares are available, indicates their type (usually "Disk" or "Print"), indicates if a drive letter matches a resource (notice that data2 corresponds to drive G in Figure 1-11), and may also provide a comment field. Figure 1-11 NET VIEW shows resources available on "srvr1".

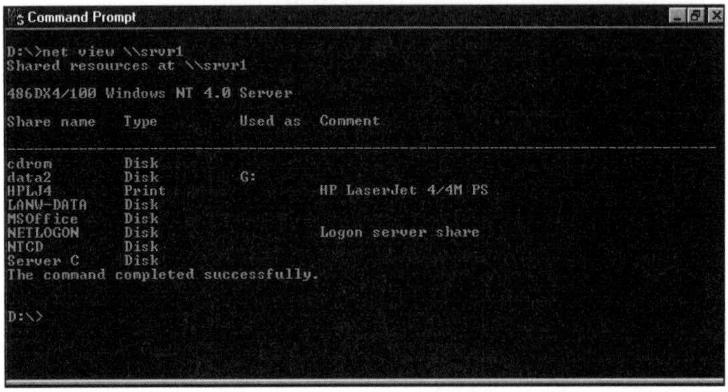

```
Command Prompt                                            _ ◻ ✕

D:\>net view \\srvr1
Shared resources at \\srvr1

486DX4/100 Windows NT 4.0 Server

Share name    Type      Used as   Comment
-------------------------------------------------------------------
cdrom         Disk
data2         Disk        G:
HPLJ4         Print                HP LaserJet 4/4M PS
LANW-DATA     Disk
MSOffice      Disk
NETLOGON      Disk                 Logon server share
NTCD          Disk
Server C      Disk
The command completed successfully.


D:\>
```

Figure 1-11   NET VIEW shows resources available on "srvr1"

5. Close the DOS window by typing **EXIT** on the command line and then pressing **Enter**, or by clicking the **Close** button in the upper-right corner of the window.

Project 1-2

Most networked operating systems support a method of making all or part of a disk drive available to the network. On Microsoft systems, this is called a directory share or sometimes (but not quite accurately) a file share. The shares in the listing in Figure 1-11 appear in the leftmost column under the heading "Share name." All of these are available to users on the network who have the correct password or permissions necessary to access them. In this project, you define a share on your own machine that others on the network can access freely.

To share a directory on your computer with the network:

1. Although there are at least three methods for creating shares on Windows 98, Windows XP, and Windows 2000, the preferred method is to open the Windows Explorer application on your desktop. For Windows 98 users, this means following the menu sequence: **Start, Programs, Windows Explorer**. Windows 2000 and Windows XP users should follow this menu sequence: **Start, Programs, Accessories, Windows Explorer**.

2. First, you create a new folder to share with the network. Begin this process by highlighting a hard drive letter icon in the left pane of your Windows Explorer window. Figure 1-12 depicts this for drive D. From the **File** menu, select **New** and then **Folder** from the submenu. A New Folder entry appears at the bottom of the rightmost pane in Windows Explorer. Type **Temp<*machine number*>**, where you substitute your computer number for <*machine number*>, and then press **Enter**. (If your machine number is 6, for instance, you'd type **Temp6**.)

Figure 1-12 Creating a new folder

Depending on the settings on your computer, your screen might differ from Figure 1-12 and Figure 1-13.

3. Once you create your Temp folder, right-click it. A shortcut menu opens, as shown in Figure 1-13. Select the **Sharing** option on the menu.

4. Once you select the Sharing option, a dialog box similar to Figure 1-14 appears. Click the **Share this folder** option button (or the **Shared As** option button in Windows 98 and Windows NT, and the **Share this folder on the network** checkbox in Windows XP) to enable this share, and then simply click the **Apply** button in the lower-right corner to turn on the share.

5. Click **OK** at the bottom of the dialog box. Your share is now ready for use.

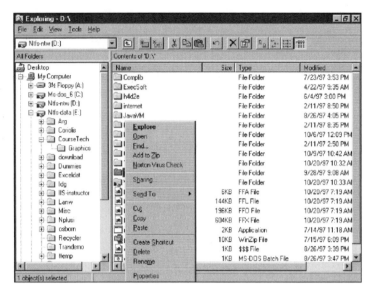

Figure 1-13   Click Sharing on the shortcut menu

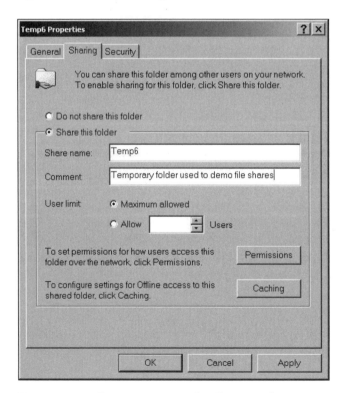

Figure 1-14   Share options on the Sharing tab

To check your work:

1. Open a DOS window (or box) on your machine. (Reread Step 1 in Project 1-1 if you don't remember how to do this.)

2. Type **NET VIEW \\<*your machine name*>**, where you substitute your actual machine name for <*your machine name*>, and then press **Enter**. (Ask your instructor for your specific machine name; for this example, the input read **NET VIEW \\Machine6**.) You should see something like that shown in Figure 1-15. Notice in the figure the appearance of a share named *Temp6*. This confirms that you created your share successfully.

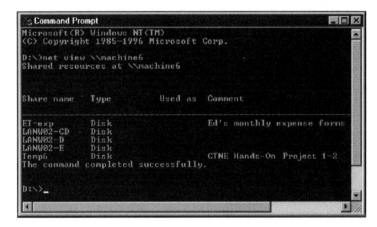

Figure 1-15   NET VIEW shows the Temp6 folder as a shared resource

To turn off (disable) a share:

1. In Windows Explorer, right-click the folder you just shared, and select the **Sharing** option again. In the properties dialog box, click the **Not Shared** option button (or the **Do not share this folder** option button in Windows 2000; uncheck the **Share this folder on the network** checkbox in Windows XP), click **Apply** in the lower-right corner, and then click **OK**. You just turned off this share.

2. [*Optional*] If you check **NET VIEW \\<*your machine name*>** again, you should no longer see the share. This is how you disable a share.

3. Close the DOS window, and Windows Explorer, if you've left it open.

Project 1-3

Working around networks means learning to swim in a cauldron of alphabet soup. That is, many of the items, elements, components, and concepts you encounter in this field don't go by their full names—they're known by the acronyms that designate them. In this chapter, you already encountered the following acronyms:

❑ CPU	❑ MAN	❑ SAN
❑ FTP	❑ NDS	❑ TCP/IP
❑ IIS	❑ NetBEUI	❑ WAN
❑ IPX/SPX	❑ NIC	❑ WWW
❑ LAN	❑ NOS	

That's a total of 14 acronyms in this first chapter alone. Other chapters in this book make this number seem small by comparison. That's why this project (which requires Internet access and a Web browser) introduces you to a tool known as "Acronym Finder." Working in a networked environment, you'll find plenty of reasons to add its URL to your bookmarks or favorites list!

To access Acronym Finder:

1. Start your Web browser at your desktop. For Windows users, this typically means following the menu sequence: **Start**, **Programs**, **Internet Explorer**. If your lab setup is different, your instructor or lab manager should be able to give you the right sequence of commands to follow.

2. Type the string **http://www.acronymfinder.com/** in the Address box in your Web browser, and press **Enter**. This should take you to the Acronym Finder home page, which looks similar to that shown in Figure 1-16.

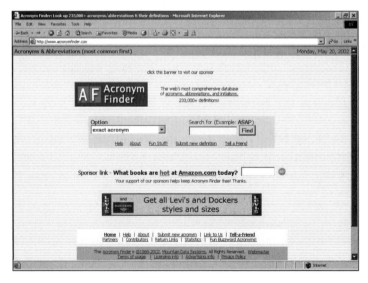

Figure 1-16   Acronym Finder home page

Web locations and Web pages change constantly! Don't worry if the Acronym Finder home page looks a little different from our example—you should still be able to navigate it in pretty much the same way. For tips on how to track down URLs that are no longer "home," see the section titled "Coping with Change on the Web" in the Introduction.

3. Once you've landed on Acronym Finder's home page, you can look up acronyms by typing them into the text box in the upper-right corner, labeled "Acronym To Find." Type the first acronym from the list in this exercise (**CPU**), and press **Enter**. This produces the listing shown in Figure 1-17. As you can see, CPU stands for a number of different things. You must know enough about what a CPU is and does to understand that the second entry that appears (Central Processing Unit) is the right one.

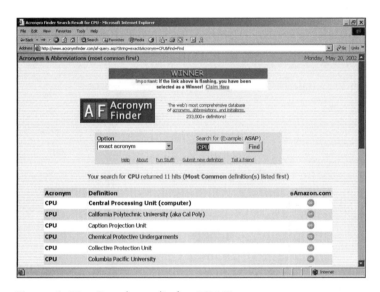

Figure 1-17   Search results for "CPU"

4. Try other entries in the list that precedes these instructions. Without checking the keyword list in this chapter, try to decide which expansion fits this book. Then, check your work by reading through the keywords to see which expansion is correct.

5. Close Internet Explorer (or whatever Web browser you're using), unless you plan to go directly to the next exercise. In that case, skip Step 1 in Project 1-4.

Project 1-4

As any interaction with Acronym Finder shows you, there is nearly always more than one possible expansion for almost any given acronym. Since we're interested in how this information applies to networking topics, it's often necessary to look up such acronym expansions to see what they really mean (and see if a likely looking expansion is indeed the correct expansion).

This Hands-on Project (which requires Internet access and a Web browser) introduces some tools you can use to decide which acronym expansion is most likely the correct one. Working in a networked environment, you'll find plenty of reasons to add one or more of these URLs to your bookmarks or favorites list!

To access networking information online:

1. Start your Web browser at your desktop. For Windows users, this typically means following the menu sequence: **Start**, **Programs**, **Internet Explorer**. If your lab setup is different, your instructor or lab manager should be able to give you the right sequence of commands to follow.

2. Type **http://www.techweb.com** into the Address box of your web browser, and then press **Enter**. This should take you to the *TechWeb* home page, as shown in Figure 1-18.

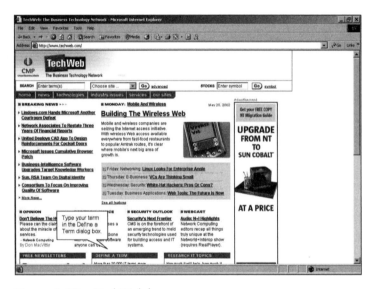

Figure 1-18   *TechWeb* home page

3. Locate the DEFINE A TERM section on this page. Type **central processing unit** into the text box, and then click the **Search** button. Your screen should resemble Figure 1-19. Click the **CPU** hyperlink to view a lengthy description.

4. Based on what you wrote for various acronym expansions, try some entries for other acronyms.

5. Close Internet Explorer (or whatever Web browser you're using).

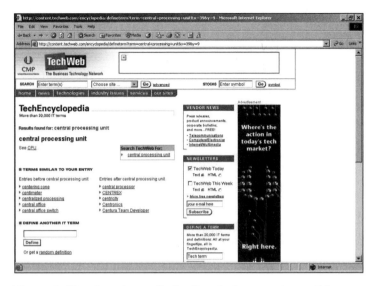

Figure 1-19 Search results for "central processing unit"

Project 1-5 [Optional]

Sometimes, you just can't get to the Internet. Whatever the reason, don't let it stop you from furthering your education in networking terms, concepts, and topics. If your instructor can furnish one or more copies of the following reference materials, you can look up most networking topics, acronyms, and technologies on the CDs that accompany these books (or even flip through the pages and look up things the old-fashioned way).

❑ Fiebel, Werner: *The Network Press Encyclopedia of Networking*, 3rd Edition, Sybex Books, San Francisco, 1999. List price: $84.99, hardcover. ISBN: 0-7821-2255-8.

❑ Sheldon, Tom: *Encyclopedia of Networking*, Electronic Edition, Osborne/McGraw-Hill, Berkeley, 2000. List price: $69.99, softcover. ISBN: 0-07-882350-1.

This Hands-on Project requires access to one of the CDs included with the two titles mentioned in the preceding bulleted list. It introduces you to some likely tools you can use to research a vast majority of networking topics, techniques, technologies, and acronyms.

To use the Sheldon book's CD:

1. Insert the CD into your CD player, then launch Windows Explorer in Windows 98 using the menu sequence: **Start**, **Programs**, **Windows Explorer**. For Windows 2000 and Windows XP, choose **Start**, **Programs**, **Accessories**, **Windows Explorer**. In Windows Explorer, double-click the icon for the CD player in the left pane to display its contents in the right pane. Your window should look similar to that shown in Figure 1-20. Notice that the CD contains two folders: Setup16 and Setup32. Use Setup16 in the next step if you're running Windows 98; use Setup32 if you're running Windows XP or Windows 2000.

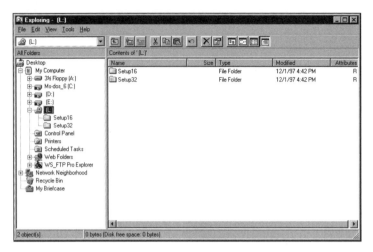

Figure 1-20   Setup folders for *Encyclopedia of Networking*

2. Double-click the folder that matches your operating system's requirements in the right pane, and then double-click the file named **SETUP.EXE** in the right pane to install the CD.

3. In the Windows environment, SETUP.EXE invokes a Windows service that's sometimes called the Windows Installation Wizard. This wizard guides you through the installation process. The only input necessary is the directory where the encyclopedia CD should be installed; your instructor will tell you if you should use the **Browse** button to specify a directory other than the default directory supplied by the Installation Wizard. Otherwise, you can simply click the **Continue** button until you get all the way through the process. Once installation completes, a Windows Explorer window like the one shown in Figure 1-21 appears.

Figure 1-21   *Encyclopedia of Networking* launch icon

4. Double-click the **Encyclopedia of Networking** icon to start the CD interface. Click the **I Agree** button to accept the user licensing conditions. Use the scroll bar on the front pane and the alphabetic tabs on the right side of the screen to look up several of the acronyms that appear in the list at the beginning of Project 1-3.

1

5. If your instructor asks you to uninstall the program, close the *Encyclopedia of Networking* window, and then double-click the **Uninstalling this E-DOC** icon in the Windows Explorer window.

6. Close the Windows Explorer window.

To use the Feibel book's CD:

1. Insert the CD into your CD player, and then start Windows Explorer using the menu sequence: **Start**, **Programs**, **Accessories**, **Windows Explorer**. (This sequence works for Windows 98, Windows 2000, and Windows XP.)

2. In Windows Explorer, double-click the icon for the CD player in the left pane to display its contents in the right pane. Your window should look similar to that shown in Figure 1-22. Notice that the CD contains two folders: Encyclop and Readers. The encyclopedia appears as an Adobe portable document format (.pdf) file, so reading it requires that your machine have a PDF reader installed. If you need to install one in your classroom, your instructor will give you supplementary directions on how to do so.

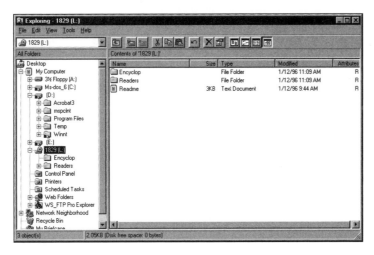

Figure 1-22 Folders for *Encyclopedia of Networking*

3. Double-click the **Encyclop** folder, and then double-click the file named **ENCYCLOP.PDF** in the right pane to access the electronic version of the book. A display like that shown in Figure 1-23 appears.

Figure 1-23   *Encyclopedia of Networking* menu interface

4. Use the alphabetic listing in the left pane, and scroll within the pages that appear on the right side of the screen to look up several of the acronyms that appear in the list at the beginning of Project 1-3.

5. Close the Acrobat Reader window.

CASE PROJECTS

1. XYZ Corporation currently employs eight people but plans to hire 10 more in the next four months. Users will work on multiple projects, and only those users assigned to any one project should have access to the project files. You're instructed to set up the network to make it easy to manage and back up. Would you choose a peer-to-peer, a server-based, or a combination network? Why?

2. Widgets Inc. hired you as a productivity consultant. Currently, they employ six people who routinely exchange information via sneakernet. They want the cheapest possible solution and only minimal training for employees. Individual employees also must be able to control resources on their own machines. Would you choose a peer-to-peer, a server-based, or a combination network? Why?

3. American Tool and Die operates two machine shops, one in Towson, Maryland, and the other in Beltsville, Maryland. The company wants the two locations to share a single database, so that managers at each facility can exchange work orders and monitor inventory on demand. Individual users need some control over individual resources, but they also want network faxing and dial-in services at each location. Would you choose a peer-to-peer, a server-based, or a combination network? Why?

4. What kind of specialized servers do you need to install at American Tool and Die, based on the information presented in the previous Case Project?

5. Windows .NET Server is the latest Microsoft server product. Research the new features of this operating system and compare the features and available versions to Windows 2000 server. Write a short explanation of what advantages an organization might realize by upgrading to this operating system.

2

NETWORK DESIGN ESSENTIALS

After reading this chapter and completing the exercises, you will be able to:

♦ Design a network layout

♦ Understand the various networking topologies

♦ Integrate the use of hubs into your network

♦ Integrate the use of switches into your network

♦ Explore the variations of the standard networking topologies

♦ Select the best network topology for your environment

♦ Construct your network layout

A network's basic design plays an integral part in its operation and performance. The topology of the network dictates the media used, the type of channel access, and the speed at which the network operates.

It is important to have an understanding of the basic network topologies and the hybrids of those topologies as a firm foundation for designing your network. When you understand the topologies, you can use this knowledge in subsequent chapters dealing with media, channel access, and network architecture.

NETWORK DESIGN

In this section, you explore the basics of good network design. This includes analyzing network requirements and selecting a network topology and the equipment to fit that topology. Following that information are pointers on how to map out your design.

DESIGNING A NETWORK LAYOUT

Before designing a network layout, it is important to understand some basic networking concepts. When you implement a network, you must first decide how to best situate the components in a topology. A network's **topology** refers not only to the physical layout of its computers, cables, and other resources, but also to how those components communicate with each other. Topology, **layout**, **diagram**, and **map** are some of the many terms used to describe this basic design.

When discussing the arrangement of cabling in a network, we are discussing a network's physical topology. When discussing the path that data travels between computers on the network, we are discussing a network's logical topology. As you will see, a network may be wired using one physical topology but pass data from machine to machine using a different logical topology.

A network's topology has a significant effect on its performance as well as its growth potential. In addition, the topology impacts such decisions as the type of equipment to purchase and the best approach to network management.

When designing a network, you must have a firm grasp on its topologies' uses as well as their limitations. Your design should provide room for growth and meet your defined security requirements. A solid design grows and adapts to the network as needs change, whereas a poor design limits growth potential and must eventually be replaced.

STANDARD TOPOLOGIES

All network designs in use today are based on three topologies: bus, star, and ring. The topologies are simple. A **bus** consists of a series of computers connected along a single cable segment. The topology of computers connected via a central concentration point, or **hub**, is a **star**. Computers connected to form a loop create a **ring**.

Bus

Also known as a linear bus, the bus topology is by far the simplest and was at one time the most common method for connecting computers. See Figure 2-1. Inherent in this simplicity, however, is a weakness: a single cable break can halt the entire network. All components of the bus topology connect via a **backbone**, a single cable segment that (theoretically) interconnects all the computers in a straight line.

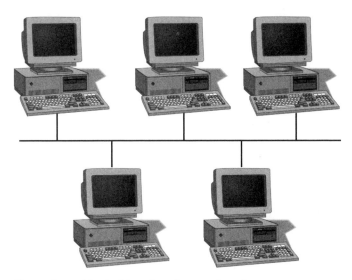

Figure 2-1   Typical bus topology network

Thinnet (Ethernet 10Base2) is the most common cable type used in a bus topology. It supports simple network expansion.

Bus Communications

To understand fully the impact of choosing a bus topology, you must understand how computers communicate with each other across a network.

All computers, regardless of their topology, communicate in the same way: they address some data to one or more computers and then transmit that data across the cable in the form of electronic signals. To understand bus communications, you must be familiar with how a signal is sent, how a signal bounces, and cable termination.

Sending the Signal.   When a computer has data to send, it addresses that data, breaks it into packets (discussed in detail in Chapter 6), and sends it across the network as electronic signals. These signals travel the length of the cable segment, and all connected computers receive them. However, because of the address given to the packets, only those computers for which these signals are destined accept the data.

In a bus environment, only one computer at a time can send information. Therefore, all network users must share the available amount of transmission time. Because of this limitation, the number of computers attached to a bus network can affect network performance. The more computers that are ready to send data at the same time, the longer some computers must wait to send their data. This slows overall network performance.

It is important to note that a bus topology is a **passive topology**. This means that computers on the bus only listen for data being sent; they are not responsible for moving data from one computer to the next. If one computer fails, it has no effect on the rest of the network. In an **active topology** network, computers and other devices attached to the network regenerate signals and are responsible for moving data through the network.

Signal Bounce.   As a signal travels across the network medium, it moves from the point of transmission to both ends of any bus. If allowed to continue undamped, such a signal would travel across the network continuously, bouncing back and forth, preventing other computers from sending data, as shown in Figure 2-2. This causes a **signal bounce**. Because of this, all signals must stop when they reach the end of any segment in a bus topology.

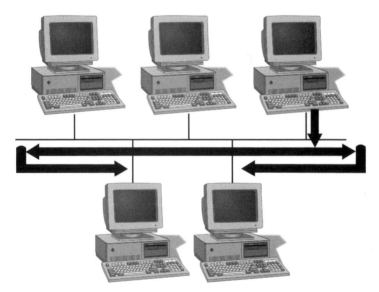

Figure 2-2   Signal bounce on an unterminated network

Cable Termination.   A **terminator** attached to each end of a cable prevents signals from bouncing. This terminator absorbs all signals that reach it, thus clearing the network for new communications. On a bus network, each cable segment end must attach to something. Open ends—ends not attached to a computer—must be terminated to prevent signal bounce. Figure 2-3 shows cable terminators absorbing an electronic signal.

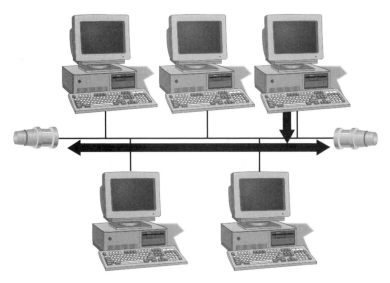

Figure 2-3   Terminated bus network

Cable Failure.   A cable break in a bus network occurs when the cable is physically cut or one end becomes disconnected. Whenever a cable break occurs, that cable is no longer terminated and signals can then bounce, halting all network activity. The computers attached to that bus can still function as standalone systems, but no network communications are possible. Figure 2-4 demonstrates signal bounce resulting from a cable break.

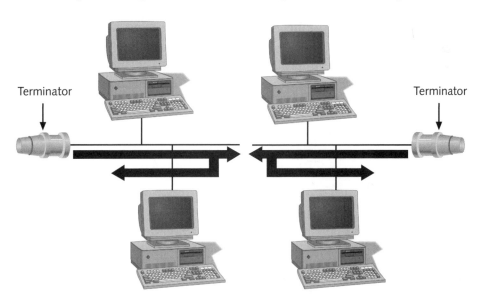

Figure 2-4   Cable break and subsequent signal bounce

Bus Network Expansion.   When using Ethernet 10Base2 (thinnet), it's easy to expand networks by attaching a BNC barrel connector between cable segments.

 Although expansion via barrel connectors is easy to install, the resulting cable segment (which consists of the combined length of all actual cable segments, less insertion loss for connectors) cannot exceed the maximum allowed cable length for the type of network medium used. Chapter 3 covers specific cable limitations in detail.

As network segments lengthen, however, the distance that signals must travel across those segments also increases, which can cause signals to weaken. This phenomenon is called **attenuation**. A **repeater** can eliminate the effects of signal attenuation on a large network. It boosts signal strength by regenerating incoming signals on one side of the device before transmitting them out the other side of the device. A repeater cannot, however, correct any errors in incoming signals and can, in fact, exacerbate such errors.

Because of the problems inherent with troubleshooting and managing a bus network, and because a single cable failure can bring down an entire bus network, the bus topology has lost popularity in favor of the star topology.

Star Topology

Because of the weaknesses in other topologies, the star has become the dominant topology in today's networks. A star topology, shown in Figure 2-5, describes computers connected by cable segments to a central hub. When a computer sends a signal, the hub receives and retransmits it down every other cable segment to all other computers or other devices attached to that hub. All computers hear the signal and check the destination address, but only the computer to which the data is addressed processes the data further. This topology got its start in the early days of mainframe computing when all nodes were attached to a central point, which was a front-end processor, itself attached to the mainframe.

2

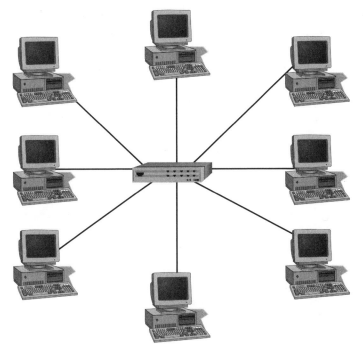

Figure 2-5   Typical star topology network

One benefit of a star topology is its inherent centralization of resources. However, because all computers connect at one location, the star topology requires a more intricate cable installation. Another drawback is that the hub defines a single, central point for failure: if a hub fails, all other computers and devices attached to that hub lose network access. On the other hand, if one computer or cable fails, it has no effect on the rest of the network. This is an important point because, unlike in a bus topology, a user cannot bring down the entire network simply by disconnecting the cable from his or her computer. Another advantage of the star topology is the relative ease of troubleshooting. Because all computers connect at a central location, an administrator can quickly and easily isolate network problems involving a single station or cable segment, without affecting other stations.

The centralization of resources and the management capabilities available on hubs (which form the center of a star) have elevated the star topology to the top choice among networking topologies.

Ring Topology

When each computer connects directly to the next computer in line, a circle of cable forms to create a ring topology network. As a computer receives a signal, it either acts on it or regenerates it and passes it along. Signals travel in only one direction around the ring.

Figure 2-6 shows the direction a signal travels in a ring network. Because the circle has no end, termination is not required.

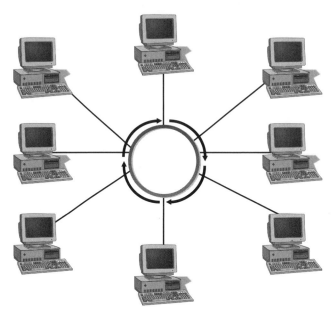

Figure 2-6   Typical ring topology network

Token passing is one method for sending data around a ring. A small packet, called a **token**, passes around the ring to each computer in turn. If a computer has information to send, it modifies the token, adds address information and the data, and sends it around the ring. That information travels around the ring until it either reaches its destination or returns to the sender. When the intended destination computer receives the information, it returns a message to the sender to acknowledge its safe arrival. The sender then creates a new token and sends it around the ring.

 A ring topology network can be wired as a star. A central hub may pass the token through the network in a virtual ring, which supports the benefits of both topologies.

Because every computer in a ring is responsible for retransmitting the token or data, a ring topology is an active topology. Surprisingly, it is still very fast. A token can make a complete circuit in a 200-meter ring 10,000 times per second. More advanced ring networks may use multiple tokens or dual counter-rotating rings.

 Although IBM's token ring networks use single rings, **Fiber Distributed Data Interface (FDDI)** uses dual counter-rotating rings for speed and redundancy, as discussed in Chapter 7.

A typical single-ring network can fail if one computer in the ring fails, but a dual-ring network can operate around any such failure. Modern ring topologies use "smart hubs" that recognize a computer's failure and automatically remove the computer from the ring. (This is one profound advantage of using a ring topology with star wiring.) Another advantage of the ring topology lies in its ability to share network resources fairly. Each computer has an equal opportunity to send data, so no single computer can monopolize the network.

Wireless Topologies

Wireless networks eliminate the need for a visible physical topology, which is one reason for their growing popularity. There are no cables to run, terminate, and test. However, wireless networking does have a topology associated with it. Wireless LANs require a centralized device to control communications, much like a hub, so in this respect, wireless LANs use a star topology because all the signals travel through one central device.

HUBS

As mentioned, a hub is a central point of concentration for a star network. There are two types of hubs: active and passive. Figure 2-7 shows a typical hub layout and its method of communication.

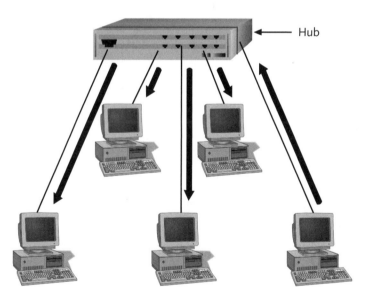

Figure 2-7   Hub communications

Active Hubs

The majority of hubs installed in networks today are **active hubs**. They regenerate the signals as they receive them and send them along. Generally, active hubs have many ports—eight or more—and so are sometimes called multiport repeaters. Because they regenerate the signal, active hubs require electrical power to run. One drawback of these multiport repeaters is that, like a bus topology, they require that the cable bandwidth be shared among all connected stations. This means that for a 10-Mbps Ethernet network using a multiport repeater with 10 stations connected, the effective bandwidth for each computer is only 1 Mbps. Until recently, this bandwidth sharing was not a big problem because the number and frequency of data transfers in a typical LAN was comparatively small. However, in today's LANs, where large multimedia data files are frequently being transferred, the need for additional, dedicated bandwidth has become paramount. The solution to this is switches, which are discussed later in this chapter.

For wireless networks, the hub is referred to as a **wireless access point (WAP)**. Wireless hubs share bandwidth just as traditional wired hubs do.

Passive Hubs

In a **passive hub**, such as a wiring panel or punchdown block, the signal passes through the hub without any amplification or regeneration. A passive hub is simply a central connection point. Because no electronic signaling occurs, a passive hub requires no power.

Hybrid Hubs

Used to interconnect different types of cables, **hybrid hubs** help maximize a network's efficiency, interconnect different topologies, and thus, realize the benefits of combining network topologies.

SWITCHES

A **switch**, like a hub, is the central connecting point in a star topology network. However, unlike a hub, the switch does more than simply regenerate signals. Yes, a switch does look just like a hub in that it has several ports for connecting workstations in a star topology. However, rather than simply regenerating an incoming signal and repeating that signal out all other ports, a switch actually determines to which port the destination device is connected and forwards the message to only that port. This capability allows a switch to handle several conversations at one time, thereby providing the full network bandwidth to each station rather than requiring that bandwidth be shared.

The performance advantage provided by switches has made them the device of choice in corporate networks, even if at a somewhat higher price. Due to the popularity of switches and the decrease in their manufacturing costs, switch prices have dropped to where the extra performance a LAN enjoys from their use has justified the slight additional cost (when compared to hubs).

A detailed discussion on hubs, switches, and other network devices can be found in Chapter 11.

VARIATIONS OF THE MAJOR TOPOLOGIES

There are three typical variations, or combinations, of the major network topologies: mesh, star bus, and star ring. These combinations may be implemented to get the most from any network. Both the star bus and star ring topologies use the biggest benefit of the star topology—its central connection point.

Mesh Topology

A **mesh** network topology is the most fault tolerant but also the most expensive. Connecting each device in a network to every other device in the network creates a mesh network topology. As Figure 2-8 shows, this configuration is very intricate.

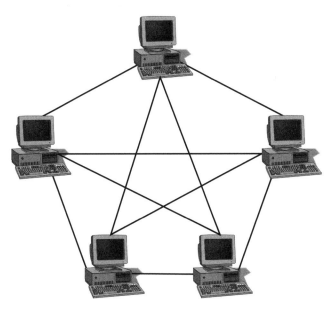

Figure 2-8   Typical mesh topology network

Any single cable or device failure in a mesh configuration affects network performance only minimally because multiple connections exist to each device. However, costs greatly increase because more cable and hardware are required. Most often, a mesh topology is used in wide area networking to ensure that all sites remain able to communicate, even in the event of a cable failure. One of the best examples of a mesh topology is the Internet. Although the entire Internet is not designed as a mesh, the critical pathways are, providing fault tolerance to the key junction points.

Star Bus Topology

The **star bus** topology, as its name states, combines a star and a bus. For example, a star bus topology is implemented when a bus backbone interconnects two or more hubs. The star configuration minimizes the effect of any single computer's failure on the network. If a hub fails, the computers attached to it cannot communicate, but other hub-computer connections remain intact and communication continues. See Figure 2-9.

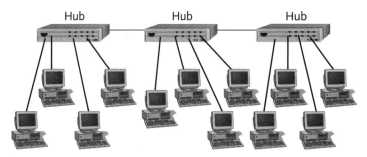

Figure 2-9   Typical star bus network

Star Ring Topology

A network that is wired as a star but that handles network traffic like a ring is a **star ring** topology. Again, a single computer failure does not affect network traffic. Several outer hubs can connect to the inner hub, extending the inner ring. See Figure 2-10.

2

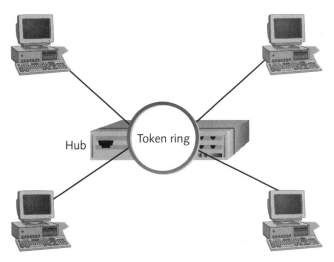

Figure 2-10   Typical star ring network

SELECTING A TOPOLOGY

Many factors deserve consideration when selecting a network topology. Tables 2–1 through 2–3 outline some of the advantages and disadvantages of each topology.

Table 2-1   Advantages and disadvantages of the bus topology

Advantages	Disadvantages
A bus network is simple and reliable.	Heavy traffic slows the network down.
Its cabling is inexpensive, easy to work with, and easy to extend.	Any (broken or unterminated) cable can bring the network down.
Because all computers are arranged in a line, it uses cable very economically.	Problems can be difficult to isolate.

Table 2-2   Advantages and disadvantages of the ring topology

Advantages	Disadvantages
All computers have equal access to the rest of the network.	A single computer failure can impact the network.
Even with many users, network performance is steady.	Isolating problems is sometimes difficult. Adding or removing computers disrupts network operations.

Table 2-3   Advantages and disadvantages of the star topology

Advantages	Disadvantages
It is easy to add new computers or modify the network.	If the central hub fails, the network fails.
Centralization enhances network monitoring and management.	Requires more cable and results in a more intricate installation.
A single computer failure does not affect the rest of the network.	

CONSTRUCTING A NETWORK LAYOUT

Now that you have reviewed the major topologies' benefits and limitations, you are ready to design a simple network. The first step in any network design is to evaluate the underlying requirements.

Begin this evaluation process by determining how the network will be used. Some of the most important questions to ask before constructing your network layout include:

- How many client computers will be attached?

- How many servers will be attached?

- What are the company's plans for expansion?

- What kind of applications will run?

- Will this be a peer-to-peer or server-based network?

- How much fault tolerance do the applications require?

- How much money is available for building this network?

Once you answer these questions, the next step is to begin sketching a network layout. To do this effectively, obtain a copy of your building's blueprints, and mark all planned locations for network resources (such as computers, printers, and so forth), so that all users have access to the resources they need. By sketching a rough design for your network, you can immediately answer many questions about its topology.

After you determine a basic layout, it is time to put your network map into a computer. Many third-party applications are available to make this step easier. One such program, netViz from netViz Corporation, allows you to map any network easily, from a small peer-to-peer network to a global WAN. Figure 2-11 shows a sample network diagram.

2

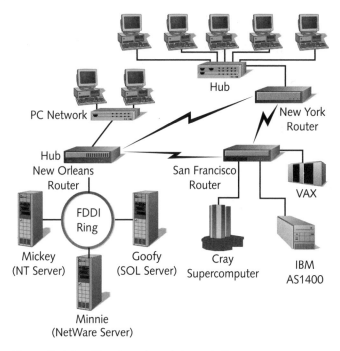

Figure 2-11   Simple network layout diagram

You should include enough detail in your network diagram so anyone can easily understand your network's construction. You may need more than one drawing. For example, the network diagram might include a high-level view of the overall network, followed by detailed maps of office layouts, cable numbers, and patch panels. Any technician should be able to take this map and troubleshoot problems. To be effective, a network diagram must be kept up to date. If you do not immediately document changes made to the network, the map becomes worthless.

CHAPTER SUMMARY

❏ All networks build upon one of three basic topologies. Knowledge of these topologies and their limitations helps ensure informed decisions when designing a network.

❏ The bus topology, the most basic of the topologies, is easy to install but is an outdated topology that should normally not be used for new installations.

❏ The star topology offers centralized management and a higher degree of fault tolerance; a single cable or computer failure does not affect the rest of the network. The star topology is the topology of choice in today's networks.

❏ The ring topology offers computers equal time on the network, but adding computers significantly degrades network performance.

❏ A hub is a central point of concentration for a star network and passes electronic signals to the network. An active hub regenerates the signals; a passive hub simply passes them along. Similar to a hub, a switch offers greater bandwidth and intelligence and provides significant performance advantages over hubs. Due to these advantages and decreasing prices on switches, they have become the device of choice in corporate star topology networks.

❏ Variations on the major topologies allow even greater fault tolerance and flexibility. The mesh is the most tolerant of all network topologies; it allows every computer to communicate with every other computer. A star bus or star ring lends the advantages of star—its centralized management—and the best of the bus and ring topologies.

❏ A network layout should be consistent with the existing network and accurately maintained as the network changes. Many third-party tools are available to assist in design and maintenance.

KEY TERMS

active hub — A network device that regenerates received signals and sends them along the network.

active topology — A network topology in which the computers themselves are responsible for sending the data along the network.

attenuation — The degradation or distortion of an electronic signal as it travels from its origin.

backbone — A single cable segment used in a bus topology to connect computers in a straight line.

bus — A major network topology in which the computers connect to a backbone cable segment to form a straight line.

diagram — A term used to describe a network's design.

Fiber Distributed Data Interface (FDDI) — A high-speed LAN technology that uses dual counter-rotating rings.

hub — The central concentration point of a star network.

hybrid hub — A device used to interconnect different types of cables and to maximize network efficiency.

layout — A term used to describe a network's design.

map — A diagram of a network's layout, including the locations of servers, workstations, computers, jacks, hubs, switches, and so forth, and the type of cabling along segments.

mesh — A hybrid network topology used for fault tolerance, and one in which all computers connect to each other.

passive hub — A central connection point through which signals pass without regeneration.

passive topology — A network topology in which the computers listen to the data signals being sent but do not participate in network communications.

repeater — A device that regenerates electronic signals, so that they can travel a greater distance or accommodate additional computers on a network segment.

ring — Topology consisting of computers connected in a circle, forming a closed ring.

signal bounce — A phenomenon that occurs when a bus is not terminated and signals continue to traverse the network.

star — Major topology in which the computers connect via a central connecting point, usually a hub.

star bus — A network topology that combines the star and bus topologies.

star ring — A network topology wired like a star, which handles traffic like a ring.

switch — A special networking device that manages networked connections between any pair of star-wired devices on a network.

terminator — Used to absorb signals as they reach the end of a bus, thus freeing the network for new communications.

token — Used in some ring topology networks to ensure fair communications between all computers.

token passing — A method of passing data around a ring network.

topology — The basic physical layout of a network.

wireless access point (WAP) — The central device, or hub, through which signals pass in a wireless network.

REVIEW QUESTIONS

1. The term _____ refers to the physical layout of a network's computers, cables, and other resources.

2. Joining together the computers in a network at a central point creates a star topology. Which of the following statements is true of a star topology network?

   a. A cable break can cause all network communications to cease.

   b. Each computer in the network transmits data as it receives it.

   c. It requires significantly more cabling than a bus network.

   d. Due to its configuration, it is difficult to troubleshoot.

3. A bus topology network does not require terminators. True or false?

4. Which of the following statements is true of a ring topology network?

   a. It requires less cabling than a bus topology network.

   b. It provides equal access to all computers on the network.

   c. It must be terminated at each computer.

   d. A single computer failure does not affect network performance.

5. The ___Star___ topology is the most fault tolerant of the hybrid designs.

6. What are two advantages of a star topology network? _fault tolerant / add more ok_

7. What cable type is most often associated with a bus topology network? _backbone segment_
   thin net

8. A cable break in a bus network does not affect network communications. True or false?

9. In a bus network, if the ends of the cable are not terminated, _signal bounce_ occurs.

10. Connecting computers to form a straight line creates a(n) _bus_ topology network.

11. How do switches provide better performance than hubs? _reduces collision Faster! act as a router/link_

12. Because of its central connection point, a(n) _star_ topology network requires a more intricate cable installation.

13. What is the central connecting point in a wireless network called? _antenna/hub_

14. What are two disadvantages of a ring topology network? _single comp failure impact network_
    isolating problem is sometime difficult

15. A bus network is referred to as a(n) _passive_ topology network.

16. List three reasons to keep a network diagram current. _what hub/what comp locate cables obtain more quickly_

17. The term _attenuation_ describes the loss of a signal's strength over distance.

18. What term describes the special packet used in ring networks? _token_

19. A cable break in a star topology network does not affect network communications for the entire network. True or false?

20. FDDI is a form of which standard topology? _Ring_

21. A ring network is a(n) _active_ topology network because the computers are responsible for regenerating the signal.

22. Mainframe computers first used the _Star_ topology.

23. A(n) _active_ hub regenerates the signals it receives and sends them down all other ports.

HANDS-ON PROJECTS

Several of the following projects can be enhanced by students using a network drawing program. A simple-to-use program that can be downloaded for evaluation is SmartDraw. The program can be downloaded at *www.smartdraw.com* and can be installed on individual student workstations.

Project 2-1

Joe's Brokerage House currently has 25 standalone computers and five laser printers fairly evenly distributed across two floors of a building. A print-sharing device lets users share the laser printers, but the computers do not connect to each other. Because of good profits, the network administrator plans expansion and upgrades. The company founder, Joe, thinks that all the computers should be able to communicate, but doesn't want to spend a lot of money. He does, however, want an easily expandable network design. Wiring closets are available on both floors and have conduit between them. The computers must share sensitive data, yet control access to the files. Aside from new brokerage software, which runs on the server, the computers will run standard word-processing and spreadsheet programs.

Use the worksheet that follows to evaluate the requirements for this network.

After you have completed the worksheet, determine the best network topology, or topology combination, for the company. On a blank piece of paper, sketch the network design you think best suits Joe's needs.

Network evaluation worksheet for Hands-on Project 2-1

Will this be a peer-to-peer or a server-based network?

If it is server-based, how many servers will be attached to the network?

How many computers will be attached to the network?

What applications will the computers run?

How many printers will be attached to the network?

Project 2-2

Old-Tech Corporation currently has 10 computers in their main office area, which is networked in a bus topology using 10Base2 Ethernet. They want to add five computers in their manufacturing area. The problem with the existing network is that it keeps going down whenever an employee tinkers with their computer cable. The owner of Old-Tech understands that a bus network is outdated and he wants to upgrade to keep up with technology. The computers they want to add in the manufacturing area present another problem. There is no easy way to run cables to the computers because the ceiling is over

30 feet high, and it would be next to impossible to provide a secure pathway for cables. Provide a solution to this company's networking problems. As part of your solution, answer the following questions.

What topology should be used to make this company's network more up-to-date?

What changes in cable and equipment are required to make this change in topology?

What type of device will connect the computers in the main office area, providing optimum use of the cable bandwidth?

What topology and which type of device can be used in the manufacturing area to solve the problem of difficult cabling?

Project 2-3

EBiz.com currently has 250 networked computers and five servers, and uses a star-wired network to reach employees' offices, with a bus interconnecting three floors in its office building. Because of a staggering influx of Internet business, the network administrator's task is to boost network performance and availability as much as possible. The company also wants a network design that is easy to reconfigure and change, because workgroups continually form and disband, and their membership also changes on a regular basis. All computers must share sensitive data and control access to customer files and databases. Aside from the customer information and billing databases, which run on all servers, workers' desktop computers must run standard word-processing and spreadsheet programs.

Use the worksheet that follows to evaluate the requirements for this network.

After you complete the worksheet, determine the best network topology, or topology combination, for the company. On a blank piece of paper, sketch the network design you think best suits EBiz.com's needs. Remember: High performance and easy reconfiguration are your primary design goals!

Network evaluation worksheet for Hands-on Project 2-3

Will this be a peer-to-peer or a server-based network?

If it is server-based, how many servers will be attached to the network? 5

How many computers will be attached to the network? 255

What applications will the desktop computers run? The servers?

What kind of networking device is easiest to reconfigure? What kind offers the best access to the network medium's bandwidth between pairs of devices? Fiber optical.

Project 2-4

ENormInc currently has two sites in Pittsburgh. Each site consists of a large factory with office space for 25 users at the front of the factory and up to 20 workstations located in two work cells on each factory floor. All office users need access to an inventory database that runs on a server at the Allegheny Street location; they also need access to a billing application whose data resides on a server at the Monongahela site. All factory floor users also need access to the inventory database at the Allegheny Street location. The two locations are four miles apart.

Office space is permanently finished, but ENormInc must tear down and reconfigure before each new manufacturing run begins. There are wiring closets available in the office space. Nothing but a concrete floor and overhead girders stay the same in the work cell areas. The computers must share sensitive data and control access to the files. Aside from the two databases, which run on the two servers, all office computers must run standard word-processing and spreadsheet programs. All work cell machines are strictly used for updating inventory and quality control information for the Allegheny Street inventory database. Workstations in the manufacturing cells are switched on only when they're in use, which may occur during various phases of a manufacturing run. Seldom will a machine be constantly in use on the factory floor.

Use the worksheet that follows to evaluate the requirements for this network.

Once you complete the worksheet, determine the best network topology, or topology combination, for the company. On a blank piece of paper, sketch the network design you think best suits ENormInc's needs.

Network evaluation worksheet for Hands-on Project 2-4

Will this be a peer-to-peer or a server-based network?

If it is server-based, how many servers will be attached to the network?

How many computers will be attached to the network?

What applications will the office computers run? The factory floor computers?

What topology works best for the offices, given the availability of wiring closets? What topology works best for the factory floor, given its need for constant reconfiguration?

What kind of connection must you use to link the Allegheny Street and Monongahela locations?

CASE PROJECTS

1. Henderson & Associates, a mid-sized engineering firm, hired you as a consultant to design their network. The company occupies three floors in a building downtown. There are PCs on all 40 desks and three servers. The company management wants access to all 40 PCs on all floors. The management also wants to keep costs

down but needs a reliable network. Select a topology, or combination of topologies, to service this company. Draw a map of this network.

2. The database manager for your company wants to implement a "server farm" (a collection of servers that communicate via a high-speed link) for the database servers. These servers will be replicated; the network must operate reliably and quickly, yet still be able to connect to other devices (PCs and so forth). Develop two plans, with different topologies, for implementing this server farm; discuss the advantages and disadvantages of each concept.

3. Design networks for two classroom environments—a permanent facility and a traveling classroom. They must have connectivity for 20 PCs and a server, and be inexpensive and easy to set up. Present both versions of this design to the class, and discuss the benefits of each.

4. Design a network for a 3-D imaging firm. It must have connectivity for 40 high-speed imaging workstations and two servers. This network must support high performance and easy reconfiguration into as many as eight workgroups, any of which may have as many as a dozen members. Explain the kind of networking device required to create such an environment and why it's the only choice for this particular kind of networking implementation.

3

NETWORKING MEDIA

After reading this chapter and completing the exercises, you will be able to:

♦ Define and understand technical terms related to cabling, including attenuation, crosstalk, shielding, and plenum

♦ Identify three major types of network cabling and of wireless network technologies

♦ Understand baseband and broadband transmission technologies and when to use each

♦ Decide what kinds of cabling and connections are appropriate for particular network environments

♦ Describe wireless transmission techniques used in LANs

♦ Describe signaling technologies for mobile computing

Most networks today use cables to interconnect various devices. Employing a variety of signaling techniques, network cables ferry signals among computers, allowing them to communicate with one another. Cables are comparable to a highway system, in that each carries payloads from place to place; the payloads on roads are tangible, whereas those on cables consist of sequences of electrical or optical signals.

Although network cables play a vital role in most networks, many different kinds of cables may be used to build networks, each with its own distinguishing set of signal-carrying characteristics. In fact, many major cable manufacturers, such as Belden or Allied Signal, offer thousands of different cable types to their customers. Fortunately, you need to be concerned only with those suitable for network use, which you learn about in this chapter.

Not all computers or networked devices attach to networks by cables. A growing portion of the networking population uses wireless technologies, either because physical obstructions or distance limitations make cables unsuitable or because users are mobile.

Although wireless networking technologies remain more expensive than wired ones, wireless is becoming increasingly attractive for certain uses. Even though wireless components may appear on networks in increasing numbers, this doesn't imply that cable-based networks are waning. On nearly all networks that incorporate wireless components, cable-based components continue to play a major role. Wireless technologies provide a way for members of the networking community who might otherwise be unable to partake of networking's benefits to access the same resources and devices that wired network users have enjoyed for years.

 When designing a network, you must also consider the installation cost of wireless technology, which can often make the total cost of the project lower than using cable.

In this chapter, you learn about the most common options for both cabled and wireless networking and for mobile computing, as well as where such options make sense. You find out about the kinds of transmission technologies involved when making wireless network links, where the majority of a network may be wired but interconnected using wireless links. Finally, you discover the transmission technologies that are most appropriate for users and devices that must be constantly on the move—which is what mobile computing is all about.

NETWORK CABLING: TANGIBLE PHYSICAL MEDIA

Regardless of the kind of media in use, data must enter and leave a computer at some point to allow networked communication to occur. Cabling and wireless communication are at the heart of networked communications because these media supply the network's "glue."

Recall that the interface between a computer and the medium to which it attaches defines the translation from digital information that's native to a computer into whatever form is needed to send outgoing messages. The process is reversed for incoming messages. Therefore, since all media must support the same basic tasks of sending and receiving signals, you can view all networking media as logically equivalent. Because there are so many different types of media, both wired and wireless, it's necessary to thoroughly understand the physical characteristics and limitations of each kind so that you know how best to utilize each type.

As you investigate the various schemes of network cabling in the sections that follow, pay special attention to the tables summarizing each type's fundamental cost and performance characteristics, as well as its device and distance limitations. All these factors play a role when you choose cabling for your own networks.

PRIMARY CABLE TYPES

Fundamentally, all forms of cabling are similar in that they provide a medium across which network information can travel in the form of a physical signal, whether it is a type of electrical transmission or some sequence of light pulses. Given the many types of cable available in today's marketplace, you should be relieved that you need to investigate and understand only three, which represent the vast majority of cabling types used to interconnect networks:

- Coaxial cable

- Twisted-pair (TP) cable, both in unshielded (UTP) and shielded (STP) varieties

- Fiber-optic cable

Each of these types of cabling comes in a variety of forms, and each has unique design and usage characteristics, with associated cost, performance, and installation criteria. The following sections begin with a general discussion of cable characteristics, rating schemes, and common elements of information, and then provide salient details for each of the cabling types.

General Cable Characteristics

All cables share certain fundamental characteristics; studying these characteristics facilitates your understanding of their function and appropriate use. Even though wire-based (or con-ductive) cables differ radically from fiber-optic cables in terms of composition and the types of signals they carry, the following characteristics apply equally to both types of cabling:

- *Bandwidth rating.* Each type of cable can transport only so much data over a given period of time; this is measured in terms of **bandwidth**, which describes how many bits or bytes of information a cable can carry over a unit of time. Typically this is measured in some number of bits per second (for example, megabits per second, or Mbps).

- *Maximum segment length.* Each type of cable can transport data only so far before its signal begins to weaken beyond where it can be read accurately; this phenomenon, as you learned in Chapter 1, is called attenuation. When rating maximum cable segment lengths, the **maximum segment length** value falls within a range where signals can be regenerated correctly and retransmitted accurately. So, an internetwork can be constructed of several such cable segments, provided the hardware interconnecting them can capture and regenerate the incoming signal at full strength.

- *Maximum number of segments per internetwork.* Each type of cable is also subject to a measure called **latency**, which measures the amount of time a signal takes to travel from one end of the cable to another. Most networks are subject to some kind of maximum tolerable delay, after which it's assumed signals can no longer arrive. A network of networks is therefore subject to a maximum number of interconnected segments, simply because of the latency when signals travel from one physical end of the network to another. By arranging cable segments in a hierarchy, a network's span can be quite large, even within these limitations, because the limitations apply to the maximum number of segments between any two particular network segments.

- *Maximum number of devices per segment.* Each time a network device is attached to a cable, a phenomenon called **insertion loss** occurs—that is, each physical connection adds to the attenuation of signals on a cable segment. Therefore, it is necessary to restrict the maximum number of devices so the signals that traverse it are kept clean and strong enough to remain intelligible to all devices. When calculating maximum legal segment lengths, the real formula for distance equals the rated maximum minus the sum of the insertion losses for all devices attached to that segment:

true maximum = rated maximum − (insertion losses)

- *Interference susceptibility.* Each type of cable is more or less susceptible to other signals present in the environment, where such interference may be electromagnetic (called **electromagnetic interference [EMI]**) or may result from other **broadcast signals** (called **radio frequency interference [RFI]**). Motors, transformers, fluorescent lights, and other sources of intense electrical activity can emit both EMI and RFI, but RFI problems are also associated with the proximity of strong broadcast sources in an environment (such as a nearby radio or television station). For the discussion in this chapter, it's necessary to distinguish only four levels of susceptibility: none, low, moderate, and high.

- *Connection hardware.* Every type of cable has associated connectors that influence the kinds of hardware to which the cable can connect and affect the costs of the resulting network. This chapter also describes whether such connectors are easy to attach, if attaching them requires specialized equipment, and whether building such cables should be left to professionals.

- *Cable grade.* Building and fire codes both include specific cabling requirements, usually aimed at the combustibility and toxicity of the **cladding** (sheath material) and insulation that cover most cables. Polyvinyl chloride (PVC) covers the cheapest and most common cables (for example, the 120V cord found on most lamps and other household appliances). Unfortunately, when this material burns it gives off toxic fumes, which make it unsuitable for cables strung in ceilings or inside walls.

  The space between a false ceiling and the true ceiling in most office buildings, called the **plenum**, is commonly used to aid air circulation for heating and cooling. Any cables used in this space must be **plenum-rated**, which typically means they're coated with Teflon because of that material's low combustibility and the relatively nontoxic fumes it produces when burned. Such cables can be used in the plenum area or within walls without being enclosed in conduit. Because it makes installing network cabling significantly cheaper, use of plenum-rated cable is common. All local fire and building codes must be checked since requirements vary greatly in this area.

- *Bend radius.* Although some types of cabling are less prone to damage from bending than others, bending many types beyond a prescribed **bend radius** damages or destroys them. This is particularly true of the most expensive types of cable; for networks, this means primarily that fiber-optic and heavy-duty coaxial cables must be treated with care. Most of the more sensitive cable types cannot be bent more than 60 degrees in a one-foot span without sustaining some damage. The key is to understand the limitations of the cabling itself and not to bend it past its limits.

- *Material costs.* Each type of cable has an associated cost per unit length. This is a good way to compare cables of the same type to one another. However, it's important to understand that building or fire codes may prohibit the use of cheaper cables in many instances, and that the cost of the cable itself is usually less than half the cost of a total installation. Also note that leaving room for faster technologies may mandate buying more expensive cabling to begin with; but it's always cheaper to reuse existing cable than it is to reinstall, so it may save money in the long run.

- *Installation costs.* Labor and auxiliary equipment can easily cost more than the cable when installing a network. That's why it's important to cost out the design, installation, and troubleshooting of your cabling (sometimes called the "cable plant"), as well as to budget for the necessary cabling, connectors, wall plates, patch panels or punchdown blocks, and other items required for a complete and functioning network. These items are discussed later in this chapter.

Now that you understand the general characteristics of cabling, as well as which characteristics influence selection of a particular cable type (or collection of cable types for larger networks), you should appreciate the significance of the strengths and weaknesses of the various cabling types discussed in this chapter. Before you learn the details about coaxial, twisted-pair, and fiber-optic cable, however, you also must understand the two primary techniques for sending signals across a cable, namely, baseband and broadband transmission.

Baseband and Broadband Transmission

Baseband transmission uses a digital encoding scheme at a single, fixed frequency, where signals take the form of discrete pulses of electricity or light. In a baseband system, the entire bandwidth of the cable is used to transmit a single data signal. This means that baseband systems use only one channel on which all devices attached to the cable can communicate. Baseband transmission also limits any single cable strand to half-duplex transmission (where only one sender consumes the entire cable's bandwidth); full-duplex implementations that use baseband transmission must therefore use two strands of cable and two network interfaces for each device—one for sending data, the other for receiving data.

As a signal travels along a network cable, its strength decreases as the distance from the signal transmitter increases. Likewise, the degree of distortion also increases as the distance from the transmitter increases. The reason each cabling type has a maximum segment length is to ensure that signals on a cable remain intelligible across its entire length. Signal flow on a baseband cable can also be bidirectional, so that computers can use a single cable for both transmission and reception. (But on a single cable, only one role may be played at any given time.)

Baseband systems—such as Ethernet—use special devices called **repeaters** that receive incoming signals on one cable segment and refresh them before retransmitting them on another cable segment. That way, they can restore the signal to its original strength and quality before shipping it out on another cable, thereby extending the span that a network can cover. As with maximum segment lengths and devices per segment, most cabling is limited by the number of such repeaters which can separate any two cable segments on an internetwork.

Broadband transmission systems use a different kind of signaling to transmit information across a cable. Instead of digital pulses, broadband systems use **analog** techniques to encode information across a continuous range of values, rather than using the binary zeros and ones that characterize digital data in a baseband environment. Broadband signals move across the medium in the form of continuous electromagnetic or optical waves, rather than in discrete pulses. On broadband systems, signal flow is one-way only, which makes two channels necessary for computers to send and receive data. (This arrangement also makes full-duplex communications much easier to arrange on broadband systems.)

Where the cabling supports sufficient bandwidth, multiple analog transmission channels may operate on a single broadband cable. This capability permits your cable television company to send such a large number of television channels across a single wire. But where multiple channels are used, the sending and receiving equipment must be able to "tune in" the correct channel to permit senders and receivers to communicate with one another.

Because of the differences between analog and digital signaling technologies, broadband cable segments are interlinked with devices called **amplifiers** that detect weak signals, strengthen those signals, and then rebroadcast them. Because two channels are needed for computers to send and receive data on broadband cabling, there are two primary approaches to supporting two-way broadband communications:

- So-called **mid-split broadband** uses a single cable but divides the bandwidth into two channels, each on a different frequency. Here, one channel transmits, and the other receives network communications.

- **Dual-cable broadband** uses two cables; each computer or networked device must connect to both simultaneously. Here, one cable transmits, and the other receives network communications. (This works for broadband the same way that it does for baseband when full-duplex communications must occur.)

Traditionally, broadband systems offered higher bandwidths than baseband systems. For example, original Ethernet cable supports 10 Mbps, but ordinary TV cable supports the equivalent of 250 Mbps or more. Today, higher-speed networking alternatives for both technologies blur this distinction, but broadband systems remain generally more expensive than baseband systems (of comparable bandwidth), because of the broadband system's need for multiple cables or channels and for tuners and amplifiers for each channel.

The Importance of Bandwidth

Anyone who's ever spent any time online knows the faster the connection, the better. Because accessing information and services is the name of the game in networking, and more, faster access is clearly better than less, slower access, it's impossible to overstate the importance of bandwidth when making any kind of network connection.

The trend in networking is to offer more complex, more comprehensive, and more powerful services—including services such as real-time video teleconferencing, voice-only networking services, streaming video and audio, and other high-bandwidth applications. While all of these services permit users to get more from their networks than ever before, they also require much higher bandwidth to deliver an acceptable quality of service. Thus, a set of parallel trends in networking is for technologists to deliver ever-higher amounts of bandwidth, and for application developers to build software that requires more bandwidth to operate. Users demand access to such applications and are increasing their use of existing networked applications, consuming still more bandwidth.

As you make your way through this chapter, notice that newer networking technologies are invariably faster and often more powerful than older ones. At the same time, technologists keep finding ways to stretch the bandwidth limits of existing technologies—especially networking media—so that older, difficult-to-replace networking components (such as cabling) can often remain in place, yet still support higher bandwidth than originally rated. Now that you understand basic cabling characteristics and the primary transmission systems, you're ready for the details of the various cabling types, which follow.

Coaxial Cable

For many years, **coaxial cable**—often called "coax" for short—was the predominant form of network cabling. Relatively inexpensive and reasonably easy to install, coaxial cable was the networker's choice. Recent improvements in electronics and signaling technologies conspired to knock coax off its pedestal, however, as the next section describes.

Simply put, coaxial cable consists of a single conductor at the core, surrounded by an insulating layer, braided metal **shielding** (called **braiding**), and an outer cover (usually called the **sheath**, or jacket), as shown in Figure 3-1. The networking signals carried by the coax cable travel over the central conductor; the remaining elements protect coax cable from external influences, whether they are electrical, mechanical, or environmental.

Some versions of coax, called dual-shielded, surround the braided metal shield with an additional layer of metallic foil. An even more robust version of coax, called quad-shielded, is also available; as its name suggests, quad-shielded coax incorporates four layers, two of foil insulation and two of braided metal shield. Obviously, more shielding translates into greater cable costs; it also translates into lowered susceptibility to interference.

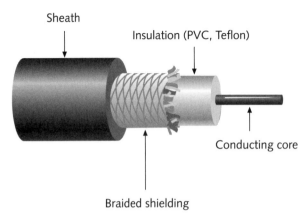

Sheath

Insulation (PVC, Teflon)

Conducting core

Braided shielding

Figure 3-1   Coaxial cable

Shielding refers to any protective layers wrapped around a cable used to protect the cable from external interference (EMI or RFI). Shielding increases the viability of the signals that pass through a cable. It does so by absorbing stray electronic signals or fields, so that they do not impinge on the data that the conductor (or conductors) within the cable itself must carry. Shielding works like a form of built-in **conduit**, a type of metal or plastic pipe built specifically to contain cabling. In a sense, conduit represents the ultimate form of shielding.

In a coaxial cable, an insulating layer surrounds the core that carries networking signals, isolating it from the shielding. If that insulation is absent or gets damaged, the conductor may make contact with the shielding (or some other conductive material); when this happens, a short (for short circuit) results, which prevents the cable from carrying any network traffic at all.

Coaxial cable is less susceptible to interference and attenuation than twisted-pair cabling, but more susceptible than fiber-optic cable. This is due in part to the beneficial influence of coax cable's shielding, which absorbs environmental interference and diminishes its impact on coax cable's ability to transport information. Nevertheless, when coax cable must pass through especially noisy environments—that is, near transformers or large electrical motors—it's wise to run the cable through metal conduit to provide extra shielding.

Types of Coaxial Cable

For Ethernet, there are two types of coaxial cable, called thin Ethernet (also known as **thinnet**, **thinwire**, or **cheapernet**) and thick Ethernet (also known as **thicknet** or **thickwire**). The **Institute of Electrical and Electronics Engineers (IEEE)** designates these cable types as **10Base2** and **10Base5**, respectively, where this notation indicates:

- *Total bandwidth for the technology.* In this case, 10 means 10 megabits per second (Mbps) and applies equally to both thin and thick varieties.

- *Base.* The network uses baseband signaling for both types of cable.

- *2 or 5.* Roughly indicates maximum segment length, measured in hundreds of meters. Thinwire (10Base2) originally supported 200 meters but was reduced to a maximum segment length of 185 meters to compensate for patch cables; thickwire (10Base5) supports a maximum segment length of 500 meters.

Thinwire Ethernet (a.k.a. Thinnet)

Thinwire Ethernet cabling is a thin, flexible cable approximately 0.25" (0.64 cm) in diameter. Thinwire cabling is easy to work with and relatively inexpensive to build or buy. (Prefabricated cables in many lengths are widely available.) Thinwire is especially well suited for small or constantly changing networks. Using **BNC** T-connectors, thinwire cables attach more or less directly to networking devices and to each computer's network adapter card, as shown in Figure 3-2.

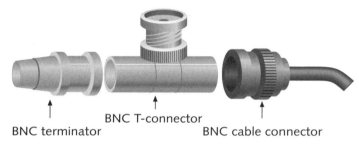

BNC terminator   BNC T-connector   BNC cable connector

Figure 3-2   BNC cable connector

Working with the U.S. military, cable manufacturers have designated so-called **Radio Government (RG)** specifications for various types of cable, including many varieties of coax. Thinnet belongs to a group called the RG-58 family and has a characteristic impedance of 50 ohms. (**Impedance**, measured in ohms, is the electrical resistance to current flowing in this type of cable.) The main differences among the various members of the RG-58 family lie with the center conductor. For some members of the family, this conductor is solid wire; in others, it has a braided core. Table 3-1 compares some members of the RG cable family.

Table 3-1   Well-known types of RG cable

Designation	Type	Impedance	Description
RG-58/U	Thinwire	50 ohms	Solid copper core (U stands for utility grade; **not** recognized as valid thinwire cable by IEEE 802.3 specifications)
RG-58 A/U	Thinwire	50 ohms	Stranded copper core (A/U indicates a tinned copper braid as the center conductor with foam dielectric insulator)
RG-58 C/U	Thinwire	50 ohms	Military version of RG-58 A/U (uses a solid dielectric insulator)

Table 3-1   Well-known types of RG cable (continued)

Designation	Type	Impedance	Description
RG-59	CATV	75 ohms	Broadband cable; used for cable television (CATV) and sometimes for ARCnet
RG-6	Broadband	75 ohms	Larger diameter, higher bandwidth than RG-59; used as CATV drop cable
RG-62	Baseband	93 ohms	Used for ARCnet and IBM 3270 terminals
RG-8	Thickwire	50 ohms	Solid core; approximately 0.4" in diameter
RG-11	Thickwire	75 ohms	Stranded core; approximately 0.4" in diameter; used for CATV trunk lines

Table 3-2 summarizes the key characteristics of thinwire Ethernet cable.

Table 3-2   Thinwire Ethernet characteristics

Characteristic	Value
Maximum cable length	185 meters (607 feet)
Bandwidth	10 Mbps
Bend radius	360 degrees/ft
Installation/maintenance	Easy to install and reroute; flexible
Cost	Cheapest form of coax cable; prefabricated cables average $1/foot
Connector type	British Naval Connector* (BNC)
Security	Susceptible to eavesdropping
Interference rating	Good: lower than thicknet, higher than TP

*   Research reveals numerous decodings for the BNC acronym that names thinwire Ethernet and thicknet connectors. These include British Naval Connector (preferred Microsoft usage), bayonet nut connector, bayonet navy connector, and bayonet Neill-Concelman.

Thickwire Ethernet (a.k.a. Thicknet)

Thickwire Ethernet is a rigid coaxial cable about 0.4" (approximately 1 cm) in diameter. It's often covered with a bright-yellow Teflon coating and commonly described as "frozen yellow garden hose," which accurately conveys its rigidity. You may sometimes hear thicknet described as Standard Ethernet because it was the first type of cable used for this kind of networking technology. However, its expense and lack of ductility, or flexibility, ensure that it's now the least commonly used type of Ethernet cable.

Thickwire's increased diameter does confer some advantages, namely, even greater resistance to interference and better conductivity. This translates into a longer maximum cable segment length and an increase in the number of devices that may attach to a single segment. In fact, thickwire's ability to carry signals over longer distances, coupled with its superior interference resistance, helps explain why this type of cable is most commonly used for backbones—heavy-duty, long-run cables—that interconnect smaller thinnet- or twisted-pair-based network segments.

Whereas thinwire Ethernet cables connect directly to network interfaces, as shown in Figure 3-3, attaching to thickwire Ethernet takes a different approach, as shown in Figure 3-4. For thickwire, it's most common to use a device called a **vampire tap** to attach a device to the cable, which in turn attaches to a **transceiver** (an abbreviation for **transmitter/receiver**). Installation of the TAP needs to be done carefully since it involves actually drilling into the wire, which can result in a short. The transceiver then attaches to a drop or transceiver cable that plugs into an **attachment unit interface (AUI)** on the computer NIC or on other devices to be attached to the network.

Figure 3-3   BNC T-connector

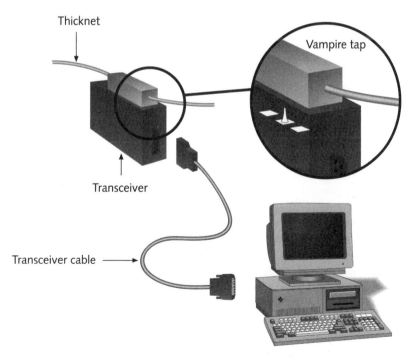

Figure 3-4   Thicknet cable transceiver with detail of a vampire tap piercing the core

Because transceiver cables can be up to 50 meters long (approximately 164 feet), this gives some latitude when running thickwire cable; its path does not have to snake from system to system. Thinwire, on the other hand, must go from system to system because the network cable attaches directly to the network interface on the computer or other device. As long as the distance between the cable and the computer remains under 50 meters, thickwire Ethernet requires less network cable than thinwire. On the other hand, the necessary transceivers and transceiver cables make thickwire more expensive than thinwire. The increased expense of using thickwire, its larger diameter, and its lack of flexibility all explain its rare use for new network installations today. Table 3-3 summarizes the characteristics of thickwire.

Table 3-3   Thickwire Ethernet characteristics

Characteristic	Value
Maximum cable length	500 meters (1640 feet)
Bandwidth	10 Mbps
Bend radius	30 degrees/ft
Installation/maintenance	Hard to install and reroute; rigid
Cost	More expensive than thinwire, cheaper than fiber
Connector type	BNC
Security	Susceptible to eavesdropping
Interference rating	Good: lowest of all electrical cable types

All the various types of Ethernet coaxial cable also have one additional requirement to create a working network. A connector (a female BNC for thinwire and thickwire) must cap each end of a cable, and a terminator must screw into each end connector. Terminators essentially "soak up" signals that arrive at the end of the cable; otherwise, they would bounce and reflect back up the cable, interfering with network traffic. Without proper termination, a coax-based Ethernet network cannot work.

The two features that make coaxial cable an attractive medium are its ability to carry signals a relatively long distance and its resistance to interference. However, its relatively low bandwidth capability, coupled with its expense, makes coaxial cable in LAN applications a dying breed of media. As you will see, twisted-pair, fiber-optic, and wireless media rule in the majority of today's applications.

Coaxial Cable in Cable Modem Applications

Whereas coaxial cable's use as the primary medium in LAN applications is becoming obsolete, the use of coaxial cable to access the Internet is exploding. The standard cable (75 Ohm, RG-59) that delivers cable television (CATV) to millions of homes nationwide is also being used to deliver Internet access to those homes.

A typical configuration for a home Internet connection using **cable modem** is depicted in Figure 3-5. Cable modem Internet access uses broadband technology to carry Internet data signals and cable television channels on the same medium. Typical cable modem connections provide 256 Kbps or 512 Kbps bandwidth to home users, but the technology is capable of carrying data at much higher rates. Because cable modem uses a shared medium, the bandwidth that any one connection receives depends on the number of active connections in a particular neighborhood. The more active connections on a cable segment, the less total bandwidth any one modem will receive.

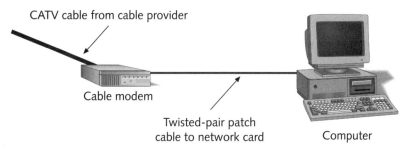

Figure 3-5   Typical cable modem connection

Other Coaxial Cable Types

As you may have noticed in Table 3-1, coaxial cable works for other types of networks besides Ethernet and CATV. Other applications for coax include ARCnet and computer terminal attachments to mainframes and minicomputers.

ARCnet is an acronym for **attached resource computing network**. ARCnet is an older networking technology developed at DataPoint Corporation in the early 1980s. It supports bandwidth of only 2.5 Mbps, which probably explains why it has faded from use on modern networks. It is interesting that one type of coaxial cable that works for ARCnet—namely, 93 ohm RG-62—was originally developed to support IBM 3270 terminals attached to a mainframe. This is a historical example of reusing an existing slower technology for what was a much faster form of networking when it was introduced. ARCnet also works with 75-ohm RG-59 coaxial cable, still widely used for CATV drop cables (the cables that run from the telephone pole or junction box into your house). Finally, ARCnet implementations that use fiber-optic and twisted-pair cable are also available.

Twisted-Pair Cable

The most basic form of **twisted-pair (TP)** wiring consists of one or more pairs of insulated strands of copper wire twisted around one another. These twists are important because they cause the magnetic fields that form around a conducting wire to wrap around one another and improve TP's resistance to interference, while also limiting the influence of signals traveling on one wire over another (called **crosstalk**). In fact, the more twists per unit length, the better these characteristics become. It's safe to say, therefore, that more expensive TP wire is usually more twisted than less expensive kinds.

There are two primary types of TP cable: **unshielded twisted-pair (UTP)**, which simply contains one or more pairs of insulated wires within an enclosing insulating sheath, and **shielded twisted-pair (STP)**, which encloses each pair of wires within a foil shield, as well as within an enclosing insulating sheath. Figure 3-6 depicts both types of wire.

Shielded twisted-pair (STP)

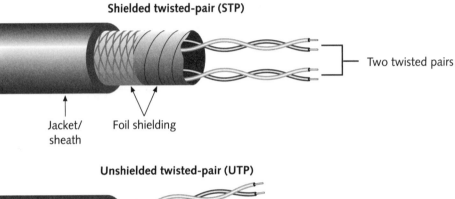

Two twisted pairs

Jacket/
sheath   Foil shielding

Unshielded twisted-pair (UTP)

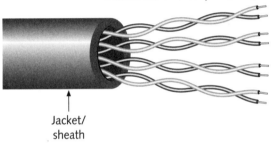

Jacket/
sheath

Figure 3-6   STP and UTP cable

TP wiring, whether shielded or unshielded, comes in many forms. Many networks commonly use one-, two-, four-, six-, and eight-pair wiring; some forms of TP wiring may bundle as many as 50 or 100 pairs within a single cable.

Unshielded Twisted-Pair (UTP)

Another version of the IEEE Ethernet specification is called **10BaseT**; here, T stands for UTP and represents another type of Ethernet cabling. In fact, 10BaseT is now the most popular form of LAN cabling, even though the maximum length of a 10BaseT segment is 100 meters, or 328 feet.

The UTP cable used for networking usually includes one or more pairs of insulated wires. UTP specifications govern the number of twists per foot (or per meter), depending on the cable's intended use. Because it's the type of cable used for telephone systems, UTP is common in most office buildings and other work environments. But voice telephony is much less demanding than networking in terms of bandwidth and signal quality. Thus, even though it may be tempting to try to turn unused telephone wiring into network connections, it's not worth attempting this unless a cable technician tests those lines and pronounces them fit for network use.

UTP cabling is rated according to a number of categories devised by the **Electronic Industries Alliance (EIA)** and the **Telecommunications Industries Association (TIA)**; since 1991, the **American National Standards Institute (ANSI)** has also endorsed these standards. A document known as the *ANSI/EIA/TIA 568 Commercial Building Wiring Standard* defines standards that apply to the kinds of wiring used in commercial environments. This set of standards helps ensure consistent performance from wiring products that adhere to its requirements. The ANSI/EIA/TIA 568 standard currently includes five categories for unshielded twisted-pair wiring, as follows:

- *Category 1*. Applies to traditional UTP telephone cabling, which is designed to carry voice but not data. Most UTP installed prior to 1982 falls into this category.

- *Category 2*. Certifies UTP cabling for bandwidth up to 4 Mbps and consists of four pairs of wire. Since 4 Mbps is slower than most networking technologies in use today (except for original token ring installations and ARCnet), Category 2 is rarely encountered in networking environments.

- *Category 3*. Certifies UTP cabling for bandwidth up to 10 Mbps, with signaling rates up to 16 MHz. This includes most conventional networking technologies, such as 10BaseT Ethernet, 4 Mbps token ring, ARCnet, and more. Category 3 consists of four pairs, each pair having a minimum of three twists per foot (10 twists per meter). 100VG-AnyLAN is also rated to work on Category 3 cable, but testing is recommended for older installations. Cat 3 remains in use in many older networks, but should be replaced as the networks are upgraded. Most networks are migrating towards 100 Mbps speeds for which Cat 3 is not suitable.

- *Category 4*. Certifies UTP cabling for bandwidth up to 16 Mbps, with signaling rates up to 20 MHz. This includes primarily 10BaseT Ethernet and 16 Mbps token ring. This is the first ANSI/EIA/TIA designation that labels the cables as **datagrade** rather than **voicegrade**. Category 4 consists of four pairs.

- *Category 5*. Certifies UTP cabling for bandwidth up to 100 Mbps, with signaling rates up to 100 MHz. This includes 100BaseX, Asynchronous Transfer Mode (ATM) networking technologies at 25 and 155 Mbps, plus FDDI at 100 Mbps, as governed by the Twisted-pair, Physical Media Dependent (TP-PMD) specification. Some experimental implementations of Gigabit Ethernet use Category 5 cable, but standards are yet undefined for this technology. Category 5 also uses four pairs.

- *Category 5E*. Category 5 Enhanced UTP cabling, as the name suggests, is an enhancement to Category 5 UTP. It differs primarily in the tests it must undergo and was designed to correct some of the shortcomings in Category 5 cabling, particularly in the areas of Gigabit Ethernet and full-duplex operation. Category 5E is the current acceptable cabling standard for new installations, as specified by EIA/TIA 568A.

- *Category 6*. This standard, while not completely defined as of this writing, is expected to be the accepted UTP cabling standard for Gigabit Ethernet over copper. Category 6 cabling will use the same type of modular jack as lower categories and will be backward compatible with Category 5 and Category 5E cabling plants.

- *Category 7*. While still in the early stages, this standard specifies a fully shielded twisted-pair cable (each wire pair is shielded, as is the outer jacket) with performance characteristics well above earlier cabling standards. Due to a different connecting hardware design, Category 7 cable and connectors will not likely be backward compatible.

Of the categories of UTP cabling listed, Category 5 and Category 5E are by far the most popular types of cable in use today. Their huge installed base guarantees that developers of new high-speed networking technologies will strive to make their technologies compatible with these categories of UTP cable. This is evident in the fact that Category 5 cable, which originally was designed for 10 Mbps Ethernet, is capable of running at speeds up to 1 Gigabit.

UTP is particularly prone to crosstalk, and the shielding included with STP is designed specifically to mitigate this problem.

Shielded Twisted-Pair (STP)

As its name indicates, STP includes shielding to reduce crosstalk as well as to limit the effects of external interference. For most STP cables, this means that the wiring includes a wire braid inside the cladding or sheath material, as well as a foil wrap around each individual wire pair. This shielding improves the cable's transmission and interference characteristics, which, in turn, support higher bandwidth over longer distances than UTP. Unfortunately, no set of standards for STP corresponds to the ANSI/EIA/TIA 568 Standard for UTP, yet it's not unusual to find STP cables rated according to those standards. STP uses two pairs of 150 Ohm wire as defined by the IBM cabling system and was not designed to be used in Ethernet applications, but it can be adapted to do so using special impedance matching transformers.

Another type of shielded twisted pair is Screened Twisted Pair (ScTP) or Foil Twisted Pair (FTP). Both use 100 ohm, four-pair cabling, just like UTP. The cabling is wrapped in a metal foil or screen. This type of cabling can be used in place of UTP in electrically noisy environments.

Whether STP or UTP, twisted-pair network cabling most commonly employs **RJ-45**, or **registered jack (RJ)** #45, telephone connectors to plug into computer network interfaces or other networked devices. This connector looks very much like the **RJ-11** connector seen on modular telephone jacks, except that it's larger and contains eight wire traces rather than the four housed in an RJ-11. Figure 3-7 depicts the RJ-45 connector.

3

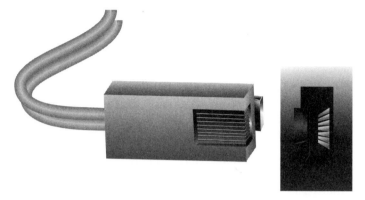

Figure 3-7   RJ-45 connector and jack

The longevity of telephone wire management systems and components, and the fact that twisted-pair networks can use the same kinds of equipment, help explain the burgeoning popularity of twisted-pair network cabling schemes of all kinds. Such systems typically include the following elements, often in a **wiring center**.

- Distribution racks, **punchdown blocks**, and modular shelving help organize cables and permit them to be arranged vertically to conserve floor space. In many companies, phone closets are used for both telephone and network wire management.

- Modular **patch panels** permit nearly arbitrary arrangements of connections. Many such panels for bandwidth up to 100, and even 155, Mbps are available today. The increasing use of Gigabit Ethernet (1000 Mbps) promises that even higher-bandwidth solutions for this kind of equipment should be forthcoming.

- **Wall plates** are special built-in receptacles that appear in many offices. Like electrical outlets, such plates supply access to voice and network connections and sometimes even to fiber-optic or private broadcast video outlets. Modular wall plates make it much easier to wire offices and also provide a single point of access for all kinds of communications (typically, voice, data, and video).

- **Jack couplers** are special RJ-45-terminated TP cables that permit modular cables to stretch between wall plates (where built-in wiring terminates) and equipment (where the cables span the gap from wall to network interface).

All this specialized technology keeps unsightly wiring out of the way and lets network configuration be handled behind the scenes at a punchdown block or a patch panel (both depicted in Figure 3-8) without requiring cables to be rerouted. In fact, many organizations choose to run lots of unused wiring pairs when cabling offices to allow for easy growth.

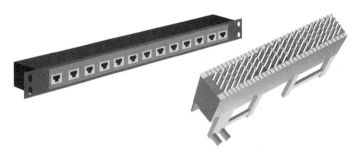

Figure 3-8   Patch panel (left) and punchdown block (right)

Twisted-pair cabling is usually the first consideration when deciding on a network cabling scheme. It's also often the final choice, provided that its use isn't precluded. Most office environments include a place for TP wiring schemes, if only as a way to bring network connections to individual offices or workspaces, even when coax or fiber backbones interlink vast internetworks behind the scenes.

Normally, the only reasons that twisted-pair would not play at least some role in a network would be if bandwidth or distance requirements rule out TP, or in signal-rich environments (such as power plants or factory floors), where TP's high susceptibility to interference renders it unsuitable for networking use. For easy reference, Table 3-4 summarizes 10BaseT's networking characteristics.

Table 3-4   10BaseT Ethernet characteristics

Characteristic	Value
Maximum cable length	100 meters (328 feet)
Bandwidth	10 Mbps
Bend radius	TP not subject to bend radius limitations
Installation/maintenance	Easy to install, no need to reroute; the most flexible
Cost	Least expensive of all cabling options
Connector type	RJ-45 for device and wall-plate connections
Security	Moderately susceptible to eavesdropping
Interference rating	Low: most susceptible of all electrical cable types

Fiber-Optic Cable

Fiber-optic cable trades electrical pulses for their optical equivalents, which are pulses of light. Because no electrical signals ever pass through the cable, fiber-optic media is as immune to interference as any medium can get. This also makes fiber-optic cables highly secure. They emit no external signals that might be detected, unlike electrical or broadcast media, thereby eliminating the possibility of **electronic eavesdropping**. In particular, fiber-optic cable is a good medium for high-bandwidth, high-speed, long-distance data transmissions because of its lower attenuation characteristics and vastly higher data-handling capacities.

Fiber-optic cable consists of a slender cylinder of glass fiber, or a bundle of glass fibers, called the core, surrounded by a concentric layer of cladding material and then by an outer sheath. Figure 3-9 depicts fiber-optic cable. Sometimes, the core may consist of plastic rather than glass fibers; plastic is more flexible and less sensitive to damage than glass, but more vulnerable to attenuation. It cannot span the enormous distances that glass fiber-based cables can.

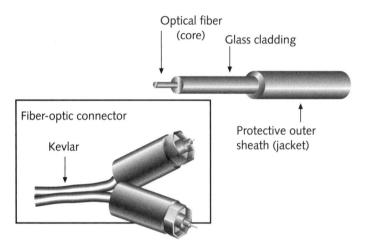

Figure 3-9   Fiber-optic cable

In any fiber-optic cable, each light-conducting core can pass signals in only one direction (so that one end is always the sender and the other always the receiver). This means that most types of fiber-optic cable incorporate two strands, each contained within separate cladding; but such cables may be enclosed within a single sheath, or **jacket**, or may be two separate cables, each with its own sheath or jacket. In most forms of fiber-optic cable, an insulating layer of plastic or glass surrounds the light-conducting fibers at the core for reinforcement and to maintain a consistent diameter. Kevlar fibers are used as sheathing because they are extremely strong and resist shearing.

Fiber-optic cable is not subject to likely forms of electrical interference. Also, fiber-optic cable supports extremely high bandwidth. Today, commercial implementations at 1 gigabit per second (Gbps) are available, and experimental 10 Gbps implementations are already in use.

Some testing has shown that glass fibers can carry as much as 200 Gbps. Best of all, the maximum segment length for fiber is best measured in miles (or kilometers), as shown in Table 3-5.

Table 3-5   Fiber-optic cable characteristics

Characteristic	Value
Maximum cable length	2 km (6562 feet)–100 km (62.14 miles)
Bandwidth	100 Mbps–1 Gbps
Bend radius	30 degrees/ft
Installation/maintenance	Difficult to install and reroute, sensitive to strain and bending
Cost	Most expensive of all cabling options
Connector type	Several types: ST, SC, MIC, MT-RJ, and SMA
Security	Not susceptible to eavesdropping
Interference rating	None: least susceptible of all cable types

Notice the wide variety of connectors for fiber-optic media. The number of options is related to the number of different kinds of light-emitting sources used to generate, and the corresponding light-detecting sensors used to detect, light pulses traveling across the medium. Their definitions follow:

- *(Straight tip) ST*. ST connectors join individual fibers at interconnects or to optical devices. They appear most often in Ethernet networks that use fiber-optic cable as backbones. Like a BNC connector, an ST connector locks onto the jack when twisted.

- *(Straight connection) SC*. SC connectors push on, which makes them easy to install and requires less space for an attachment. SC connectors make a strong connection and may be used when splicing fiber-optic cables. An SC connector is a one-piece component, with two receptacles for sending and receiving fibers. A notch in its jacket ensures proper orientation when inserted.

- *(Medium interface connector) MIC*. MIC connectors are used for the Fiber Distributed Data Interface (FDDI). Like SC connectors, MIC connectors are one-piece constructions.

- *(Subminiature type A) SMA*. A company called Amphenol originally designed SMA connectors for microwave use and later modified them for fiber-optic use. Two SMA versions are widely available: the 905 uses a straight ferrule, which is a metal sleeve used to strengthen the connector, whereas the 906 uses a stepped ferrule with a plastic sleeve to ensure precise alignment of the fibers. Like ST connectors, SMAs use two individual connectors for each fiber strand.

- *MT-RJ*. The MT-RJ connector, as the name implies, looks a little like an RJ-45 connector. It provides a high-density fiber-optic connection utilizing two fiber-optic cables. Compared to other connector types, the use of MT-RJ connectors takes only half the space for the same number of cable terminations. Besides saving space, the MT-RJ advantages include ease of installation and the requirement of only one connector for a two-fiber termination.

Installation of fiber-optic networks is somewhat more difficult and time-consuming than copper media installation, but this is changing. Advances in connector technology make field termination of fiber-optic cables almost as fast and easy as copper terminations. Whereas the connectors and test equipment required for proper termination are still considerably more expensive than their copper counterparts, the trend toward easier, more affordable fiber-optic networks is continuing to where fiber-optic cable to the desktop is a feasible option.

Fiber-optic cables come in two primary types: single-mode cables, which include only one glass fiber at the core; and multimode cables, which incorporate two or more glass fibers at their cores. Single-mode cable costs more and generally works with laser-based emitters but spans the longest distances; multimode cables cost less and work with **light emitting diodes (LEDs)** but span shorter distances.

Historically, fiber-optic cable's high cost and difficult installation meant that it was used only when a network required extremely high bandwidth or to span long distances between individually wired network segments. However, because of the falling costs of fiber and the inherent advantages of this medium with respect to interference immunity, high bandwidth capability, and security, fiber-optic cable is being used almost exclusively for all network backbone connections. Likewise, it is the medium of choice for cable-based, long-haul telecommunications, where large amounts of voice and data traffic are routinely aggregated.

Cable Selection Criteria

Given so many different kinds of networking cable from which to choose, making a selection may seem daunting. But as you consider the following criteria for any particular network installation, the corresponding choices emerge:

- *Bandwidth: How fast must the network be?* Higher bandwidth means more expensive cable and higher installation costs. The higher the bandwidth requirements, the more likely you are to use a less flexible, more heavily shielded, if not fiber-optic, cable.

- *Budget: How much money can you spend on cabling?* Can the network be deployed piecemeal? Sometimes, budget alone dictates a choice. Since all the cabling types have been ranked by cost, it should be easy to tell what the budget dictates.

- *Capacity: How much traffic must the network carry? How will the traffic flow?* Planning a network layout to separate light-to-moderate users from heavy users, and to separate the backbone traffic from local user traffic is generally a good idea. Such considerations can also affect cable choices and equipment requirements.

- *Environmental considerations: How noisy is the deployment environment? How important is data security?* Sometimes signal-rich environments or security requirements can dictate cable choices, regardless of other factors. The higher either factor weighs, the more likely it becomes that you choose fiber-optic cable.

■ *Placement: Where will the cables run? How tight are the spaces?* Requirements for cable flexibility, access, and routing also weigh heavily on cable selection, particularly where there are tight spaces or it's necessary to avoid obstacles. The higher the need for sharp bends or high flexibility, the more likely the selection of thinwire Ethernet or TP cable becomes.

■ *Scope: How many devices must connect to the network?* By itself, this can sometimes dictate cable selection, but when the number exceeds 50 to 100, multisegment networks are generally necessary. For single-segment networks, you need to weigh the ability to attach more devices against thickwire's higher costs.

■ *Span: What kind of distance must the network span?* Longer spans need more expensive, higher-bandwidth cables, if not more exotic options. (This chapter covers more exotic options later in the section, "Wireless Extended LAN Technologies.") Strategic placement of small hubs for use with TP wiring, interlinked by either fiber or coax cable, gives TP surprising reach in many office environments where workers tend to cluster in groups, even if those groups are widely scattered.

■ *Local requirement:* Local building and fire code officials must approve any new installation and should be consulted before installation decisions are made.

■ *Existing cable plant:* For a new installation, only the previously listed criteria need be considered, but for an upgrade, the existing cable plant must be considered. For example, if some of the existing cable is to remain, is it compatible with the speeds and new equipment that are planned?

At one extreme, where money is no object and the need for speed or long spans is great, fiber-optic cable is an obvious choice. At the other end of the spectrum, where quick, cheap, and easy networking is desirable, either UTP with a small, inexpensive hub or thinwire Ethernet does the job. Hybrid networks are also common, where coax or fiber-optic cables provide a backbone that ties together individual clusters of devices networked with TP cable through hubs and wiring centers.

Table 3-6 condenses the most important cabling information for the various cable types covered so far in this chapter.

Table 3-6 Comparison of general cable characteristics

Type	Maximum Length	Bandwidth	Installation	Interference	Cost
UTP	100m	10–100 Mbps	Easy	High	Cheapest
STP	100m	16–1000 Mbps	Moderate	Moderate	Moderate
10Base2	185m	10 Mbps	Easy	Moderate	Cheap
10Base5	500m	10 Mbps	Hard	Low	Expensive
Fiber	2–100 km	100 Mbps–10 Gbps	Moderate	None	Most expensive

The IBM Cabling System

IBM has developed its own cabling system, which includes its own cable ratings, with corresponding standards, designations, and specifications. This system first became available in 1984 to help IBM define cable types, distribution panels (wiring centers), face plates, and connectors for their wiring needs. Nevertheless, you may be familiar with much of this information, especially in light of the ANSI/EIA/TIA 568 UTP standard this chapter already covered.

Of all the elements in this collection of cables, connectors, and related hardware, the feature unique to the IBM system is the IBM cable connector. Unlike most other such connectors, IBM designed theirs as neither male nor female but, rather, made any two connectors able to plug into each other. While convenient, this means that IBM connectors require special face plates and distribution panels.

The **IBM cabling system** designates cables in terms of types numbered from 1 to 9. The corresponding definitions indicate which type is appropriate for specific applications or environments. As for most electrical wiring, the wires specified in the IBM system use the **American Wire Gauge (AWG)** standards that specify the diameter of the conductor in terms of a specific gauge that equates to a specific width. For more information on the IBM cabling system, see *www.techfest.com/networking/cabling/ibmcs.htm*.

 As the diameter of the conductor increases, the AWG rating decreases. Thus, 10-gauge wire is much thicker than 20-gauge wire. Ordinary voicegrade telephone wire is rated 22 AWG.

WIRELESS NETWORKING: INTANGIBLE MEDIA

Wireless technologies continue to play an increasing role in all kinds of networks. Since 1990, especially, the number of wireless options has increased, while the cost of these technologies continues to decrease. As wireless networking becomes more affordable, demand increases, and economies of scale come increasingly into play. Most experts anticipate that wireless networking of all kinds will become more prevalent, if not commonplace, in the years to come.

The very adjective "**wireless**" sometimes connotes more than it means—that is, you may infer that wireless networks have no cabling of any kind. Nothing is further from the truth, however. Wireless networks appear most frequently in conjunction with wired networks, often to interconnect physically disjointed LANs or groups of mobile users with stationary servers and resources on a wired LAN. Microsoft calls networks that include both wired and wireless components **hybrid networks**.

The Wireless World

Wireless networking has considerable appeal in many circumstances. Related technologies can provide the following capabilities:

- Create temporary connections into existing wired networks

- Establish back-up or contingency connectivity for existing wired networks

- Extend a network's span beyond the reach of wire- or fiber-optic-based cabling, especially within older buildings in which rewiring may be too expensive

- Permit certain users to roam with their machines, within certain limits (so-called "mobile networking")

Each of these capabilities supports uses that expand or extend the benefits of networking beyond conventional limits. Although wireless networking is invariably more expensive than cable-based alternatives, sometimes these benefits can more than repay the extra costs involved. Today, commercial applications for wireless networking technologies include the following:

- Ready access to data for mobile professionals, such as doctors or nurses in hospitals or delivery personnel in their vehicles. For instance, United Parcel Service (UPS) truck drivers maintain ongoing connections to a server at their home office; their handheld computers send and receive delivery updates and status information to a network server over a wireless telephone connection.

- Delivery of network access into isolated facilities or even into disaster-stricken areas. For example, the Federal Emergency Management Agency (FEMA) uses battery-powered, wireless technologies to install field networks in areas where power and connections may be unavailable.

- Access in environments in which layout and settings change constantly. For instance, the shooting set areas at animation and film studios often include wireless network components so that information is always available, no matter how the stage area configuration changes.

- Improved customer services in busy areas, such as check-in or reception facilities. For example, Hertz employees use handheld units to check in returned rental vehicles right in the parking lot.

- Network connectivity in facilities, such as historical buildings, where in-wall wiring would be impossible to install or prohibitively expensive.

- Home networks where the installation of cables is inconvenient. An increasing number of homes with multiple computers are installing inexpensive wireless networks in order to share Internet connections and files among family members. An example of using wireless in a home network is depicted in Figure 3-10.

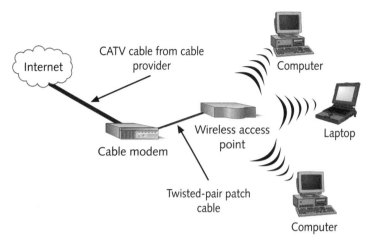

Figure 3-10   A typical home wireless network

In fact, as wireless technologies decrease in cost, their number of uses grows correspondingly.

Types of Wireless Networks

Depending on the role that wireless components play in a network, wireless networks can be subdivided into three primary categories:

- *Local area networks (LANs).* In LANs, wireless components act as part of an ordinary LAN, usually to provide connectivity for roving users or changing environments or perhaps to provide connectivity across areas that might not otherwise be networkable. Examples include older buildings where installing wiring would be impractical or across right-of-ways where cabling might not be permitted.

- *Extended LANs.* In extended LANs, an organization might use wireless components to extend the span of a LAN beyond normal distance limitations for wire- or fiber-optic-based cables.

- *Mobile computing.* With mobile computing, individual users communicate using a wireless networking medium, such as radio or cellular telephone frequencies that permit them to move while remaining attached to a network.

An easy way to differentiate among these uses is to distinguish in-house from carrier-based facilities. Both LAN and extended LAN uses of wireless networking involve equipment that an organization owns and controls. However, mobile computing typically involves a third party that supplies the necessary transmission and reception facilities to link the mobile part of a network with the wired part. Most often, the company that provides such services is a **communications carrier** (such as GTE, MCI, or AT&T) that offers wireless communications for data, as well as voice, to its customers.

Wireless LAN Applications

The wireless components of most LANs behave like their wired counterparts, except for the media and the related hardware involved. The operational principles are much the same: it's still necessary to attach a network interface of some kind to a computer, but the interface attaches to an **antenna** and an emitter, rather than to a cable. Users can still access the network just as if cable connects them to it.

An additional item of equipment is required to link wireless users with wired users or resources. That is, at some point on a cabled network, it is necessary to install a transmitter/receiver device, called a transceiver or an access point, that translates between the wired and wireless networks. This access point broadcasts messages in wireless format that must be directed to wireless users and also relays messages sent by wireless users to resources or users on the wired side of its connection. An **access point device** includes an antenna and transmitter to send and receive wireless traffic, but also connects to the wired side of the network. This permits the device to shuttle traffic back and forth between the wired and wireless sides of a network.

Some wireless LANs use small individual transceivers, which may be wall-mounted or freestanding, to attach individual computers or devices to a wired network. This permits some limited mobility with an unobstructed view of the transceiver for such devices. Although such attachments are indeed wireless, some experts contend that this approach does not represent wireless networking, because each individual component has its own separate wireless connection. Regardless, you may still see such technologies advertised as "wireless LANs."

Wireless LAN Transmission

All wireless communications depend on sending and receiving signals broadcast through the atmosphere to ferry information between network devices. Such signals take the form of waves somewhere in what physicists call the electromagnetic spectrum. This spectrum is measured in terms of the frequency (or frequencies) of the wave forms used for communication, measured in cycles per second, usually expressed as **Hertz (Hz)**, in honor of Heinrich Hertz, one of the inventors of radio. The spectrum starts with low-frequency waves, such as those used for electrical power (60 Hz in the United States) and telephone (0-3 KHz for traditional voice systems), and goes all the way through the spectra associated with visible light, to the highest frequencies in existence—those at which gamma rays and other high-energy particles operate.

In wireless communications, frequency affects the amount and speed of data transmission. The strength or power of the transmission determines the distance that broadcast data can travel and still remain intelligible. In general, though, the principles that govern wireless transmissions dictate that lower-frequency transmissions can carry less data more slowly over longer distances, while higher-frequency transmissions can carry more data faster over shorter distances.

The middle part of the electromagnetic spectrum is commonly divided into several named frequency ranges, or bands. These are the most commonly used frequencies for wireless data communications.

- Radio: 10 KHz to 1 GHz

- Microwave: 1 GHz to 500 GHz

- Infrared: 500 GHz to 1 THz (TeraHertz)

The important principles to remember about a broadcast medium are those which focus on the inverse relationship between frequency and distance and the direct relationship between frequency and data transfer rate and bandwidth. It's also important to understand that higher-frequency technologies often use tight-beam broadcasts and require a clear line of sight between sender and receiver to ensure correct delivery.

Wireless LANs make use of four primary technologies for transmitting and receiving data:

- Infrared

- Laser

- Narrowband, single-frequency radio

- Spread-spectrum radio

Infrared LAN Technologies

Infrared wireless networks use infrared light beams to send signals between pairs of devices. These devices typically generate reasonably strong signals to prevent interference from light sources present in most office environments. Infrared works well for LAN applications because of its high bandwidth, which makes 10 to 100 Mbps transmission rates easy to deliver.

The four primary kinds of infrared LANs include:

- *Line-of-sight networks* require an unobstructed view, or a clear **line of sight**, between the transmitter and receiver.

- *Reflective wireless networks* broadcast signals from optical transceivers near individual devices to a central hub, which then forwards the signals to their intended recipients.

- *Scatter infrared networks* bounce transmissions off walls and ceilings to deliver signals from sender to receiver. This approach limits maximum reception distances to approximately 30 meters (100 feet). Because bounce technologies introduce signal delays, scatter infrared offers less bandwidth than line of sight.

- *Broadband optical telepoint networks* provide broadband services. This technology offers high speed and wide bandwidth, can handle high-end multimedia traffic, and matches the capabilities of most modern wired networks.

There is an increased use of infrared transmissions for **virtual docking** connections that permit laptops or other portable computing devices to communicate with individual wired computers or with peripheral devices such as printers. Even though infrared offers reasonable networking speeds and convenience, infrared LANs are hampered by the 100-foot distance limitation typical for most such devices. Because infrared light is close in frequency to visible light (and most visible light sources also emit strongly in infrared frequencies), infrared is prone to interference problems in most work environments. Such devices are often called **IrDA** devices, named after the Infrared Device Association, a trade association that represents designers and manufacturers of such equipment.

Laser-Based LAN Technologies

Laser-based transmissions also require a clear line of sight between sender and receiver. Any solid object or person blocking a beam blocks data transmissions. To protect humans from injury and to avoid excess radiation, laser-based LAN devices are subject to many of the same limitations as infrared, but are not as subject to interference from visible light sources.

Narrow-Band, Single-Frequency Radio LAN Technologies

Narrow-band radio or **single-frequency radio** LANs use low-powered, two-way radio communications, much like those used in taxi-cabs, police communications, and other private radio systems. Receiver and transmitter must be tuned to the same specific frequency to handle incoming and outgoing data. Unlike light-based communications, such as infrared or laser, narrow-band radio requires no line of sight between sender and receiver, as long as both parties stay within the broadcast range of these devices—typically, a maximum range of approximately 70 meters (230 feet).

In the United States, government agencies, such as the **Federal Communications Commission (FCC)**, regulate nearly all radio frequencies. Organizations that want to obtain frequencies for their exclusive use within specific locales must complete a time-consuming, expensive application process before being granted the right to use them. Because of the onus involved in securing exclusive use, the FCC also sets aside certain frequencies for unregulated use. (These include the frequencies at which cellular telephones and remote-control toys operate, for instance.) As wireless networking and other forms of wireless communications become more popular, these frequencies face crowding.

Depending on the frequency used, walls or other solid barriers also can block such signals and prevent successful transmission and reception. Interference from other radio sources is also possible, particularly if the devices broadcast in the unregulated frequency ranges, as do most wireless LAN technologies. As with any broadcast technology, anyone who comes within range of the network devices could eavesdrop on networked communications. For narrow-band radio technologies, this range is quite short. Table 3-7 summarizes the characteristics of narrow-band wireless LAN technologies.

Table 3-7   Narrow-band, single-frequency wireless LAN characteristics

Characteristic	Value
Frequency ranges	Unregulated: 902–928 MHz, 2.4 GHz, 5.72–5.85 GHz
Maximum distance	50–70 meters (164-230 feet)
Bandwidth	1–10 Mbps
Installation/maintenance	Easy to install and maintain
Interference	Highly susceptible
Cost	Moderate
Security	Highly susceptible to eavesdropping within range

Other single-frequency LAN technologies operate at higher power ratings. Networks of this type can usually transmit as far as the horizon and even farther using repeater towers or signal bouncing techniques. This kind of technology is well suited for communicating with mobile users, but significantly more expensive than lower-powered alternatives. Likewise, transmission equipment is more expensive and usually requires FCC licensing. Most end users of such technology, even in the largest organizations, choose to purchase this service from a communications carrier such as AT&T or GTE, rather than operate their own facilities.

Security can be a profound concern with this kind of networking technology. Anyone with an appropriate receiver can eavesdrop on these communications; this helps explain why encryption of traffic is common for networks that operate at these frequencies. Table 3-8 summarizes the characteristics of high-powered, single-frequency radio networks.

Table 3-8   High-powered, single-frequency LAN characteristics

Characteristic	Value
Frequency ranges	Unregulated: 902–928 MHz, 2.4 GHz, 5.72–5.85 GHz
Maximum distance	Line of sight, unless extension technologies are used
Bandwidth	1–10 Mbps
Installation/maintenance	Difficult, highly technical, requires licensing
Interference	Highly susceptible
Cost	Expensive to very expensive
Security	Highly susceptible to eavesdropping

Spread-Spectrum LAN Technologies

Spread-spectrum radio addresses several weaknesses of single-frequency communications, whether high or low power. Rather than using a single frequency, spread-spectrum uses multiple frequencies simultaneously, thereby improving reliability and reducing susceptibility to interference. Also, using multiple frequencies makes eavesdropping more difficult because of how individual frequencies are used together for spread-spectrum communications.

The two main kinds of spread-spectrum communications are called frequency-hopping and direct-sequence modulation. **Frequency-hopping** switches data among multiple frequencies at regular intervals. Transmitter and receiver must be tightly synchronized to keep communications ongoing. The hardware handles the timing of hops and chooses the next frequency without sending any information about such activity, so eavesdropping is nearly impossible. But because they only use one frequency at a time, frequency-hopping technologies' effective bandwidth is usually 1 Mbps or less and seldom exceeds 2 Mbps.

Direct-sequence modulation breaks data into fixed-size segments called **chips** and transmits the data on several different frequencies at the same time. The receiving equipment knows what frequencies to monitor and understands how to reassemble the arriving chips into properly arranged sequences of data. It's even possible to transmit dummy data on one or more channels, along with real data on other channels, to make it even more difficult for eavesdroppers to re-create the original data as sent. Direct-sequence networks typically operate in unregulated frequencies and provide bandwidths from 2 to 6 Mbps, depending on the number of dummy channels used. Table 3-9 summarizes the characteristics associated with spread-spectrum LAN technologies.

Table 3-9   Spread-spectrum LAN characteristics

Characteristic	Value
Frequency ranges	Unregulated: 902–928 MHz or 2.4 GHz
Maximum distance	Limited to cell boundaries, but often extends over several miles
Bandwidth	1–2 Mbps for frequency-hopping, 2–6 for direct-sequence
Installation/maintenance	Depends on equipment; ranges from easy to difficult
Interference	Moderately resistant
Cost	Inexpensive to moderate
Security	Not very susceptible to eavesdropping

802.11 Wireless Networking

The 802.11 Wireless Networking Standard, which was completed in 1997, has continued to be developed. With it, manufacturers of wireless networking devices have brought inexpensive, reliable, wireless LANs to homes and businesses. The current standards include 802.11b, which specifies bandwidth of 11 Mbps at a frequency of 2.4 GHz, and 802.11a, which specifies bandwidth of 54 Mbps at a 5 GHz frequency. Another high-speed wireless standard, 802.11g, is slated to be ratified by the first quarter of 2003. It operates at speeds up to 54 Mbps at a frequency of 2.4 GHz.

Of these competing standards, 802.11b is by far the most prevalent and has been in use the longest. Of the two higher-speed standards, 802.11g is backward compatible with 802.11b and therefore provides a convenient bandwidth upgrade path. 802.11a, on the other hand, due to its higher frequency, presents problems for upgrades from 802.11b, but provides for a more reliable and more flexible transmission.

802.11 wireless is essentially an extension to Ethernet using the airwaves as the medium. In fact, most 802.11 networks incorporate some wired Ethernet segments. The 802.11b networks can extend from several feet to several hundred feet depending on environmental factors, such as obstructions and radio frequency interference. For a wealth of information on the 802.11 standards, see *http://www.80211-planet.com*.

3

Wireless Extended LAN Technologies

Certain kinds of wireless networking equipment extend LANs beyond their normal cable-based distance limitations or provide connectivity across areas where cables are not allowed (or able) to traverse. For instance, **wireless bridges** can connect networks up to three miles (4.4 km) apart.

Such LAN bridges permit linking of locations, such as buildings or facilities, using line-of-sight or broadcast transmissions. LAN bridges also may make it unnecessary to route dedicated digital communications lines from one site to another through a communications carrier. Normally, up-front expenses for this technology are as much as 10 times higher, but eliminate recurring monthly service charges from a carrier that can quickly make up (and exceed) this difference. Spread-spectrum radio, infrared, and laser-based equipment is readily available on the commercial market.

Longer-range wireless bridges are also available, including spread-spectrum solutions that work with either Ethernet or token ring over distances up to 25 miles. As with shorter-range wireless bridges, the communications cost savings realized over time may justify the cost of a long-range wireless bridge. Where appropriately connected, such equipment (in both long- and short-range varieties) can transport both voice and data traffic. Table 3-10 summarizes the characteristics of wireless extended LAN technologies.

Table 3-10   Wireless extended LAN characteristics

Characteristic	Value
Frequency ranges	Spread-spectrum, infrared, laser
Maximum distance	1–3 miles for short-range, up to 25 miles for long-range
Bandwidth	1–6 Mbps for spread-spectrum, 2–100 for infrared and laser
Installation/maintenance	Depends on equipment; ranges from easy to difficult
Interference	Highly resistant
Cost	Inexpensive to moderate
Security	Not very susceptible to eavesdropping

Wireless bridges always appear in pairs, and both such devices function together as a repeater—that is, whatever comes in on the wired side of one device is transmitted out the wired side of the other. These devices are sometimes called "half-repeaters," a reference to the frequency ranges they use. Thus, you may sometimes hear this equipment called "optical half-repeaters" (for laser or infrared versions) or "radio half-repeaters" for their spread-spectrum counterparts.

Microwave Networking Technologies

Microwave systems deliver higher transmission rates than do radio-based systems, but because the frequencies are so high, transmitters and receivers must share a common, clear line of sight. Microwave communications usually require FCC approval and licensing and also are more expensive than radio systems. Experts distinguish between two types of microwave systems: terrestrial and satellite.

Terrestrial means "of the earth" and refers to line-of-sight transmissions between special microwave towers or between transmitters and receivers mounted on tall buildings, mountaintops, or other locations with long, clear lines of sight to desirable locations. **Terrestrial microwave** systems use tight-beam, high-frequency signals to link sender and receiver. By using relay towers, microwave systems can extend a signal across continental-scale distances.

In fact, many communications carriers use microwave towers to send traffic across sparsely populated areas where traffic is moderate and distances make laying cable expensive. The tight-beam nature of microwave systems means that transmitters and receivers must align precisely for best results. Some low-powered microwave systems are available for short-range LAN use, but these, too, require a clear line of sight between transmitters and receivers. Table 3-11 summarizes the characteristics of terrestrial microwave networks.

Table 3-11   Terrestrial microwave LAN/WAN characteristics

Characteristic	Value
Frequency ranges	4–6 GHz or 21–23 GHz
Maximum distance	Typically from 1–50 miles
Bandwidth	1–10 Mbps
Installation/maintenance	Difficult
Interference	Varies with respect to power and distance; longer distances more prone to weather disturbances
Cost	Expensive
Security	Highly susceptible, but signals usually encrypted

The other primary alternative for microwave transmission is satellite. Instead of aiming at transmitters or receivers within a clear line of sight on the ground, **satellite microwave** systems send and receive data from geosynchronous satellites that maintain fixed positions in the sky. This is how television signals and some long-distance telephone signals travel from one side of the world to another: the sender beams the signal to a satellite visible on the horizon, the satellite relays the signal to one or more satellites until it comes onto the receiver's horizon, and then the satellite redirects the signal to the receiver.

Geosynchronous satellites orbit 50,000 km (23,000 miles) above Earth. The distances involved are therefore great enough to incur measurable transmission delays (called "propagation delays") that vary between 0.5 and 5 seconds, depending on the number of hops (jumps across network segments) involved between sender and receiver.

Launching satellites is an activity that most organizations cannot fund; therefore, most satellite microwave systems must lease frequencies on satellites operated by global communications carriers. Since this approach also is prohibitively expensive, even multinational companies with legitimate needs to send data around the globe typically choose to pay for their communications time, rather than pay for exclusive use of their own frequency.

Even more than terrestrial microwave, satellite communications cover a broad area and can be received by anyone who has the right reception equipment. That's why microwave transmissions are routinely encrypted—to make sure only their intended recipients can access their contents. Table 3-12 summarizes the characteristics of satellite microwave communications.

Table 3-12 Satellite microwave WAN characteristics

Characteristic	Value
Frequency ranges	11–14 GHz
Maximum distance	Global reach
Bandwidth	1–10 Mbps
Installation/maintenance	Prohibitively difficult
Interference	Prone to EM interference, jamming, atmospheric disturbances
Cost	Prohibitive
Security	Not very susceptible to eavesdropping

When it comes to extending the reach of a network to its ultimate dimensions, microwave technologies currently provide the broadest reach. That's why they are labeled LAN/WAN (terrestrial) or WAN (satellite) technologies.

Other Wireless Networking Technologies

Because it is so desirable to break the wire tether that anchors users to most networks, wireless technologies continue to evolve and expand, yet simultaneously grow cheaper and significantly faster. Recently, some key wireless networking developments have occurred. We have discussed the IEEE's **802.11b Wireless Networking Standard**, along with its higher-speed enhancements. This standard promises to continue evolving, making wireless LANs commonplace in homes and in corporate environments.

On the technology side, there have been numerous developments as well. Metricom Inc., a wireless service provider based in Los Gatos, CA, now offers **cellular packet radio** networking in three areas in the United States—the San Francisco Bay area; Washington, DC; and Seattle, WA—where users in these metropolitan areas can carry laptops anywhere within the coverage area and establish a 2 Mbps connection at will. Likewise, **Cellular Digital Packet Data (CDPD)** connections at 19.2 Kbps are already available in most major U.S. metropolitan areas. CDPD technology is being used in handheld and palmtop PDAs for wireless Internet and e-mail access, further expanding the capabilities of these devices.

Motorola and other satellite communications vendors envision entire armadas of low-orbit satellites blanketing the United States with high-bandwidth wireless connectivity at a fraction of the cost of today's microwave satellites. Rather than precisely aiming at geosynchronous satellites for connectivity, these new approaches aim to launch into orbit enough satellites so that at least one is within broadcast range at all times all over the country. Such technologies should support affordable bandwidth of up to 10 Mbps for all kinds of mobile computing applications. Unfortunately, many of the companies experimenting with these satellite systems (for example, Motorola's Iridium LLC) found the actual costs of implementation much higher than expected and, therefore, scaled down their efforts or pulled out of the market, at least for now.

In a different vein, Intel, Nokia, and Unwired Planet have collaborated on a **narrow-band sockets** specification that permits pagers, cell phones, and wireless computers to communicate readily with the Internet. This specification accommodates the unique requirements of cellular and other wireless communications much more readily than does plain-vanilla IP (Internet Protocol), and provides a way to bridge the wireless world into Internet information and resources.

Finally, technology companies all over the United States—such as Winstar Communications Inc. of New York, NY, and ArrayComm Inc. of San Jose, CA—are positioning themselves to cash in on an emerging trend toward higher-bandwidth mobile and wireless networking technologies. Winstar significantly raised bandwidth limitations (up to 6 Gbps, in fact) for short- to medium-haul, line-of-sight infrared and microwave communications. Winstar's high-speed technology permits the company to provide high-speed alternatives to converting what telephony experts call the "last mile"—that is, the cable from the nearest central office where high-bandwidth lines converge and the homes or businesses that want access to that bandwidth. ArrayComm offers an adaptive antenna technology that extends the broadcast ranges for a wide variety of mobile wireless technologies. (This offers no increase in speed, but does offer increases in broadcast reach.) Clearly, the wireless marketplace is growing furiously, and that growth promises to accelerate in years to come.

CHAPTER SUMMARY

◻ Working with network media—whether wired or wireless—requires careful attention to user requirements, as well as consideration of budget, distance, bandwidth, and environmental factors. Choosing an appropriate technology depends on weighing all these factors, meeting immediate needs, and leaving room for growth and change.

◻ For wired networks, the primary choices are between twisted-pair and coaxial conductive cables, and fiber-optic cables. Coaxial cable comes in two primary forms, thinwire and thickwire Ethernet. Both types surround a copper core with insulation and a wire braid that deflects noise and reduces crosstalk. Coaxial cable remains a good choice for transmitting network data over medium to long distances.

3

❑ Twisted-pair cable comes in unshielded (UTP) and shielded (STP) varieties. UTP is commonly rated according to the ANSI/EIA/TIA 568 standard in six categories, of which Category 5/5E is the most commonly used in modern networks. STP has no similar rating scheme, but its shielding supports higher bandwidth and longer network spans than UTP. IBM also has its own cabling system, which rates cables in a nine-type hierarchy; here, IBM Type 2 cabling is a voice and data cable designed to bring both network and telephone connections to users' desktops.

❑ New UTP categories include Category 6 and Category 7. Category 6 cabling promises to be the new standard for Gigabit Ethernet, while Category 7, due to its lack of backward compatibility with older standards, will likely be used only in special situations.

❑ Fiber-optic cable supports the highest bandwidth and offers the best security and resistance to interference of any type of cable, but it's also the most expensive. Fiber-optic cable is more sensitive to stress and bending and requires considerable expertise to attach connectors and install in general. Connector types include ST, SC, and a newer type called MT-RJ.

❑ Cabled networks typically use one of two transmission schemes: broadband or baseband. Broadband transmissions use analog signals to carry multiple channels on a single cable, where one channel is required to send and another to receive signals on most networks. Baseband transmission uses only a single channel to send digital signals that occupy the cable's entire carrying capacity.

❑ Alongside cabled-based networks, wireless networking assumes an increasing portion of the networking load. Wireless technologies work well to provide cable-free LAN access, to extend the span of LANs (called extended LANs), to provide wide area network (WAN) links, and to support mobile computing needs.

❑ A typical wireless network acts like its wired counterpart—that is, a network adapter transfers communications across the networking medium, except that wires are not needed to carry the signals involved. Otherwise, users communicate as they would on any other network.

❑ Wireless networks use a variety of electromagnetic frequency ranges, including narrow-band and spread-spectrum radio, microwave, infrared, and laser transmission techniques. A pair of devices called a wireless bridge can also extend LANs. Short-range wireless bridges can span distances up to three miles; long-range wireless bridges can span up to 25 miles.

❑ The 802.11b wireless standard and its higher-speed successors promise to make wireless networking commonplace in homes and in the corporate environment. The 802.11b standard specifies bandwidth of 11 Mbps, whereas two new standards, 802.11a and 802.11g, specify bandwidth up to 54 Mbps.

❑ Mobile computing involves using broadcast frequencies and communications carriers to transmit and receive signals using packet-radio, cellular, or satellite communications techniques. Finally, wireless networking appears poised to grab an increasing share of networking installations as newer and more powerful technologies and standards start to come online.

KEY TERMS

10Base2 — A designation for 802.3 Ethernet thin coaxial cable (also called thinnet, thinwire, or cheapernet). The 10 indicates bandwidth of 10 Mbps, the Base indicates it's a baseband transmission technology, and the 2 indicates a maximum segment length of 185 meters for this cable type.

10Base5 — A designation for 802.3 Ethernet thick coaxial cable (also called thicknet or thickwire). The 10 indicates bandwidth of 10 Mbps, the Base indicates it's a baseband transmission technology, and the 5 indicates a maximum segment length of 500 meters for this cable type.

10BaseT — A designation for 802.3 Ethernet twisted-pair cable. The 10 indicates bandwidth of 10 Mbps, the Base indicates it's a baseband transmission technology, and the T indicates that the medium is twisted-pair. (Maximum segment length is around 100 meters, or 328 feet, but the precise measurement depends on the manufacturer's testing results for the particular cable.)

802.11 Wireless Networking Standard — An IEEE standard for wireless networking. A version of the 802.11 standard appeared late in 1997.

access point device — The device that bridges wireless networking components and a wired network. It forwards traffic from the wired side to the wireless side and from the wireless side to the wired side as needed.

American National Standards Institute (ANSI) — The U.S. representative in the International Standardization Organization (ISO), a worldwide standards-making body. ANSI creates and publishes standards for networking, communications, and programming languages.

American Wire Gauge (AWG) — A numeric classification and naming scheme for copper wiring: the higher the gauge, the narrower the diameter of the wiring.

amplifier — A hardware device that increases the power of electrical signals to maintain their original strength when transmitted across a large network.

analog — The method of signal transmission used on broadband networks. Creating analog waveforms from computer-based digital data requires a special device called a digital-to-analog (d-to-a) converter; reversing the conversion requires another device called an analog-to-digital (a-to-d) converter. Broadband networking equipment must include both kinds of devices to work.

antenna — A tuned electromagnetic device that can send and receive broadcast signals at particular frequencies. In wireless networking devices, an antenna is an important part of the devices' sending and receiving circuitry.

ARCnet (attached resource computing network) — A 2.5 Mbps LAN technology created by DataPoint Corporation in the early 1980s. ARCnet uses token-based networking technology and runs over several kinds of coaxial cable, twisted-pair, and fiber-optic cable.

attachment unit interface (AUI) — A standard Ethernet connector, also called a DIX connector.

3

bandwidth — The range of frequencies that a communications medium can carry. For baseband networking media, the bandwidth also indicates the theoretical maximum amount of data that the medium can transfer. For broadband networking media, the bandwidth is measured by the variations that any single carrier frequency can carry, minus the analog-to-digital conversion overhead.

baseband transmission — A technology that uses digital signals sent over a cable without modulation. It sends binary values (0s and 1s) as pulses of different voltage levels.

bend radius — For network cabling, the bend radius describes the maximum arc that a segment of cable may be bent over some unit length (typically, one foot or one meter) without incurring damage.

BNC — Bayonet nut connector or British Naval Connector (preferred Microsoft usage); also known as bayonet navy connector or bayonet Neill-Concelman connector. This is a matching pair of coaxial cable connectors, male and female. The female connector consists of a ferrule around a hollow pin with a pair of guideposts on the outside. The male connector consists of a rotating, locking wire nut, with an inner sleeve with two channels that match the female connector's guideposts. A pin projects from the center of the male connector and mates with the hollow pin in the center of the female connector, while the guideposts and locking wire nut ensure a tight, well-seated connection.

braiding — A woven mesh of metallic wires, usually either copper or steel, wrapped around the outside of one or more conductive cables. It provides shielding against EMI, RFI, and crosstalk from other cables.

broadband optical telepoint network — An implementation of infrared wireless networking that supports broadband services equal to those provided by a cabled network.

broadband transmission — An analog transmission technique which may use multiple communication channels simultaneously. Each data channel is represented by modulation on a particular frequency band, for which sending or receiving equipment must be tuned.

broadcast signal — A technique that uses a transmitter to send signals, such as network data, through a communications medium. For wireless networks, this involves sending signals through the atmosphere, rather than over a cable.

cable modem — A special-purpose networking device that permits a computer to send and receive networking signals, primarily for Internet access, by using two data channels on a broadband CATV network (one to send outgoing data, the other to receive incoming data). Cable modems can support bandwidth up to 1.544 Mbps, but it's more typical to observe upstream traffic (from computer to network) between 100 and 300 Kbps and downstream traffic (from network to computer) between 300 and 600 Kbps.

Category 1–5E — The EIA/TIA designations for unshielded twisted-pair cable, described in terms of categories, labeled Category 1, Category 2, and so on. Often, these are abbreviated as Cat 1, Cat 2, and so on.

Cellular Digital Packet Data (CDPD) — A cellular communications technology that sends packets of digital data over unused cellular voice channels at a rate of 19.2 Kbps. CDPD is one member of an emerging family of mobile computing technologies.

cellular packet radio — A communications technology that sends packets of data over different radio frequencies than those used for cellular telephones; a generic term for an emerging family of mobile computing technologies.

cheapernet — A synonym for 10Base2, also known as thinnet or thinwire Ethernet.

chip — A fixed-sized element of data broadcast over a single frequency using the spread-spectrum radio networking technology called direct-sequence modulation.

cladding — A nontransparent layer of plastic or glass material inside fiber-optic cable; cladding surrounds the inner core of glass or plastic fibers. Cladding provides rigidity, strength, and a manageable outer diameter for fiber-optic cables.

coaxial cable — A type of cable that uses a center conductor, wrapped by an insulating layer, surrounded by a braided wire mesh and an outer jacket or sheath, to carry high-bandwidth signals such as network traffic or broadcast television frequencies. The word "coax" is often used as a shortened form of "coaxial cable."

communications carrier — A company that provides communications services for other organizations, such as your local phone company and the long-distance telephone carriers. Most mobile computing technologies rely on the services of a communications carrier to handle the wireless traffic from mobile units to a centralized wired network of some kind.

conduit — Plastic or metal pipe laid specifically to provide a protected enclosure for cabling of any kind.

crosstalk — A phenomenon that occurs when two wires lay against each other in parallel. Signals traveling down one wire can interfere with signals traveling down the other, and vice versa.

datagrade — A designation for cabling of any kind; datagrade indicates that cabling is suitable for transporting digital data. When applied to twisted-pair cabling, datagrade indicates that the cable is suitable for either voice or data traffic.

direct-sequence modulation — The form of spread-spectrum data transmission that breaks data into constant length segments called chips and transmits the data on multiple frequencies.

dual-cable broadband — A broadband technique in which two cables are used; one is for transmitting, and one is for receiving.

electromagnetic interference (EMI) — A form of electrical interference caused by emissions from external devices, such as transformers or electrical motors, and which can disrupt network transmissions over an electrical medium.

electronic eavesdropping — The ability to "listen" to signals passing through some communications medium by detecting its emissions. Eavesdropping on many wireless networking technologies is especially easy, because they broadcast their data into the atmosphere.

3

Electronic Industries Alliance (EIA) — An industry trade group of electronics and networking manufacturers that collaborates on standards for wiring, connectors, and other common components.

extended LAN — The result of certain wireless bridges' ability to expand the span of a LAN up to 25 miles. Microsoft calls the resulting networks "extended LANs."

Federal Communications Commission (FCC) — Among other responsibilities, the FCC regulates access to broadcast frequencies throughout the electromagnetic spectrum, including those used for mobile computing and microwave transmissions. Where these signals cover any distance (more than half a mile) and require exclusive use of a particular frequency, FCC requires a broadcast license. Many wireless networking technologies make use of so-called unregulated frequencies set aside by the FCC. These frequencies do not require such licensing, but they must be shared with others.

fiber-optic — A cabling technology that uses pulses of light sent along a light-conducting fiber at the heart of the cable to transfer information from sender to receiver. Fiber-optic cable can send data in only one direction, so two cables are required to permit any two network devices to exchange data in both directions.

frequency-hopping — The type of spread-spectrum data transmission that switches data across a range of frequencies over time. Frequency-hopping transmitters and receivers must be synchronized to hop at the same time, to the same frequencies.

geosynchronous — An orbital position relative to Earth where a satellite orbits at the same speed as Earth rotates. This permits such satellites to maintain a constant, fixed position relative to Earth stations and represents the positioning technique used for microwave satellites.

Hertz (Hz) — A measure of broadcast frequencies, in cycles per second; named after Heinrich Hertz, one of the inventors of radio communications.

hybrid network — A network that includes both wired and wireless components.

IBM cabling system — Numeric cable designations (Type 1 through Type 9) representing the grades of cabling recognized by IBM's Cabling System. Types 2 and 9 are the most commonly used networking cables; Type 3 is voicegrade only, which is unsuitable for networking use.

impedance — The resistance of a cable to the transmission of signals. Impedance accounts for attenuation in a cable.

infrared — That portion of the electromagnetic spectrum immediately below visible light. Infrared frequencies are popular for short- to medium-range (tens of meters to 40 km) point-to-point network connections.

insertion loss — The weakening of signals that occurs on a cable segment each time a network device is attached. Necessary restrictions on the maximum number of devices keep the signals that traverse the network clean and strong enough to remain intelligible to all devices.

Institute of Electrical and Electronics Engineers (IEEE) — An engineering organization that issues standards for electrical and electronic devices, including network interfaces, cabling, and connectors.

IrDA — A device that is compliant with the Infrared Device Association's specifications for infrared components and devices.

jack coupler — The female receptacle into which a modular TP cable plugs.

jacket — The outermost layer of a cable.

latency — The amount of time a signal takes to travel from one end of a cable to the other.

light-emitting diode (LED) — A lower-powered alternative for emitting data at optical frequencies. LEDs are sometimes used for wireless LANs and for short-haul, fiber-optic-based data transmissions.

line of sight — A term which describes the requirement that narrow-band, tight-beam transmitters and receivers have an unobstructed path between them. If you can see from sender to receiver, they can also exchange data with one another.

line-of-sight networks — Networks that require an unobstructed view, or clear line of sight, between the transmitter and receiver.

local area network (LAN) — A small network that is limited to a single collection of machines and one or more cables and other peripheral equipment.

maximum segment length — The longest legal segment of cable permitted by a particular networking technology. This limitation helps network designers and installers make sure that the entire network can send and receive signals properly.

medium interface connector (MIC) — One of a number of fiber-optic cable connector types. MIC connectors feature a separate physical connector for each cable in a typical fiber-optic cable pair.

mid-split broadband — A broadband technique in which two channels on different frequencies are used to transmit and receive signals using a single cable.

mobile computing — A form of wireless networking that uses common carrier frequencies to permit networked devices to be moved freely within the broadcast coverage area yet remain connected to the network.

MT-RJ — A fiber-optic connector that provides a high-density connection utilizing two fiber-optic cables.

narrow-band radio — A type of broadcast-based networking technology that uses a single, specific radio frequency to send and receive data. Low-powered, narrow-band implementations do not usually require FCC approval, but are perforce limited to a 250-foot or so range; high-powered, narrow-band implementations do require FCC approval and licensing.

narrow-band sockets — An emerging programming interface designed to facilitate communication between cellular data networks and the Internet.

patch panel — An element of a wiring center where individual cable runs are brought together. By making connections between any two points on the patch panel, the physical path of individual wires can be controlled and the sequence of individual wires managed. The so-called data path is particularly important in token ring networks, where patch panels are frequently found.

plenum — The area between a false ceiling and the true one in most commercial buildings. Used to circulate heating and cooling air; it's sometimes called the plenum space. Many types of cable, including networking cable, also run through this space.

plenum-rated — Cable that has been burn-tested to make sure it does not emit toxic fumes or large amounts of smoke when incinerated. Most building and fire codes require this designation for any cable to be run in plenum space.

punchdown block — A wiring center used for telephone and network TP cable, where bare wire ends are inserted (punched down) into specific connectors to manage wiring layout and the data path. In effect, a punchdown block is the equivalent of a patch panel.

Radio Government (RG) — The coaxial cable designation that reflects coaxial cable's original use as a conveyance for radio frequency data and signals. The cable designation for thinnet is RG-58; for CATV, RG-59; for ARCnet, RG-62; and for thickwire, either RG-8 or RG-11.

radio frequency interference (RFI) — Any interference caused by signals operating in the radio frequency range. This term has become generic for interference caused by broadcast signals of any kind.

receiver — A data communications device designed to capture and interpret signals broadcast at one or more frequencies in the electromagnetic spectrum. Receivers are necessary for both cable- and wireless-based transmissions.

reflective wireless network — An infrared wireless networking technology that uses a central optical transceiver to relay signals between end stations. All network devices must have an unobstructed view of this central transceiver, which explains why they're usually mounted on the ceiling.

repeater — Networking device used to strengthen a signal suffering from attenuation.

registered jack (RJ) — Used for modular telephone and network TP jacks.

RJ-11 — The four-wire modular jack commonly used for home telephone handsets. *See* registered jack.

RJ-45 — The eight-wire modular jack used for TP networking cables and also for PBX-based telephone systems. (Take care which connector you plug into an RJ-45 coupler.) *See* registered jack.

satellite microwave — A microwave transmission system that uses geosynchronous satellites to send and relay signals between sender and receiver. Most companies that use satellite microwave lease access to the satellites for an exorbitant fee.

scatter infrared network — An infrared LAN technology that uses flat reflective surfaces such as walls and ceilings to bounce wireless transmissions between sender and receiver. Because bouncing introduces delays and attenuation, this variety of wireless LAN is the slowest and supports the narrowest bandwidth of any of the infrared technologies.

sheath — The outer layer of coating on a cable; sometimes also called the jacket.

shielded twisted-pair (STP) — A variety of TP cable, wherein a foil wrap encloses each of one or more pairs of wires for additional shielding, and where a wire braid or an additional layer of foil may enclose the entire cable for further shielding.

shielding — Any layer of material included in cable to mitigate the effects of interference on the signal-carrying cables it encloses.

single-frequency radio — A form of wireless networking technology that passes data using only a single broadcast frequency, as opposed to spread-spectrum, which uses two or more frequencies.

spread-spectrum radio — A form of wireless networking technology that passes data using multiple frequencies simultaneously.

straight connection (SC) — A type of one-piece fiber-optic connector that is pushed on, yet makes a strong and solid contact with emitters and sensors.

straight tip (ST) — The most common type of fiber-optic connector used in Ethernet networks with fiber backbones. These connectors come in pairs, one for each fiber-optic cable.

subminiature type A (SMA) — Yet another fiber-optic connector, this connector twists on and also comes in pairs.

Telecommunications Industries Association (TIA) — An industry consortium of telephone equipment, cabling, and communications companies, that together formulate hardware standards for equipment, cabling, and connectors used in phone systems and on networks.

terrestrial microwave — A wireless microwave networking technology that uses line-of-sight communications between pairs of Earth-based transmitters and receivers to relay information. The large distances the signals must extend requires that microwave transmitters and receivers be positioned well above ground level, on towers, on mountaintops, or atop tall buildings. Such equipment is usually expensive.

thicknet — A form of coaxial Ethernet that uses a rigid cable about 0.4" in diameter. Because of its common jacket color and its rigidity, this cable is sometimes called "frozen yellow garden hose." Also known as thickwire and 10Base5.

thickwire — A synonym for thicknet and 10Base5.

thinnet — A form of coaxial Ethernet that uses a thin, flexible cable about 0.2" in diameter. Also known as thinwire, 10Base2, and cheapernet.

thinwire — A synonym for 10Base2 and thinnet.

transceiver — A compound word made from the beginning of the word *transmitter* and the end of the word *receiver*. Thus, a transceiver combines the functions of a transmitter and a receiver and integrates into a single device the circuitry needed to emit and receive signals on a medium.

transmitter — An electronic device capable of emitting signals for delivery through a particular networking medium.

twisted-pair (TP) — A type of cabling where two copper wires, each enclosed in some kind of sheath, are wrapped around each other. The twisting permits narrow-gauge wire, otherwise extraordinarily sensitive to crosstalk and interference, to carry higher-bandwidth signals over longer distances than would traditionally be possible with straight wires. TP cabling is used for voice telephone circuits as well as for networking.

unshielded twisted-pair (UTP) — A form of TP cable that includes no additional shielding material in the cable composition. This cable encloses one or more pairs of twisted wires inside an outer jacket.

vampire tap — A two-piece apparatus with a set screw on the upper half that permits the pointed end of the screw to penetrate thickwire coax to a precise depth, where it taps into the center conductor without breaking it. This permits a transceiver to connect to the cable, thereby enabling devices to attach to the thickwire segment. The set screw that penetrates the cable is called, in keeping with the name of the tap, the "fang."

virtual docking — One of numerous point-to-point wireless infrared technologies that permit laptops to exchange data with desktop machines or permit data exchange between a computer and a handheld device or a printer. Since this capability replaces a cable between the two devices, this technology is sometimes called "virtual docking."

voicegrade — A designation for cable (usually TP) that indicates it's rated only to carry telephone traffic. Voicegrade cable is not recommended for network use.

wall plate — A module that includes couplers for telephone (RJ-11) and network (RJ-45, BNC, or other female connector) jacks.

wireless — Indicates that a network connection depends on transmission at some kind of electromagnetic frequency through the atmosphere to carry data transmissions from one networked device to another.

wireless bridge — A pair of devices, typically narrow-band and tight beam, that relay network traffic from one location to another. Wireless bridges that use spread-spectrum radio, infrared, and laser technologies are available and can span distances from hundreds of meters up to 25 miles.

wiring center — A set of racks with associated equipment that generally includes hubs, punchdown blocks or patch panels, backbone access units, and other network-management equipment, which brings TP-wired network cables together for routing, management, and control.

REVIEW QUESTIONS

1. Of the following cabling elements, which does not commonly occur in coaxial cable?
   a. wire braid
   b. center conductor
   c. outer sheath
   d. optical fiber

2. If the center conductor and the wire braid make contact in a coaxial cable, the resulting condition is called a:

   a. fault

   b. open

   c. short

   d. dead circuit

3. What surrounds the center conductor in a coaxial cable to separate it from the wire braid?

   a. vacuum

   b. conductive mesh

   c. piezoelectric material

   d. insulating layer

4. The type of fiber-optic connector that provides high density and requires only one connector for two cables is the _____.

   a. SC

   b. ST

   c. MT-RJ

   d. RJ-45

5. The condition that requires cables not to exceed a recommended maximum length is called _____.

   a. diminution

   b. resistance

   c. carrying capacity

   d. attenuation

6. What component of a coaxial cable actually carries data?

   a. core

   b. insulating layer

   c. wire braid

   d. sheathing or jacket

7. The space between a false ceiling and the true ceiling where heating and cooling air circulates is called _____.

   a. duct-equivalent airspace

   b. conduit

   c. return air

   d. plenum

8. Cable sheathed with _____ material should not be routed in ceiling or walls.

    a. Teflon

    b. Kevlar

    c. foil

    d. PVC (polyvinyl chloride)

9. The fire-resistant cable specified by fire and building codes is rated as _____.

    a. fire-resistant

    b. fire-retardant

    c. inflammable

    d. plenum

10. To build the network in your New York City headquarters, you must run a cable through the elevator shaft from the customer service center on the second floor, all the way up to the corporate offices on the 37th floor. The distance is 550 meters. What type of cable must you use?

    a. unshielded twisted-pair (UTP)

    b. thinwire coax (10Base2)

    c. thickwire coax (10Base5)

    d. fiber-optic cable

11. Which of the following cables is not suitable for network use of any kind?

    a. Category 1

    b. Category 2

    c. Category 3

    d. Category 4

12. Name the type of connector most commonly used with TP network wiring.

    a. RJ-11

    b. RJ-45

    c. BNC

    d. MT-RJ

13. Both thinwire and thickwire Ethernet use a form of BNC connector. True or false?

14. You are hired to install a network at the Central Intelligence Agency (CIA). The agency wants zero chance of electronic eavesdropping on their network. What kind of cable should you use?

    a. UTP

    b. STP

    c. coaxial

    d. fiber-optic

15. You're preparing to install a conventional Ethernet network in your new office building, but your boss tells you to be ready to handle a switchover to 1 Gbps Ethernet in 2004. What two types of cable could you install?

    a. thinwire

    b. thickwire

    c. Category 4

    d. Category 6

    e. Category 3

16. When two cables run side-by-side, signals traveling down one wire may interfere with signals traveling on the other wire. What is this phenomenon called?

    a. RFI

    b. attenuation

    c. impedance

    d. crosstalk

17. XYZ Corp. operates a thinnet network. When the network administrator goes to the supply room looking for some network cable, he finds a suitable length that ends in BNC connectors. It's labeled RG-62. Will this cable work?

    a. Yes, it's exactly the right cable.

    b. No, it won't work at all.

    c. Yes, it will work but not as well as RG-58.

    d. Yes, but only if the TIA wiring is geosynchronous.

18. Which of the following cabling elements does not occur in fiber-optic cable?

    a. glass or plastic fiber core

    b. glass or plastic cladding

    c. wire braid

    d. Kevlar sheathing

    e. plastic or Teflon jacket

19. What benefits does shielding confer on shielded twisted-pair cable? (Choose all that apply.)

   a. improves flexibility

   b. lowers susceptibility to interference

   c. increases maximum segment length

   d. decreases cost

3

20. If you want to share an Internet connection among three home computers, but find it difficult to run cables, what type of network should you use?

   a. 802.3

   b. 10Base2

   c. 802.12b

   d. 802.11b

21. You currently are using 11 Mbps wireless in your LAN but are considering an upgrade to 54 Mbps speed. For best compatibility, which wireless standard should you choose for this higher bandwidth?

   a. 802.11g

   b. 802.11a

   c. 802.11b

   d. 802.11c

22. Baseband transmission sends signals in which of the following forms?

   a. analog

   b. digital

   c. spread-spectrum

   d. frequency-hopping

23. Broadband transmission sends signals in which of the following forms?

   a. analog

   b. digital

   c. spread-spectrum

   d. frequency-hopping

24. The devices used to manage transmission and reception of data between a wired LAN and wireless components are:

   a. access points

   b. gateways

   c. wireless interfaces

   d. antennae

25. The device used to link buildings without cable is a:

    a. wireless hub

    b. wireless router

    c. wireless gateway

    d. wireless bridge

26. Which of the following technologies might be used in a wireless LAN? (Choose all that apply.)

    a. narrow-band radio

    b. microwave transmission

    c. infrared

    d. laser

27. Spread-spectrum transmissions occur in which of the following forms? (Choose all that apply.)

    a. channel-hopping

    b. frequency-hopping

    c. multiplexed sequencing

    d. direct-sequence

28. Which of the following wireless technologies would not be appropriate to link two buildings? (Choose all that apply.)

    a. reflective infrared

    b. point-to-point infrared

    c. spread-spectrum radio

    d. terrestrial microwave

    e. low-power, single-frequency radio

29. To support a population of mobile computing users, which wireless technology is most appropriate?

    a. point-to-point infrared

    b. satellite microwave

    c. terrestrial microwave

    d. spread-spectrum radio

HANDS-ON PROJECTS

When it comes to working with networking media, it's important to be able to distinguish among as many types of media—and the connectors that go with them—as possible. The first Hands-on Project in this chapter consists of some show-and-tell from your instructor, giving you an opportunity to touch and examine several different types of networking media. The remaining Hands-on Projects ask you to consider a variety of methods for combining networking media using pencil and paper, rather than the real thing. Don't worry—when the time comes to work on a real network, you'll have more opportunities to work with its media than you can imagine.

Project 3-1

For this exercise, your instructor will pass around several different types of networking media, along with the connectors that go with each kind. Examine each one closely, and learn to recognize each by its shape and size. Here are some hints to help you:

❑ The RJ-45 connector used with twisted-pair Ethernet looks just like a conventional telephone jack, only slightly larger. Close examination reveals that it incorporates eight wire traces, whereas the RJ-11 jacks used for regular telephone handsets incorporate only four such traces.

❑ The BNC connectors and coaxial cable used for thinwire Ethernet are relatively small. The cable itself is flexible and often appears insubstantial. Examine the cable's outer jacket. You should see some kind of code printed at regular intervals, such as "20 AWG CL2 RG-58A/U E111378A (UL)."

❑ The BNC connectors and coaxial cable used for thickwire Ethernet are more substantial: the cable is about 0.4" in diameter, and the female BNC connectors are nearly 0.5" in diameter. The rigid cable, if properly jacketed, lives up to its common name of "frozen yellow garden hose." This type of medium also requires external transceivers and transceiver cables, which your instructor may also pass around. Because transceiver cables may be up to 50 feet long, this leaves considerable distance between the coax and whatever computer must attach to it.

❑ The IBM media connectors look more like devices than connectors, with their heavy external shells and outer clips. The cable used with such connectors varies from moderately thin (like thinwire) to somewhat less thick and rigid than thickwire but containing two or more twisted pairs of wire.

Remember, you must be able to recognize and distinguish among these types of cables and connectors. Also, be aware that the kind of coaxial cable used for thinwire closely resembles cable TV cable and the kind of coax used for ARCnet or IBM 3270 terminal-based networks. That's why learning to read the jacket codes is so important: it may keep you from trying to use the wrong medium on some particular network connection. Always check the jacket codes!

Project 3-2

In this project, you practice making a Category 5/5e UTP patch cable. You will need the following tools and materials to complete this project:

❑ Wire cutter and stripper

❑ RJ-45 crimp tool

❑ 3-4 feet of Category 5 or Category 5e cable

❑ Two RJ-45 plugs

❑ Patch cable checker (optional)

1. Strip approximately two inches of the outer jacket off one end of the cable. Be careful not to nick the inner wires.

2. Untwist the four pairs of wires.

3. Here comes the tricky part. Arrange the wires from left to right (as you are looking down on them) so that the wires are in the following order: white/orange, orange, white/green, blue, white/blue, green, white/brown, brown. (This order of wires adheres to the 568-B wiring standard. Another wiring standard, 568-A, is also commonly used, and switches the orange and green wires.)

4. Clip the eight wires so that there is about 3/4" of wire extending beyond the outer jacket.

5. While holding the RJ-45 connector in one hand with the key facing away from you, insert the eight wires into the connector, being sure that the tops of the wires extend to the front of the connector and that the cable jacket goes far enough into the connector so that the jacket will be caught by the crimp bar. See Figure 3-11.

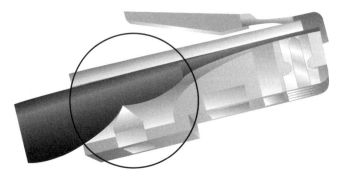

Figure 3-11   Correct RJ-45 plug installation

6. Now, insert the RJ-45 into the crimping tool while making sure that the wires do not slip. Close the handle on the crimp tool firmly.

7. Repeat the process for the other side of the cable and test using a patch-cable tester if available. Congratulations, you have made a network patch cable!

Projects 3-3 Through 3-7

During the design of most real-world networks, you'll discover that it is commonplace to use more than one type of networking medium. The usual reasons for needing more than one type of medium include the following:

▫ Two or more areas must be interconnected, where the distance that separates them is greater than the maximum segment length for the type of medium used in (or best-suited for) each area.

▫ A connection must pass through an interference-rich environment (across some large transformers, near heavy-duty electrical motors, and so on). Failure to use a different type of medium increases the risk of impeding the data flow. This is an especially popular reason thickwire or fiber-optic cable appears in many networks, especially when multiple floors in an office building must be interconnected and the only available pathway is the elevator shaft.

▫ Certain parts of a network of networks (also known as an internetwork) may have to carry more traffic than other parts. Typically, the segment or segments where traffic aggregates is the backbone, a common cable segment that interconnects two or more subsidiary networks. (Think of a tree trunk as the backbone and the major branches as individual cable segments.) Often, a higher-capacity cable is used for a backbone (for example, fiber-optic cable or Category 5 cable rated for 100 Mbps Ethernet), along with a higher-speed networking technology for attachments to the backbone. This means that outlying segments might use conventional 10 Mbps Ethernet, while the backbone uses 100 Mbps Ethernet or switched Ethernet.

Using the information just presented, suggest solutions that involve at least two types, if possible, of networking media to address the following five projects.

Project 3-3: A Noisy Stretch

XYZ Corp. is planning a new network. Engineers in the design shop must be connected to the accountants and salespeople in the front office, but all routes between the two areas must traverse the shop floor, where arc welders and metal-stamping equipment create potent sources of EMI and RFI. Given that both the engineering and the front office areas will use 10BaseT (twisted-pair Ethernet), how might you interconnect those two areas? What medium guarantees immunity from such interference?

Project 3-4: Going the Distance

Once the front office gets networked at XYZ Corp., an accountant realizes that if the loading dock connects to the network, the dock workers could log incoming and outgoing shipments and keep the inventory much more current. Even though the loading dock is nowhere near the shop floor, the dock is 1100 feet from the front office. What kinds of cable will work to make this connection? What kind would you choose and why?

Project 3-5: Build a Better Backbone

ABC Company occupies three floors in a 10-story building, where the elevator shaft provides the only path to all three. In addition, users on the ninth and tenth floors must all access a collection of servers on the eighth floor. Explain what kind of connections would work in the elevator shaft. If more than one choice is possible, pick the best option and explain the reasons for your choice. Assuming that interfloor connections might someday need to run at significantly higher speeds, reevaluate your choice. What is the best type of medium for open-ended bandwidth needs? Explain your answer.

Project 3-6: More Bandwidth, No Cables

Very Big ISP Corporation (VBISP) wants to increase the bandwidth it can access at its downtown location in New York City. Bringing in new fiber-optic cables for the kinds of high-speed connections the corporation wants is out of the question, because the expense is millions of dollars. Given that cost dictates a high-bandwidth alternative to fiber-optic cable, what kind of solution makes sense? (*Hint*: Check the final section of the chapter, on high-speed wireless networking technologies, for the answer.)

Project 3-7: Extreme Long-Distance Networking

Following a year of major sales increases in the Pacific Rim, MarTexCo decides to open a second plant in Malaysia. The company wants the new plant to be able to access the headquarters database in Des Moines, IA, in real time, but long-haul telephone connections are not possible, owing to the lack of communications infrastructure at the Malaysia location. What kind of wireless networking alternative makes the most sense when considering network links that span an appreciable portion of the globe? Explain why laying cable might not be feasible.

CASE PROJECTS

1. XYZ Corp.'s Nashua, NH, facilities are two office buildings located 400 feet apart, each with its own LAN. To connect the two networks, you plan to dig a trench and lay cable in conduit between the two buildings. You want to use fiber-optic cable, but your budget-conscious facilities manager wants to use thinwire Ethernet. What's the best reason you can use to justify fiber-optic cable in this case?

   a. Thinnet will not span a 400-foot distance.

   b. Fiber-optic cable is cheaper and easier to work with than thinnet.

   c. Thinnet is a conductive cable and can therefore carry current based on the difference in ground potential between the two buildings.

   d. Fiber-optic leaves more room for growth, and for future needs for increased bandwidth, than thinnet does.

3

2. TVBCA is moving to new facilities. Its new campus includes three buildings, each no more than 100 meters apart from the others. The network should link all the buildings together. Each building is to be remodeled, so there's plenty of space to run cable and put the network together.

   Required result: The network must support speeds of up to 100 Mbps.

   Optional desired results: The network should be as secure as possible from electronic eavesdropping. To stay within TVBCA's budget, the network should also be as inexpensive as possible.

   Proposed solution: The network staff suggests using a fiber-optic backbone to link all three buildings. Which results does this solution deliver? Why?

   a. The proposed solution delivers the required result and both of the optional desired results.

   b. The proposed solution delivers the required result and only one of the two optional desired results.

   c. The proposed solution delivers the required result, but neither of the optional desired results.

   d. The proposed solution does not deliver the required result.

3. An advertising firm decides to install a network to link all employees' computers together. The company plans to introduce some video teleconferencing software across the board and plans heavy use of e-mail and database applications. Because of the anticipated load on the network, you want it to be as fast as possible.

   Required result: The network must operate at speeds of up to 100 Mbps.

   Optional desired results: The cabling should be as inexpensive as possible. Also, since you have to do the work yourself, you want installation to be easy.

   Proposed solution: You suggest using Category 5 UTP and hubs to connect all the workstations. Which results does this proposed solution produce? Explain your answer.

   a. The proposed solution delivers the required result and both of the optional desired results.

   b. The proposed solution delivers the required result and only one of the two optional desired results.

   c. The proposed solution delivers the required results, but neither of the optional desired results.

   d. The proposed solution does not deliver the required result.

4. XYZ Corp. decides to provide mobile computing to its field engineers. Each field engineer is to be supplied with a laptop, a portable fax/printer, and some kind of wireless transmission device.

   Required result: Field engineers must be able to send e-mail to and receive it from employees at the headquarters operation.

   Optional desired results: The wireless technology chosen should be as cheap as possible. It should also be secure from electronic eavesdropping.

   Proposed solution: The network manager recommends leasing a cellular link from GTE MobilNet for $2500 a month, plus air-time charges and encryption fees. Which results does this solution deliver? Explain your answer.

   a. The proposed solution delivers the required result and both of the optional desired results.

   b. The proposed solution delivers the required result and only one of the two optional desired results.

   c. The proposed solution delivers the required result, but neither of the optional desired results.

   d. The proposed solution does not deliver the required result.

5. TVBCA has just occupied an old historic building in downtown Pittsburgh in which 15 employees will work. Due to historic building codes, TVBCA is not permitted to run cables inside walls or ceilings.

   Required result: Employees must be able to share files and printers as in a typical LAN environment without the use of cables.

   Optional desired results: Employees must be able to use their laptops and move freely throughout the office while maintaining a network connection. Due to the size of some of the Computer-aided design (CAD) files employees frequently use, data transfer speeds should be well over 10 Mbps.

   Proposed solution: Install an 802.11b wireless access point and configure each computer and laptop with a wireless network card. Which results does the proposed solution deliver? Explain your answer.

   a. The proposed solution delivers the required result and both of the optional desired results.

   b. The proposed solution delivers the required result and only one of the two optional desired results.

   c. The proposed solution delivers the required result, but neither of the optional desired results.

   d. The proposed solution does not deliver the required result.

4

NETWORK INTERFACE CARDS

After reading this chapter and completing the exercises, you will be able to:

♦ Describe the role a network adapter card plays in networked communications

♦ Explain how network adapters prepare data for transmission, accept incoming network traffic, and control how networked communications flow

♦ Understand the variety of configurable options for network adapters, and describe common settings

♦ Describe important characteristics for selecting adapter cards

♦ Recount network adapter enhancements that can improve performance

♦ Explain the role of driver software in network adapters

Attaching a computer to a network requires a physical interface between the computer and the networking medium. For most PCs, this interface resides in a special **network interface card (NIC)**, also known as a **network adapter** or a **network card**, that plugs into an **adapter slot** inside the computer's case. Laptops and other computers may include built-in interfaces or use special modular interfaces, such as the PC Card interface (PCMCIA cards), to accommodate a network adapter. In any case, special hardware to mediate the connection between a computer and the networking medium—the focus of this chapter—must be present.

As a network administrator, you must understand what a network interface does and how it works. It's also important to understand what's involved in installing and configuring such hardware because network adapters are key ingredients in assembling a network. Therefore, you must understand how to install and configure PC adapters and know how to select an appropriate adapter for your situation. This knowledge is critical to your ability to manage any network.

NETWORK INTERFACE CARD (NIC) BASICS

For any computer, a NIC performs two crucial tasks: (1) it establishes and manages the computer's network connection; and (2) it translates digital computer data into signals (appropriate for the networking medium) for outgoing messages, and translates signals into digital computer data for incoming messages. In other words, the NIC establishes a link between a computer and a network and then manages that link on the computer's behalf.

From Parallel to Serial, and Vice Versa

Because of the nature of the connection between most NICs and the computers to which they're attached, network adapters also manage transformations in the form that network data takes. Most computers use a series of parallel data lines, called a computer bus (or **bus**, for short), to send data between the CPU and adapter cards. This allows the computer and adapters to exchange data in chunks equal to the number of lines that extend between them. Because data travels along multiple lines at the same time, and those lines run parallel, both metaphorically and physically, this type of data transmission is called **parallel transmission**.

However, for nearly all forms of networking media, the signals that traverse the media consist of a linear sequence of information that corresponds to a linear sequence of bits of data (or their analog equivalents on nondigital media). Because these bits of data follow one another in a straight line, or a series, this type of transmission is called **serial transmission**. Thus, one of the most important jobs a network adapter performs is to grab outgoing transmissions from the CPU in parallel form and recast them into their serial equivalents. For incoming messages, the process reverses: the network adapter grabs an incoming series of signals, translates them into bits, and distributes those bits across the parallel lines that communicate with the CPU. Figure 4-1 depicts this process.

An analogy may help clarify the difference between parallel and serial forms of data. A parallel transmission works like a multilane highway: each lane carries part of a stream of traffic—information between sender and receiver—at the same time. The larger the number of lanes, the more traffic—or information—the highway can carry at any given moment.

Using the same analogy, serial transmission resembles a one-lane road. Obviously, a serial line is inherently slower than a parallel line, because the speed of the line alone limits the amount of data a serial line can transmit; for a parallel set of lines, both the number and the speed of the lines play a role in how fast data can travel. Consequently, one of the most important components on a network adapter is memory, which acts as a holding tank, or **buffer**. The data going out in large parallel chunks must be serialized for output; incoming data arrives one bit at a time and must be distributed across all the parallel lines before a single set of bits can be delivered to the CPU.

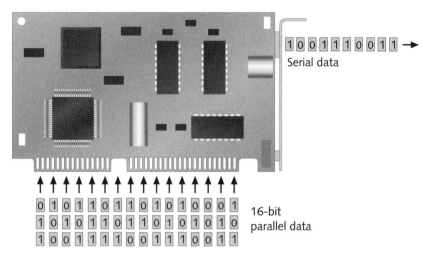

Figure 4-1   NICs mediate communication between a computer and the network cable

The collection of parallel lines that links elements inside a computer is called a bus. When data moves from one component to another, it moves along the bus. Most of the early-generation PCs used 8-bit buses—they used eight lines for data in parallel and could move eight bits' worth of data in a single bus transfer. The number of parallel lines that make up a particular kind of computer bus is called its **bus width**. For example, ISA supports 8- and 16-bit bus widths, EISA and MCA support 16- and 32-bit bus widths, and PCI supports 32- and 64-bit bus widths.

One significant improvement in the IBM PC/AT (AT stands for Advanced Technology) was its 16-bit bus. This bus became so prevalent that it is called the **Industry Standard Architecture (ISA)** bus. For years, this was the primary bus found on PCs. While some new PCs still include it, use of the ISA bus is waning and should disappear altogether from new PCs by 2004. The late 1980s to early 1990s witnessed the introduction of 32-bit buses, of which the 64-bit-capable **Peripheral Component Interface (PCI)** is the fastest and most popular in use today. Each of these bus types is explained later in the section titled "PC Buses."

To transmit data across the network medium, a network adapter must include or access a device called a **transceiver** that is designed for the specific medium in use. For common networking technologies such as Ethernet that work over a variety of media, it's common to find multiway NICs that can be configured to use one of several media attachments built into the card.

Figure 4-2 shows an Ethernet NIC that includes a female BNC connector, where the base of the T-connector attaches for a thinnet network, along with an AUI for thicknet and an RJ-45 for 10BaseT. With the appropriate setting chosen, the card can be told which attachment to use and brings the appropriate circuitry to bear. For both thinnet and 10BaseT, such NICs include a built-in, on-board transceiver; for thicknet, an external transceiver must be connected to the card through the AUI port on the back. With most newer cards only one type media connector is supported.

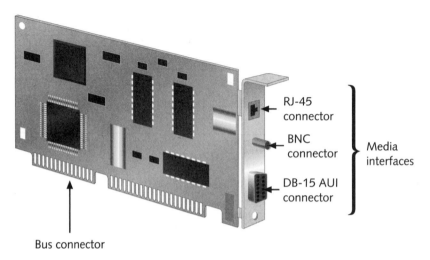

Figure 4-2   Ethernet NIC with interfaces for thinnet (BNC), thicknet (AUI), and 10BaseT (RJ-45)

Network adapters that use more exotic media—for example, certain wireless technologies or fiber-optic cable—usually support only that one medium. In that case, it's necessary to make the right connections to the card to establish a network connection, whether wired or wireless.

Network adapters also handle important data-packaging functions as they serialize outgoing parallel data streams from the CPU and translate incoming serial data streams from the network medium into parallel data. The NIC packages all the bits into orderly collections called **packets** and then transmits individual packets serially onto the network medium. For incoming messages, the NIC creates packets of data from incoming signals and then extracts the contents of each packet for parallel translation and delivery to the CPU. Packets are the fundamental unit of data for network transmission and reception. Much of the important processing that network adapters perform not only involves creating, sending, and receiving packets, but also dealing with packet-level errors and incomplete, or unintelligible, packet structures.

Other important roles a NIC plays are packaging and preparing data for transmission across the medium and managing access to the medium to know when to send data. Network adapters examine incoming network packets and check to find any addressed to the computer where the adapter resides. The NIC acts as a gatekeeper and permits inbound communications aimed only at its computer to pass through the interface and on to the CPU. Some NICs can operate in what's called "promiscuous mode"—this essentially turns off the gatekeeper functions and enables the NIC to forward any packets it sees to the computer. This functionality is important when it interacts with network scanning or sniffing software that analyzes overall traffic flow or permits detailed inspection of individual packets. For ordinary users, though, such functionality is usually unnecessary.

The NIC's role as gatekeeper points to another important function network adapters provide—determining whether the computer is the appropriate recipient of data sent across the wire. Each card has a unique identifier, called a **MAC address**, that takes the form of data programmed onto Read-Only Memory (ROM) on the interface. The IEEE sponsors a manufacturers' committee that designed an addressing scheme for network adapters and assigns unique blocks of addresses to NIC manufacturers. Each new NIC built has a unique, identifiable address encoded onto it, guaranteeing each computer its own network address. The gatekeeper function simply looks for an address bit string in the decoded packet that matches its own address or that corresponds to a valid "general delivery" address.

The address on any NIC is called the MAC address because the **Media Access Control (MAC)** functions in the NIC handle it. These addresses take the form of six two-digit **hexadecimal** numbers separated by colons—for example, 00:60:97:33:90:A3 is a MAC address. The first three numbers identify the manufacturer; the second three numbers define a unique network address.

By now, it should be clear that the NIC is intimately involved in managing and controlling network access, and its role goes beyond creating a physical link between a computer and a network medium. The NIC also handles data transfers to and from the network and CPU and translates which forms such data can take between parallel and serial representations. In addition, the NIC interacts with the medium to determine when data transmission is permissible.

PC Buses

When PCs were introduced, only a single bus design existed: an 8-bit bus of limited speed and capability, but as the technology evolved, other buses came along (and some have already left the scene). Today, a variety of PC bus types, also known as bus architectures, appear in modern PCs. Each bus differs in its layout and configuration (with a single exception, as you'll soon learn); therefore, it's imperative that any adapter card you want to use matches the bus type of the socket. Fortunately, as Figure 4-3 illustrates, distinguishing among these bus architectures is straightforward.

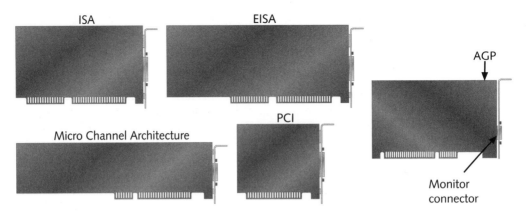

Figure 4-3   Primary PC bus architectures

Note the following facts about PC bus architectures:

- **Industry Standard Architecture (ISA).** The ISA bus originally appeared in the first PCs in an 8-bit form. With the introduction of the IBM PC/AT in 1984, the bus size doubled to 16 bits. Even so, the top end of rated bus speed for ISA remains a leisurely (by today's standards) 10 MHz, the same speed a "blazingly fast" 80286 PC/AT processor had when it was introduced in 1982. Although today's computers can still be found with ISA bus slots, many newer computers forgo the ISA bus altogether in favor of the newer bus standards.

- **Extended Industry Standard Architecture (EISA).** By 1988, a 16-bit bus was no longer sufficient to handle the demands that high-end network servers put on a PC bus. A consortium of PC clone vendors, led by Gary Stimac of Compaq Computer, developed the 32-bit EISA bus. Through mechanical and electrical trickery, EISA slots can accommodate either 16-bit ISA or 32-bit EISA adapters. Built with deeper edge connectors than ISA, EISA cards plug into a 32-bit socket beneath the 16-bit connector that ISA cards can reach. EISA runs at the same bus speeds as ISA, up to 10 MHz. EISA cards support more sophisticated bus controls than ISA, including bus mastering, which permits circuitry on the adapter to coordinate data transfers with other devices without requiring that the CPU do the job. (This chapter covers bus mastering later in the section titled "Choosing Network Adapters for Best Performance.") For the same reasons that ISA is rapidly disappearing from the PC landscape, new computers supporting EISA bus have gone the way of the dodo.

- **Micro Channel Architecture (MCA).** At around the same time EISA came along, IBM introduced its PS/2 computers, which feature the 32-bit MCA bus. MCA can work in 16- or 32-bit mode and supports a variety of bus speeds. MCA runs faster than ISA—up to 66 MHz in some non-PC implementations, from 5 to 20 MHz in PCs—and supports bus mastering as well. But IBM never opened its MCA specifications to the marketplace as it did with ISA.

Consequently, even IBM supports ISA and PCI in its PCs, but still uses MCA in its RISC/6000 and ES/9370 computer families. Some operating systems such as Windows 2000 no longer offer support for MCA, which significantly limits its future use.

- **Peripheral Component Interface (PCI).** The introduction of ever-faster CPUs brought about a parallel need for faster buses. Manufacturers created the idea of a local bus, which uses the same technology the CPU uses to communicate with RAM, and that co-processors use to communicate with peripherals. Several local bus standards appeared in the early 1990s, but by 1995, Intel's PCI bus became the default 32-bit bus standard. PCI is also widely available in a 64-bit version, and a 128-bit version is under development as faster buses continue to chase ever-speedier CPUs. PCI operates at 33 MHz and 66 MHz. A new PCI specification, PCI-X 1.0, is backward compatible to PCI, but supports 133 MHz speeds, providing data transfers in excess of 1 GB/s. This high speed will accommodate new developments in networking cards (such as Gigabit and 10 Gigabit Ethernet) and disk controllers (such as Ultra3 SCSI and Fibre Channel). As of this writing, both PCI and PCI-X NICs support Gigabit Ethernet running on fiber-optic or Cat 5 and Cat 5e cabling. PCI supports bus mastering and was the first bus to accommodate the Microsoft **Plug and Play** architecture as well. Finally, PCI supports interrupt sharing on a PC, so that any and all PCI adapters can share a single **Interrupt Request Line (IRQ)** without requiring a unique IRQ for each adapter. (Thus, only a single free IRQ is required for all PCI cards on a PC.) Due to the advances in the PCI technologies, some PC manufacturers are building PCs with only PCI slots.

- **PC cards.** Also known as **PCMCIA cards**, these credit-card size expansion cards are used primarily to add functionality to laptop computers. A variety of network interface cards are available in this format, including wireless.

- **Accelerated Graphics Port (AGP).** An Intel-developed, high-speed connection that links a display device directly to a computer's memory, AGP is a special-purpose bus that works only for computer displays. AGP operates at 33 MHz and can transfer data between memory and a computer display at up to 1 Gbps. It's not used for networking at present, and most AGP-equipped PCs include only a single AGP bus slot on the motherboard.

- **Developing bus standards.** As of this writing, new standards in development include PCI-X 266 and PCI-X 533 that will transfer data at 2.1 GB/s and 4.3 GB/s, respectively. Also in development is a serial-based bus called PCI Express (formerly named 3GIO) that is expected to operate at .5 GB/s initially, but will ramp up to 1, 2, 4, and 8 GB/s fairly quickly. Although PCI-X bus slots will be backward compatible with existing PCI boards, PCI Express hardware will maintain only some backward compatibility.

Although it's important to understand the characteristics and capabilities of these PC buses, it's not necessary to memorize their chronology or the companies that introduced them.

When working with PC buses, the most important requirement to remember is that the adapter you install in a PC—whether a network interface or some other peripheral device—matches the socket in the PC where you wish to put it. As you become more familiar with what's inside most PCs, you'll quickly recognize that most incorporate slots for more than one bus type. At the time of this writing, a quick review of current computer ads illustrates that the three most popular buses for desktop machines and network servers are ISA, AGP, and PCI.

For network servers, where fast network access is a key component in network performance, use 32-bit or 64-bit PCI NICs whenever possible. Because traffic aggregates at the server, spending extra money on a faster network card pays for itself quickly.

Other PC Interfaces Used for Networking

Although the following interface technologies don't replace the buses found inside most typical PCs, they do offer other ways to attach computers to networks. As with bus types, a computer must be equipped to accommodate devices built for any specific interface for that interface to be successfully attached to that machine. Typically, such interfaces may be added to a PC by inserting an adapter card for that interface into a bus. The interface is then made available on the "back side" of the adapter card and communicates with the PC through the bus connector on the adapter card. Today, the two most common such interfaces are:

- **Universal Serial Bus (USB) 1.0.** USB 1.0 is a relatively low-speed serial interface that operates at a maximum bandwidth of 12 Mbps. It's primarily used for low-speed peripheral devices such as mice, keyboards, or joysticks, but may also be used to attach printers, scanners, telephones, or some video devices to a computer. USB is now a standard interface both on PCs and Macintoshes for such uses. In networking, you most likely will find USB being used as an interface for wireless network adapters, or as the attachment for cable or DSL modems.

  USB 2.0 is the successor to USB 1.0 and can operate up to 480 Mbps—40 times faster than USB 1.0. This interface is being used for external hard drives, CD/DVD burners, high-speed scanners, and digital cameras.

- **FireWire** (also known as IEEE 1394). FireWire is a high speed serial bus, jointly developed by Apple Computer and Texas Instruments, that operates at bandwidths up to 400 Mbps. A newer version of the governing IEEE standard, 1394b, supports transfer rates up to 3200 Mbps. FireWire is used for high-bandwidth multimedia applications and can reserve guaranteed bandwidth for streaming video and multimedia. It's also used for networking and to attach digital cameras and video devices to computers. The popularity of FireWire and the new USB 2.0 standard has prompted many manufacturers to offer combo cards that sport both a FireWire interface and a USB 2.0 interface.

Principles of NIC Configuration

Once you match a network adapter to a slot in a PC, or plug it into a serial bus, your next step is to configure it to work with your computer. In a perfect world, this might mean opening the PC, seating (positioning) the network adapter in a bus slot, closing the PC box, and turning on the system. Alternately, it might only require plugging an external network interface into a serial bus port (very handy for laptops). As soon as the computer boots up, the network would be available. Unfortunately, it isn't usually this easy.

In an effort to approach this level of perfection, Microsoft introduced its Plug and Play architecture with the Windows 95 operating system. Plug and Play attempts to define a set of configuration protocols so a computer can communicate with its peripherals during the **power-on self-test (POST)** sequence and negotiate a working configuration without requiring human intervention. If the motherboard, operating system, and all adapters support Plug and Play, this works well. But if some devices do not support Plug and Play (these types of devices are referred to as legacy devices), or if any device fails to conform precisely to Plug and Play requirements, manual (human) intervention is required. For computer systems that do not precisely fit the Plug and Play model, or for PCs that run operating systems other than Windows 95, 98, 2000, or XP, manual configuration is essential to make any NIC work properly.

Typically, NIC configuration involves working with three types of PC settings:

- Interrupt request line (IRQ)
- **Base I/O port**
- **Base memory address**

You can be thankful that today's operating systems and PCI-bus Plug and Play NIC cards make manual configuration largely unnecessary. However, older NICs or older operating systems may make manual configuration a necessity from time to time. For a thorough treatment of expansion card configuration details, see *Enhanced A+ Guide to Managing and Maintaining Your PC, 3rd Ed.,* from Course Technology.

Making the Network Attachment

Network adapters perform several vital roles to coordinate communications between a computer and a network, including:

- Establishing a physical link to the networking medium
- Generating signals that traverse the networking medium

- Receiving incoming signals
- Implementing controls for when to transmit signals to or receive signals from the network medium

Because the network medium attaches directly to the network adapter, or through a transceiver attached to the adapter, it's important to match the adapter you choose with the medium to which it must attach. Every networking medium has its own physical characteristics that the adapter must accommodate. That's why NICs are built to accept certain kinds of connectors that match the media involved.

For common networking technology—for example, Ethernet—a network adapter usually can accommodate two or three media types (usually, two or more of thinnet, thicknet, and 10BaseT). But when a network adapter supports more than one media type, selecting the one to use becomes another configuration option. Normally, selecting the media type on such cards involves changing DIP switches or shifting a jumper block if the card isn't software-configurable. Whenever you encounter such a card, read the manual to get the information you need to configure the card correctly.

CHOOSING NETWORK ADAPTERS FOR BEST PERFORMANCE

As the focus of network traffic on workstations, and of large volumes of traffic on network servers (even those with more than one network interface), NICs can exert significant influence on network performance. If a NIC is slow, it can limit network performance. Particularly on networks with shared media, slow NICs anywhere on the network can decrease performance for all users.

When selecting a network adapter, you must first identify the physical characteristics the card must match. These include the type of network technology in use and the kind of connector or physical attachment the adapter must accommodate. Once you determine these basic characteristics, it's equally important to consider other options available for purchase that can seriously affect a card's speed and data-handling capabilities. Some of these options suit servers better, whereas others work equally well for servers and clients; all help improve overall network performance. These hardware-enhancement options include:

- **Direct Memory Access (DMA)** allows an adapter to transfer data directly from its on-board buffers into the computer's memory, without requiring the CPU to coordinate memory access.
- **Shared adapter memory** means the adapter's buffers map directly into RAM on the computer. When the computer thinks it's writing to its own memory, it's writing to the buffers on the NIC. In this instance, the computer treats adapter RAM as its own.

- **Shared system memory** means a NIC's on-board processor selects a region of RAM on the computer and writes to it as if it were buffer space on the adapter. In this instance, the adapter treats computer RAM as its own.

- **Bus mastering** permits a network adapter to take control of the computer's bus to initiate and manage data transfers to and from the computer's memory, independent of the CPU. This lets the CPU concentrate on other tasks and can improve network performance 20% to 70%. Such cards are more expensive than other NICs, but are worth the price, especially for servers.

- **RAM buffering** means a NIC includes additional memory to provide temporary storage for incoming and outgoing data that arrives at the NIC faster than it can be shipped out. This speeds overall performance because it lets the NIC process data as quickly as it can, without having to pause occasionally to grab (or send) more data.

- **On-board co-processors** included on some NICs permit the card to process data (that is, packetize outgoing data or depacketize incoming data) without requiring service from the CPU. Today, most NICs include such processors to speed network operations.

- **Security features** may be available on some high-end NICs. These permit the card to handle several protocol functions, including IPSec and other encryption services related to authentication and payload protection. **IPSec (IP Security)** is a secure transport mechanism that's gaining broad acceptance as a way to protect network traffic from unwanted snooping.

- **Traffic management** may also be available on some high-end NICs. These services include improved abilities to guarantee levels of access to the network (called **Quality of Service (QoS)** when applied to streaming video or multimedia or other applications that require bandwidth guarantees) to support remote management software and services, and more.

- Improved **fault tolerance**, in the form of redundant NICs with failover capabilities, may be available on some high-end NICs. By installing a second such NIC in a PC, failure of the primary NIC shifts network traffic to the second NIC, rather than cutting off the PC from the network. Hot-plug-capable NICs are also an option for fault tolerance because a NIC can be installed or removed without turning off the server. NICs with dual ports provide added bandwidth and fault tolerance. These NICs have two media connectors, both of which may be active, providing double the bandwidth and fault tolerance in the event that one media connection fails.

- **Improved management**, by way of features such as wake-on-LAN, which allows an administrator to power-on a PC remotely by accessing the NIC through the network. This is a useful feature for tasks such as maintenance. Simple Network Management Protocol (SNMP) comes built-in on some NICs, allowing the NIC to be configured and managed remotely.

When you select the number of such options on any network interface you must weigh carefully how much network traffic the adapter must handle and how important its continued functioning is. The more traffic, the bigger the payback speed-up options can provide. For servers, this means buying the fastest network interface you can find (or afford, as the case may be); usually, this means 64-bit, bus-mastering PCI-X NICs with shared memory and substantial on-board buffer space. For workstations, slower cards may be acceptable on machines that use the network lightly, but any machine that accesses the network heavily for demanding applications, such as database management systems (DBMSs) or CAD, benefits from any speed-up options a quality network adapter can provide. Increased availability, reliability, and manageability have obvious payoffs for servers that may not apply to workstations.

SPECIAL-PURPOSE NICs

In addition to straightforward network adapters, several types of cards deliver specialized capabilities. These include interfaces for wireless networks as well as a special type of interface for so-called diskless workstations (a.k.a. thin clients), which must access the network to load an operating system as they boot up. For that reason, such cards are said to support remote boot or remote initial program load.

Wireless Adapters

Wireless network adapters usually include more gear than conventional cabled NICs. Nevertheless, wireless NICs are available for most major network operating systems, including Windows NT, Windows XP/2000, Windows .NET Server, and NetWare, among others. Such interfaces usually incorporate some or all of the following components:

- Indoor antenna and antenna cable
- Software to enable the adapter to work with a particular network environment
- **Diagnostic software** to check initial installation or to troubleshoot thereafter
- Installation software

Although it's unusual, such adapters can be used to build entirely wireless local area networks (LANs). More commonly, they are used with a wireless access point device to add wireless elements to an existing wired network.

Remote Boot Adapters

In some situations, organizations want to use workstations without disk drives, whether for security reasons, kiosks, or other public-access uses. It's not surprising that such computers are often called **diskless workstations**. But because most computers start themselves (in a process called **boot up**) by reading information from a disk of some kind, the network must be the source of access to the programs needed to boot up a diskless workstation.

For such uses, some network adapters include a chip socket for a special bit of circuitry called a **Boot PROM** (programmable read-only memory), which is referred to as PXE compliant. The Boot PROM contains just enough hardwired code (usually 0.5 MB or less) to start the computer and access the network to download an operating system and other software that, when complete, permits the machine to perform its assigned tasks. Once a diskless workstation finishes booting, it can use the network to read and write any additional needed data. Most manufacturers also offer bootable floppies to support this type of diskless environment.

Remote boot adapters offer several advantages. First, there is cost savings because no hard drive is required. This provides an added benefit of better reliability because hard drives are a common source of problems in PCs. Second, there is increased security. Without a hard drive, no sensitive data can be stored with the computer. Additionally, virus attacks prove useless on a diskless workstation because the virus has neither a place to reside nor files to infect. For these reasons, diskless workstations using remote boot adapters are becoming popular in situations that do not require the workstation to maintain local long-term data storage.

DRIVER SOFTWARE

At first, a network adapter appears to be entirely physical. It's a piece of hardware that connects to some networking medium and provides the signaling circuitry necessary to use that medium to send and receive information across a network. Before a network adapter can become more than an inert hunk of metal, plastic, and silicon, a software **driver**—more formally, a **device driver**—for the card must be installed on your computer. Incorrect drivers or poorly written drivers can have a detrimental impact on the overall performance of a network or even prevent the user's PC from booting. The proper installation of correct drivers is extremely important. Installation should be done only by experienced personnel.

In the earliest days of networks, each NIC vendor custom built its own drivers. But it quickly became apparent that tracking every software change and every hardware revision was a difficult (and thankless) task. Consequently, operating system (OS) vendors developed a way to define device drivers to permit their operating systems to communicate with hardware devices installed in a computer. Thus, the driver is a small, specialized program that knows how to represent a particular device to some operating system and how to manage communications between the operating system and the adapter card.

You should become familiar with three major vendor standards that apply to drivers: NDIS, WDM, and ODI. Explanations of these vendor standards follow:

- The **Network Device Interface Specification (NDIS)** defines a communications interface (called the NDIS interface) between the MAC sublayer and the network interface driver. The main benefit of NDIS is that it allows NICs to use multiple protocols simultaneously. It applies to most Windows operating systems in use today, including Windows 9x, Windows NT, and Windows 2000/XP.

- The **Win32 Driver Model (WDM)** defines a complete adapter card driver interface for PCs that run modern 32-bit Windows operating systems. (Today, this means Windows 98 and Windows 2000/XP machines.) The WDM architecture divides drivers into various bus and device classes by function, enabling generic class drivers to handle common details for the adapter bus and for the type of device to which it attaches (such as Ethernet card, token ring card, printer, and scanner). Therefore, developers who create device drivers can concentrate on writing only the most device-specific portion of the driver code. This improves overall driver quality, since it subjects class drivers to intense scrutiny and testing, and allows manufacturers to concentrate on writing code specific to the devices that they want to sell. The WDM also interfaces with the Plug and Play manager in Windows 98 and Windows 2000/XP, allowing maximum automation for most devices and their drivers.

- Apple Computer and Novell defined the **Open Data-link Interface (ODI)**, not only to allow a NIC to use multiple protocols but also to simplify driver development for NIC manufacturers. Thus, ODI is quite similar to NDIS (but different enough to require a separate driver architecture).

These standards apply to more than network interfaces. Printers need printer drivers, tape drives need tape drivers, disk controllers need controller drivers, and so on. In short, the driver mediates between an operating system and some kind of external device. As a result, the operating system can communicate with that device without implementing all the specifics inherent in sending and receiving data from some piece of hardware.

Installing a driver for a network adapter is usually easy. Many operating systems, including Windows 9x and Windows 2000/XP, ship with drivers for a broad range of devices—including most popular NICs—as part of their release packages. Also, most NICs include one or more disks with drivers for the most widely available operating systems—again, including the current Windows operating systems. Although the details of installing a driver are operating-system specific, most installation programs provide a graphical interface with built-in help to make the job as easy as possible.

Although driver installation for NIC cards on modern operating systems is fairly straightforward, this has not always been the case. Windows NT, for example, provides limited support for NIC cards during installation and often does not recognize the NIC. This is problematic for novice installers of NT. It is critical to have the NIC drivers available on floppy disk during NT installation.

Figure 4-4 shows how to install a new network connection on Windows 2000, including the software driver. To perform this action, click the Start button, select Settings, select Network and Dial-up Connections, and then double-click the Make New Connection option.

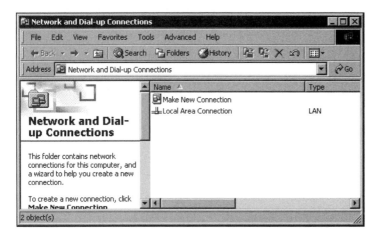

Figure 4-4 Network and Dial-up Connections dialog box in Windows 2000

 Although it's tempting to assume that manufacturers supply all necessary drivers with their adapters, you should make sure a driver is available for your operating system before you purchase a NIC. If, as with Windows 2000/XP and Windows NT, the OS vendor supplies a **Hardware Compatibility List (HCL)**, choosing a NIC from such a list nearly guarantees a flawless installation.

During the driver installation, you are prompted to supply necessary configuration information, which usually includes the card's IRQ and its base I/O port ID, at a minimum. This configuration information usually is necessary with legacy NICS due to resource conflicts. Most plug and play NICS will install and use available computer resources without any user intervention.

It is crucial that the information you supply to the installation program agrees with the settings on the adapter. That's why, when you install the hardware, you should record your configuration data for later reference. This information also comes in handy if you need to troubleshoot that machine's network connection in the future.

NIC driver software continually evolves. Whenever you plan to install any NIC, try to determine if newer software is available. Good places to check for such information usually are documented in the NIC's manual and often include the vendor's Web site and its technical support line, or the Web site of the operating system manufacturer. The NIC and operating system manufacturer Web sites are also good places to find troubleshooting information for a NIC installation and operation. The larger manufacturers have a searchable database of problems and their resolutions in what is called a **knowledgebase**.

A knowledgebase allows you to enter a keyword or an error code to search for a problem. If the problem or error has been encountered before, it is likely that the resolution will be posted.

Likewise, you should check one or more of these resources from time to time just to see if drivers changed since your installation. If so, it's usually just as easy to update a NIC driver as it is to install one—the only necessity is a copy of the latest and greatest driver. In fact, easy driver upgrades are often touted as yet another benefit of modern operating systems, which treat drivers as independent software components that you can change at a moment's notice. If the driver were built into the operating system, you'd have to wait for the operating system to change before the driver could change.

CHAPTER SUMMARY

❑ Network interface cards (NICs) supply the interface between a computer and the networking medium. Network adapters also prepare, send, and control data flow across the network.

❑ When sending data, a NIC must reformat outgoing data from the parallel form that arrives via the computer's bus to the serial form used over most networking media; to receive data, this process is reversed. Each NIC incorporates a unique hardware network address to distinguish it from all other NICs on a network.

❑ NICs include configurable options that must be properly set for an adapter to make a working network connection; these options are usually automatically selected by the Plug and Play process, but sometimes they require specifying a unique interrupt request line (IRQ), base I/O port, and base memory address.

❑ For compatibility, the NIC's edge connector must match the PC slot into which it plugs; likewise, the NIC's media attachment must match the network medium and connector type to which it will connect.

❑ Network adapters can exert a profound effect on overall network performance. Numerous performance-improving options, including Direct Memory Access (DMA), shared adapter or system memory, and bus mastering, can enhance the capabilities of such cards. Other useful enhancements include RAM buffering or incorporating an on-board co-processor to offload data-handling chores from the computer's CPU. Network adapters can even incorporate specialized capabilities, including hot-plug, dual ports, security settings, management interfaces, wireless communications, and remote boot support.

❑ When purchasing a network adapter, consider the following checklist:

- Bus width (16-bit is slower than 32-bit; pick PCI or PCI-X)
- Bus type (pick PCI-X for servers whenever possible)
- Memory transfer (shared memory outpaces I/O or DMA)

- Special features required (security, management, protocol handling, hot-plug capable)

- Bus mastering (important for servers)

- Vendor factors (quality, reliability, staying power, reputation)

❏ The driver software is the key ingredient that permits a network adapter to communicate with a computer's operating system. It's essential to ensure that a valid driver is available for your operating system before purchasing an adapter; even better, always obtain the latest driver versions before installing any network adapter. It's also a good idea to make regular driver upgrades part of your network maintenance routine.

4

KEY TERMS

adapter slot — The sockets built into a PC motherboard that are designed to seat adapter cards. *See also* Accelerated Graphics Port, Industry Standard Architecture, Extended Industry Standard Architecture, Micro Channel Architecture, and Peripheral Component Interface. (All represent specific types of adapter slots.)

Accelerated Graphics Port (AGP) — A special-purpose bus used solely to interconnect PCs with a graphics adapter and one or more display devices. AGP is a high-speed, 64-bit-wide bus capable of bandwidth from 0.25 to 1.0 Gbps.

base I/O port — The memory address where the CPU and an adapter check for messages that they leave for each other.

base memory address — The memory address at which the transfer area between the computer's main memory and a NIC's buffers begin, bounded by the size of its extent, which is the size of an area that describes the upper limit of a memory region on a PC named by a base address that indicates the starting point (upper bound = base address + extent).

Boot PROM — A special programmable chip that includes enough software to permit a computer to boot sufficiently and access the network. From there, it can download an operating system to finish the boot process. This is also known as PXE compliant.

boot up — The process a computer goes through when starting, also called booting.

buffer — A temporary storage area that a device uses to contain incoming data before it can be processed for input or to contain outgoing data before it can be sent as output.

bus — Also called the bus architecture, a specialized collection of parallel lines in a PC used to ship data between the CPU and peripheral devices and, occasionally, from one peripheral device to another. One or both adapters involved must have bus-mastering capabilities.

bus mastering — The quality of an adapter card's circuitry that allows it to take possession of a computer's bus and coordinate data transfers without requiring any service from the computer's CPU.

bus width — The number of parallel lines that make up a particular kind of computer bus. For example, ISA supports 8- and 16-bit bus widths, EISA and MCA support 16- and 32-bit bus widths, and PCI supports 32- and 64-bit bus widths.

device driver — A software program that mediates communication between an operating system and a specific device for the purpose of sending and/or receiving input and output from that device. These drivers are operating-system dependent. They also need to be kept up to date per the information on the manufacturer's Web site.

diagnostic software — Specialized programs that can probe and monitor a system (or a specific system component) to determine if it works properly and, if not, to try to establish the cause of the problem.

Direct Memory Access (DMA) — A technique for addressing memory on some other device as if it were local memory directly available to the device accessing that memory. This technique lets a CPU gain immediate access to the buffers on any NIC that supports DMA.

diskless workstations — Network computers that require a special type of ROM because they have no built-in hard or floppy drives.

driver — An abbreviation for "device driver," a small program that mediates between an operating system and the hardware device it knows how to access.

Extended Industry Standard Architecture (EISA) — A 32-bit PC bus architecture that is backward compatible with the older, slower 16-bit ISA bus architecture.

fault tolerance — A system feature which allows it to continue working after an unexpected hardware or software failure.

FireWire — A high-speed, external serial bus that supports bandwidths up to 400 Mbps and can connect up to 63 devices. Also known as IEEE 1394. FireWire is used for streaming video and multimedia, networking, and to attach video devices to computers.

Hardware Compatibility List (HCL) — A vendor-maintained list of all hardware compatible with a particular operating system. In practice, it is the name of a document maintained by Microsoft that lists all hardware compatible with Windows NT or Windows 2000.

hexadecimal — A mathematical notation for representing numbers in base 16. The numbers 10 through 15 are expressed as A through F; 10h or 0x10 (both notations indicate the number is hexadecimal) equals 16.

Industry Standard Architecture (ISA) — Originally an 8-bit PC bus architecture, but upgraded to 16-bit with the introduction of the IBM PC/AT in 1984.

Interrupt Request Line (IRQ) — Any of 16 unique signal lines between the CPU and the bus slots on a PC. IRQs define the mechanism whereby a peripheral device of any kind, including a network adapter, can stake a claim on the PC's attention. Such a claim is called an "interrupt," which gives the name to the lines that carry this information.

IPSec (IP Security) — An Internet security protocol that's gaining acceptance as a way to protect network traffic from unwanted snooping.

knowledgebase — A searchable database that contains problems and errors, along with their solutions, related to a manufacturer's product.

Media Access Control (MAC) — A level of data communication where the network interface can directly address the networking media; also refers to a unique address programmed into network adapters to identify them on any network where they might appear.

MAC address — The number that identifies the physical address of a computer on a network. This address is hard wired into the computer's NIC.

4

Micro Channel Architecture (MCA) — IBM's proprietary 16- and 32-bit computer buses. Originally developed for its PS/2 PCs, MCA is now popular on its midrange RISC/6000 computers.

network adapter — A synonym for network interface card (NIC). It refers to the hardware device that mediates communication between a computer and one or more types of networking media. *See also* network interface card.

network card — Synonym for network interface card.

Network Device Interface Specification (NDIS) — A standard for providing an interface between a network interface card and the network medium that enables a NIC to use multiple protocols.

network interface card (NIC) — The hardware device that mediates communication between a computer and one or more types of networking media.

on-board co-processor — A special- or general-purpose microprocessor that appears on an adapter card, usually to offload data from a computer's CPU. NICs with on-board co-processors usually employ the special-purpose variety.

Open Data-link Interface (ODI) — A specification developed by Apple Computer and Novell that simplified driver development and enabled the use of multiple protocols from a single NIC.

packet — A specially organized and formatted collection of data destined for network transmission; alternately, the form in which network transmissions are received following conversion into digital form.

parallel transmission — The technique of spreading individual bits of data across multiple, parallel data lines to transmit them simultaneously, rather than according to an ordinal and temporal sequence.

PC cards — Credit-card size expansion cards used to add functionality to laptop computers.

PCMCIA cards — *See* PC cards.

Peripheral Component Interface (PCI) — The 32- and 64-bit PC bus architecture that currently prevails as the best and fastest of all available bus types, operating at 33 and 66 MHz. PCI-X supports 64-bits at 133 MHz for 1 GB/s data transfers.

Plug and Play — The Microsoft requirements for PC motherboards, buses, adapter cards, and operating systems which let a PC automatically detect and configure hardware on a system. For Plug and Play to work properly, all system components must conform rigorously to its specifications; currently, only Windows 95, Windows 98, and Windows 2000 support this architecture.

power-on self-test (POST) — The set of internal diagnostic and status-checking routines a PC and its peripheral devices perform each time the computer is powered on.

Quality of Service (QoS) — A networking term that specifies a guaranteed level of service when applied to applications that require high bandwidth.

RAM buffering — A memory-access technique that permits an adapter to use a computer's main memory as if it were local buffer space.

security feature — In terms of NICs, a feature that allows the card to handle security-related protocols, including encryption services.

serial transmission — A technique for transmitting data signals, which set each bit's worth of data (or its analog equivalent) one at a time, one after another, in sequence.

shared adapter memory — A technique for a computer's CPU to address memory on an adapter as if it were the computer's own main memory.

shared system memory — A technique for an adapter to address a computer's main memory as if it were resident on the adapter itself.

traffic management — In terms of NICs, features that improve network accessibility for remote users, especially those using applications that require higher bandwidth, such as streaming video or multimedia.

transceiver — A device that transmits and receives network information.

Universal Serial Bus (USB) 1.0 — A hot-pluggable Plug and Play serial interface that operates at a maximum data transfer rate of 12 Mbps. USB ports support peripheral devices such as mice, keyboards, and other pointing devices, in addition to some printers, scanners, telephony equipment, and monitors. USB 2.0 supports up to 480 Mbps.

Win32 Driver Model (WDM) — A unified driver architecture that allows a single driver to be written for both Windows 98 and Windows 2000/XP.

REVIEW QUESTIONS

1. Of the following PC bus types, which supports 32-bit data transmission? (Choose all that apply.)

   a. PCI

   b. MCA

   c. EISA

   d. ISA

2. Which of the following statements is true?

   a. A driver is a small program that mediates between the computer's operating system and a hardware device.

   b. A driver is part of the operating system.

   c. Only one driver is needed to handle communications between the computer's operating system and all peripheral devices.

   d. Operating systems usually include all the drivers you need to install for any NIC.

   e. You need a driver only if the NIC does not support Plug and Play.

3. When installing a NIC driver, the configuration information you supply to the installation software must _____ the way you configured the hardware.

   a. agree with

   b. differ from

4. A network adapter card converts serial data from the computer into parallel data from the network for transmission and reverses that process on reception. True or false?

5. Today's most popular PC bus widths are:

   a. 16-bit and 24-bit

   b. 24-bit and 48-bit

   c. 8-bit and 32-bit

   d. 16-bit and 32-bit

6. The PCI-X bus standard pushes data transfer rates to _____.

   a. 1 MB/s

   b. 10 GB/s

   c. 1 GB/s

   d. 10 MB/s

7. Where is temporary data stored on a network adapter to act as a buffer for excess input or output?

   a. transceiver

   b. physical attachment

   c. on-board co-processor

   d. on-board RAM

4

8. To work properly, which characteristics of a network adapter must match those of the network medium? (Choose all that apply.)

   a. network technology

   b. connector type

   c. transmission speed

   d. media type

9. If two devices share a common IRQ, the most likely outcome is that
   _____.

   a. each device takes a turn talking to the CPU

   b. service requests are handled first-come, first-served

   c. neither device works

   d. the device inserted into the lowest slot ID works; the other does not

10. Which of the following methods may be used to configure a multiway NIC for a particular media interface? (Choose all that apply.)

    a. jumper settings

    b. DIP switches

    c. software configuration

    d. boot configuration files

11. Which of the following PC buses can function in 16- or 32-bit mode and also accommodate independent functioning from multiple bus masters? (Choose all that apply.)

    a. ISA

    b. EISA

    c. MCA

    d. PCI

12. Which of the following Microsoft operating systems support Plug and Play? (Choose all that apply.)

    a. DOS 6.22

    b. Windows 3.11

    c. Windows 95

    d. Windows NT Workstation 4.0

    e. Windows XP Professional

13. A 16-bit ISA adapter works in which of these types of PC bus slots? (Choose all that apply.)

    a. ISA

    b. EISA

    c. MCA

    d. PCI

14. Which of the following NIC performance enhancements is recommended for use in a server? (Choose all that apply.)

    a. bus-mastering

    b. DMA

    c. shared memory

    d. 32-bit bus or higher

15. Of the following items, which are most likely to be required when manually configuring a NIC? (Choose all that apply.)

    a. DMA address

    b. IRQ

    c. base I/O port

    d. base memory address

    e. transceiver setting/media type selection

16. The NIC device that translates digital data into signals for transmission, and signals into digital data on receipt, is called a(n) _____.

    a. media attachment unit (MAU)

    b. transceiver

    c. emitter

    d. MAC address

17. Which of the following roles does a network adapter play in connecting a computer to a networking medium? (Choose all that apply.)

    a. formats outgoing data into data packets for transmission and translates incoming signals into data packets on receipt

    b. provides a physical link to the network medium

    c. acts as a gatekeeper to control access to the medium for transmission and to direct incoming traffic on receipt

    d. converts parallel bus data into serial form for transmission and serial data packets into parallel form on receipt

    e. provides a unique hardware-level network address specific to the network adapter

18. Which of the following factors contributed to the development of new data buses in PCs? (Choose all that apply.)

a. Networks got faster, so buses did too.

b. Increased CPU speeds demanded faster, wider buses.

c. Increased application sophistication increased users' demands for data.

d. More applications needed network support.

e. Bigger operating systems bred bigger buses.

19. The POST sequence is intended to perform which of the following tasks?

a. check the CPU, motherboard, and peripherals at PC boot time

b. provide built–in diagnostics when system errors occur

c. support Microsoft Plug and Play functionality

d. develop an ongoing set of performance and operations data for PCs

20. Which of the following driver architectures is supported only in Windows 98, Windows 2000, and Windows XP?

a. Plug and Play

b. WDM

c. NDIS

d. ODI

21. A special circuitry device that can be inserted into some NICs to support booting the system across the network is called a _____.

a. bootstrap loader

b. boot chip

c. Boot PROM

d. Boot ROM

22. Which of the following buses or serial interfaces supports the highest bandwidth? (*Hint:* To calculate bandwidth, multiply maximum speed in MHz by bus width.)

a. ISA

b. USB

c. PCI

d. PCI-X

e. FireWire

23. Which serial standard improves on the older version by up to 40 times the existing data transfer rate?

    a. 1394

    b. PCI-X

    c. 3GIO

    d. USB 2.0

24. Which emerging serial bus technology will bring data transfer rates up to 8 GB/s?

    a. 1394b

    b. USB 3.0

    c. PCI Express

    d. ISA-X

25. The address burned into ROM on a NIC is called the _____.

26. Advantages of a remote boot adapter include which of the following? (Choose all that apply.)

    a. increased reliability

    b. better security

    c. higher performance

    d. virus protection

27. The ODI drive model was defined by _____.

    a. Microsoft

    b. Novell

    c. IBM

    d. Digital Equipment Corporation

28. Choosing a NIC from the _____ almost guarantees that the NIC will install without errors in the Windows 2000 operating system.

29. The type of connector used for a 10BaseT network is the _____.

    a. AUI

    b. transceiver

    c. RJ-45

    d. BNC

30. The type of connector used for a thinnet network is the _____.

    a. AUI

    b. transceiver

    c. RJ-45

    d. BNC

HANDS-ON PROJECTS

Installing a network interface card (NIC) in a PC involves several steps. In this series of Hands-on Projects, you start by checking your PC's current configuration to determine what kinds of IRQs, base I/O addresses, and other configuration elements are available. If you know what settings are already taken, you may be able to install a network interface card in your PC within the various configuration elements that remain available.

Although the Hands-on Projects do not pose situations as complex as those you're likely to encounter in a real-world production environment, they help you develop the skills necessary to make your PCs network ready. If the machines in which you install network adapters run Windows 98, Windows 2000, or Windows XP, and all system elements are fully Plug and Play compatible, the systems probably require no effort. Because this is a far from perfect world (and not all PCs run these Windows versions), you will probably take the same series of steps when performing a real installation as you must to complete these projects.

 These projects assume that in the computer lab you have ready access to copies of all the manuals for all of the adapters already installed in the PC, as well as the manual for the network adapter you're about to install. This may not be true in the workplace. This project requires you to document settings on your PC. In the real world, you'd start by gathering all the documentation for system components before documenting a PC's IRQs, DMA settings, base I/O addresses, and so forth.

End-user machines often have more (and more exotic) adapters installed than do many servers. Sometimes all the common IRQs, or base I/O addresses, or other settings, are occupied. Because network connectivity is usually a necessity rather than a luxury, you must find some way to install a NIC in the PC. This usually leads to one of two solutions, each of which can be painful to execute:

❑ Checking other adapter manuals to see which unoccupied settings might work for the adapters. If you can switch other adapters to other settings to make room for the NIC, you've solved your problem.

❑ Deciding which of the other adapters is least important and removing it from the system. Elements of the preceding solution may still be required, because this does not always free the entire range of configuration settings a network adapter may require.

Project 4-1

To document your PC's configuration:

1. Microsoft includes a system documentation tool with Windows 98, Windows NT, and Windows 2000/XP. Unless your instructor informs you otherwise, assume you'll use one of these built-in utilities. For Windows 98, and Windows 2000/XP, use the **Start**, **Run** menu sequence to invoke the Run dialog box. Enter **msinfo32.exe**. For Windows NT, use **winmsd.exe**. See Figure 4-5 for an example of launching the System Information utility from the Run dialog box on Windows 2000.

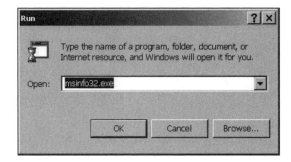

Figure 4-5   Running msinfo32.exe diagnostic utility on Windows 2000

2. Whichever version of the program you use, you must explore its various sources of information. The Windows 2000 version appears in Figure 4-6; it organizes everything neatly under graphical folders. (*Hint*: The Hardware Resources folder contains what you're interested in, including IRQ, I/O port, DMA settings, and more.)

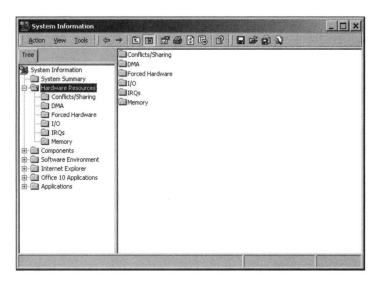

Figure 4-6   Windows 2000 System Information utility

3. Using the System Information utility, find out as much as you can about the IRQ status, base I/O addresses, and DMA settings (if applicable) of your machine. Fill out the following chart for your system to help determine what's available:

IRQ	Typical Assignment	Current Assignment	DMA	Other
0	PC system timer			
1	Keyboard			
2	IRQ controller/video adapter			
3	Unassigned (COM2/COM4, bus mouse)			
4	COM1/COM3			
5	Unassigned			
6	Floppy disk controller			
7	Parallel port LPT1			
8	Real-time clock			
9	IRQ controller, sound card			
10	Unassigned (SCSI controller)			
11	Unassigned (secondary SCSI controller)			
12	PS/2 mouse			
13	Math co-processor			
14	Primary IDE controller			
15	Secondary IDE controller			

Project 4-2

Once you map your PC's occupied IRQs, base I/O addresses, DMA settings, and other configuration items, you can determine whether or not the system can accommodate a network adapter based on the current settings available. Only when you establish that some sequence of settings available on the PC will work with the network adapter should you begin the installation. Consult your instructor to obtain any additional information you may need before proceeding with this project. This project assumes you have access to a PC, the requisite tools (flat- and Phillips-head screwdrivers usually suffice), an adapter card to insert, a driver disk (or access to drivers on a CD-ROM or other media), and some kind of network medium, ready to plug into the network adapter, once it's been installed.

To install a network adapter:

1. Always begin with a preinstallation checklist. For this project, make sure you have all of the elements just mentioned: tools, the adapter, a driver disk, access to the network medium, and a copy of the adapter manual.

 Before working on any computer, be sure you have observed proper safety precautions and have a proper ground strap.

4

2. Read the adapter manual. Determine the factory default settings for the adapter. Will they fit within available, open settings on the PC? If so, you're over the hardest part. If not, you must check alternate settings that the card supports against what's available on your machine. If you find a match, you must then make necessary adjustments to the hardware (DIP switches, jumper settings, or perhaps altering the configuration information in the card's setup software for software-configurable adapters) to accommodate them. Write down the settings you plan to use (on the chart from the previous project, if you like). Then make sure you understand how to make whatever changes are necessary before moving to the next step.

3. If your PC is turned on, turn it off. Note which cable fits into which connector before you take the whole PC apart. You can tape small labels onto the back of the machine and place corresponding labels on the cords and cables themselves. If you cannot put things back together properly when you finish, you cannot restore the computer to operating condition. Don't proceed until you feel comfortable that you can do this. Standing on an antistatic floor covering, remove the power cord, then unplug all other cords and cables that attach to the machine.

4. Remove the screws or pins that anchor the computer's external case to its internal chassis. You must remove the case (or some portion of it, depending on what kind of computer you're using) to access the location of the adapter slots in your PC. If you're unsure how to proceed, ask your instructor for help.

5. When the computer case is open, inspect the available unoccupied adapter slots and locate one that matches the slot type on your network adapter card. Unless you have an EISA slot and an ISA card, the edge connector on the card and the available slot must both be of the same type; otherwise, you cannot install the network adapter.

6. Before you can insert the card, you must properly configure it (and double-check it for correctness). Examine the jumper or DIP switch settings, if applicable, and make sure they match the configuration needed to make your card work. (If you have a software-configurable card, you can skip this step.) Typical items to check include IRQ, DMA, base I/O address, and media type. Make sure these match what works, and what is needed, for your PC.

7. Once you locate an available slot of the right type, prepare it for installation. If a placeholder (shown in Figure 4-7) covers the access hole in the case for that slot, you must remove the placeholder before you can insert the network adapter.

Figure 4-7   Placeholders keep dust and dirt out of the PC case

8. To insert the adapter, grab the card by the upper corners, then position the edge connector directly over the empty PC slot where you will insert it. Gently rock the adapter back and forth, while pushing down gently, until the card is firmly seated. Screw the case edge of the card onto the chassis, using the screw you removed from the placeholder (or one of the proper size and threading).

9. Once the card is properly seated, close the case and test your work. The proper way to do this is to reattach the case to the chassis and reinsert all cables and cords. You also want to plug the network medium into the newly installed network adapter, perhaps for the first time. As your final step, insert the power cord.

Project 4-3

To check the hardware installation:

1. Check that you have properly put the machine back together. Turn on the power and see what happens.

 If you hear funny noises or smell smoke, turn off the power immediately!

2. Check to see if the machine boots properly. If the operating system boots without any problems, continue to Hands-on Project 4-4. If not, continue to Step 3.

3. If the machine won't boot, turn off the power, unplug the power cord, open the case, and remove the network adapter. Reseal the case without the network adapter installed, plug in the power cord, and try again. If the system works without the adapter, you've just discovered a hardware conflict. Check your IRQ, DMA, and base I/O address settings again; something on the network adapter is interfering with another device. If the machine still won't boot, repeat Hands-on Project 4-1.

4. If the machine won't boot without the NIC, something more serious is wrong. Consult with your instructor. Chances are you omitted something important, or something is broken. You may end up finishing this project on another machine.

5. Acquire a new network adapter from your instructor and repeat Hands-on Projects 4-2 and 4-3. Once your computer (or another computer) boots with the new network adapter inside, you're ready to install the software. Continue to Hands-on Project 4-4.

Project 4-4

To install the network adapter software:

1. Windows 98 and Windows NT are both network-friendly operating systems. In fact, their network adapter installation routines are similar. To begin the process, click the **Start** button, select **Settings**, select **Control Panel**, and then click the **Network** icon.

> Because Windows 2000 and Windows XP automatically detect an installed network adapter and create and activate a network connection, this project does not cover NIC software installation in detail. Should you need to update a network adapter driver in Windows 2000/XP at some point in the future, the sequence is: Start, Settings, Control Panel, Network and Dial-up Connections, Local Area Connection, Properties button, Configure button on the General tab, Driver tab, and then the Update Driver button.

2. For Windows 98, select the **Configuration** tab in the Network window. Click the **Add** button beneath the list of installed components to see a list that reads "Client, Adapter, Protocol, Service." Because you want to install an adapter, highlight **Adapter**, and then click the **Add** button to the right. This invokes a Select Network adapters window with a scrolling list of manufacturers on the left and a list of known adapters on the right, as shown in Figure 4-8.

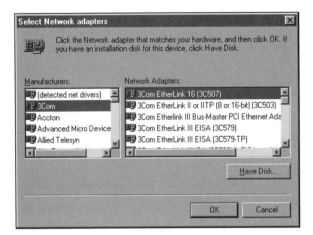

Figure 4-8   Windows 98 Select Network adapters window

For Windows 2000 and XP, you must use the Add/Remove Hardware Wizard to add a NIC if it is not detected using Plug and Play. If you are using a legacy device, you will eventually encounter a dialog box similar to that shown in Figure 4-8. For Windows NT, click the Adapters tab from among the folder tabs, then click the Add button beneath the list of installed adapters. This invokes a dialog box similar to that shown in Figure 4-9.

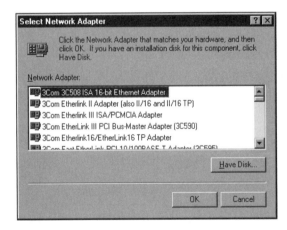

Figure 4-9   Windows NT Select Network Adapter window

For Windows 98 and Windows NT, you must select the adapter that matches the manufacturer, make, and model of the one you installed in your machine. On Windows 98, that means identifying the manufacturer on the left and the make and model on the right; on Windows NT, you pick all three characteristics from one long list.

3. Once you select the card you wish to install, click the **Add** button again. If built-in drivers are available, they install automatically; if not, you are asked to provide a disk (or access to some available medium) where the driver software and other information files reside. Your instructor can provide the necessary details (and disk).

4. If you're using Windows 98 or Windows 2000, and Plug and Play is working, you may be finished. Windows NT users need to supply some additional information during the driver installation. This usually consists of matching the IRQ, DMA, and base I/O address, plus any other settings you made for the adapter itself before installing it in the PC. Follow the steps that the software takes, and be sure the information you supply here matches the hardware settings you noted in Hands-on Project 4-1.

5. Once you finish the adapter software installation, reboot the machine.

Project 4-5

To check your work:

1. When the computer reboots, if all has gone well, you can access the network. Type a **NET VIEW** command after the DOS prompt, and see what happens: you either see a list of network resources, or one of several possible error messages telling you that the network is unreachable or the network interface is uncommunicative; you might receive any of a number of sundry messages. All these messages signal troubleshooting time. (If you are not connected to a network, you will not see any network resources).

2. Many network adapters include diagnostic programs on their installation disks. If your adapter offers such software, run this software next—in many cases, it can tell you precisely what's wrong. Check the most obvious things first: Is the proper media type selected? Is the network medium properly connected to the adapter card?

   ❐ Many 3Com network interfaces revert on rebooting to the factory settings for media type, so even if you switch to thinwire (10Base2) during installation, you may find that the card reverted to 10BaseT. In that case, double-click the driver name inside the Network window's adapter listing to invoke the configuration program, which lets you reselect the correct media type.

   ❐ Other common causes of problems include mismatched hardware settings and software configuration or an improperly selected driver. (Be especially sensitive to version numbers; we use a 3Com 589C in our teaching laptop, and the default driver is for the 589/589B. We learned the hard way that the 589C works only with the 589C driver, available only on disk.) Always check the Internet to see if an updated driver is available.

3. If you investigate these common causes and still cannot resolve your problems, consult your instructor.

Project 4-6

If you cannot find a manual for a network interface card, you will be pleased to learn that many NIC manufacturers make the same information available online through their Web sites. In this project, you visit the 3Com Web site to read about a 3C900B NIC. (If this card becomes obsolete, your instructor can provide details on a newer model for you to investigate).

Web locations and Web pages change constantly! The steps in this Hands-on Project might not be exactly applicable by the time this book is in print.

1. On an Internet-connected machine, open a Web browser (**Start, Programs, Internet Explorer** or **Start, Programs, Netscape Navigator**, or whatever your instructor directs).

2. Type **www.3com.com** in the Address box. Under the Products menu, click **Product Support**. On the Product Support page, find the Quick Search dialog box, click and then type **3C900B**, and then click the **Quick Search** button.

3. To download documentation for the 3C900B Combo card, click the **Documentation** link. From the resulting page, you can view or download a variety of documents describing this card.

4. To download drivers for the 3C900B, repeat Steps 2 and 3, click the **Drivers** link, and select the driver for the appropriate operating system.

5. Close the Web browser to conclude this project. Now you know how to find a 3Com NIC driver; most other vendors provide access in a similar fashion.

CASE PROJECTS

1. Your company just decided to install a network for the first time. Your manager asks you to specify configurations for 120 clients. Because of heavy data load anticipated on the network, it's essential that the servers keep up with significant amounts of traffic. Your manager asks you to put together a "killer server" to keep up with demand.

   Required Result: The server must be able to handle all the network traffic it receives "with reasonable response time."

   Optional Desired Results: Because some network segments are busy and others are relatively idle, you must keep the hardware costs to a minimum. You also need to make sure the server won't slow down the network.

   Proposed Solution: Because of high demand on one segment, you get approval to buy 64-bit bus-mastering NICs with additional RAM for all segments. Which result does the proposed solution produce? Why?

a. The required result and both of the optional desired results

b. The required result, but only one of the optional desired results

c. The required result, but neither of the optional desired results

d. The proposed solution does not produce the required result.

2. On an Ethernet coaxial network, all users share the medium. Bob just moved to your group (and network) from manufacturing, and he brought his ancient 80286 10 MHz PC/AT with him. Bob's system includes an equally decrepit NE1000 Ethernet NIC. Knowing the snail's space speed of Bob's computer will influence overall performance of the network, which of the following solutions makes the most sense, assuming you cannot replace his PC with a newer, faster model? Justify your choice.

a. Replace the 8-bit NE1000 with a 16-bit NE2000.

b. Replace the 8-bit NE1000 with a 32-bit NE3200 EISA card because EISA is backward compatible with ISA, and you can enjoy the extra performance boost.

c. Run a dedicated cable from the server to Bob's machine, and put him on his own network segment. That way, his laggard performance won't affect anyone else.

d. Buy a 32-bit PCI bus-mastering card and get Bob's machine moving on the network as fast as possible.

3. You are in the process of purchasing new computers for a new wing of your building. You want these machines to be as management friendly as possible—and that includes the network interface cards. You know that there are new features available to meet this goal. What features might you look for on the NICs for these new computers?

4. You are in the process of choosing an enterprise server for your organization. Primary requirements of this server include high availability, fault tolerance, and high performance. List some of the features you will look for on the NIC you select for this server. Do some research on the Internet by checking some of the major NIC manufacturers to see what features are available. To give you a start, try *www.3com.com*, *www.intel.com*, and *www.transition.com* for some ideas. Write a report, providing some of the key features available that meet this server's requirements.

5

MAKING NETWORKS WORK

> **After reading this chapter and completing the exercises, you will be able to:**
> ♦ Understand and explain the OSI reference model
> ♦ Understand and explain the IEEE 802 networking model and related standards
> ♦ Explain the OSI reference model's layers and their relationships to networking hardware and software

This chapter spans the entirely theoretical to the profoundly practical aspects of networking. Here, you learn about two different, but complementary, theoretical models for what networks are and how they work (or should work). First you explore the Open Systems Interconnection (OSI) reference model for networking, which explains how networks behave within an orderly, seven-layered model for networked communications. Then you learn more about the IEEE 802 networking model and the standards that surround the 802 designation. Finally, you match the two models against each other to see how they fit together and note where networking hardware plugs into each model.

OSI AND 802 NETWORKING MODELS

The concept of networking is almost as important as the real thing. Several proposed models sought to create an intellectual framework within which to clarify network concepts and activities. Of all these models, none has been as successful as the **Open Systems Interconnection (OSI)** reference model proposed by the **International Organization for Standardization (ISO)**. This model is sometimes referred to as the ISO/**OSI reference model**.

ISO is neither an acronym nor an abbreviation. (ISO comes from the Greek prefix "iso-", which means "same.") The ISO is a network of national standard institutes from 140 countries. The expanded name differs from language to language. For example, in France the organization is called the Organisation Internationale de Normalisation. The term ISO is used to give the network of institutes a common name.

Because it's so widely used and supplies so much important network terminology, the OSI reference model has become a key part of networking. The full-blown OSI scheme for networking was intended to elaborate from the reference model into a completely open systems approach to networking. However, the OSI reference model took an unrivaled place in networking, while the rest of the OSI effort was discontinued. This chapter covers the model's organization and its capabilities.

This chapter also describes the IEEE 802 networking model, sometimes perceived as an enhancement to the OSI model and sometimes as a family of specifications for networks of many kinds. This is one of the most influential sets of networking standards in use anywhere. In fact, the 802 specification encompasses most types of networking and is open-ended, allowing the addition of new types of networks (such as Gigabit Ethernet) as necessary.

Role of a Reference Model

You might wonder why a reference model for networking is needed in general, and why the layer concept in particular is so valuable. To illustrate the value of the layers, consider the process of purchasing mobile telephone service. All the functionality of each option and feature involved in mobile phone service can be broken into layers. At the most basic level or layer, there is the type of communication, such as analog or digital. From there, you can decide on calling features such as forwarding and conferencing. Then you can focus on the features of the phone itself. After you choose a phone, you can select some high-level features such as alphanumeric paging and Internet access.

While many of the details of how mobile phone service works may be unclear to you, you know what it can do for you and basically how to use it. You also know that even though there are many mobile telephone services, it is possible to communicate with users of other services. Furthermore, even if you travel outside the area where your particular service is provided, you can usually continue using your phone. All of this interoperability among layers is possible because of reference models and standards.

This analogy is to show that in its entirety, the process of buying a mobile phone can be confusing at best because there are so many options. But, once it is broken down into steps or layers, the process becomes more clear and easy to understand. Furthermore, because you know that mobile services are generally compatible, you do not have to focus on the details of how mobile phone service works. All you have to do is pick a mobile phone package that best meets your communication requirements.

Just like cellular phone service, computer networking, computer compatibility, and networking features and functions can be a daunting subject to grasp. However, it would be much more difficult to comprehend if not for the fact that networking is built on a common framework and the process is broken into layers. This is the idea of the OSI Model and its 7-layer approach to networking.

OSI Reference Model

During the latter half of the 1970s, the ISO began to formulate a theoretical model for networks of all kinds. In the late 1970s, the organization drafted what became known as the Open Systems Interconnection (OSI) reference model. By 1983, the draft became ISO Standard 7498, which forever enshrines this model for networking. The real value of the OSI reference model is that it provides a useful way to describe—and think about—networking.

It is interesting to note that ISO formulated its standards deliberately to avoid proprietary vendor requirements. Although the grand vision of OSI was never realized, it did bring debate about open systems to the forefront. Like the reference model, this consciousness is also an enduring legacy of the OSI effort.

One word—**layers**—conveys the essence of the OSI reference model. Essentially, this model's foundation rests on the idea that networking can be broken into a series of related tasks, each of which can be conceptualized as a single aspect, or rather a layer, of the communication process. This approach breaks the complexity of networked communications, from applications to hardware, into a series of interconnected tasks and activities. Then, even though the relationship among these tasks and activities persists, each individual task or activity can be handled separately and its issues solved independently. Computer scientists like to call this approach "divide and conquer" because it creates a method to solve big problems by deconstructing them into a series of smaller problems with individual solutions.

Understanding Layers

To understand how layering applies to communications, consider the following real-world example based on a telephone call. Let's say Mary, an executive at XYZ Software Corporation, wants to schedule a conference call with several of her staff members. Handling the call probably works something like this:

1. Mary reviews her calendar and picks four dates when she's available. She calls Sally, her assistant, and gives her the list of call participants and the dates.

2. Sally calls all the participants, tells them she wants to schedule a conference call, and determines their availability on the dates listed.

3. Sally lets Mary know that two of the dates work. Mary picks the date.

4. Sally calls the phone company and schedules the call for 10 a.m. on the fourth of the next month. The phone company provides Sally with an 800 call-in number for all participants, along with an ID for the scheduled conference.

5. Sally calls the participants and lets them know the call is scheduled for 10 a.m. on the fourth of the next month; she also provides the 800 number and the conference ID.

6. On the first of the next month, Sally sends e-mail and calls all participants to remind them of the call, the ID number, and the call-in number. She also sends an agenda and a list of scheduled discussion items to permit participants to prepare for the call.

7. On the fourth, Sally calls in at 9:50 a.m. She contacts the operator, who connects her to her conference. Then she listens as the invited parties call, identify themselves, and wait for the conference to start. At 10 a.m. sharp, Mary begins the conference call with a review of the agenda, and the other callers begin to participate.

8. As the call progresses, Sally informs the attendees when only 15 minutes of scheduled talk time remain. They wrap up outstanding items and assign action items to the participants.

9. At the conclusion of the call, the phone company operator breaks in. She indicates the call is about to end, waits while the participants say their good-byes, and then ends the conference.

10. Sally follows up the meeting with e-mail of the minutes and a list of outstanding action items for all attendees. Another successful conference has been completed.

Considerable effort behind the scenes specified and handled the following tasks:

- Negotiating a time to hold the conference call
- Identifying all parties invited to participate
- Obtaining a dial-in number and a conference ID
- Broadcasting the time, number, ID, and agenda
- Conducting the call, including welcoming and orienting participants, monitoring activity, and shutting down the call when it ended
- Following up with actions once the call is completed

Of course, participants must share access to a common telephone system. Thus, even farther behind the scenes, the telephone network, with its ubiquitous wires, handsets, and switches, provides the low-level hardware and software necessary for placing calls and routing them to bring the conference callers together. The key point, however, remains that successful networked communications, like successful conference calls, demand several carefully orchestrated activities and communications for information to pass between a sender and a receiver. Layering helps clarify the process, as the next section of this chapter illustrates.

The OSI reference model for networking makes explicit many communications activities and related tasks and requirements. This frame of reference clarifies what networks are and how they work. For the conference call, several activities (for example, planning whom to involve, when the call should occur, and setting the agenda) happened well before the event itself; likewise, some data handling must occur in a networked environment before any electrical signals traverse an electronic medium. The structure of the OSI reference model should help make this clear.

OSI Reference Model Structure

Simply put, the OSI reference model breaks networked communications into seven layers, as depicted in Figure 5-1.

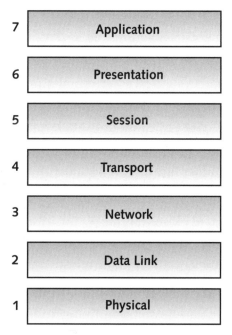

Figure 5-1   Seven layers of the OSI reference model

Uppermost in the reference model, the Application layer provides a set of interfaces that permit networked applications—such as Windows Explorer, an e-mail package, or a Web browser—to access network services. Thus, applications reside above the reference model and communicate with its top layer. At the bottom of the reference model, the Physical layer is where the networking medium and the signals that traverse it reside. All the activities necessary to handle networked communications occur between the top and bottom layers.

To fully comprehend the model's function, it's necessary to understand how it behaves as a whole. Although you have a chance to learn about each layer separately, it's important to appreciate how most computers implement the kinds of services and functions embraced within the OSI reference model. At the outset, any computer that can access a network must be endowed with a **protocol stack** (also known as a **protocol suite** because it usually consists of a collection of related software elements and services that correspond to the layers specified by the OSI model, rather than a single massive program).

Protocol stacks provide the software that enables computers to communicate across a network. Currently, the most common protocol stacks include the following:

- **Transmission Control Protocol/Internet Protocol (TCP/IP)**, the protocol suite used on the Internet, also the default protocol for Windows 2000, Windows XP, .NET, and Novell NetWare 5 and later

- **Internetwork Packet Exchange/Sequenced Packet Exchange (IPX/SPX)**, the protocol suite most commonly used with NetWare versions 4.*x* and below; NetWare 5.*x* and above use TCP/IP as the default protocol

- **NetBIOS Enhanced User Interface (NetBEUI)**, a protocol suite developed by IBM for PC networking and traditionally used in IBM and Windows products, such as Windows NT, Windows 9*x*, and Windows for Workgroups

- **AppleTalk**, the protocol suite developed by Apple for its Macintosh computers and still commonly used in Macintosh-based networks

- **Systems Network Architecture (SNA)**, the protocol suite developed by IBM for use with its mainframe computers

These protocol stacks, combined with drivers for whatever network devices are attached to a computer, provide the crucial software link that permits applications to communicate with a network. Taken as a whole, protocols plus drivers equal network access. Looking further into the model helps explain the activities and functions involved; not coincidentally, it also uncovers why layering is a powerful concept for software developers as well as model builders.

Each individual layer in the OSI model has its own set of well-defined functions, and the functions of each layer communicate and interact with the layers immediately above and below it. (The Physical layer, where transmission of outgoing signals to the networking medium or decoding of incoming signals constitutes its "lower-layer" handoff, is an exception.) For example, the Transport layer works with the Network layer below it and with the Session layer above it.

In the broadest sense, Layers 1 and 2 (Physical and Data Link) define a network's physical media and those signaling characteristics necessary to send and receive information across the network medium and to request access to the medium for transmission. Layers 3 and 4 (Network and Transport) move information from sender to receiver and handle the data to be sent or received. Layers 5 through 7 (Session, Presentation, and Application) manage "conversations," or ongoing communications, across a network and deal with how data is to be represented and interpreted for use in specific applications or for delivery across the network.

It's sensible to look at each layer's role as one of handling data for delivery over the network to another computer. Each layer concerns itself with a different aspect of the data, or with the information exchanged between sender and receiver. However, each layer puts an electronic envelope around the data it sends down the stack for transmission; conversely, it removes the envelope holding data that travels up the stack for delivery to an application.

Rigidly specified boundaries called interfaces separate layers in the OSI reference model. Any request from one layer to another must pass through the interface. Each layer builds on the capabilities and activities of the layers below it and acts to support the layers above. Any layer can communicate directly with its one or two adjacent layers.

In general, the purpose of any layer in the model is to provide services to the adjacent higher layer but also to shield that higher layer from the details of how its services are implemented. In the reference model, layer construction follows an abstract concept called "peer layers"—that is, each layer on one computer behaves as if it were communicating with its twin on the other computer. This is sometimes called logical, or virtual, communication between peer layers, as shown in Figure 5-2.

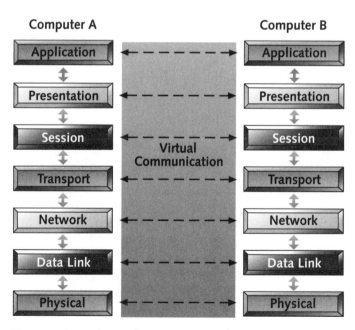

Figure 5-2   Relationships among OSI layers

In reality, communications pass up and down the protocol stacks on both machines. Operations that occur on the way down the stack on the transmitting machine are largely reversed on the way up the stack on the receiving machine, so data on one layer of the sender is nearly identical to the data that arrives on that layer for the receiver. That's why it seems as if peer layers communicate directly; but at each layer, specific software provides specialized network functions defined by the set of protocols in use.

 Here are two good mnemonics to remember the seven layers of the OSI reference model. From the bottom up, starting with the Physical layer, the acronym is "Programmers Do Not Throw Sausage Pizza Away." From the top down, starting with the Application layer, it's "All People Seem To Need Data Processing."

On its way down the stack, before data gets passed from one layer to the next, it is broken down into data units, sometimes called **packets** or **payloads**. The official OSI acronym is **PDU**, sometimes interpreted as **protocol data unit**, **packet data unit**, or even **payload data unit**. The PDU is a unit of information passed as a self-contained data structure from one layer to another on its way up or down the stack. In the preceding discussion, it would have been more accurate to say that, within reason, an outgoing PDU for the sender at any given layer should substantially agree with the incoming version of that same PDU on the receiver. At each layer in the stack, the software adds its own special formatting or addressing to the PDU to allow successful delivery of its payload across the network.

When data arrives at the receiving end, the packet travels up the stack from the Physical layer through the Application layer. At each layer, the software reads its specific PDU data and performs any additional processing required. It then strips its specific information from the PDU and passes the PDU to the next-higher layer. When the packet leaves the Application layer, the data is in a form that the receiving application can read and has been stripped of all the network addressing and packaging instructions necessary to move the data from sender to receiver.

Except at the bottom layer of the reference model, no layer can pass information directly to its counterpart on another computer. Even then, the Physical layer instructs the driver and interface what signals to send across the medium, and a corresponding set of signals must be received and decoded on the receiving end of the transmission. Thus, if the Network layer includes addressing information in its PDU components for transmission across the network, that data must pass down through the Data Link and Physical layers on the transmitting computer, across the network medium, and back through the Physical and Data Link layers on the receiving computer before that machine can "read" the address information provided by the sender. This information might include network addresses for sender and receiver as well as error-checking information that would be recalculated on the receiving end and compared to the value sent. (It is assumed that if the value calculated equals the value sent, data transmission occurred without errors.)

The following sections describe the individual layers of the OSI reference model and the specific services each one provides for its adjacent layers. After reading this material, you should have a good idea about the functions of each layer in the model and how they interact with the adjacent layer or layers.

Application Layer

The **Application layer** (also called Layer 7) is the top layer of the reference model. It provides a set of interfaces for applications to obtain access to networked services as well as access to the network services that support applications directly, including services such as networked file transfer, message handling, and database query processing. The Application layer also handles general network access, the movement of data from sender to receiver, and error recovery for applications, where applicable.

Presentation Layer

The **Presentation layer**, Layer 6, handles data format information for networked communications. For outgoing messages, it converts data into a generic format that can survive the rigors of network transmission; for incoming messages, it converts data from its generic networked representation into a format that makes sense to the receiving application. The Presentation layer also handles protocol conversion, data encryption or decryption, character set issues, and graphics commands.

In some cases, data managed by the Presentation layer may be compressed to reduce the volume of data to be transmitted. (This requires decompression on the receiving end to restore the data to its original form.) A special software facility known as a **redirector** operates at this layer. The redirector intercepts requests for service from the computer; requests that cannot be satisfied locally are redirected across the network to whichever networked resource can handle the request.

Session Layer

Layer 5, the **Session layer**, permits two parties to hold ongoing communications—called a session—across a network. This means applications on either end of the session can exchange data for as long as the session lasts. The Session layer handles session setup, data or message exchanges, and teardown when the session ends. It also monitors session identification, so only designated parties can participate, and monitors security services to control access to session information (or to permit only authorized parties to establish sessions). Some of the common network functions handled by this layer include name lookup and user login and logout.

In keeping with its role to help manage ongoing communications over time, the Session layer also provides synchronization services between tasks on both ends of a connection. It can place checkpoints in the data stream so that if communications fail at some point, only data after the most recent checkpoint needs retransmission. The Session layer also manages the mechanics inherent in any ongoing conversation, including identifying which side may transmit data when and for how long, and maintaining a connection through transmission of so-called keep-alive messages designed to keep inactivity from shutting down an open connection.

Transport Layer

The **Transport layer**, Layer 4, manages the conveyance of data from sender to receiver across a network. It segments arbitrarily long data payloads into chunks that match the maximum packet size for the networking medium in use, includes error checks to ensure error-free delivery, and handles resequencing of chunks into the original data on receipt. The Transport layer also handles **flow control**. Flow control ensures that the recipient of transmitted data is not overwhelmed with more data than it can handle.

Network Layer

Layer 3, the **Network layer**, handles addressing messages for delivery, but also translates logical network addresses into their physical counterparts, which are known as the MAC addresses. The Network layer also decides how to route transmissions from sender to receiver. To determine how to get from point A to point B, the Network layer considers factors based on network conditions, quality of service information, cost of alternate routes, and delivery priorities. This layer is also the traffic cop for network activity and handles **packet switching**, data **routing**, and **congestion control**.

When moving data from one kind of network medium to another, the Network layer also handles segmentation and reassembly functions based on disparities between dissimilar media. This means the Network layer downsizes packets coming from a medium that handles larger PDUs to a medium that handles smaller packets. (This process is called **fragmentation** or **segmentation**.) When the data arrives at the receiving end (its final destination), the Network layer **reassembles** the downsized pieces into their original packets. This action is much like what the Transport layer does for arbitrarily long messages; however, at this layer packets from one kind of medium (with larger PDUs) are permitted to traverse another kind of medium (with smaller PDUs).

Data Link Layer

Layer 2, the **Data Link layer**, sends special PDUs, called **data frames** or sometimes just **frames**, from the Network layer to the Physical layer. On the receiving side, Layer 2 packages the raw data from the Physical layer into data frames for delivery to the Network layer. A data frame is the basic unit for network traffic "on the wire" (as sent across the medium, in more general terms); it's a highly structured format within which payload data from upper layers is placed for sending and from which payload data from upper layers is taken on receipt.

Figure 5-3 shows the contents of a typical data frame. Notice that it includes IDs for both sender and receiver as well as control information and a data integrity check, in addition to its data payload.

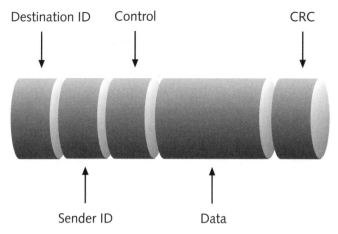

Figure 5-3   Data frame

The destination ID provides a network address for the frame's intended recipient; the sender ID provides the "return address" for the frame's sender.

Control information covers a multitude of topics from identifying specific frame types to providing routing and segmentation data. The payload is the information that origi-nated from an application, segmented and labeled for networked delivery. The data integrity check, called a **Cyclical Redundancy Check (CRC)**, is a special mathe-matical function based on the bit patterns in the frame; sent as part of the frame itself, the CRC is recalculated on the receiving end. If the recalculated and sent values agree, the assumption is that the data was received in the same form it was sent.

The Data Link layer handles delivery of frames from sender to receiver through the Physical layer (and across the network medium). Its error-checking and address-handling facilities permit the Network layer to assume that only explicit errors need handling; otherwise, it's safe to assume that the network delivered its transmissions error free.

In the majority of networking technologies, the Data Link layer is responsible for detect-ing errors in the transmission of frames and discarding those frames that arrive containing errors. However, it is the responsibility of the upper layers (usually the Transport layer) to retransmit data that has been discarded due to errors.

Physical Layer

Layer 1 is the **Physical layer**; its job is to convert bits into signals for outgoing messages and signals into bits for incoming ones. In other words, the Physical layer orchestrates the transmission of whatever form a data frame's bits take when dispatched across the net-work medium. In this capacity, the Physical layer manages the computer's interface to the network medium and instructs the driver software and the network interface what to send across the medium. It also translates and screens incoming data for delivery to the receiving computer.

The Physical layer is where specification of all the details for creating a network connection occurs; this includes how the medium attaches to (or communicates with) the NIC. It also governs the type of connector used and regulates the transmission technique used to send signals across the networking medium.

Ultimately, the Physical layer handles the intricacies of transmitting the pattern of bits that represents a data frame from the sending to the receiving computer, even though those bits are arbitrary at this layer (and a digital format may not even represent them). The Physical layer attempts to guarantee that the pattern of bits translated into signals at the sending end matches the pattern of bits those signals translate into at the receiving end. It specifies how to encode ones and zeros, the timing and interpretation of signals sent across the medium, and the form those signals must take. **Encoding** is the representation of zeros and ones as a physical signal, such as electrical voltage or a light pulse. For example, a one bit may be represented on a copper wire as a 5-volt signal, whereas a zero bit may be represented as a signal that is less than 2 volts.

From top to bottom, and reverse, the OSI reference model provides a compelling way to categorize and compartmentalize the activities involved in networking. (See Table 5-1.) It's a testament to the model's explanatory powers that most discussions of protocol stacks and networking software invoke its terminology and categories. Even though most protocol stacks do not strictly adhere to this model (perhaps because so many of them were already implemented in some form before the model's development), they still invoke its outlook on networking.

Although the OSI model is not strictly adhered to by all networking protocols, a network administrator's clear understanding of the functions at each layer is paramount to the troubleshooting process and to understanding how networking devices operate. Many networking devices are described in terms of the OSI model. For example, you may hear the term Layer 3 switch or Layer 4-7 load-balancing switch. A solid comprehension of what goes on in each of the layers significantly aids an administrator in his or her understanding and support of networks and network equipment.

Table 5-1   Actions for each layer of the OSI reference model

OSI Layer	Function
Application	Transfers information from program to program
Presentation	Handles text formatting and displays code conversion
Session	Establishes, maintains, and coordinates communication
Transport	Ensures accurate delivery of data
Network	Determines transport routes and handles the transfer of messages
Data Link	Codes, addresses, and transmits information
Physical	Manages hardware connections and handles sending and receiving of signals

No protocol suite developed after introduction of the OSI reference model has been free from its influence. Pay close attention to the AppleTalk discussion in Chapter 6 to see how the OSI model guides the shape and functions of the entire stack. In Chapter 6, you also learn how each of the most popular protocol suites stacks up against the OSI model.

IEEE 802 Networking Specifications

By the late 1970s, it was clear that local area networks (LANs) would take an important place in business computing environments. Spurred by this realization, the Institute of Electrical and Electronic Engineers (IEEE) launched an effort to define a set of LAN standards to ensure that network interfaces and cabling from multiple manufacturers would be compatible as long as they adhered to the same IEEE specification. This effort was called **Project 802** to indicate the year (1980) and month (February) of its inception. Since then, the IEEE 802 specifications have taken firm root in the networking world.

Because the OSI reference model was not standardized until 1983-1984, the IEEE 802 standards predate the model. Nevertheless, the two were developed in collaboration and are compatible with one another. (The IEEE is one of the U.S. participants in ISO, the standards organization that formulated OSI.)

Project 802 concentrates its efforts on standards that describe the physical elements of a network, including network adapters, cables, connectors, signaling technologies, Media Access Controls (MACs), and the like. Most of these reside in the lower two layers of the OSI model, in the Physical or Data Link layers. In particular, the 802 specification documents describe how NICs may access and transfer data across a variety of networking media. They also describe what's involved in attaching, managing, and detaching such devices in a networked environment.

IEEE 802 Specifications

IEEE codified the various efforts undertaken as part of Project 802 in a number of standards categories, numbered **802.1** through **802.18**, as shown in Table 5-2.

For the purposes of this book, Standards 802.1 through 802.5 are of the greatest interest, with some attention devoted to 802.11 and 802.12. These categories are the focus of ongoing development and extension efforts at the IEEE through its working groups; these categories also are the repository of a large body of existing standards. For more information on the IEEE standards documents, visit the Web site at *http://www.ieee.org/*.

Table 5-2   IEEE 802 standards

Standard	Name	Explanation
802.1	Internetworking	Covers routing, bridging, and internetwork communications
802.2	Logical Link Control	Relates to error control and flow control over data frames
802.3	Ethernet LAN	Covers all forms of Ethernet media and interfaces, from 10 Mbps to 1 Gbps (Gigabit Ethernet)
802.4	Token Bus LAN	Covers all forms of token bus media and interfaces
802.5	Token Ring LAN	Covers all forms of token ring media and interfaces
802.6	Metropolitan Area Network	Covers MAN technologies, addressing, and services
802.7	Broadband Technical Advisory Group	Covers broadband networking media, interfaces, and other equipment
802.8	Fiber-Optic Technical Advisory Group	Covers use of fiber-optic media and technologies for various networking types
802.9	Integrated Voice/Data Networks	Covers integration of voice and data traffic over a single network medium
802.10	Network Security	Covers network access controls, encryption, certification, and other security topics
802.11	Wireless Networks	Sets standards for wireless networking for many different broadcast frequencies and usage techniques
802.12	High-Speed Networking	Covers a variety of 100 Mbps-plus technologies, including 100VG-AnyLAN
802.13	Unused	This standard number was never used
802.14	Defunct working group	This defunct working group was involved in specifying data transports over cable TV
802.15	Wireless PAN	Covers the emerging standards for wireless personal area networks
802.16	Wireless MAN	Covers Wireless Metropolitan Area Networks
802.17	Resilient Packet Ring	Covers emerging standards for very-high-speed, ring-based LANs and MANs
802.18	Wireless Advisory Group	This technical advisory group monitors radio-based wireless standards

IEEE 802 Extensions to the OSI Reference Model

The two lowest layers of the OSI reference model—the Physical and Data Link layers—define how computers attach to specific networking media and how such computers can access those media without impeding one another from communicating across the media. Project 802 took this work further to create the specifications (primarily, 802.1 through 802.5) that define the most successful LAN technologies, including Ethernet and token ring, which together dominate the networking world.

The IEEE 802 specification expanded the OSI reference model at the Physical and Data Link layers, which define how more than one computer can access the network without causing interference with other computers on the network. Figure 5-4 shows how the 802 standards provide more detail at these layers by breaking the Data Link layer into the following **sublayers**:

- **Logical Link Control (LLC)** for error recovery and flow control
- **Media Access Control (MAC)** for access control

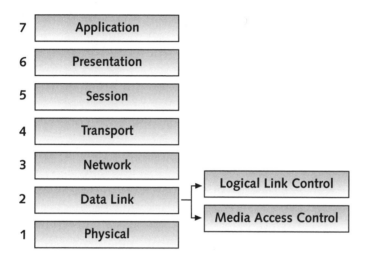

7	Application
6	Presentation
5	Session
4	Transport
3	Network
2	Data Link
1	Physical

Logical Link Control

Media Access Control

Figure 5-4   IEEE 802 standard divides the OSI Data Link layer into two sublayers

The Logical Link Control sublayer (as defined by 802.2) controls data-link communication and defines the use of logical interface points, called **Service Access Points (SAPs)**, that other computers can use to transfer information from the LLC sublayer to the upper OSI layers. The LLC is also responsible for error recovery in some situations. There are several modes of LLC operation; some modes require the LLC to detect and recover from errors in transmission. This function is largely implemented in hardware on the NIC.

The Media Access Control (MAC) sublayer provides shared access for multiple NICs with the Physical layer. The MAC directly communicates with a computer's NIC and is responsible for ensuring error-free data transmission between computers on a network. The data-link address burned into every NIC's PROM is called a MAC-layer address because it operates at this sublayer of the 802.2 specification.

As Figure 5-5 shows, the IEEE 802 specifications map to the LLC and MAC sublayers to provide specifications for LLC, CSMA/CD networking, token bus networking, token ring networking, and Demand Priority. These networking technologies are discussed in detail in Chapter 6.

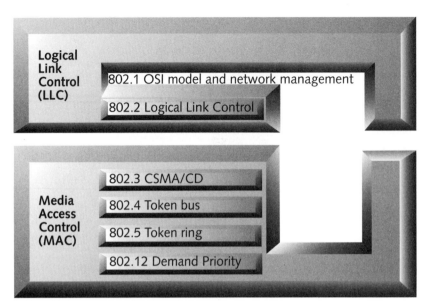

Figure 5-5   IEEE 802.x specifications map to the OSI reference model

CHAPTER SUMMARY

- ◻ The OSI reference model and the IEEE Project 802 define a frame of reference for networking and specify the lower-layer behaviors for most networks in use today. Together, these models describe the complex processes and operations involved in sending and receiving information across a network.

- ◻ The OSI reference model breaks networking across seven layers, each with its own purposes and related activities, from the bottom up: Physical, Data Link, Network, Transport, Session, Presentation, and Application. This reference model explains most networks, even those that predate its introduction. Most network products and technologies are also positioned in terms of the layers they occupy; the layers help describe the features and functions that the products and technologies deliver.

- ◻ The IEEE 802 project further elaborates on the functions of the Physical and Data Link layers of a network by breaking the Data Link layer into two sublayers: the Logical Link Control (LLC) sublayer and the Media Access Control (MAC) sublayer. Together, these sublayers handle media access, addressing, and control (through the MAC sublayer) and provide reliable, error-free delivery of data frames from one computer to another (through the LLC sublayer).

KEY TERMS

802.1 — The IEEE specification within Project 802 for the OSI reference model and for internetworking and routing behavior at the Data Link layer (where logical addresses must be translated into their physical counterparts, and vice versa).

802.2 — The IEEE specification within Project 802 for the Logical Link Control (LLC) sublayer within the Data Link layer of the OSI reference model.

802.3 — The IEEE specification within Project 802 for Collision Sense Multiple Access/Collision Detection (CSMA/CD) networks. Ethernet users can attempt to access the medium any time it's perceived as "quiet," but they must back off and try to transmit again if they detect any collisions once transmission begins. More commonly called Ethernet.

802.4 — The IEEE specification within Project 802 for token bus LANs, which use a straight-line bus topology for the networking medium, yet circulate a token to control access to the medium.

802.5 — The IEEE specification within Project 802 for token ring LANs, which map a circulating ring structure onto a physical star and circulate a token to control access to the medium.

802.6 — The IEEE specification within Project 802 for metropolitan area networks (MANs).

802.7 — The IEEE specification within Project 802 for the Broadband Technical Advisory Group's findings and recommendations for broadband networking technologies, media, interfaces, and equipment.

802.8 — The IEEE specification within Project 802 for the Fiber-Optic Technical Advisory Group's findings and recommendations for fiber-optic networking technologies, media, interfaces, and equipment.

802.9 — The IEEE specification within Project 802 that addresses hybrid networks, which combine voice and data traffic within the same networking environment.

802.10 — The IEEE specification within Project 802 for network security.

802.11 — The IEEE specification within Project 802 for wireless networks.

802.12 — The IEEE specification within Project 802 for high-speed networks, including Demand Priority and 100VG-AnyLAN technologies.

802.13 — Unused. This standard number was never used.

802.14 — This defunct working group was involved in specifying data transports over cable TV.

802.15 — Covers the emerging standards for wireless personal area networks (PANs).

802.16 — Covers wireless metropolitan area networks (MAN).

802.17 — Resilient Packet Ring; covers emerging standards for very high-speed, ring-based LANs and MANs.

802.18 — Wireless Advisory Group; a technical advisory group to monitor radio-based, wireless standards.

AppleTalk — The protocol suite/stack native to the Macintosh operating system.

5

Application layer — Layer 7 in the OSI reference model. The Application layer provides interfaces to permit applications to request and receive network services.

congestion control — A technique for monitoring network utilization and manipulating transmission or forwarding rates for data frames to keep traffic levels from overwhelming the network medium; gets its name because it avoids "network traffic jams."

Cyclical Redundancy Check (CRC) — A mathematical recipe that generates a specific value, called a checksum, based on the contents of a data frame. The CRC is calculated before transmission of a data frame and then included with the frame; on receipt, the CRC is recalculated and compared to the sent value. If the two agree, it is assumed that the data frame was delivered intact; if they disagree, the data frame must be retransmitted.

data frame — The basic package of bits that represents the PDU sent from one computer to another across a networking medium. In addition to its contents (payload), a data frame includes the sender's and receiver's network addresses as well as some control information at the head and a CRC at the tail.

Data Link layer — Layer 2 in the OSI reference model. This layer is responsible for managing access to the networking medium and for ensuring error-free delivery of data frames from sender to receiver.

encoding — The representation of zeros and ones as a physical signal, such as electrical voltage or a light pulse.

flow control — An action designed to regulate the transfer of information between a sender and a receiver. Flow control is often necessary when a speed differential exists between sender and receiver.

fragmentation — The process of breaking a long PDU from a higher layer into a sequence of shorter PDUs for a lower layer, ultimately for transmission as a sequence of data frames across the networking medium.

frame — Used interchangeably with "data frame," the basic package of bits that represents a PDU sent from one computer to another across a network. In addition to its contents, a frame includes the sender's and receiver's network addresses, control information at the head, and a CRC at the tail.

International Organization for Standardization (ISO) — The international standards-setting body, based in Geneva, Switzerland, that sets worldwide technology standards.

Internetwork Packet Exchange/Sequenced Packet Exchange (IPX/SPX) — The protocol stack Novell developed for use with its NetWare networking operating system software.

layers — The functional subdivisions of the OSI reference model. The model defines each layer in terms of the services and data it handles on behalf of the layer directly above it, and the services and data it needs from the layer directly below it.

Logical Link Control (LLC) — The upper sublayer of the IEEE Project 802 networking model for the Data Link layer (Layer 2) of the OSI reference model. It handles error-free delivery and controls the flow of data frames between sender and receiver across a network.

Media Access Control (MAC) — The lower sublayer of the IEEE Project 802 networking model for the Data Link layer (Layer 2) of the OSI reference model. It handles access to the networking media and mapping between logical and physical network addresses for network adapters.

NetBIOS Enhanced User Interface (NetBEUI) — An enhanced set of network and transport protocols that carry NetBIOS information. Built in the late 1980s, when earlier implementations became too limiting for continued use, NetBEUI remains popular on many IBM and Microsoft networks.

Network layer — Layer 3 of the OSI reference model. The Network layer handles addressing and routing of PDUs across internetworks in which multiple networks must be traversed between sender and receiver.

Open Systems Interconnection (OSI) — The family of ISO standards developed in the 1970s and 1980s and designed to facilitate high-level, high-function networking services among dissimilar computers on a global scale. The OSI initiative was unsuccessful, owing to a fatal combination of an all-inclusive standards-setting effort and a failure to develop standard protocol interfaces to help developers implement its manifold requirements.

OSI reference model — ISO Standard 7498. It defines a frame of reference for understanding and implementing networks by breaking down the process across seven layers. By far, the OSI reference model remains the OSI initiative's most enduring legacy.

packet — The data unit associated with processing at any layer in the OSI reference model.

packet data unit (PDU) — A data unit associated with processing at any layer in the OSI reference model; sometimes identified by the particular layer, as in "a Session or Layer 5 PDU."

packet switching — A transmission method that sends packets across a networking medium which supports multiple pathways between sender and receiver. Transmissions may follow any available path, and multiple packets may travel simultaneously across the network. Thus, packets may arrive in an order that differs from that in which they were sent. X.25 (discussed in Chapter 12) is a common type of packet-switched network.

payload — The data content within a PDU.

payload data unit (PDU) — The combination of the data content plus the header and trailer information that make up an entire PDU.

Physical layer — Layer 1, the bottom layer of the OSI reference model. The Physical layer transmits and receives signals, and specifies the physical details of cables, adapter cards, connectors, and hardware behavior.

Presentation layer — Layer 6 of the OSI reference model. Here data may be encrypted and/or compressed to facilitate delivery. Platform-specific application formats are translated into generic data formats for transmission, or from generic data formats into platform-specific application formats for delivery to the Application layer.

5

Project 802 — The IEEE networking initiative that produced the 802.x networking specifications and standards.

protocol data unit (PDU) — A packet structure as formulated by a specific networking protocol. Such a structure usually includes specific header and trailer information in addition to its data payload.

protocol stack — An ordered collection of networking protocols that, taken together, provide end-to-end network communications between a sender and a receiver.

protocol suite — A family of related protocols in which higher-layer protocols provide application services and request handling facilities, while lower-layer protocols manage the intricacies of Layers 1 through 4 from the OSI reference model.

reassembles (reassembly) — Reconstructing a larger, upper-layer PDU from a collection of smaller, lower-layer PDUs. Resequencing and recombining may be required to reassemble the original PDU.

redirector — A software component that intercepts requests for service from a computer and redirects requests that cannot be satisfied locally across the network to whichever networked resource can handle the request.

routing — A network-layer service that determines how to deliver an outgoing packet of data from sender to receiver. Routing entails several methods for managing delivery and requires error and status reporting so that senders can determine if they are reaching their receivers.

segmentation — Decomposing a larger, upper-layer PDU into a collection of smaller, lower-layer PDUs. It includes sequencing and reassembling information to permit restoration of the original upper-layer PDU on receipt of all the smaller, lower-layer PDUs.

Service Access Points (SAPs) — Logical interface points used to transfer information from the LLC sublayer to the upper OSI layers.

Session layer — Layer 5 of the OSI reference model. The Session layer is responsible for setting up, maintaining, and ending ongoing sequences of communications (called sessions) across a network.

sublayers — The two components of Layer 2, the Data Link layer (DLL), of the OSI reference model. Elaborated upon by the IEEE 802 project, they are the Logical Link Control (LLC) sublayer and the Media Access Control (MAC) sublayer.

Systems Network Architecture (SNA) — IBM's native protocol suite for its mainframes and older minicomputers. SNA is still one of the most widely used protocol suites in the world.

Transmission Control Protocol/Internet Protocol (TCP/IP) — A protocol suite that supports communication between heterogeneous systems. TCP/IP has become the standard communications protocol for the Internet.

Transport layer — Layer 4 of the OSI reference model. The Transport layer is responsible for fragmenting large PDUs from the Session layer for delivery across the network, and for inserting sufficient integrity controls and managing delivery mechanisms to allow for their error-free reassembly on the receiving end of a network transmission.

REVIEW QUESTIONS

1. The OSI reference model divides networking activity into how many layers?

   a. four

   b. five

   c. seven

   d. eight

2. With the OSI reference model, the job of each layer is to provide services to the next-higher layer and to make accessible the details of how its services are implemented. True or false?

3. Which two of the following types of information are added at each layer as a PDU makes its way down a protocol stack? (Choose two answers.)

   a. formatting

   b. data conversion

   c. data compression

   d. addressing

4. Layers that act as if they communicate directly with each other across the network are called _____.

   a. partners

   b. synchronous

   c. interchangeable

   d. peers

5. Write the number that corresponds to each of the following layers in the OSI reference model (for example, 7 = top, 1 = bottom):

   a. Presentation

   b. Data Link

   c. Session

   d. Physical

6. The _____ layer handles the creation of data frames.

7. Which layer handles general network access, flow control, and recovery from network failures?

   a. Application

   b. Physical

   c. Transport

   d. Data Link

8. The _____ layer governs how a network adapter must be attached to the networking medium.

9. Which layer determines the route a packet takes from sender to receiver?

   a. Application

   b. Physical

   c. Network

   d. Data Link

10. The _____ layer handles conversion of data from platform-specific application formats to a generic, network-ready representation (and vice versa).

11. Which layer is responsible for setting up, maintaining, and ending ongoing exchanges of information across a network?

   a. Application

   b. Presentation

   c. Session

   d. Transport

12. The ___Network___ layer handles fragmentation of long packets for transmission and reassembly of fragmented packets on receipt.

13. A family of related networking protocols is called a _____.

   a. protocol stack

   b. protocol suite

   c. protocol family

   d. protocol package

14. Which of the following elements might occur within a data frame? (Choose all that apply.)

   a. network addresses for sender and receiver

   b. control information for frame type, routing, and segmentation

   c. payload data

   d. CRC, a data integrity check

   e. a special bit pattern to mark the beginning and end of the frame

15. CRC is an acronym for _____.

   a. Circular Redundant Checksum

   b. Cyclical Redundancy Check

   c. Convex Recalculation Check

   d. Computed Recursive Count

16. How many times is a CRC calculated?

    a. once before transmission

    b. once after receipt

    c. twice; once before transmission and again on receipt

    d. three times; once before transmission, once on receipt, and a third time immediately prior to delivery to the application

17. Of the following Project 802 specifications, which belong at the MAC sublayer? (Choose all that apply.)

    a. 802.1

    b. 802.2

    c. 802.3

    d. 802.4

    e. 802.5

    f. 802.12

18. Which layer of the OSI reference model does Project 802 break into two sublayers?

    a. Physical

    b. Data Link

    c. Network

    d. Session

19. What are the names of the two sublayers specified as part of Project 802? (Choose two answers.)

    a. Data Link Control (DLC)

    b. Logical Link Control (LLC)

    c. Collision Sense Multiple Access/Collision Detection (CSMA/CD)

    d. Media Access Control (MAC)

20. Which IEEE 802 sublayer communicates directly with a network adapter and handles error-free data delivery between two computers on a network?

    a. Data Link Control (DLC)

    b. Logical Link Control (LLC)

    c. Collision Sense Multiple Access/Collision Detection (CSMA/CD)

    d. Media Access Control (MAC)

21. Which IEEE 802 standard applies to Ethernet?

    a. 802.2

    b. 802.3

    c. 802.4

    d. 802.5

    e. 802.11

22. Which IEEE 802 standard applies to token ring?
    a. 802.2
    b. 802.3
    c. 802.4
    d. 802.5
    e. 802.11

23. Which IEEE 802 standard applies to token bus?
    a. 802.2
    b. 802.3
    c. 802.4
    d. 802.5
    e. 802.11

24. Which IEEE 802 standard applies to wireless networks?
    a. 802.2
    b. 802.3
    c. 802.4
    d. 802.5
    e. 802.11

25. Under which 802 sublayer are access methods such as CSMA/CD and Demand Priority found?
    a. Transport
    b. MAC
    c. LLC
    d. Data Link

26. Which of the following acronyms represent popular protocol suites? (Choose all that apply.)
    a. IPX/SPX
    b. TCP/IP
    c. SMB
    d. NetBIOS

27. Which of the following definitions best describes a redirector?
    a. a software service that handles only network access requests
    b. a software service that handles both local and network access requests
    c. a software service that handles resource requests, passes on local requests for local service, and redirects network access requests to the appropriate network server or service
    d. none of the above

28. Which IEEE standard governs Gigabit Ethernet?

    a. 802.1

    b. 802.2

    c. 802.3

    d. 802.4

29. At which Data-Link sublayer does the network address burned into every NIC reside?

    a. Media Access Control (MAC) sublayer

    b. Logical Link Control (LLC) sublayer

    c. Data Access Control (DAC) sublayer

    d. Network Access Control (NAC) sublayer

30. The Logical Link Control (LLC) sublayer handles data-link communications. True or false?

HANDS-ON PROJECTS

Unfortunately, you cannot do much in the lab to observe the OSI network reference model at work. The same is true for the IEEE 802 family of specifications. Therefore, the Hands-on Projects in this chapter show you how to take advantage of the standardization of those unique IDs programmed into firmware on network interface cards as a part of the 802.2 MAC-layer address specification from the IEEE.

In this two-part exercise, you first use a command-line utility to obtain the MAC-layer address for the network interface in your machine, you visit the IEEE Web page to download its list of public manufacturer IDs, and then you look up the manufacturer who built that NIC. (The first three bytes of the MAC-layer address identify the board's manufacturer.)

Project 5-1

To obtain your NIC's MAC address:

Microsoft includes command-line utilities in its Windows operating systems to display a machine's TCP/IP configuration. For Windows 98, that command is named **winipcfg**; for Windows NT and Windows 2000, it's named **ipconfig**. In this Hands-on Project, you run this command to produce a listing that includes the MAC address as part of its output.

    1. In a GUI operating system such as Windows 98, Windows NT, or Windows 2000, you must execute command-line utilities in a so-called DOS box. For Windows 98, access the DOS prompt with this sequence of menu selections: **Start**, **Programs**, and **MS-DOS Prompt**. For Windows NT, the sequence is **Start**, **Programs**, **Command Prompt**. For Windows 2000, the sequence is **Start**, **Programs**, **Accessories**, **Command Prompt**.

2. After the DOS command prompt, for Windows 98 type **winipcfg /all**; for Windows NT, Windows 2000, or Windows XP type **ipconfig /all**. Press the **Enter** key. (*Note*: For Windows 98, you may have to select **Ethernet Adapter** from a drop-down list.) Output like that shown in Figure 5-6 should appear for Windows NT and Windows 2000/XP.

```
Command Prompt                                                    _ □ ×
(C) Copyright 1985-1999 Microsoft Corp.

D:\>ipconfig /all

Windows 2000 IP Configuration

        Host Name . . . . . . . . . . . . : w2kp-21-et
        Primary DNS Suffix  . . . . . . . :
        Node Type . . . . . . . . . . . . : Broadcast
        IP Routing Enabled. . . . . . . . : No
        WINS Proxy Enabled. . . . . . . . : No

Ethernet adapter Local Area Connection:

        Connection-specific DNS Suffix  . :
        Description . . . . . . . . . . . : 3Com EtherLink III ISA (3C509/3C509b
) in Legacy mode
        Physical Address. . . . . . . . . : 00-60-97-1B-7B-01
        DHCP Enabled. . . . . . . . . . . : No
        IP Address. . . . . . . . . . . . : 172.16.1.21
        Subnet Mask . . . . . . . . . . . : 255.255.255.0
        Default Gateway . . . . . . . . . :
        DNS Servers . . . . . . . . . . . :

D:\>
```

Figure 5-6   Output of the ipconfig /all command

3. Look for a line that begins with the words "Physical Address" (or "Adapter Address" in Windows 98), and then write down the first three sets of numbers in the corresponding value to the right. In Figure 5-6, that value is 00-60-97.

4. Type **exit** after the DOS prompt, and then press **Enter** to exit the DOS window.

Project 5-2

To look up the manufacturer's ID for your NIC:

The IEEE operates a Web page for the collection of Organizational Unique IDs (OUIs) that it maintains. Here, you visit that page, download the list of IDs, and try to locate the manufacturer's ID in that list. Note that not all such IDs are made public, but you should be able to find IDs for most commercially available NICs.

1. Start your Web browser at your desktop. For Windows users, this typically means following the menu sequence **Start**, **Programs**, **Internet Explorer**. If your lab setup differs, your instructor or lab manager should be able to give you the right sequence of commands to follow.

2. Type the string **http://standards.ieee.org/regauth/oui/index.shtml** into the Address box in your Web browser, and then press the **Enter** key. This should take you to the IEEE OUI and Company_id Assignments page shown in Figure 5-7. (Remember that Web pages change over time, so the page you see probably varies from the page in Figure 5-7.)

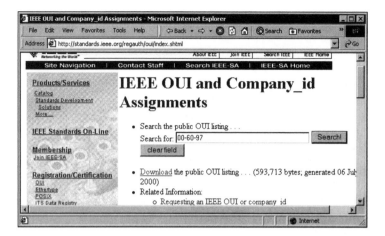

Figure 5-7   IEEE OUI and Company_id Assignments Web page

3. Click the first text box on the page, and then type the three sets of digits for the manufacturer's ID that you wrote down in Project 5-1, including the hyphens. In Figure 5-6, that value is 00-60-97. Click the **Search** button to the right. This produces a result like that shown in Figure 5-8. (Note that this also agrees with the card identification that appears in the Description line in Figure 5-6.)

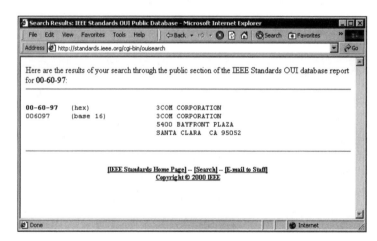

Figure 5-8   Search results for 00-60-97

4. Close your Web browser to end this exercise.

CASE PROJECTS

1. You have learned plenty about the OSI model, but haven't seen a networking protocol that actually contains components at all seven layers. However, after doing some research on *www.protocols.com*, you are pleased to discover that there is a protocol that has components at each layer—the ISO Protocol Suite. Research this protocol and make a table showing which ISO components are found at each OSI model layer. You can find details on the ISO protocol at *www.protocols.com/pbook/iso.htm*. (*Hint*: This is an excellent Web site for researching protocols of all types.)

2. You just took a job as a network administrator at ABC Toy Company, which operates a large toy factory. The current network is an ancient Allen-Bradley broadband technology that barely limps along at 1 Mbps. You believe that upgrading to Ethernet is worth the expense and will result in an explosion of productivity on the shop floor. What reasons could you use to persuade management to fund a new network? (Choose all that apply.)

   a. Ethernet adheres to the IEEE 802.3 standard and is likely to be supported for the foreseeable future.

   b. Basic 10 Mbps Ethernet runs up to ten times faster than the Allen-Bradley network and permits much more data to move among the shop-floor workstations; faster versions (100 Mbps and 1 Gbps) are also available for high-performance use and for high-traffic backbones.

   c. Ethernet supports fiber-optic cable as well as coaxial and twisted-pair, so even the most interference-ridden parts of the factory can get on the network. (The Allen-Bradley network is not installed in those areas because it works only on a special type of coaxial cable.)

   d. Even though the Allen-Bradley networking technology is about the same age as Ethernet, drivers, adapters, cables, and other devices are much easier to find for Ethernet than for the Allen-Bradley network. In fact, you even had trouble finding drivers that would work with newer PCs. Ethernet makes much more sense for that reason.

3. Back on the premises of ENormInc, you ponder what type of twisted-pair cable to use for the office computers. Current specifications call only for 10 Mbps Ethernet, but you are sure that bandwidth requirements will increase over time. You want to leave room for a future upgrade to 100 Mbps Ethernet for those office computers. Which of the following will most likely help you justify to management the extra expense of installing Category 5 twisted-pair cable? (Choose all that apply.)

   a. Although interface cards and hubs may need upgrading, the cable itself will be ready to carry the higher bandwidth. Since installing new cable in the future would be quite expensive, it's worth spending the extra money now. (Remember, most of the costs associated with cabling relate to labor charges for its installation, not the cost of the medium itself.)

b. Because 10 Mbps and 100 Mbps Ethernet are part of the same IEEE 802.3 specification, the 10 Mbps setup for the factory floors can be left as is, and will interoperate with a new 100 Mbps setup in the offices.

c. The savings on a single cable installation will ultimately offset the costs of new NICs and hubs.

d. Improved productivity in the offices from higher network speeds will offset the costs of new NICs and hubs.

4. The original commercial version of Ethernet supported 10 Mbps bandwidth; a newer version introduced in the early 1990s supports 100 Mbps; in 1998 a 1000 Mbps (1 Gbps) version called Gigabit Ethernet was introduced. All versions use the same data frame formats, with the same maximum PDU sizes, and therefore can interoperate freely.

The original commercial version of token ring supported 4 Mbps bandwidth; a newer version introduced in the late 1980s supports 16 Mbps; in the late 1990s a 100 Mbps version was discussed. Each version uses a similar data format but supports a different maximum PDU size. Interoperation requires segmentation of PDUs when stepping down in speed.

Given this information, which two of the following statements represent the best choices for a multi-technology network?

a. Ethernet is superior to token ring because it offers a broader range of bandwidths for multi-technology deployment.

b. Token ring is superior to Ethernet because it offers a broader range of bandwidths for multi-technology deployment.

c. Ethernet is superior to token ring because it can interoperate across all of its implementations without requiring payload segmentation at any step along the way.

d. Token ring is superior to Ethernet because it can interoperate across all of its implementations without requiring payload segmentation at any step along the way.

5

6

NETWORK COMMUNICATIONS AND PROTOCOLS

> **After reading this chapter and completing the exercises, you will be able to:**
>
> ♦ Understand the function and structure of packets in a network, and analyze and understand those packets
>
> ♦ Understand the function of protocols in a network
>
> ♦ Discuss the layered architecture of protocols, and describe common protocols and their implementation
>
> ♦ Understand channel access methods

For effective communication across a network, computers must be able to transmit their data completely and safely. To design and troubleshoot a network, it is important to understand how this communication takes place. This chapter discusses the numerous prerequisite steps that enable network communications.

FUNCTION OF PACKETS IN NETWORK COMMUNICATIONS

Computer communications usually involve long messages. Because networks don't do a good job of handling large chunks of data, they reformat the data into smaller, more manageable pieces, called packets or frames. In many cases, the terms packet and frame can be used interchangeably. In different types of networks, however, the terms have slightly different meanings. For this discussion, the term packet suffices.

Networks split data into small pieces for two reasons. First, large units of data sent across a network hamper effective communications by saturating that network, as shown in Figure 6-1. If a sender and receiver use all the available bandwidth, other computers cannot communicate. This frustrates users.

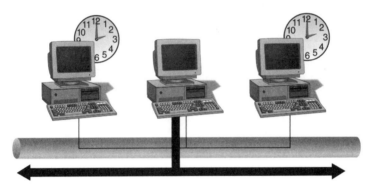

Figure 6-1 Large blocks of data sent by one computer tie up the network

Second, networks can be unreliable. If errors occur during transmission of a large packet, the entire packet must be re-sent. If that same data is split into numerous smaller packets, only those packets in which errors occur need to be re-sent. Packets are, therefore, more reliable and make error-recovery easier. With data split into packets, individual communications are faster and more efficient, which allows more computers to use the network. When those packets reach their destination, the receiving computer collects and reassembles them into their proper order to re-create the original data, and also requests retransmission of packets that may have been damaged or lost in transmission.

Packet Structure

All packets have three basic parts: header, data, and trailer. (See Figure 6-2.)

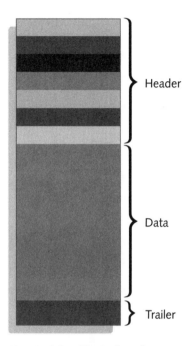

Figure 6-2   Typical packet structure

The **packet header** usually contains the source and destination addresses of the packet, an alert signal to indicate data transmission, and clocking information to synchronize the transmission.

The **data section** of a packet consists of the actual data being sent. The size of this section can vary from 512 bytes to 16 kilobytes, depending on the network type. The data section is also known as the **payload**.

The **packet trailer** contains information to verify the validity of the packet's contents. This usually involves a Cyclical Redundancy Check (CRC) value, as mentioned in Chapter 5. The CRC value is a number associated with the packet that the sending computer first calculates and adds to the trailer. When the receiving computer gets the packet, it recalculates the CRC independently and compares the calculated value to the CRC value embedded in the trailer. If the two CRCs match, the receiver accepts the packet as undamaged. If the CRCs don't match, the receiving computer discards the packet and requests that the packet be re-sent.

Packet Creation

Chapter 5 covered the OSI model, a theoretical structure that helps define how data is transmitted across a network. As data moves through the OSI model, first down through the sender's layers and then up through the receiver's layers, each layer adds or removes its header or trailer information, as shown in Figure 6-3. For example, information added at the Session layer on the sending computer is read in the Session layer on the receiving computer.

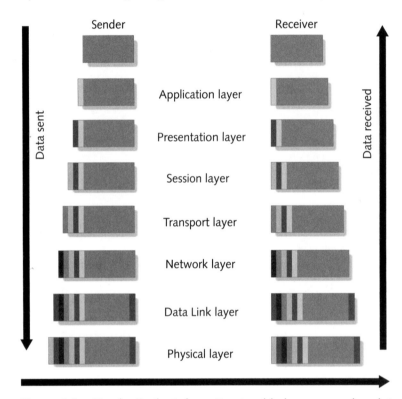

Figure 6-3   Header/trailer information is added or removed as data passes from layer to layer

When an outgoing data stream enters the OSI model, it is a complete message. The Transport layer splits it into segments. The protocol used by the two computers defines that transport segment structure. As the Transport layer splits the data into segments, it includes sequence information that allows the Transport layer on the receiving computer to put those segments back together in the right order. When the segment reaches the Network layer, the Network layer adds its own header information and the data is called a packet. When the data reaches the Physical layer, it includes information from all six of the other layers.

Understanding Packets

As mentioned earlier, any packet's header information includes the source and destination addresses for that packet. A packet is usually addressed to only one computer, and is called a unicast packet. Network adapters in the computers on a network see all packets as they pass through the network. However, the adapters read such packets and pass them to higher layers only if the destination address inside the packet header matches their own addresses.

In some cases, special packets—called **broadcast packets**—are created for all computers on a network. In this case, the destination address of the packet allows every computer to read and act on the packet. Likewise, special packets—called **multicast packets**—are created for any computers on a network that "listen" to a shared network address. This approach works particularly well for traditional broadcast applications on a network, such as video or audio broadcasts, where a single sender emits data streams that may be of interest to multiple receivers. Here again, a special kind of network address allows any receiver interested in listening to the broadcast to read such multicast data streams.

6

PROTOCOLS

Strictly speaking, **protocols** are the rules and procedures for communicating. When people travel to other countries, they must be familiar with the proper way to meet, greet, and communicate with the locals. This need to adapt applies to computers as well. For two computers to communicate, they must speak the same language and agree on the rules of communication.

The Function of Protocols

Computers use many protocols today; although every protocol provides basic communications, each one has a different purpose and function. As protocols serve their functions in the OSI model, they may work at one or many layers. The higher the layer at which a protocol operates in the OSI model, the more sophisticated that protocol is.

When a set of protocols works cooperatively, it's called a protocol stack, or protocol suite. Two of the most common protocol stacks are TCP/IP, the Internet protocol suite, and IPX/SPX, the Novell NetWare protocol suite. Within any protocol stack, the different levels map, or correspond, to their functions in the OSI model. Together, such related collections of protocols constitute a complete communications method.

Connectionless Versus Connection-Oriented Protocols

There are two methods for delivering data across a network: connectionless and connection-oriented.

Protocols that use **connectionless** delivery place the data on the network and assume it will get through, much the same way we rely on the U.S. Postal Service to deliver our mail when we drop it in a mailbox. However, much like the Postal Service, delivery is not always guaranteed, so connectionless protocols are not entirely reliable. However, connectionless protocols are fast because they require little overhead and don't waste time establishing, managing, and tearing down connections. When a connectionless protocol transports data across a network, higher layers handle packet sequencing and sorting, thereby allowing faster communications. Often, packets in a connectionless communication are referred to as **datagrams**.

On the other hand, **connection-oriented** protocols are more reliable and, consequently, slower. When a connection-oriented protocol is used, two computers establish a connection before communications begin. With the connection established, the data is sent in an orderly fashion. As each packet reaches the destination, its receipt is acknowledged. This type of communication can be related to using certified delivery for a U.S. Postal Service letter. If errors occur during the transmission, the packet is re-sent. After the communication is completed, the connection terminates. This procedure ensures that all data is received and is accurate, or that suitable error messages are generated when successful communications do not occur within a reasonable time period. With such assurances, upper-layer protocols can rely on connection-oriented delivery to handle matters of sequencing, data integrity, and delivery timeouts.

Routable Versus Nonroutable Protocols

As mentioned in Chapter 5, the Network layer—Layer 3—of the OSI model is responsible for moving data across multiple networks. Devices called routers are responsible for this process, called **routing**. However, not all protocol suites operate at the Network layer. Protocol suites that do function at the Network layer are called **routable**, whereas protocol suites that do not encompass the Network layer are called **nonroutable**. Because routing operates at Layer 3 of the OSI model, the routable/nonroutable attribute primarily applies to individual protocols that operate at Layer 3 (perhaps among other layers), but this characteristic also applies to the protocol suites of which such Layer 3 protocols are important parts.

In fact, a protocol suite's ability to be routed (or not) has a major impact on its effectiveness in a large-scale network, commonly called an **enterprise network**. TCP/IP and IPX/SPX are routable protocols well suited for large networks. NetBEUI, however, is a nonroutable protocol that works well in small networks, but its performance drops considerably as a network grows. When choosing the protocol suite for your network, consider the current size of the network and the possibilities for future expansion.

Protocols in a Layered Architecture

Most protocols can be explained or positioned in terms of the OSI model's layers, even though they may not map exactly onto that model layer for layer. As mentioned earlier, a protocol suite or stack is a combination of protocols that work cooperatively to accomplish network communications. Because each protocol performs a specific function and has its own rules, a protocol stack often has a different protocol for each layer. Figure 6-4 recaps the functions of each layer of the OSI model.

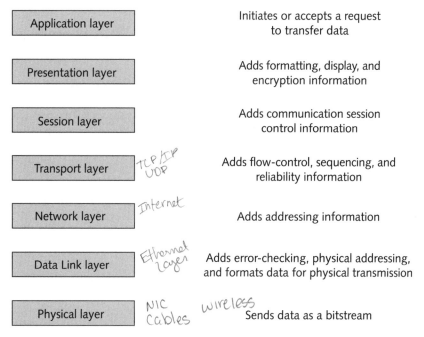

Figure 6-4   Functions of the OSI model layers

Figure 6-5 shows how the tasks required for network communication combine to form three major protocol types—application, transport, and network.

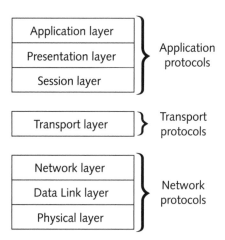

Figure 6-5   Three main protocol types

Network Protocols

Network protocols provide addressing and routing information, error checking, retransmission requests, and rules for communicating in some particular networking environment. The services provided by network protocols are called link services. Some popular network protocols, discussed in detail later in this chapter, include:

- **Internet Protocol (IP)**: The TCP/IP network protocol, which provides addressing and routing information

- **Internetwork Packet Exchange (IPX)** and NWLink (or **Novell IPX ODI Protocol**): Novell's protocol and the Microsoft implementation of Novell's protocol, respectively, for packet routing and forwarding (Windows 95 and Windows 98 identify this protocol explicitly as a Novell protocol, while Windows NT and Windows 2000 include NWLink as all or part of the same protocol's name.)

- **NetBEUI**: A network protocol developed by IBM and Microsoft specifically to provide transport services for **Network Basic Input/Output System (NetBIOS)**

- **Delivery Datagram Protocol (DDP)**: Apple's data transport protocol used in AppleTalk

- **Data Link Control (DLC)**: A network protocol used mainly by Hewlett-Packard printers attached to a network and IBM terminals attached to mainframes

Transport Protocols

Transport protocols handle data delivery between computers. Recall that connection-oriented transport protocols ensure reliable delivery, whereas connectionless transport protocols provide only best-effort delivery. Some of the most widely used transport protocols are:

- **Transmission Control Protocol (TCP)**: The TCP/IP protocol responsible for reliable delivery of data

- **Sequenced Packet Exchange (SPX)** and NWLink (the Microsoft implementation of SPX): Novell's connection-oriented protocol used to guarantee data delivery

- **AppleTalk Transaction Protocol (ATP)** and **Name Binding Protocol (NBP)**: AppleTalk's session and data transport protocols

- **NetBIOS/NetBEUI**: NetBIOS establishes and manages communications between computers; NetBEUI provides data transport services for such communications.

 NetBIOS also runs over TCP/IP and IPX/SPX, so using NetBIOS does not require also using NetBEUI.

Application Protocols

Application protocols operate at the upper layers of the OSI model and provide application-to-application services. Some of the more prevalent application protocols include:

- **Simple Mail Transport Protocol (SMTP)**: A member of the TCP/IP protocol suite responsible for transferring e-mail

- **File Transfer Protocol (FTP)**: Another member of the TCP/IP protocol suite used to provide file transfer services

- **Simple Network Management Protocol (SNMP)**: TCP/IP protocol used to manage and monitor network devices

- **NetWare Core Protocol (NCP)**: Novell's client shells and redirectors

- **AppleTalk File Protocol (AFP)**: Apple's remote file-management protocol

Common Protocol Suites

Because most protocols contain a combination of components to make communications work properly, these components are usually bundled as a protocol suite. As noted earlier, a protocol suite is a combination of protocols that work cooperatively to accomplish network communications.

Many protocols are available for communication, and each has its own strengths and weaknesses, which are discussed later in this section. Some protocols are used for computer-to-computer communications, whereas others connect local area networks (LANs) over a wide area network (WAN). The most common of these protocols are:

- TCP/IP
- NWLink (IPX/SPX)
- NetBIOS/NetBEUI
- AppleTalk
- DLC
- XNS
- DECNet
- X.25

Transmission Control Protocol/Internet Protocol (TCP/IP)

The TCP/IP suite, sometimes called the Internet Protocol (IP), is the most commonly used protocol suite in the networking world. TCP/IP enables easy communications across platforms and provides the basis for the global Internet.

Internet development began in 1969 as part of the U.S. Department of Defense's Advanced Research Projects Agency (ARPA, which later became DARPA) to provide internetwork communications. TCP/IP gained popularity when it was adopted by UNIX as the protocol for its systems. TCP/IP's scalability and superior functionality over WANs made TCP/IP the standard for connecting different types of computers and networks. Because of its wide acceptance, TCP/IP is the default protocol in Novell NetWare (starting with version 5.0), Windows XP/2000, and Windows NT and is incorporated into other Microsoft operating systems.

Although the TCP/IP suite predates the OSI model by nearly a decade, its protocols and functions are quite similar. Figure 6-6 shows TCP/IP's relation to the OSI model.

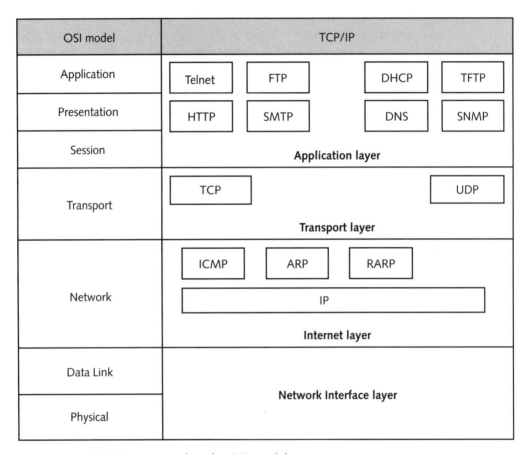

Figure 6-6   TCP/IP compared to the OSI model

More than any other protocol suite, TCP/IP utilizes highly compartmentalized and specialized protocols. The following sections discuss some of TCP/IP's many constituent protocols.

Internet Protocol (IP) is a Network layer protocol that provides source and destination addressing and routing for the TCP/IP suite. IP is a connectionless datagram protocol; like all connectionless protocols, it is fast but unreliable. IP assumes that other protocols used by the computer ensure reliable delivery of the data.

Internet Control Message Protocol (ICMP) ICMP is a Network layer protocol used to send control messages (such as error messages, flow control instructions, and confirmations). The PING utility may be used to request a response from a remote host. PING uses ICMP to return messages about remote responses, such as whether the initial query was received (and if so, how long the round trip lasted), or if the query timed out or the host was unreachable.

Address Resolution Protocol (ARP) ARP is another Network layer protocol used to associate a logical (IP) address to a physical (MAC) address. When a system begins a conversation with a host for which it lacks a physical address, it sends an ARP broadcast packet requesting the physical address that corresponds to the host's logical address. Then, the Data Link layer can correctly send the packet through the network.

 Communication using the ARP protocol can occur only between two systems on the same cable segment; holding a conversation with a remote host actually means sending a packet to the nearest IP gateway or router, which forwards it to its final destination.

Transmission Control Protocol (TCP) TCP is the primary Internet transport protocol. It accepts messages of any length from an upper-layer protocol and provides transportation to a TCP peer on a remote network station. TCP is connection oriented, so it provides more-reliable delivery than IP does. When a connection is established, a TCP port address determines for which connection a packet is destined. TCP is responsible for message fragmentation and reassembly. TCP uses a sequencing function to ensure that received packets are reassembled in the correct order. Most higher-level layer TCP/IP services use TCP as their transport protocol.

User Datagram Protocol (UDP) UDP is a connectionless Transport layer protocol. Its reduced overhead makes it generally faster, although less reliable, than TCP. Only a few higher-level layer TCP/IP services use UDP as their transport protocol (for example, the Network File System (NFS) uses UDP for transport).

Domain Name System (DNS) DNS is a Session layer, name-to-address resolution protocol. A DNS server keeps a list of systems' names and their associated IP addresses. Through a properly configured workstation, a user can use a remote system's logical name—for example, microsoft.com rather than a numerical address such as 207.46.131.30—to communicate with that remote system.

File Transfer Protocol (FTP) FTP, an upper-layer protocol, works cooperatively at the Session, Presentation, and Application layers. FTP provides services for file transfer as well as directory and file manipulation services (DIR, Delete, and so forth). Each upper layer provides its specific service to FTP; for example, the Session layer provides connection establishment and release.

Telnet Surprisingly, Telnet is not an acronym for anything. **Telnet** is a remote terminal emulation protocol that operates on all three upper layers and is used mostly to provide connectivity between dissimilar systems (for example, PC and VMS, PC and router, UNIX and VMS). Through Telnet, remote equipment (such as routers and switches) can be monitored and configured and remote systems can be operated.

Simple Mail Transport Protocol (SMTP) SMTP is another protocol that operates at all three upper layers. As its name implies, SMTP provides messaging services to the TCP/IP suite. SMTP is the basis for most e-mail that travels across the Internet.

Routing Information Protocol (RIP) RIP, a distance-vector protocol used for route discovery, represents the simplest IP-based routing protocol. As with other routing protocols, RIP operates at the Network layer to gather and exchange information about network routes and status. The current implementation of RIP, known as RIPv2, offers substantial performance and reliability improvements to the original RIP. Still widely used on smaller TCP/IP networks, RIP is not suitable for large, complex TCP/IP networks (which generally use OSPF for routing inside an organization or a site, and some kind of border protocol for routing among sites or organizations).

Open Shortest Path First (OSPF) OSPF is a link-state routing protocol used by routers running TCP/IP to determine the best path through a network. Chapter 11 discusses different methods for route discovery.

IP Addressing

As you learned earlier, IP is responsible for addressing and routing in the TCP/IP environment. IP addresses are logical addresses, which are 32 bits (4 bytes) long. A decimal number from 0 to 255, separated by periods, represents each byte or octet, for example, 172.24.206.18.

Although eight bits have 256 possible combinations, the numbers 0 and 255 are reserved; 0 represents the local network address, and 255 is used for broadcasts to all nodes on the local network. Real address values use only numbers 1 through 254.

Part of the address assigned to a computer designates on which network the computer is located, whereas the remainder of the address represents the host ID for that computer. For example, a computer with the address shown earlier might reside on the 172.24 network with a host address of 206.18. In this case, the complete network address is 172.24.0.0, where the trailing zeros indicate a network address. The computer next to it may have the address 172.24.208.192; both computers are on the same network because they share the same network address (172.24), even though their host IDs are quite different.

In a TCP/IP network, individual computers are referred to as hosts.

Originally, IP addresses were broken into classes, with classes A, B, and C available for normal networking use. A number of public and private companies around the world, known as IP **address registries**, cooperatively manage the total collection of valid IP addresses. This activity occurs under the control of IANA (the Internet Assigned Numbers Authority), a public, nonprofit agency responsible for Internet addressing and address management.

Although the IP address class system is not used universally today, it provides an easy way to describe a network's TCP/IP implementation. The first octet of an address denotes its class.

Note the following facts about addresses:

- Class A addresses were intended for use by extremely large corporations such as IBM and Hewlett-Packard. An IP address registry assigns the first octet, leaving the last three octets to be assigned arbitrarily to hosts. This allows for 16,777,214 hosts per network address. These addresses begin with ID numbers between 1 and 126.

- Class B addresses begin with network IDs between 128 and 191 and are intended for use in medium-sized networks. An IP address registry assigns the first two octets, creating 65,534 hosts per network address.

- Class C addresses were intended for small networks. An IP address registry assigns the first three octets, ranging from 192 to 223. These networks are limited to 254 hosts per network.

- Class D addresses are reserved for a special function called multicasting in which a packet is addressed so that it can be received by more than one destination. Applications that use this feature include videoconferencing and streaming media. In a class D address, the first octet is in the range of 224 to 239.

- Class E addresses have a first-octet value in the range of 240 to 255. This range of addresses is reserved for experimental use and cannot be used for address assignment.

Notice that a few addresses are missing. These addresses are used for special services. For example, the network beginning with 127 is called the **loopback** address. A packet sent to any host address starting with 127 is sent to the local device without reaching the media. Likewise, the reserved name **localhost** always corresponds to the IP address 127.0.0.1 so that a local machine may always be referenced using this name.

Due to the popularity of TCP/IP and the Internet, IP addresses are rapidly becoming scarce. To help alleviate this problem, TCP/IP's technical governing body reserved a series of addresses for private networks, that is, networks *not* connected to the Internet. The organization is called the Internet Engineering Task Force (IETF). It's public, nonprofit, and responsible for TCP/IP standards and characteristics.

6

The reserved addresses are:

- Class A addresses beginning with 10 (one Class A address)
- Class B addresses from 172.16 to 172.31 (16 Class B addresses)
- Class C addresses from 192.168.0 to 192.168.255 (256 Class C addresses)

In addition, the IETF is working on a new implementation of TCP/IP, known as IPv6. (The current version is called IPv4 using the same notation.) IPv6 uses IP addresses that are 16 bytes long but retain backward compatibility with IPv4 4-byte addresses. In the long term, switching to this newer version of TCP/IP should solve any potential address limitations because it will provide 3.4×10^{38} addresses, which, for all practical purposes, is a limitless supply.

Classless Inter-Domain Routing (CIDR)

As mentioned earlier, addressing by class has been abandoned. To use all available addresses more efficiently, the Internet now uses a different addressing scheme called **Classless Inter-Domain Routing (CIDR)**. Now, when an address is assigned, the network and host demarcation is not always made on octet boundaries, but, rather, may be made any specific number of bits from the beginning of the address.

For example, a Class C address's network section is 24 bits. Using CIDR, an address registry can assign an address whose network section is 26 bits. Because this technique involves "stealing" bits from the host portion of the address for use in the network portion, this technique is sometimes called subnetting. Subnetting provides fewer hosts on each network but more networks overall. When these addresses are assigned, a slash denotes the number of bits in the network section. For example, if your company had two networks and 60 hosts per network to attach to the Internet, your ISP might give you network addresses something like 192.203.187.64/26 and 192.203.187.128/26.

Subnet Masks

As already mentioned, an IP address consists of two sections, one that defines on which network a computer is located, and one that defines the host ID for a computer. IP uses an address's **subnet mask** to determine which part of the address denotes the network portion and which part denotes the host. In a subnet mask, the network section of the address (the **subnet**) is signified by the binary number 1 that blocks a bit position in the IP address. The host ID section uses 0 to indicate that such zero bit positions are available for host use.

Each of the three address classes has what's called a default subnet mask that uses the decimal number 255 for each octet in the address that corresponds to the network portion of the IP address. (The number 255 is 11111111 in binary, which fills all 8-bit positions in an IP address octet.) Thus, the default Class A subnet mask is 255.0.0.0, the default Class B subnet mask is 255.255.0.0, and the default Class C subnet mask is 255.255.255.0.

For example, if a computer has an IP address of 153.92.100.10 and a mask of 255.255.0.0 (a Class B mask), its host ID is 100.10 and the network is 153.92. However, if the computer uses the address 192.92.100.10 and the mask is 255.255.255.0 (a Class C mask), the host ID is 10; the network is 192.92.100.

 All devices on any single physical network (also called a network segment) must share the same network address, and therefore, must also use the same subnet mask.

Some Simple Binary Arithmetic

Working with IP addresses, especially for subnetting and supernetting—which you tackle later in this section—is a lot easier if you understand the basics of binary arithmetic. For the purposes of this class, you need to master four different kinds of binary calculations:

1. Converting between binary and decimal

2. Converting between decimal and binary

3. Understanding how setting high-order bits to the value of 1 in 8-bit binary numbers corresponds to specific decimal numbers

4. Recognizing the decimal values for the numbers that correspond to low-order bits when they're set to the value of 1

Before we tackle each of these two subjects, you must understand another apparent anomaly before binary counting makes sense. A sample question best illustrates this: How many numbers are there between 0 and 3 (or 00 to 11, in binary)? To find the answer, subtract the lower number from the higher number, and then add one. Thus $3 - 0 = 3 + 1 = 4$. Enumerating the binary digits from 0 to 3 demonstrates this (numbers in parentheses are decimal equivalents: 00 (0), 01 (1), 10 (2), 11 (3). If you count the numbers in the list, you'll find there are four, so our formula does not lie! Another apparent anomaly is that any number raised to the zero power always equals one. (You use that fact when converting decimal to binary and binary to decimal.)

Converting Decimal to Binary This is extremely easy, if you don't mind thinking mathematically. If you find this approach too challenging, we suggest an alternate approach as well. This method has the advantage of working for any number. The recipe is to divide the decimal number by two, write down the remainder (which must be zero or one), write down the dividend, and repeat until the dividend is 0.

The decimal number 125 is converted to binary in the following example:

125 divided by 2 equals 62, remainder 1

62 divided by 2 equals 31, remainder 0

31 divided by 2 equals 15, remainder 1

15 divided by 2 equals 7, remainder 1

7 divided by 2 equals 3, remainder 1

3 divided by 2 equals 1, remainder 1

1 divided by 2 equals 0, remainder 1

To produce the binary number that corresponds to 125, you must now write the digits starting from the bottom of the remainder column and work your way up: 1111101. Now, let's check the work involved. The exponential expansion of 1111101 is $1*2^6 + 1*2^5 + 1*2^4 + 1*2^3 + 1*2^2 + 0*2^1 + 1*2^0$.

The other way to convert the number depends on what mathematicians like to call a "step function." This approach depends on knowing the powers of two, and then applying a recipe similar to the one above, but more formal. The following example is based on powers of two:

125 is less than 128 (2^7) and more than 64 (2^6)

125 minus 64 is 61

61 is less than 64(2^6) and more than 32(2^5)

61 minus 32 is 29

29 is less than 32(2^5) and more than 16(2^4)

29 minus 16 is 13

13 is less than 16(2^4) and more than 8(2^3)

13 minus 8 is 5

5 is less than 8(2^3) and more than 4(2^2)

5 minus 4 is 1

The next lower power of 2 (2 itself) does not "fit," so it shows up as a zero when converted to binary. One is always 1, even in binary. Thus, 125 = 1*26 + 1*25 + 1*24 + 1*23 + 1*22 + 0*21 + 1*20. Read the multipliers from left to right to convert to binary, or 1111101. Choose some numbers and practice to make sure you understand how to do this.

Converting Binary to Decimal This is extremely easy, if you know your powers of two. Here's the recipe, using 11011011 as our example number:

1. Count the total number of digits in the number (11011011 has eight digits).

2. Subtract one from the total (8 - 1 = 7).

3. That number (7) is the power of 2 to associate with the highest exponent for two in the number.

4. Convert to exponential notation, using all the digits as multipliers.

5. 11011011 therefore converts to:

$$11011011 = 1*2^7+1*2^6+0*2^5+1*2^4+1*2^3+0*2^2+1*2^1+1*2^0$$
$$= 128+64+0+16+8+0+2+1 = 219$$

Choose some numbers and practice to make sure you understand how to do this.

High-Order Bit Patterns Sometimes, we block off bits in 8-bit numbers from the top down. (These are called the most significant bits because they represent the highest numeric values.) In an 8-bit number, there's little or no value in blocking less than 2 bits, or more than 6 bits, so the bit patterns you care about are the second through the sixth in the list in Table 6-1:

Table 6-1   High-order bit patterns

Binary	Decimal
10000000	128
11000000	192
11100000	224
11110000	240
11111000	248
11111100	252
11111110	254
11111111	255

Simply memorize these correlations to become well equipped to deal with subnet masking problems when you see them in a later section.

Low-Order Bit Patterns In Table 6-2, we stand the previous example on its head and start counting up through the 8-bit numbers from right to left, adding ones as we increment. Note that each of these numbers is the same as 2 raised to the power of the number of bits showing, minus 1. If you memorize the values of the powers of 2, from 1 through 8, you can calculate this table in a flash!

Table 6-2   Low-order bit patterns

Binary	Decimal	Exponent
00000001	1	$2^1 - 1$
00000011	3	$2^2 - 1$
00000111	7	$2^3 - 1$
00001111	15	$2^4 - 1$
00011111	31	$2^5 - 1$
00111111	63	$2^6 - 1$
01111111	127	$2^7 - 1$
11111111	255	$2^8 - 1$

Memorize these numbers, or how to calculate them, to become well equipped to deal with supernet masking problems when you see them later in this section as well. As with subnet masks, you seldom deal with supernet masks of more than 4 to 6 bits. These numbers are easy enough to calculate on demand, so you should force yourself to learn how to do so.

Now you are ready to tackle the intricacies of IP subnetting and supernetting, which follow in the next two sections of this chapter.

Calculating a Subnet Mask To decide how to build a subnet mask, you must follow this recipe:

1. Decide how many subnets you need.

2. Because a binary bit pattern must represent the number of subnets needed, add two to the number of subnets needed (one for the network address, the other for the broadcast address). Then jump to the next higher power of 2.

3. Reserve bits from the top of the host portion of the address down (that is, from the left side).

4. Be sure that enough host addresses to be usable are left over.

5. Always use the formula $2^b - 2$ to calculate the number of usable subnets from a mask, where b is the number of bits in the subnet mask, and 2 is subtracted to account for the network (all zeros) and broadcast (all ones) addresses that every IP network and subnetwork requires.

Here's an example to help you put this recipe to work:

1. ABC Inc. wants 12 subnets for their Class C address: 200.10.10.0. No subnet needs more than 10 host addresses.

2. Add 2 (for network and broadcast addresses) to 12 to get 14. The nearest power of 2 is 16, which equals 2^4. This means your subnet requires a 4-bit subnet mask.

3. Reserving 4 bits from the top down creates a subnet mask with the pattern 11110000. The decimal value for this number is 128+64+32+16, or 240. This extends the default subnet mask for the Class C address from 255.255.255.0 to 255.255.255.240 (because we're "stealing" 4 bits from the host portion of the address).

4. To calculate the number of host addresses for each subnet, reverse the logic from the subnet mask. In English, this means that any bit used for the subnet mask cannot be used for host addresses. Count the number of zeros remaining in the subnet mask to determine the number of bits left for the host address. In this case, that number is 4. The same formula used to calculate the number of subnets works to calculate the number of hosts, where b becomes the number of bits in the host address—namely $2^b - 2$, or $2^4 - 2$, which equals 14.

5. Remember, the purpose of this exercise is to compare the number of hosts needed for each subnet to the number you just calculated. In other words, if you need more than 14 hosts per subnet, this subnet mask cannot produce the desired results. But since you need only 10 hosts per subnet, as stated in the requirements for ABC Inc., this design works as intended.

Here's a quick summary of what you just did: based on the requirements for 12 subnets in a Class C address, where no individual subnet needs more than 10 host addresses, you calculated that a 4-bit subnet mask would be required. Because the corresponding bit pattern, 11110000, equates to 240 in binary, the default subnet mask for Class C, 255.255.255.0, must be changed to steal those 4 bits from the host portion of the address, so the actual subnet mask becomes 255.255.255.240. Because the remaining 4 bits for the host portion allow up to 14 host addresses per subnet, and the requirements call for no more than 10 addresses per subnet, the design works as intended. But always remember this last step: check your work—renumbering IP networks is a messy, tedious business, and you don't want to be forced to do this work over!

Another Subnet Mask Example Let's pick a more ambitious design this time: one that shows how subnet masks or host addresses can extend across multiple octets.

1. XYZ Corporation wants 300 subnets for its ClassB address: 178.16.10.0. No subnet needs more than 100 host addresses.

2. Add 2 (for network and broadcast addresses) to 300 to get 302. The nearest power of 2 is 512, which equals 2^9. This means you require a 9-bit subnet mask.

3. Reserving 9 bits from the top down creates a subnet mask with the pattern 11111111 10000000. Because this subnet mask extends across two octets, you must calculate the subnet separately for each octet. For the first host portion octet, the value is 255 because all the bits are set to ones. For the second octet, the first bit (which equals 2^7) is the only one set to a one; this translates to a decimal value of 128. This extends the default subnet mask for the Class B address from 255.255.0.0 to 255.255.255.128 (because we're "stealing" 9 bits from the host portion of the address).

4. To calculate the number of host addresses for each subnet, reverse the logic from the subnet mask. In English, this means that any bit used for the subnet mask cannot be used for host addresses. Count the number of zeros remaining in the subnet mask to determine the number of bits left for the host address. In this case, that number is 7. The same formula used to calculate the number of subnets works to calculate the number of hosts, where b becomes the number of bits in the host address—namely $2^b - 2$, or $2^7 - 2$, which equals 128 - 2 or 126.

5. Remember, the purpose of this exercise is to compare the number of hosts needed for each subnet to the number you just calculated. In other words, if you need more than 126 hosts per subnet, this subnet mask cannot produce the desired results. But since you need only 100 hosts per subnet, as stated in the requirements for XYZ Corporation, this design works as intended.

If you want to read more about this topic and access an outstanding "cheat sheet" to help you calculate subnets (and supernets, for that matter), please consult Joe Rudich's article from the June 1999 issue of *Windows NT Systems* magazine. To access this article online or print your own copy for later use, visit *www.ntsystems.com/db_area/archive/1999/9906/306fe1.shtml*. Another good source for learning to subnet is *www.learntosubnet.com*.

Calculating Supernets The act of **supernetting** "steals" bits from the network portion of an IP address to "lend" those bits to the host part. As part of how they work, supernets permit multiple IP network addresses to be combined and make them function as a single logical network. Incidentally, this permits many more hosts to be addressed on a supernet than the combination of multiple addresses might suggest. Here's why:

1. Combining seven Class C addresses steals 3 bits from the network portion of the address and adds it to the host portion of the address (in binary 7 = 111, which occupies all three bit positions with a 1).

2. Thus, instead of supporting only 8 bits for the host address portion, the supernet now supports 11 bits (8 + 3) for host addresses. The resulting subnet mask looks like this: 255.255.248.0 (instead of the default 255.255.255.0).

3. There are two ways to calculate a supernet mask. The first is to recognize that you're stealing 3 bits from the right side of the third octet. Note that the resulting bitmask for that octet becomes 11111000, which calculates to 248. The other way to calculate this value is to recognize that the largest number that can be represented in 3 binary bits is 111, which calculates to $2^3 - 1$, or 7 in decimal. If you subtract that number from 255, you get 248, which gives the same answer more quickly than the other formula. Because both methods work, use whichever one is easiest for you. The number of usable hosts for this supernet, using the old familiar $2^b - 2$ formula, is $2^{11} - 2$, which calculates to 2,046.

4. Each individual Class C address has 254 ($2^8 - 2$) hosts. Seven times 254 is 1,778. Supernetting gives access to an additional 268 hosts, for an overall increase of 15% as compared to the original number (15% of 1,778 is approximately 268, in other words). Supernetting also lets all host addresses in the seven combined Class C addresses be treated as a single routing domain, and it also improves network access efficiencies (especially among the network segments that the combined address pool denotes).

We hope this helps illustrate why supernetting is a useful tool for Internet Service Providers who can combine multiple Class C addresses to serve much larger populations than might seem possible. In the next section, we leave IP address calculation behind and discuss a service that makes network administrators' lives easier by helping them manage IP address allocation.

Network Address Translation (NAT)

Although subnetting and supernetting can help alleviate the IP address shortage problem, they only help make more efficient use of the existing addresses. **Network Address Translation (NAT)** helps considerably more by allowing the private IP addresses to be used by an organization while being connected to the Internet.

Using NAT, an organization can, for example, assign all its workstations addresses in the 10.*x.x.x* private network. Assume that the organization has 1000 workstations. Although these addresses cannot be used on the Internet, the NAT process translates the workstation address as it leaves the corporate network to some valid Internet address. When data returns to the workstation, the address is translated back to the original 10.*x.x.x* address. NAT is usually done by a network device that connects the organization to the Internet, such as a router. Figure 6-7 depicts the process.

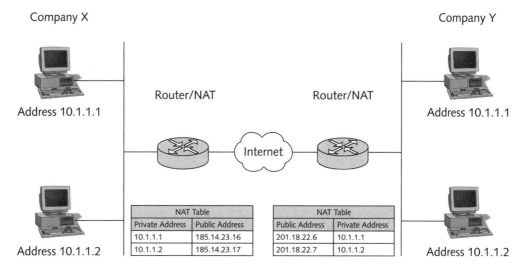

Figure 6-7   Network Address Translation (NAT)

Notice that the workstations in Company X are assigned the same IP addresses as the workstations in Company Y. These addresses in the 10.*x.x.x* network are used within the corporate network, but as soon as a workstation attempts to access the Internet, the address is translated to a valid public Internet address. This process allows any number of companies to use private IP addresses within their own network but only requires a public IP address when a workstation attempts to access the Internet. This reduces the number of public IP addresses required because a public address is only required if a workstation accesses the Internet. In fact, some NAT processes allow several hundred workstations to use a single public IP address to access the Internet. You can see how NAT has gone a long way toward extending the life of IPv4 and 32-bit IP addresses.

For an excellent tutorial on NAT, see *www.howstuffworks.com/nat.htm*.

Dynamic Host Configuration Protocol (DHCP)

Some drawbacks to using TCP/IP in a large network include the detailed configuration of all devices, keeping track of assigned addresses and to which machine they were assigned, and so forth. To make this process easier, the **Dynamic Host Configuration Protocol (DHCP)** was developed.

To utilize DHCP, a server must be configured with a block of available IP addresses and their subnet masks. Then, to receive its address from the server, each computer must be configured to request its address configuration. From that point on, each time the computer starts, it sends a broadcast message requesting an IP address from a DHCP server. Each time a computer requests an address, the server assigns one until it has no more addresses to assign.

A computer leases the IP address the server assigns to it. During the length of the lease, the computer has the address. When the lease expires, the computer can renew it and keep the address.

One major benefit of using DHCP is the ease with which computers can be moved. When a computer is moved to a new network segment and turned on, it requests its configuration from a DHCP server on that segment. Of course, this type of address assignment does not work for systems that require a static address, such as Web servers.

All major operating systems today include a DHCP client service, and most server operating systems include the DHCP server component.

NetBIOS and NetBEUI

In the early 1980s, IBM hired a third-party company named Sytek to build a simple, basic set of network programming interfaces. The result became NetBIOS. This interface persisted much longer than anyone expected and remains in broad use today. Its initial deployment occurred in a basic networking product that IBM called PC-Net and that Microsoft later remarketed as MS-Net.

By the mid-1980s, Microsoft, 3Com, and IBM together developed a protocol suite for use with OS/2 and LAN Manager. Using NetBIOS to provide application-layer capabilities, this consortium developed a lower-layer protocol known as NetBEUI (NetBIOS Extended User Interface) that spans Layers 2, 3, and 4 of the OSI model. From their inception, NetBIOS and NetBEUIwere designed to work in small- to medium-sized networks of two to 250 computers. NetBIOS is still going strong today, and Microsoft still supports NetBEUI across its Windows product family, even in Windows 2000.

Although NetBIOS and NetBEUI work closely together and are often confused with each other, in fact they are neither inseparable nor the same. Figure 6-8 shows the Microsoft protocol suite and its relationship to the OSI model.

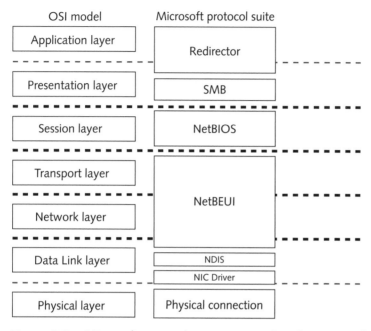

Figure 6-8   Microsoft protocol suite compared to the OSI model

As shown in Figure 6-8, the Microsoft protocol suite defines four components above the Data Link layer. Because of this, the Microsoft protocols can run on any network card or physical medium.

The redirector interprets requests from the computer and determines whether requests are local or remote. The redirector passes a local request to the local operating system and passes a request for remote network service to the protocol below, in this case the **Server Message Block (SMB)**.

The SMB passes information between networked computers. The redirector is responsible for repackaging SMB requests for transmission to other devices for processing.

As mentioned in Chapter 5, the Session layer is responsible for managing communications between applications on two computers. NetBIOS works at this layer to establish and maintain those connections.

NetBEUI works at the Transport layer to manage communications between two computers. Figure 6-8 shows NetBEUI operating at the Network layer, but it is, in fact, a nonroutable protocol and skips this layer. A NetBEUI packet has no fields for source or destination network information.

NetBIOS NetBIOS, as mentioned earlier, operates at the Session layer to provide peer-to-peer network application support. A unique 15-character name identifies each computer in a NetBIOS network. A NetBIOS broadcast advertises a computer's name. Periodically, a computer broadcasts its NetBIOS name so other computers can communicate with it. All computers on the network keep a cache of names and hardware addresses of computers from which they received broadcasts. If a computer wants to communicate with a computer whose name is not in its cache, it sends a broadcast requesting the hardware address for that computer.

NetBIOS is a connection-oriented protocol responsible for establishing, maintaining, and terminating network connections. Also, NetBIOS can use connectionless communications, if necessary.

Although closely related to NetBEUI, NetBIOS can utilize a number of other lower-layer protocols, including TCP/IP and IPX/SPX, for transport and lower-layer services. NetBIOS is a nonroutable protocol, but it can be routed when using a routable protocol for transport.

NetBEUI NetBEUI is a small, fast, nonroutable Transport and Data Link layer protocol designed for use with NetBIOS on small networks. NetBEUI 3.0 is the Microsoft improvement on IBM's version of NetBEUI (and therefore works only on Microsoft networks). All members of the Windows product family include it, from Windows for Workgroups through Windows 2000. Its low overhead makes NetBEUI ideal for DOS-based computers that require network connectivity. NetBEUI's speed and size also make it a good choice for slow serial links. Because NetBEUI is not routable, its use is limited to small networks in most cases. (However, this protocol can be bridged, as Chapter 11 explains.)

Server Message Block (SMB) The Server Message Block (SMB) protocol operates at the Presentation layer. Microsoft networks use it for communication between the redirector and the server software; for example, when a client computer requests a file list from the file server. SMB is also used if a client requires a connection to a Microsoft LAN Manager server.

IPX/SPX

IPX/SPX is the original protocol suite developed for use with Novell's NetWare network operating system software. Novell continues to support this protocol suite, even in its latest version of NetWare (version 6.0 as of this writing), but does so primarily for backward compatibility with older NetWare implementations. Currently, as is also the case with Microsoft products, TCP/IP is the protocol suite of choice for networking, even with NetWare.

NWLink is the Microsoft implementation of the IPX/SPX protocol suite used by Novell's NetWare and intraNetWare. Figure 6-9 shows the protocols that compose the NWLink suite and their corresponding layers in the OSI model. In Windows 98,

Microsoft changes its terminology. Rather than calling the IPX/SPX protocols "NWLink," it calls them "Novell IPX ODI Protocol" (Windows 98, Release 2) or "IPX/SPX-Compatible Protocol" (Windows 98, Release 1).

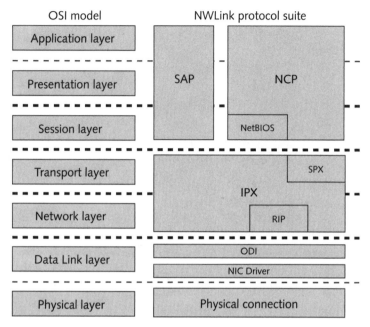

6

Figure 6-9 NWLink compared to the OSI model

Windows NT and Windows 2000 include NWLink, mostly to support connections to older NetWare servers. However, NWLink can also provide transport for NetBIOS. Because it is a routable protocol suite, network expansion is easier with IPX/SPX than with NetBEUI.

One major consideration when using IPX/SPX or NWLink is which Ethernet frame type to use. Chapter 7 discusses the various Ethernet frame types and their applications. For now, it is important to remember that all computers on a network must use the same frame type to communicate successfully. If computers on a network use IPX/SPX and communication does not occur, verify that all computers use the same frame type.

Open Data-link Interface (ODI) ODI is similar to the Microsoft Network Device Interface Specification (NDIS) discussed in Chapter 4. It allows a single network driver to support multiple protocols, thereby enabling a computer to use multiple protocols for network communications through a single network interface card.

Internetwork Packet Exchange (IPX) IPX is a Transport and Network layer protocol that handles all addressing and routing on a network. Workstations utilize the hardware (MAC) address of the NIC for identification. IPX is a connectionless protocol that provides fast, but unreliable, services.

IPX Routing Information Protocol (IPX RIP) Roughly based on TCP/IP's RIP protocol, servers and routers use IPX RIP to exchange information about network addresses and topology. IPX RIP (Routing Information Protocol) is a distance-vector protocol that uses the number of hops between points to determine the best path for a packet to take from sender to receiver. In addition to hops, IPX RIP uses ticks, a value based on the expected delay between routers, to determine the best path. Chapter 11 discusses RIP and other routing protocols in greater detail.

Sequenced Packet Exchange (SPX) SPX works in conjunction with IPX to provide connection-oriented services. As with all connection-oriented protocols, transmission is slower, but more reliable than with a similar connection-oriented protocol.

NetWare Core Protocol (NCP) NCP functions at the Transport layer and all upper layers (Session, Presentation, and Application) to provide a broad range of client/server functions. NCP handles client redirection through IPX/SPX or NWLink, including printing and file sharing.

Service Advertising Protocol (SAP) File and print servers use SAP to advertise their services to computers on the network. Broadcast periodically (usually every 60 seconds), SAP packets ensure that all computers know the services available and the addresses of those servers. Newer NetWare implementations tend to avoid SAP, choosing instead to use Novell Directory Services and related protocols. That's because the once-per-minute update interval for SAP can become problematic on large networks with a multitude of service advertisers.

Service Lookup Protocol (SLP) In the modern NetWare world (versions 4.0 and later), Novell Directory Services provide the preferred methods for servers to advertise services and for clients to look up such services. SLP is a new IP-based NetWare protocol that applies when clients want to look up the services available on an IP-only network. SLP packets locate the nearest identifiable directory tree and ensure that all directory-enabled computers can easily inquire about available network services.

AppleTalk

Although the AppleTalk standard defines the physical transport in Apple Macintosh networks, it also establishes a suite of protocols those computers use to communicate. Apple created AppleTalk Phase II to allow connectivity outside the Macintosh world. Rather than define networks, AppleTalk divides computers into zones.

Xerox Network Systems (XNS)

Xerox created the **Xerox Network Systems (XNS)** for use in its Ethernet networks. The basis for Novell's IPX/SPX, XNS is seldom found in today's networks.

DECNet

Digital Network Architecture (DNA) uses DECNet, which was Digital Equipment Corporation's proprietary protocol. **DECNet** is a complete, routable protocol suite generally used only by Digital systems. Its current iteration, Phase IV, closely resembles the OSI model. Digital Equipment Corporation was purchased by Compaq Computers, which was later purchased by Hewlett Packard. The Digital Equipment Corporation name no longer exists.

X.25

X.25 is a set of wide-area protocols created to connect remote terminals to mainframes and is used in packet-switching networks. Although many other wide-area communications types are now available in the United States, X.25 is still widely used in Europe.

For more information on these protocols and others, see *www.protocols.com*.

Implementing and Removing Protocols

In most operating systems, adding or removing protocols is relatively easy. For example, in Windows 2000/XP Professional and Server machines, and in most versions of UNIX, TCP/IP automatically loads when the operating system is installed. More protocols can be added during installation, such as IPX/SPX or NetBEUI. Also, they can be added or removed later using the Network and Dial-up Connections control panel in Windows 2000/XP, as shown in Figure 6-10, or using a similar utility in other operating systems.

While it may be tempting to install several protocols on a machine to ensure interoperability with any and all operating systems, adding unnecessary protocols can have a detrimental effect on network performance. Furthermore, when multiple protocols are installed, the operating system must be carefully configured to properly prioritize the use of each protocol. This priority is referred to as the protocol binding order. Typically, the most frequently used protocol should be first in the binding order.

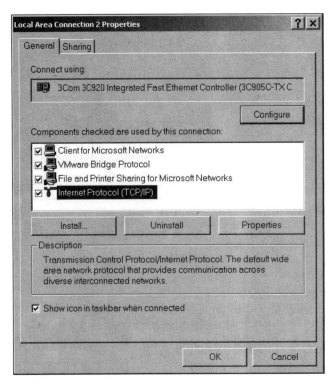

Figure 6-10 Network and Dial-up Connections in Windows 2000

PUTTING DATA ON THE CABLE: ACCESS METHODS

Given that computers communicate in a number of ways, some factors must be considered in network communications, including how computers put data on the cable and how they ensure that the data reaches its destination undamaged.

Function of Access Methods

When multiple computers are attached to a network, the way those computers share the cable must be defined. When computers have data to send, they transmit data across the network. However, when two computers send data at the same time, a data **collision** can occur, destroying both messages. As discussed earlier in this chapter, splitting the data into smaller chunks is one way to ensure that the data reaches its destination, but often this is not enough.

In addition to reformatting the data into packets, computers must have a way to ensure that the data they send is not corrupted. A number of rules have been defined to prevent collisions. These rules specify when the computers can access the cable, or **data channel**.

These **channel access methods** provide additional assurance that the data reaches its destination by preventing two or more computers from sending messages that might collide on the cable. Allowing only one computer at a time to send data, or preventing collisions in some other way, gives the data a much higher chance of reaching its destination intact.

As with all other network communication parameters, every computer on a network must use the same access method. If not, the data is not received, and, depending on the method used, all network communications might be interrupted.

Major Access Methods

Channel access is handled at the Media Access Control (MAC) sublayer of the Data Link layer in the OSI model. There are five major types of channel access:

- Contention
- Token passing
- Demand priority
- Polling
- Switching

Contention

Have you ever attended a meeting without a moderator? Effective communication is difficult in such a situation because everyone talks at the same time.

In early networks based on **contention**, computers sent data whenever they had data to send. This might work well in a small environment where computers send little data along the cable. But as more computers send data, outgoing messages collide more frequently, must be re-sent, and then collide again. The network becomes a useless jumble of electronic signals.

In Figure 6-11, packets from two computers collide when they try to send data at or near the same instant.

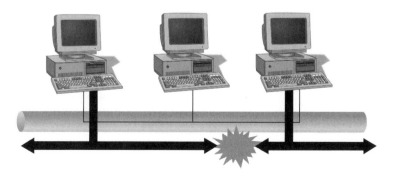

Figure 6-11   Data collision

To organize contention-based networks, two carrier access methods were created: Carrier Sense Multiple Access with Collision Detection (CSMA/CD), and Carrier Sense Multiple Access with Collision Avoidance (CSMA/CA).

CSMA/CD

Carrier Sense Multiple Access with Collision Detection (CSMA/CD) is one of the most popular ways to regulate network traffic. Used by Ethernet, this access method prevents collisions by listening to the channel to see if another computer is sending data, as shown in Figure 6-12.

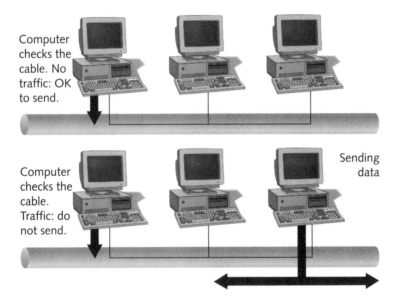

Computer checks the cable. No traffic: OK to send.

Computer checks the cable. Traffic: do not send.

Sending data

Figure 6-12   With CSMA/CD, computers check for cable traffic

If the computer senses no data on the line, it sends its message. If another computer is using the channel, the computer waits a random amount of time and then checks again. This process continues until the channel is free and the computer can send its data. In the event that two or more stations do send data simultaneously, a collision occurs. The sending stations involved in the collision then send a jamming signal to alert all stations to the collision. The stations involved in the collision then wait a random period of time before attempting to resend their data.

CSMA/CD does not allow traffic from a server to take precedence over traffic from a workstation. All computers on the network have an equal chance to control the channel.

Although this may seem like a good way to prevent collisions, limitations remain, for example:

- CSMA/CD is not effective at distances over 2500 meters because of attenuation and signal length restrictions.

- The more computers on a network, the more collisions are likely to occur. Adding computers places higher demands on the network, increases the likelihood of collisions, and requires retransmission of data. This can dramatically slow network transmissions.

- Computers have unequal access to the media. A computer with large amounts of data to send monopolizes the network channel, slowing transmission for all other computers on the network.

CSMA/CA

Carrier Sense Multiple Access with Collision Avoidance (CSMA/CA) is another channel access method that uses Carrier Sense Multiple Access. However, it uses collision avoidance, rather than detection, to prevent collisions. With CSMA/CA, once the computer senses that no other computer is using the network, it signals its intent to transmit data. Any other computers with data to send wait when they receive the "intent-to-transmit" signal and send their intent-to-transmit signals when they see that the channel is free.

Although this method more reliably avoids collisions than CSMA/CD, the additional overhead created by the "intent-to-transmit" packets significantly reduces network speed. Therefore, it is not used nearly as much as CSMA/CD. In fact, Apple's LocalTalk is the only major network type that uses CSMA/CA.

Token Passing

Chapter 2 discussed **token passing** as a function of the ring topology. Using this channel access method, a special packet called the token passes sequentially from one computer to the next. Only the computer holding the token can send data. A computer can keep the token only a specific amount of time. If the computer with the token has no data to send, it passes the token to the next computer. Figure 6-13 shows communication in a token-passing network.

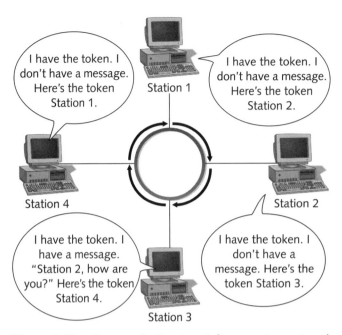

Figure 6-13   Communication in a token-passing network

Because only the computer with the token can transmit data, this method prevents collisions. Computers no longer spend time waiting for collisions to be resolved, as they do in a contention-based environment. All computers have equal access to the media, which makes token-passing networks best suited for time-sensitive environments; for example, banking transactions and databases that require precise timestamps. Also, because traffic moves in a specific "direction" around a ring topology, faster access methods (such as 16 Mbps token ring) can actually circulate two tokens at the same time, without fear of collision. (By keeping the two sets of messages from overlapping, both tokens can circulate in order.)

Two disadvantages of a token-passing environment follow:

- Even if only one computer on the network has data to send, it must wait to receive the token. If its data is large enough to warrant two or more "turns" at the token, the computer must wait until the token makes a complete circuit before starting its second transmission.

- The complicated process of creating and passing the token requires more expensive equipment than that used by contention-based networks.

Demand Priority

Demand priority is a channel access method used solely by the 100VG-AnyLAN 100Mbps Ethernet standard (IEEE 802.12), discussed in more detail in Chapter 7. As shown in Figure 6-14, 100VG-AnyLAN runs on a star bus topology. The demand priority channel access method relies on this design.

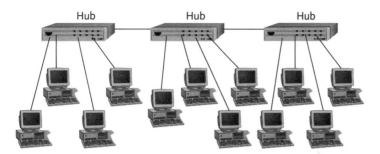

Figure 6-14 Demand priority uses the star bus topology

Intelligent hubs control access to the network. The hub searches all connections in a round-robin fashion. When an end node—a computer, bridge, router, or switch—has data to send, it transmits a **demand signal** to the hub. The hub then sends an acknowledgment that the computer can start transmitting its data.

Unlike other channel access methods, demand priority allows certain computers to be assigned a higher priority than others. If multiple computers make simultaneous demands, the computer with the highest priority transmits first. Demand priority makes the most efficient use of the available network media. Rather than wasting time addressing computers that have no data to send, hubs using demand priority channel access respond only when computers signal for service. Also, packets are not broadcast in a demand priority network as they are in CSMA/CD and CSMA/CA networks but, instead, are sent from the computer to the hub and from the hub directly to the destination. This eliminates extraneous traffic on the network.

The major disadvantage of demand priority is price. To work, this access method requires special hubs and other equipment.

Polling

Polling is one of the oldest ways of controlling access to the network. A central controller, often referred to as the **primary device**, asks each computer (the **secondary device**) on the network if it has data to send. If so, the computer may send up to a certain amount of data; then it is the next computer's turn, as shown in Figure 6-15.

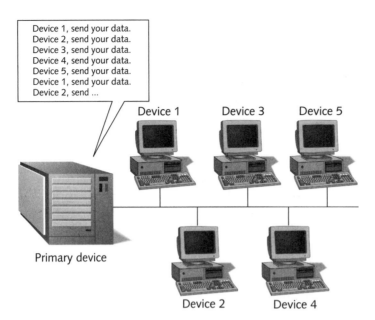

Figure 6-15   Primary device controls polling

Polling has many advantages. First, like token passing, it allows all computers equal access to the channel; no single computer monopolizes the media. The central controller allows centralized management, and certain computers (for example, file servers) can receive priority over other computers; they can be polled more often or be allowed to send for a longer period of time than the remaining computers.

Like token passing, however, polling does not make efficient use of the media. Another major drawback to polling is that if the primary device fails, the network fails. For this reason, it is difficult to find networks using this method today, other than IBM SNA networks.

Switching

When networks interconnect individual nodes through a special device called a switch, the switch itself controls access to the media. This method of channel access control is called **switching**. Contention occurs on a switch only when two or more senders ask to reach the same receiver simultaneously, or when the number of simultaneous transmission requests exceeds the switch's total ability to handle multiple connections.

Except in these special circumstances, contention is not a problem for a network switch, because it can interconnect any pair of nodes that want to exchange data on demand. Furthermore, since each connection between two machines that want to exchange data is reserved for their exclusive use, that connection can use the entire available bandwidth for whatever networking technology may be in use. (Because collisions cannot occur, this is true even for Ethernet or other contention-based networking technologies, where performance normally degrades as network utilization increases.)

Switching also has many advantages. First, it is fairer than strict contention-based technologies. Switches permit multiple, simultaneous conversations. Thus, a computer need not wait to access the media, as is required in contention-based methods. In addition, no single computer can monopolize the network media. Second, switching also supports centralized management, and certain computers (routers or servers, for example) can receive priority over other computers; they can get preferential access to a channel because of priority settings or because of quality of service guarantees (which essentially offer access to minimum guaranteed bandwidth for certain time-sensitive network services such as video or audio streams).

One drawback to switching is higher cost (particularly for the switch itself). Another major drawback to switching is that if the switch itself fails, the network fails. Despite these drawbacks, switching is an increasingly popular networking technology, especially for high-speed networking technologies like ATM and Gigabit Ethernet, which usually require a switch to make that bandwidth available to a local area network.

Choosing an Access Method

The access method is an integral part of your network. The biggest factor in the choice of access methods is the network topology. A ring topology network generally uses the token-passing channel access method. Switching is an exception to the topology constraint, because switches support nearly arbitrary node groupings and can manage traffic circulation when necessary. Switches can emulate all the common networking topologies (and sometimes even combine them within a single device).

Tables 6-3 through 6-7 outline the advantages, disadvantages, and typical network architectures of each channel access method.

Table 6-3   Summary of the contention access method

Typical Network Architecture	Advantages	Disadvantages
Ethernet (CSMA/CD)	Inexpensive to implement	Slow in a large network with high traffic
LocalTalk (CSMA/CA)	Fast in a small network with low traffic	Does not support priority; a single computer can monopolize the network

Table 6-4   Summary of the token-passing access method

Typical Network Architecture	Advantages	Disadvantages
Token ring	Guaranteed equal access for all computers on the network	Slow in low-traffic environments
FDDI	Fast and reliable; suited to critical campus backbones	Very expensive because more-sophisticated equipment is required

Table 6-5   Summary of the demand priority access method

Typical Network Architecture	Advantages	Disadvantages
100VG-AnyLAN	Very fast in high- and low-traffic environments Provides guaranteed channel access; allows certain computers to be given higher priority over others on the same network	Expensive because special equipment is required

Table 6-6   Summary of the polling access method

Typical Network Architecture	Advantages	Disadvantages
IBM SNA	Guaranteed access for all computers Supports priority assignment	Inefficient use of network media

Table 6-7   Summary of the switching access method

Typical Network Architecture	Advantages	Disadvantages
Ethernet (from 10 Mbps to 1 Gbps)	Higher levels of access for all users	Slightly more expensive equipment
Token ring (4 Kbps, 16 Kbps)	Support for guaranteed bandwidth (quality of service)	Configuration and setup often time-consuming and difficult
Other architectures, including ATM, voice and data traffic, etc.	Provides highest bandwith inter-connections between senders and receivers	

CHAPTER SUMMARY

- The data stream on a network is divided into packets, which provide more-reliable data delivery and ease network traffic. With the data split into smaller pieces, if errors occur during transmission, the receiving computer can request only the packet with errors be re-sent.

- As the data travels through the layers of the OSI model, each layer adds its own header or trailer information to the packet. Then, as the receiving computer processes the packet, each layer strips its header or trailer information and properly resequences segmented messages so that when the application receives the data, the packet is in its original form.

- Many protocols are available for network communications. Each protocol has its own strengths and weaknesses. A suite, or stack, of protocols allows for a number of protocols to work cooperatively to achieve maximum performance. The major protocol suites are TCP/IP, IPX/SPX, and NetBEUI. Many smaller protocols constitute each of these; each smaller protocol has its own network function.

❐ IP addressing involves several concepts, including address classes, subnetting, supernetting, and subnet masks. The current method for Internet addressing is called CIDR, which uses all available addresses more efficiently. Other IP addressing concepts include DHCP, which is a method for the automatic assignment and management of IP addresses, and NAT, which allows companies using private IP addresses to access the Internet and use public IP addresses more efficiently.

❐ Once a computer is ready to send its data, it must be assured that the data will reach its destination. In a perfect environment, all computers would have a dedicated channel over which to send information. However, this environment does not exist, so rules have been established to ensure that all computers have time on the channel.

❐ Token passing and polling allow for guaranteed time for each computer to send its data. Demand priority allows a computer to send data after it notifies the controlling hub that it has data to send.

❐ In contention channel access methods, computers vie for network time. They listen to the network to determine whether any other computer is sending data; if not, they send their data immediately (CSMA/CD) or broadcast their intention to send data (CSMA/CA).

❐ Switching can emulate all other access methods and offers the greatest total available bandwidth to its users.

6

KEY TERMS

address registries — Any of a number of IP address registry organizations worldwide. (Some are governmental, especially outside the United States and Europe; many are private, for-profit companies.) These organizations dole out IP addresses, manage IP address ranges, and handle DNS domain name registration under the auspices of the IANA (Internet Assigned Numbers Authority, the suborganization of the Internet Society, or ISOC).

Address Resolution Protocol (ARP) — A protocol in the TCP/IP suite used to associate logical addresses to physical addresses.

AppleTalk File Protocol (AFP) — Apple's remote file-management protocol.

AppleTalk Transaction Protocol (ATP) — AppleTalk's session protocol.

application protocol — A type of protocol that works in the upper layers of the OSI model to provide application-to-application interaction.

broadcast packet — A packet type whose destination address specifies all computers on a network or network segment.

Carrier Sense Multiple Access with Collision Avoidance (CSMA/CA) — A contention-based channel access method in which computers avoid collisions by broadcasting their intent to send data.

Carrier Sense Multiple Access with Collision Detection (CSMA/CD) — A contention-based channel access method in which computers avoid collisions by listening to the network before sending data. If a computer senses data on the network, it waits and tries to send its data later.

channel access method — The rules used to determine which computer can send data across the network, thereby preventing data loss due to collisions.

Classless Inter-Domain Routing (CIDR) — A more efficient way to assign IP addresses than using IP address "classes."

collision — Occurs when two computers put data on the cable at the same time. This corrupts the electronic signals in the packet and causes data loss.

connectionless — A type of protocol that sends the data across the network to its destination without guaranteeing receipt.

connection-oriented — A type of protocol that establishes a formal connection between two computers, guaranteeing the data will reach its destination.

contention — A channel access method in which computers vie for time on the network.

data channel — The cables and infrastructure of a network.

Data Link Control (DLC) — A network protocol used mainly by Hewlett-Packard printers and IBM mainframes attached to a network.

data section — The actual data being sent across a network. The size of this section can vary from 512 bytes to 16 kilobytes, depending on the network type.

datagram — The term used in some protocols to define a packet.

DECNet — Protocol suite of a company known at the time as Digital Equipment Corporation.

Delivery Datagram Protocol (DDP) — Data transport protocol for AppleTalk.

demand priority — A high-speed channel access method used by 100VG-AnyLAN in a star hub topology.

demand signal — A signal sent by a computer in a demand priority network that informs the controlling hub it has data to send.

Domain Name System (DNS) — A TCP/IP protocol used to associate a computer's IP address with a name.

Dynamic Host Configuration Protocol (DHCP) — A TCP/IP protocol that allows automatic IP address and subnet mask assignment.

enterprise network — A large-scale network usually connecting many LANs.

File Transfer Protocol (FTP) — A TCP/IP protocol used for file manipulation.

Internet Control Message Protocol (ICMP) — A TCP/IP protocol used to send information and error messages.

Internet Protocol (IP) — TCP/IP's primary network protocol, which provides addressing and routing information.

Internetwork Packet Exchange (IPX) — IPX is a Transport and Network layer protocol that handles all addressing and routing on a network. IPX is a connectionless protocol that provides fast, but unreliable, services.

IPX Routing Information Protocol (IPX RIP) — IPX RIP is a distance-vector protocol that uses the number of hops between points to determine the best path for a packet to take from sender to receiver.

localhost — A special DNS host name that refers to whatever IP address is assigned to the machine where this name is referenced. (Think of this as a special way to access your current IP address on any computer.)

loopback — A special DNS host name that refers to the reserved Class A address 127.0.0.1, used to confirm that a computer's IP configuration works.

multicast packet — A packet that uses a special network address to make itself readable to any receiving computer that wants to read its payload. Multicast packets usually transport streaming broadcast data, such as video programs, teleconferences, or live audio broadcasts, where many receivers want to access data from the same sender.

Name Binding Protocol (NBP) — AppleTalk's data transport protocol.

NetBEUI — A network protocol developed by IBM and Microsoft specifically to provide transport services for Network Basic Input/Output System (NetBIOS).

NetWare Core Protocol (NCP) — Novell's upper-layer protocol, which provides all client/server functions.

Network Address Translation (NAT) — A process by which an organization may assign private IP addresses to workstations; those addresses are translated to public IP addresses when access to the Internet occurs.

Network Basic Input/Output System (NetBIOS) — A connection-oriented protocol used by Windows 98, Windows NT, Windows 2000, and LAN Manager; closely related to NetBEUI.

nonroutable — A protocol that does not include network layer or network address information.

Novell IPX ODI Protocol — The name that Windows 98, Release2, gives to the Microsoft implementation of the IPX/SPX protocol suite for that operating system.

Open Data-link Interface (ODI) — ODI allows a single network driver to support multiple protocols, thereby enabling a computer to use multiple protocols for network communications through a single network interface card.

Open Shortest Path First (OSPF) — TCP/IP's link-state routing protocol used to determine a packet's best path through an internetwork.

packet header — Information added to the beginning of the data being sent, which contains, among other things, addressing and sequencing information.

packet trailer — Information added to the end of the data being sent, which generally contains error-checking information such as the CRC.

payload — The data section of a network packet. This portion contains all or part of the information being passed from sender to receiver. Because this information represents the primary "information value" of the transmission, it is called the payload.

polling — A channel access method in which a primary device asks secondary devices in sequence whether they have data to send.

6

primary device — Used in a polling network to manage data transmission. The primary device asks each secondary device if it has data to send and controls the data transmission.

protocol — The rules and procedures for communicating.

routable — A protocol that includes network layer information and can be forwarded by a router.

routing — The process of moving data across multiple networks via routers.

Routing Information Protocol (RIP) — Used by TCP/IP and IPX/SPX; a distance-vector routing protocol used to determine a packet's best path through an internetwork.

secondary device — A device, such as a computer, in a polling network where the primary device controls communications.

Sequenced Packet Exchange (SPX) — Novell's connection-oriented protocol that supplements IPX by providing reliable transport.

Server Message Block (SMB) — A block of data comprising client/server requests or responses. All areas of Microsoft network communications use SMBs.

Service Advertising Protocol (SAP) — Used by file and print servers on Novell networks to inform computers of the services available.

Service Lookup Protocol (SLP) — SLP is a new IP-based NetWare protocol that applies when clients want to look up the services available on an IP-only network.

Simple Mail Transport Protocol (SMTP) — A TCP/IP protocol used to send mail messages across a network. SMTP is the basis for e-mail on the Internet.

Simple Network Management Protocol (SNMP) — A TCP/IP protocol used to monitor and manage network devices.

subnet — A portion of an IP address that identifies the network portion of that address.

subnet mask — The "all ones" bit pattern that masks the network portion of an IP address. For a Class A address, the default subnet mask is 255.0.0.0; for Class B, 255.255.0.0; for Class C, 255.255.255.0.

supernetting — The operation of "stealing" bits from the network portion of an IP address to extend the host address space for a group of contiguous IP addresses. For supernetting to work properly, the group of IP addresses must be contiguous and consist of a binary number made entirely of ones (11 or 3; 111 or 7; 1111 or 15; and so on).

switching — Using a network switch to manage media or channel access. It helps increase overall bandwidth, provides greater bandwidth to senders and receivers, and can emulate other access methods based on the switch's built-in capabilities.

Telnet — A TCP/IP protocol that provides remote terminal emulation.

token passing — A channel access method used mostly in ring topology networks. It ensures equal access to all computers on a network through the use of a special packet called the *token*.

Transmission Control Protocol (TCP) — The core of the TCP/IP suite. TCP is a connection-oriented protocol responsible for reformatting data into packets and reliably delivering those packets.

transport protocol — A protocol type responsible for providing reliable communication sessions between two computers.

User Datagram Protocol (UDP) — A connectionless TCP/IP protocol that provides fast data transport.

X.25 — An international standard for wide-area packet-switched communications. X.25 offers 64-Kbps network connections and error checking for users.

Xerox Network Systems (XNS) — A protocol suite developed by Xerox for its Ethernet LANs. The basis for Novell's IPX/SPX.

REVIEW QUESTIONS

1. Novell's IPX/SPX protocols are based on the IBM SNA protocol suite. True or false?

2. Which of the following terms describe data being sent across a network? (Choose all that apply.)

   a. packet

   b. token

   c. frame

   d. datagram

   e. protocol

3. The subnet mask of an IP address _____.

   a. provides encryption in a TCP/IP network

   b. allows automated IP address configuration

   c. defines which part of the address specifies the network and which part specifies the host ID

   d. allows users to use a computer's given name rather than its address

4. A network protocol operates in which layers of the OSI model? (Choose all that apply.)

   a. Presentation

   b. Data Link

   c. Transport

   d. Physical

   e. Network

5. Which of the following IP addresses cannot be sent across the Internet?

   a. 192.156.90.100

   b. 172.19.243.254

   c. 11.200.99.180

   d. 221.24.250.207

   e. 12.12.12.12

6. As data travels through the OSI model, the _____ layer is responsible for splitting the data into packets.

7. The _____ channel access method is generally used in ring topology networks.

8. NetBEUI is well suited for large enterprise networks because it is very fast. True or false?

9. Which of the following is *not* a benefit of the contention-based channel access method? (Choose all that apply.)

   a. works well in high-traffic environments

   b. ease of installation

   c. price

   d. allows certain computers to be assigned a higher priority than others

10. Logical-address-to-physical-address resolution is performed by the _____ protocol.

    a. DHCP

    b. XNS

    c. IP

    d. DNS

    e. ARP

11. Which of the following protocols provide connectionless service? (Choose all that apply.)

    a. IPX

    b. UDP

    c. TCP

    d. SMTP

    e. NetBIOS

12. Which of the following are advantages of polling? (Choose all that apply.)

    a. price

    b. equal access to the medium for all computers on the network

    c. efficient use of network media

    d. allows for priority assignment

13. The _____ channel access method is best suited for time-critical communications.

14. A packet trailer contains which of the following information?

    a. source and destination address information

    b. error-checking information

    c. clocking information

    d. alert signal

15. Which of the following protocols provides client/server functionality in a Novell NetWare environment?

    a. NCP

    b. SPX

    c. IPX

    d. ODI

16. When using TCP/IP, computers on the same network segment must have the same _____. (Choose all that apply.)

    a. network number

    b. host ID

    c. subnet mask

    d. computer name

17. Which of the following channel access methods is used in 100VG-AnyLAN networks?

    a. CSMA/CD

    b. polling

    c. demand priority

    d. CSMA/CA

    e. token passing

18. A connection-oriented protocol provides fast, but unreliable, service. True or false?

19. When two computers using IPX/SPX cannot communicate, what is likely to be the cause?

    a. duplicate computer names

    b. different subnet masks

    c. different network cards

    d. different IPX frame types

20. Which protocol can automatically configure a computer's IP address and subnet mask?

    a. TCP

    b. IP

    c. ARP

    d. DNS

    e. DHCP

21. Which access control mechanism uses a device to check each potential sender to see if it wants to transmit data?

    a. token ring

    b. Ethernet

    c. polling

    d. demand priority

    e. switching

22. Which access control mechanism circulates one or more special transmission tickets to control media access?

    a. token ring

    b. Ethernet

    c. polling

    d. demand priority

    e. switching

23. Which access control mechanism uses Collision Sense Multiple Access/Collision Detection hardware to control media access?

    a. token ring

    b. Ethernet

    c. polling

    d. demand priority

    e. switching

24. Which access control mechanism provides the highest bandwidth to the senders and receivers it interconnects?

    a. token ring

    b. Ethernet

    c. polling

    d. demand priority

    e. switching

25. For the Class C network address 192.168.10.0, which of the following subnet masks delivers 30 subnets?

 a. 255.255.255.252

 b. 255.255.255.248

 c. 255.255.255.240

 d. 255.255.255.224

26. For the Class C network 192.168.10.0 subnet mask described in Question 25, how many hosts are available on each resulting subnet?

 a. 2

 b. 6

 c. 14

 d. 30

27. For the Class C network 192.168.220.0, what subnet mask supports up to 14 subnets?

 a. 255.255.255.252

 b. 255.255.255.248

 c. 255.255.255.240

 d. 255.255.255.224

28. For the Class C network mask for 192.168.220.0 described in Question 27, how many hosts are available per subnet?

 a. 2

 b. 6

 c. 14

 d. 30

29. If you create a supernetted subnet mask for seven contiguous Class C IP addresses, how many bits worth of additional address space for host addresses do you create?

 a. 2

 b. 3

 c. 4

 d. 5

30. Which IP addressing scheme permits workstations to use private IP addresses to access the Internet?

 a. supernetting

 b. NAT

 c. DHCP

 d. subnetting

6

HANDS-ON PROJECTS

Adding, configuring, and removing protocols in a Windows environment is handled by a variety of means. For these projects, you view the properties for TCP/IP and add (and remove) the DLC protocol to a Windows 98, Windows 2000, or Windows XP machine. Remember, Windows systems sometimes use the DLC protocol to print to certain HP printers directly connected to the network. You learn about several command-line utilities, including PING and NETSTAT, that help you examine your local TCP/IP networking environment. Finally, you discover an easy method to calculate IP subnets using a subnet calculator downloaded from the Internet.

Project 6-1

To view a Windows 98 TCP/IP configuration:

1. Right-click the **Network Neighborhood** icon on the desktop, and select the **Properties** option.

2. Double-click a component that starts with **TCP/IP ->** on the **Configuration** tab to open the Properties window. Click **OK** if a warning dialog box appears.

3. Select the **IP Address** tab. It contains address and subnet mask information for the computer. There are two options for assigning an address to a computer in Windows 98. If the network uses a DHCP server, select **Obtain an IP address automatically**. Otherwise, select the **Specify an IP address** option, which allows you to set the IP address and subnet mask for the computer. (In the classroom, this information is already configured.)

   The WINS Configuration tab is used to configure a WINS server for name resolution. Clicking the option button enables WINS resolution. You can then specify primary and secondary WINS server addresses, an option to use DHCP for Windows resolution, and the Scope ID, used for NetBIOS over TCP/IP communications.

   The Gateway tab allows you to specify the IP Gateway to forward packets out of the local network segment. (You must supply a value for this field if you want to access any resources outside your local cable segment, such as the Internet.)

   The DNS Configuration tab covers the computer's name (Host Name) and TCP/IP domain. The DNS Service search order contains the address(es) of DNS servers on the network, and the Domain Suffix Search Order box contains the domain suffixes appended to host names during resolution.

   The NetBIOS tab enables use of NetBIOS over TCP/IP (often abbreviated as NetBT or NBT). Checked by default for Windows 98, you need not alter it.

   The Advanced tab allows you to invoke advanced Windows98 TCP/IP capabilities (currently limited to Allow Binding to ATM). This is seldom necessary.

   The Bindings tab establishes a relationship between the Client for Microsoft Networks (which uses NetBIOS) and TCP/IP in Windows 98. Here again, this is the default, so changing this selection is necessary only if your Windows 98 machine runs on a non-Microsoft network (the Sun Microsystems PC-NFS, for example).

4. Click the **Cancel** button twice to ensure that the existing TCP/IP configuration remains unchanged.

For Windows XP Professional machines:

1. Right-click the **My Network Places** icon on the desktop, and select the **Properties** option. If my Network Places is not on the desktop, go to **Start**, **Control Panel**, and double-click the **Network Connections** icon.

2. Double-click the **Local Area Connection** icon in the Network Connections window.

3. In the Local Area Connection Status dialog box, click the **Properties** button.

4. In the Local Area Connection Properties dialog box, select the **Internet Protocol (TCP/IP)** entry in the This connection uses the following items: list box, and then click the **Properties** button.

5. A pair of option buttons controls the top section. They allow you to obtain an IP address from a DHCP server or elect to use a static IP address. If the second option button is selected, you can assign an IP address, a subnet mask, and gateway information to the computer. Another pair of option buttons controls the lower section. They allow you to obtain a DNS server address automatically or elect to define one or more static DNS server addresses. If you select the second option button, you can define IP addresses for a preferred and an alternate DNS server.

6. If you click the Advanced button in this window, an Advanced TCP/IP Settings dialog box opens. It contains four tabs: one for IP settings, one each for DNS and WINS settings, and a fourth (Options) for managing IP security settings.

   The DNS tab contains DNS server information, such as the address(es) of DNS servers on the network and the domain suffixes appended to host names during resolution.

   Use the WINS Address tab to configure a WINS server for name resolution. This tab includes a dialog box to add WINS server addresses in order of use, options to enable LMHOSTS Lookup, and an option to enable or disable NetBIOS over TCP/IP (this option should be disabled only in a network that includes either Windows 2000 or Windows XP machines.)

   The Options tab permits you to set IP security settings and IP address filtering settings.

7. Click the **Cancel** or **Close** button four times to ensure that you do not change the existing configuration, and then close the Network Connections window.

For Windows 2000 machines:

1. Right-click the **My Network Places** icon on the desktop, and select the **Properties** option.

2. Double-click the **Local Area Connection** icon in the Network and Dial-up Connections window.

6

3. In the Local Area Connection Status dialog box, click the **Properties** button.

4. In the Local Area Connection Properties dialog box, select the **Internet Protocol (TCP/IP)** entry in the **Components checked are used by this connection** list box, and then click the **Properties** button.

5. A pair of option buttons control the top section. They allow you to obtain an IP address from a DHCP server, or elect to use a static IP address. If the second option button is selected, you can assign an IP address, a subnet mask, and gateway information to the computer. Another pair of option buttons controls the lower section. They allow you to obtain a DNS server address automatically, or elect to define one or more static DNS Server addresses. If you select the second option button, you can define IP addresses for a preferred and an alternate DNS server.

6. If you click the Advanced button in this window, an Advanced TCP/IP Settings dialog box opens. It contains four tabs: one for IP settings, one each for DNS and WINS settings, and a fourth (Options) for managing IP security settings. The DNS, WINS, and Options settings tabs are similar to those for Windows XP. (See Step 6 in the Windows XP Professional steps that precede these instructions.)

7. Click the **Cancel** or **Close** button four times to ensure that you do not change the existing configuration, and then close the Network and Dial-up Connections window.

Project 6-2

To add the DLC protocol to a computer's configuration:

For Windows 98:

1. Right-click the **Network Neighborhood**, icon on the desktop, and select the **Properties** option.

2. Click the **Add** button beneath the first pane on the **Configuration** tab in the **Network** window.

3. Select the **Protocol** option, then click the **Add** button.

4. Select the **Microsoft** option in the left pane, select the **Microsoft DLC** option, and click the **Have Disk** button.

5. When prompted to supply the path to the installation files for Windows 98, enter the directory name indicated by your instructor. Windows 98 then installs the necessary files to support the DLC protocol.

6. From the main Network screen, click the **Close** button. You are prompted to restart the computer. For the new configuration to take effect, click the **Yes** button. (Your instructor may tell you to click the No button instead, since you remove this protocol in the next project anyway.)

For Windows XP Professional:

The DLC protocol is no longer supported in Windows XP.

For Windows 2000:

1. Right-click the **My Network Places** icon on the desktop, and select the **Properties** option.

2. Double-click the **Local Area Connection** icon in the Network and Dial-up Connections window. Click the **Properties** button in the Local Area Connection Status dialog box.

3. In the Local Area Connection Properties window, click **Install**.

4. In the Select Network Component Type window, select **Protocol** and then click **Add**.

5. When the Select Network Protocol window appears (this may take a while), select the **DLC Protocol** entry in the Select Network Protocol pane, and then click **Have Disk**.

6. When prompted to supply the path to the installation files for Windows 2000, enter **C:\I386** (or the directory indicated by your instructor). Windows 2000 then installs the necessary files to support the DLC protocol.

7. Click **Close** repeatedly until you close all network configuration windows.

Project 6-3

To remove the DLC protocol from the computer's configuration:

For Windows 98:

1. Right-click **Network Neighborhood**, and select the **Properties** option.

2. Select **Microsoft DLC** in the installed components list.

3. Click **Remove**.

4. When asked to confirm your action, click **Yes**.

5. Click **Close**.

6. After Windows 98 finishes the configuration, it asks if you want to restart the computer. Click **Yes**.

For Windows XP Professional:

The DLC protocol is no longer supported in Windows XP.

For Windows 2000:

1. Right-click the **My Network Places** icon, and select the **Properties** option.

2. Double-click the **Local Area Connection** icon in the Network and Dial-up Connections window. Click the **Properties** button in the Local Area Connection Status dialog box.

3. Select the **DLC Protocol** entry in the Components checked are used by this **connection** list box.

4. Click the **Uninstall** button.

5. When asked to confirm your action, click **Yes**.

6. Click **Close**.

Project 6-4

For all Windows systems (98, XP, and 2000), we assume that you know how to open a DOS box on your desktop to use the command prompt. Start this project by doing so. (If you can't remember, check the Hands-on Projects for Chapter 1 in this book.)

To use the PING utility to check your computer's IP configuration:

1. Enter **ping loopback** on the command line. This shows you output for the special IP address 127.0.0.1, as shown in Figure 6-16. If it executes properly, ping loopback confirms that your IP stack is properly configured.

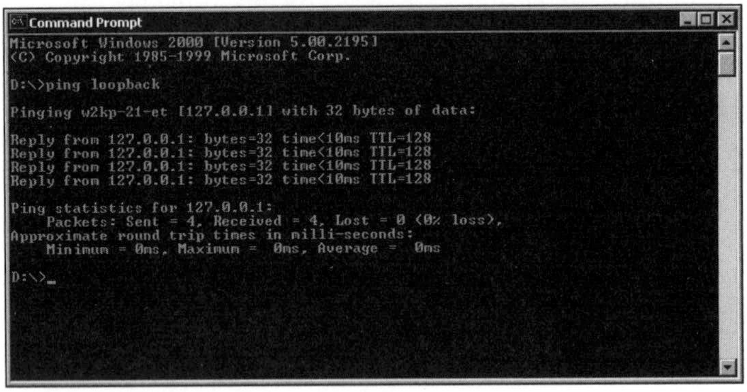

```
Command Prompt                                          _ □ X
Microsoft Windows 2000 [Version 5.00.2195]
(C) Copyright 1985-1999 Microsoft Corp.

D:\>ping loopback

Pinging w2kp-21-et [127.0.0.1] with 32 bytes of data:

Reply from 127.0.0.1: bytes=32 time<10ms TTL=128
Reply from 127.0.0.1: bytes=32 time<10ms TTL=128
Reply from 127.0.0.1: bytes=32 time<10ms TTL=128
Reply from 127.0.0.1: bytes=32 time<10ms TTL=128

Ping statistics for 127.0.0.1:
    Packets: Sent = 4, Received = 4, Lost = 0 (0% loss),
Approximate round trip times in milli-seconds:
    Minimum = 0ms, Maximum = 0ms, Average = 0ms

D:\>_
```

Figure 6-16   Ping loopback results

2. Type **ipconfig** on the command line (Windows XP or Windows 2000) or **winipcfg** (Windows 98). Write down the IP address for your local machine. Enter **ping xx.xx.xx.xx** on the command line, where xx.xx.xx.xx is your local machine's IP address. The output should be similar to Figure 6-17, except that it displays your computer's current IP address.

Figure 6-17   Ping results for the local IP address

3. Repeat Hands-on Project 6-4 to obtain your computer's default IP gateway address (or get the IP gateway address from your instructor), and write it down. Then enter **ping yy.yy.yy.yy** where yy.yy.yy.yy is the actual gateway address you wrote down. The output should resemble that shown in Figure 6-18. If it executes properly, ping yy.yy.yy.yy confirms that you can access your default IP gateway (and thus, send packets outside your local cable segment).

Figure 6-18   Ping results for the gateway IP address

4. Type **exit** on the command line, and press **Enter**. (If you plan to proceed directly to the next Hands-on Project, omit this step.)

Project 6-5

Unless you're continuing from the preceding project, begin by opening a DOS box to access a command prompt. (If you can't remember how, see the Hands-on Projects for Chapter 1 in this book.)

To use the netstat utility to observe your computer's IP communications statistics:

1. Enter **netstat /?** on the command line. This displays the online help file for this command. Read the file so you understand the commands that you enter in the next three steps of this project.

2. Enter **netstat -a** on the command line. This should display output similar to that shown in Figure 6-19, customized for your local circumstances.

Figure 6-19 Netstat -a results

3. Enter **netstat -e** on the command line. This should display output similar to Figure 6-20, customized for your local circumstances. If you're not using Ethernet in your computer lab, your instructor will tell you to skip this step.

Figure 6-20 Netstat -e results

4. Enter **netstat -s** on the command line. This should display output similar to that shown in Figure 6-21, customized for your local circumstances.

```
Command Prompt                                           _ □ ×

D:\>netstat -s

IP Statistics

    Packets Received                      = 152505
    Received Header Errors                = 0
    Received Address Errors               = 65
    Datagrams Forwarded                   = 0
    Unknown Protocols Received            = 0
    Received Packets Discarded            = 0
    Received Packets Delivered            = 152440
    Output Requests                       = 122540
    Routing Discards                      = 0
    Discarded Output Packets              = 0
    Output Packet No Route                = 0
    Reassembly Required                   = 0
    Reassembly Successful                 = 0
    Reassembly Failures                   = 0
    Datagrams Successfully Fragmented     = 0
    Datagrams Failing Fragmentation       = 0
    Fragments Created                     = 0

ICMP Statistics

                                 Received      Sent
    Messages                     41            63
    Errors                       0             0
    Destination Unreachable      1             23
    Time Exceeded                0             0
    Parameter Problems           0             0
    Source Quenches              0             0
    Redirects                    0             0
    Echos                        20            20
    Echo Replies                 20            20
    Timestamps                   0             0
    Timestamp Replies            0             0
    Address Masks                0             0
    Address Mask Replies         0             0

TCP Statistics

    Active Opens                          = 4937
    Passive Opens                         = 318
    Failed Connection Attempts            = 1
```

Figure 6-21   Netstat -s results

5. Type **exit** on the command line, and then press **Enter** to close the command window.

Project 6-6

This chapter teaches you to calculate IP subnets by hand, should you ever need to do so. But if you have access to the Internet, we recommend that you instead take advantage of the subnet calculator software tool.

To access a subnet calculator on the Internet:

1. Open your Web browser and enter **www.wildpackets.com/products/ ipsubnetcalculator** in the Address text box.

2. Click the **Free Download** link and follow the instructions to download and install the IP Subnet Calculator software. (Your instructor may provide alternate instructions, especially if the software has already been downloaded and is available from a local server or on your local machine.)

3. From the Start menu, select **Programs**, **WildPackets IP Subnet Calculator**. (In Windows XP, choose **All Programs** from the Start menu rather than Programs.) WildPacket's IP Subnet Calculator provides numerous handy tools to calculate subnet masks and the resulting number of hosts and subnets.

6

4. Click the **Subnet Info** tab in the IP Subnet Calculator window. Investigate how selecting a value for the Max # of Subnets field controls the Max # of Hosts/Subnet field, and vice versa.

5. Type the IP address **192.168.10.0** in the IP Address text box, and then click the Subnets/Hosts tab to see how it displays usable host addresses within individual subnets.

6. Explore the **CIDR** tab to see how varying the number of mask bits changes the Supernet Mask, Max # of Supernets, and Max # of Addresses fields.

7. Click the **Close** button in the upper-right corner of the IP Subnet Calculator to exit the application.

CASE PROJECTS

1. As the network administrator for a growing firm, you want to design your network to run efficiently now and in the future. You plan to implement a server-based Windows 2000 network. Although you currently support only 20 users on one floor of one building, management is rumored to be planning an acquisition that would effectively double your company's network size. Highlight your current and future requirements, and choose the protocol(s) and channel access method best suited to this situation. Then, explain why you chose those protocols and access methods.

2. A local bank just hired you to completely redesign its network. Money is no object, but its database transactions are time-critical, and PCs throughout the bank must be able to access the databases, which are on UNIX systems. Choose the best protocol(s) and channel access method for this situation.

3. A special-effects company works on high-resolution computer graphics and animation projects for the film industry. It decides to upgrade its networks so that its artists and editors can work together, not only to move extremely large graphics files across the network, but also to permit workers to view video clips streamed from a multicast server on their desktops. What kind of channel access method works best for this situation? Explain why high bandwidth is important under these circumstances.

4. Mercy Hospital decides to install a network to service its various wards and operating rooms, partly to permit professional staff to manage shared schedules for the emergency room (ER) and operating rooms in real time. Although each operating room (OR) and ER theater has its own computer, the machines total fewer than 10. (There are more than 100 computers on the wards.) Nevertheless, the ORs and ER theaters need preferential access to the server that manages schedules. What kind of channel access method works best for this situation? Explain how a different network topology for Ethernet could also produce the same effect.

7

NETWORK ARCHITECTURES

After reading this chapter and completing the exercises, you will be able to:

♦ Understand the different major network architectures, including Ethernet, token ring, AppleTalk, ARCnet, FDDI, and ATM

♦ Understand the standards governing network architectures

♦ Understand the limitations, advantages, and disadvantages of each standard or architecture

Anetwork's architecture generally refers to its overall structure, including topology, physical media, and channel access method. This chapter explains network architectures, as well as the specifics of different network architecture standards, including Ethernet, token ring, AppleTalk, ARCnet, FDDI, and ATM. To properly assess network technology implementation requirements, you must understand these topics.

ETHERNET

During the late 1960s and early 1970s, many organizations worked on methods to connect several computers and share their data. One of these projects was the ALOHA network at the University of Hawaii. From this research, Robert Metcalf and David Boggs, researchers at Xerox's **Palo Alto Research Center (PARC)**, developed an early version of Ethernet in 1972. Then in 1975, PARC released the first commercial version, which allowed users to transmit data at approximately 3 Mbps (megabits per second) to up to 100 computers with a maximum of 1 km of total cable.

Xerox teamed with Intel Corporation and Digital Equipment Corporation, in an industry group known as **DIX (Digital, Intel, Xerox)**, to develop a standard based on Xerox Ethernet, and raised the transfer rate to 10 Mbps. In 1990, the IEEE used this version of Ethernet as the basis for its 802.3 specification, which defines how Ethernet networks operate at the Physical and Data Link layers of the OSI model.

Overview of Ethernet

Ethernet is the most popular network architecture. Its many advantages include ease of installation and low cost. Ethernet is generally easier to install and use and less expensive than other network architectures. Another reason for Ethernet's popularity is its support for many different kinds of networking media. Each of these architectures (such as AppleTalk, ARCnet, and FDDI) shares similar methods for packaging data into frames and uses baseband signaling; most use the CSMA/CD channel access method. Nearly all versions of Ethernet transmit at 10 Mbps or 100 Mbps, but newer standards support transmission at 1 Gbps (or 1000 Mbps).

All Ethernet standards use the hardware address of the NIC to address packets. This hardware address is "burned in" to the read-only memory (ROM) on the NIC when it is created and is universally unique. When a packet is sent, the hardware (MAC) addresses of both the source and the destination computers are added to the packet header.

Ethernet is divided into three categories based on transmission, speed, and media. The sections that follow cover these categories.

10 Mbps IEEE Standards

There are four major implementations of 10 Mbps Ethernet:

- **10Base5:** Ethernet using thicknet coaxial cable
- **10Base2:** Ethernet using thinnet coaxial cable
- **10BaseT:** Ethernet over unshielded twisted-pair (UTP) cable
- **10BaseF:** Ethernet over fiber-optic cable

Although it may seem cryptic, IEEE's naming scheme is straightforward. The first section represents the speed of transmission in Mbps (10, 100, or 1000 for Ethernet). The middle section describes the signal transmission type (baseband or broadband). Originally, the last section represented the distance the network could cover in hundreds of meters; for example, a 10Base5 network transmits data at 10 Mbps using baseband transmission over a maximum distance of 500 meters. However, as new technologies developed, the last section was changed to describe the media type, such as fiber-optic (F) or twisted-pair (T) cable.

10Base5

As discussed in Chapter 3, 10Base5 uses transceivers attached to thicknet by a vampire tap. When vampire taps are installed, a special jig fixture is used to drill through the covering and mesh. The "tap" makes contact only with the center conductor. The vampire tap has small teeth that keep the tap/transceiver from moving after it is installed. A drop cable connects the transceiver to the NIC's AUI or DIX port (standard Ethernet connectors). Each computer connected to the thicknet cable must have a transceiver and drop cable.

The distance limitations for 10Base5 Ethernet are more stringent than for other implementations of Ethernet. Transceivers must be at least 2.5 meters (about 8 feet) apart. Each cable segment can be a maximum of 500 meters (1640 feet) long. Up to five cable segments can be attached using repeaters, creating a network with a total length of 2500 meters; the drop cable connecting the computer to the transceiver must be less than 50 meters (164 feet). However, the length of the drop cables is not figured into the total network length. Figure 7-1 shows a typical 10Base5 network.

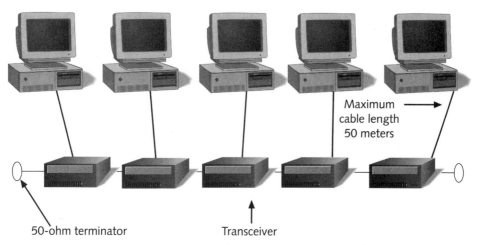

Figure 7-1   10Base5 network using transceivers connected to thicknet cable

All coaxial Ethernet networks (10Base5 and 10Base2) are subject to the **5-4-3 rule**, which states that a coaxial Ethernet network can consist of a maximum of five segments with four repeaters with devices attached to three of the segments, as shown in Figure 7-2. This prevents signal loss due to attenuation.

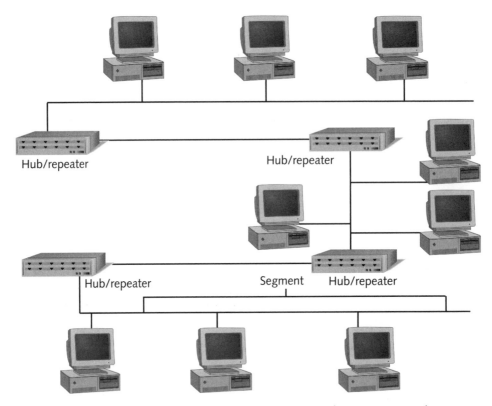

Figure 7-2   Ethernet 5-4-3: 5 segments, 4 repeaters, and 3 segments with devices attached

Note that the 5-4-3 rule is an "end to end" rule, not a "total population" rule. The difference has to do with how many segments and repeaters exist between any two machines, rather than stipulating the total number of elements that an entire network may involve. This rule applies only to individual pairs of segments where a node on one segment seeks to transmit data to a node on another segment. Thus, the 5-4-3 rule does not mean that a 10Base5 or 10Base2 network may have only five segments, four repeaters, and so forth in total; this rule applies only when tracing a route from a node on one segment to a node on any other segment. Plenty of networks with hundreds of segments and numerous repeaters do not violate the 5-4-3 rule because they are designed not to, as shown in Figure 7-3.

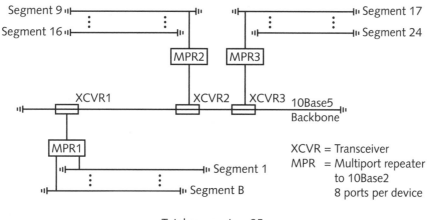

Total segments = 25

Figure 7-3   No pathway violates the 5-4-3 rule

As mentioned earlier, 10Base5 networks represent the original Ethernet architecture. However, 10Base5's limitations and the difficulties of working with thicknet cable have essentially eliminated it as an option for new installations in most networking environments. Table 7-1 lists the specifics for 10Base5 Ethernet.

Table 7-1   10Base5 Ethernet summary

Category	Specification
IEEE specification	802.3
Advantages	Long maximum cable length
Disadvantages	Difficult to install; cost
Topology	Linear bus
Cable type	50-ohm thicknet
Channel access method	CSMA/CD
Transceiver location	Connected to cable at vampire tap
Maximum cable segment length	500 meters (1640 feet)
Maximum total network length	2500 meters (8200 feet)
Maximum drop cable length	50 meters (164 feet)
Minimum distance between transceivers	2.5 meters (8 feet)
Maximum number of segments	5 connected by 4 repeaters
Maximum number of populated segments	3
Maximum devices per segment	100
Maximum devices per network	1024
Transmission speed	10 Mbps

10Base2

10Base2 was the second version of Ethernet introduced. Strictly following the IEEE naming convention, you would think that 10Base2 could support a single 200-meter cable segment. The original IEEE specification for 10Base2 *did* permit a 200-meter cable segment, but that distance was shortened to 185 meters to improve performance and to account for patch cables. Like 10Base5, 10Base2 uses coaxial cable, but rather than thicknet, it uses thinnet, which is flexible and much easier to manipulate. Also, unlike 10Base5, the transceiver is part of the NIC, so the cable attaches directly to the device. As mentioned in Chapter 3, 10Base2 uses a BNC connector to connect the NIC to the cable, and uses the bus topology with terminators at each end of the cable segment. The minimum cable length for 10Base2 is .5 meters (about 20 inches).

It is important to note that although thinnet cable looks remarkably like the coaxial cable used for television, they are not interchangeable. The IEEE specification states that thinnet must use RG-58A/U or RG-58C/U. As noted in Chapter 3, thinnet uses 50-ohm coaxial cable, while the cable used for cable TV is 75-ohm cable. In addition, other RG-58 cable types (RG-58U, for example) cannot support Ethernet 10Base2.

Like its 10Base5 predecessor, 10Base2 follows the 5-4-3 rule. The 10Base2 limitations on cable length from end to end on a network, allow for five 185-meter segments connected by four repeaters, with three segments populated. This creates a maximum total network length of 925 meters from any one end to any other end of the network. In each of those five cable segments, a BNC **barrel connector** can be used to connect two shorter thinnet cables. Its use should be limited, however, because each barrel connector degrades the signal as it travels across the network. 10Base2 supports up to 30 devices per cable segment.

Because of its ease of installation and lower price, thinnet rapidly replaced thicknet as the preferred network medium. As new Ethernet standards developed, thinnet, too, was eventually replaced, but has not disappeared entirely. It is still being used in networks that were installed in the late 1980s and early 1990s, and you can still readily purchase NICs and cabling that support thinnet. However, its use is strongly discouraged for new installations. Table 7-2 summarizes the 10Base2 Ethernet standard.

Table 7-2 10Base2 Ethernet summary

Category	Specification
IEEE specification	802.3
Advantages	Inexpensive; easy to install and configure
Disadvantages	Difficult to troubleshoot
Topology	Linear bus
Cable type	50-ohm thinnet—RG-58A/U or RG-58C/U
Channel access method	CSMA/CD
Transceiver location	On NIC
Maximum cable segment length	185 meters (607 feet)
Maximum total network length, end to end	925 meters (3035 feet)
Minimum distance between devices	.5 meters (20 inches)
Maximum number of segments	5 connected by 4 repeaters
Maximum number of populated segments	3
Maximum devices per segment	30
Maximum devices per network	1024
Transmission speed	10 Mbps

7

The authors learned from experienced network engineers at 3Com that, although the IEEE 802.3 specification stipulates a maximum of 1024 devices on a thinnet network, a more practical maximum occurs at around 900 devices. This is seldom a problem nowadays, even at sites that have many more than 900 devices (such as college campuses or large office buildings), because it's so routine to use routers to divide large networks into smaller subnetworks. In fact, only subnetworks are subject to the kinds of maximum values that appear in the tables (Tables 7-1, 7-2, and so forth) in this chapter.

10BaseT

10BaseT Ethernet usually uses unshielded twisted-pair (UTP) cable but also can transmit with shielded twisted-pair (STP) cable. The exceptionally low cost of both the media and the equipment make 10BaseT the most popular Ethernet architecture currently used. Figure 7-4 shows a 10BaseT Ethernet network wired in a star topology, but 10BaseT Ethernet networks use a bus signaling system internally.

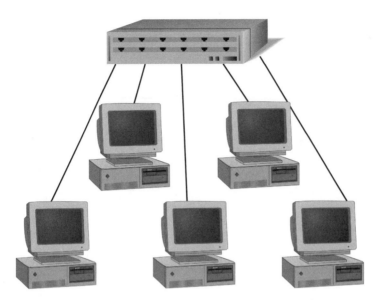

Figure 7-4   10BaseT network uses a star wiring topology

In this configuration, active hubs act as repeaters to amplify signal strength. Because a 10BaseT network uses a star topology in which each computer is attached to a repeater, the 5-4-3 rule is somewhat modified for 10BaseT networks. The rule for expanding a 10BaseT network simply states that no more than five cabling segments and no more than four hubs may lie between two communicating workstations. The IEEE 802.3 specification allows for a total of 1024 computers on a 10BaseT network connected with multiple hubs. Each computer is an end-node on a cable segment, which eases troubleshooting because any cable failure affects only one computer.

10BaseT Ethernet works on Category 3, 4, or 5 UTP. The 10BaseT standard lists a minimum of Category 3. However, most newer installations use Category 5 UTP to support 100 Mbps Ethernet discussed later in the section, "100 Mbps IEEE Standards."

The biggest limitation of 10BaseT is distance. The maximum cable segment length is only 100 meters for any twisted-pair cable segment. Therefore, it's typical to see 10BaseT hubs connected to each other by 10Base2, or even 10Base5, as shown in Figure 7-5.

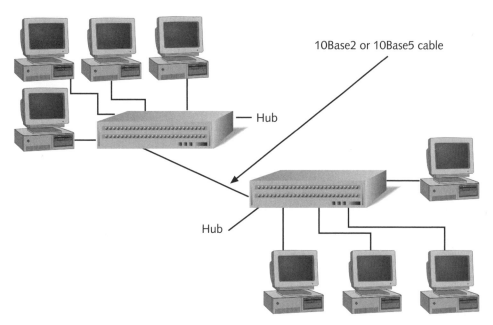

Figure 7-5   10BaseT implementations use media with greater distance allowances to connect 10BaseT hubs

Table 7-3 outlines the 10BaseT Ethernet specifications.

Table 7-3   10BaseT Ethernet summary

Category	Summary
IEEE specification	802.3
Advantages	Very inexpensive; easy to install and troubleshoot
Disadvantages	Small maximum cable segment length
Topology	Star
Cable type	Category 3, 4, or 5 UTP
Channel access method	CSMA/CD
Transceiver location	On NIC
Maximum cable segment length	100 meters (328 feet)
Minimum distance between devices	N/A
Maximum number of segments	1024
Maximum devices per segment	2
Maximum devices per network	1024
Transmission speed	10 Mbps

10BaseF

The IEEE specification for running Ethernet over fiber-optic cable is 10BaseF and is generally divided into three subcategories:

- 10BaseFL is used to link computers in a LAN environment (fiber to the desktop).
- 10BaseFP is used to link computers using passive hubs rather than repeaters. This category has a maximum cable segment length of 500 meters.
- 10BaseFB uses fiber-optic cable as a backbone between hubs.

Each of the 10BaseF implementations uses a star topology. Like 10BaseT, the specification lists 1024 as the maximum number of nodes on a single network connected by repeaters. Because of its high cost, 10BaseF generally is reserved for connections between hubs or for situations in which security requires cabling not easily affected by electromagnetic interference (EMI). Although fiber-optic cable can support much higher speeds, as discussed later in the section, "FDDI," its high cost and difficult installation prevent its wide use.

Table 7-4 summarizes 10BaseF Ethernet.

Table 7-4   10BaseF Ethernet summary

Category	Summary
IEEE specification	802.3
Advantages	Long distance
Disadvantages	High cost; difficult installation
Topology	Star
Cable type	Fiber-optic
Channel access method	CSMA/CD
Transceiver location	On NIC
Maximum cable segment length	2000 meters (6561 feet), except for 10BaseFP at 500 meters (1635 feet)
Maximum number of segments	1023
Maximum devices per segment	2
Maximum devices per network	1024
Transmission speed	10 Mbps

100 Mbps IEEE Standards

The most widely accepted Ethernet standards today are the 100 Mbps Ethernet standards—100VG-AnyLAN (the topology for this was discussed in Chapter 6) and 100BaseT, which is also called **fast Ethernet**. Higher speeds make these technologies well suited for applications such as video, CAD (computer-aided design), CAM (computer-aided manufacturing), and imaging.

100VG-AnyLAN

The Ethernet Standard 100VG-AnyLAN—also called 100BaseVG, 100VG, VG, or AnyLAN—was developed by Hewlett-Packard and AT&T. It combines elements of Ethernet and token ring architectures and uses a demand priority channel access method in which intelligent hubs control network communication. When a computer has data to transmit, it sends a demand packet to the hub, which then tells the computer when the channel is free for it to send its data. These hubs can cascade, as shown in Figure 7-6, much like 10BaseT, creating a star topology network. A **root hub** or **parent hub** connects to multiple hubs, each of which can connect to other hubs.

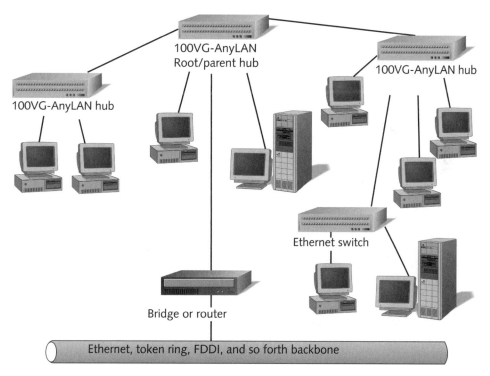

Figure 7-6   In 100VG-AnyLAN networks, hubs can be connected to form a star topology

100VG-AnyLAN is designed to run over any data-grade UTP cable and can be used with Category 3 or higher. In older facilities, it is an attractive option because existing cabling can be reused. However, one caveat is that 100VG requires all four pairs or wires in a typical UTP cable, two to transmit and two to receive, whereas 10BaseT uses only two pairs. In some existing 10BaseT installations, two pairs of wires may be used for data, whereas the other two pairs on the same cable may be used for voice. In this case, the cabling must be upgraded before 100VG-AnyLAN can work. (And further, it may make even more sense to use a different, less-expensive 100 Mbps Ethernet technology.)

The biggest limitation of 100VG-AnyLAN is its cost. The requirements for special NICs and hubs for demand priority channel access and for all four pairs of wires in UTP make costs significantly higher than those of other 100 Mbps Ethernet implementations. Due to these detractors, 100VG-AnyLAN is a networking technology that came and went without making a significant impact on the networking world.

Table 7-5 summarizes the 100VG-AnyLAN standard.

Table 7-5   100VG-AnyLAN summary

Category	Summary
IEEE specification	802.12
Advantages	Fast, easy to configure and troubleshoot; supports token ring and Ethernet packets
Disadvantages	High cost; limited distance over UTP
Topology	Star
Cable type	Category 3 or higher UTP and STP, fiber-optic
Channel access method	Demand priority
Transceiver location	On NIC
Maximum cable segment length	100 meters (328 feet) Category 3 UTP; 150 meters (492 feet) Category 5 UTP; 2000 meters (6561 feet) fiber-optic
Maximum number of segments	1023
Maximum devices per segment	1
Maximum devices per network	1024
Transmission speed	100 Mbps

100BaseT

100BaseT, also called fast Ethernet or 100BaseFX, is an extension of the 10BaseT standard. Grand Junction Networks, 3Com, Intel, and others modified the 802.3 Ethernet standard to support 100 Mbps transmission over Category 5 UTP. The current IEEE standard for 100BaseT is 802.3u.

The 100BaseT standard has three subcategories that define cable types:

- **100BaseT4:** four-pair Category 3, 4, or 5 UTP

- **100BaseTX:** two-pair Category 5 UTP

- **100BaseFX:** two-strand fiber-optic cable

When considering implementing fast Ethernet, it is important to remember the cabling requirements for each category. 100BaseTX *requires* Category 5 UTP but uses only two pairs of wires, whereas 100BaseT4 can operate over Category 3 or higher but uses all four pairs. Because 10BaseT operates over Category 3 or higher UTP, it may be necessary to upgrade the cabling in an existing building to support 100 Mbps Ethernet. Although three cable types are available for 100BaseT, 100BaseTX is the most widely accepted and, therefore, is the standard generally referred to as fast Ethernet.

An important consideration when designing a 100BaseT network is the total number of hubs allowed between end stations. There are two types of 100BaseT hubs: class I and class II. Class I hubs may have only one hub between communicating devices, whereas class II hubs may have a maximum of two hubs between devices. Typical 100BaseT networks use switches to interconnect multiple hubs. Figure 7-7 illustrates this concept.

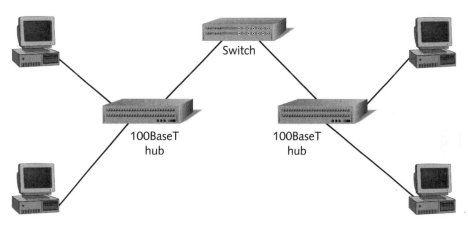

Figure 7-7   Using a switch to interconnect 100BaseT hubs

Table 7-6 summarizes the 100BaseT Ethernet standard.

Table 7-6   100BaseT Ethernet summary

Category	Summary
IEEE specification	802.3u
Advantages	Fast; easy to configure and troubleshoot
Disadvantages	High cost; limited distance
Topology	Star
Cable type	Category 3 or higher UTP—100BaseT4; Category 5 UTP—100BaseTX; Fiber-optic—100BaseFX
Channel access method	CSMA/CD
Transceiver location	On NIC
Maximum cable segment length	100 meters (328 feet)—100BaseT4, 100BaseTX 2000 meters (6561 feet)—100BaseFX
Maximum number of segments	1023
Maximum devices per segment	1
Maximum devices per network	1024
Transmission speed	100 Mbps

GIGABIT ETHERNET: 1 GBPS IEEE 802.3Z STANDARDS

Collectively, the IEEE identifies various **Gigabit Ethernet** standards under the general heading 1000BaseX. Because signaling methods at 1 Gbps are so fast, they are also quite different from methods used for slower Ethernet technologies. In fact, the specifications for Gigabit Ethernet are based on the ANSI X3.230-1994 standard for Fiber Channel (a high-speed, fiber-optic-based networking technology developed specifically for Storage Area Networks, or SANs, as mentioned in Chapter 1). In fact, 1000BaseX uses the 8B/10B coding scheme (where 8 bits of actual data are packaged with 2 bits of error-correction data) just as Fiber Channel does, with nearly identical optical and electrical characteristics. Building 1000BaseX around Fiber Channel's physical layer specifications made it faster and easier to bring Gigabit Ethernet to market.

 1000BaseT represents a different Gigabit Ethernet standard from 1000BaseX. 1000BaseT does not adhere to the Fiber Channel physical layer specifications, nor does it belong to the 1000BaseX standards. It is the subject of a distinct 1000BaseT standard instead.

Two separate extensions to the 802.3 specification cover 1000BaseX and 1000BaseT:

- 802.3z-1998 covers 1000BaseX specifications, including the L (long wavelength laser/fiber-optic), S (short wavelength laser/fiber-optic), and C (copper jumper cables) discussed in the following sections.

- 802.3ab-1999 covers 1000BaseT specifications, which require four pairs of 100-ohm Category 5 cable or better.

The following sections describe 1000BaseX and 1000BaseT standards.

Doing the Duplex Thing   Most Gigabit Ethernet implementations—including network interfaces, switches, and other equipment—work in full-duplex mode. Remember that two interconnections between a sender and a receiver are required when fiber-optic media are in use because each cable links an emitter (sender) on one end to a sensor (receiver) on the other end. Two connections make it possible for both parties to send and receive. Because this capability is inherent in the medium, it makes sense to use full-duplex communications with such equipment so that both parties can send (and receive) data at the same time. This doubles the theoretical maximum throughput in many cases, which is why you see numbers that are double the rated throughput for full-duplex communications rates in some tables in this chapter.

1000BaseLX   1000BaseLX uses fiber-optic media; the "L" stands for "long wavelength," the kind of laser used to send signals across the medium. These long wavelength lasers operate at wavelengths between 1270 to 1355 nanometers and work with single mode and multimode optical fibers. Long wavelength lasers cost more than short wavelength lasers, but can also drive their signals over longer lengths of cable.

Table 7-7 summarizes 1000BaseLX Ethernet.

Table 7-7   1000BaseLX Ethernet summary

Category	Summary
IEEE specification	802.3z
Advantages	Fast; supports full-duplex communications
Disadvantages	High cost; hard to deploy and install
Topology	Star
Cable type	Two strands of fiber-optic cable per connection; Multimode (MMF): 62.5/125 or 50/125 cable; Single mode (SMF): 10 micron cable
Channel access method	Switched
Transceiver location	On NIC
Maximum cable segment length	Half-duplex MMF, SMF: 316 meters (1036 ft); Full-duplex MMF: 550 meters (1804 ft); Full-duplex SMF: 5000 meters (16,404 ft)
Maximum number of segments	1023
Maximum devices per segment	2
Maximum devices per network	1024
Transmission speed	1000 Mbps (uses 8B/10B encoding); 2000 Mbps in full-duplex mode

7

Although the 1000BaseLX standard specifies a maximum cable segment length of 5000 meters, it is important to realize that some manufacturers have extended that distance using specialized and proprietary optical transceivers. Cisco Systems, for example, provides a product called 1000BaseLH (where LH stands for long-haul) that provides a maximum cable segment length of 10,000 meters over single-mode fiber. For extremely long-distance Gigabit communications, a product called 1000BaseZX is capable of distances up to 100,000 meters over single-mode fiber. These long-range Gigabit products clearly have important implications for high-speed metropolitan area networks and Internet Service Provider (ISP) connections to the Internet backbone.

1000BaseSX   1000BaseSX uses fiber-optic media; the "S" stands for "short wavelength," the kind of laser used to send signals across the medium. These short wavelength lasers operate at wavelengths between 770 to 860 nanometers and work only with multimode optical fibers. Short wavelength lasers cannot cover as much distance as long wavelength lasers, but they are cheaper (and also use cheaper MMF cable).

Table 7-8 summarizes the 1000BaseSX standard.

Table 7-8   1000BaseSX Ethernet summary

Category	Summary
IEEE specification	802.3z
Advantages	Fast; supports full-duplex communications
Disadvantages	High cost; hard to deploy and install
Topology	Star
Cable type	Two strands of fiber-optic cable per connection; Multimode (MMF): 62.5/125 or 50/125 cable
Channel access method	Switched
Transceiver location	On NIC
Maximum cable segment length	Half-duplex 62.5 MMF: 275 meters (902 ft); Half-duplex 50 MMF: 316 meters (1036 ft); Full-duplex 62.5 MMF: 275 meters (902 ft); Full-duplex MMF: 550 meters (1804 ft)
Maximum number of segments	1023
Maximum devices per segment	2
Maximum devices per network	1024
Transmission speed	1000 Mbps (uses 8B/10B encoding); 2000 Mbps in full-duplex mode

1000BaseCX   1000BaseCX uses specially shielded, balanced, copper jumper cables; the "C" stands for "copper," the kind of electrical signaling in use. Jumper cables are normally used for interconnections between devices or to interlink VLANs on a switch; such jumper cables may also be called twinax or short-haul copper cables. Segment lengths for 1000BaseCX cables top out at 25 meters, which means they're used primarily in wiring closets or equipment racks.

Table 7-9 summarizes 1000BaseCX Ethernet.

Table 7-9   1000BaseCX Ethernet summary

Category	Summary
IEEE specification	802.3z
Advantages	Fast; supports full-duplex communications
Disadvantages	High cost; short-haul only
Topology	Star
Cable type	Two strands of copper cable (twinax); sold in pre-fabricated lengths only
Channel access method	Switched
Transceiver location	On NIC or switch
Maximum cable segment length	Half-duplex: 25 meters (82 ft); Full-duplex: 25 meters (82 ft)
Maximum number of segments	1023 (normally, far fewer are used)
Maximum devices per segment	2
Maximum devices per network	1024
Transmission speed	1000 Mbps (uses 8B/10B encoding); 2000 Mbps in full-duplex mode

1000BaseT   1000BaseT was formally released as IEEE Standard 802.3ab in June 1999. It supports Gigabit Ethernet over 100-meter segments of balanced Category 5 copper cabling and requires four pairs of wires. The 1-Gbps aggregate data rate results from sending data at 250 Mbps over each of the four pairs of wires in the Category 5 cable. 1000BaseT also employs special equipment, called hybrids and cancellers (to combine multiple signals and to cancel interference) to support full-duplex transmission. 1000BaseT supports two signaling methods already used in other IEEE standards for 100 Mbps Ethernet; these methods were chosen to make it possible to build the same kind of hybrid circuitry for 100/1000 Ethernet devices that proved so popular for 10/100 devices.

Unlike 10BaseT and 100BaseT Ethernet, 1000BaseT Ethernet does not dedicate a wire pair to transmitting or receiving. Each wire pair is capable of both transmitting and receiving data simultaneously, thereby providing the 1000 Mbps data rate in both half-duplex and full-duplex modes. Similarly to 100BaseT, 1000BaseT permits only one hub or repeater between end stations when using half-duplex communications. The majority of installations will use switches that automatically detect the speed of the connected device, be it 10 Mbps, 100 Mbps, or 1000 Mbps. Thus, the one-repeater limitation is unlikely to be a problem for most organizations.

1000BaseT Ethernet is gaining wide acceptance in corporate data centers to connect servers to the corporate backbone and as the primary connection type for storage area networks (SANs). Because 1000BaseT works over standard Category 5 cable, the upgrade path for companies that currently run 100BaseT should be relatively simple. NICs and hubs or switches must be replaced, but the cabling infrastructure will not require replacement. Although Category 5 cable is the minimum requirement, 1000BaseT will work over Category 5E and the proposed Category 6 cable.

Table 7-10 summarizes 1000BaseT Ethernet.

Table 7-10   1000BaseT Ethernet summary

Category	Summary
IEEE specification	802.3ab
Advantages	Fast; supports full-duplex communications
Disadvantages	High cost; short-haul cable segments only
Topology	Star
Cable type	Four-pair, balanced Category 5 cable; 100-ohm impedance
Channel access method	CSMA/CD or switched
Transceiver location	On NIC
Maximum cable segment length	Half-duplex: 100 meters (328 ft); Full-duplex: 100 meters (328 ft)
Maximum number of segments	1023
Maximum devices per segment	2
Maximum devices per network	1024
Transmission speed	1000 Mbps 2000 Mbps in full-duplex mode

10 Gigabit Ethernet: 10 Gbps IEEE 802.3ae Standard

As of this writing, the 10 Gbps Ethernet standard (IEEE 802.3ae) was still under development, with an anticipated ratification in mid to late 2002. This version of Ethernet is essentially like all the other, slower versions of Ethernet with respect to the frame formats and media access method, but it's faster. However, it does have some important technical differences. It is defined to run only on fiber-optic cabling, both single-mode and multi-mode, but the 10-Gbps Ethernet standard specifies a maximum distance of 40km, compared to just 5km for Gigabit Ethernet over fiber-optic. This distance has important implications for wide area and metropolitan area networks. Another design difference is that 10-Gbps Ethernet is defined to run in full-duplex mode only, so the CSMA/CD technology required in other Ethernet standards is not necessary.

Initially, the primary use of 10 Gigabit Ethernet will likely be as the network backbone, interconnecting servers and network segments that are running 100-Mbps and 1000-Mbps Ethernet technologies. However, it will also have its place in Storage Area Networks (SANs) and eventually as the interface for enterprise-level servers. Whatever the applications, it is safe to say that Ethernet will be with us for a long time due to its extraordinary ability to scale from 10-Mbps to 10-Gbps speeds.

 For the latest news on 10 Gigabit Ethernet, see *www.10gea.org*.

Ethernet Frame Types

One major distinction between Ethernet and other network architectures is that Ethernet can structure data a number of different ways before placing it on the network medium. As discussed in Chapter 6, a computer places data on the network in packets, or frames, which define that data's structure. Ethernet supports four **frame types**, each of which is unique and does not work with the others. For communications to take place between any two Ethernet devices, their frame type settings must match.

- Ethernet 802.3 is generally used by IPX/SPX on Novell NetWare 2.x and 3.x networks.

- Ethernet 802.2 is the default frame type used by IPX/SPX on Novell NetWare 3.12 and 4.x networks. This is also the native frame type supported by default when Microsoft NWLink is installed.

- Ethernet SNAP is used in EtherTalk and mainframe environments.

- Ethernet II is used by TCP/IP.

All Ethernet frame types support a packet size between 64 and 1518 bytes and can be used by all network architectures mentioned previously. In most cases, a network requires only one frame type, but occasionally particular devices, such as file or database servers, must support multiple frame types (for instance, when some clients use one frame type, but other clients use another).

When running a protocol, such as IPX/SPX, that can use more than one frame type, there must be a method to select the desired frame type. In Windows, this is accomplished through the network control panel by selecting the properties for the IPX/SPX protocol. Windows defaults to auto-detection of the frame type; this may cause undesirable results as non-server versions of Windows will support only the first frame type detected. If there are resources on the network using different frame types, some resources will not be available to those workstations that auto-detect a different frame type. Therefore, it is very important to ensure that either only a single frame type is used or that all workstations have been set to a common frame type that allows access to all necessary resources.

Always remember that mismatched frame types stymie network communication.

Ethernet 802.3

Sometimes called **Ethernet raw**, the **Ethernet 802.3** frame type was developed before completion of the IEEE 802.3 specification. Therefore, the 802.3 frame does not completely comply with the 802.3 specification—despite its name! Generally, Ethernet 802.3 frames occur only on networks that use Novell's NetWare 2.x or 3.x.

Figure 7-8 is a diagram of an Ethernet 802.3 frame. It begins with a preamble and a **start frame delimiter (SFD)** statement, which indicates the beginning of the frame. The destination and source addresses of the packet follow. Because Ethernet supports variable length packets (64 to 1518 bytes), the next field specifies the length of the data portion of the packet. Then, a 4-byte Cyclical Redundancy Check (CRC) follows the data itself. As described in Chapter 6, the CRC verifies that the data reached its destination undamaged.

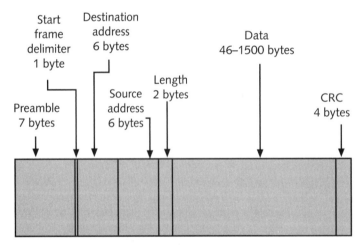

Figure 7-8 Ethernet 802.3 frame

Ethernet 802.2

Ethernet 802.2 frames completely comply with the Ethernet 802.3 standard. The IEEE 802.2 group was totally unconcerned with Ethernet, but only with the Logical Link Control (LLC) sublayer of the Data Link layer of the OSI model. However, because Novell had already decided to use the term *Ethernet 802.3* to describe Ethernet raw, it is generally accepted that Ethernet 802.2 means a fully 802.3-and 802.2-compliant Ethernet frame. Ethernet 802.2 frames contain similar fields to 802.3, with three additional LLC fields.

Ethernet SNAP

Ethernet SNAP (SubNetwork Address Protocol) is generally used on the AppleTalk Phase 2 networks discussed later in the section, "AppleTalk Environment." It contains enhancements to the 802.2 frame, including a **protocol type field**, which indicates the network protocol used in the data portion of the frame.

Ethernet II

Ethernet II frames are used in TCP/IP networks. As Figure 7-9 shows, Ethernet II frames differ only slightly from 802.3 frames. Rather than using a separate SFD field, the preamble includes that data. The Type field replaces the length field and is used much the same way it is used in Ethernet SNAP—to identify which network protocol is in the data section of the frame.

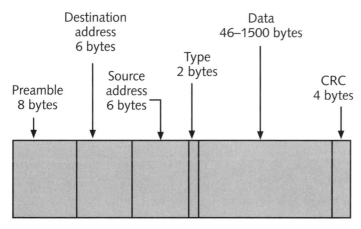

Figure 7-9   Ethernet II frame uses a Type field

Segmentation

Greater numbers of computers and increased traffic bog down most network implementations. One way to ease this problem is by **segmenting** the network into manageable pieces. By inserting a switch or router between network segments, you direct traffic more efficiently to its destination and reduce traffic on each segment. Also, because fewer computers vie for time on a single segment, the chances of a computer sending its data in a timely manner are greater, as illustrated in Figure 7-10.

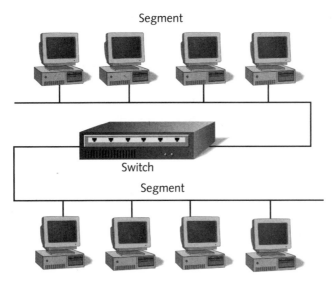

Figure 7-10 Adding a switch reduces network traffic

 Segmenting networks with routers requires a fairly high degree of understanding of network protocol addressing and routing and must be done by experienced administrators. Incorrect addressing can isolate an entire segment of your network. Refer to Chapter 6 for proper addressing techniques.

Wireless Ethernet: IEEE 802.11b

Although the details of 802.11b networking are beyond the scope of this book, it is valuable to understand how wireless networking differs from traditional wired networks because your understanding will facilitate the installation and support of wireless technologies. 802.11b uses a wireless access point (WAP) that serves as the center of a star topology network. Workstations equipped with wireless NICs send packets to the WAP, which then sends the packets to the destination workstation.

We discussed the use of CSMA/CD as the access method used in wired forms of Ethernet, but wireless networks have a special problem regarding this access method. CSMA/CD requires that all stations can hear each other so that each station knows when another station is sending data. This is reasonable, but if two stations try to send at the exact same time, a collision can occur. Fortunately, in a wired network, the sending stations hear the collision and attempt to resend the data. However, 802.11b stations cannot send and receive at the same time, so if a collision does occur, it would not be detected by the sending stations. For this reason, 802.11b specifies a CSMA/CA access method in which an acknowledgement is required for every packet sent. With this requirement, if a collision occurs, the sending stations know the packet did not arrive safely because there is no acknowledgement.

Consider another problem that exists in wireless networks but does not exist in wired networks. It is quite possible that in a three-station network, all workstations can communicate with the WAP—workstation A can hear workstation B and workstation B can hear workstation C, but workstation A cannot hear workstation C, perhaps because they are out of range. This is called the hidden node problem. In this situation, CSMA/CA will not work because workstation A will never know if workstation C is sending and vice versa. To counteract this, 802.11b specifies an optional feature that uses handshaking before transmission. In this implementation, a station must send the WAP a Request to Send (RTS) packet requesting transmission. If it is okay to transmit, the WAP sends a clear to send (CTS) message and the workstation commences with its communication.

The 802.11b standard specifies a transmission rate of 11 Mbps, but this is not an absolute value. Environmental conditions may prevent transmission at that speed. Therefore, transmission speeds may be dropped incrementally from 11 Mbps to 5.5 Mbps to 2 Mbps, and finally to 1 Mbps, to make a reliable connection. Note also that there is no fixed segment length for wireless communication because reliable communication relies heavily on the environment, for example, the number of walls between stations and the WAP.

Note further that, in general, an 802.11b network has a maximum distance of 300 feet with no obstructions. However, this distance can be extended using large, high-quality antennas. Keep in mind that the data rate may suffer as the distance increases and as more obstructions are present. For an excellent tutorial on wireless networking and 802.11b, visit *www.networkcomputing.com/1115/1115ws22.html*.

TOKEN RING

Developed by IBM in the mid-1980s, the **token ring** network architecture provides users with fast, reliable transport. Its design uses a simple wiring structure with twisted-pair cable that connects the computer to the network through an outlet in the wall; the majority of the wiring is in a central location.

Based on the IEEE 802.5 standard, token ring networks are cabled in a physical star topology but function as a logical ring, as shown in Figure 7-11. The token-passing channel access method, rather than the physical layout of the network, gives token ring its name.

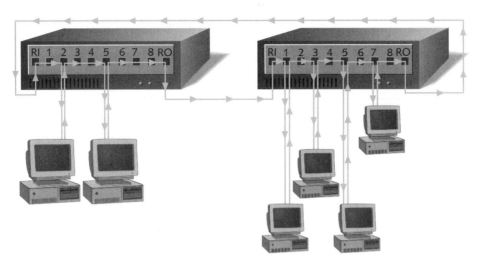

Figure 7-11   Token ring networks have a physical star topology but function as a logical ring

Token Ring Function

By using the token-passing channel access method, token ring networks ensure that all computers get equal time on the network. As discussed in Chapter 6, a small frame, called the token, passes around the ring. A computer receives the token from its **Nearest Active Upstream Neighbor (NAUN)**. If the token is not in use at the time—no nearby computer is sending data—and the computer has data to send, it attaches its data to the token and sends it to its **Nearest Active Downstream Neighbor (NADN)**. Each computer thereafter receives the token, determines that it is in use, and verifies that the data's destination is not itself. If not, the computer re-creates both the token and the data exactly as it received them and sends them to its NADN.

When the data reaches its destination, the receiving computer sends the data to the upper-layer protocols for processing. Then the receiving computer toggles two bits in the data packet to indicate it received the data and sends the token and data along the network to its NADN. Eventually, both token and data reach the original sender; the sender sees that the data was received successfully, frees the token, and then passes it along.

Although this process seems laborious, it is fairly efficient. Unlike Ethernet, there are no collisions, so data seldom has to be re-sent. Because all computers on the network have equal access to the token, traffic is consistent, and token ring gracefully handles increases in network size and bandwidth utilization.

The original version of token ring operated at 4 Mbps, but newer versions increased that speed to 16 Mbps.

If a 4 Mbps NIC is used in any workstation in an otherwise 16-Mbps token ring network, the entire network will operate at 4 Mbps.

Another advantage of token ring over Ethernet is the size of the data in the packet. Because collisions never occur in token ring, it can send much larger data packets—between 4000 and 17,800 bytes.

Like Ethernet, token ring addresses are burned into the NIC when it is created.

Beaconing

One unique aspect of the token ring network architecture is its capability to automatically isolate faults by using a process called **beaconing**. The first computer powered on in a token ring network is assigned the responsibility of ensuring that data can travel along the ring. This computer, the **active monitor**, manages the beaconing process. All other computers on the network are **standby monitors**.

Every seven seconds, the active monitor sends a special packet to its nearest downstream neighbor announcing the address of the active monitor and the fact that it is the upstream neighbor. The station examines the packet and passes it along to its NADN, changing the upstream address. The third station, then, has a packet that lists the active monitor's address and the address of its upstream neighbor. The third station repeats the process, sending to its downstream neighbor a packet containing the active monitor's address and its own address. When the active monitor receives the packet, it knows that the packet has successfully navigated the ring and the ring is intact. In addition, all stations know the address of their upstream neighbor.

As shown in Figure 7-12, if a station does not hear from its upstream neighbor in seven seconds, it sends a packet down the ring that contains its address, the address of its NAUN (from which it received no packet), and a beacon type. As the other computers in the network receive this packet, they check their configurations. If the NAUN does not answer, the ring can reconfigure itself to avoid the problem area. Beaconing allows some level of automatic fault tolerance in the token ring network, something many other network architectures lack.

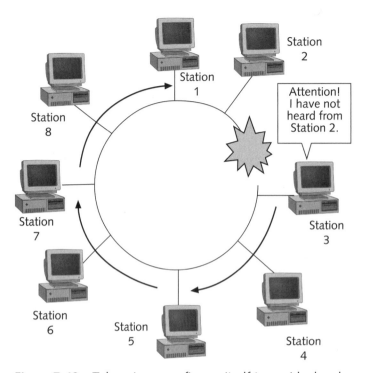

Figure 7-12   Token ring reconfigures itself to avoid a break

Hardware Components

In a token ring network, a hub can be referred to as a **Multistation Access Unit (MAU or MSAU)**, or **Smart Multistation Access Unit (SMAU)**. IBM's implementation of token ring is the most popular adaptation of the IEEE 802.5 standard. Although some minor differences, such as the maximum number of computers on an STP ring, exist between IBM's specifications and the IEEE's specifications, the specifications are virtually synonymous. When discussing hardware components of the token ring architecture, IBM equipment is most often used.

A typical IBM token ring hub, such as the 8228 MSAU, has 10 connections, eight of which can be used for connecting computers. As previously shown in Figure 7-11, the other two ports are used to connect the hubs in a ring. The Ring Out (RO) port on one hub connects to the Ring In (RI) port on the next hub, and so on to form a ring among the hubs. New hubs must also be added to the ring in this manner. IBM's implementation of token ring allows 33 hubs to be connected in this fashion. With the original token ring hubs, this provides a total of 260 stations per network. However, newer hubs that allow 16 computers per hub double this number.

Cabling in a Token Ring Environment

In 1984, IBM defined a comprehensive cabling system that specified cable types, connectors, and all other components required for computer networking. This cabling system breaks cables into different types based on the American Wire Gauge (AWG) standards that specify wire diameters. When token ring was introduced, it followed these standards for cabling and equipment.

 AWG numbers are inversely related to the diameter of the cable—larger AWG numbers indicate smaller diameters. For example, standard telephone wire has a thickness of 22 AWG, whereas thicknet cable is 12 AWG.

Table 7-11 shows the cable types included in the IBM system and used by the token ring.

Table 7-11   IBM/Token ring cabling

Cable Type	Description
Type 1	STP with two pairs of 22-AWG solid copper wire surrounded by a braided shield and casing. This cable is used to connect computers to MAUs and can be run through conduit or inside walls.
Type 2	STP with two pairs of 22-AWG solid copper wire for data and four pairs of 26-AWG wire for voice. This cable is used to connect both data and voice without running two cables.
Type 3	UTP voice-grade cable with 22 AWG or 24 AWG, each pair twisted twice every 3.6 meters (12 feet). It is a cheaper alternative to Type 1, but limited to 4 Mbps.
Type 5	Fiber-optic cable, 62.5- or 100-micron diameter; it is used for linking MAUs over distance.
Type 6	STP cable with two twisted pairs of 26-AWG stranded wire surrounded by braided shield and casing. Similar to Type 1, except that the stranded wire allows greater flexibility but less distance (two-thirds that of Type 1). This cable is generally used as a patch cable or for extensions in wiring closets.
Type 8	STP cable for use under carpets. It is similar to Type 6, except it is flat.
Type 9	Plenum-rated Type 6 cable.

Table 7-12 summarizes the token ring network architecture.

Table 7-12   Token ring summary

Category	Summary
IEEE specification	802.5
Advantages	Fast and reliable
Disadvantages	More expensive than Ethernet; difficult to troubleshoot
Topology	Ring; cabled as star
Cable type	IBM cable types (STP and UTP)
Channel access method	Token passing
Maximum cable segment length	45 meters (150 feet)—UTP; 101 meters (330feet)—STP
Maximum number of segments	33 hubs
Maximum devices per segment	Depends on hub
Maximum devices per network	72 with UTP, 260 with STP
Transmission speed	4 Mbps or 16 Mbps

APPLETALK AND ARCNET

This section discusses two other prevalent network architectures: AppleTalk and ARCnet. Apple Computer, Inc. designed the AppleTalk architecture for use in its Macintosh networks, whereas PC-based networks use ARCnet. Given the speed and affordability of Ethernet, ARCnet is seldom used anymore; the same is true for Apple's LocalTalk physical implementation of AppleTalk (because AppleTalk also runs over Ethernet, token ring, and other network architectures, it is not as deeply affected as ARCnet).

AppleTalk Environment

First introduced in 1983, AppleTalk is a simple, easy-to-implement network architecture designed for use with Apple Macintosh computers. Because all Macintoshes have a built-in network interface, implementing AppleTalk is as easy as attaching all the computers with cable. Therefore, AppleTalk networks were popular in early Macintosh environments.

At its introduction, "AppleTalk" referred to the networking protocols and the hardware used to connect computers. In 1989, Apple changed AppleTalk's definition to refer to the overall architecture of the network and added the term **LocalTalk** to refer to the cabling system.

Unlike Ethernet and token ring, which use the address of the NIC, AppleTalk applies a dynamic scheme to determine the address of a device. When the computer is powered on, it chooses a numeric address—generally, the last address it used. It then broadcasts this address to the network to determine if the address is available. If the address is not taken, it starts transmitting from that address. If, however, another device on the network is using the address, the computer randomly chooses another address and broadcasts that address to the network. This process continues until the computer finds an unused address.

The original version of AppleTalk, now referred to as AppleTalk Phase 1, supported only 32 computers per network, and even those could use only LocalTalk cabling. Including hubs and repeaters increased the number of computers to 254. When Apple introduced AppleTalk Phase 2 in 1989, it introduced **EtherTalk** and **TokenTalk**, which allow AppleTalk protocols to operate over Ethernet and token ring networks, respectively. This increased the number of computers that an AppleTalk network can include to more than 16 million. In practice, standards governing AppleTalk networks, the token ring, or Ethernet limit the number of computers to well below 16 million. It is important to remember, however, that for a Macintosh running AppleTalk Phase 2 over a LocalTalk network, the maximum number of computers is still 254.

To put it most simply, the underlying network architecture sets the maximum number of computers on an AppleTalk Phase 2 network—254 for LocalTalk, 1024 for EtherTalk, 72 for TokenTalk over UTP, and 260 for TokenTalk over STP. Most newer Macintoshes (those manufactured in 1996 or later) support Ethernet interfaces, in addition to LocalTalk. For obvious reasons, the Ethernet option is currently exercised far more often than LocalTalk.

LocalTalk

Apple Computer, Inc. designed the **LocalTalk** network architecture, which uses STP in a bus topology, to allow users to share peripherals and data in a small home or office environment. The LocalTalk connector consists of three connectors: one to the computer and two like the one in Figure 7-13 that join the devices.

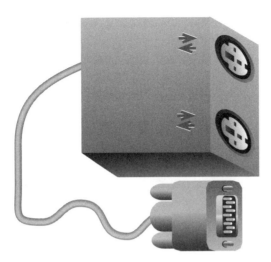

Figure 7-13   LocalTalk connector

Because of the connector's configuration, a LocalTalk network more often resembles a tree rather than a bus. See Figure 7-14.

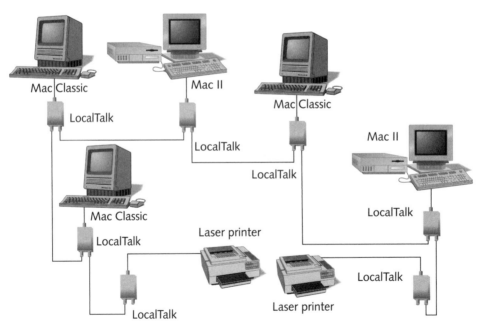

Figure 7-14   LocalTalk bus networks sometimes resemble trees

LocalTalk uses the CSMA/CA channel access method discussed in Chapter 6. Recall that before a computer begins transmitting data on the network, it listens to determine if anyone else is transmitting. If the lines are clear, the computer sends a packet informing the other computers that it will send data on the network, letting the other computers know the media will be in use. The original computer then sends its data to its destination. This method of channel access avoids more collisions. This process is, however, cumbersome. Imagine if every time you sent a letter, you first had to mail a postcard announcing you were sending a letter.

The maximum transmission speed of a LocalTalk network is only 230.4 Kbps. When compared to other network architectures' speeds (10, 100, or 1000 Mbps for Ethernet and 4 or 16 Mbps for token ring), it is easy to see why this architecture is primarily used in small, Macintosh-only environments.

EtherTalk and TokenTalk

In an effort to overcome the speed limitation of LocalTalk, Apple created EtherTalk and TokenTalk. EtherTalk is the AppleTalk protocol running over a 10 Mbps IEEE 802.3 Ethernet network. TokenTalk is principally the same thing—the AppleTalk protocol running over a 4 or 16 Mbps IEEE 802.5 token ring network.

Both implementations require that a different NIC be used on the computer. Such NICs include all drivers and protocols required to run EtherTalk or TokenTalk. Both of these protocols support AppleTalk Phase 2 and its extended addressing. In addition, with extra software, each protocol can be used to connect Macintosh computers to a PC Ethernet or token ring environment. Since 1996, Apple Computer has offered systems with built-in Ethernet interfaces or with options to add Ethernet or token ring to its systems at a low cost.

Table 7-13 summarizes the LocalTalk standard.

Table 7-13   LocalTalk summary

Category	Summary
IEEE specification	None
Advantages	Very simple; easy to configure
Disadvantages	Slow
Topology	Bus
Cable type	STP
Channel access method	CSMA/CA
Maximum cable segment length	300 meters (1000 feet)
Maximum overall network length	2400 meters (7200 feet)
Maximum number of segments	8
Maximum number of devices per segment	32
Maximum number of devices per network	254
Transmission speed	230.4 Kbps

ARCnet Environment

Introduced by Datapoint Corporation in 1977, the **Attached Resource Computer Network (ARCnet)** provides transmission speeds up to 2.5 Mbps using the token-passing channel access method. Like token ring, ARCnet operates in a virtual ring but, as Figure 7-15 shows, is physically wired in a bus or star topology, or a combination of both. ARCnet also can operate over a combination of media such as UTP, coaxial cable, and fiber-optic cable.

While ARCnet can run on coaxial cable, it is not the same type of cable used in thinnet applications. ARCnet uses RG-62 coaxial cable and thinnet uses RG-58 cable.

Data transmission in an ARCnet network is similar to data transmission in an Ethernet network. Data is broadcast to the entire network; each computer listens for data directed to its address and processes that data, ignoring other data on the network. Although ARCnet uses the token-passing channel access method, the hubs in an ARCnet environment are wired similarly to Ethernet star networks, not as logical rings similarly to a token ring network.

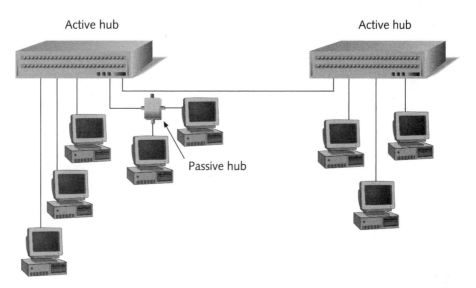

Figure 7-15 ARCnet network

The token-passing method used by ARCnet differs from that used by token ring. As mentioned earlier, the token passes through a token ring environment from one station to the station closest to it, usually the next populated port on the hub. In an ARCnet environment, the token passes between computers based on their **station identifiers (SIDs)**. ARCnet NIC addresses are not burned in during their manufacture, as are Ethernet and token ring addresses. Rather, they have a bank of DIP switches used to set the SID for each computer. When the adapter is installed in a computer, its SID is set to a number from 1 to 255. In essence, the token passes between the computers in the order of their SIDs; the computer with SID 1 sends data and passes the token to the computer with SID 2, which sends it to SID 3, and so forth. Regardless of how many computers are in the network, the "last" computer must have SID 255. When that computer receives the token, it sends it back to SID 1. Figure 7-16 illustrates this process.

In the ARCnet environment, SID refers to the station identifier for a device on the network. However, on a Microsoft Windows network, SID refers to the security identifier assigned to a user or group, or other secured object stored in a domain database or under Active Directory. (See Chapter 8 for a discussion of directory services in general, and of Microsoft Active Directory.)

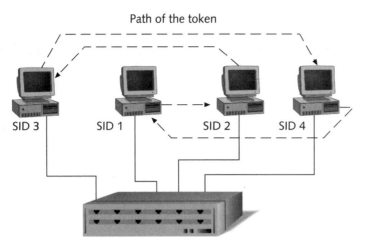

Figure 7-16   Token passing in an ARCnet network is in SID order

Although this token-passing method is easy to understand and works well, it has several drawbacks. Figure 7-16 illustrates the first (and probably most obvious). Because the token passes solely based on the SID, the next computer in the passing order may be on the other side of the network; this dramatically decreases the network's efficiency. However, careful planning of SID numbers can eliminate this problem. Assigning SID numbers based on proximity helps ease network traffic.

The manual configuration of SID numbers is one major drawback to using ARCnet. Whereas with Ethernet and token ring, you can insert a new NIC into a computer and be guaranteed it has a unique address, ARCnet does not offer this guarantee; therefore, duplicate addresses are common. Consequently, administration of an ARCnet network is more tedious.

Because ARCnet uses token passing, it does guarantee equal access to all computers on the network. It is an inexpensive and simple network architecture to implement. Also, it can transmit data over greater distances than other architectures, and it can use various physical media.

The biggest drawbacks to standard ARCnet use today are low speed and inability to connect easily with other network architectures. Standard ARCnet transmits data at 2.5 Mbps. A new version of ARCnet, **ARCnet Plus**, transmits at speeds of up to 20 Mbps, and has been discussed for years; however, it has not made any impact on today's network marketplace.

Table 7-14 summarizes the ARCnet network architecture.

Table 7-14 ARCnet summary

Category	Summary
IEEE specification	No IEEE, ANSI 878.1
Advantages	Inexpensive; easy to install; reliable
Disadvantages	Slow; does not connect well to other architectures
Topology	Bus and star
Cable type	RG-62 A/U coaxial; UTP; fiber-optic
Channel access method	Token passing
Maximum cable segment length	600 meters (2000 feet)—RG-62 A/U; 121 meters (400 feet)—UTP; 3485 meters (11,500 feet)—fiber-optic; 30 meters from passive to active hub
Maximum number of segments	Depends on topology
Maximum number of devices per segment	Depends on topology
Maximum number of devices per network	255
Transmission speed	2.5 Mbps

7

FDDI

The Fiber Distributed Data Interface (FDDI) uses the token-passing channel access method while also using dual counter-rotating rings for redundancy, as shown in Figure 7-17. FDDI transmits at 100 Mbps and can include up to 500 nodes over a distance of 100 km (60 miles). Like token ring, FDDI uses token passing; however, FDDI networks are wired as a physical ring, not as a star. An FDDI network has no hubs; devices generally connect directly to each other. However, devices called **concentrators** can serve as a central connection point for buildings or individual sites in a campus setting.

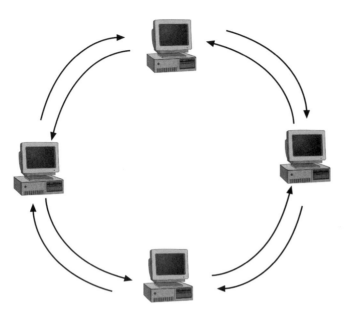

Figure 7-17   FDDI networks operate two counter-rotating rings

An FDDI network handles token passing differently than token ring or ARCnet. As in token ring, an FDDI token passes around the ring. However, unlike token ring, when the computer possessing the token has more than one data frame to send, it can send the next frame before the initial data frame fully circles the ring. This is possible because the sender possesses the token, so no other senders can become active. The computer can avoid data collision by calculating the network latency and waiting an appropriate interval before sending the next packet. This process transmits data more quickly around the network. Also, once a computer finishes sending its data, it can immediately pass along the token; it need not wait for confirmation of the data's receipt; the data doesn't need to completely circuit the ring before the token may be passed on.

Unlike token ring, FDDI supports the capability to assign a priority level to a particular station or type of data. For example, a server can receive higher priority than workstations, while video or time-sensitive data can receive even higher priority.

As mentioned earlier, FDDI uses two physical rings operating in different directions to avoid cable problems. In a token ring network, beaconing and network reconfiguration resolve cable breaks. In an FDDI network, all data transmission occurs along the **primary ring**, while the **secondary ring** circumvents a cable break. When a computer determines it cannot communicate with its downstream neighbor, it sends the data along the secondary ring. When the data reaches the other end of the ring where the cable break is located, the data is transferred to the primary ring where it continues its journey, as shown in Figure 7-18.

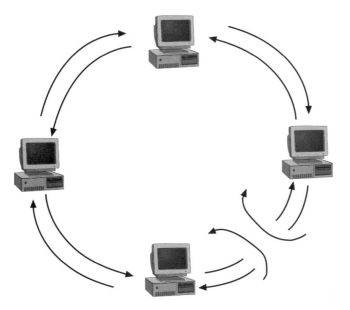

Figure 7-18   Dual rings in FDDI ensure that data reaches its destination

An FDDI uses two types of NICs: **Dual Attachment Stations (DAS)** and **Single Attachment Stations (SAS)**. DAS attached to both rings are intended for use in servers, concentrators, and other devices that require full reliability. SAS connected to only one ring are intended for individual workstations that are attached to concentrators. These stations still benefit from the reliability of the dual rings in FDDI because the concentrators to which they are attached are usually also attached to both rings.

Table 7-15 outlines the FDDI architecture.

Table 7-15   FDDI summary

Category	Summary
IEEE specification	No IEEE; ANSI X3T9.1
Advantages	Very fast; reliable; long distance; highly secure
Disadvantages	Expensive; difficult to install
Topology	Ring
Cable type	Fiber-optic
Channel access method	Token passing
Maximum total network length	100 km (60 miles)
Maximum number of devices per network	500
Transmission speed	100 Mbps

OTHER NETWORKING ALTERNATIVES

Many other network architectures are available. Some are good for specialized applications, and others are emerging as new standards.

Broadband Technologies

The earlier discussion of the IEEE naming convention briefly mentioned broadband as a signal transmission type. Chapter 3 described the two techniques for sending data along a cable: baseband and broadband. Baseband systems use a digital encoding scheme at a single, fixed frequency, where signals take the form of discrete pulses of electricity or light. In a baseband system, the entire bandwidth of the cable transmits a single data signal. This means baseband systems use only one channel on which all devices attached to the cable communicate.

However, broadband systems use analog techniques to encode information across a continuous range of values, rather than using binary zeros and ones that characterize digital data in a baseband environment. Broadband signals move across the medium in the form of continuous electromagnetic or optical waves, rather than in discrete pulses. On broadband systems, signals flow one way only, so two channels are necessary for computers to send and receive data. When trying to conceptualize broadband, think of your cable television connection. A single cable delivers dozens or hundreds of channels. This is possible because each channel uses a different frequency and the television tuner is used to capture only the data traveling on the channel which is currently set. Historically, broadband technology was limited to special applications. However, the Internet's rapid growth pushed broadband to the forefront again. New networking products use broadband transmission for extremely high-speed, reliable connectivity.

Cable Modem Technology

Cable modem networking is a broadband technology used to deliver Internet access to homes and businesses over standard cable television coaxial cable. Because it is a broadband technology, data delivered to a cable modem shares the same cable as the television channels delivered to your TV set. In fact, the Internet data simply travels on a television channel that is not used by the cable company to deliver television video.

The official standard governing cable modem operation is called Data-Over-Cable Service Interface Specifications (DOCSIS). Although considerably more complicated than a dial-up modem, cable modems are true modems in the sense that they modulate and demodulate signals.

Cable modem networks share some properties of traditional 10Base2 Ethernet. Cable modem networks are shared media, bus topology networks at the point where the data is delivered to a home. Other parts of a cable modem network utilize high-speed wide area network technologies such as ATM or SONET (discussed later in this chapter), as depicted in Figure 7-19.

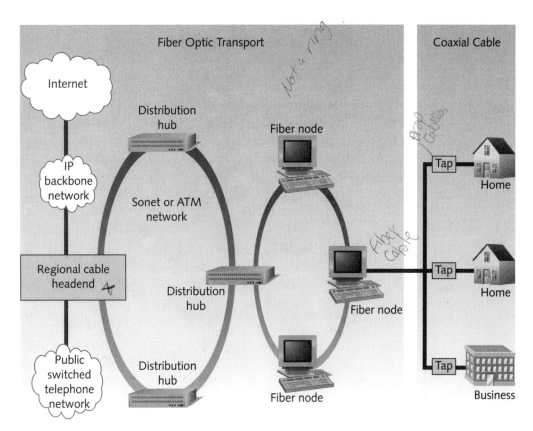

Figure 7-19 Typical cable modem network

The exploding popularity of cable modems is due to the high speeds that Internet data can be delivered to homes and businesses. Internet data can be delivered at up to 27 Mbps, but most providers limit the data rate to between .5 Mbps and 2.5 Mbps. Cable modem uses an asymmetrical communication scheme—the data rates going to the home (referred to as downstream) are different from data rates coming from the home (referred to as upstream) to the cable provider. Upstream data rates may be as much as 10 Mbps but are usually limited to between 256 Kbps and 1 Mbps. Additional information on cable modem and other modem technologies can be found in Chapter 11 when we discuss enterprise and distributed networks.

 For a wealth of information on cable modem technologies, see *www.cablemodem.com* and *www.cabledatacomnews.com*.

Digital Subscriber Line (DSL)

Digital subscriber line (DSL) bears special mention in this section as it competes with cable modem technologies for Internet access. DSL is a broadband technology that uses existing phone lines to carry voice and data simultaneously. There are many flavors of DSL available; the most prominent one for home Internet access is Asymmetric DSL (ADSL). ADSL is so named because the download and upload speeds differ significantly, so the data rates are not symmetrical. ADSL splits the phone line into two frequency ranges: frequencies below 4Khz are used for voice transmission, and frequencies above 4Khz are used to transmit data. Typical connection speeds for downloading data range from a modest 256 Kbps to a snappy 8 Mbps; upload speeds are typically much slower, in the range of 16 Kbps to 640 Kbps. Chapter 11 provides additional information on DSL technology.

Broadcast Technologies

By definition, broadcast technologies are one-way transmissions. However, the advent of the Internet changed this too, most evidently in the case of Internet access by satellite television systems.

These systems work on the principle that most traffic a user generates is to receive files, text, and graphics. The average user's computer sends very little traffic. A user taking advantage of satellite service connects to a service provider through a regular modem. Then, the service provider sends the data by satellite to the user's home at speeds up to 400 Kbps. This can be a much more efficient way to use the available technology. One satellite TV vendor that offers Internet access using its broadcast network is DirectTV, through its family of DirectPC add-on products.

Asynchronous Transfer Mode (ATM)

Unlike the rest of the network architectures covered in this chapter, ATM is a high-speed network technology designed for both LAN and WAN use. ATM uses connection-oriented switches to permit senders and receivers to communicate over a network. A **dedicated circuit**, an ongoing (but possibly transient) link between two end systems must be set up before communications between those systems can begin.

In an ATM environment, data travels in short, 53-byte cells, of which 5 bytes contain header information and 48 bytes contain the data payload. All ATM transmissions consist of such cells, so that a final cell in a data stream is padded with empty payload bytes whenever there are less than 48 bytes of payload to send. ATM's use of fixed-length cells enables it to work at extremely high speeds, because no single transmission is ever larger (or smaller) than the required cell size.

ATM works with network switches, which permit ATM cells to transit such switches quickly and efficiently. Fixed-cell sizes help make traffic flow predictable because transfer time is a strict function of the amount of data to be transferred and the bandwidth available for its transfer. This also enables ATM to guarantee quality of service (QoS) and deliver time-sensitive information, such as multimedia, audio, videoconferencing, and so forth, within a specified delay period. Quality of service features in ATM also permit certain types of network traffic to receive priority; time-sensitive data is always processed and forwarded before other, less time-sensitive traffic.

ATM originated as a telephone company technology and is used quite heavily for the backbone and infrastructure in large communications companies such as AT&T, WorldCom, the Regional Bell Operating Companies, and so forth. Since the mid-1990s, there has been a strong impetus to use ATM for both voice and data traffic, and to make lower-speed ATM implementations available for LAN use as well. To a certain extent, the delivery and broad acceptance of Gigabit Ethernet somewhat blunted this initiative, because Gigabit Ethernet retains the same basic frame structure and packet level characteristics as slower forms of Ethernet. As a result, it integrates more easily with existing LANs (most of which already use Ethernet). ATM's cell structure and its connection-oriented switching requirements mean that some form of LAN emulation (LANE) is required to use ATM for LAN applications. Likewise, the same characteristics mean that using ATM for WAN backbones with conventional LAN technologies requires a special-purpose gateway device (or router interface) to permit ATM to ferry LAN traffic from one location to another.

Because of Gigabit Ethernet's popularity, ATM is best suited for LAN applications in situations where voice, data, and time-sensitive information (video, audio, multimedia, and so forth) travel on the same media. Also, ATM is the overwhelming choice for long-haul, high-bandwidth applications of just about any kind.

ATM and SONET Signaling Rates

ATM bandwidths are rated in terms of an optical carrier level that takes the form OC-x, where x is some number that represents a multiplier of the basic OC-1 carrier rate of 51.840 Mbps. The Exchange Carriers Standards Association (ECSA), working under the auspices of ANSI (American National Standards Institute), originally defined this rate for the Synchronous Optical Network (SONET). Since ECSA is a consortium of communications carriers—primarily long-distance telephone companies—ATM and SONET both have strong roots in the telephone company community. Likewise, both ATM (the underlying signaling technology and transmission medium) and SONET (the overlying communications standards) represent state-of-the-art, all-digital, high-bandwidth communications designed to mix and match data, voice, and all kinds of time-sensitive information through a single, high-capacity networking technology.

The various signaling rates associated with SONET are the same as those associated with ATM. Table 7-16 lists common SONET optical carrier rates, which range from OC-1 (51.840 Mbps) to OC-768 (39.813 Gbps). Typical ATM signaling rates available in today's market range from OC-3 to OC-12, but slower and faster implementations are both available.

Table 7-16   Optical carrier signaling rates from OC-1 to OC-768

Optical Carrier Designation	Signaling Rate
OC-1	51.84 Mbps
OC-3	155.52 Mbps
OC-9	466.56 Mbps
OC-12	622.08 Mbps
OC-24	1.244 Gbps
OC-36	1.866 Gbps
OC-48	2.488 Gbps
OC-96	4.976 Gbps
OC-192	9.953 Gbps
OC-255	13.271 Gbps
OC-768	39.813 Gbps

As of early 2000, the biggest commercially deployed ATM backbone in the world (on the East Coast of the United States) operated many hundreds of miles of fiber at OC-192. By the time you read this, this rate probably will have increased to OC-255 or perhaps even OC-768.

High Performance Parallel Interface (HIPPI)

Developed in the late 1980s, HIPPI is a high-speed communication interface originally developed to serve super-computers and high-end workstations. Serial HIPPI is a fiber-optic version of the original HIPPI, which uses a series of point-to-point optical links to provide network bandwidth up to 800 Mbps. In the early 1990s 800 Mbps was blazingly fast, and HIPPI enjoyed some popularity as a network backbone and for interconnecting super-computers. HIPPI networking products are still available in the form of NICs and switches, but with the advent of Gigabit Ethernet, interest in HIPPI as a LAN backbone decreased significantly. In 1998 HIPPI extension, HIPPI-6400, was developed that provides up to 6.4 Gbps data transfer rates. HIPPI-6400 is now known as Gigabyte System Network (GSN). While these speeds are impressive, HIPPI and GSN are considered exotic networking products and are not frequently found in typical corporate networks. For more about HIPPI and GSN, point your Web browser to *www.hnf.org*.

CHAPTER SUMMARY

◻ A network's architecture defines how data is placed on the network, how that data is transmitted and at what speed, and how problems in the network are handled.

❏ Beginning with its first version in 1972, Ethernet provided a stable method for sending data between computers. Digital, Intel, and Xerox teamed to introduce a viable version for public use that eventually became the basis for the IEEE Ethernet 802.3 standard, which transmits data at 10 Mbps. This standard originally defined the standards for transmission over thicknet cable (10Base5). Later revisions to the standard included thinnet (10Base2), twisted-pair (10BaseT), and fiber-optic (10BaseF) cables. 100 Mbps Ethernet standards have been developed using the existing 802.3 standard. These standards encompass two cable types—twisted-pair and fiber-optic—and two twisted-pair cable configurations.

❏ Gigabit Ethernet is defined by two standards: 802.3Z and 802.3ab. 802.3z defines 1000BaseX, which has standards based on another high-speed technology called Fiber Channel. 1000BaseX includes 1000BaseLX, 1000BaseSX, and 1000BaseCX, which define Gigabit Ethernet on different media types ranging from single-mode fiber-optic cable to twin-ax copper cable. 802.3ab defines 1000BaseT, which is Gigabit Ethernet running on Category 5 twisted-pair cable. An emerging technology, 10 Gigabit Ethernet, is underway and is specified to run only on fiber-optic cabling.

❏ The 100VG-AnyLAN network architecture was developed by AT&T and Hewlett-Packard as an alternate 100 Mbps standard. It uses intelligent hubs and the demand priority channel access method for network communications. It is an attractive alternative for many reasons, mostly because it supports Ethernet and token ring frames. Through the use of a bridge, a 100VG-AnyLAN network can easily connect to other network types, including FDDI, token ring, and ATM. Due to the high costs to implement 100VG-AnyLAN and the dominance of Ethernet, 100VG-AnyLAN is rarely found in today's networks.

❏ Developed by IBM in the early 1980s, token ring networks are reliable, fast, and efficient. Capable of transmitting at either 4 Mbps or 16 Mbps, token ring networks automatically reconfigure themselves to avoid cabling problems. Although wired as a physical star, the token ring architecture operates as a logical ring. One of the biggest benefits of token ring is that all computers have equal access to the network—this enables the network to grow gracefully.

❏ AppleTalk and ARCnet are no longer popular. Macintosh computers use AppleTalk to communicate over a network. AppleTalk Phase 2 includes the capability to use Ethernet and token ring networks for transporting AppleTalk. ARCnet is an extremely reliable token-passing architecture, but not a terribly fast one. Unlike token ring and Ethernet, ARCnet NICs must be addressed manually. Also unlike token ring, ARCnet tokens pass through the network according to the computers' addresses, not their proximity to each other. Therefore, ARCnet is not as efficient as other available architectures.

7

❑ FDDI is an extremely reliable, fast network architecture that utilizes dual counter-rotating rings in a token-passing environment. The dual rings enable FDDI to route traffic around problems in the network. However, it's an expensive network architecture usually reserved for installations where speed and security are paramount.

❑ Cable modem technology is used to deliver high-speed Internet access to homes and businesses over existing cable television cable. Cable modem provides data rates typically ranging from 256 Kbps to 2.5 Mbps.

❑ ATM, a high-speed network technology designed both for LANs and WANs, uses connection-oriented switches to permit senders and receivers to communicate over a network. A dedicated circuit between two end systems must be set up before communications between those systems can begin. ATM is best suited for long-haul, high-bandwidth applications, although Gigabit Ethernet is still more popular because of the ease of incorporating it into existing Ethernet networks.

KEY TERMS

5-4-3 rule — Applies to Ethernet running over coaxial cable. The rule states that a network can have a maximum of five cable segments with four repeaters, with three of those segments being populated. It is an "end-to-end" rule, which means that it governs the number of segments, devices, and so forth between any two nodes on a network. It is not a "total population" rule: you can have more than five cable segments, four repeaters, and three populated segments on an Ethernet network, but no more than those numbers between any two possible senders and receivers on that network.

active monitor — A computer in a token ring network responsible for guaranteeing the network's status.

Attached Resource Computer Network (ARCnet) — An inexpensive and flexible network architecture created by Datapoint Corporation in 1977. It uses the token-passing channel access method.

ARCnet Plus — The successor to ARCnet. It supports transmission up to 20 Mbps.

barrel connector — Used in Ethernet 10Base2 (thinnet) networks to connect two cable segments.

beaconing — The signal transmitted on a token ring network to inform networked computers that token passing has stopped due to an error.

cable modem — A device used to receive data from the Internet by a cable television cable.

concentrator — Used in an FDDI network to connect computers at a central point. Most concentrators connect to both available rings.

dedicated circuit — An ongoing (but possibly transient) link between two end systems.

digital subscriber line (DSL) — A broadband-based technology that delivers Internet data over existing phone lines.

DIX (Digital, Intel, Xerox) — The group that introduced the first Ethernet connector.

Dual Attachment Stations (DAS) — Computers or concentrators connected to both rings in an FDDI network.

Ethernet 802.2 — Ethernet frame type used by IPX/SPX on Novell NetWare 3.12 and 4.x networks.

Ethernet 802.3 — Ethernet frame type generally used by IPX/SPX on Novell NetWare 2.x and 3.x networks.

Ethernet II — Ethernet frame type used by TCP/IP.

Ethernet raw — Ethernet frame type, also called Ethernet 802.3.

Ethernet SNAP (SubNetwork Address Protocol) — Ethernet frame type used in Apple's EtherTalk environment.

EtherTalk — The standard for sending AppleTalk over Ethernet cabling.

fast Ethernet — The 100 Mbps implementation of standard Ethernet.

frame type — One of four standards that defines the structure of an Ethernet packet: Ethernet 802.3, Ethernet 802.2, Ethernet SNAP, or Ethernet II.

Gigabit Ethernet — An IEEE standard (802.3z) that allows for 1000-Mbps transmission using CSMA/CD and Ethernet frames.

LocalTalk — The cabling system used by Macintosh computers. Support for LocalTalk is built into every Macintosh.

Multistation Access Unit (MAU or MSAU) — An active hub in a token ring network.

Nearest Active Downstream Neighbor (NADN) — Used in a token ring environment to describe the computer to which a computer sends the token.

Nearest Active Upstream Neighbor (NAUN) — Used in a token ring environment to describe the computer from which a computer receives the token.

Palo Alto Research Center (PARC) — A Xerox research center where Robert Metcalf and David Boggs developed an early version of Ethernet in 1972.

parent hub — The central controlling hub in a 100VG-AnyLAN network to which child hubs are connected.

primary ring — The FDDI ring around which data is transmitted.

protocol type field — Field used in the Ethernet SNAP and Ethernet II frames to indicate the network protocol being used.

root hub — *See* parent hub.

secondary ring — An FDDI ring used for the sole purpose of handling traffic in the event of a cable failure.

segmenting — The insertion of a bridge or router between two cable segments to direct traffic more efficiently to its destination and reduce traffic on each part of the network.

Single Attachment Stations (SAS) — Computers or concentrators in an FDDI network that are connected only to the primary ring.

Smart Multistation Access Unit (SMAU) — An active hub in a token ring network.

standby monitor — A computer in a token ring network that monitors the network status and waits for the signal from the active monitor.

start frame delimiter (SFD) — A field in the Ethernet 802.3 frame that defines the beginning of the packet.

station identifier (SID) — The hardware address for a computer in an ARCnet network.

token ring — A network architecture developed by IBM, and which is physically wired as a star but uses token passing in a logical ring topology.

TokenTalk — The standard for sending AppleTalk over token ring cabling.

REVIEW QUESTIONS

1. What are the different implementations of 100 Mbps Ethernet? (Choose all that apply.)
   a. 100BaseT4
   b. 100BaseTX
   c. 100BaseFX
   d. 100VG-AnyLAN

2. Which channel access method does ARCnet use?
   a. polling
   b. CSMA/CD
   c. CSMA/CA
   d. token passing

3. How many rings exist in an FDDI network?
   a. one
   b. two
   c. three
   d. four

4. Which Ethernet frame type does TCP/IP use?
   a. Ethernet 802.2
   b. Ethernet II
   c. Ethernet 802.3
   d. Ethernet SNAP

5. The function of the active monitor is _____.

6. How many cable segments can be populated in a coaxial network?

7. How are ARCnet NICs addressed?

   a. jumpers

   b. software

   c. automatically

   d. dynamically

8. What is the maximum transmission speed for a LocalTalk network?

9. What is the function of the CRC in Ethernet?

10. What device serves as the central point of connection in an FDDI network?

   a. hub

   b. router

   c. concentrator

   d. bridge

11. To what devices can passive hubs be connected in an ARCnet environment? (Choose all that apply.)

   a. active hubs

   b. computers

   c. passive hubs

   d. routers

12. Which standards did IBM use to define its cabling system?

   a. IEEE 802

   b. OSI

   c. American Wire Gauge (AWG)

   d. ISO

13. How many rings are used in a token ring environment?

   a. one

   b. two

   c. three

   d. four

14. The _____ Ethernet frame type complies with the IEEE standard.

15. The _____ network architecture uses the demand priority channel access method.

16. In what order is the token passed in an ARCnet network?

17. Which Ethernet standard uses thicknet cable?

    a. 10Base2

    b. 10Base5

    c. 10BaseT

    d. 10Broad30

18. What is the transmission speed for ARCnet?

    a. 10 Mbps

    b. 100 Mbps

    c. 2.5 Mbps

    d. 1.44 Mbps

19. Which token ring cable type is used to connect computers to MAUs through conduit or inside walls?

    a. Type 1

    b. Type 2

    c. Type 3

    d. Type 4

20. Which network architecture can automatically correct for cable failures? (Choose all that apply.)

    a. ARCnet

    b. Ethernet

    c. token ring

    d. FDDI

21. Data is sent on the _____ ring in an FDDI network.

22. A vampire tap performs what function in a network?

23. What are hubs called in a token ring network? (Choose all that apply.)

    a. MAU

    b. MSAU

    c. AUI

    d. DIX

24. What are two advantages of FDDI?

25. Which channel access method does AppleTalk use?

    a. polling

    b. CSMA/CD

    c. CSMA/CA

    d. token passing

26. What kind of connections does ATM establish before commencing network communications?

    a. virtual circuit

    b. permanent virtual circuit

    c. short circuit

    d. connection-oriented circuit

27. Which of the following IEEE specifications applies to 1000BaseX?

    a. 802.3

    b. 802.3z

    c. 802.3ab

    d. 802.3ac

28. Which two of the following optical carrier signaling rates represent the upper and lower end of ATM's normal operating bandwidth?

    a. OC-1

    b. OC-3

    c. OC-12

    d. OC-24

    e. OC-48

29. 1000BaseT and 1000BaseX both fall under the same IEEE specification. True or false?

30. Which of the following capabilities does ATM's fixed-length (53-byte) cell structure enable? (Choose all that apply.)

    a. By making all traffic elements the same size, it makes traffic flow more predictable.

    b. It makes it possible to offer quality of service guarantees for time-sensitive data.

    c. It helps make traffic prioritization possible.

    d. It makes cell-switching fast and efficient.

    e. It is required to support connection-oriented services such as phone calls.

31. What is the proposed standard for 10GB Ethernet?

    a. 802.3g

    b. 802.11b

    c. 802.3ae

    d. 802.5

32. The document governing cable modem standards is _____.

7

33. The maximum number of Class I Fast Ethernet repeaters allowed between stations is
    a. 5-4-3
    b. 3
    c. 2
    d. 1

HANDS-ON PROJECTS

The rate of change in networking technology is truly amazing. In the mid-1990s, networking at 100 Mbps was considered astonishingly fast; today, 10/100 Ethernet NICs and devices are the most commonly purchased networking components. Currently, Gigabit Ethernet is becoming increasingly affordable, and 10 Gbps implementation is already under development. Networks' speed and complexity grow at an ever-increasing pace.

This set of Hands-on Projects helps you learn how to locate current information about networking architectures and technologies. As you step through these projects, be aware that learning how to search for information is becoming as important as reading and absorbing the information you find. Likewise, identifying what is worth your time and effort amidst the many possible sources of information a search engine provides is just as important as mastering the information itself. (In fact, you can find information more quickly and easily if you work with the best possible sources.)

Project 7-1

This project requires a computer with a Web browser and Internet access. You access the IEEE Web site to download an IEEE 802 standard. Feel free to spend some time exploring the site after you complete the required steps.

To download the IEEE 802 standards:

1. Open your Web browser and type **standards.ieee.org/getieee802/portfolio.html** in the Address box. (For explicit instructions on how to start a Web browser and enter an address, please refer to Hands-on Project 1-3 in this book.)
2. Click the link that says **IEEE 802.11®: Wireless**.
3. Next click the link that says **IEEE 802.11b-1999**.
4. Read the license agreement and click the Accept button if you want to download the document. You can follow these directions to download any of the listed 802 documents.
5. Click the **Close** button in the upper-right corner of your browser window to close your Internet connection, unless you plan to proceed immediately to the next project.

Project 7-2

This project requires a computer with a Web browser and Internet access. You access a search engine to look for usable Ethernet references. In this project, you have the advantage of the Yahoo! editing staff, which combs the Internet on your behalf to locate and identify readable resources. Feel free to spend some time exploring this site, once you complete the steps for this project.

To investigate Ethernet resources:

1. Open your Web browser and type **www.yahoo.com** in the Address box.
2. Type **Ethernet** in the text box, and then click the **Search** button to the right.
3. From the list below Yahoo! Category Matches, click the term **LANs and WANs > Ethernet**.
4. Click the link labeled **Ethernet Technical Summary**.
5. Read the "TechFest Ethernet Technical Summary" at the TechFest Web site (*www.TechFest.com*), an extremely good source for computer technical information of all kinds, and a great source for networking information. Updated regularly, this summary of Ethernet technical information is worth reading once in its entirety and skimming every six months or so thereafter. Pay special attention to the information on 100 Mbps and 1000 Mbps Ethernet; it's some of the best on the Web!
6. Close your Internet connection, unless you plan to proceed immediately to the next project.

Project 7-3

This project uses Windows 2000 or Windows XP and requires a network connection. In this project, you will display the status of your network connection and view the current speed of the connection.

For Windows XP:

1. Right-click **My Network Places** on your desktop and select **Properties**.
2. In the Network Selections box, right-click the **Local Area Connection** icon and select **Properties**.
3. In the Connect Using box of the Local Area Connection Properties dialog box, note the type of NIC installed for this connection. At the bottom of the Local Area Connection Properties dialog box, check the **Show icon in notification area when connected** check box.
4. Click **OK** and then close the Network Connections windows.
5. Now look in your System Tray located in the lower-right corner of your desktop. You should see an icon that looks like two monitors stacked together. Place your mouse pointer over the icon and an information box pops up and shows the speed of your connection. What is that speed?

6. Click the network connection icon to bring up more details about your connection. This dialog box shows the status of your connection (connected, disconnected, or disabled) and the duration of your connection as well as the speed. Write down these values.

7. Close the Local Area Connection Status box.

For Windows 2000:

1. Right-click **My Network Places** on your desktop and select **Properties**.

2. In the Network and Dial-up Connections box, right-click the **Local Area Connection** icon and select **Properties**.

3. In the Connect Using box of the Local Area Connection Properties dialog box, note the type of NIC installed for this connection. At the bottom of the Local Area Connection Properties dialog box, check the **Show icon in taskbar when connected** check box.

4. Click **OK**, and then close the Network and Dial-up Connections windows.

5. Now look in your System Tray located in the lower-right corner of your desktop. You should see an icon that looks like two monitors stacked together. Place your mouse pointer over the icon, and an information box pops up and shows the speed of your connection. What is that speed?

6. Click the network connection icon to bring up more details about your connection. This dialog box shows the status of your connection (connected, disconnected, or disabled), the duration of your connection, and the speed. Write down these values. In this dialog box, you can also disable a connection or enable a connection that is currently disabled.

7. Close the Local Area Connection Status box.

Project 7-4

This project requires a computer with a Web browser and Internet access. You access a Web-based encyclopedia to look for information about FDDI.

To find an industry association:

1. Open your Web browser and type **webopedia.internet.com** in the Address box. (For explicit instructions on how to launch a Web browser and enter an address, please refer to Hands-on Project 1-3 in this book.)

2. Type **FDDI** in the By/ keyword search text box, and then click **Go!**

3. Scroll to the Links! section near the bottom of the page. Note that it provides a link to FDDI Tutorials and Resources. Click the hyperlink for the tutorial. You will be presented with another page that includes several links. Browse these links to learn more about FDDI.

4. Close your Internet connection, unless you plan to proceed immediately to the next project.

Start your search for technical information at a site that specializes in explaining such content, for example, TechFest, Webopedia, and CMP's TechWeb (*www.techweb.com*). These sites help you find the information you need much faster than a conventional search engine. We recommend that you build your own list of such resources and that you skip general-purpose search engines except when specialized tools don't help you find what you need.

Project 7-5

This project teaches you how to select the correct frame type in an IPX/SPX environment. This project uses Windows XP Professional or Windows 98.

For Windows XP:

1. Right-click **My Network Places** on your desktop and select **Properties**.

2. In the Network Selections box, right-click the **Local Area Connection** icon and select **Properties**.

This project assumes that the NWLink IPX/SPX protocol is not already installed on the computer. If it is installed, skip to Step 5.

3. Click the **Install** button. In the Select Network Component Type dialog box, select **Protocol** and click the **Add** button.

4. Select **NWLink IPX/SPX/NetBIOS Compatible Transport Protocol** and click **OK**.

5. In the Local Area Connection Properties box, find and select the **NWLink IPX/SPX/NetBIOS Compatible Transport Protocol** (do not click the check box next to the protocol description). Click the **Properties** button.

6. In the Adapter section of the Properties dialog box, find the Frame Type drop-down box. What is the current Frame Type selected? Click the down arrow beside the drop-down box to see the available frame type selections. List the available frame types.

7. Click **OK** and close the Local Area Connection Properties dialog box.

For Windows 98:

1. Right-click **Network Neighborhood** on your desktop and select **Properties**.

This project assumes that the IPX/SPX-compatible protocol is not already installed on the computer. If it is installed, skip to Step 4.

2. In the Network control panel, click the **Add** button. In the Select Network Component Type dialog box, select **Protocol** and click the **Add** button.

3. In the Manufacturer box, select **Microsoft**. In the Network Protocol box, select **IPX/SPX–compatible protocol**. Click **OK**.

4. In the Network control panel, select **IPX/SPX–compatible protocol** and click the **Properties** button.

5. Select the Advanced tab. In the Property box, select **Frame Type**. In the Value drop-down box, what is the current frame type selected? Click the down arrow beside the Value drop-down box to see the available frame type selections. List the available frame types.

6. Click **Cancel**, and then click **Cancel** again to close the Network control panel without making any changes.

Case Projects

1. Handy Widgets, Inc. operates in an office park in three buildings that are not currently connected to each other. Each building has four floors and is occupied by 50 to 60 Handy employees, all of whom have computers. Each floor has four printers that all employees on that floor use. The cabling closet on each floor of each building is centrally located, with no desktop run past 50 meters. You're hired to design a new network which must support high-speed connections between the buildings, which are 500 to 700 meters apart, with some fault tolerance.

Two of the buildings (buildings 1 and 3) are prewired to the desktop with Category 3 UTP. Currently, they run in a workgroup environment. Building 2 is new, ready for cabling to your specification. The IT (Information Technology) steering committee wants the network to have the ability to easily move from 10 Mbps to 100 Mbps and asks you to design the network with this in mind.

Building 3 houses all servers in a computer control center, which occupies the entire second floor; speed and fault tolerance are imperative there as well.

Outline the specifications you will use to design this network, including the network architectures involved, transmission speeds, cabling changes, and so forth. Draw the network you design, including media types, distances, numbers of hubs, locations, and so forth. Your drawing might resemble Figure 7-20.

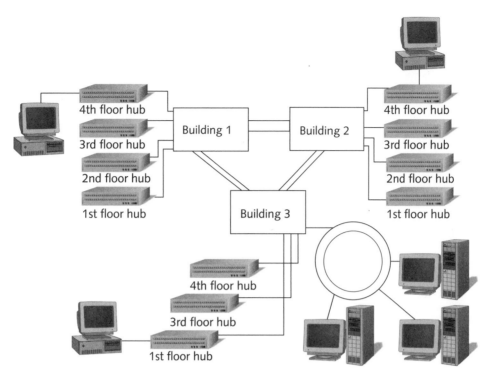

Figure 7-20   One possible Case Project solution

2. As administrator for your group's Macintosh network, you're asked to help upgrade and connect the network to the existing PC network. Your department has grown rapidly, raising concerns about whether the network can handle the expansion. With these considerations in mind, develop a plan to upgrade and connect the networks. Outline the specifications you will use to design this network, including the network architectures involved, protocols, transmission speeds, cabling changes, and so forth. Draw the network you design.

3. Your company expanded recently to include two new buildings for a total of three, roughly arranged in a triangle with each building about 500 meters apart. Previously, these buildings were wired with Category 3 UTP. The IT director mandates that your company be among the first to use 100 Mbps Ethernet to the desktop. Define a comprehensive network architecture that fulfills the director's requirements and allows for future growth.

4. You're asked to design a network for use in a training environment. It should be mobile, easy to set up, and simple to tear down. Speed is not an issue. Develop a network design that accommodates these requirements and keeps costs down.

CHAPTER

8

SIMPLE NETWORK
OPERATIONS

> **After reading this chapter and completing the exercises, you will be able to:**
>
> ♦ Explain the operation fundamentals of network operating systems
> ♦ Understand the various networking software components
> ♦ Describe the basic steps required for network operating system installation
> ♦ Define network services
> ♦ Understand network application installation and configuration concepts

The subject of network operations spans many aspects of network computing, including the types of applications and services present, how an administrator installs or enables these services for access by users, and how the network is managed. Before anything actually occurs on a network, however, a few prerequisites must be satisfied. First, a **network operating system (NOS)** must be installed; then the network must offer some type of resource or service, such as shared files or directories, or software applications. This chapter discusses the issues involved in installing a NOS, connecting network printers, sharing files and directories, and accessing network applications.

NETWORK OPERATING SYSTEMS

Before providing the setup instructions for a generic network operating system (NOS), first this chapter introduces and discusses numerous concepts and terminology. Previous chapters focused on the hardware and communications aspects of networking. The next few sections introduce important network software concepts.

Network Operating Systems Overview

The addition of NOSs to the personal computing world occurred during the mid 1980s. Initially, the ability to communicate over a network was added to existing operating systems. Therefore, the original NOSs were not true network operating systems; rather, they were communication software packages or additions to standalone operating systems. Both the main operating system and the NOS extensions had to be present on a single computer before it could communicate over the network. One significant example of this is the Microsoft LAN Manager, an add-on that enabled network communications on computers with the MS-DOS, Windows 3.x, UNIX, or OS/2 operating systems.

True network operating systems quickly replaced this solution. These systems handled the standalone computer activities as well as communications over the network. The most notable examples of such NOSs include NetWare (from Novell), Windows .NET Server, Windows 2000 Server, Windows NT Server, UNIX, and Linux.

You may recall that a computer's operating system (OS) directs the activities of that computer's hardware components. The operating system controls memory, CPU, storage devices, and peripherals (such as printers). Without an OS, a computer is a nonfunctional pile of expensive metal and plastic. The OS coordinates the interaction between software applications and the computer hardware so precisely that, although applications can operate on multiple versions of a particular operating system (such as Windows 98, Linux, and Windows XP), many applications must be written to the control parameters for a specific OS and cannot be used on different OSs. For example, Microsoft Word written for Windows XP does not function on a computer running Linux OS.

NOS Demands

The client and server sections that follow explain that the activities of a NOS are broad, numerous, and complex. Therefore, a NOS demands a significant amount of computing power from its hardware. Multitasking is one technique used by most network operating systems, and some non-network operating systems, to squeeze the most power out of a hardware configuration.

Multitasking is the ability of an OS to support numerous processes at one time. The support for a process includes maintaining memory pointers, offering access to I/O data, and providing cycles of the CPU for computations. In other words, a multitasking OS can simultaneously control more than one task. A true multitasking OS can support as many simultaneous processes as there are CPUs. However, when only a single CPU is present, time slicing can simulate multitasking.

Time slicing occurs when the CPU's computing cycles (of which there are hundreds to millions per second) are divided between more than one task. Each task receives a limited number of process cycles before the CPU halts it and activates the next task. This activity repeats until each task is completed. We perceive this activity as many applications operating simultaneously, because each time slice is an imperceptibly small increment. Thus, our inability to distinguish milliseconds from microseconds creates the illusion of multitasking.

There are two types of multitasking:

- **Preemptive multitasking:** The OS controls what process gets access to the CPU and for how long; when the assigned time slice expires, the current process halts and the next process gets its computing time.

- **Cooperative multitasking:** The OS cannot stop a process; once a process receives control of the CPU, it maintains control until it satisfies its computing needs. No other process can access the CPU until the current process releases it.

It is obvious that a true high-performance NOS must be a preemptive multitasking system. Otherwise, it could not complete many time-dependent tasks and would repeatedly fail to complete tasks.

SOFTWARE COMPONENTS OF NETWORKING

A true NOS is a single entity that manages the activities of the local computer and enables communication over the network media. This is just the initial requirement, though; other important features of a NOS include the following:

- Connects all machines and peripherals on a network into an interactive whole

- Coordinates and controls the functions of machines and peripherals across the network

- Supports security and privacy for both the network and the individual users

- Controls access to resources on a user authentication basis

- Advertises and manages resources from a centralized directory

- Gives the ability to share resources such as printers, files, and Internet access

These criteria clarify the definitions of general NOS components, including client network software and server network software.

General NOS Components

When it comes to implementing the wide range of functions that a modern network operating system supports, it is no surprise that because several functions and services need support, several software components are needed to provide those functions and services. In the sections that follow, you learn more about the two sides of the networking equation—client and server—and the various software components and services that balance this equation on a network.

Naming Services

On most networks, a name is necessary to identify and access resources of all kinds. Because humans recognize symbolic names more easily than numeric names, modern networks generally include one or more naming services to translate symbolic names (such as "HP4M-2nd Floor") into corresponding network addresses (such as 172.16.12.23). In the NetBIOS discussion in Chapter 6, you learned some of the functions of NetBIOS names on a Microsoft network. Here, you learn the rest of the story, which includes the relationship between how Microsoft uses NetBIOS names and how the TCP/IP-based Domain Name System uses domain names.

More About NetBIOS Names   Until the release of Windows 2000, Microsoft networking depended almost completely on using NetBIOS names to identify computers, shared drives and directories, printers, and other network resources. But proper use of NetBIOS names depends on understanding the following rules for their construction:

- NetBIOS names may be no longer than 15 characters. (A sixteenth character is always included, but the operating system manages it outside user control. On networks with DOS and Windows 3.x client machines, the DOS 8.3 short file-name limitation makes NetBIOS names longer than 8 characters invisible to such older clients.)

- Certain characters may not appear anywhere in a legal NetBIOS name. See Table 8-1.

- Ending a NetBIOS name with a dollar sign ($) prevents that name from appearing on a browse list. You use this character to hide computer and share names; Windows NT, Windows 2000, and Windows XP use this technique to create *administrative drive shares* by default; any administrator may access the share by adding a dollar sign after the drive letter. (That is, \\Ntw009\C$ accesses the C: drive on the machine named Ntw009.) Nevertheless, these hidden shares do not appear in any network browse list.

Table 8-1 Illegal characters in a NetBIOS name

/	right slash	<	left angle bracket
\	left slash	>	right angle bracket
[	left square bracket	+	plus sign
]	right square bracket	=	equals sign
"	double quotation mark	,	comma
'	apostrophe/single quotation mark	?	question mark
:	colon	*	asterisk
;	semicolon	(	open (left) parenthesis
		vertical slash	)	close (right) parenthesis

Microsoft's Universal Naming Convention Mapping a drive, or **drive mapping**, the process of associating a network drive resource with a local drive letter, is not the only way to access network resources. Windows 2000, Windows XP, Windows 98, Linux (running Samba), and most other modern NOSs recognize UNC names. A **Universal Naming Convention (UNC)** name is a standard method for naming network resources. UNC names usually take the form \\servername\sharename; for example, the Accounting share on the FINANCE server is \\FINANCE\Accounting. In UNC-aware applications and from many command-line activities, a UNC name can be used instead of a drive-letter mapping.

Domain Names and DNS In Chapter 6, you learned about the IP-based Domain Name System (DNS), which makes it possible to translate symbolic domain names such as microsoft.com into numeric IP addresses such as 207.46.131.30. The NetBIOS-based naming services used by Microsoft permit users to access resources and services through symbolic names on a Microsoft network. In much the same way, DNS permits users to access resources and services using symbolic domain names on the Internet (and other TCP/IP-based networks where DNS is available).

Beginning with Windows 2000 Server, Microsoft supports a naming service called Dynamic DNS (DDNS), which eventually will replace the NetBIOS-based naming service in Microsoft networks.

When used with a roster of well-known UDP and TCP port addresses (which identify specific services), the combination of a domain name and a port address is all that it takes to invoke services that range from newsgroups to file transfers on a TCP/IP host. This simple but powerful approach to accessing services (and the resources that go along with them) on TCP/IP-based networks helps explain why "the Internet is the only net" from a global networking perspective. Any computer or device with a valid IP address and using the TCP/IP protocol simply connects to the Internet to make its services, such as Web or file services, available to all other computers connected to the Internet.

Directory Services

The disadvantage of name services, such as those supported on Microsoft networks and through DNS, is that you must know—or guess—a name before you can ask for a resource or browse a list of available resources by network and node. A newer approach to handling network names, especially for resources, is to take advantage of a special class of network service called a directory service. A **directory service** works for a network much like the white and yellow pages in a phone book work for their area of coverage. You look up things by name (if you know what name to look for), but you can also look up things by type of service or resource (such as printer, file system, share, FTP e-mail server, and so forth). Users may request services or resources in a generic way and let the underlying directory server figure out which printer is closest to their desk (or give users directions on how to find the chosen printer), or which server they should use for file services, Internet access, remote access, and so forth. However, in most cases users don't care which server they use, as long as they get the services they request soon after they request them!

Windows 2000 is the first Microsoft NOS that includes Active Directory, a comprehensive directory service, just as NetWare (starting with version 4.0) includes an equally comprehensive directory service called Novell Directory Services (a.k.a. NDS). Both services use a "tree and forest" metaphor to organize directory contents. The local network neighborhood appears within some kind of container (such as a subdirectory inside the left pane of Windows Explorer), where all neighborhood resources are organized and listed for easy inspection and access. Although Linux does not include a built-in directory service, add-on directory services from companies like Sun Microsystems and Netscape Communications, among others, are readily available for that network operating system.

Better still, the servers that store directory information—directory servers—do so in a database that contains a list of the shared resources available over the network, against which users or programs can make queries. Thus, if a user or a program wants to use a color laser printer, for example, a quick query to the directory server determines if the server can honor that request and if the user is allowed to use the color laser printer. The server redirects the print job without requiring further user or program action.

In addition, directory servers store access control information about services and resources as part of the record that represents these devices to the directory. Therefore, directory services can prevent users from seeing resources or services they're not allowed to access. In fact, most directory services perform routine access control checks as a part of granting access to the services and resources that users are allowed to see. Thus, directory services help centralize security information for a network, as well as coordinate and advertise the network's available resources and services.

Both Novell's NDS and Microsoft Active Directory were patterned after a vendor-independent directory service called X.500. The X.500 directory service is built around the OSI protocol stack. Because of X.500's considerable overhead, another directory service, Lightweight Directory Access Protocol (LDAP), was developed.

LDAP is similar to X.500, but is far easier to implement. LDAP runs on TCP/IP and is making inroads as a directory service for the entire Internet. With the addition of LDAP, many remote devices such as Palmtops and handheld PDAs can access the NOS directory without running the actual NOS locally. Directory services are becoming more and more critical in today's information-intensive computing environments; their importance will only increase in the future.

In the section that follows, we investigate the software components that operate on the client side of client-server connections to make networking possible under the auspices of a network operating system. Strictly speaking, naming and directory services both belong under the heading "Server Services," but because they are so important to the proper functioning of modern networks, we made them a preamble to the other software components covered in the following sections.

Client Network Software

Client network software, a portion of the NOS installed on computers, is what network users are intended or required to use. This type of networking software is called the client because it represents the component of the networking system that requests resources from a server. From the user's point of view, a NOS simply offers a wider range of resources to access. However, a lot more goes on inside a NOS than inside a non-network-enabled OS. The most important of these software components is a redirector.

A redirector is a software component operating at the Presentation layer of the OSI model and found both on client and on server network operating systems. Whenever a user or an application requests a resource—be it a printer or a data file—a redirector intercepts that request. Then the redirector examines the request to determine if the resource is local (on this computer) or remote (on the network). If the resource is local, the redirector sends the request to the CPU for immediate processing. If the resource is remote, the redirector sends the request over the network to the server or host of that particular resource.

 Although Microsoft documentation uses the term *redirector*, Novell refers to the same component with the term **requester**. In the Linux arena (and other operating systems as well), the term **shell** sometimes refers to this component.

Redirectors route resource requests either to computers or directly to a peripheral device. Redirector resource routing most commonly occurs when the local printer port, LPT1, is mapped to a network printer instead of to a locally attached printer. In such cases, the redirector intercepts the print request, recognizes the LPT1 port is mapped to a network peripheral rather than assigned locally, and then routes that request directly to the printer.

The beauty of a redirector is its ability to hide from users the complicated tasks involved in accessing network resources. Once a network resource is properly defined, users never have to think about its location: access to network resources works the same as access to local resources.

A **designator** is another NOS software component that aids in network resource inter-action. A designator keeps track of the drive letters assigned locally to remote or shared drives (a shared drive is known as a **share**). When a drive is mapped, the designator notes the drive letter assigned to each network resource. When a user or an application attempts to access the assigned drive letter, the designator substitutes the real network address of the resource before letting the request go to the redirector.

Redirectors and designators make up the client portion of a client/server operating system used in a corporate environment for file and print sharing. Today, because of the burgeoning use of the Internet and TCP/IP, client software can refer to a Web browser, an e-mail pro-gram, an FTP client, or several other Internet access applications. In addition, new forms of client software are being developed for the exploding handheld and palmtop OS markets, and provide the unique requirements these types of devices demand.

Server Network Software

Server network software, a NOS portion installed on computers, handles resources and services to be distributed to clients. This type of networking software is called a server because it is the networking system component that hands out resources. While a client computer can function with only a redirector, server computer components are much more complex. The purpose of a server is to allow the sharing of resources, as shown in Figure 8-1.

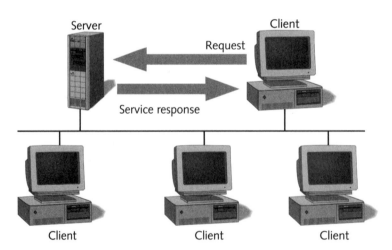

Figure 8-1   Server's function

Part of resource sharing is the ability to restrict access to those resources. This type of security controls which resources users are permitted to access, what type of access they are allowed, and how many simultaneous users may access any single resource at any given time. These are access controls—they provide data privacy and protection, and help maintain a productive computing environment.

The following example demonstrates why access controls are important. A shared folder on the network contains an organization's financial statement. Users in the finance department have full control over that report, so they can change, replace, or delete it. Users in the sales department have read-only access to the report, so they can only examine its contents. Users in the data-entry department have no access to the report, so they cannot even open the file. Thus, only authorized users have access to private, sensitive data, and even authorized access can be fine-tuned.

In addition to protecting and doling out resources, a NOS usually has numerous other responsibilities, such as:

- Management of users and groups
- Resource advertisement, name services, and directory services
- Logon authentication of individual users
- Management, control, and auditing tools to administer the network
- Fault-tolerance to protect the integrity of the network and the data it supports

In addition to these features, most server operating systems also contain or support the same features found in client OSs. These include a redirector, designator, and UNC name support. Servers use these features to host and offer resources to clients and to access resources from other servers elsewhere on the network.

Client and Server

Many NOSs, such as Windows 2000 and Windows XP, include client and server capabilities in the Server and the Professional versions. This enables both types of computers to host and use network resources. It is not recommended, or even possible, to host all your network resources from a single workstation running Windows 2000 Professional or XP Professional. Generally, the workstation version of the NOS (for example, Windows 2000 Professional or XP Professional) is not as powerful or as robust as the product's server version (for example, Windows .NET Server or Windows 2000 Server).

Note, however, that an important resource located on a workstation can be shared with the rest of the network. Where Linux is concerned, workstations and servers run the same version of the operating system software, but workstations generally have far fewer network services installed or available to other clients, whereas servers offer a wide range of such services to clients.

 If a single workstation hosts more than two heavily accessed resources, seriously consider transferring these resources to a real server, because accessing such resources can impose a performance hit on a workstation.

INSTALLING A NETWORK OPERATING SYSTEM

Installing a NOS is not much different from installing a standard desktop standalone operating system. There are only a few additional steps, and these focus on the configuration of the network and the server services. Later sections in this chapter review the major steps required in the installation process of Microsoft Windows NT Server or Windows 2000 Server, Red Hat Linux 7.3, and Novell NetWare 6.0. Before the installation of a NOS can begin, however, you must complete a few preparatory steps.

Installation Preparation

You must understand many important aspects of the network before you begin the NOS installation. Not all of these issues are addressed during the installation, but they help you understand the final result you are attempting to achieve. These items are:

- Type of network (topology)
- Size of network
- Job requirements of the server
- File systems to be used
- Identification or naming convention
- Types of OSs found on servers and clients
- Organization of storage devices

Let's examine some of these issues in more detail.

Job Requirements

The services and resources hosted by a server often determine what components or add-ons are installed. It is important to know a particular machine's job requirements before installing the NOS. This information can simplify installation and guide configuration later by having the proper components present and active on the system. Some of the services you may evaluate and install include DNS, DHCP, Web services, and remote access services, among others.

The responsibilities of a server do not end with what services and resources it hosts. You must resolve many other server-related issues. In the world of Windows networking, you can configure a server as a domain controller or a member server. A domain controller authenticates users and maintains the directory services and security database for a domain. A **member server** simply hosts a service or resource and does not participate in maintaining the directory and security database. In general, it's a good idea to install at least two domain controllers in any given domain, so that if one server fails, the other continues to provide access to the directory and security database. Thus, an additional domain controller provides built-in data redundancy to avoid loss of access to a key data resource for a Windows domain. NetWare servers require that you decide whether to install the server into an existing NDS tree (typically the choice for all servers except for the first server installed in the organization) or whether a new NDS tree is created (typically the choice when this is the first NetWare server installed in the organization).

Windows and NetWare servers support other fault-tolerant features, such as disk mirroring or disk duplexing, which provide an exact duplicate of a server's hard drive, so that data can be rebuilt in the event of a disk failure. This technology is referred to as RAID (Redundant Array of Inexpensive Disks). RAID technology is used widely through the server environment; its understanding is critical for an administrator. For more information on RAID and levels of RAID, go to *www.acnc.com/04_01_00.html*. In the Linux world, similar fault-tolerant features are available, but more often are implemented by hardware solutions or through the use of special-purpose, fault-tolerant software or subsystems.

Naming Conventions

A **naming convention** is simply a predetermined process to create names for use on a network (or a standalone computer). A good naming convention incorporates a scheme for user accounts, computers, directories, network shares, printers, and servers. In addition, these names should be descriptive enough so that anyone can decipher which names correspond to what objects. This applies equally to Windows and Linux networks, because regardless of the network in use, names provide the tools that users employ to identify and access resources of all kinds.

Employing a formal naming convention may seem pointless for a single computer or for small networks. However, small networks seldom stay small. In fact, most networks expand at an alarming rate. If you begin naming network objects or resources randomly, you soon forget which name corresponds to what resource. Even with excellent management tools, without a standard way to name things within a network's namespace, you can quickly lose track of important resources.

The naming convention your organization chooses ultimately doesn't matter, as long as it provides useful names for new network objects. To get an idea of a naming scheme, read these three common rules:

- Construct user names from the first and last name of the user, plus a code identifying their job title or department, for example, BobSmithVP.

- Construct group names from resource types, department names, location names, project names, and combinations of all four; for example, Printer01, Accounting, Austin, MegaDeal, and AustinAccountingMegaDeal, respectively.

- Construct computer names for servers and clients from their department, location, and type, for example, SalesTexas01.

No matter what naming convention you deploy, it must be:

- Consistent across all objects

- Easy to use and understand

- Simple to construct new names by mimicking the composition of existing names

- Able to clearly identify object types

Thus, before you install a new server, you must construct its name. Identifying a server's name (and a corresponding network address) are key steps in any server's installation.

Storage Device Organization

The organization of storage devices is crucial to the ultimate success of a network—where accessibility, performance, and fault-tolerance determine success. The most important organization decision about storage devices is how to organize the drive containing or hosting the NOS, especially regarding partitions. A **partition** is a logical organization of disk space, in which each portion (partition) appears as a separate logical drive. There are three schools of thought on the best way to organize a NOS host drive:

- *Multiple-boot.* A multiple-boot configuration enables the operator to select among many OSs/NOSs at boot up. Although good for testing and learning purposes, multiboot systems can compromise security in networks that are in actual business use.

- *Single-partition, single-NOS.* A single-partition, single-NOS configuration is a drive that has a single primary partition completely reserved for the NOS. This is the most secure configuration.

- *Multiple-partition, single-NOS.* A multiple partition, single-NOS configuration is a drive with two or more partitions, one partition for the NOS and the other partition(s) for data storage. This configuration is useful for separating data from OS files on large drives, but increases the level of drive activity and can more quickly degrade the life of the drive.

- *Fault-Tolerant Storage.* Most server computers today come equipped with two or more drives that can be configured for fault-tolerance. The simplest form of fault-tolerance is disk mirroring, which requires two identical disk partitions on two separate drives. Although most NOSs include the capability to provide fault-tolerant disk configuration, computers that are designed as servers frequently come equipped with disk controllers called RAID controllers that provide fault-tolerance in hardware. Whichever way it is done, the fault-tolerant configuration of your storage systems is a critical part of the NOS installation.

The organizational method you choose for your network should reflect and support your security needs as well as your hardware availability.

A second important issue regarding storage organization is the file system used. Many NOSs include special high-performance file systems that provide object-level security and a "common" format such as FAT (File Allocation Table) or FAT32 (a higher-capacity, 32-bit version of the older 12- and 16-bit FAT that originates from DOS). High-performance file systems such as NTFS (New Technology File System) offer security and control, whereas FAT offers full compatibility with other OSs (especially on the same machine). Linux, and some versions of UNIX, use their proprietary file system formats but resemble NTFS in their support for file- and directory-level security and access controls. Always use the most secure file systems on a server unless only an insecure file system format can meet your specific deployment and network needs.

Network Adapter Configuration

The network interface card (NIC) is the primary communication device between a computer and the rest of the network. It is important to properly configure a NIC before installing the NOS. You usually do this through a manufacturer-supplied BIOS configuration utility that is launched from a boot floppy. Be sure to define and test all possible NIC settings. Don't forget to set the cable type and the bus slot number, if appropriate. Many experts recommend that you start by installing your NIC on a server PC under DOS (which you can boot from a single floppy), just to make sure it works properly before you install a NOS on that machine. If you're setting up a server, it must have network access by definition—without at least one working NIC, the machine is isolated from the network and cannot do its job. That's why making sure the NIC works is such an important installation issue!

Protocol Selection

Selecting a protocol is key to the installation of a NOS. Simply stated, all computers on a network must communicate using the same protocol. A more complicated explanation follows. Within each protocol are special designations for subnets, network addresses, frame types, and so forth. Each of these items must either match exactly or be compatible for computers to communicate.

For example, the TCP/IP protocol—the world's most commonly used network protocol—requires the following pieces of information before NOS installation begins:

- *IP address.* A 32-bit address used to identify each individual computer on the network. An example of a valid IP address is 206.224.95.1.

- *Subnet mask.* A logical division mechanism to define small networks within larger networks (a subnet). A valid subnet mask is 255.255.0.0.

- *Default gateway.* Because computers communicate only with other computers within the same subnet without additional help, the default gateway is the IP address of a routable computer or device that gives access to other computers in other subnets.

- *DNS.* The Domain Name System (DNS) is a server-based service that resolves host names, such as *www.lanw.com*, into IP addresses. Internet access often requires the IP address for a DNS server.

- *WINS.* The Windows Internet Naming Service (WINS) is a server-based service that resolves NetBIOS names into IP addresses. Large intranets often require the IP address of a WINS server. WINS applies only to Windows networks that use NetBIOS names. Linux-based networks, except when Samba is in use, do not require NetBIOS names—and WINS.

- *DHCP.* When DHCP is the selected option for TCP/IP configuration, the IP address, subnet mask, and default gateway for the workstation, along with DNS and WINS server addresses, are automatically configured by the network. When the DHCP option is chosen, the computer simply broadcasts a DHCP request to the network. A DHCP server (which must be previously configured) responds with an IP address and subnet mask, and optionally, a default gateway WINS server address and DNS server address. The workstation then uses these values for its TCP/IP settings.

Hardware Compatibility

For a NOS to operate completely, if at all, the hardware components of the computer must be compatible with the NOS. Most NOS vendors publish and maintain lists of compatible hardware that they have tested with their software. (Microsoft calls their list a **Hardware Compatibility List (HCL)**; most Linux distributors publish similar lists that identify compatible hardware components and incompatible or problematic components.) If you use incompatible hardware, the vendor may not provide technical support. Always double-check that your computer's hardware components are fully compatible with the NOS being installed—doing so can prevent much grief and frustration.

Installing Microsoft Windows Servers

Whether you work with Windows 2000 Server, Windows .NET Server, or Windows NT Server 4.0, each NOS is relatively easy to install. With the proper preparation—as described in the previous sections—the Setup Wizard makes the installation process as simple as clicking the mouse and entering a few key data items. You need not know every detailed step involved in the setup process, especially because you are studying networking essentials and not NOS specifics. However, the major steps or sections of the installation included here give you insight into the architecture and simplicity of Windows 2000 and Windows NT 4.0 (the installation process for Windows .NET Server is not described because it was not available as of this writing).

Beginning the Installation

The first step of the installation is the most difficult because you can employ a plethora of methods which include:

- *Complete baseline installation or use existing OS?* New computers without an existing operating system require drive partitioning and a fully compatible CD-ROM. An existing OS may require no new partitioning and can employ an unsupported CD-ROM. (Such devices are now incredibly rare and seldom encountered.)

> There are many older proprietary CD-ROM drives for which DOS drivers are available, but not Windows NT or Windows 2000 drivers. The only way you can use the contents of the Windows installation CD on such a system is to boot under DOS, copy the files from the CD to a hard drive, and then begin the installation using the copied files. This limitation occurs because once the Windows install program reaches the point where the Windows kernel starts running the computer (this occurs partway through the installation process), the install program can no longer access the CD-ROM drive because there's no driver!

- *Floppy-assisted or floppyless setup?* You can begin setup with the four setup floppies (or three floppies, for Windows NT); this is especially useful for computers without an existing OS. The floppyless install is simpler for systems with network access or an accessible CD-ROM, especially a bootable CD-ROM. (In the latter situation, you can boot to the CD and run the installation directly from its files.)

- *Network or local installation?* You can store the Windows distribution files on a network-shared CD-ROM or directory; however, this requires that the computer have a network-compatible OS already running. A local install forces the distribution files to be pulled from a local CD-ROM drive or to be copied to a local hard drive.

No matter which installation type you use, all these options require launching WINNT.EXE (or WINNT32.EXE if you are launching the installation from Windows 95 or a later version of Windows) to start the setup process. (The floppy-based installation launches this utility as part of the boot process.) After launching WINNT or WINNT32 from the Run dialog box, the installation begins with a text-based phase. See Figure 8-2.

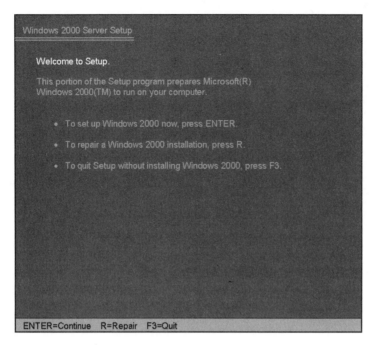

Figure 8-2   Windows 2000 Server text-based setup screen

Text-Based Portion

You perform the initial portion of Windows Server setup in a text-only mode. During this phase, you configure hard drives, format file systems, confirm the license agreement, and define the name of the system directory. Figure 8-3 shows the hard drive configuration screen. Once this has been completed, the distribution files are copied temporarily into a directory on the destination partition. The computer then reboots into the Graphical User Interface (GUI) portion of setup.

Graphical User Interface Portion

You control the GUI portion of setup with a mouse or with keystrokes (tab, arrows, and Enter). During the GUI phase, you define the computer and domain names, enter the identification key from the installation CD-ROM, select the server type as a domain controller (Primary or Backup for Windows NT) or a member server, assign a password to the Administrator account, and select environment and desktop components. Setup copies some files from the temporary folder to the destination folder and then moves into the network setup phase.

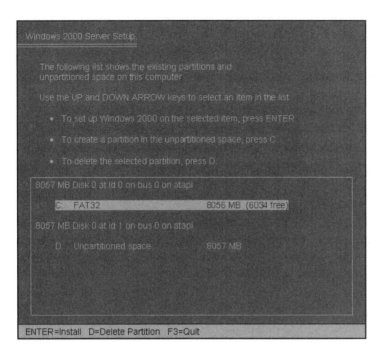

Figure 8-3   Windows 2000 Server hard-drive configuration screen

Networking Portion

The next portion of setup installs and configures the network communication components. During the networking phase, you install drivers for the NIC, select and configure the protocols, and review bindings. After this section is completed, setup copies numerous files to the final destination folder and deletes the temporary folder.

After the files are moved to the system folder, you define the time zone and display settings. Then, the computer reboots. After it reboots and the Administrator logs on, the Configure Server Wizard runs. This portion of the setup allows the server to be configured as a domain controller, member server, or standalone server. If the server is to act as a domain controller, Active Directory is installed and configured.

Installing Novell NetWare 6.0

Installing NetWare is not too different from the Windows Server installation process. In fact, installation of any NOS involves similar steps. You can install NetWare using one of two methods:

- *Over the network.* If a NetWare server is already online within your network and a network-enabled OS is already present on the current machine, you can launch the installation of NetWare across the network.

■ *From a CD-ROM.* You can start most NetWare installations from the CD-ROM; this usually involves a CD-ROM-enabled OS or a bootable disk with the proper drivers.

No matter which installation method you use, the primary install utility is INSTALL.NLM. After you start this utility (it is automatically started if you boot from the CD-ROM installation disk), the character-based setup screen appears. Select the Simple installation method; it requests only a few specific configuration items, and the process proceeds quickly.

Like Windows, NetWare is installed in two phases—initially in character mode, and then in GUI mode. During the character portion of the installation, you create partitions, accept the license agreement, copy files, install storage device drivers, and select drivers for the NIC. During the GUI portion, you assign the server name, set up protocols (such as TCP/IP or IPX), and install NDS. After these items are completed, the machine reboots, and the NetWare installation is completed.

Installing Red Hat Linux 7.3

Installing Red Hat Linux 7.3 is not too different from the other NOS installations previously covered. You can install Red Hat Linux most easily from the CD-ROM; this usually involves a CD-ROM-enabled OS or a bootable disk with the proper drivers.

 Before installing any Linux OS to an existing partition, you must defragment your hard drive and verify that it contains no dead clusters. You can use the MS-DOS utilities CHKDSK and DEFRAG to accomplish these tasks.

The Red Hat Linux CD-ROM distribution comes on three CD-ROM disks. Two additional disks are available, but are not required for installation. To begin the installation process, boot the computer with the Red Hat Linux CD-ROM disk 1 inserted. The character-based setup screen appears. Two installation modes are available, text and graphical. Graphical is the default mode and is started by pressing the Enter key. To use text mode, type "text" at the boot prompt.

Although the Linux installation contains many of the same elements as a Windows or NetWare server installation, there are important differences. Linux does not have a combined server and a workstation version. During the installation, you are asked to choose the type of installation you want, as shown in Figure 8-4. Note in the figure that your choices are not limited to Workstation or Server, but include Laptop, Custom, and Upgrade. Based on your choice, the installation program will install the most appropriate services for that type of installation.

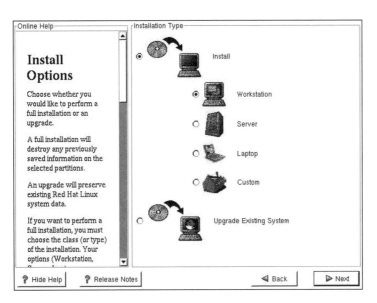

Figure 8-4   Linux Install Options dialog box

The Linux installation includes a step for the boot loader choice—something you will not find in a Windows or NetWare installation. A boot loader is a small program that executes when the computer first boots, allowing the user to choose which operating system to load, or to change the default manner in which Linux boots. Figure 8-5 depicts the Boot Loader Installation dialog box.

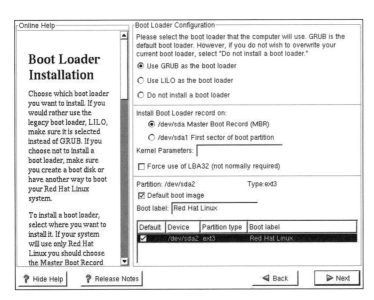

Figure 8-5   Linux Boot Loader Installation dialog box

Linux developers have always been concerned about security. In keeping with that sentiment, they have developed a built-in firewall for the Linux OS. During installation of Linux, you can select the level of security you desire and can customize the operation of the included firewall, as shown in Figure 8-6.

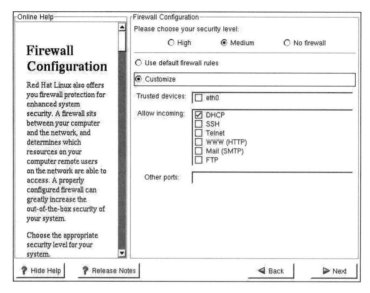

Figure 8-6   Linux Firewall Configuration dialog box

Most other Linux installation tasks are similar to those found in Windows and NetWare server installations and include disk partitioning, network configuration, administrator password assignment, and selection of optional operating components.

NETWORK SERVICES

Network services, the basic resources found on all networks, are the foundation of network applications. Without these basic services, networks cannot exist. Earlier chapters described a network's central purpose: to share resources. The two most basic shared network resources (a.k.a. network services) are printers and directory shares.

A network is not limited to these two primary services; in fact, the range of possible network services is broad. You can add numerous abilities, resources, and delivery methods to a default NOS installation to extend its usefulness. These can include groupware applications, mail packages, shared whiteboard applications, Web servers, and so forth.

Installing, Removing, and Configuring Network Services

Setting up network services is similar to configuring hardware device drivers. In a way, a network service (or the software that creates or enables a network service) is a driver for software or the network itself. Most NOSs have an administrative tool for the installation and removal of network services. In Windows 2000 and Windows XP, network services are installed by using the Windows Add/Remove Programs control panel. From this control panel, you select the Add/Remove Windows Components option, which brings up the Windows Components Wizard shown in Figure 8-7.

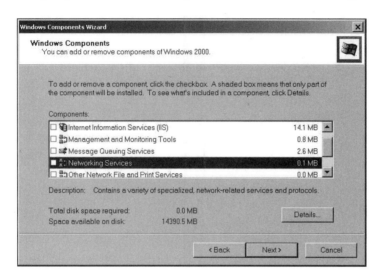

Figure 8-7   Windows Components Wizard in Windows 2000

Once a network service is in place, you can control its operation parameters in one of two ways. The first is through a global services administrative tool, such as the Windows Services applet in the Control Panel, where you can start and stop all active network services and modify basic operational parameters. For the second method, in some cases the installation of a network service adds a new administrative tool or console plug-in for the exclusive management of the new service, such as RAS (Remote Access Service) for Windows NT or (RRAS) Routing and Remote Access Service for Windows 2000. This tool is referred to as the Microsoft Management Console (MMC). These consoles must be custom built, and they are extremely valuable tools.

Network Bindings

Another issue related to network services and the operation of a network in general is **binding**, the process of linking network components from various levels of the network architecture to enable communication between those components. Bindings associate upper-layer services and protocols to lower-layer network adapter drivers. Many NOSs enable all valid bindings by default, but this often results in some performance degradation.

Your binding order should enhance the system's use of the network. For example, if your network has both TCP/IP and NetBEUI installed (most network devices use TCP/IP), you should set bindings to access TCP/IP first and NetBEUI second. In other words, you should bind the most frequently used protocol, service, or adapter first because this speeds network connections. A timeout period must elapse after each unsuccessful connection attempt before trying the next possible connection; these delays add up and slow system performance.

Network Printing

Network printing, one of the two essential network services, is the ability for a client located anywhere on the network to access and use a printer hosted by a server (if that user's access permission levels are appropriate). The redirector plays a major role in network printing by intercepting print requests and forwarding them to the proper print servers or network-connected printers.

Network printing begins with the installation of a printer on a server (or with installing a workstation to act as a server for the printer) or as a direct network-connected device. Once you properly install the printer and it is functioning, the logical representation of the printer within the NOS can be shared. The process of sharing on a network is what enables remote access of a local resource.

 This chapter does not discuss the issues of user access, security, and auditing; Chapter 10 covers these. You address these issues simply by taking additional steps in the share-establishment process, both for printers and for directories.

In some cases, a workstation or client computer must have local printer drivers installed, while in other cases, a workstation can access the printer drivers from the print server itself. Whichever the case, a new logical printer that points to the printer share, as shown in Figure 8-8, is installed. Once this logical device is constructed, users send print jobs to the printer simply by directing any application to print to the defined redirected port. The redirector handles all the complicated network communications involved with transferring the print job to the remote printer.

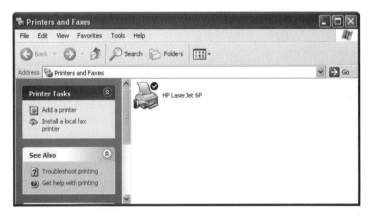

Figure 8-8   Windows XP printer share

Printer Management

On most networks, you manage printers from either local direct access or through the network printer share. Windows 2000 also gives you the ability to manage the printers through your Web browser using the Internet printing protocol. Obviously, management and administration can be performed only when the proper level of access is granted to a user, but this is the only limitation to printer share management.

Printer management covers a wide range of activities, including:

- Granting and restricting user access to printers
- Monitoring the print queue for proper function, including stopping, restarting, reordering, and deleting print jobs
- Limiting access by time frame, department, or priority
- Updating local and remote printer drivers
- Maintaining printers
- Managing printers remotely

This is just a short list of the responsibilities of printer management; many other abilities are NOS-specific as well.

Sharing Fax Modems

Just as printers can be shared across the network, so can fax modems. Although this feature is not often found as a default component in a NOS, many third-party vendors offer add-on products, such as FACSys from Optus Software, to share a fax modem over a network. This gives every client the ability to fax documents from the desktop. You can manage and administer fax shares just like a printer share. Usually, it takes additional client-installed software to connect to a fax share, but this is only a sign that the drivers and setup utility are not native to the NOS. Once the proper drivers are installed, there is no significant difference between using a printer share and a fax share.

Network Directory Shares

A network directory share, the second primary network service, offers clients the ability to access and interact with storage devices located anywhere on the network. Figure 8-9, for example, shows three shared folders, indicated by the "offering hand" icons for those folders. Once again, the redirector, as well as the designator, plays a major role in the directory share service.

You often access a shared directory (also a network share or just share) in three ways:

- By mapping an unused local drive letter to the directory share
- By using a UNC name to reference the directory share
- By selecting the directory share from a list of available shares

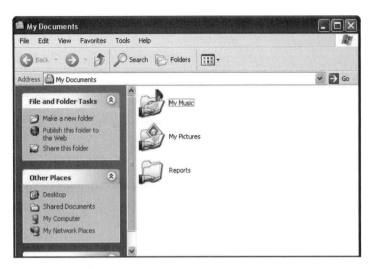

Figure 8-9   Windows XP folder shares

Like a printer share, you can manage and administer a directory share by granting and restricting specific access levels to users.

NETWORK APPLICATIONS

Most computer applications originally were electronic versions of existing data-management tools, such as typewriters, and calculators. You probably worked with many of these applications. However, most of these software tools are designed for a single user on a single computer. **Network applications** are designed for multiple simultaneous users on numerous computers connected over a network. Initially, the single-user applications were enhanced to accommodate multiple users. Soon, completely new applications were developed that could exist only as network applications.

Three types of network applications are quickly becoming essential tools on any network:

- E-mail or messaging
- Scheduling or calendaring
- Groupware

The benefits of network applications go beyond improved communication. Network applications are much easier to administer and manage than their standalone counterparts, especially on large networks. They simplify the headache of version control because a single server-based software update brings the entire network up to date. Network applications also save money. Standalone software requires purchasing a complete version for each user, whereas a network application can host multiple users with a single installation of the software through user licenses. However, even with these benefits, network applications do have drawbacks. Poor network performance or limited bandwidth degrades application performance accordingly. Also, when the network is down, the application is often unusable. Another service, called clustering, is available to correct the problem of network applications being unavailable, but this also requires advanced hardware and administrative skills. Even with these drawbacks, network applications offer previously unachievable communication solutions.

Not all network applications operate in the same manner. There are at least three types of architectures for network applications:

- *Centralized.* The application operates exclusively on a server. All clients interact with the central application through a simple terminal interface.

- *File-system sharing.* The application resides on each client, but all clients share a common database file or a storage directory.

- *True client/server.* Some aspects of the application reside on the server and some on the client. This enables group activities to be processed on the server separately from local processing.

The next sections discuss the three common network applications in more detail.

E-Mail or Messaging

E-mail (electronic mail), the most popular network application, is simply a tool that distributes messages from one person to one or more other people on the same network or across the Internet. E-mail is fast, asynchronous, and can contain more than just plain text. Most e-mail applications have common abilities, such as deleting messages, storing messages in folders, and replying to messages. This easy-to-use communication tool has many powerful and sophisticated abilities, including attaching files, filtering, and using distribution lists.

In addition to message delivery, many e-mail software products offer a versatile address book to store names, addresses, phone numbers, and more, for each contact you maintain. Also, if the e-mail application is based on the Internet standards known as SMTP, POP3, and/or IMAP, then communication outside the local network over the Internet is possible.

There is more to e-mail than just typing a message, attaching a file, and sending it to a colleague. E-mail is based on a common protocol and standards for communication. You really need to be familiar with only a few of the numerous e-mail communication protocols:

- **X.400.** A hardware- and software-independent message-handling protocol.

- **Internet Message Access Protocol (IMAP).** This is the standard that may someday replace POP3 on the Internet. It has advanced message controls, including the ability to manage messages locally yet store them on a server, plus numerous fault-tolerance features.

- **Message Handling System (MHS).** This Novell-developed standard is similar to X.400.

- **Post Office Protocol, version 3 (POP3).** This is what e-mail clients use to download incoming e-mail messages from an e-mail server to their local desktops. POP3 clients must manage messages locally (not on the server, as they can using IMAP).

- **Simple Mail Transfer Protocol (SMTP).** This is the current (as of this writing) standard protocol for Internet and other TCP/IP-based e-mail.

- **X.500.** This improved message-handling protocol from CCITT is closely linked to the X.400 standard but offers improved directory services. The X.500 protocol communicates across networks and maintains a global database of addresses.

Scheduling or Calendaring

One of the newest network applications to gain widespread popularity is **scheduling**. A network scheduler (sometimes known as a calendar) is an electronic form of the commonly used personal information and appointment book. The real benefit of this application is easy coordination of meetings, appointments, and contact details. Most schedulers offer private and public calendars, appointment books, task lists, and contact/address books. In addition to recording information, the network scheduler can notify users about an upcoming meeting, warn about overlapped schedules, and offer reminders of special events or of the need to contact someone.

Most scheduler programs offer integration into e-mail programs and office-productivity suites. This simplifies the exchange of information to and from each of the most commonly used applications on a user's desktop. To further supplement the paper-based personal information manager, users can print daily, weekly, monthly, and yearly schedules in a variety of formats, layouts, and styles.

Groupware

Groupware enables multiple users to simultaneously interact with a single file, document, or project. Using groupware, an entire department can contribute to a document's production and watch as the groupware combines everyone's input into a single entity. Some examples of groupware include multiuser multimedia authoring tools, Lotus Notes, Novell's GroupWise, and DEC's TeamLinks.

Groupware products make good use of networking's inherent abilities to keep dispersed users synchronized and to coordinate distributed data and activities. Today, many companies focus their research and development activities on creating new technologies to permit them to exploit groupware capabilities across the Web, thereby opening their collaboration to the entire Internet (with appropriate access controls, of course).

CHAPTER SUMMARY

❑ A network operating system (NOS) is software that controls the operations of a computer, including local hardware activity as well as communication over network media. Because they must support both local and remote activities, most NOSs are multitasking systems.

❑ A NOS also enables sharing resources, managing peripherals, maintaining security, supporting privacy, and controlling user access. Naming services on networks provide a way for users to identify services and resources by name. On Microsoft networks, UNC names provide a standard method of naming a shared resource; on TCP/IP-based networks, domain names and well-known port addresses provide much the same capability. Modern NOSs—especially Windows 2000 and NetWare (version 4.0 and later)—include built-in directory services that permit users simply to request resources and services, and do the work of locating and providing access to resources and services on the user's behalf.

❑ Client network software on workstation computers allows users to take advantage of network resources. Two components or conventions—redirectors and designators—simplify network access and hide the details from the user. A redirector intercepts a request for resources, interprets the request, and then guides the request to local devices or network shares accordingly. A designator is associated with drive mappings of network directory shares. It replaces a local drive letter with the appropriate network share name. The designator acts on behalf of, or in coordination with, the redirector.

❑ Client software does not always mean redirectors and designators. Many Internet services have separate client software components, such as Web browsers, e-mail clients, and FTP clients, that access server services without the use of a redirector and designator.

❑ Server network software on server computers is designed to host resources so multiple clients can access them. Part of a server's responsibility in hosting resources is controlling proper access to those resources, managing users and groups, administering the network, and protecting the data integrity.

❑ Workstation and server versions of a NOS both commonly contain client and server components. Thus, servers can access network resources, and workstations can host resources.

❑ Installing a NOS is similar to installing any OS. However, because a network is more complicated than a standalone computer, you must specify additional items, such as a naming convention, the requirements of the server, and configuration of storage devices, NICs, and network protocols, before installing a NOS.

8

❑ The steps required for installing Windows NT Server 4.0, Windows 2000 Server, Novell's NetWare 6.0, and Red Hat Linux 7.3 are similar. The overall process is simple. However, proper preparation and a clear understanding of the required data items, such as system requirements, are essential to a successful installation.

❑ There are two fundamental network services—sharing printers and sharing directories. However, networks are not limited to just these two services; networked applications such as groupware and e-mail extend network capabilities.

❑ Some standalone applications have been revised to function as cross-network applications. A network application offers numerous benefits to networks, including improved communication, simplified application maintenance, and lower storage requirements. Some examples of network applications include e-mail, scheduling, and groupware.

KEY TERMS

binding — The OS-level association of NICs, protocols, and services to maximize performance through the correlation of related components.

client network software — A type of software designed for workstation computers, and that enables the use of network resources.

cooperative multitasking — A form of multitasking in which each individual process controls the length of time it maintains exclusive control over the CPU.

designator — Associated with drive mappings. Working in coordination with a redirector, it exchanges the locally mapped drive letter with the correct network address of a directory share inside a resource request.

directory service — A comprehensive network service that manages information about network services, resources, users, groups, and other objects, so that users may access resources and services by browsing for them, or asking for them by type, along with maintaining and enforcing access control information for directory objects.

drive mapping — The convention of associating a local drive letter with a network directory share to simplify access to the remote resource.

groupware — A type of network application in which multiple users can simultaneously interact with each other and with data files.

Hardware Compatibility List (HCL) — A list of hardware devices compatible with a particular Microsoft operating system.

Internet Message Access Protocol (IMAP) — An Internet e-mail standard that may someday replace POP3 because of its advanced message controls and fault-tolerance features. The appeal of IMAP (a more modern client message transfer protocol) is that it permits clients to read and manage messages locally, while leaving them stored on the server.

member server — Any server on a Windows NT or Windows 2000 network that is not responsible for user authentication.

Message Handling System (MHS) — A Novell-developed standard that is similar to X.400.

multitasking — A mode of CPU operation where a computer processes more than one task at a time. In most instances, multitasking is an illusion created through the use of time slicing.

naming convention — A predetermined schema for naming objects within network space. It simplifies the location and identification of objects.

network applications — Enhanced software programs made possible through the communication system of a network. Examples include e-mail, scheduling, and groupware.

network operating system (NOS) — A type of software that controls both the local hardware activities of a computer and the network communications across a NIC.

network services — Those resources offered by a network, and not normally found in a standalone OS.

partition — A logical separation of disk space that is viewed as a separate logical drive.

Post Office Protocol version 3 (POP3) — An Internet message transfer protocol that e-mail clients use to copy messages from an e-mail server to a client machine to be read and managed on the local desktop.

preemptive multitasking — A form of multitasking where the NOS or OS retains control over the length of time each process can maintain exclusive use of the CPU.

requester — The term used by Novell for a redirector.

scheduling — A type of network application in which multiple users share a single appointment book, address book, and calendar.

server network software — A type of software designed for a server computer; this software enables the hosting of resources for clients to access.

share — A network resource made available for remote access by clients.

shell — The command-line interpreter on a UNIX or Linux system. The shell also includes built-in redirector functions.

Simple Mail Transfer Protocol (SMTP) — The current standard protocol for Internet and other TCP/IP-based e-mail.

time slicing — A method of granting different processes CPU cycles by limiting the amount of time each process has exclusive use of the CPU.

Universal Naming Convention (UNC) — A standard method for naming network resources; it takes the form \\servername\sharename.

X.400 — A hardware- and software-independent message-handling protocol.

X.500 — An improved message-handling protocol from CCITT. Able to communicate across networks and maintain a global database of addresses.

8

REVIEW QUESTIONS

1. NOSs were originally add-ons to standalone operating systems. True or false?

2. Regarding Windows NT Server or Windows 2000 Server, what is the most important aspect of a server's responsibilities or purpose that must be decided before installation?

   a. the names of clients within the network it supports

   b. whether or not it serves as a domain controller or a member server

   c. the number of users it will support

   d. whether to allow remote

3. Which of the following are examples of true NOSs? (Choose all that apply.)

   a. Windows NT Workstation

   b. Windows 95

   c. Microsoft LAN Manager

   d. Novell NetWare

   e. Windows 2000 Server

4. Which of the following storage device organizational schemes is the most secure and fault-tolerant?

   a. multiple boot

   b. single-partition, single NOS

   c. multiple-partition, single NOS

   d. single-partition, multiple NOS

5. Multitasking is _____ .

   a. the installation of more than one protocol

   b. the illusionary method of computing where multiple processes operate simultaneously by sharing the CPU

   c. the act of binding two or more services to a single protocol

   d. the activity of accessing a directory share over a network link

6. It is important to preconfigure all NICs in a server before initiating NOS installation. True or false?

7. Cooperative multitasking is the method of computing where the NOS/OS maintains control of the CPU by assigning specific time slices to processes. True or false?

8. If TCP/IP is one of the protocols installed on your network, which of the following items are important to define before installation? (Choose all that apply.)

   a. IP address

   b. e-mail address

    c. subnet mask

    d. Web server name

9. Which of the following are features of a NOS? (Choose all that apply.)

    a. connect all machines and peripherals on a network into a conglomerate inter-active whole

    b. coordinate and control the functions of machines and peripherals across the network

    c. support security and privacy for both the network and the individual users

    d. control access to resources on a user-authentication basis

    e. control local hardware activity and network communications

10. Verifying hardware compatibility prior to NOS installation is important because _____.

    a. not all hardware is supported by the high-performance requirements of a NOS

    b. a NOS vendor limits what equipment can be used to improve its advertising expenditures

    c. high-speed CPUs do not support some protocols

    d. all of the above

11. Client networking software has a primary purpose of _____.

    a. supporting local resources

    b. distributing text messages to other users within the network

    c. accessing network shares

    d. offering local resources to other users

12. Which of the following installation methods do Windows 2000 Server and Novell NetWare have in common? (Choose all that apply.)

    a. CD-ROM based

    b. over the network

    c. floppy-based only

    d. EPROM based

13. What is the function of a redirector?

    a. to maintain a group appointment list

    b. to map directory shares to local drive letters

    c. to associate protocols, NICs, and services in order of priority

    d. to forward requests to local or remote resource hosts

8

14. What is the benefit of having an existing operating system on a computer when you are planning to install a NOS?

    a. It enables a boot floppy to function correctly.

    b. It removes the need to repartition the storage devices.

    c. It provides an alternate boot OS for security purposes.

    d. It can provide access to a CD-ROM otherwise not supported by the NOS itself.

15. Which of the following are components of client network software? (Choose all that apply.)

    a. requester

    b. resource–hosting protocols

    c. designator

    d. DNS server

16. Which of the following installation tasks are found in a Linux Red Hat 7.3 installation, but not found in a Windows or NetWare server installation?

    a. boot loader selection

    b. network configuration

    c. disk partitioning

    d. administrator password assignment

17. Which of the following is the proper format for a UNC name?

    a. (sharename)->servername

    b. \\servername\sharename

    c. sharename://servername/path

    d. servername, sharename

18. Printer shares and directory shares are considered _____.

    a. network applications

    b. groupware

    c. network services

    d. network protocols

19. What are common features in server network software for the management of resources? (Choose all that apply.)

    a. access limitations

    b. user authentication

    c. auditing tools

    d. fault-tolerance

20. Managing a network printer remotely can encompass what administrative tasks? (Choose all that apply.)

    a. deleting print jobs

    b. restricting user access

    c. reordering the print queue

    d. setting access by priority

    e. updating drivers

21. Typically, NOSs include features of client networking software and server networking software to enable workstations and servers both to access and host resources. True or false?

22. Which of the following is not an e-mail protocol?

    a. POP3

    b. MAPI

    c. IMAP

    d. MHS

    e. SMTP

23. Which of the following are important issues to address before initiating the setup of a NOS? (Choose all that apply.)

    a. responsibilities of the server

    b. personnel manager responsible for the IS department

    c. naming conventions

    d. client applications

    e. organization of storage devices

24. Windows directory shares can be mapped to local drive letters. True or false?

25. A naming convention should be applied to which objects within a network's namespace? (Choose all that apply.)

    a. servers and clients

    b. users

    c. directory shares

    d. passwords

    e. printer shares

26. To hide a NetBIOS name, you must begin that name with a dollar sign ($). True or false?

8

27. Which of the following NetBIOS names are legal? (Choose all that apply.)

    a. ComputerSeventeen

    b. Computer17

    c. Computer/17

    d. Computer+17

    e. Computer&17

28. Directory services perform the same kinds of functions on a network as UNC names or domain names. True or false?

29. Which of the following network operating systems do(es) not include a built-in directory service? (Choose all that apply.)

    a. Linux

    b. NetWare 6.0

    c. Windows NT 4.0

    d. Windows 2000

30. Which of the following statements about UNC or NetBIOS names are true? (Choose all that apply.)

    a. Users may not define UNC names longer than 15 characters.

    b. The 16th (or final) character of a UNC name is a system-supplied suffix.

    c. NetBIOS names must begin with an alphanumeric character (an uppercase or lowercase letter or a number).

    d. NetBIOS names that end in a dollar sign ($) do not appear in a browse list.

    e. Linux does not include built-in support for NetBIOS names.

HANDS-ON PROJECTS

Project 8-1

This project walks you through the process of creating a shared folder in Windows 2000 or Windows XP. The File and Print Sharing for Microsoft Networks service must be installed.

1. Log on.

2. Open Windows Explorer by going to **Start/Run** and typing **explorer** in the Run dialog box. Click **OK**.

3. In the left pane of Explorer, select the **My Documents** folder.

4. From the Explorer menu bar, choose **File/New** and click **Folder**. A new folder named New Folder is created and appears in the bottom of the right pane of Explorer.

5. Right-click the **new folder** and select **Rename** from the menu. Type **MyShare** and press **Enter** to rename the new folder.

6. Right-click the **MyShare** folder that you just created and select **Sharing** from the menu (in Windows XP the menu choice is named **Sharing and Security**).

7. To share this folder, click the **Share this folder** option button, as shown in Figure 8-10. At this point, you may change the name of the share so that users on the network see this folder with a different name. For the purposes of this exercise, you can leave the name as is.

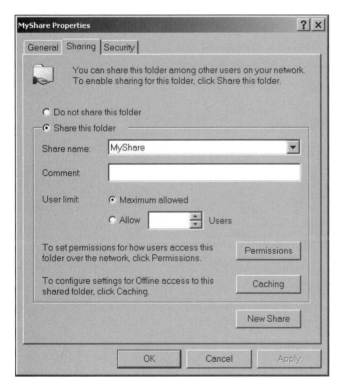

Figure 8-10   Windows 2000 Properties dialog box—Sharing tab

8. Click **OK**.

9. Look for the folder in Windows Explorer. You will see that an offering hand icon has been added to the folder icon. Your folder is now ready for access from the network. The next projects show you how to access shared resources.

Project 8-2

This project assumes a network printer share has been created and named "HP LaserJet 5L."

To connect to a printer share:

1. Log on.

2. For Windows 98 or Windows 2000, click **Start**, **Settings**, **Printers** to open the Printers dialog box. For Windows XP, click **Start**, **Printers and Faxes**.

3. For Windows 98 or Windows 2000, double-click the **Add Printer** icon. For Windows XP, click the **Add a printer** button under the Printer Tasks menu. The Add Printer Wizard opens. See Figure 8-11, which shows the Wizard in Windows XP.

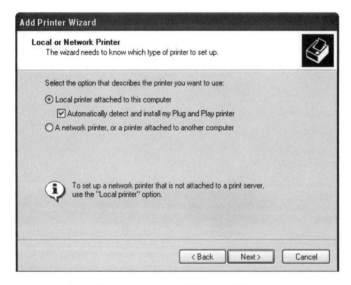

Figure 8-11   Windows XP Add Printer Wizard

4. Click **Next**. For Windows 98, click **Network printer server**, for Windows 2000, click the **Network printer** option button, and for Windows XP, click the **A network printer, or a printer attached to another computer** option button.

5. Click **Next**. For Windows 98, the Connect to Printer dialog box opens. For Windows 2000, the Locate Your Printer window opens, and for Windows XP, the Specify a Printer window opens; click **Next** to make Windows 2000 or Windows XP browse the network for the UNC names for shared printers.

6. Select the printer share **HP LaserJet 5L** (or the printer specified by your instructor) from the Shared Printers list, and click **Next**.

7. Click **No** to the inquiry about setting this as the default printer.

8. Click **Next**.

9. Click **Finish**. The new logical printer should appear in the Printers folder. If not, press the **F5** key or select **View**, **Refresh** to update the display.

 To remove a network printer, highlight it in the Printers folder, right-click, and select **Delete** from the menu.

 ## Project 8-3

 This lab assumes a directory share named USERS has been created.

8

To map a drive letter to a directory share for Windows 98 or Windows NT:

1. Log on.

2. Double-click the **Network Neighborhood** icon on the desktop.

3. Traverse the network browser list hierarchy to locate and select the **USERS** share located in the machine indicated by your instructor. Figure 8-12 shows the shares on a computer named Ntw1.

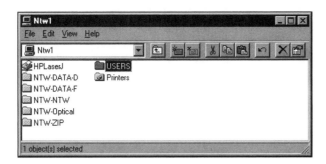

Figure 8-12   Network shares on computer Ntw1

4. Select **File**, **Map Network Drive** from the menu bar.

5. In the **Map Network Drive** dialog box, select the drive letter to assign to this directory share. (In Figure 8-13, drive I is selected in the Map Network Drive dialog box.)

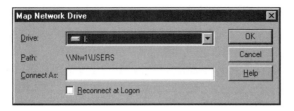

Figure 8-13   Map Network Drive dialog box

6. Click the **OK** button.

7. Close Network Neighborhood.

8. Open **My Computer**.

9. Locate and open the drive letter you assigned to the network share.

> To disconnect a mapped drive, right-click the assigned drive icon in My Computer, and then select **Disconnect** from the shortcut menu.

To map a drive letter to a directory share for Windows 2000:

1. Log on.

2. Double-click **My Network Places** on the desktop. This produces a display like that shown in Figure 8-14.

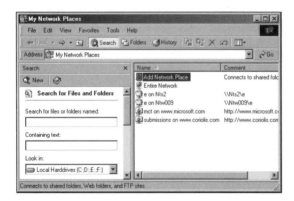

Figure 8-14   My Network Places window in Windows 2000

3. Double-click **Add Network Place**. The Add Network Place Wizard opens, as shown in Figure 8-15.

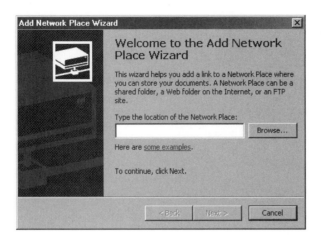

Figure 8-15   Add Network Place Wizard in Windows 2000

8

4. Click the **Browse** button to open the Browse For Folder window (a browse list for your local network), and ask your instructor to help you navigate to the Users share. This usually means double-clicking a network icon and then expanding the shares on a particular machine, as shown in Figure 8-16.

Figure 8-16   Browse For Folder window in Windows 2000

5. Click the **Users** share in the Browse window, and then click the **OK** button. You return to the Add Network Place Wizard window. Notice that the UNC name for the share you selected now appears inside the Type the location text box.

6. Click the **Next** button to proceed. The default name for a Windows 2000 share is <*sharename*> on <*machinename*>, where <*sharename*> is the name of the share, and <*machinename*> is the NetBIOS name for the computer on which it resides. This

is *Users on Ntw009* in the Add Network Place Wizard window shown in Figure 8-17. (You can replace this default with a different name of your own choosing.)

Figure 8-17   Naming a share in the Add Network Place Wizard in Windows 2000

7. Click the **Finish** button. An Explorer window opens displaying the share's contents.

8. Click the **Close** button in the upper-right corner to close the window. Notice how the new share appears in the My Network Places window.

9. Click the **Tools** menu and select **Map Network Drive**. Notice how Windows 2000 picks the next available drive letter to assign to this share. (Your instructor will tell you if you need to select a different letter; in these instructions, we assume it's OK to use the default selection.)

10. Click the **Browse** button to produce another browse list, navigate to the correct network and machine as in Step 4, select the **Users** share, and then click the **OK** button at the bottom of the Browse window.

11. If you want a drive mapping to be persistent (that is, to show up each time you log on to that machine), you must check the box labeled **Reconnect at logon** beneath the Drive and Folder text boxes. In this case, you're making a temporary assignment, so make sure that the **Reconnect at logon** check box is empty, and click the **Finish** button at the bottom of the window.

12. Click the **Close** button in the upper-right corner of the Explorer window that opens for the share. (Notice the drive letter that appears to the right of the share name in parentheses.) Then click the **Close** button for the My Network Places window.

To disconnect a mapped drive, right-click the assigned drive icon in My Computer, and then select **Disconnect** from the shortcut menu.

To map a drive letter to a directory share for Windows XP:

This method does not use a Wizard as does the method described for Windows 2000. However, if need be, this method can be used on Windows 2000.

1. Log on.
2. Double-click **My Network Places** on the desktop.
3. Select **Tools**, **Map Network Drive** from the menu bar. You will see a display like the one in Figure 8-18.

8

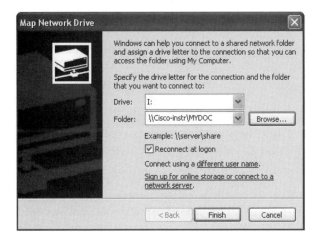

Figure 8-18   Map Network Drive dialog box in Windows XP

4. From the Drives drop-down box, select **I:** (or a drive specified by your instructor).
5. Click the **Browse** button to open the Browse For Folder window (a browse list for your local network), and ask your instructor to help you navigate to the Users share.
6. After you have selected the folder, click **OK**. The UNC name of the folder appears in the Folder box that was shown in Figure 8-18.
7. Click the **Finish** button. An Explorer window opens displaying the share's contents. If you open My Computer on your desktop, you will see a new drive listed there that represents the drive mapping you just completed.

Project 8-4

This lab assumes that you have access to a Web browser on a machine that's connected to the Internet.

Part of the ritual of preparing to install any modern NOS on a PC is a step that we like to call "prequalifying the hardware." This consists of two sets of activities:

❑ Record a complete list of the PC's components—motherboard make and model, CPU make and model, RAM size and make, hard disk(s) manufacturer, model, and size, and so forth. In some cases, you find all this information on the sales receipt and documentation you received when you purchased your PC. If you don't have this documentation or if it doesn't contain the information, you have to crack the case and start hunting; sometimes you have to unplug or dismount components to obtain this information. Make sure you know how to put things back together before you start taking them apart!

❑ For each component, check a hardware qualification list of some kind to see if it works with the operating system you want to install. For this project, you use the Microsoft Windows Hardware Compatibility List on the Microsoft Web site.

To use the Microsoft Windows Hardware Compatibility List (HCL):

1. Launch your Web browser.

2. In the Address box, type **http://www.microsoft.com/hcl/** and then press **Enter** to access the home page for the Microsoft Windows HCL.

You might also be able to download text-based versions of the various HCL files at this site. At the time of this writing the site contained a hyperlink, "HCL Information," to one exhaustive file for each of the following Windows operating systems: Windows XP, Windows 2000, Windows Millennium (Me), Windows NT 4.0, Windows 98, and Windows 95. You may prefer to use these files instead of the Web site to complete this task, if they are still available.

3. Look up the items that appear in Table 8-2 in the HCL. Enter the manufacturer's name in the Search for the following text box, select the category name from the In the following types pull-down menu, and then click the **Search Now** button to initiate a search for each item. If the item appears in the list with a "compatible" or a "logo" graphic in the Windows 2000 column in the HCL, it's compatible; if not, check with the manufacturer or the manufacturer's Web site to see if a Windows 2000-compatible driver is available for the item you seek.

Table 8-2 System compatibility lookup items

Category	Manufacturer	Make/Model	Project 8-4 Notations	Project 8-5 Notations	Project 8-6 Notations
Audio	Creative Labs	CT4780 Sound-Blaster Live!			
CPU	AMD	Athlon 750 MHz			
Input/Keyboard	Microsoft	Internet Keyboard PS/2			
Display	Acer	V771 Value 17" CRT color SVGA display			
Network/Ethernet	3Com	3C918 Fast Ethernet			
Storage/CD-ROM	Toshiba	XM6401B CD-ROM player			
Input/Pointing/Drawing	Microsoft	Intellimouse 1.1A PS/2			
Storage/SCSI controller	Adaptec	29160LP Ultra 160 Controller			
Storage/Hard disk	IBM	DMVS 18GB Ultra 160 hard disk			
Storage/Tape drive	Aiwa	TD-20001 [SCSI] tape drive			

4. Check each item in the list, and record a check mark for each one that appears in the HCL. If all entries appear with a "logo" or "compatible" entry in the Windows 2000 column, the machine is compatible. Is the machine, in fact, compatible with Windows 2000?

5. Close your Web browser by clicking the **Close** button in the upper–right corner, unless you plan to proceed immediately to the next project.

Project 8-5

This lab assumes that you have access to a Web browser on a machine that's connected to the Internet.

As with Windows 2000, part of the ritual of preparing to install any modern NOS on a PC is prequalifying the hardware. For Linux, this is normally performed on a per-distribution basis. Therefore, hardware qualified for use with Debian Linux may differ somewhat from that qualified for use with Red Hat Linux. In this project, you check the components in Table 8-2 against the Red Hat Hardware Compatibility lists.

To check the Red Hat Hardware Compatibility Lists:

1. Launch your Web browser.

2. In the Address box, type **http://www.redhat.com/support/hardware/**, and then press **Enter** to access the home page for the Red Hat Hardware Compatibility Lists.

3. Scroll down the page and click the link for the Red Hat Linux 7.1 (Seawolf) release.

 At this writing, Red Hat Linux 7.1 is the latest release for which a Hardware Compatibility List exists.

4. On the resulting Web page, click the **Hardware Compatibility List** link. Click the **Complete Listing** link, and select the manufacturer from the list. Next click the Audio Device/Controller category, and look for the make and model in the resulting list. Again, put a check mark for each entry if it appears in the list. How does this configuration fare for Linux compatibility?

5. When you finish, click the **Close** button to close your Web browser unless you plan to go on to the next project.

Project 8-6

 This lab assumes that you have access to a Web browser on a machine that's connected to the Internet.

As with Windows 2000, part of the ritual of preparing to install any modern NOS on a PC is prequalifying the hardware. For NetWare, you must visit Novell's Solutions Search Web page, where certified systems, hardware, and software all appear for easy lookup. In this project, you check the same list in Table 8-2 against the hardware categories that appear near the bottom of this Web page.

To check NetWare hardware compatibility:

1. Launch your Web browser.

2. In the Address box, **type http://developer.novell.com/nss/category.html**, and then press **Enter** to access the home page for Novell's various compatibility listings.

3. Scroll down the page to the hyperlinks under the "Hardware" heading; use the list from Table 8-2 to drive your lookup efforts by category.

4. On the various Web pages attached to the category links, look for the items listed in Table 8-2. Again, place a check mark in the appropriate column if it appears in the list. How does this configuration fare for NetWare compatibility?

5. When you finish, close your Web browser by clicking its **Close** button.

CASE PROJECTS

1. You work for a small consulting firm. When you introduce the idea of implementing a client/server network, your manager says that she is wary of using a server because she heard they are vulnerable to crashes. What could you tell your manager about modern networking technologies that might alleviate her fears?

2. You manage a network for a small firm. Upper management changed accountants and wants to make sure that the former accountant cannot access sensitive financial data. What can you do to ensure your firm's financial security?

3. You notice that your network server is experiencing slow performance. You check the server and find plenty of storage space and the fastest CPU available. However, you surmise that the bottleneck occurs at the CPU. What can you do to improve the CPU's performance?

4. In your lab, you plan to build a dual-boot Windows 2000 and Linux test server. The PC has a single 8 GB hard disk. Windows 2000 requires a minimum of 1 GB of disk space, whereas Linux requires about 1.5 GB for a server installation. For Windows 2000 and Linux operating system files, you want to use their native file systems. (Note that Linux requires a separate swap partition for its virtual memory swap file, in addition to a primary partition for the operating system files.) You want the two operating systems to share some common files, so you decide to install a FAT16 partition on the drive as well. Describe a possible partition scheme for the hard disk on your test machine; the scheme should include the number of partitions and each partition's type and size. Explain why you chose the size you did for each partition.

5. As you learned in this chapter, TCP/IP-based e-mail clients use either POP3 or IMAP to read and manage e-mail messages. XYZ Company's salespeople are out of the office three days a week on average, during which time they access e-mail from their laptops. The two days a week they're in the office they access e-mail on separate desktop machines. Select the client e-mail protocol (POP3 or IMAP) most appropriate for these circumstances, and justify your selection.

9

UNDERSTANDING COMPLEX NETWORKS

After reading this chapter and completing the exercises, you will be able to:

♦ Discuss interconnectivity issues in a multivendor environment

♦ Define the various options to implement a multivendor network environment

♦ Discuss the differences between centralized and client/server computing

♦ Define the client/server networking environment

♦ Discuss the basics of Web-based computing environments

Network management is a complex and intricate subject. However, understanding how networks function assists you not only in network-management issues, but also in planning and troubleshooting networks. This chapter examines aspects of complex network management from the standpoint of clients and servers. In this chapter, you explore the issues involved in getting various vendors' products to interoperate, as well as the differences between centralized and distributed client/server computing.

Interconnectivity in Multivendor Environments

Typically, in today's networking environments, you must connect computers and networks from different vendors and provide remote as well as local network access. This section discusses networking vendors and provides suggestions that should help you overcome typical interconnectivity challenges.

One of the biggest dilemmas in networking involves connecting systems that use different vendors' network operating systems (NOSs), or, still more challenging, implementing a single network that makes use of multiple NOSs. To make this work effectively, the server's operating system, the clients' operating systems, and the redirectors must be compatible. A good example of this is an environment in which one computer runs Windows 98 with the client for Microsoft networks, one computer runs the client for Novell NetWare, one client is an Apple Macintosh, and the server runs Windows 2000 Server. In this scenario, the computer running Windows 2000 Server can support all clients on the network, as shown in Figure 9-1.

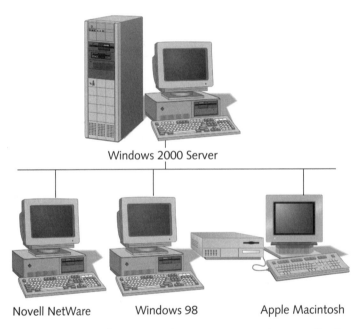

Windows 2000 Server

Novell NetWare   Windows 98   Apple Macintosh

Figure 9-1   Windows 2000 Server can support many clients

Implementing Multivendor Solutions

There are two basic ways to handle multivendor connectivity: from the client end and from the server end. The solution you choose depends on which vendors' products you seek to interconnect.

Client-Based Solutions

As discussed in Chapter 8, it is the job of the client's redirector to intercept messages from the client and forward those messages to the correct server if a request cannot be fulfilled locally. In a multivendor environment, multiple redirectors may be loaded onto a single client to facilitate connections to different vendors' servers. This is called a **client-based multivendor solution**.

For example, if a Windows 98 client requires access to a Windows 2000 server and a Novell NetWare server, you can load a redirector for each operating system onto that client. Each such redirector redirects a request to the appropriate server, as shown in Figure 9-2. For Windows 98, Windows 2000, and Windows XP, in fact, clients can use Microsoft client software that can redirect requests both to Windows and to NetWare servers, or they can use client software from Novell that can do the same thing.

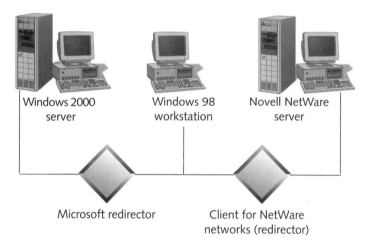

Figure 9-2 Redirectors make multivendor connectivity possible

The vendor of choice in this situation is often the vendor to which access is most frequently requested or whose applications are most mission critical.

Server-Based Solutions

To implement a **server-based multivendor solution**, software must be loaded on the server to provide services for a particular client. For example, if a Windows 2000, Windows .NET, or Windows NT network includes Apple Macintosh computers, the administrator can add Services for Macintosh to any of the Windows Server operating systems. Windows 2000, Windows .NET, and Windows NT network operating systems include this service, which supplies a simple solution for Macintosh connectivity. (You practice installing client services in the Hands-on Projects at the end of this chapter.)

With Services for Macintosh installed on a Windows server, Macintosh clients can connect to resources on the Windows server. This service also automatically converts files to Macintosh format when retrieving them from the server, as depicted in Figure 9-3. This enables Macintosh users to share files with any other user connected to the Windows server where Services for Macintosh is installed.

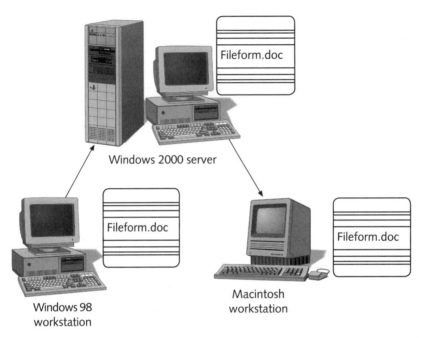

Figure 9-3 File conversion is automatic with Services for Macintosh on the Windows 2000 server

Another benefit of using Services for Macintosh is that Macintosh users can access the resources on a Windows server in the same way they access resources on a Macintosh server. This feature, which allows easy transition from a Macintosh-only network, is also present in other Windows server services, such as the Gateway (and Client) Services for NetWare.

Vendor Options

Many NOSs are available from vendors such as Sun, Banyan, SCO, and IBM. This chapter focuses on the four most popular networking product vendors: Microsoft, Novell, Linux, and Apple.

Throughout this chapter we refer to Linux as a "vendor" for ease of explanation, but Linux is actually a freely available operating system that comes in many different versions from a variety of distributors.

In an effort to ease connectivity between different NOSs, the respective companies or organizations include utilities in their operating systems to allow simple connectivity between clients and servers from different vendors, as shown in Figure 9-4. The following sections outline these companies' or organizations' interconnectivity options.

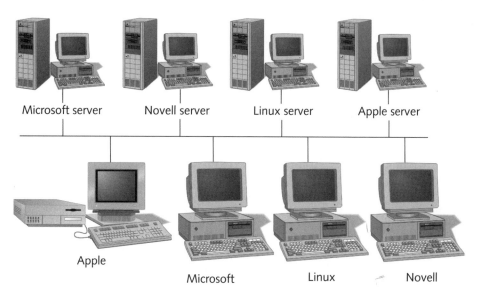

Figure 9-4 Major networking vendors provide easy client and server connectivity

Microsoft Redirector

The following Microsoft operating systems include the Microsoft redirector, which recognizes Microsoft networks: Windows .NET, Windows XP, Windows 2000, Windows NT, Windows Me, Windows 98, Windows 95, and Windows for Workgroups.

Installing the operating system automatically installs the Microsoft redirector. The installation process loads all required drivers and edits the startup files, so that when the computer reboots, the redirector is in place, ready for immediate use.

In addition to allowing clients to access Microsoft network resources, these various implementations all allow users to share their own resources—local hard drive, printer, CD-ROM, and so on—with other users on the network. (This is what makes peer-to-peer networking possible, in fact.)

Microsoft in a Novell Network

To connect a Windows 2000 Professional or Windows XP Professional client to a Novell NetWare network, NWLink and the Client Service for NetWare (CSNW) must be loaded on that Windows machine. When connecting a Windows 2000 or Windows .NET Server to a NetWare network, the NWLink protocol, as well as the Gateway Service for NetWare (GSNW), must be loaded on the Windows server. NWLink is the Microsoft implementation of the IPX/SPX protocol suite. CSNW is the Microsoft implementation of a NetWare requester.

A Windows 98 or Windows Me client can connect to a NetWare network by loading IPX/SPX or NWLink and the Client for NetWare Networks. An enhanced client, the Microsoft Service for NetWare Directory Services, supports Windows 98 connectivity to a NetWare 4.x or 6.x network, as well as connections to all types of NetWare servers, from 2.x to 6.x.

The NetWare client that comes with Windows operating systems will connect only to NetWare servers that are running the IPX/SPX protocol. If a NetWare 5.x or 6.x server is running only the default protocol of TCP/IP, you must install the Novell Client on the Windows PCs. The Novell Client is available from the Novell Web site. The Novell Client is also required to run the Novell management program, which is NWAdmin.

MS-DOS Clients

Each of these NOS vendors offers utilities to allow MS-DOS clients to connect to servers of all four types—Microsoft, Novell, Linux, and Apple. Also, each utility can coexist with the other utilities to provide MS-DOS client connections to all servers.

In an Apple Macintosh network, MS-DOS clients must have AppleShare PC software to use file and print services offered by Apple servers. A LocalTalk card, which includes firmware that controls the link between the AppleTalk network and the PC, may also be installed on a PC to allow the computer to communicate on a LocalTalk network.

In a Linux-based network, an MS-DOS client typically uses some kind of UNIX-derived client software, such as Sun Microsystem's PC-NFS. In this case, PCs participate in a TCP/IP-based network as if they were a "junior version" of Linux or UNIX. On many networks where PC clients need to access Linux servers, particularly when these PCs run some form of DOS or Windows, the popular add-on Linux server known as **Samba** may be installed. It makes Linux servers look and act like Windows Servers instead. In that case, a native Microsoft networking client may be used. (The section "Linux Networks" later in this chapter explains Samba in more detail.)

Novell Networks

The Novell NetWare NOS provides file and print services for the following clients:

- MS-DOS-based clients
- Windows 95, 98, and Me clients
- Windows 2000, Windows XP, and Windows NT clients
- Apple Macintosh clients
- UNIX/Linux clients in the form of UNIX print services and NFS

NetWare 6, Novell's latest version as of this writing, also includes a platform-independent method for accessing file and print services. NetWare's WebAccess provides an interface to server services that is available through any Web browser. This means that users can log on and access their files and printers, regardless of the client operating system they are running and without the need for a NetWare redirector. Figure 9-5 shows the NetWare WebAccess screen. This type of Web-based access to traditional file and print services is expected to grow in popularity and extend to handheld and palmtop computing devices as our workforces become more and more mobile.

9

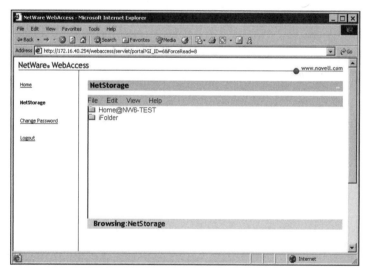

Figure 9-5   NetWare WebAccess screen

Linux Networks

Nearly every distribution of Linux includes a veritable cornucopia of network services. These encompass an implementation of the **Network File System (NFS)**, which is a distributed file system native to UNIX. NFS permits networked machines to export portions of their local file systems and make them available to authorized users elsewhere on the network.

After an exported NFS file system portion, known as a **mount point** or **NFS volume**, is published on the network, authorized users with NFS client capability can install, or mount, that mount point within their local file systems. To these users, this networked NFS volume becomes an extension of their local file systems, accessible the same way as local files. NFS also supports printer sharing, but its file and print services appear most commonly in multivendor networks where PCs are in the minority and the UNIX or Linux operating system predominates.

Because enabling PC clients to access NFS requires adding software to those clients, many Linux administrators prefer to add the Samba service to their Linux servers instead. Samba is named after the Server Message Block (SMB) services it adds to a UNIX or Linux host. Using Samba to permit DOS or Windows machines to access Linux- or UNIX-based file systems and services makes sense for three reasons:

1. Because Samba is a server-based solution, software and services need to be installed only on a relatively small number of servers, rather than a relatively large number of clients.

2. Because Samba is an **open source** software product, you can download it for free from the Internet and install and use it without charge. By contrast, PC-NFS, a commercial software product, costs as much as $300 per machine on a network.

3. Because Samba allows a Linux or UNIX machine to masquerade as a native Microsoft network server, Windows clients need no extra software to access its services. Samba-based resources appear in a Windows browse list along with other network nodes and their file and print shares.

For these reasons, Samba is the preferred service to interconnect Microsoft Windows clients with UNIX or Linux hosts. Samba also permits Linux hosts to connect to Windows shared folders. Users simply create a directory on their Linux drive and then connect that directory to the Windows network share using a utility called smbmount.

Apple Macintosh

Included in every Macintosh are the OS files and the hardware required to communicate in an AppleTalk network. The AppleShare networking software automatically provides file sharing and includes a print server that allows computers to share printers.

Mac OS-X

The newest of the Macintosh operating systems, OS-X is a major departure from previous Mac OS versions. This Mac OS includes network client software to run in a Macintosh, Windows, or UNIX environment. In short, OS-X negates the need for Windows servers to install special services for Macintosh computers or AppleTalk protocols because OS-X provides support for native Windows file sharing through SMB services. In addition, because Mac OS-X is built upon a UNIX core, OS-X is right at home in a UNIX environment. Backward-compatible support is provided for traditional

Macintosh file sharing through other Macs or through Windows or NetWare servers providing Macintosh services.

Handheld Computing Environment

The handheld computing market is somewhat fragmented—there is no clear hardware or software standard on which users can rely. The lack of compatibility between competing manufacturers presents a particular challenge for network administrators who must integrate these devices into the corporate computing environment.

 The two operating systems that are leading the way in the handheld arena are the Palm OS, by Palm OS, and the Microsoft PocketPC.

One of the key challenges of managing handheld computers on a LAN is that, unlike desktop computers, the handheld computers are rarely connected to the corporate LAN. In addition, while most handheld devices offer some type of Ethernet connection, other options for connecting include modem, infrared communications, and serial links. Maintaining a working environment for these handhelds while also maintaining security and data integrity is the latest challenge posed to network administrators.

Desktop computers connect to the corporate network to access shared resources on a continuous basis, but the normal operating mode of a handheld computer is disconnected and mobile. Thus, the primary reason for connecting to the corporate LAN is to synchronize data between the network and the handheld. This synchronization is often accomplished with a software program loaded on a user's desktop computer. The handheld device then is connected to a cradle that has a connection to the desktop.

In recognition that handheld computing is here to stay and is an integral part of the corporate computing environment, enterprise software companies have developed server-based software that handles synchronization, backup, and even application loading for all handheld computers in a company. This sector of the computing industry is growing rapidly as the technology matures, and before long, managing and configuring handheld computers will be just another trick in the network administrator's bag of magic.

CENTRALIZED VERSUS CLIENT/SERVER COMPUTING

The client/server model for computing evolved from the centralized computing environment. In **centralized computing**, mainframes perform all processing and "dumb" terminals connect directly to the mainframe. PCs, and so-called "thin clients" attached to a terminal server of some kind can also access a mainframe. In essence, all these approaches behave much the same: the terminal requests information from the mainframe, and the mainframe retrieves and displays the information on the terminal. Generally character-based, these applications require little input from the PC, thin client, or terminal.

When a central computer performs processing in a network environment, traffic increases greatly, because for every keystroke a user makes, a packet is sent across the network to the mainframe. Then the mainframe sends a response, which can be quite voluminous.

This type of network generates a large amount of data and does not efficiently use the PCs available today. As a result, client/server computing is replacing many centralized computing applications.

Understanding Terminal Services

Halfway through the Windows NT Server product cycle and with the release of Windows 2000 Server, Microsoft included a software subsystem called Terminal Services. Essentially, **Terminal Services** provides support for a specialized kind of network processing that is quite useful under certain circumstances.

Terminal Services permits clients to run large or complex applications on older, less-capable clients or on minimal computers, called thin clients, by transferring the burden of client processing to the server. A **thin client** is a bare-bones PC that includes little more than a local keyboard, display device, network interface, and sufficient memory and processing power to access the network to connect to a server running Terminal Services.

Terminal Services is well suited for certain uses, including:

- Providing access to modern Windows applications on older PCs or thin clients that otherwise might not be able to run those applications

- Providing access to centralized applications or services that otherwise would have to be installed on client machines

- Permitting remote clients using narrow bandwidth connections (usually dial-up to the Internet or a private network) to access modern, powerful Windows applications without imposing bandwidth-related performance delays

Terminal Services makes it possible for older, less-capable PCs, thin clients, or narrow bandwidth remote users to run modern, demanding Windows applications in an interesting way. For each user, the server that runs Terminal Services runs a software-based "virtual PC" that actually runs the services or applications on the user's behalf. The client runs a small program that intercepts keystrokes and mouse activity on the local machine, and then sends that information to the virtual PC running on the server, where all real processing takes place. The server then sends only screen updates to the client machine in response to user input.

Because the only processing that the local client handles is user input and displaying program output, the client doesn't require much power or capability. This explains how older PCs, thin clients, and remote users on slow connections can operate like fully functional, heavily loaded modern PCs—the virtual PCs that work on their behalf do indeed deliver state-of-the-art capabilities.

Of course, this means that the servers that run Terminal Services must be heavily configured, with large amounts of RAM and disk space, and one or more (but usually four or more) powerful CPUs, to provide the horsepower required to create and operate multiple virtual PCs. However, sometimes companies must support older PCs (for embedded systems on a factory floor, for instance, where removing and replacing machines is often difficult). Using special-purpose, single-use applications, such as point of sale (cash register) or data entry stations, means that providing general-purpose PCs to users does not always make sense. Finally, when remote users must communicate through low-bandwidth connections, it is more effective to put as much processing activity and power on the client or remote side of the connection as possible. This limits the amount of traffic that must travel across the remote connection. In all of these cases, Terminal Services provides a useful solution for such computing needs.

In addition to Microsoft Terminal Services, which supports PCs that run DOS or some form of Windows, other vendors offer terminal server products. Some, like those from Citrix (the well-known WinFrame and MetaFrame products), support multiple-client operating systems and may make sense when UNIX or Linux and Macintosh machines require terminal services along with Microsoft-based PCs. In addition, Linux includes support for Telnet services and X Window System graphical clients, so any TCP/IP-based computer can obtain the same services that Terminal Services provides, except access to Windows-based applications.

Thin-Client Computing

Some operating systems include capabilities for thin clients to connect to the server, to access resources, and to run applications, all with considerably fewer resources than the typical desktop computer. Thin clients add the following benefits to the computing environment:

- *No removable storage.* Without a floppy drive or ZIP disk, employees cannot copy sensitive files from the corporate server to a floppy or ZIP disk to take home. In addition, viruses cannot be brought into the corporate LAN via these media types.

- *No hard drive.* Without a hard drive, there are few configuration tasks necessary on the local thin-client computer. This means that when the operating system or applications must be upgraded, they need to be upgraded only at the server. This significantly decreases problems caused by old or incompatible software. Not having a hard disk saves money and provides better reliability. The lack of a hard disk also means that viruses have no place to live on the machine.

- *Lower total cost of ownership.* Thin clients typically cost less than a full-blown desktop PC. In addition, because these computers can be managed completely from a centralized server, the support costs are dramatically lower. Thus, the total cost of ownership of thin clients is considerably less than desktop PCs.

Back to the Future: The Mainframe Environment

As you already learned, the mainframe computers originally introduced to users in the late 1950s and early 1960s also introduced the centralized computing model, which is the basis of terminal services. Even today, certain transaction-intensive applications—such as large-scale airline, hotel, and rental car applications—work well with mainframes and terminals (or terminal emulation, which temporarily transforms a fully functional PC into a simple terminal). Although computing currently comes in many forms, the centralized mainframe, with huge numbers of terminals accessing its large-scale, heavily trafficked data collections, remains a viable processing model for applications. Despite many predictions of their demise, mainframes continue to be important computing resources today and for the foreseeable future.

CLIENT/SERVER ENVIRONMENT

The client/server method of network communications is currently the most popular. Its ease of implementation and scalability make it a good choice in many different networking environments.

A client is a computer that requests access to shared network resources from a server, a computer that provides shared resources (files and directories, printers, databases, and so on) in response to client requests. **Client/server computing** generally refers to a network structure in which the client computer and the server computer share the processing requirements.

Note that some services provided by file servers are often not considered client/server. One such service is shared-file storage. For example, many popular e-mail programs, such as Microsoft Exchange Server and Outlook or Eudora, use the file server as a central location to store messages. When users access the e-mail program, they retrieve the data from a specific directory on the server. Many other programs, such as scheduling programs, database management systems, and personal information managers, use this kind of data retrieval.

A shared-file network configuration makes better use of the power of the PC but does not fully utilize a server's potential. This implementation also does not solve the problem of network traffic. Unlike a terminal-based application that sends each keystroke, client-side applications on the PC retrieve large amounts of data across the network. Such applications then process that data locally (on the client machine) before re-sending updated data files back to the server.

One of the most prominent uses of the client/server model today is the World Wide Web (WWW). When you type the name of a particular Web site in the Address text box of your Web browser, your computer sends a request to the server that's responsible for that site. That server processes your request and returns the corresponding page. Your browser receives the file, formats it for your screen, determines if any other data, such as graphics, are required, and displays the page. At this point, the server is no longer responsible for communication. If you use a hyperlink to jump to another page, click a graphic to view it, or click a link to send e-mail, your computer then sends the request to the server (the same server or another), and the process begins again.

Client/Server Model in a Database Environment

Database management systems (DBMSs) are another example of efficient use of the client/server model. The client in a DBMS environment uses the **Structured Query Language (SQL)** to translate what the user sees into a request that the database can understand. IBM designed SQL to provide a relatively simple way to manipulate data using language based on English rather than using a cryptic programming language. Its ease of use prompted many database vendors to adopt SQL as their query language as well, and it is now a de facto standard for database queries in general.

Figure 9-6 illustrates the two major components in a client/server SQL environment:

- The application, often referred to as the **front end** or client
- The database server, also referred to as the **back end** or server

9

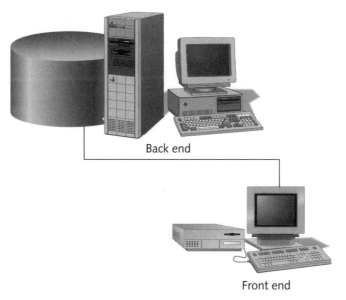

Back end

Front end

Figure 9-6 Front-end and back-end systems in a DBMS

Requesting data from a server in SQL is a six-step process:

1. The user requests the data.
2. The client software translates that request into SQL.
3. The SQL request is sent across the network to the server.

4. The server processes the request.

5. The results are sent back across the network to the client software.

6. The results are presented to the user.

In this type of DBMS environment, the server does not contain user interface software. The client is responsible for presenting the data in a usable form, both with user interfaces and report writing. It accepts instructions from the user, formats them for the server, and sends its requests to the server.

The server in this environment is usually dedicated to storing and managing data, so most database functions occur within the server. The server receives requests from clients, processes them, and returns the information to the client. The back-end processing that takes place to fulfill a user's request includes sorting data and extracting the requested data from the database.

Client/Server Architecture

There are a number of ways to implement a client/server environment. Figure 9-7 illustrates two of the most-often used:

- Single database server

- Multiple database servers (distributed or multitiered database)

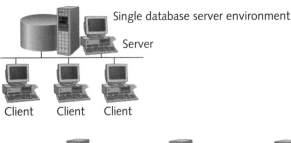

Single database server environment

Server

Client   Client   Client

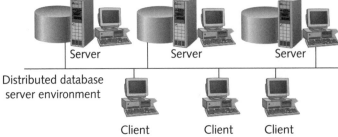

Server   Server   Server

Distributed database
server environment

Client   Client   Client

Figure 9-7   Single versus multiple servers in a database environment

Advantages of Working in a Client/Server Environment

The client/server networking environment has many advantages over centralized computing. It more efficiently uses the computers, both front end and back end, as well as the network.

By using the superior processing power of the server for functions such as database queries, the client computer's configuration can be less extensive. It can have a smaller processor and less RAM than the server because it does not have to search for the data. Drive space on the client can be reserved for local applications, rather than for storage of large amounts of database information.

One additional benefit of the client/server environment in general is centralized location. Because all file services and data reside on servers, the servers are easy to secure and maintain in one location. Centralization also simplifies the back-up process and ensures that security can be maintained for all users across all servers.

WEB-BASED COMPUTING ENVIRONMENTS

9

Having a connection to the Internet used to be considered a luxury; today it is a necessity, and Internet connections can be found almost anywhere: work, home, the library, hotels, even the airport. Because of this, many traditional operating systems are making their file and print services available over a standard Web browser. We already discussed how Novell provides this capability in NetWare 6. An emerging technology called WebDAV is attempting to go one step further by providing a single framework that can be used on all client and server computing platforms.

WebDAV is an extension to HTTP (the protocol used for transferring Web pages) that allows a Web browser to exercise traditional file system tasks, including file reads, file writes, file locking, and version control. Initially, the applications for WebDAV included document collaboration and Web publishing, but its potential is limitless. For instance, e-mail, calendaring, and a host of other applications can be accomplished with a single client. Because WebDAV capabilities are expandable, it might be possible in the future to do away with traditional redirectors, FTP, and e-mail clients in favor of a single client/server technology based on the WebDAV protocol. Whether WebDAV lives up to its promise, it is clear that the direction client/server networking is taking is one of providing simple-to-use, vendor-independent access to all of your networking resources. For more information on WebDAV, see *www.webdav.org*.

CHAPTER SUMMARY

- Interconnectivity between multiple-vendor operating systems is becoming increasingly necessary in networking. Two ways to connect multivendor environments ease the stress of making these connections.

- A client-based multivendor network environment relies on the client computer's redirectors to decide which server should be sent the request. For example, a computer that requires connections to both a NetWare server and a Windows 2000 server loads software to connect to both servers.

- In a server-based solution, the server supports multiple client types. For example, a computer running Windows 2000 Server can support Microsoft, Novell, or Apple clients.

- The four major networking product vendors and organizations—Microsoft, Novell, Linux, and Apple—support connectivity to each others' NOSs.

- Using the processing power of a mainframe computer creates a centralized computer environment. This type of computing can generate large amounts of network traffic and does not fully exploit the power available in PCs today. It is not well suited for typical user productivity applications, such as word processing, spreadsheets, e-mail, and so forth. Mainframes still play a valid role on modern networks, especially for large-scale, transaction-oriented applications, such as airline, hotel, and rental car reservation systems, and financial trading applications.

- Server-based terminal services can provide useful access to networks and centralized server-based resources for remote users away from the network, or for single-use workstations (such as point of sale or data entry terminals).

- The handheld computing environment is growing in leaps and bounds. The non-standardized hardware and software used for these devices poses particular challenges for the network administrator.

- In a client/server computing environment, the PC and the server share processing and more efficiently use the resources of both machines. The WWW is a good example of a client/server networking environment. When you ask for a Web page, your browser (the client) asks the server to send you the page. This type of computing environment reduces network traffic.

- Most database management systems use SQL as their query language. The database application resides on the client, or front end, while the server, or back end, stores and maintains the data.

- The trend in today's networking environment is to remove the obstacles and incompatibilities of working in a multivendor environment. To that end, a promising new technology, WebDAV, hopes to make any Web-enabled device a client to file-sharing, e-mail, and calendaring applications.

KEY TERMS

back end — A server in a client/server networking environment.

centralized computing — A computing environment in which all processing takes place on a mainframe or central computer.

client-based multivendor solution — When multiple redirectors are loaded on a client, the client can communicate with servers from different vendors.

client/server computing — A computing environment in which the processing is divided between the client and the server.

database management system (DBMS) — A client/server computing environment that uses SQL to retrieve data from the server.

front end — A client in a client/server networking environment.

mount point — Terminology that describes a portion of a file system published for access through NFS to users who are authorized to add that file system portion to their local file systems. NFS originated in the UNIX world and is still common on UNIX and Linux hosts.

Network File System (NFS) — A distributed file system originally developed at Sun Microsystems. It supports network-based file and printer sharing using TCP/IP-based network protocols.

NFS volume — An NFS mount point that functions as a standalone local drive on a user's desktop; it may also sometimes refer to an NFS mount point situated at the root of a drive on the machine where the mount point is exported.

open source — Software that's always available at no charge, even after modifications to its source code.

Samba — An open source software suite that makes Linux servers look and act like Windows Servers. It permits DOS or Windows clients to access Linux- or UNIX-based file systems and services without special software on the client end.

server-based multivendor solution — A server, such as one running Windows 2000 Server, that can readily communicate with clients from multiple vendors.

Structured Query Language (SQL) — Standard database query language designed by IBM.

Terminal Services — A software subsystem for Windows NT and Windows 2000 Server that permits clients to run large or complex applications on computers with minimal processing power by transferring the burden of client processing to the server.

thin client — A networked computer with keyboard, pointing device (mouse), display, network interface, and sufficient processing power to access terminal services or a mainframe, where the real application processing occurs.

9

REVIEW QUESTIONS

1. _____ must be loaded on any Windows 2000 or Windows NT system to enable it to connect to a Novell network.

2. The four major networking product vendors are:

    a. Microsoft

    b. Novell

    c. Banyan

    d. Apple

    e. Linux

3. Of the two computing environments, _____ generates more network traffic.

4. A _____-based multivendor network solution provides connectivity by loading multiple redirectors.

    a. client

    b. server

    c. workstation

    d. peer

5. The _____ translates the request from the user into SQL in a DBMS environment.

6. A(n) _____ computer provides shared resources in a client/server network.

    a. client

    b. server

    c. workstation

    d. application

7. In a DBMS environment, the _____ is generally used for data storage.

8. In a client/server environment, the client must have as much or more RAM than the server. True or false?

9. _____ computing is replacing _____ computing today.

10. A(n) _____ computing environment uses the processing power of only one system.

11. The _____ is the Microsoft implementation of a NetWare requester.

12. The NetWare operating system includes requesters for what types of clients?

13. Mac OS-X provides client software capable of accessing server resources in a Windows, Macintosh, or UNIX environment. True or false?

14. A(n) _____ computer uses shared resources on a network.

   a. client

   b. server

   c. workstation

   d. application

15. By using a _____-based multivendor solution, different clients are easily connected to a server.

   a. client

   b. server

   c. network

   d. WAN

16. In a DBMS environment, the application is sometimes called the _____.

17. The Microsoft redirector that is included with the _____ operating system(s) allows users to share local resources.

18. _____ is an enhanced redirector from Microsoft that connects Windows 95 computers to NetWare 4.x and higher networks.

19. _____ is a database language based on English.

20. The WWW is an example of a _____ computing environment.

   a. workstation

   b. client/server

   c. peer-to-peer

   d. all of the above

21. Terminal services permit clients to run applications locally and access data remotely. True or false?

22. Which of the following types of clients are most likely to benefit from terminal services? (Choose all that apply.)

   a. older, less-capable PCs

   b. thin clients

   c. network-attached PCs with high-bandwidth connections

   d. remotely-attached PCs with narrow-bandwidth connections

   e. none of the above

9

23. When sharing files and printers on a Linux machine, the best solution is
     _____.

    a. Services for Macintosh

    b. PC-NFS

    c. Samba

    d. Client Service for NetWare

24. In which one of the following operating systems did NFS originate?

    a. Windows NT

    b. Macintosh OS

    c. UNIX

    d. Windows for Workgroups

25. A new Web-based technology, called _____, promises to permit any
    Web-enabled client to access shared network resources.

HANDS-ON PROJECTS

Services for Macintosh and Gateway Services for NetWare can be added to a
Windows 2000 Server system to allow easy connectivity for Macintosh and NetWare
clients. For a Windows 98, Windows NT, or Windows 2000/XP client, the Client for
NetWare Networks (or Client Service for NetWare, depending on the OS) and
IPX/SPX must be loaded to connect to a NetWare network. In Hands-on Project 9-1,
you install the Services for Macintosh on a Windows NT or Windows 2000 server,
view the available properties, and then remove the service. In Hands-on Project 9-2, you
install the NetWare client service on a Windows 98, Windows NT, or Windows 2000
workstation, view its available properties, and remove the client.

Project 9-1

To install, view, and remove Services for Macintosh on a Windows NT Server 4.0 computer:

1. Right-click the **Network Neighborhood** icon on the Windows desktop, and
   select the **Properties** option.

2. Select the **Services** tab, which looks similar to that shown in Figure 9-8.

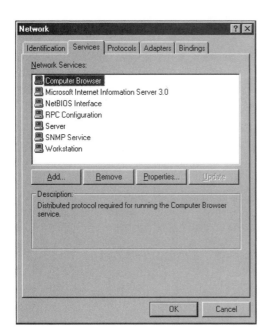

Figure 9-8   Services tab in Windows NT

3. Click the **Add** button.

4. From the list of available services, select **Services for Macintosh** and click **OK**.

5. A prompt asks you to supply the path to the installation files for Windows NT, which, in this case, is **E:\I386** (or the location specified by your instructor). Click the **Continue** button.

6. When the system finishes updating the files, click the **Close** button.

7. For the changes to take effect, you must restart the computer. When prompted, click the **Yes** button.

8. Once the system finishes rebooting, start the Network applet again by right-clicking **Network Neighborhood** and selecting **Properties** from the menu.

9. Select the **Services** tab.

10. Select **Services for Macintosh**, and click the **Properties** button.

11. Examine the properties of the service. The General tab defines in which AppleTalk Default Zone the computer is located, or, for a multihomed computer (a computer with multiple NICs), the AppleTalk Default Zone for each NIC. In a multihomed computer, use the Routing tab to route AppleTalk traffic.

12. Click the **OK** button.

13. Click **Remove** to remove the Services for Macintosh from the computer.

14. When asked to confirm the deletion of this service, click the **Yes** button.

15. Click the **Close** button.

16. For the changes to take effect, you must restart the system. When prompted, click the **Yes** button.

To install, view, and remove File Services for Macintosh and Print Services for Macintosh on a Windows 2000 Server computer:

1. Right-click the **My Network Places** icon on the Windows desktop, and select the **Properties** option. The Network and Dial-up Connections dialog box opens. See Figure 9-9.

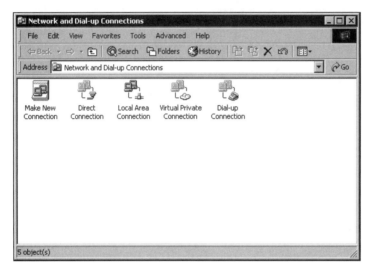

Figure 9-9   Network and Dial-up Connections dialog box in Windows 2000 Server

2. Click **Advanced** on the menu bar, and select **Optional Networking Components**. The Windows Optional Networking Components Wizard opens. See Figure 9-10.

3. Select **Other Network File and Print Services**.

4. Click **Details**. The Other Network File and Print Services dialog box opens.

5. Click the **File Services for Macintosh** and **Print Services for Macintosh** check boxes. See Figure 9-11.

6. Click **OK**.

7. Click **Next**.

8. Wait while Windows 2000 Server installs the necessary files for these networking components. If your Windows 2000 Server CD is not available, you are prompted to provide the path to the distribution files. If not already installed, AppleTalk installs automatically along with the Macintosh network services.

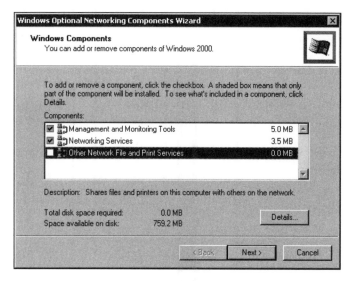

Figure 9-10   Windows Optional Networking Components Wizard in Windows 2000 Server

9

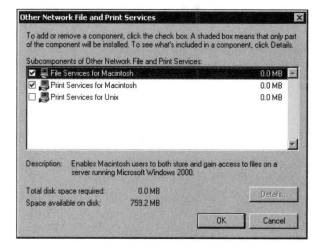

Figure 9-11   File Services for Macintosh and Print Services for Macintosh subcomponents

9. Rebooting is usually not necessary. However, if prompted, reboot your system.

10. If the Network and Dial-up Connections dialog box is not open, open it by right-clicking the **My Network Places** icon on the Windows desktop and selecting the **Properties** option.

11. Right-click the **Local Area Connection** icon that Macintosh clients will use, and select the **Properties** option.

12. Select the **AppleTalk Protocol** from the Local Area Connection Properties dialog box.

13. Click the **Properties** button. The AppleTalk Protocol Properties dialog box opens.

14. From this dialog box, you can select the AppleTalk zone in which this system will appear.

> The Macintosh systems connected to the network segment define the selections in this pull-down list. Windows 2000 does not define or control AppleTalk zones; it can only join or communicate with an existing zone.

15. Click **OK** to close this dialog box.

16. Click **Close** to return to the Network and Dial-up Connections dialog box.

17. To remove Macintosh support, you must first remove all Macintosh services (whether File Services and/or Print Services) and then remove the AppleTalk protocol itself. To do this, select **Advanced** on the menu bar in the Network and Dial-up Connections dialog box, and then select the **Optional Networking Components** option.

18. Select **Other Network File and Print Services**.

19. Click **Details**.

20. Deselect **File Services for Macintosh and Print Services for Macintosh**.

21. Click **OK**.

22. Click **Next**. Windows 2000 removes the networking components.

23. Right-click the **Local Area Connection** icon that Macintosh clients use, and select the **Properties** option.

24. Select **AppleTalk Protocol**.

25. Click **Uninstall**.

26. Click **Yes** to confirm removal. Windows 2000 removes the protocol.

27. Click **OK** or **Close** to close the Local Area Connection Properties dialog box.

28. Click **Yes** to restart the computer.

Project 9-2

Microsoft includes NetWare Client software that coexists with the Client for Microsoft Networks installed by default on all of its modern Windows operating systems—namely Windows 98, Windows Me, Windows NT, and Windows 2000. In this project, you step through its installation on Windows 98, Windows 2000, or Windows NT.

To install the Client for NetWare Networks on a Windows 98 workstation, view its available properties, and remove the client:

1. Right-click the **Network Neighborhood** icon on the desktop, and select the **Properties** option.

2. Click the **Add** button.

3. Select the **Client** option and click **Add**.

4. Select **Microsoft** from the leftmost list.

5. Select **Client for NetWare Networks** from the rightmost list. Click the **OK** button. (This automatically adds the IPX/SPX-compatible protocol to the list of installed network components.)

6. Click the **OK** button.

7. You may be asked for the path to the Windows 98 installation files. In this case, they are in **C:\WINDOWS\OPTIONS\CABS** (or the location specified by your instructor). Click **OK** to complete the operation.

8. When asked to restart the computer, click the **Yes** button.

9. After the computer restarts, start the Network applet again by right-clicking **Network Neighborhood** and selecting the **Properties** option.

10. Select the **Client for NetWare Networks**, and click the **Properties** button.

11. Examine the properties tabs. The General tab includes fields for preferred server, first network drive, and a check box to enable login script processing. The Advanced tab includes advanced Novell functions.

12. Click the **Cancel** button.

13. Select the **IPX/SPX-compatible Protocol** (for your network card), and click the **Properties** button.

14. Examine the properties of this protocol. The NetBIOS tab allows you to enable NetBIOS over IPX/SPX. The Advanced tab includes options for Frame Type, Maximum Connections, Source Routing, and manual Network Address configuration. The Bindings tab displays which network components can use IPX/SPX. This should include Client for Microsoft Networks, as well as the Client for NetWare Networks.

15. Click the **Cancel** button.

16. With IPX/SPX still highlighted, click the **Remove** button. Notice that this automatically removes Client for NetWare Networks as well.

 If an IPX/SPX protocol remains, remove it also.

17. Click the **OK** button.

18. For the changes to take effect, you must restart the computer. When prompted, click the **Yes** button.

To install the Client Service for NetWare on a Windows NT workstation and then remove the client:

1. Right-click the **Network Neighborhood** icon on the desktop, and select the **Properties** option.

2. Select the **Services** tab.

3. Click the **Add** button.

4. Select **Client Service for NetWare**, and click the **OK** button.

5. You are asked for the path to the Windows NT installation files. In this case, they are in **E:\I386** (or the location specified by your instructor). Click **Continue** to complete the operation.

6. Click **Close**.

7. When asked to restart the computer, click the **Yes** button.

8. After the computer restarts, start the Network applet again by right-clicking **Network Neighborhood** and selecting the **Properties** option.

9. Select the **Services** tab.

10. Select the **Client Service for Netware** service. Notice that you cannot access any properties (the button is dimmed) unless you actually establish a connection to a real NetWare server on your network.

11. To remove Client Service for NetWare, highlight **Client Service for Netware**, and then click the **Remove** button.

12. When asked if you want to permanently remove the service, click the **Yes** button. (This automatically removes the Client Service for NetWare.)

13. Click the **Close** button.

14. For the changes to take effect, you must restart the computer. Click the **Yes** button.

To install the Client Service for NetWare on a Windows 2000 workstation and remove the client:

1. Right-click the **My Network Places** icon on the desktop, and select the **Properties** option.

2. Right-click the **Local Area Connection** icon, and then select the **Properties** option.

3. Click the **Install** button in the Local Area Connection Properties window, and then make sure the Client entry in the Select Network Component Type window is highlighted. (If not, click it once to highlight it.) Click the **Add** button.

4. Wait until the next window, labeled Select Network Client, appears; highlight the **Client Service for NetWare** entry, and then click the **OK** button.

5. You may be prompted for a path to the installation files. (Please obtain this information from your instructor.) After the files are loaded and installed, you are prompted to restart your computer. Click **Yes** in the Local Network window to

restart your computer. (This is one of a few situations in which you must restart a Windows 2000 computer for configuration changes to take effect.)

6. Before the restart operation completes, you are asked to supply information to the Select NetWare Logon window. Ordinarily, you use this to supply a preferred NetWare server for bindery-based NetWare networks, to designate a default NDS directory tree and directory context, and to indicate if login scripts should execute at login. In this case, type **Server1** (or another NetWare server name provided by your instructor) in the Preferred Server text box, and then click the **OK** button. Unless Server1 or the alternate server exists on your local network, Windows 2000 cannot locate that server and asks if you want to use it as your preferred server. Click **OK** to close this dialog box and continue rebooting.

7. After the computer restarts, the Network and Dial-up Connections window should appear on your desktop. Right-click the **Local Area Connection** icon, and then select the **Properties** option.

8. When the Local Area Connection Properties window appears, the Client Service for NetWare entry should be checked and highlighted. Notice that you cannot access any properties (the button is dimmed) unless you actually establish a connection to a real NetWare server on your network.

9. Click the **Uninstall** button to remove the Client Service for NetWare, and then click **Yes** in the removal confirmation dialog box.

10. Click **Yes** to permit Windows 2000 to restart your machine and remove the NetWare client code from your system. When your machine finishes rebooting, you've completed this project.

Project 9-3

Samba, an open source implementation of an SMB server for Linux and UNIX, permits such hosts to masquerade as Windows servers on a Microsoft network. Samba has the undeniable advantages of no cost and no required changes to modern Windows clients to permit access to file and print shares. (Its status as an open source software product means that anyone may download it at no charge. In fact, Samba is now included with numerous Linux distributions, having proven its worth on many networks.) In this project, you visit Samba's home at *www.samba.org*, inspect the various download sites available, and read some documentation about this useful software product.

To view the official Samba download sites on the Web and learn more about Samba's capabilities:

1. Open your Web browser, and then type **www.samba.org** in the Address text box. Press **Enter** to visit this site.

2. The home page contains pointers to Samba Web sites (where information about the product resides) and to Samba download sites (where you can download the executable code for Samba). Click the first **USA** entry beneath the "Web Sites" heading (or whichever link your instructor tells you to select).

9

3. Click the **documentation** link in the left column, scroll down the resulting page, and then click **An Introduction to Samba** in the right column labeled "Other Documentation."

4. Read the document. Expand the acronym CIFS and determine why it's important on networks with multiple types of servers.

5. Close your Web browser unless you plan to proceed immediately to the next Hands-on Project.

Project 9-4

Microsoft includes Terminal Services with Windows 2000 Server and Windows .NET Server and makes a special release of Windows NT Server (called Terminal Server Edition) available to its customers. Both versions of this service are based on code originally developed by Citrix, a leading vendor of terminal services software and solutions. In this project, you visit the Citrix Web site to learn more about its Nfuse product that makes applications available through any Web browser (that's about as platform-independent as you can get). You'll also learn about Citrix's multiplatform terminal services products.

To learn more about state-of-the art remote application access and about a leading terminal services software products family:

1. Open your Web browser, and then type **www.citrix.com** in the Address text box. Press **Enter** or click **Go** to visit this site.

2. The Citrix home page appears. Click the **Products** hyperlink, and then find and click the Citrix **Nfuse Classic** link under "Portal Products" on the left menu.

3. Read the resulting page, and then click the **Demo Room** link under the "Resources" heading. Click the **Login** button. Feel free to click **Skip Intro** to bypass the animated flash graphics that appear. As you read through each page, click the > symbol to proceed to the next page. Notice the variety of products and services that Citrix offers for Windows 2000. (These explain why Citrix products remain popular and are widely purchased, even though Microsoft bundles a scaled-down version as its Terminal Services in Windows 2000.)

4. Write a memo to your instructor explaining the concept of a "server farm." Why do you think it's important for the Citrix MetaFrame application?

5. Read through the demo and feel free to explore more of this site. Then close your Web browser.

Project 9-5

This project walks you through the process of installing and configuring Terminal Services on Windows 2000 Server for the purposes of remote administration.

To install and configure Terminal Services:

1. Log on to Windows 2000 Server.

2. Open the Control Panel by clicking **Start**, **Settings**, and **Control Panel**.

3. From the Control Panel, double-click **Add/Remove Programs**.

4. From the left column, click **Add/Remove Windows Components**.

5. Scroll down the list of components until you see Terminal Services. Click the **Terminal Services** check box. Then click **Next**.

6. Click the **Remote Administration** option button, and then click **Next**.

7. You will be asked to insert the Windows 2000 Server CD. Insert the CD and click **OK**.

8. When the files have finished copying, click **Finish**. When asked if you would like to restart your computer, remove the CD from the drive and click **Yes**.

9. When the server reboots, log on. Terminal services is now running.

10. To check Terminal Services configuration, go to **Start**, **Programs**, **Administrative Tools**, and select **Terminal Services Configuration**. Browse the configuration options available, and then close Terminal Services Configuration.

9

Project 9-6

This project walks you through connecting to a Windows Terminal Services server using the Remote Desktop applet in Windows XP Professional. Your instructor will provide you with the server name and username and password needed to connect.

To connect to a Windows Terminal Services server:

1. To open a remote desktop connection to a Windows Terminal Services server, go to **Start**, **Programs**, **Accessories**, and **Communications**, and select **Remote Desktop Connection**.

2. When the Remote Desktop Connection dialog box opens, type the server name in the Computer text box and click **Connect**.

3. When prompted for a username and password, type the user name and password provided by your instructor.

4. You are now connected to the server desktop through Terminal Services.

5. Change from full-screen mode to window-mode. Click the **Maximize** button on the tab at the top of the screen so that you can see both your Windows XP desktop and your Windows 2000 Server desktop. At this point, you can perform any tasks on the Windows 2000 Server as if you were sitting at its keyboard.

6. To close the connection, close the Remote Desktop window.

CASE PROJECTS

1. Your company just merged with another similarly sized organization. Your network consists of two Windows NT servers, five Windows NT Workstation computers, 10 Macintosh computers of various shapes and sizes, and 25 Windows 98 systems. All of your computers, including the Macintoshes, currently communicate in an Ethernet environment.

   Your new partner company runs a Novell NetWare network. It has two servers and 20 client workstations, both Windows 98 and MS-DOS, also on Ethernet. The new company decides to link the two networks using a T1 line.

   Develop a plan that allows clients from both networks to access servers on both networks. Outline any software that must be changed or added to the clients and/or the servers.

2. Three divisions in your company—accounting, advertising, and engineering—have each run in their own workgroup environment for over a year. Engineering runs a NetWare Lite network with no server, but has nine NetWare clients. The Advertising department uses LocalTalk, which is built into its Macintosh computers. Accounting uses Windows 98 to share its files and printers. The MIS department's task is to connect these three workgroups, and purchase a server if necessary.

   Develop a solution that allows these three divisions to share resources easily.

3. We've Got Parts Inc. distributes industrial machine replacement parts to its clients worldwide. The company's network includes 40 workstations and a single server. The president wants all employees to access a new order/inventory database that will interface with the accounting database currently residing on its server. Choose either a client/server or a client-based computing model and an appropriate database architecture. Explain your choices. How could the company improve the availability and fault tolerance of its implementation?

4. At XYZ Corp., the sales staff carries laptops and sometimes requires access to the corporate network to read e-mail, access a customer contact database, place orders, and check their status. In most cases, salespeople dial in using 28.8-Kbps modems. They complain that it takes an inordinately long time to access the customer contacts database and to interact with the order-handling system. What kind of remote access could they use instead of Dial-up Networking, if they go through a properly configured Windows 2000 Server, that would speed their access? Explain how this performance improvement is achieved.

5. BlueSkies Inc., a regional airline based in Des Moines, decided to go nationwide, open at least two reservation counters in every U.S. city with a population over 800,000, and create a Web site where customers can make reservations online. The company expects to handle over 200,000 transactions per day. Select either a terminal services- or mainframe-based architecture for the implementation, and defend your choice. Be sure to explain why your solution is superior to the alternate architecture.

10

NETWORK ADMINISTRATION AND SUPPORT

After reading this chapter and completing the exercises, you will be able to:

♦ Manage networked accounts

♦ Enhance network performance

♦ Create a network security plan

♦ Protect your servers from data loss

Network administration involves much more responsibility than simply installing and troubleshooting hardware. After the hardware is installed and configured, the network administrator must ensure that the network performs to specifications, verify that users can easily access the resources they are authorized to use, monitor network traffic, and be responsible for security issues.

Management of **user accounts** and **groups** is a critical aspect of fulfilling the responsibilities of network management. A user account is a collection of information known about an individual user, including an account name, associated password, and a set of access permissions for network resources. A group, on the other hand, is a named collection of user accounts, usually created for resource sharing specific to that group's needs. For example, assume that the Design group needs access to the ColorLaser1 printer. Rather than adding printer permissions for each user account in the Design department, you need to create and assign print permission to the Design group only once. You can grant **rights**—the access to and control over various objects and functions on the network—to individual user accounts or to groups. This chapter explains how to set up and manage user accounts and groups, how to monitor network performance, and how to provide network security.

MANAGING NETWORKED ACCOUNTS

The main task of network management is basic: make sure all users can access resources they are allowed to access, and prevent users from accessing resources they don't have permission to access (or shouldn't be allowed to access). This seemingly simple concept isn't always easy to apply, but there are ways to assign users and groups permissions to the resources they need without threatening system security. The following sections discuss user and group accounts and how to set up and maintain them.

The principles of user management for Windows and Linux systems are quite similar, but the management utilities that operate in both environments are quite different. Windows operating systems use graphical interfaces, such as the User Manager for Domains (in Windows NT) and the Active Directory Users and Computers utilities (in Windows 2000 Server and .NET Server after Active Directory is enabled). In Linux, as in Windows systems, this information resides in specially formatted files buried deep within the system. In Linux, you are much more likely to open and operate on such files directly, while a graphical interface mediates access in Windows systems. As you read through the sections that follow, note that most customary administrative activities (such as creating and managing users or groups) are common to nearly all network operating systems. The differences, of course, lie in the details, but the principles and practices are largely the same. To simplify the discussion that follows, focus is placed on the Windows 2000 Server operating system. Most concepts apply equally to Windows NT Server and Windows .NET server, but any differences will be indicated.

Creating User Accounts

Windows server operating systems come with two predefined accounts: the Administrator account, for management duties; and the Guest account, for users who have no personal account in the local domain. It's unlikely, however, that you will regularly use either of these accounts. It is unclear who's doing what to a system if everybody with administrative access to a machine uses the default account "Administrator." Therefore, employees who will have administrator duties should no longer use the Administrator account after they receive their own uniquely named accounts, each with administrative privileges. After that, if anyone attempts to use the Administrator account, you'll know a break-in is probably being attempted.

That being said, it is still important to provide the Administrator account with a strong password and to guard it carefully. The Administrator account cannot be disabled or deleted. Therefore, if you forget the password to your personal account or your personal account is disabled, you can still access the system using the Administrator account. It is also suggested that you rename the Administrator account so if anyone tries to access the computer, they will be foiled if they try to use Administrator as the user name.

The Guest account provides only limited access to the local domain and is disabled by default in Windows 2000.

Before you begin to create accounts, you must make some network administration decisions:

- *User Names*: What type of naming convention should be used for user login names? How many letters should they be? Should the user name be based on the user's real name, or should the administrator create it so that it is hard to guess? Remember, a person trying to break into the system needs both a user name and a password. If the user name is difficult to guess, that makes breaking in more difficult.

- *Passwords*: Should users be able to change their passwords? How often should passwords be changed? How many letters should the password contain? How often should users be able to reuse passwords? Should failed attempts to log on lead to **account lockouts**?

- *Logon hours*: Should users be restricted to logging on during certain hours of the day or only on certain days?

- *Auditing*: Should user actions (for example, log on, log off, object access, and policy changes) be tracked? To what degree?

The following sections cover some of these topics in detail.

Passwords

For security reasons, users should change **passwords** regularly, but as an administrator, you should limit the frequency of change to some extent. One reason to limit changes is so users don't forget which password they're using. It is fairly simple, though, to remedy a forgotten password within Linux or Windows 2000: Open the user's account information, assign a new password, and then change the settings so that the user must change the password at the next network logon. It is more important that you adjust passwords so that they cannot be reused too frequently; changing passwords is futile if an enterprising user cycles through eight passwords to arrive at "GoFish" yet again.

This raises another point: Most server-based passwords are case sensitive—including on Windows 2000 and Linux—so take advantage of this fact to make them harder to guess (for example, TrumpeT09). Passwords also can include numbers or higher-order characters (which don't appear on the keyboard) to make them less susceptible to **dictionary attacks** (password-guessing programs that run through an entire dictionary to guess a password).

Many security experts recommend that, when generating passwords, you pick two dictionary terms plus a punctuation mark and string them together; for example, separate the words "bear" and "cat" with a plus sign, as in "bear+cat." Alternately, use a combination of lowercase and uppercase letters and combine that with two or more numbers. These techniques make passwords more or less immune to dictionary attacks because they greatly increase the number of possible combinations. However, be careful not to make passwords so difficult to remember that users start writing them on sticky notes attached to their monitors.

Note that it's also a good idea to limit the number of times in a row a user can unsuccessfully try to log on. It might seem unfriendly to lock out a user after a certain number of failed logon attempts (perhaps three). However, doing so slows down dictionary or other brute force attacks because attackers can only try a limited number of entries before they are timed out and must wait before trying again. The Administrator account can be locked out only by using a program called Passprop, which is available with the Windows 2000 Resource Kit.

Windows 2000 can handle passwords of up to 128 characters, but Windows NT passwords are limited to only 14 characters. Linux, on the other hand, can handle passwords up to 256 characters. Without making passwords so long that they become difficult to remember and type accurately, longer is generally better, especially because passwords must not include spaces. In practice, a minimum of eight characters seems to work well.

Logon Hours

Restricting users' logon hours isn't always necessary, and in some work environments might be undesirable. In a tightly regulated office, time restrictions are another way of ensuring that intruders can't break in and log on after working hours. Locking an account except during certain periods when its owner is present to use it limits opportunities for unauthorized users to log on with stolen passwords.

In most NOSs, you can restrict logon hours by days of the week or hours in the day, or both. If a user is logged on when restricted logon hours begin, the results of the logon hours expiration differ, depending on the option selected. Windows 2000 logon hours can be set to disconnect the user from all network resources after the logon hours expire, or, less dramatically, simply disallow connections to new resources.

Auditing

One way to keep track of what's happening on the network (or, more accurately, on the server) is **auditing**, that is, configuring the server so that it records certain actions—such as object accesses, changes to the security information, logons and logoffs, and the like—for later review.

How much you should audit depends on how much information you can efficiently store. Although you could conceivably log every activity on the network, a huge volume of information would result. Also, recognizing patterns that point to intrusions or incursion might be difficult amidst all the successful (and perfectly legal) activities logged. Often, recording only failed access attempts is enough; that way, you know which people are trying, but failing, to access the network. Of course, if you suspect unauthorized access attempts, then you should record successful accesses (at least, for suspect objects or resources) as well. In all cases, however, you must use auditing sparingly because auditing can adversely affect the availability of system resources.

Setting User Rights

Another responsibility of network administrators is assigning user rights, the actions that particular accounts have permission to perform. Most network operating systems, including Windows 2000 and Linux, come with predefined default groups to which you can assign users.

In addition, there are two general kinds of groups: **local groups** (those intended for use only on a single machine) and **global groups** (those intended for use within or across domain boundaries). Windows 2000 also offers a new type of group called **universal group** in Active Directory native mode. Universal groups offer yet another layer to help with cross-domain resource management. Assignment of rights on a group basis greatly simplifies network management. Default groups have preassigned rights that apply to all group members. For example, Table 10-1 shows the default local groups and the rights assigned to those groups for Windows 2000 Server.

Table 10-1   Windows 2000 Server default local groups

Group	Rights
Administrators	Have complete control over the computer and domain
Account Operators	Can administer user and group accounts for the local domain
Backup Operators	Can back up and restore files that users normally cannot access
Guests	Are permitted guest access to domain resources
Print Operators	Can add, delete, and manage domain printers
Server Operators	Can administer domain servers
Users	Are allowed ordinary user accounts

 Table 10-1 does not include the Replicator group (a default Windows 2000 Server group) because it's not a user group; instead, the Replicator service uses it to dynamically replicate specified folders across the network.

In addition to local groups, Windows 2000 Server has numerous default global groups. These include Domain Admins, Domain Users, and Domain Guests. Essentially the same as the local groups with similar names, these groups apply to entire domains rather than to a single machine. The next section, "Managing Group Accounts," covers some caveats about group membership.

The network administrator also has the option of assigning extra rights to users on an individual basis. For example, you could add the right to create printers to Carla's account, although as a member of the Users group, Carla ordinarily would not have such a right. You can assign a user to more than one group to extend that user's rights. You could assign Carla both to Users and to Print Operators, and she would acquire the rights for both groups. Remember that rights are cumulative; when rights conflict (for example, one group has the right to do something but another group does not), the widest-reaching right normally applies. The exception is when No Access is assigned to a group; in that case, No Access means no access.

In addition to the groups to which you can assign them, users are automatically added to certain groups when they log on and you cannot change these memberships. Table 10-2 lists these automatic groups.

Table 10-2   Windows 2000 automatic groups

Group	Membership
Everyone	Everyone currently belonging to the domain
Authenticated Users	All users who logged on to the domain using a valid account and password (added to Windows NT in Service Pack 4; part of Windows 2000 from its first version)
Interactive	Everyone logged on to the domain locally
Network	Everyone logged on to the domain through the network

It's important to remember that these groups exist. For example, all members of the group Everyone have full control over some objects, which means they can add, delete, and change those objects. Sometimes this is exactly what you want, but recall that Everyone's membership includes everyone from the network administrator to the intern who started last week. The default permission for all new shares is Full Control to Everyone; this is not a good idea for an Accounting share. Always be aware of who has what rights on your network.

Every change you make to a Windows user account or group is reflected in one of two ways:

1. For Windows NT domains, changes are written to the Registry database (which stores all system information) on the primary domain controller and recorded in the two files that make up the Registry's security information: SECURITY and **Security Accounts Manager (SAM)**.

2. For Windows 2000/.NET domains, changes are written to a domain controller's Active Directory database, under the control of a directory system agent. This information is deliberately spread across multiple domain controllers to increase redundancy and availability of directory data. When user or group information changes in Active Directory, those changes are written to the directory database immediately. Although some Active Directory data does indeed wind up in the Windows 2000 Registry, the Registry no longer acts as the sole repository for such information in Windows 2000.

Managing Group Accounts

Of course, you can add and delete rights for groups just as you can for users, and even create entirely new groups to provide exactly the rights needed. You can even add groups to other groups. For Windows NT, adding one group to another must adhere to the following guidelines:

- Global groups can include individual users.

- Local groups can include individual users and global groups.

 It is not recommended to have users in the local groups. Local groups should be reserved for resource management only.

The Windows 2000 and Linux rules for placing groups within groups are a great deal more flexible. Linux supports arbitrary nesting of groups within groups and does not recognize a local-global distinction. (Add-on directory services, however, are different and work somewhat like Windows 2000 Active Directory.) For Windows 2000 to support nesting of groups within groups, you must configure the domain to operate in **native mode**, which means that no Windows NT Servers may act as domain controllers in that domain. (When NT Servers do function as domain controllers with Windows 2000 Active Directory Servers, the network is said to operate in **mixed mode**.)

When your network expands beyond a single domain, you can use groups to make other domains accessible to your users.

At first it seems confusing that local groups can include global groups but not the other way around. Why, you might ask, would you want to add a global group to a local one? The answer is for cross-domain communication. As you know, Windows networks are organized into administrative units called domains for security reasons and to manage resources and accounts from a central point. By default, the resources for one domain are not accessible to those whose accounts are in another domain. Although generally this is preferred, it is sometimes desirable to let members of one domain access resources on another. This communication is known as a trust relationship.

Trust Relationships

In Windows domains, a **trust relationship** manages cross-domain communications. For Windows NT, trust relationships are governed in the Trust Relationships dialog box (Figure 10-1) and accessed through the Policies, Trust Relationships menu selection in the NT User Manager for Domains. In Windows 2000, trust relationships are automatically extended to interrelated domains based on the structure of the directory tree in use. A trust relationship is an arrangement in which one domain permits members of another domain to access its resources.

In Microsoft domain terminology, there are three types of trusts: one-way, two-way, and universal. A one-way trust establishes a relationship in which users on Domain A can access resources on a Domain B, but the users on Domain B cannot access the resources on Domain A. A two-way trust is a relationship in which users on Domain A can access Domain B resources and vice versa. A universal trust is one in which all domains trust one another and all users can access resources on all domains.

With a trust relationship in Windows NT, you must establish "trust" (one-way or two-way) between domains so that members of a given domain can access resources of another domain. In Windows 2000, automatic trust relationships are all two-way and transitive trusts. In addition, all domains within an Active Directory tree engage in a universal trust by default. These can be modified by the administrator as needed.

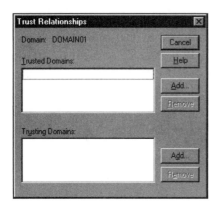

Figure 10-1   Trust Relationships dialog box for Windows NT

For the members of two domains to use each other's resources, the domains must establish a two-way trust, with each domain trusting the other as a separate action. In Windows NT, trust must be explicitly granted: If Domain A trusts Domain B and Domain B trusts Domain C, then Domain A does not trust Domain C until a separate trust relationship is built. This proved unwieldy and hard to manage, so in Windows 2000, trust relationships are indeed transitive—if Domain A trusts Domain B, and Domain B trusts Domain C, then Domain A also trusts Domain C.

Why are local and global groups concerned with domains and trusts? Well, you can establish a trust relationship, but until you give the members of Domain A some kind of account on Domain B, trust means nothing. There are three potential methods for doing this:

- *Method 1*: Add each user individually to Domain B's user account database.
- *Method 2*: Add each user's Domain A account to a global group on Domain A, and give that group rights on Domain B.
- *Method 3*: Add the Domain A user accounts to a global group, and then add that group to a local group on Domain B.

Although Method 3 is the easiest choice for obvious reasons, let's quickly walk through the decision-making process. Method 1 works, but it's slow and painful. Also, if you add new users to Domain A, you must remember to add them to Domain B as well. Because the account databases are not shared, Domain B's is not updated to reflect the change.

Method 2 makes a little more sense because you don't have to make as many changes, but it still includes the *additional* step of assigning the global group rights on Domain B.

Method 3, on the other hand, is the simplest from an administrative standpoint. Add the users of Domain A to Domain Users (a global group), and then add that group to the Users group on Domain B. Domain B immediately reflects any changes to the membership of Domain A, as long as the accounts belong to the global group.

Disabling and Deleting User Accounts

You won't want to keep every account you create active forever. Windows 2000 provides two options to make any user account inactive: disabling it or deleting it.

Disabling an account is like turning it off: The account hasn't gone anywhere; the security identifiers that determine its assigned rights and permissions don't change. It's unusable while disabled, but still works when you turn it back on. You might want to disable temporarily inactive accounts, for instance, when a summer intern leaves but plans to return next year. This is also useful when an individual leaves a company and you plan to hire a replacement at a later time. The administrator needs only to disable the departing employee's account. When the replacement employee is hired, the account is enabled and renamed. This gives the new employee the exact same privileges and group membership as the employee who left. It also saves the company administrative time.

Deleting an account is final. A deleted account is gone; you cannot restore it even if you create a new account with the same name and same group memberships. You can create an account almost exactly identical to the one deleted, but the security identification information must change. Then the new account does not reflect any adjustments you made to the account group membership or to its individual rights. Deleting an account is advisable only if you're sure that no one will ever again need the account, or if you want to be absolutely certain that no one can ever again use that account. Remember, disabling or deleting the default Administrator account is not permitted.

Renaming and Copying User Accounts

If, however, a new user is replacing an existing user, you have two choices: Rename the old account; or copy the existing account to a new one named for the new user, and then disable the old account. After you rename (or copy) the old user's account, be sure to change its password as well. In Windows 2000 and XP Professional, you do this through the Users and Passwords utility in the Control Panel; in Windows 2000 Server, you use the Active Directory Users and Computers management console. The Users and Passwords utility is shown in Figure 10-2, and the Active Directory Users and Computers

10

management console is shown in Figure 10-3. In Windows NT Server, you use the User Manager for Domains tool.

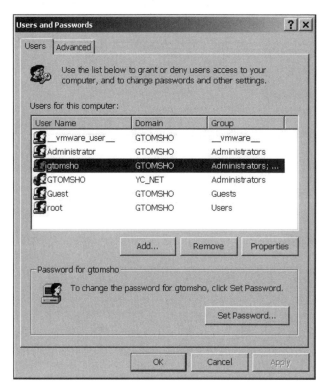

Figure 10-2 Users and Passwords utility in Windows 2000

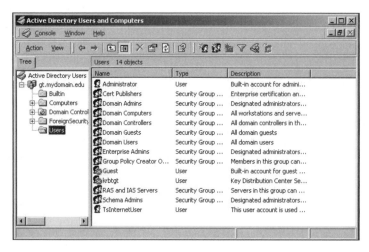

Figure 10-3 Active Directory Users and Computers management console

MANAGING NETWORK PERFORMANCE

Obviously, when monitoring your network, you want to ensure that the cables are operational and the network cards don't conflict. But beyond the minimum of making sure that the hardware works, you need to monitor additional parameters, such as:

- Data read from and written to the server each second
- Queued commands
- On an Ethernet network, the number of collisions per second
- Security errors (errors accessing data)
- Connections currently maintained to other servers (server sessions)
- Network performance

Data Reads and Writes

The number of bytes read from and written to a server provides a useful measure of the server's activity, particularly if these counts increase over time.

As well as counting the amount of data read from and written to the server, you can also count the amount of data that *cannot* be read or written. On a Windows network, the server attempts to take large data streams, not as sets of packets, but as streams of **raw data** unbroken by header information. The server's refusal to accept many such streams of raw data is a possible indication of server memory problems because a certain buffer is needed to accept the stream.

Queued Commands

One measure of a server's traffic is the number of **queued commands**, or commands awaiting execution. This number should never be much more than the number of network cards in the server, or a bottleneck occurs.

Collisions per Second

Only one node on an Ethernet segment can transmit at a time. When more than one node attempts to do so, the two packets collide and both must be re-sent. Although the time to resend is fairly short for the first failed attempt, it increases exponentially with each additional failed attempt. It is unlikely that two stations will repeat a collision on the second attempt, but the more stations there are on the network, the more likely it is that there will be multiple collisions. The point is that collisions slow down network throughput. Collisions are normal and some are to be expected, but high collision rates are not good.

The rate of collisions per second can indicate something about your network's physical topology. One of the main causes of network collisions is a segment that is too long for

10

nodes on one end to "hear" that another node at the other end is already transmitting. On an Ethernet network, nodes usually listen to make sure that the lines are clear before transmitting data.

Note that if too many repeaters exist between the sending and receiving computer, causing excessive delay between the sender and receiver, the signal will not be heard in time. Then, another machine might transmit, causing a collision. In this case, you may need to redesign your network using switches. Of course, the most common reason for high collision rates is too many workstations transmitting a lot of network data on a single Ethernet segment.

Security Errors

Although there may be an innocent explanation, a high rate of failed logons, failed access to objects, or failed changes to security settings may indicate a security risk on your network. A hacker might be attempting to break into the system, or a user might be trying to use objects to which he or she has been denied access. Either way, errors are something to watch for, and auditing helps you see who's causing the errors. It is also useful to employ a protocol analyzer, a combination of hardware and software that can capture network traffic and create reports and graphs from the data it collects. It helps you find the source of errors, in case someone is being "spoofed" (for example, when an unauthorized user acts as an authorized user).

Server Sessions

You can tell something about server activity by observing details about **server sessions**. Such details include connections between network devices and the server, for example, the rate at which connections to the server are made and how those connections are broken, whether by a normal logoff or by an error or server timeout. The latter conditions may indicate that the server is overloaded and either refusing connections or unable to service them quickly enough. More RAM in the server may solve the problem, or you may need to update other hardware.

Network Performance

If your network runs Windows NT or Windows 2000 Server, you already have three tools you can use to monitor your system's performance: the Event Viewer, the Performance Monitor, and the Network Monitor. For Linux servers, numerous comparable open source (free) or shareware (low cost) utilities are available as well.

Event Viewer

Event Viewer is a utility available in Windows NT, Windows 2000, Windows XP, and Windows .NET Server. This utility permits an administrator to view and manage three log files that maintain information related to system operation, security, and application activities. These logs are named, aptly enough: System Log, Security Log, and Application Log.

Of the three logs that Event Viewer maintains, the first two—the System Log and the Security Log—are most important to this discussion. The Security Log records security events based on the audit filters you set up in the User Manager for Domains (Windows NT) or in a policy setting (Windows 2000), so it's the most useful for getting more information about failed attempts to log on or access data. Be aware that the Security Log starts recording information only after auditing has been enabled and configured. The System Log records events by Windows system components and, therefore, provides basic information about how your operating system services are running and whether all hardware works properly. For example, if you recently installed a new network card and it's not working, you can check the System Log in the Event Viewer to see whether it recorded an interrupt conflict. In the Event Viewer, you can also see the times when services stopped or started, so you can be sure that all necessary services are running. The Event Viewer for Windows 2000 is shown in Figure 10-4.

Note that with Active Directory, additional logs are created. They are Directory Service, DNS Server, and File Replication Service.

10

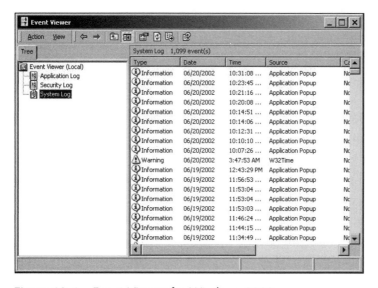

Figure 10-4   Event Viewer for Windows 2000

Performance Monitor

Unlike the Event Viewer, which records individual events, the **Performance Monitor** is best for recording and viewing trends. In Windows 2000, this tool may be accessed in the menu hierarchy as Start, Programs, Administrative Tools, Performance.

The Performance Monitor keeps track of certain counters for system objects. An **object** is a portion of software that works with other portions to provide services. Any system component or resource that's accessible to a user program in Windows 2000 is considered an object. A **counter**, on the other hand, is a certain part of an object that tracks some particular aspect of its behavior. For example, the Processor object has counters such as % Processor Time and % Interrupt Time per second. (See Figure 10-5.)

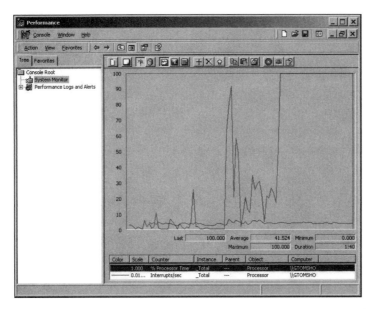

Figure 10-5   Tracking processor time and interrupts per second in Performance Monitor

For the purposes of monitoring your server, you'll be most interested in collecting data for the following system objects:

- Logical or physical disk on the server
- Network interface
- Any of the protocol counters (for example, IP packets per second)
- Redirector
- Server
- Server work queues

Monitoring these types of objects can give you insights, such as what hardware needs upgrading and where system bottlenecks occur. When you monitor a system that's behaving normally under normal loads, you produce a snapshot of its behavior known as a system baseline. You can refer to this baseline as changes or errors occur to compare what's normal against what's happening at any given moment.

Because running the Performance Monitor takes resources that you probably want to save for servicing client requests, it's a good idea to monitor a server remotely, perhaps from a Windows 2000 Professional machine. This increases network traffic, but the degradation in performance won't be as intrusive as running Performance Monitor directly from the server being monitored. It's the user interface portion of running Performance Monitor that requires resources, not the gathering of counter data for Performance Monitor objects.

Network Monitor

Unlike the Event Viewer and Performance Monitor, the **Network Monitor** is not installed automatically during Windows setup, but must be installed separately as a network service. Perform the following steps to install Network Monitor from the NT Server distribution CD-ROM:

1. Right-click the Network Neighborhood icon.

2. Select the Properties menu item.

3. Click the Services tab.

4. Click the Add button, select Network Monitor Tools and Agent from the list of available services, and click OK.

5. Provide the path to the NT CD-ROM, then click Continue. NT copies the needed files.

6. After the files are copied, click Close. NT then stores the new binding information.

7. Click Yes when NT asks whether to restart the computer.

The process for installing Network Monitor on Windows 2000 is fairly straightforward. You must start with the Add/Remove Programs utility in Control Panel, and then select the Add/Remove Windows Components button to access the component installation routines, which list Network Monitor beneath the Management and Monitoring Tools entry. To install Network Monitor, simply click the check box to its left in the Management and Monitoring Tools window, and provide a location for the system files so that installation may proceed. No further configuration is required.

After you install it, the Network Monitor becomes part of the Administrative Tools menu. Network Monitor is a capable software-based protocol analyzer (which, as mentioned, is software that can capture network traffic and create reports and graphs from the data it collects). The Network Monitor oversees the network data stream by recording the source address, destination address, headers, and data for each packet, as shown in Figure 10-6. Network Monitor can capture as many frames as will fit in physical memory (with 8 MB free for other programs). However, it's best not to fill memory with extraneous data; you can specify various filters to select only the data you want. For example, you can filter data packets based on the transport protocol used to transmit them, by source and destination address, or by data pattern, looking for specific ASCII or hexadecimal streams in the data at a certain point.

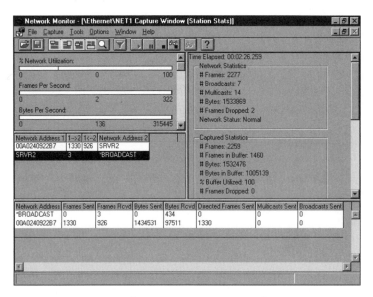

Figure 10-6   Network Monitor session specifics

For security reasons, Network Monitor detects other installed instances of Network Monitor agents on the network, showing the name of the computer on which the agent runs, the name of the account logged in, what the monitor is doing at the moment, the adapter address, and the version number. Some instances of Network Monitor may not be detected if there is a router between those agents and your part of the network. If other instances can detect you, however, you can detect them. Note that if Network Monitor is being used to get a reading on overall network performance, it is necessary to install Network Monitor on at least one server per network segment so that the overall network picture is represented.

Total System Management

Although events on the network constitute a major network performance concern, they are not the only influence. In addition to network conditions, it's also important to consider what's happening on the server side in regard to hard drive and memory usage.

Hard Drive Performance

Of the three tools that come with Windows 2000 Server, the Performance Monitor is most useful for monitoring hard drives on a Windows network. To monitor hard drive performance, look at the following:

- Disk space remaining

- Speed at which requests are serviced (throughput and the amount of data being transferred)

- How often the disk is busy (how often it runs and the average number of requests queued)

When monitoring drives, notice whether you're viewing the physical disk object or the logical disk object—they may not represent the same thing when a physical hard disk consists of only a single disk partition. Also, notice that not all disk-related counters add up precisely to 100%, even if totaled on a percentage basis for a single drive. That's because readings for multiple logical drives, all of which reside on a single physical drive, may add up to more than 100% for the entire physical drive, especially if file compression is in use. Sometimes you must average the results across multiple logical or physical drives to obtain more meaningful results.

To use the disk performance counters under Windows NT, you must first run DISKPERF -y from the command prompt; otherwise, the counters register zero. Be sure to run DISKPERF -n to disable this feature after the monitoring is completed—monitoring counters on physical drives is resource intensive. In Windows 2000, logical disk counters are enabled by default, but you must enable physical disk counters if you want to use them.

Memory Use

Another major server issue concerns the amount of memory available to service incoming requests. Windows 2000 is designed to page data out of memory (that is, store information in a separate file, called a paging file) when not in use or when the memory is needed for other, more recently used data. If paged-out data is needed again, a page fault occurs to get the data back in memory. When the server has to page too much data (when contrasted to a baseline performance), consider installing more memory.

There are two kinds of page faults. **Soft page faults** occur when data is removed from a program's **working set** (the set of data actively in use by the process), but moved to another area in physical memory. Then, when that data is needed, it's a very fast operation to get it back into the working set. **Hard page faults**—when the data has gone unused for so long or there's such a shortage of physical memory that program data is stored on the hard disk—are another matter entirely. Reading data from disk takes considerably longer than reading it from memory, so if too many hard page faults occur, the response time slows considerably. Thus, the best measure of memory shortages is the rate of hard page faults.

CPU Utilization

A computer's central processing unit, or CPU, is where its real work takes place. That's why monitoring CPU utilization (or the percentage of time the CPU stays busy on average) provides such an important statistic. It's possible to measure CPU utilization at any given moment or over a longer period of time. The natural rhythm of computing is such that activities like starting a program, triggering an event, or fielding an interrupt can cause the CPU to show utilization rates of 100%. Don't let peaks at that level surprise or upset you.

When evaluating the health of a system, it's best to monitor on the % Processor Time counter for the Processor object. This provides an average utilization figure over the past second, rather than an instantaneous reading. Constant rates of 90% or over on this counter (along with a queue length of two or more) might indicate that the machine is overloaded. As with any potential bottleneck, you must evaluate other counters to make sure that high utilization isn't a secondary symptom of insufficient memory, of a device that's generating spurious interrupts, or of other causes that can manifest as high CPU utilization on a system.

Network Statistics

You can monitor network statistics in either the Performance Monitor or the Network Monitor on a Windows system. In Performance Monitor, you want to check statistics for the Network Interface and protocol stack objects—that is, the TCP and IP objects keep track of TCP- and IP-related protocol statistics, and the Network Interface object tracks bytes read from or written to the network. Network Monitor allows you to track the same data, but shows error rates and also lets you investigate individual packets or errors. (Performance Monitor only counts events and monitors data rates; it cannot capture any data as Network Monitor can.)

Utilization rates can also be meaningful on networks, so monitoring network utilization in Network Monitor or Bytes Total/Sec in Performance Monitor (Network Interface object) can give you a crude measure of a network's health. Remember that healthy utilization rates vary from networking technology to networking technology. An average 80% utilization over time on a token ring network is perfectly acceptable, while the same utilization on an unswitched Ethernet network is decidedly unacceptable. (On Ethernet, significant data collisions occur when utilization creeps past the 56–60% range.)

Maintaining a Network History

Both the Performance Monitor and the Event Viewer can prepare log data that you can use to keep long-term records of network performance and events. This is mostly so that you can determine trends or notice when a new problem arises. Just as with any other form of troubleshooting, to recognize "sick" you must know how "healthy" looks.

 Be selective about the data you retain. One of the principal errors made by novice network administrators is archiving data overenthusiastically. When the time comes to review this material, there's an impossible amount of data to wade through and the history is useless.

MANAGING NETWORK DATA SECURITY

Data security has two elements: ensuring that data is safe from intruders and ensuring that you can replace destroyed data. The next sections describe these elements.

Planning for Network Security

The initial stage of planning for network security is a process of threat identification. As a network administrator, you should ask yourself the following questions:

- What am I trying to protect?

- Whom or what do I need to protect data from?

- How likely is it that this threat will manifest itself?

- What is the cost of breached security?

- How can I protect the data in a cost-effective manner?

Network security is *not* the same in every situation and for every piece of data. If it were, then the optician's office with a three-node network and a customer database would need to implement the same security measures to protect data as the U.S. National Security Agency does. Thus, it's important to identify the threat, to note how likely the threat is to be acted upon, to note potential damage if the threat *does* become a problem, and then to determine how much to spend protecting the data from the threat.

Considering the cost-effectiveness of security might sound picky, but, as with backups, at some point it costs more to protect data than it does to lose it. You can always invest in additional data security, but doing so might not make financial sense.

When developing a security system, communicating with other managers in the office is a good idea—to be certain that your security system meets the needs of those who must put it in place, and to be certain that the other managers understand the methods you're using to make the network secure, and why you made the choices you did.

Security Models

You can view the problem of network security from two standpoints: physical security, based on hardware, and data security, based on software. Implementing physical security is fairly straightforward: Keep intruders away from cables that they could tap, physically isolate servers and keep them locked up, and generally limit physical access to your network.

 One advantage to protecting cables is that the steps taken to keep them safe from tapping also might help protect them from radio-frequency interference (RFI) noise, which can disrupt network transmissions.

10

From a software standpoint, there are two main security models: share-oriented and user-oriented. In **share-oriented security**, the security information is attached to the object (a network resource of some kind) and applies to everyone who might access that object. For example, if you share a folder as read-only, then *everyone* who accesses that folder has read-only permission. The share does not differentiate based on who's doing the accessing. The Windows 95 security model runs along these lines.

User-oriented security focuses on the rights and permissions of each user. A table attached to every object lists who can do what to the object. The Windows NT and Windows 2000 security models are user-oriented.

Implementing Security

Implementing a security model is a two-stage process: (1) setting up the security system and making it as foolproof as possible; and (2) training network users about why the system is in place, how to use it, and the consequences of failing to comply with it. For example, one aspect of network security is password protection. Stage 1 of implementing passwords consists of setting passwords for everyone or setting a standard to which passwords must conform. Stage 2 includes explaining this standard to the network users, expressing why it's necessary to follow this standard, and outlining any consequences of creating passwords that don't follow the standard. Making sure that users understand why certain policies are in place should make the implementation process easier.

New Security Features in Windows 2000

Some of the most significant changes introduced with Windows 2000 relate to security: from the protocols and related controls supported, to the introduction of powerful IP-based services such as Kerberos for logon authentication, to Public Key Infrastructure for reliable exchange of digital proofs of identity called "digital signatures" and "digital certificates." It's interesting to note, however, that all the security items Microsoft includes with Windows 2000 were available on UNIX and Linux servers several years before they were available on Windows operating systems.

Although the many and interesting security features available in Windows 2000 (note that these features are not available on Windows NT) are too numerous to describe in detail here, the following items deserve mention:

- *Kerberos v5 authentication*: On modern networks, Kerberos uses a three-step method to make sure that users and servers can identify themselves to each other properly and exchange information safely and securely. (The v5 indicates that it is based on version 5, the most current version of this software.) The biggest advantages that Kerberos authentication provides for Windows 2000 networks are secure, encrypted mechanisms for computers to establish their identities and equally secure methods for computers to exchange data (by using session-specific encryption keys) across the network. For Windows 2000 computers and domains, Kerberos v5 authentication is the preferred authentication mechanism; mixed-mode networks must also support older authentication mechanisms for Windows NT, Windows 98, and other Windows machines. Because older Windows authentication mechanisms are notoriously not secure, it is highly recommended that new client software specifically designed to work with Kerberos v5 be installed on machines running older software. Windows 2000 Active Directory can also interoperate with third-party Kerberos servers, but extra configuration effort is required to do so.

■ **_Public Key Infrastructure (PKI)_**: As long as two computers reside on the same network, they can easily use a service like Kerberos to establish authentication and to manage secure exchange of data. In a nutshell, PKI extends the capabilities that Kerberos provides locally to the Internet at large, where public certificate authorities (CAs) such as VeriSign or Thawte can issue and revoke digital certificates for users or businesses to use to establish their identities and manage secure exchanges of data. The difference here is that trusted third parties—the CAs—must act as neutral authorities that verify each party's identity to the other party when two parties in different organizations want to communicate or exchange information. Windows 2000 includes support for PKI for a variety of users, including Certificate Server software, so that organizations can set up and use their own private CAs and a variety of mechanisms to allow Windows 2000 networks to interoperate with third-party, external CAs.

■ **_Enhanced security policy mechanisms_**: Windows 2000 consolidates almost all of its security settings and features within the Group Policy mechanism managed in Active Directory. The functionality covered in one consistent interface captures data that had to be entered across a handful of utilities in Windows NT. In addition, Windows 2000 supports more advanced protocol filtering and more secure networking protocols (covered in the next list item). They make Windows 2000 easier to manage from a security perspective and more able to be made secure in many more ways than Windows NT supports.

■ **_Improved IP security mechanisms and protocols_**: The Windows 2000 TCP/IP configuration includes the ability to filter IP traffic on the basis of protocols, port addresses, and IP addresses, and also includes wild-card mechanisms that simplify allowing or denying access by matching patterns related to specific protocols, ports, or addresses. In addition, Windows 2000 includes support for numerous application programming interfaces (APIs), for numerous IP protocols, including the Layer 2 Tunneling Protocol (L2TP) and the IP Security (IPSec) protocol, and for Transport Layer Security (TLS) protocol enhancements. Because TCP/IP is the protocol of choice on modern networks and Microsoft has adopted modern, secure protocols from this suite (as well as upgraded its TCP/IP implementation, primarily to improve security), Windows 2000 networks can be made considerably more secure than Windows NT networks.

Once again, remember that Linux has had many of these capabilities for years or soon after their introductions to the standards-oriented networking community.

10

Maintaining Security

Maintaining security is similar to any other kind of maintenance; you take the plan you implemented based on your initial identification of needs and make sure that the plan accomplishes its goals and works as intended. Typically, you must modify the plan after you see how the security system works in practice and you note any omissions.

Security Against Viruses

Maintaining physical security and data security through password protection and encryption/decryption methods is indeed important. However, in recent years, one of the biggest security threats network administrators have faced is software attacks in the form of the computer virus.

Virus protection used to be an afterthought on most networks, implemented by careful attention to not using floppy disks that may have been exposed to viruses. However, in today's world of always-on Internet connections and advanced capabilities of Web browsers and e-mail programs, viruses are a constant threat. A computer network without comprehensive virus protection is ripe for an attack.

Virus protection can be implemented at the computer workstation, at the network server, and at the Internet gateway. Workstation virus scanners protect a single computer from infection and can be set to constantly monitor files read from and written to the server drives. Workstation virus scanners can also be set to scan all incoming e-mail messages, which is useful because e-mail viruses are so common today.

Server-based virus scanners can scan data as it is read from or written to the server. This protects against a server infection that could quickly spread throughout an entire organization.

The latest in virus scanners are Internet gateway scanners. These scanners are installed on a computer that acts as the gateway for all Internet traffic—all traffic coming from or going to the Internet must pass through that computer. These scanners can scan all Web browser, FTP, and e-mail traffic as it passes through the gateway, stopping viruses before they even enter the corporate network.

So, which type of virus protection should you implement? The safest route is to implement all three types of protection. The developers of viruses are constantly finding ways to thwart existing protection methods, so although an Internet gateway scanner may stop all known viruses today, a clever virus developer is certain to find a way to deliver a virus that gets past the gateway scanner of tomorrow. In addition, users still carry floppy disks and ZIP disks that may infect the corporate network, so the workstation and server scanners are still needed even if your Internet gateway is fairly secure.

Using Firewalls to Prevent Internet Attacks

Today, a network administrator is courting disaster if a firewall is not between the corporate network and the Internet. Firewalls protect against outside attempts to access unauthorized resources, and they protect against malicious network packets that are intended to disable or cripple the corporate network and its resources.

A second use of firewalls placed between the Internet and the corporate network is to restrict access to Internet resources by corporate users. This type of restriction is usually intended to prevent users from accessing offensive Web sites or from accessing content such as streaming audio or video that are bandwidth intensive and that may not be the best use of an employee's time.

Firewalls installed on the corporate network are often expensive and typically complicated to configure. This type of firewall is definitely not suitable for the home Internet user trying to protect his or her computer from would-be hackers. Due to the availability of fast, always-on Internet connections for home users, a new type of firewall, dubbed a personal firewall, was developed to guard a single workstation against Internet attacks. These firewalls are programs that you install on your computer. They guard your computer from attempts to access your computer's resources and services through the Internet. Personal firewalls are not just for the home, though. Because many hacker attacks occur within corporate networks, these lightweight firewalls can also be used in the office to prevent other users from infiltrating your workstation.

10

AVOIDING DATA LOSS

Another aspect of data security involves protecting data from loss or destruction, as opposed to unauthorized access. The chances of a hard drive failing are probably higher than the risk of a break-in. This section covers the methods you can use to protect your data and reduce the chances of data loss.

In most cases, you can best accomplish data protection with a three-tiered scheme that (1) reduces the chance of data loss, (2) makes quick recovery from data loss easy, and (3) if all else fails, allows you to completely rebuild lost or corrupted data.

Tape Backup

Backups are the most obvious form of data security, and tape backups are a favorite method of creating them. Tape backups are more popular than other methods, such as optical drives or removable hard drives, because tapes offer a useful combination of respectable speed, high capacity, and cost-effectiveness. Although a tape drive cannot act as a separate drive as some other back-up media can, tape backup is otherwise an excellent back-up medium, widely supported by tape-backup software (such as the back-up programs included with Windows 2000, Windows NT, and Windows 98).

When making backups on any medium, it is key to back up regularly and often. Microsoft recognizes five types of backups:

- *Full backup*: Copies all selected files to tape
- *Incremental backup*: Copies all files changed since the last full or incremental backup
- *Differential backup*: Copies all files changed since the last full backup; does not reset the archive bit
- *Copy backup*: Copies selected files to tape without resetting the archive bit
- *Daily backup*: Copies all files changed the day the backup is made

Of the five types, full, incremental, and differential backups are most useful as part of a regular back-up schedule. A copy backup is good for copying files to a new location and a daily backup is good for collecting data to work on at home or other off-site locations.

A good model for creating a back-up schedule combines a full weekly backup with daily differential backups, so that you can perform the backups quickly on a daily basis and easily restore by restoring the contents of two tapes: the full backup overlaid with the differential backup. You can also use incremental backups for daily backup, but restoration is more difficult because of the number of tapes required to keep a full incremental set.

When creating a backup schedule, it's a good idea to post the schedule and assign one person to perform the backups and sign off on them each day. That way, you can (1) see at a glance when the last backup was done, and (2) train one person to perform backups and care for the tapes.

 If you maintain a Windows server, be sure to back up Registry data daily, so that you can restore changes to your system if the Registry information becomes corrupted.

Another important aspect of a successful back-up plan is to ensure that you can restore the data. Use the "verify data" option that comes with your back-up software to ensure that the data copied to tape matches the data on the drive. Create some test files and backup those files and then practice restoring the files to the server so that you can check that the restore operation works properly. Ensure that tapes are stored in a cool, dry, dark place to minimize the risk of damage by heat, moisture, or light. Periodically take a tape off the shelf, and make sure it's readable and its data can be restored *after* the tape has been removed from the machine. For example, it's possible for a miscalibrated tape drive to accept tapes for backup but refuse to restore their contents—a condition usually discovered only when you need to restore the data. Have a policy to rotate tapes so that no single tape set is reused within the same week. In addition, have a policy to remove tapes completely from the set after a predetermined amount of time to avoid worn tapes that might affect performance.

Tape backup is the preferred method for doing regular system backups to ensure data integrity and to allow the restoration of individual files that have been corrupted or accidentally deleted. To save an entire disk drive with a particular configuration, you can use drive copying or drive ghosting. Different products exist to perform this function, including PowerQuest's DriveImage and Norton's Ghost.

Repairing or Recovering Windows Systems

Windows systems occasionally fail to boot or manifest problems or errors at runtime that indicate the system is damaged or corrupted and possibly needs repair. These network operating systems include reasonably powerful repair utilities built into their installation routines. The first step in attempting such a repair on either platform is to boot the system from the CD-ROM for the operating system in use or from a set of boot floppies for that operating system.

Not all PCs can boot from a CD-ROM, but if the machine you're repairing can be configured to do so, you can attempt repairs directly from the Windows NT or Windows 2000 installation CD itself. This is faster and more convenient than working with setup floppies.

The Windows NT repair facility depends on the availability of an Emergency Repair Disk (or ERD) that contains copies of key Windows NT files and a snapshot of the machine's Windows Registry. The Windows NT repair facility can attempt to repair a variety of boot problems, including repairs to the Master Boot Record (MBR) and repairs to the Windows NT boot files or boot configuration information. In addition, this utility allows you to reinstall the operating system but leaves configuration files and settings intact.

The Windows 2000 repair facility is considerably more powerful than that of Windows NT. It operates a command-line console that supports 26 commands that you can use together to manipulate the system under repair from its partition table to replace specific files and folders. This utility is the recovery console and, like the Windows NT repair facility, is also started from the Windows setup program. This utility also includes specific commands to replace the Master Boot Record (fixmbr), to write a new boot sector (fixboot), to format hard disks (format), and even to manage disk partitions (diskpart).

Windows NT and Windows 2000 repair utilities and capabilities differ considerably, so be prepared to apply different approaches and strategies when repairing damaged Windows systems of both types. Note also that Windows 2000 offers greatly improved and more powerful repair tools than its predecessor.

Uninterruptible Power Supply

Of course, backups only help if they get made, and if you're making daily backups and a thunderstorm knocks out the power—and the server—at 4:00 P.M., then you've lost nearly an entire day's data. Sometimes, this kind of loss is unavoidable, but power protection can help prevent this particular mishap.

An **uninterruptible power supply (UPS)** is a device with a built-in battery, power conditioning, and surge protection. You plug the UPS into the wall and the computer (and monitor) into the UPS, so that while the AC power from the wall powers the computer, it charges the battery. Then, if the power goes out, the charged battery takes over and keeps the computer up and running long enough for you to perform an orderly shutdown, which can be important in bringing the server back up after the outage. If the users connected to the server have UPSs, they also have a chance to save their data before powering down. The amount of time you have depends on the size of the battery inside the UPS and the amount of power drain placed on it, but you should plan for at least 10 minutes to shut everything down. When choosing a UPS, explain what you plan to plug into it, and the vendor should be able to help you choose the right one for your needs.

Be aware that there are two categories of UPS: online and stand-by. A stand-by UPS normally supplies power to the plugged-in devices by passing the AC power directly from the wall outlet to the device receptacle. In the event of a power outage, the stand-by UPS detects the power failure and quickly switches to battery power to supply power to the plugged-in devices. Unfortunately, if the switch from wall power to battery power does not occur quickly enough, the plugged-in devices may lose power long enough to re-boot or cause a malfunction.

An online UPS continually supplies power to the plugged-in devices through the UPS battery. The batteries are continually recharged by the wall outlet power. In the event of a power outage, there is no need to switch to battery power because the UPS is already supplying power from the battery. Overall, an online UPS is the far better solution for computer equipment.

 Never plug a laser printer into a UPS! Laser printers draw an enormous amount of power—some as much as 15 amps (the amount an entire kitchen might require)—and can drain the battery almost immediately.

Battery backup isn't the only advantage to UPSs. In these days of overloaded power grids, power conditioning and surge protection are equally important. **Power conditioning** cleans the power, removing noise caused by other devices on the same circuit (such as the already-mentioned laser printer). **Surge protection** keeps the computer from being affected by sags or spikes in the power flow—a condition often found during thunderstorms even if the power doesn't go out, or when there's a drain on power resources, such as on a hot day when air conditioners strain power stations.

Fault-Tolerant Systems

Another method of data protection comes in the form of **fault–tolerant disk config–urations**, which may be implemented in either hardware or software. The two most popular of these configurations are disk mirroring (or duplexing) and disk striping with parity. These disk structures are based on **Redundant Arrays of Inexpensive Disks (RAID)**. In plain English, this means such disk structures may be built from standard hard disks, using specialized disk controllers to create and manage whatever special features may be associated with the type of RAID array in use. Table 10-3 describes these types of arrays.

 RAID is sometimes written out as Redundant Array of Independent Disks.

Table 10-3   RAID levels explored and explained

RAID Level	Description and Usage Information
RAID 0	Disk structure treats a group of disks as a single logical storage unit. Applies to volume sets and disk striping without parity, which have no fault-tolerance capabilities. Available in both Windows NT and Windows 2000 servers.
RAID 1	Applies to disk mirroring and disk duplexing, in which two drives are exact copies of each other, and failure of the primary drive automatically causes the secondary drive to take over. Available in both Windows NT and Windows 2000 servers.
RAID 2	Uses separate check disks, where data bits are striped on both data and check disks, to replace information from a damaged data or check disk in the array. Because the check data requirements are high and require multiple separate drives for that data, this form of RAID is seldom used. Not available for Windows NT or Windows 2000 servers.
RAID 3	Uses a single check disk for parity information (sometimes called a parity disk for that reason) for each group of drives. Because the same size chunk of data is read or written each time the array is accessed, space allocation on such drives is not very efficient, especially for small files. Not available for Windows NT or Windows 2000 servers.
RAID 4	Works much like RAID 3 but uses block or sector striping, so that a single block or sector may be accessed at any given time, rather than requiring all drives in the set to be accessed. Inefficient for writing data, since check writes must occur immediately after data writes. Not available for Windows NT or Windows 2000 servers.
RAID 5	Divides the parity data across all drives in the RAID array, so that each drive can be reconstructed from parity data stored on all other drives in the set. This array type, also called disk striping with parity, is available for both Windows NT and Windows 2000 servers.

10

RAID 1: Disk Mirroring

Disk mirroring requires two disks, configured to work in tandem. When data is written to one disk, the same data is written to the second disk, thus creating a constant backup of the data. If either disk fails, then the other disk contains a complete copy of all data. It's even possible to mirror a system disk, so that if the boot disk crashes, the second one can take over.

Disk mirroring normally involves two hard drives on a single controller. Data is mirrored between two disks, each with its own controller, thereby protecting the system not only from disk failures but controller failures as well. This is known as **disk duplexing**.

Disk mirroring is simple to set up and makes recovery from disk failures easy. Its main disadvantage is the amount of disk space it requires—twice as much as you have data.

RAID 5: Disk Striping with Parity

Disk striping with parity is a more space-efficient solution to the problem of how to create a fault-tolerant disk configuration; in keeping with standard RAID terminology, Windows 2000 calls these disk structures RAID 5 volumes. In this configuration, an array of disks—at least three, although Windows NT and Windows 2000 Server support arrays of up to 32 disks—is treated as a single logical drive. Not all of each disk must be part of an array, but every area on each disk must be the same size. Thus, if areas of free space on three disks equal 100 MB, 200 MB, and 150 MB in size, then when those areas are combined to make a stripe set, only 100 MB on each disk is used. That 100 MB section on each disk is logically divided into narrow stripes.

To the user, data written to the stripe set looks as though it's simply being sent to a single logical drive. Actually though, data, along with parity information, is written to the stripes on each disk in the array, as shown in Figure 10-7. RAID5 can recover only from a single failed disk. If more than one disk fails, data must be recovered from backup.

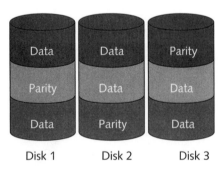

Figure 10-7   Stripe set with parity

Although disk mirroring requires a lower initial investment than disk striping (two disks instead of a minimum of three), disk striping uses space more efficiently, using only $1/n$ (where n is the number of disks in the stripe set) for redundancy information instead of half the disk space. Disk mirroring performs better than striping when it comes to writing data (all that parity calculation takes extra memory), and striping takes a big performance hit for reading if a disk in the array dies and the data must be regenerated from the parity data. Disk mirroring recovers data more quickly than does disk striping because the data on the dead disk does not need to be regenerated; only the mirror set is broken, so the second disk may function independently of the one it mirrored. In short, both mirroring and striping have their advantages, and the choice between the two depends on your particular situation. For example, if storage space is limited, disk striping is the way to go. If disk space is not a concern, then a disk mirror or duplex is the better choice.

 Most Network Operating Systems that support RAID configurations support only RAID 0, RAID 1, and RAID 5.

Intellimirror

Another interesting addition introduced with Windows 2000 is a system called Intellimirror. **Intellimirror** is a client/server application that runs on Windows 2000 machines, in which a Windows 2000 Professional or Server machine can be a client, but a Windows 2000 Server machine must be the server. Essentially, Intellimirror creates a "smart back-up copy" of a system on a server. If a user wants to log onto another machine on the network, that user's home desktop can be re-created elsewhere.

With Intellimirror, all the files, applications, and customization resident on users' home desktops can be accessed on any other Windows 2000 machine that can establish a working connection to the Intellimirror server where their home desktop images reside. This image is called a "smart back-up copy" because Intellimirror only copies items to the desktop that the user requests (or that it can infallibly predict that the user needs, such as basic desktop settings, permanent file share and network printer definitions, and so forth).

In fact, Intellimirror is more capable than a system recovery or back-up access mechanism. Intellimirror works from domain policy settings and user account permissions, and can deploy, recover, restore, or replace user data, software, and personal settings in a Windows 2000-based environment. Based on comprehensive controls over user data management, automated software and installation facilities, and user settings management, Intellimirror is part of the Microsoft Zero Administration initiative for Windows (ZAW) and intended to make lives easier for users and administrators alike.

10

CHAPTER SUMMARY

Network maintenance doesn't end with installing the hardware and software; it is a continuing process of which the network administrator must be vigilant. This chapter discusses some of the important issues pertaining to network management:

❐ The main task of network management is to ensure that all users can access what they are allowed to access but cannot access resources they don't have permission to access. Windows NT and Windows 2000 use User Manager for Domains and the Active Directory Users and Computers utilities, respectively, to manage users and groups.

❐ Groups may be either local or global. Users are automatically added to some groups, such as Everyone, at log on.

❐ Rights can be granted to individual user accounts or to groups to control access to various objects and resources on the network.

❐ Passwords should be changed regularly, and the same password should not be used repeatedly. To make a password more or less immune to dictionary attacks, pick two dictionary terms plus a punctuation mark, and string them together; for example, a plus sign could separate the words "bear" and "cat", as in "bear+cat." Alternately, and perhaps even better, is a password that combines uppercase and lowercase letters and combines the letters with two or more numbers.

❐ In Windows NT and Windows 2000, cross-domain communications are managed through a trust relationship, which is an arrangement in which one domain permits members of another domain to access its resources. In Windows NT, you can establish a one-way or two-way "trust" between domains, so that members of a given domain can access resources in another domain. In Windows 2000, automatic trust relationships are all two-way trusts.

❐ Monitor the performance of a Windows NT or Windows 2000 Server network using Event Viewer, Performance Monitor, and Network Monitor, which include various audit logs for system, driver, security, and application event information.

❐ Both physical security, based on hardware, and data security, based on software, are important network security issues. Software security comes in two flavors—share-oriented security and user-oriented security.

❐ Important new security features in Windows 2000 include Kerberos v5 authentication, Public Key Infrastructure (PKI), enhanced security policy mechanisms, and improved IP security mechanisms and protocols.

❐ A critical part of maintaining security on a network is virus protection. Virus protection can be implemented at the workstation, the server, or the Internet gateway, and preferably at all three locations.

❐ Firewalls protect corporate networks from outside intrusion and attempts to disable or cripple the corporate network. Personal firewalls can protect individual workstations that have a network connection.

❐ Avoid data loss by making regular data backups, using Intellimirror, and employing fault-tolerant system components.

Key Terms

account lockout — The process of automatically disabling a user account based on certain criteria (for example, too many failed logon attempts).

auditing — Recording selected events or actions for later review. Audits can help establish patterns and note changes in those patterns that might signal trouble.

copy backup — Copies all selected files without resetting the archive bit.

counter — A certain part of an object. For example, the Processor object has counters such as % Processor Time and % Interrupt Time per second.

daily backup — Copies all files modified on the day of the backup.

dictionary attack — A method of attempting to determine an account's password by attempting to log on using every word in the dictionary for a password.

differential backup — Copies all files modified since the last full backup.

disk duplexing — A fault-tolerant disk configuration in which data is written to two hard drives, each with its own disk controller, so that if one disk or controller fails, then the data remains accessible.

disk mirroring — A fault-tolerant disk configuration in which data is written to two hard drives, rather than one, so that if one disk fails, then the data remains accessible.

disk striping with parity — A fault-tolerant disk configuration in which parts of several physical disks link together in an array, and data and parity information is written to all disks in this array. If one disk fails, then the data may be reconstructed from the parity information written on the others.

Event Viewer — A Windows NT and Windows 2000 tool that records events in three logs based on type of event: security, system, and application.

fault-tolerant disk configuration — An arrangement of physical or logical disks such that if one disk fails, the data remains accessible without requiring restoration from backups.

full backup — A copy of data that resets the archive bit on all copied files.

global group — A group meant to be used in more than one domain.

groups — Umbrella accounts to which individual accounts may be assigned to grant them a predetermined set of rights.

hard page fault — An exception that occurs when data needed by a program must be called back into memory from its storage space on the hard drive. Hard page faults are relatively time-consuming to resolve.

10

incremental backup — Copies all files modified since the last full or incremental backup.

Intellimirror — A Windows 2000 client/server application that creates a "smart back-up copy" of a Windows 2000 system on a Windows 2000 server. All the files, applications, and customization resident on users' home desktops can be accessed by them on any other Windows 2000 machine that can establish a working connection to the Intellimirror server where their home desktop images reside.

local group — A group meant to be used in a single domain.

mixed mode — A domain configuration in which a Windows NT Server functions as a domain controller with Windows 2000 Active Directory Servers.

native mode — A domain configuration in Windows 2000 that supports nesting of groups within groups; no Windows NT Servers may act as domain controllers in that domain.

Network Monitor — A Windows NT and Windows 2000 network service that you can use to capture network frames based on user-specified criteria, such as a software protocol analyzer.

object — A portion of software that works with other portions to provide services. Each component in Windows NT and Windows 2000 is considered an object.

password — A string of letters, numbers, and other characters that's intended to be kept private and hard to guess. It identifies a particular user or controls access to protected resources.

Performance Monitor — A Windows NT and Windows 2000 tool used for graphing trends, based on performance counters for system objects.

power conditioning — A method of balancing the power input and reducing any spikes caused by noise on the power line, thus providing better power for delicate components such as computers.

queued commands — Commands awaiting execution but not yet completed.

raw data — Data streams unbroken by header information.

Redundant Arrays of Inexpensive Disks (RAID) — Two or more drives on a network server that provide fault tolerance (via disk mirroring or disk striping with parity). Also known as Redundant Array of Independent Disks.

rights — Actions that the user of a particular account has permission to perform.

Security Accounts Manager (SAM) — Part of the Windows NT Executive Services that maintains user and group account information.

server session — Connection between a network server and another node.

share-oriented security — Security information based on the object being shared.

soft page fault — An exception that occurs when data must be called back into a program's working set from another location in physical memory. Soft page faults take comparatively little time to resolve.

surge protection — Power protection that evens out spikes or sags in the main current and prevents them from affecting the computer.

trust relationship — An arrangement in which a domain permits members of another domain to access its resources.

uninterruptible power supply (UPS) — Power protection device that includes a battery backup to take over if the main current fails. Usually incorporates power conditioning and surge protection.

universal group — A group available in Active Directory native mode that adds another option for administrators to manage cross-domain resources.

user account — Collection of information known about the user; usually includes an account name, an associated password, and a set of access permissions for network resources.

user-oriented security — Security information based on the account of the user accessing an object.

working set — Data that a program actively uses at any given time. The working set is only a small subset of the total amount of data that the program *could* use.

REVIEW QUESTIONS

10

1. One Registry file that stores security information in Windows NT is named

   _____.

2. What account(s) come predefined with Windows NT and Windows 2000 Server? (Choose all that apply.)

   a. Domain Administrator

   b. Guest

   c. Administrator

   d. Users

3. A currently unusable account that retains its security information if reactivated is said to be _____.

4. Although Windows NT passwords may technically be up to _____ characters long, the dialog box only lets you enter _____ characters.

5. What is the maximum number of characters a Linux password may contain?

   a. 64

   b. 128

   c. 256

   d. 512

6. Which of the following statements is true for Windows NT? (Choose all that apply.)

    a. Only global groups may be part of another domain's groups.

    b. Global groups may not contain other global groups.

    c. There are three predefined global groups.

    d. None of the above are true.

7. In a server with a single network card, what is the maximum number of queued commands that you can have on the server without creating a bottleneck?

    a. one

    b. two

    c. three

    d. four

8. To scan for viruses as data enters the network from the Internet, you should implement a(n) _____.

    a. personal firewall

    b. Internet gateway virus scanner

    c. server-based virus scanner

    d. desktop virus scanner

9. Only Ethernet networks can experience collisions. True or false?

10. Which of the following tools best record failed logon attempts?

    a. Event Viewer

    b. Performance Monitor

    c. Network Monitor

    d. none of the above

11. The _____ log in the Event Viewer is most useful for determining which drivers have been loaded.

12. A domain relationship in which only one domain has access to another domain's resources is called a _____.

    a. reciprocal trust

    b. single-way trust

    c. one-way trust

    d. hard drive audit

13. The default trust relationship enjoyed by all domains in an Active Directory is called _____.

    a. one-way

    b. multi-way

    c. all-way

    d. universal

14. The Network Monitor uses all available memory in the server, minus _____ for use by other programs.

15. The _____ is most useful when it comes to getting detailed information about a server's hard drive.

    a. Performance Monitor

    b. Event Viewer

    c. System log

    d. Network Monitor

16. Which kind of backup does not reset the archive bit? (Choose all that apply.)

    a. copy

    b. full

    c. differential

    d. incremental

17. All other things being equal, disk duplexing has a lower initial cost than disk mirroring. True or false?

18. Membership of the Everyone group includes all _____.

    a. user accounts

    b. currently logged-on user accounts

    c. currently logged-on user accounts accessing the server from the network

    d. currently logged-on accounts

19. In a three-disk RAID 5 stripe set, where is the parity information?

    a. on the first disk

    b. on the second disk

    c. on the third disk

    d. on all disks

10

20. You created a six-disk stripe set with parity. Each disk is 100 MB in size. How much room do you have in the stripe set for user data?

    a. 600 MB

    b. 500 MB

    c. 300 MB

    d. 200 MB

21. Windows NT and Windows 2000 Server support stripe sets with parity (RAID 5) of up to _____ disks.

22. You have a data partition 500 MB in size (only 200 MB is filled) that you'd like to mirror. What size partition do you need to mirror it to?

    a. 200 MB

    b. 300 MB

    c. 400 MB

    d. 500 MB

23. For security reasons, you should delete the Everyone group. True or false?

24. You're updating your Emergency Repair Disk (ERD) on a Windows NT system. In order to back up all security data, you must enter the _____ command on the command line.

25. System recovery procedures on Windows NT and Windows 2000 (including the ERD) are exactly the same. True or false?

26. Joe Brown has an account in the SALES domain but needs to store some information in the MANAGEMENT Windows NT Server domain. Which of the following actions do you need to take to make this possible? (Choose all that apply.)

    a. Permit MANAGEMENT to trust SALES.

    b. Make Joe a member of a local group in the MANAGEMENT domain.

    c. Make SALES trust MANAGEMENT.

    d. Add Joe to a global group in the SALES domain.

27. The new network card you just installed does not work, and you suspect an interrupt conflict. Which of the following should give you the information you need to determine whether this is the case?

    a. Security log

    b. System log

    c. Network Monitor

    d. Performance Monitor

28. Which of the following Windows 2000 fault-tolerance features permits you to access user settings, data files, and applications from your home desktop on another Windows 2000 machine on a network?

    a. disk mirroring

    b. disk duplexing

    c. RAID 5

    d. Intellimirror

29. Which of the following RAID levels are available on Windows 2000 and Windows NT servers? (Choose all that apply.)

    a. RAID 0

    b. RAID 1

    c. RAID 2

    d. RAID 3

    e. RAID 4

    f. RAID 5

30. Ideally, you should keep the Administrator account the same name and make the password something easy for you to remember in case you forget your account password. True or false?

10

HANDS-ON PROJECTS

In some of these Hands-on Projects, you use the RDISK utility to update Windows NT system repair information and to create an Emergency Repair Disk (ERD) on the Windows 2000 recovery console to perform similar actions. You also create a sample network security plan, practice creating a disk stripe set with parity (RAID 5), learn more about Intellimirror and RAID technologies, and examine Event Viewer logs.

Project 10-1

Because of the differences between the recovery mechanisms for Windows NT and Windows 2000, this Hands-on Project provides separate steps to attempt repairs for each type of system.

To update a Windows NT system's repair information and its ERD:

1. Procure a blank, 1.44 MB floppy disk or use one that contains data you don't need. (This procedure erases all extant data from the disk.)

2. From the **Start** menu, choose **Run**, and enter **rdisk/s** to start the RDISK utility. (The /s option tells the rdisk program to skip the initial "Create Repair Disk?" dialog box.)

   RDISK saves your current configuration information, updating the contents of %systemroot%\system32\repair, where backup copies of your system repair files are stored. (These files are not updated unless you run RDISK.) This takes a while, but a status bar shows the progress of the save.

3. When prompted to create the ERD, choose **Yes** to create the disk.

4. Label the floppy disk. (It's a good idea to date the label so you know when you last updated the ERD.) Insert the disk in Drive A, and click the **OK** button when prompted. Setup creates the updated ERD.

To operate the Windows 2000 recovery and repair consoles:

1. Boot a Windows 2000 system, either from the Windows 2000 CD (this requires a system that can boot from a CD-ROM) or from the Windows 2000 setup disks.

2. Press **Enter** when you see the Setup Notification prompt. Next, enter **R** to start the repair process, then **C** to start the Windows 2000 recovery console.

3. If there is more than one installation of Windows 2000 on the machine, the recovery console asks you to select the one you want to repair. If more than one entry appears, ask your instructor for directions about which to select. Select that entry, then press **Enter**. (If there's only one entry, simply press **Enter**.)

4. Next you are prompted for the Administrator password. Without that password, you cannot run this utility, so type the Administrator password after the prompt, and then press **Enter**.

5. Type **help** and then press **Enter**. You see a list of commands that work inside the recovery console. Notice that you can list, copy, and delete files, and perform many other common system administration tasks at the command line inside this utility. This makes it powerful and dangerous!

6. Type **exit** and then press **Enter**. This closes the recovery console and restarts your machine.

Project 10-2

A list of questions follows each step in this Hands-on Project. Answering these questions helps you make decisions about your network security plan.

To create a network security plan:

1. Create users and groups with the rights and permissions they need, without granting more than needed.

   a. Who will create user and group accounts?

   b. Who will perform backups?

   c. Who will perform printer and print job maintenance?

   d. Who will monitor network performance?

2. Determine a password policy.

   a. What words or characters are unacceptable in passwords? Names? Obscenities? Single characters or no password at all? What's the minimum password length?

   b. How often must passwords be changed? How long must they stay in effect until they are changed? How often may passwords be reused?

3. Identify the hours during which users may log on to the network. Consider the possibility that some users may need extended hours in which to finish special projects, or that network administrators may need to work weekends.

4. Determine an auditing policy.

   a. What events will you audit, and for what purpose? Logons/logoffs? Object accesses?

   b. Will you audit failed attempts, successful attempts, or both?

   c. How often will you review these audits?

   d. How often will you review your auditing criteria to be sure you're getting the information you need?

5. Determine a backup policy.

   a. How often will backups be made? What backup type will be used?

   b. Who will be responsible for creating and verifying these backups?

   c. Where will data be stored to ensure it gets backed up?

   d. Where will backups be stored, and how many generations will be kept?

Project 10-3

In this exercise, you examine how to create a set of mirrored disks on Windows NT Server and on Windows 2000 Server. The processes differ, so this Hands-on Project provides two separate sets of steps, one for each server type.

To create a set of mirrored disks on Windows NT Server:

1. Log on to a Windows NT Server 4.0 computer with two or more hard drives using an account with Administrator privileges.

2. Click **Start**, **Programs**, **Administrative Tools (Common)**, and **Disk Administrator** to open the Disk Administrator. Make sure you are in the Disk Configuration view by clicking the **Disk Configuration** icon (second from the left) on the toolbar. You see a screen similar to Figure 10-8.

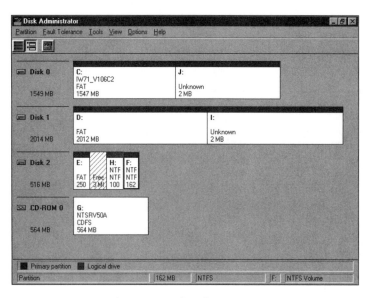

Figure 10-8   Windows NT Disk Administrator

3. Hold down the **Ctrl** key, and click to select the partition you want to mirror and an area of free space at least equal to it in size. (Any unused space on the disk becomes free space.)

4. From the **Fault Tolerance** menu, choose **Establish Mirror.** The partition and the area of free space are both color-coded, as shown in Figure 10-9.

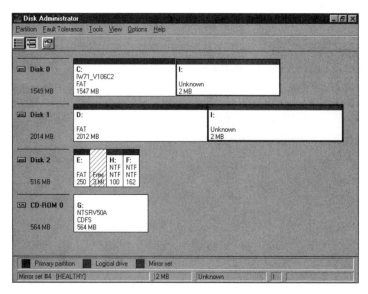

Figure 10-9   Mirror set changes appearance, but it's not yet ready to use

5. Right-click the new mirror set, and choose **Commit Changes Now** from the menu.

6. Right-click the mirror set and choose **Format** from the menu. You see a dialog box like the one shown in Figure 10-10. Click **Start**.

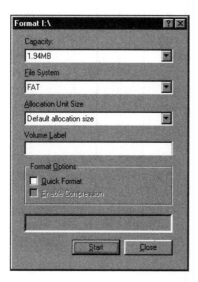

Figure 10-10 Formatting a mirror set before using it

7. Once you format the mirror set, the Disk Administrator should look something like Figure 10-11. Notice that the mirror set's status appears in the lower-left of the status bar.

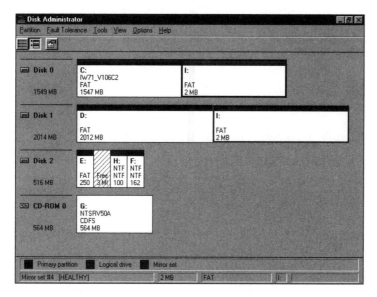

Figure 10-11 Mirror set (I:) is color-coded in the Disk Administrator

To create a set of mirrored disks on Windows 2000 Server:

1. Log on to the Windows 2000 Server computer with two or more hard drives using an account with Administrator privileges.

2. Click **Start**, **Programs**, **Administrative Tools**, and **Computer Management**, and then click the **Disk Management** folder beneath the Storage Management icon. You see a screen similar to Figure 10-12.

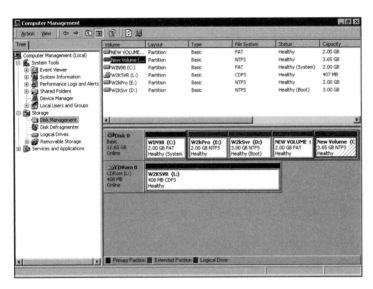

Figure 10-12   Windows 2000 Disk Management utility in Computer Management

3. Right-click the volume you want to mirror, and then select **Add Mirror** from the shortcut menu.

4. Select the dynamic volume that will act as the mirror for the original volume, and then click **OK**. This creates the necessary mirror volume for you. The newly mirrored set appears in a brick-red pattern by default in the Disk Administrator window.

5. Close this utility. (If your instructor asks you to break and remove the mirror before closing, select the mirror in the Disk Administrator pane, right-click, select **Break Mirror** from the menu, and then delete the individual partitions. Then close this utility.)

Project 10-4

In this project, you use Performance Monitor on Windows 2000 or Windows XP to check CPU performance indicators on your computer.

To use Performance Monitor:

1. Open the Performance Monitor by going to **Start**, **Program Files**, **Administrative Tools** and clicking **Performance**. (For Windows XP, replace Program Files with **All Programs**.)

2. Click the plus sign on the toolbar to bring up the Add Counters dialog box.

3. In the Performance object drop down box, select **Processor** and then click the **Select counters from** list option button.

4. Select **% Processor Time** and click the **Add** button.

5. Next select **Interrupts/sec** and click the **Add** button. Click the **Close** button.

6. You will see a vertical bar cross the graph, leaving a line histogram of the % Processor Time and the Interrupts/sec counters. If your machine is fairly idle, you will not see much movement in the histogram. To create some movement, open a Web browser window or Windows Explorer. These actions will cause the CPU to work and will create interrupts.

7. When you are finished, close Performance Monitor. Choose **No** when asked to save console settings.

Project 10-5

In this exercise, you enable auditing on a Windows 2000 Professional or Windows XP Professional computer and perform some actions that will create Security Log events. In the next project you examine the Event Logs. Note that this project requires a Windows 2000 or Windows XP Professional computer that is not part of a domain.

To enable auditing:

1. Log on to Windows. For Windows 2000, go to **Start/Programs/Administrative Tools**, and select **Local Security Policy**. For Windows XP, go to **Start/All Programs/Administrative Tools**, and select **Local Security Policy**.

2. Under Security Settings in the Tree pane of the window, expand Local Policies by clicking the plus sign.

3. Click **Audit Policy**. In the right pane, double-click **Audit account logon events**.

4. Click the **Failure** check box.

5. Click **OK** and close the Local Security Settings dialog box.

6. Log off Windows.

7. When you log back on, purposely misspell your password so that your logon fails. Then log on correctly.

Project 10-6

In this project, you examine the contents of the three Windows Event logs—the System log, the Security log, and the Applications log—to learn more about their contents and functions. Regular review of these logs is an important part of system maintenance on any Windows machine, especially a server.

To access the Windows Event Viewer:

1. For Windows NT and Windows 2000, the menu sequence is the same: **Start**, **Programs**, **Administrative Tools**, **Event Viewer**. In Windows XP, use **Start**, **All Programs**, **Administrative Tools**, **Event Viewer**. You must log on with administrative privileges to access the various Event Viewer logs. (Your instructor will tell you the appropriate password.)

2. In Windows 2000 and Windows XP, all three logs appear in the left pane of the standard management console display, and the contents of the selected log appear in the right pane of this display. Windows NT shows the system log by default, and you must access the Log entry in the menu bar to switch menu selections.

3. Items in the Event Viewer logs use colors and icons to indicate status: a red x or stop sign indicates an error, a yellow triangle indicates a warning, and a blue i indicates an informational message. You can double-click an entry in the log to view an Event Properties window that shows whatever information Event Viewer collected for this item. Select an item of each kind, if available, and double-click it to examine the associated details.

4. Repeat Step 3 for the security and application logs.

5. Close the program.

CASE PROJECTS

1. Your NT-based office network has three domains: ALPHA, BETA, and OMEGA.

   Required Result: You must give some users with accounts in the ALPHA domain access to some resources in the OMEGA domain, but you must not open the ALPHA domain to any OMEGA users.

   Optional Result: If possible, changes to the ALPHA users' accounts should be reflected in the accounts they use to access OMEGA resources.

   Proposed Solution: Set up a two-way trust relationship between ALPHA and OMEGA, add the ALPHA users to a local Users' group in ALPHA, and add that group to the global OMEGA group Domain Users. Based on your goals and your actions, which of the following statements is true? Why?

   a. You accomplished both your required result and your optional result.

   b. You accomplished your required result, but not your optional result.

   c. You accomplished your optional result, but not your required result.

   d. You accomplished neither your optional nor your required result.

2. Your network server has a UPS attached, and the server's data partition is mirrored. Each Sunday night, you perform a full backup of the mirrored partition, and each night you complete a differential backup. In the event of a power outage, can you still lose data? Why or why not?

3. On your network, all network administrators upgraded their machines to Windows 2000 Professional, and a special Windows 2000 Server with an enormous amount of disk space is available for their use. Explain what Windows 2000 fault-tolerant subsystem they should use to protect their desktop settings, applications, and data files, and how it provides such protection.

4. Explain why CompuServe's technique for creating passwords—namely to separate two words using a punctuation character—is a good idea. Table 10-4 lists the punctuation characters.

Table 10-4   CompuServe punctuation characters in passwords

Character	Name	Character	Name
~	Tilde	&	Ampersand
!	Exclamation point	*	Asterisk
@	At sign	(	Open parenthesis
#	Hash mark	)	Close parenthesis
$	Dollar sign	–	Dash (minus sign)
%	Percent symbol	+	Plus sign
^	Caret	=	Equal sign
<	Left angle bracket	>	Right angle bracket

Please note that each of the two words used is from a 25,000-entry dictionary of terms that CompuServe maintains for this purpose, and that the punctuation marks in Table 10-4 total 16. What implications does this approach have for someone who wants to try a brute force attack on a CompuServe password? What other common account control should you always use to foil brute force attacks?

5. Under normal circumstances, auditing focuses on failures to access rather than on successful accesses. Explain why it might be a good idea to audit successful access to files in a directory that contains highly confidential files.

6. Although Windows NT and Windows 2000 both support software RAID arrays for RAID 0 and RAID 5, in practice hardly anyone uses either of these RAID implementations; instead they prefer to buy a hardware RAID controller and let the hardware handle the RAID subsystem. Explain three reasons why this decision represents good judgment. (*Hint*: At least two of these reasons involve performance.)

10

11

ENTERPRISE AND DISTRIBUTED NETWORKS

> **After reading this chapter and completing the exercises, you will be able to:**
>
> ♦ Understand how modems are used in network communications
>
> ♦ Understand faster alternatives to modems for network communications
>
> ♦ Survey the different types of carriers used for long-haul network communications
>
> ♦ Explain how larger networks may be implemented using devices such as repeaters, bridges, routers, brouters, gateways, and switches

This chapter introduces some devices that allow the expansion of networks locally or across the world. First, you learn about modems, the basic communications tool that lets computers communicate using conventional telephone lines. Then the different types of communications lines or carriers are discussed. Finally, you find out about products that make it possible to expand networks and network segments.

MODEMS IN NETWORK COMMUNICATIONS

A **modem** is a tool used to connect computers over a telephone line or TV cable line, effectively extending a network beyond a local area. Because a modem can use existing telephone lines, it remains one of the most popular methods to connect remote users to a network or the Internet. As shown in Figure 11-1, a modem converts a digital signal received from a computer into an analog signal that can be sent along regular telephone lines.

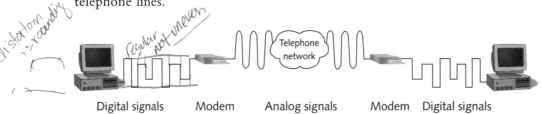

Digital signals   Modem   Analog signals   Modem   Digital signals

Figure 11-1 Modems convert digital signals to analog and vice versa

This conversion is called modulation. A modem modulates the digital signal into an analog signal. Then, at the other end of the line, another modem demodulates the analog signal back to digital. Thus, the term **MOdulator/DEModulator**, or **modem** is used.

Modems are available for use internally or externally for most computers. Internal modems are added to an expansion slot in the computer. An external modem is a separate box, with its own power supply, that connects to the serial port on a computer using the RS-232 communications interface standard. Both types of modems include RJ-11 connectors to allow easy connection to a standard telephone wall jack, using a standard modular phone cable.

Modems are sometimes described as **Hayes-compatible**. In the early 1980s, Hayes Microcomputer Products, Inc., developed a modem called the Smartmodem, which could automatically dial a number through a telephone. In much the same way that the IBM PC became the de facto standard against which PCs are measured to this day (that is, IBM-compatible), Hayes modems defined a reference standard for modems.

Modem Speed

Modem speed is measured in the number of bits per second (bps) that can be transmitted. Table 11-1 shows some of the **V-series** standards developed by the **International Telecommunications Union (ITU)** to define modem speed. The table lists standards with the terms **bis** and **ter**. These do not refer to the modem speed, but, rather, are the French terms for *second* and *third*, which indicate revisions of the original standard. As a point of reference, the V.22bis modem transmits a 1000-word document in 25 seconds, whereas the V.34 modem sends the same document in two seconds, and the V.42bis compression modem can send the document in only one second.

Table 11-1   ITU communications standards

Standard	bps	Year Introduced
V.22bis	2400	1984
V.32	9600	1984
V.32bis	14,400	1991
V.32ter	19,200	1993
V.FastClass (V.FC)	28,800	1993
V.34	28,800	1994
V.42bis	57,600	1995
V.90	115,200	1998

Note

The term **baud** is sometimes used to denote modem speed. Baud represents the oscillation of a sound wave that carries one bit of data. For earlier modems, the terms *baud* and *bps* are used interchangeably; a 300-bps modem has 300 oscillations of sound waves each second. However, with new compression technologies, the number of bits per second increased way beyond the number of oscillations per second. For example, a modem that transmits at 28,800 bps may actually be transmitting at 9600 baud.

Types of Modems

Two types of modems are used today: asynchronous and synchronous. Which type you use depends on the type of phone lines and the network requirements involved. Also, you should be aware that where continuous network connections may be desirable (as when linking a branch office to a headquarters location for a constant network connection), digital technologies such as DSL or cable modems (discussed later in this chapter in the section titled "Digital Modems") may offer higher bandwidth and better communications capabilities at little or no extra cost.

Asynchronous Modems

Asynchronous (or async) communication is the most popular method for communicating with a modem because it uses regular telephone lines. Asynchronous modems convert each data byte into a stream of ones and zeros. As shown in Figure 11-2, start and stop bits separate each byte from the next. Both the sending and receiving devices must agree on the start and stop bit sequence.

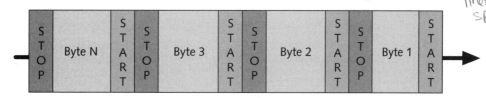

Figure 11-2   Asynchronous modems use start and stop bits

As its name implies, in asynchronous communications, there is no synchronization of communication or method for coordinating communication between two computers. The sending computer transmits data in a continuous stream, and the receiving computer receives that data and checks that it matches what was sent. In an asynchronous environment, flow control and data coordination account for 25 percent of all communication.

Many modems correct transmission errors as they occur. In addition to the start and stop bits, a parity bit is added for each byte of data. The sending computer counts the number of ones in the data stream. If the number is odd, it sets the parity bit to one. The receiving computer counts the number of ones in the data stream, determines whether the number is odd or even, and then compares the result with the parity bit. If the parity bits match, the chances are high that the data arrived intact. If not, the modem requests retransmission of the data packet.

Most modems also incorporate data compression in their transmission to achieve higher transmission speeds. One of the most common data compression standards used is MNP Class 5 compression by Microcom. When both modems use MNP 5, data transmission time can be cut in half. The ITU V.42bis standard uses hardware data compression and is one of the more efficient compression standards available. For example, a 9600-bps modem using V.42bis can achieve throughput of up to 38,400 bps.

The most current asynchronous modem standard used for connecting to the Internet is the V.90 standard. The V.90 standard makes connection speeds up to 56 Kbps possible. Eliminating one of the modulation/demodulation steps done by traditional modem communications makes these higher speeds possible. Traditional modem communications convert digital data coming out of the computer into analog data that travels on the phone lines. After the analog signal reaches the destination modem, the conversion is from analog back to digital. Figure 11-3 shows this type of communication in a typical Internet connection. After the analog signal reaches the telco, the signal is converted to digital. The telco then must convert the signal back to analog for the receiving modem at the ISP, which in turn converts the signal to digital for the Internet. This two-way conversion limited transfer speeds to 33.6 Kbps.

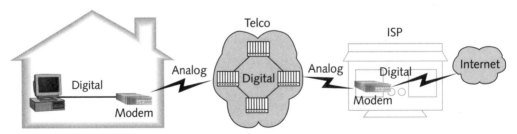

Figure 11-3   Modem communications using two analog-to-digital conversions

V.90 modems assume that the network from the phone company to the Internet Service Provider (ISP) and then out to the Internet is an all-digital network. Therefore, rather than modulating the analog data into digital data, as it is received from the phone company, the V.90 modem uses a technique called **pulse code modulation (PCM)**. PCM is a technique for digitizing analog signals. PCM introduces less noise into the signal than traditional modulation/demodulation techniques. Thus, it boosts the total number of bits per second that data can be transferred. This type of connection is depicted in Figure 11-4. Notice in the figure that there is only one analog connection—from the home to the telco. From the telco to the ISP and then to the Internet, the signal is all digital.

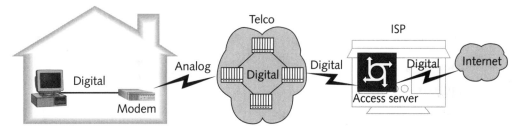

Figure 11-4 Modem communications using the V.90 standard

Two caveats with V.90 communications are that there must be only one analog circuit between the modem and the Internet, and 56 Kbps communications works only in one direction—the download direction. This means that the data from the modem to the ISP travels at the rate of only 33.6 Kbps, whereas the data from the ISP to the modem travels at the V.90 speed of 56 Kbps.

When data travels in the download direction at a speed different from the upload direction, this is what is known as **asymmetric communication**.

 Although V.90 technology is capable of data transfer speeds up to 56 Kbps, FCC regulations limit the maximum download speed to 54 Kbps. However, actual transfer rates depend on line conditions.

Synchronous Modems NOT DIALUP -

Asynchronous modems depend on the start and stop bits in the data stream to determine where data begins and ends; **synchronous** modems depend on timing. Two devices coordinate this timing scheme to separate groups of bits and transmit them in blocks known as frames. Both modems must be synchronized for communication to occur. Figure 11-5 shows how synchronous modems transmit frames of data with synchronization (or synch) bits inserted periodically to ensure accurate timing.

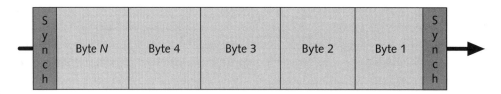

Figure 11-5   Synchronous modems send synchronization bits periodically

Cost more than Asyncs *Connect up to 128 Kbps*

If an error occurs, the modem simply requests that the frame be retransmitted. Because synchronous modems have so little overhead in terms of error checking, they are significantly faster than asynchronous modems. In addition, synchronous protocols provide a number of functions not available in asynchronous communication. They format the data into blocks, add control information, and check the information for errors. There are three primary synchronous communication protocols: **Synchronous Data Link Control (SDLC)**, **High-level Data Link Control (HDLC)**, and **Binary Synchronous (bisync) communications** protocol.

Synchronous modems were *not* designed for use over regular phone lines; instead, they are generally found in dedicated, leased-line environments. (Chapter 12 covers dedicated leased lines.) Because of this and the more expensive equipment involved, implementing a synchronous solution for network communication costs much more than implementing asynchronous solutions.

Digital Modems

Another increasingly prevalent modem type is the **digital modem**. Of course, because a modem translates a signal from digital to analog, the term digital modem is not technically accurate and most often refers to the interface for **Integrated Services Digital Network (ISDN)**. Chapter 12 describes this service in greater detail. It is important to understand that the interface used for ISDN is sometimes referred to as a digital modem. In fact, the adapters used for ISDN consist of a **network termination (NT)** device and **terminal adapter (TA)** equipment. However, because most users are familiar with the term *modem*, manufacturers of these NT/TA devices often use that term.

Since 1998, cable television operators and telecommunications companies have offered higher-speed digital connections that supplanted both ISDN and conventional asynchronous modems for small office/home office (SOHO) use. In both cases, the term modem often is used, even though these technologies may require no digital-to-analog and analog-to-digital demodulation.

Cable modems take advantage of the high bandwidth of broadband CATV cables and the wide availability of this infrastructure in many households to ferry signals to and from Internet points of presence (POP) on behalf of households. The devices that attach to a network interface card (NIC) on a computer typically feature a BNC connector, where the CATV coaxial cable attaches, and an RJ-45 connector that attaches through a modular cable to a NIC on a computer. Some CATV systems do indeed use analog signaling in their broadband environment, so the term cable modem is exactly correct in such cases. However, an increasing number of cable companies are switching to digital cable, which retains broadband's use of multiple channels on a single cable but switches from analog to digital signaling methods on a per-channel basis. In such cases, cable modems are not really modulator/demodulators. However, the terminology indicates that the devices involved (which customers usually rent from the cable company) permit a computer to attach to the Internet through the CATV infrastructure.

It's important to note that cable modems provide bandwidth to end users as a form of shared media access. That is, all users on any particular CATV cable segment (usually part of a neighborhood, subdivision, apartment complex, or large building) share the available bandwidth. Therefore, more users (or more traffic per user) means less bandwidth per user because access is shared. Maximum bandwidth for most CATV cable segments is about 1.5 Mbps (roughly equivalent to a T1 connection). One powerful advantage of cable modem access, however, is that distance limitations do not govern functionality. As long as the user has access to cable television and the cable company also offers Internet access on the local cable segment, that user can install a cable modem and access the Internet for rates as low as $30 to $50 per month.

Aside from the performance issues raised from the shared access media used in cable modem networks, security concerns also abound. These concerns stem from the fact that users who share the same cable segment may eavesdrop on other users' communications sessions. This may have been a legitimate concern for early cable networks, but networks that comply with the DOCSIS cable modem standard utilize a strong 56-bit encryption key for each user connection. This level of encryption ensures privacy for each user on the network.

Telecommunications carriers offer a competing digital technology called **Digital Subscriber Line (DSL)**. (Typically, such companies include local telephone companies and their competitors, for example, long-distance companies, local-exchange carriers, and digital-only carriers such as Covad and Rhythms.) To deliver digital services, DSL uses the same twisted-pair telephone lines that deliver voice telephone services. Unlike cable modem connections, DSL connections are not shared and thus offer their subscribers guaranteed bandwidth. But because bandwidth is guaranteed, upstream (communications from the user to the remote side of the connection) and downstream (communications from the remote side of the connection to the user) data rates are metered. Users must pay more for higher bandwidth connections. Nevertheless, DSL is a great SOHO technology because it costs less than ISDN and usually offers at least 384-Kbps upstream and downstream bandwidth. As with cable modems, most DSL implementations top out at around 1.5-Mbps bandwidth. (Even so, such connections usually cost less than a T1 line.)

DSL's primary disadvantage is its distance limitation between the end user's location and the nearest **central office (CO)** (measured as the wire runs), where a copper-to-fiber interface device links to the telecommunication carrier's digital backbone. Depending on which vendor's equipment is used, this distance limitation varies between 17,500 feet

(3.31 miles or 5.33 km) and 23,000 feet (4.36 miles or 7.01 km). Thus, it's important to measure how far a connection point is from the local CO to determine if DSL is a viable network option for any particular installation.

Although there are many flavors of DSL, the two most common types are **Asymmetric Digital Subscriber Line (ADSL)** and **Symmetric Digital Subscriber Line (SDSL)**. Its upload and download speeds differ. ADSL supports speeds up to 8 Mbps in the download direction and up to 1 Mbps in the upload direction, but typical connection speeds are less than 1.5 Mbps for download and less than 1 Mbps for upload.

ADSL is ideal for home Internet users because the bulk of traffic in home Internet connections is traveling in the download direction.

The upload and download speeds are equivalent in SDSL. This technology is often chosen for businesses where a Web site is operated because the amount of traffic uploaded and downloaded is likely to be similar.

For more information on DSL technology, see *www.dslreports.com*.

DSL and cable modems both share one significant advantage over asynchronous modems—they are "always on." Both technologies maintain constant connections to a remote server on the other side of the connection, so there's never a delay to establish a connection, as is the case with a conventional modem. Given the higher bandwidth, faster access, and relatively low cost of these digital connection types, it's no wonder that droves of users are switching from modems for SOHO connections. However, because mobile users (such as those who want to dial into the Internet or a private network from a laptop while traveling) will always remain part of the remote user base, this doesn't yet sound a death knell for conventional modems. Other digital technologies are not yet widely available to mobile users, but conventional telephone lines are.

CARRIERS – SBC, AT&T ext

Three general considerations can affect your choice of modem and connection for remote network communications:

- Throughput
- Distance
- Cost

You must consider each of these factors when deciding on the type of carrier (telephone line) to use for your network.

Four carrier options are available through the **public switched telephone network (PSTN)**: dial-up, ISDN, DSL, and dedicated leased lines. In addition, CATV-based cable access may also be an option for SOHO users.

As already noted, dial-up connections use existing telephone lines to establish a temporary connection to your network. However, because line quality varies greatly, communication speed is generally limited to 28,800 bps. New technology is pushing this limitation to 56 Kbps over some lines, and some experiments have reached speeds up to 115 Kbps. However, these newer technologies are not in wide use today. If you add a separate analog phone line for residential or business use for telecommunications, expect to pay somewhere between $18 and $35 per month in the United States for no-frills service.

ISDN, which Chapter 12 discusses in detail, provides a dial-up solution for transmitting voice and data over a digital phone line. **Basic Rate Interface (BRI)** ISDN provides two 64-Kbps B-channels for voice or data and one 16-Kbps D-channel for signal control. **Primary Rate Interface (PRI)** ISDN, which provides 23 B-channels and one D-channel, is used primarily for WAN connectivity. Although ISDN requires digital phone lines, many companies use ISDN as an effective way to connect remote offices. The BRI B-channels can be combined easily to provide throughput of 128 Kbps, significantly more bandwidth than a standard dial-up connection provides. ISDN BRI lines typically cost about $50 to $70 per month and may not include Internet access services (which may cost an additional $20 per month or more for ISDN services). ISDN PRI lines are usually priced on par with T1 connections, which vary widely by location from a low of around $300 to a high of $1500 per month in the United States.

DSL connections represent an all-digital service that local carriers provide as a lower-cost, medium-bandwidth alternative to conventional modems and dedicated leased lines. DSL connections offer guaranteed bandwidth, and prices increase along with bandwidth. A 384-Kbps upstream/downstream connection might cost anywhere from $30 to $60 per month in the United States, depending on location, and a 1.5-Mbps upstream/downstream connection might cost between $300 and $600 per month. (Note that higher bandwidth offerings are often asymmetrical—they offer higher downstream bandwidth with lower upstream bandwidth at a lower price, because download traffic-handling requirements are often higher than upload requirements.)

Dedicated leased lines provide continuous connections between two sites. More expensive than other types of connections, these are also higher speed, generally from 56 Kbps up to 45 Mbps. Given competition at the low end from DSL and cable modems, speeds above T1 remain the strongest bastion for dedicated leased lines looking into the future. At half the price, or less, of a T1 connection, equivalent DSL connections (which don't require as much expensive equipment as a T1 link does) appear poised to take over the low end of the digital communication business.

REMOTE ACCESS NETWORKING

For your network to be even more effective, you may need to allow users dial-in access from their homes, remote sites, or hotel rooms. A simple way to accomplish this in a Microsoft Windows NT network is to use the Windows NT **Remote Access Service (RAS)**; on a Windows 2000 network, the equivalent service is called Routing and Remote Access Service (RRAS).

Loaded on a Windows NT or Window 2000 server, remote access services allow up to 256 remote clients to dial in, if the hardware is available. Figure 11-6 shows Windows 2000 RRAS. In Windows 2000, RRAS includes routing software that permits a server to function as a low-end routing device. RRAS also includes local-area routing services, as well as the ability to route between one or more remote connections and one or more local connections. (This chapter covers routing services in more detail later.)

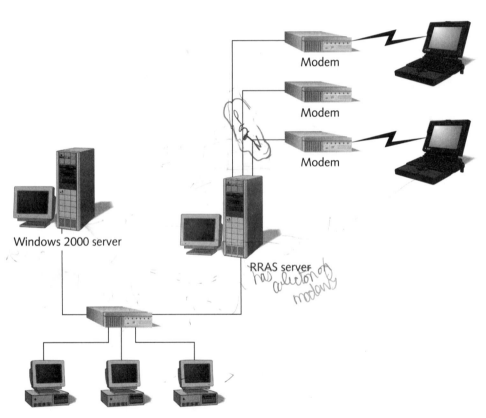

Figure 11-6   Windows 2000 RRAS provides remote connectivity to clients

Using RAS or RRAS to connect to a network, users can dial in over general-use telephone lines or cable lines. After the connection is established, the computer that is remotely connected acts exactly as if it were directly connected to the network, albeit a little slower. In addition, both RAS and RRAS also support virtual private network connections across the Internet. (You'll learn more about virtual private networks in Chapter 12.) Users only need to connect to a local Internet Service Provider (ISP) and establish a virtual private network connection to a remote access server also attached to the Internet.

 It is important to note that the ability for a user to dial into a Windows remote access server is disabled by default. This default condition is for security reasons. A user's remote access capability must be enabled in the user account information in order for that user to log into the remote server.

Windows XP, Windows 2000, Windows NT 4.0, Windows Millennium, Windows 98, and Windows 95 include **Dial-Up Networking (DUN)** software to make a RAS connection. The DUN client also connects computers to ISPs.

Two protocols are available for remote access (for RRAS, RAS, and DUN):

- Serial Line Internet Protocol (SLIP)
- Point-to-Point Protocol (PPP)

Serial Line Internet Protocol (SLIP)

Serial Line Internet Protocol (SLIP) is an older protocol used primarily by PCs to connect to the Internet using a modem. Essentially a Physical layer protocol, it provides connectivity across telephone lines and no error correction. SLIP, which relies on hardware for error checking and correction, supports connections only for TCP/IP and requires no addressing because a connection is made only between two machines. Standard implementations of SLIP provide no compression, but a version called compressed SLIP (CSLIP) does support this option. SLIP is still supported but not used much in today's environment.

Point-to-Point Protocol (PPP)

Point-to-Point Protocol (PPP) provides a much more dynamic connection between computers than SLIP does. The largest difference between SLIP and PPP is that PPP provides both Physical and Data Link layer services, which effectively turn a modem into a NIC. Therefore, PPP supports multiple protocols, including IP, IPX, and NetBEUI. In addition, PPP inherently supports compression and error checking, which makes it faster and more reliable than SLIP.

Although both SLIP and PPP allow connectivity through TCP/IP, PPP supports dynamic assignment of IP addresses. This allows the administrator to assign a block of addresses to RAS and RRAS modems. Because it is more robust and allows greater flexibility, PPP has replaced SLIP as the remote protocol of choice for TCP/IP connections. In fact, while it is possible to use a Windows computer to dial into a remote connection using SLIP, the only kinds of dial-up connections that RAS and RRAS support require PPP (or a direct Internet connection, for virtual private network connections).

IP ADDRESSES
Support DHCP

CREATING LARGER NETWORKS

As your organization grows and uses the network more heavily, the network eventually may no longer be as efficient as it should be. Perhaps you reach the physical limitations of the network, or network traffic increases so much that you must find a way to relieve congestion. A time comes in every administrator's life when the network must be changed. There are different ways you can stretch or expand network capabilities:

- Physically expanding to support additional computers
- Segmenting to filter and manage network traffic
- Extending to connect separate LANs
- Connecting two or more disjointed networking environments

Many devices are available to accomplish these tasks:

- Repeaters
- Bridges
- Routers
- Brouters
- Gateways
- Switches

The following sections discuss each device.

Repeaters   attenuation - weakening of signal

A signal that travels along a cable degrades and becomes distorted through attenuation. If the cable is long enough, the signal eventually becomes so degraded that it is unrecognizable. A repeater regenerates the signal and extends a network's reach.

As shown in Figure 11-7, a repeater accepts a signal, cleans it, regenerates it, and sends it down the line, effectively doubling the length of the network. To pass data through a repeater in a usable fashion, the packets and the Logical Link Control (LLC) protocols must be the same on both sides of the repeater. This means that you cannot use a repeater to translate data between different kinds of LAN technologies. For example, you cannot place a repeater between an Ethernet 802.3 LAN and a token ring 802.5 LAN.

Incoming signal   Repeater   Cleaned and regenerated
                                               outgoing signal

Figure 11-7   Repeaters regenerate signals

Repeaters operate at the Physical layer of the OSI model without concern for the type of data being transmitted, the packet address, or the protocol used. They cannot perform any filtering or translation on the actual data.

Although a repeater cannot connect different types of network architectures, it can connect different physical media. For example, a network running Ethernet 802.3 over thinnet coaxial cable can use a repeater to connect to a network running Ethernet 802.3 over UTP, as shown in Figure 11-8.

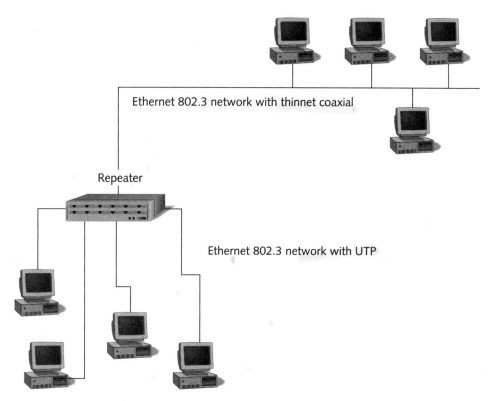

Ethernet 802.3 network with thinnet coaxial

Repeater

Ethernet 802.3 network with UTP

Figure 11-8   Repeaters can connect different physical media

Repeaters retransmit the data at the same speed as the network. However, a slight delay occurs as the repeater regenerates the signal. Using a number of repeaters in a row can create significant **propagation delay**. Propagation delay is the time it takes for a signal to travel from the source device to the destination device. Therefore, many network architectures limit the number of repeaters. For example, a 10Base2 network can have a maximum of four repeaters connecting five network segments. Table 11-2 highlights the advantages and disadvantages of repeaters.

Repeaters obsol...

B

Switches

Table 11-2 Advantages and disadvantages of repeaters

Advantages	Disadvantages
Allow easy expansion of the network over large distances	Provide no addressing information
Have very little impact on network speed	Cannot connect different network architectures
Allow connection between different media	Do not help ease congestion problems

Bridges

Like repeaters, **bridges** also connect two network segments and can connect dissimilar physical media. However, bridges can also do the following: limit the traffic on each segment; eliminate bottlenecks; connect different network architectures, such as Ethernet and token ring; and forward **frames** between them. A frame is the unit of data with which bridges work. Frames contain physical address information and are defined at layer 2 of the OSI model, which is where bridges operate.

A bridge functions primarily to filter traffic between network segments. As a network segment receives a frame, the bridge looks at the physical destination address of the frame before forwarding the frame to other segments. If, in fact, the frame's destination is on another network segment, the bridge retransmits the frame out the appropriate port. However, if the destination is on the same network segment that receives the frame, the bridge assumes the frame has already reached its destination and discards it. As a result, network traffic is greatly reduced.

This raises an interesting question: how does a bridge know which computers are on which network segments? Bridges work at the Data Link layer of the OSI model or, more specifically, at the Media Access Control (MAC) sublayer of the Data Link layer of the OSI model. Recall from Chapter 6 that the MAC sublayer is where the hardware addresses, both source and destination, are added to the packet, at which point the packet becomes a frame. Because bridges function at this layer, they have access to this address information. In Ethernet and token ring networks, this information generally is burned into the NIC when it is created. In ARCnet networks, the address is assigned using DIP switches; AppleTalk networks assign the address when the system is turned on. Through one of these methods, each computer in the network receives a unique address. Bridges analyze these MAC addresses, also called hardware addresses, to determine whether to forward a frame. Bridges use two methods to determine on which network segment a computer exists: transparent bridging and source-route bridging.

Ethernet networks most often use **transparent bridges**, or **learning bridges**. These bridges build a **bridging table** as they receive frames. When a bridge is turned on, the bridging table is empty. As it receives a frame, the bridge notes the network segment that received the frame, as well as the source and destination address of the frame. By doing this, the bridge builds a comprehensive list of MAC addresses and the network segment of each address.

When the bridge receives a frame, it compares its source and destination addresses to its bridging table. If the two addresses are on the same network segment, the bridge discards the frame. If the bridge finds the MAC address of the frame's destination in its bridging table, it sends the frame down to the particular network segment on which that MAC address resides. If, however, the destination MAC address is not in the bridging table, the bridge sends the frame to all segments except the one that received the frame. This assures that the frame reaches its destination.

Source-routing bridges are used primarily in token ring networks. These bridges rely on the frame's source to include path information. Bridges of this type require little processing power because the sending computer does most of the work. Source computers use explorer frames to determine the best path to a particular computer. The frame includes this information when it is sent across the network. When a source-routing bridge receives such a frame, it notes the path and uses it for future frames sent to that destination.

Regardless of the type of bridge used, bridges are slower than repeaters because they examine each frame's source and destination addresses. However, because they filter traffic, bridges can increase the throughput on a network.

It is important to note, however, that bridges do not reduce network traffic caused by broadcast frames (transmissions sent simultaneously to all network devices). Most traffic in a computer network is destined for a particular computer, and a bridge can send the frame to its destination. However, when a computer needs to send information to all other computers on the network, it sends a broadcast frame. When the computers receive this frame, they treat it as if it were addressed to them individually.

In many instances, a network benefits from broadcasts. For example, some network protocols, such as NetBEUI, rely on broadcasts for network communication. Of course, too many broadcast frames cause a network to bog down; this is especially problematic if a malfunctioning NIC or computer generates the broadcasts. In this situation, the NIC can flood the network rapidly, causing a **broadcast storm** during which no other data is sent across the network. Unfortunately, bridges do not help in this situation and, in fact, may exacerbate it.

As mentioned, bridges, like repeaters, can connect networks of dissimilar media because bridges can operate at the Physical layer of the OSI model. For example, a bridge can connect an Ethernet 10BaseF network to an Ethernet 10BaseT network.

Generally speaking, bridges are intended to connect similar networks at the Data Link layer of the OSI model. However, **translation bridges** can connect different types of networks. For example, a translation bridge can connect an Ethernet network to a token ring network. To Ethernet nodes, these bridges appear as transparent bridges and accept Ethernet frames. To token ring nodes, they appear as source-routing bridges and accept token ring frames. Translation bridges also are available for Ethernet-to-FDDI conversion. Table 11-3 lists the advantages and disadvantages of bridges.

11

Table 11-3   Advantages and disadvantages of bridges

Advantages	Disadvantages
Easily extend network distances	Slower than repeaters
Filter traffic to ease congestion	Pass broadcast frames
Connect networks with different media	More expensive than repeaters
Translation bridges can connect different network architectures.	

Switches

A **switch** is, in essence, a high-speed multiport bridge. A switch is an intelligent hub that maintains a switching table and keeps track of which hardware addresses are located on which network segments. Almost all of the features of bridges are present in switches.

The primary difference between bridges and switches is in the implementation details. Whereas a bridge may have only two or three ports permitting the connection of only two or three network segments, a typical switch may have between four and hundreds of ports. This allows switches to interconnect many network segments.

Another primary difference between bridges and switches is the speed at which they perform their tasks. A bridge has a general-purpose CPU that runs a software program that implements the bridging function. A switch uses a specialized processor that is preprogrammed to perform the switching function. Therefore, a bridge performs its functions in software, while a switch performs its functions in hardware.

Today, switches are replacing multiport repeaters or concentrators in a UTP environment. Like a bridge, a switch only sends a frame down the network segment on which a computer resides. Because of this, the network works more efficiently than it would with any other type of hub.

Switches accomplish the task of receiving a frame on one port and forwarding it out another port using a variety of methods. The simplest and fastest method is called **cut-through switching**. In cut-through switching, the switch reads only enough of the incoming frame to determine where to forward the frame, which in Ethernet amounts to 12 bytes. After the forwarding location is determined, the frame is switched internally from the incoming port to the outgoing port, and the switch is free to handle additional frames.

The benefit of cut-through switching is speed. A typical Ethernet frame can be up to 1518 bytes in length, whereas a Token Ring frame can be up to 18000 bytes. With cut-through switching, the switch reads only a very small portion of the total frame before sending the frame on its way. The disadvantage to this switching method is that the switch indiscriminately forwards frames that contain errors, therefore needlessly tying up bandwidth.

On the other hand, **store-and-forward switching** requires that the switch read the entire frame into its buffers before the forwarding process can occur. The switch first examines the CRC field in the frame to be sure that the frame contains no errors before it is forwarded. If a CRC error is found, the switch discards the frame.

The store-and-forward switching method has the advantage of preserving bandwidth usage when there are many frames that contain errors. The disadvantage to this method is that the entire frame must be read, stored in memory, and examined before it can be forwarded. This process takes time and slows the network.

A third popular switching method is called **fragment-free switching**. Fragment-free switching reads enough of the frame to guarantee that the frame is at least the minimum size for the network type. For Ethernet, this minimum frame size is 64 bytes.

One type of frame error that can occur in a network is a **frame fragment**, in which the frame is damaged due to either a collision or a malfunctioning device such as a NIC or hub. When this type of damage occurs, the frame may be truncated to less than the minimum allowable size. A switch operating in fragment-free mode detects this problem and discards the frame without forwarding it.

A benefit of switching technology is its ability to dedicate bandwidth to each port on the switch. For example, in an Ethernet 10BaseT environment using a regular hub, all ports of the hub share the maximum throughput of 10 Mbps. If your hub has 48 ports, all 48 ports share the 10 Mbps. However, in a switched networking environment, the switch can dedicate 10 Mbps to each port on the switch, which ensures that the maximum bandwidth is available to all computers on the network. In addition, repeaters allow only half-duplex communication, in which a device can send or receive only at a given time, but cannot do both simultaneously. A switch, however, permits full-duplex communications, allowing a connected workstation to send and receive data simultaneously, further increasing throughput.

Another important feature available on switches, and which you will not find on bridges or repeaters, is the ability to segment your network into **virtual local area networks (VLANs)**. VLANs allow network administrators to logically group users and resources irrespective of the physical location of the user or resource. With conventional networks (networks that do not use VLANs), the physical location of a user or resource dictates to which network that user or resource is assigned. This limitation sometimes makes resource sharing inefficient because, ideally, a user is assigned to the same network as the resources that the user most frequently accesses.

A switch that supports VLANs permits any one switch port or group of switch ports to be assigned to a VLAN, which can be a benefit. Suppose you have a group of employees from different departments working on a long-term project. A new server has been allocated for this project, but there's a problem—the employees are scattered in different buildings. To solve this problem, you can assign the switch port to the same VLAN to which each employee's computer is connected. You can also assign the switch port to the same VLAN to which the server is connected. In this way, these employees and the resources they share, while physically separate, are logically grouped using VLANs.

11

Each VLAN is assigned a unique network number. Because each VLAN has a different network number, a router is needed to communicate between VLANs. Figure 11-9 depicts how users and resources from different physical locations can be assigned to the same VLAN. Although the details of implementing VLANs are beyond the scope of this book, you can read a good overview on the subject at *www.howstuffworks.com/lan-switch8.htm.*

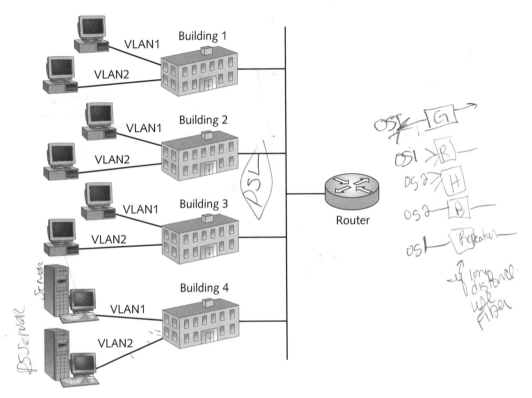

Figure 11-9   VLANs logically group users and resources from different physical locations

Routers

Routers are advanced devices that connect separate networks to form an internetwork. Connecting two or more independent networks so that they continue to function separately creates an **internetwork**. A good example of this is an Ethernet network and an FDDI network interconnected so that users on each network can access resources on the other network. Both networks continue to function separately, but users can exchange information between the networks. The best-known internetwork today is the Internet, which is, in essence, a large number of small networks connected to share information.

As networks grow and become a more integral part of an organization, multiple paths through a network are commonly requested to provide fault tolerance.

Like bridges, routers can connect multiple network segments and filter traffic; unlike bridges, routers can be used to form complex networks. As shown in Figure 11-10, routers can connect complex networks with multiple paths between network segments. Each network segment, also called a subnetwork (or subnet), is assigned a network address. Each node on a subnet is assigned an address as well. Using a combination of the network and node addresses, the router can route a packet from the source to a destination address somewhere else on the network.

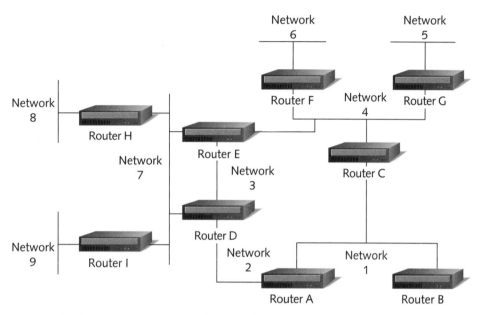

Figure 11-10   Routers can connect networks with many different paths between the networks

To accomplish this task, the router analyzes the destination network address of the packet. As you might suspect, routers operate at the Network layer of the OSI model.

To route a packet through the internetwork successfully, a router must determine the packet's path. When the router receives a packet, it analyzes the packet's destination network address and looks up that address in its **routing table**. The router then repackages the data and sends it to the next router in the path. range of IP Addresses,

Because routers operate at a higher layer of the OSI model (layer 3) than bridges do (layer 2), routers can easily send information over different network architectures. For example, routers can send a packet received from a token ring network over an Ethernet network. The router removes the token ring frame, examines the packet to determine the network address, repackages the data into Ethernet frames, and sends the data onto the Ethernet network.

This kind of translation, however, affects network speed. For instance, refer to the previous example. Ethernet frames have a maximum data frame size of approximately 1518 bytes,

11

whereas token ring frames range in size from 4000 to 18,000 bytes. So, for a single token ring frame of maximum size (18,000 bytes), routers must create 12 Ethernet frames. Although routers are very fast, this type of translation affects the network's speed.

One of the primary differences between bridges and routers, aside from a router's ability to select the best path, is what routers do with broadcasts and unknown addresses. As mentioned, when a bridge receives a packet with an unknown destination address, it forwards that packet to all connected network segments. When a router receives a packet with a destination network address it does not know, however, it discards that packet. This also applies to corrupted packets and broadcasts. A router discards any packet that it does not understand or for which it has no route.

Routing Tables

The routing tables maintained by routers vary from the bridging tables maintained by bridges. A bridge keeps track of the hardware address of each device on a particular network segment, while a router's table contains only network addresses and addresses of the routers that handle those networks. Figure 11-10 shows Router A, and Table 11-4 shows Router A's sample routing table. The table lists the next hop (that is, where transmissions go next) and cost (that is, number of hops the data must take).

Table 11-4   Router A's routing table *router name = IP address*

Network	Next Hop	Cost in Hops
1	Directly connected	0
2	Directly connected	0
3	Router D	1
4	Router C	1
5	Router C	2
6	Router C	2
7	Router D	1
8	Router D	2
9	Router D	2

The router's type is defined by the way its routing tables are populated. The routing tables can be populated in two ways: static routing or dynamic routing.

If a router uses **static routing**, the administrator must manually update the routing table, adding each individual route. The router always uses the same path to a destination, even if it is not necessarily the shortest or most efficient route. If the table has no route to a particular destination, the router drops the packet.

A router using **dynamic routing** uses a **discovery** process to find information about available routes. Dynamic routers communicate with each other and constantly receive updated routing tables from other routers. If multiple routes are available to a particular network, the router decides which route is best and enters that route in its routing table.

A router chooses the best path for a packet in two ways:

- Using a **distance-vector algorithm**, the router calculates the cost of a particular route based on factors such as the number of routers between the two networks (hop count), the bandwidth of the lines between networks, network congestion, and delays. It determines the path a given packet takes by identifying the route with the lowest cost. Distance-vector algorithms communicate with each other by periodically exchanging copies of their routing tables. Routing Information Protocol (RIP), used by both TCP/IP and IPX/SPX, is a distance-vector routing protocol.

- When using a **link-state algorithm**, the router relies on the speed of the links between networks to determine the lowest cost path. Routers using link-state algorithms communicate by sending the status of all their interface links to the other routers in the internetwork. This exchange of information occurs only when a change occurs in the network. This type of algorithm requires more processing power but delivers the packets more efficiently. Open Shortest Path First (OSPF) is a TCP/IP routing protocol that uses a link-state algorithm.

Dynamic routers are easier to maintain and provide better route selection than static routers, but the routing table updates and discovery generate additional network traffic. This is especially true of distance-vector protocols such as RIP, which sends its entire routing table across the network every 30 seconds.

11

Routable Versus Nonroutable Protocols

As Chapter 6 discusses, not all protocols operate at every layer of the OSI model. Routers work with protocols that include Network layer information. These **routable protocols** include:

- TCP/IP
- IPX/SPX
- DECNet
- OSI
- DDP (AppleTalk)
- XNS

Also, there are many **nonroutable protocols** that do not have Network layer information, including:

- NetBEUI
- DLC (used with HP printers and IBM mainframes)
- LAT (Local Area Transport, part of the DEC networking structure)

Table 11-5 shows the advantages and disadvantages of routers.

Table 11-5   Advantages and disadvantages of routers

Advantages	Disadvantages
Connect networks of different physical media and network architectures	More expensive and more complex than bridges or repeaters
Choose the best path for a packet through an internetwork	Work only with routable protocols
Reduce network traffic by not forwarding broadcasts or corrupt packets	Dynamic routing updates create network traffic
	Slower than bridges because they must perform more intricate calculations on the packet

Brouters

As their name implies, **brouters** combine the best features of bridges and routers. When a brouter receives a routable packet, it operates as a router by choosing the best path for the packet and forwarding it to its destination. However, when a brouter receives a nonroutable packet, the brouter functions as a bridge, forwarding the packet based on hardware address. To do this, brouters maintain both a bridging table, which contains hardware addresses, and a routing table, which contains network addresses.

Brouters are especially helpful in hybrid networks using a mixture of routable and non-routable protocols. For example, if you want to filter traffic on a network running both TCP/IP and NetBEUI, neither a bridge nor a router is the best solution. Using a brouter, you can route the TCP/IP packets to their destination, while the NetBEUI packets are bridged. This uses the network more efficiently, despite the fact that NetBEUI broadcasts are sent down all segments. You will not typically find the term brouter in a network equipment manufacturer's catalog. A brouter is usually a router that has bridging capabilities as well.

Gateways

A **gateway** is an intricate piece of networking equipment that translates information between two dissimilar network architectures or data formats. For example, a gateway can allow network communication between a TCP/IP LAN and an IBM mainframe system using Systems Network Architecture (SNA). Another example of a gateway is a system that converts Microsoft Mail to Simple Mail Transport Protocol (SMTP) for transmission over the Internet.

Although routers work at the Network layer of the OSI model and can route packets of the same protocol (such as TCP/IP) over networks with dissimilar architectures (such as Ethernet to token ring), gateways can route packets over networks with different proto-cols. Gateways can change the actual format of the data, whereas routers only repackage the data into different frames.

Gateways often connect PCs to mainframe computers, as in the TCP/IP to SNA example. However, many other types of gateways are found in smaller networks. For example, as Chapter 9 discusses, the Windows NT Server and Windows 2000 Server operating systems include Services for Macintosh, which allows Microsoft Windows clients to communicate with Macintosh clients through the Windows 2000 server. This gateway software allows Macintosh file servers and printers to appear to Microsoft clients as though they were on the Windows networks, and vice versa. The gateway handles all the translations between NetBEUI or TCP/IP and AppleTalk.

When packets arrive at a gateway, the software strips all networking information from the packet, leaving only the raw data. The gateway then translates the data into the new format and sends it back down the OSI layers using the networking protocols of the destination system, as shown in Figure 11-11.

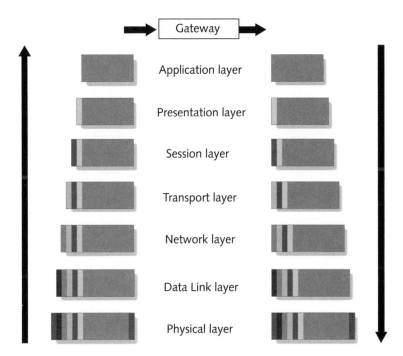

Figure 11-11   Gateways translate data between different protocols

Because gateways translate data, they generally operate at the upper layers of the OSI model. Usually, this takes place at the Application layer, but some gateways can translate at the Network or Session layer.

Gateways generally are harder to install, slower, and more expensive than other networking equipment. They are usually a separate computer with only one task, such as translating MS Mail to SMTP.

Table 11-6 displays the advantages and disadvantages of gateways.

Table 11-6   Advantages and disadvantages of gateways

Advantages	Disadvantages
Connect completely different systems	More expensive than other devices
Dedicated to one task and perform that task well	More difficult to install and configure
	Greater processing requirements mean less speed than other devices

CHAPTER SUMMARY

□ As your network usage increases, it may become necessary to support remote connections to your network. Analog modems are a simple and effective way to provide users with connectivity. Using various technologies, modems can transmit up to 56 Kbps, and their speeds are increasing.

□ At times, however, remote connections require even greater speeds. In such cases, ISDN, DSL, cable modem, or dedicated leased-line environments may be the best solution. (Chapter 12 covers ISDN and leased lines in more detail.) ISDN provides a dial-up digital network connection up to 128 Kbps from a single installation. Cable modems and DSL both typically deliver bandwidth that varies between 384 Kbps and 1.5 Mbps. A leased line provides continuous point-to-point connectivity between sites and may be the best solution for connecting a remote office when you need bandwidth higher than 1.5 Mbps.

□ Windows NT Server and Windows 2000 Server include support for remote access services, which permit up to 256 users to dial in to a server to obtain remote access to the network to which the server is attached.

□ A repeater increases the length of your network by eliminating the effect of attenuation on the signal.

□ A bridge installed between two network segments filters traffic according to hardware destination address. By placing computers that communicate most often on the same side of the bridge, you greatly reduce network traffic. You can also use a bridge to connect networks of different physical media, such as 10BaseT and 10Base2.

□ Switches are similar to bridges, but their advanced technology allows them to handle more network segments and switch frames much faster than bridges. Three primary switching methods are cut-through, store-and-forward, and fragment-free.

□ A router connects several independent networks to form a complex internetwork. Able to connect networks with different physical media like a bridge, a router can also connect networks using the same protocols but different network architectures, such as Ethernet and token ring. In a network with multiple paths, a router can determine the best path for a packet to take to reach its destination.

❐ Using static routes, a router always sends the packet along the same path; but if a router uses dynamic routing, it makes a decision on which path to send the packet based on the cost of the packet traveling a particular path. RIP is one protocol through which routers learn and advertise the paths available to them. RIP is a distance-vector protocol that uses the number of routers (hops) along a path to determine cost. OSPF is a link-state routing protocol that determines a packet's best path by taking other factors into account, including line speed and network congestion.

❐ Brouters incorporate the best functions of bridges and routers. Brouters route protocols that have Network layer information and bridge protocols that do not.

❐ Gateways are the most intricate networking devices. They translate information from one protocol to another. They generally operate at the upper layers of the OSI model.

KEY TERMS

asymmetric communication — Communication in which data travels in the download direction at a speed different than the upload direction.

Asymmetric Digital Subscriber Line (ADSL) — A digital telecommunications technology that uses different speeds for downloading and uploading data.

asynchronous — A communication method that sends data in a stream with start and stop bits indicating where data begins and ends.

Basic Rate Interface (BRI) — An ISDN implementation that provides two 64-Kbps B-channels. Generally used for remote connections.

baud — A measurement of modem speed that describes the number of state transitions that occur in a second on an analog phone line.

Binary Synchronous (bisync) communications — A synchronous communications protocol.

bis — A French term for *second*, which describes the second version of an ITU standard.

bridge — A networking device that works at the Data Link layer of the OSI model. It filters traffic according to the packet's hardware destination address.

bridging table — A reference table created by a bridge to track hardware addresses and to track on which network segment each address is located.

broadcast storm — Phenomenon that occurs when a network device malfunctions and floods the network with broadcast packets.

brouter — A networking device that combines the best functionality of a bridge and a router. It routes packets that include Network layer information and bridges all other packets.

central office (CO) — A phone company's or communications provider's local facility where copper local telephone cables (sometimes called the subscriber loop or the "last mile" of cable in the telecommunications infrastructure) link to long-haul, all-digital, fiber-optic communications lines.

11

cut-through switching — The fastest switching method, in which the switch reads only enough of the incoming frame to determine where to forward the frame.

Dial-Up Networking (DUN) — The program included with Windows 95, Windows 98, Windows Millennium, Windows NT, and Windows 2000 that allows connectivity to servers running RAS or RRAS.

digital modem — A hardware device used to transmit digital signals across an ISDN link.

Digital Subscriber Line (DSL) — A digital technology that uses specially tuned telephone lines to deliver network and Internet access, at bandwidths from 384 Kbps to 1.5 Mbps.

discovery — The process by which dynamic routers learn the routes available to them.

distance-vector algorithm — One method of determining the best route available for a packet. Distance-vector protocols count the number of routers (hops) between the source and destination. The best path has the least number of hops.

dynamic routing — The process by which routers dynamically learn from each other the available paths.

fragment-free switching — A switching method in which the switch reads in enough of the frame to guarantee that the frame is not less than the minimum frame size allowed for the network type.

frame — The unit of data with which bridges and switches work. Frames contain physical address information and are defined at layer 2 of the OSI model.

frame fragment — A frame error that occurs because the frame is less than the allowable size for the network type. A frame fragment usually occurs due to a collision or a device malfunction.

gateway — A networking device that translates information between protocols or between completely different networks, such as from TCP/IP to SNA.

Hayes-compatible — The modem standard based on the Hayes Smartmodem.

High-level Data Link Control (HDLC) — A synchronous communication protocol.

Integrated Services Digital Network (ISDN) — A WAN technology that offers increments of 64-Kbps connections, most often used by SOHO (small office/home office) users.

International Telecommunications Union (ITU) — The standards body that developed the V-series modem standards.

internetwork — A complex network created when two or more independent networks are connected using routers.

learning bridge — Another term for a transparent bridge that learns the hardware addresses of the computers connected to each network segment.

link-state algorithm — A method used by routers to determine a packet's best path. In addition to the number of routers involved, routers using link-state algorithms take network traffic and link speed into account to determine the best path.

modem (MOdulator/DEModulator) — Used by computers to convert digital signals to analog signals for transmission over telephone lines. The receiving computer then converts the analog signals to digital signals.

network termination (NT) — Part of the network connection device in an ISDN network.

nonroutable protocol — A network protocol that does not contain Network layer information, but instead relies only on Data Link layer addressing. A nonroutable protocol cannot be routed in an internetwork.

Point-to-Point Protocol (PPP) — A remote access protocol that supports many protocols, including TCP/IP, NetBEUI, and IPX/SPX.

Primary Rate Interface (PRI) — An ISDN implementation that provides twenty-three 64-Kbps B-channels.

propagation delay — Signal delay created when a number of repeaters connect in a line. To prevent this, many network architectures limit the number of repeaters on a network.

public switched telephone network (PSTN) — Another term for the public telephone system.

pulse code modulation (PCM) — A technique for digitizing analog signals. PCM introduces less noise into the signal than traditional modulation/demodulation techniques, therefore boosting the total number of bits per second.

Remote Access Service (RAS) — Service available in Windows NT to allow dial-in connections to the network.

routable protocol — A network protocol that contains Layer 3 (Network layer) addressing information, which permits packets to be routed throughout an internetwork.

router — A networking device that operates at the Network layer of the OSI model. A router connects networks with different physical media and also translates between different network architectures, such as token ring and Ethernet.

routing table — A reference table that includes network information and the next router in line for a particular path.

Serial Line Internet Protocol (SLIP) — The dial-up protocol originally used to connect PCs directly to the Internet.

source-routing bridge — A type of bridge used in IBM token ring networks that learns its bridging information from information included in the packet's structure.

static routing — A type of routing in which the router is configured manually with all possible routes.

store-and-forward switching — A switching method in which the switch reads the entire frame to check for errors before forwarding the frame.

switch — A hardware device that opens and closes electrical circuits, completes or breaks an electrical path, and selects paths or circuits.

Symmetric Digital Subscriber Line (SDSL) — Uses equivalent speeds for downloading and uploading data.

synchronous — Communications type in which computers rely on exact timing and sync bits to maintain data synchronization.

Synchronous Data Link Control (SDLC) — A synchronous communication protocol.

11

[handwritten: subnet mask splits into host/network]

ter — A French term for *third*, which describes the third version of an ITU standard.

terminal adapter (TA) — Part of the ISDN network interface. Sometimes called a digital modem.

translation bridge — A bridge that can translate between network architectures.

transparent bridge — Generally used in Ethernet networks, these bridges build their bridging tables automatically as they receive packets.

Virtual local area network (VLAN) — A feature of switches that allows network administrators to logically group users and resources, irrespective of the physical location of the user or resource.

V-series — The ITU-T standards that specify how data communications can take place over the telephone network.

REVIEW QUESTIONS

1. A router using a _____ algorithm sends updates to other routers only when the network status changes.

   a. spanning tree

   b. distance-vector

   c. link-state

   d. triggered-vector

2. The term *propagation* refers to the phenomenon created when too many repeaters are interconnected in a network.

3. _____C_____ bridges populate their bridging tables from information included in the frame specifically for bridging.

   a. Asynchronous

   b. Synchronous

   c. Transparent

   d. Source routing

4. A _____ operates at the Physical layer of the OSI model and effectively doubles the length of the network.

   a. repeater

   b. gateway

   c. router

   d. switch

5. A subnet is created when two or more independent networks are connected using routers. True or false?

6. A(n) _____ protocol does not include Network layer information.

7. The ___PPP___ remote access protocol supports many network layer protocols, including TCP/IP and IPX/SPX.

8. At which layer of the OSI model do bridges operate?

    a. Physical

    b. Network

    c. Transport

    d. Data Link

9. Asynchronous communications take place when a start bit and a stop bit surround each byte of data. True or false?

10. What occurs when a network device malfunctions and the network floods?

    a. beacon

    b. broadcast storm

    c. bottleneck

    d. none of the above

11. Modem speed is measured in _____.

    a. bits per second

    b. baud rate

    c. megabits per second

    d. gigabits per second

12. A router using the _____ algorithm periodically exchanges its entire routing table with other routers.

    a. spanning tree

    b. distance-vector

    c. link-state

    d. triggered-vector

13. A _____ converts digital signals to analog signals and back again.

    a. bridge

    b. router

    c. modem

    d. gateway

14. The _____ remote access protocol is used to connect computers to a network remotely and only supports TCP/IP.

15. The term *baud* is synonymous with the bit rate on an analog phone line. True or false?   false

16. Which of the networking devices defined in this chapter causes the least delay?

17. When a router is manually configured, it is using _____ routing.
    a. static
    b. dynamic
    c. predefined
    d. spanning

18. A _____ can translate data from different physical media and network architectures.
    a. router
    b. repeater
    c. gateway
    d. switch

19. A(n) _____ protocol includes Network layer addressing information.

20. The _____ modem standard uses hardware compression.

21. Which bridges populate their bridging table from the source and destination hardware addresses in the packet?
    a. Transparent
    b. Source-routing
    c. Translation
    d. none of the above

22. _____ communications rely on exact timing between the sending and receiving units.
    a. Asynchronous
    b. Synchronous
    c. Static
    d. Dynamic

23. _____ Digital Subscriber Line uses different speeds for uploading and downloading data.

24. Placing a bridge on the network easily remedies a broadcast storm. True or false?

25. Which networking device can translate data from one protocol to another?
    a. bridge
    b. repeater
    c. gateway
    d. switch

26. A _____ modem is a network interface device that allows Internet access through CATV lines.

27. Which method of switching provides for the fastest performance but might forward frames that contain errors?

    a. store-and-forward

    b. fragment-free

    c. cut-through

    d. fast-CRC

28. Which of the following limitations applies to cable-based access to network services?

    a. A connection is only possible within 17,500 to 23,000 feet of the local point of presence (POP).

    b. All users on the local CATV cable segment share the bandwith.

    c. Only one user may access the network at a time, at any given moment.

    d. Service is scarce and extremely expensive.

29. Which of the following limitations applies to DSL-based access to network services?

    a. A connection is only possible within 17,500 to 23,000 feet of the local point of presence (POP).

    b. All users on the local CATV cable segment share the bandwith.

    c. Only one user may access the network at a time, at any given moment.

    d. Service is scarce and extremely expensive.

30. Switches are faster than bridges because switches use hardware to make forwarding decisions, whereas bridges use software. True or false?

11

HANDS-ON PROJECTS

As mentioned earlier, the Remote Access Service (RAS) available in Windows NT Server allows computers to dial in to the network or connect via the Internet; likewise, the Routing and Remote Access Service (RRAS) is available in Windows 2000 Server, in part to support the same kind of dial-in services. In the first Hands-on Project, you add RAS to a Windows NT 4.0 Server; because you automatically install RRAS when you install Windows 2000 Server, the Hands-on Project for Windows 2000 Server involves enabling and configuring RRAS. In the second project, you add a dial-up networking client to a Windows 98 computer. In Hands-on Projects 11-3 through 11-5, you research modems and internetworking devices, and measure the speed of your Internet connection.

Project 11-1

For this Hands-on Project, you need a Windows NT 4.0 Server computer with an installed modem and access to an account with Administrator privileges. This project walks you through the steps required to add the remote access server (RAS) service to a Windows NT 4.0 server. This service is necessary if a company wants employees to dial into the corporate network.

To add RAS service to a Windows NT 4.0 Server:

1. Click **Start**, **Settings**, **Control Panel**, and double-click the **Network** icon.

2. Click the **Services** tab, and click the **Add** button.

3. Scroll to **Remote Access Service** in the Select Network Service dialog box, highlight it as shown in Figure 11-12, and click the **OK** button.

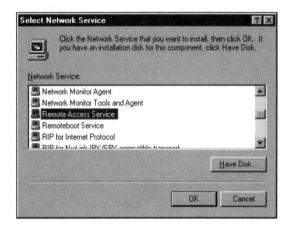

Figure 11-12   Adding RAS

4. Provide file and path information for the Distribution files.

5. Confirm the RAS Capable device found by NT, and click the **Continue** button.

6. Specify whether the **Entire network** or **This computer only** can access services.

7. Select the communications port for RAS.

8. Add an installed modem as a RAS device.

9. You must configure the port for one of the following:

   ◻ Dial out only

   ◻ Receive calls only

   ◻ Dial out and Receive calls

10. You must select the LAN network protocols:

   ◻ If you selected Dial out, you can choose only the outbound protocols.

   ◻ If you selected Receive calls, you can configure only the inbound protocols.

   ◻ If you selected Dial out and Receive calls, you can configure both outbound and inbound protocols.

11. Each inbound protocol requires protocol-specific configuration. Ask your instructor if he or she wants you to carry out any further configuration activities.

 Once you've installed RAS on a Windows NT Server, your attempts to uninstall then reinstall it will not succeed. You're better off reinstalling Windows NT Server and installing RAS on a "clean copy" of the operating system than trying to remove and reinstall RAS on any Windows NT Server installation.

 ## Project 11-2

In this hands-on project, you enable and configure RRAS on Windows 2000 Server.

To enable and configure RRAS:

1. Log on to the Windows 2000 Server computer.
2. Go to **Start/Programs/Administrative Tools** and click **Routing and Remote Access**.
3. Select the name of the server in the Tree column.
4. Click the **Action** menu, and select **Configure and Enable Routing and Remote Access**.
5. When the Routing and Remote Access Server Wizard appears, click **Next**.
6. You will see the list of options for configuring the server. Click the **Remote Access Server** option button.
7. Click the **Yes, all of the required protocols are on the list** option button and click **Next**.
8. Click the **Automatically** option button, and click **Next**.
9. Click the **No** option button, and click **Next**.
10. Click **Finish**.

You have successfully configured RRAS to accept incoming connections. To disable RRAS and try a different configuration, follow Step 11.

11. Click **Action** and select **Disable Routing and Remote Access**. Click **Yes** when prompted.

 ## Project 11-3

For this Hands-on Project, you need a Windows 98 computer with a modem already installed.

To add a dial-up networking client to a Windows 98 computer:

1. Double-click **My Computer** on the desktop.
2. Double-click the **Dial-Up Networking** folder.

11

3. Double-click the **Make New Connection** icon, as shown in Figure 11-13.

Figure 11-13 Adding a dial-up networking connection

4. Name the connection, and click the **Next** button.

5. Provide the number to be dialed, including area code, telephone number, and country code, if necessary. Click the **Next** button.

6. Click the **Finish** button.

Project 11-4

For this Hands-on Project, you need a Windows XP Professional computer with a modem already installed.

To add a dial-up networking client to a Windows XP Professional computer:

1. Go to **Start/Control Panel** and double-click the **Network Connections** icon.

2. Under Network Tasks on the left side of the screen, click **Create a new connection**. (If a dialog box pops up asking you to enter your area code, do so, and click **OK**.)

3. At the New Connection Wizard, click **Next**.

4. Click the **Connect to the Internet** option button, and click **Next**.

5. Click **Set up my connection manually**, and click **Next**.

6. Click the **Connect using a dial-up modem** option button, and click **Next**.

7. Enter a name for your ISP, and click **Next**.

8. Enter the phone number for your ISP, and click **Next**. (If you do not plan to actually dial an ISP, you can put anything you want here.)

9. Enter the username and password (you need to enter the password twice) for your ISP account. (If you do not plan to actually dial an ISP, you can put anything you want here). Click **Next**.

10. Click **Finish**. Congratulations! You have just added a dial-up connection to Windows XP.

11. Close the Network Connections dialog box.

Project 11-5

In this project, you visit a Web site that sends data to your browser and measures the delivery time required to determine the effective bandwidth—that is, the actual speed at which your connection works. You also have a chance to determine, by experiment, if other students in the laboratory share Internet bandwidth with you, by observing the bandwidth reported for independent and simultaneous access to the same Web site.

To measure the effective bandwidth of your Internet connection:

1. Start your Web browser using **Start**, **Programs**, **Internet Explorer**, or whatever sequence of steps your instructor tells you to follow.

2. Type **http://computingcentral.msn.com/internet/speedtest.asp** in the Address text box in your Web browser, and then press **Enter**.

3. Type your area code in the box indicated, and then select the type of connection you have to the Internet (most likely LAN/WAN if you are doing this in a classroom). Click the **Test it!** button. Your effective bandwidth reading will be indicated in red. You can click the Back button any time to redo the test and get a new reading. What do you think accounts for different results each time you do the test?

4. Place your insertion point over the **Back** button, and count down out loud with your fellow students, so that everyone clicks the Back button at more or less the same time. What do you think accounts for any variance between the readings that show up in this case, with respect to the independent readings conducted earlier? If you aren't sure how to answer these questions, read the note and follow the link on this page.

5. Close your Web browser.

11

CASE PROJECTS

1. As network administrator for a growing company, you are asked to solve a remote access dilemma. The 12 employees who work out of their homes complain about not being connected to the network except by e-mail. The company also has a number of employees who travel and would benefit from dial-up network connections. The director of marketing is responsible for part of the cost and wants only the best solution. Currently, you run a combination Windows NT and NetWare network, and the users want access to all systems.

   Develop a plan to connect your remote users. Your solution may involve more than one remote access type. Make a drawing of your plan for remote access.

2. Recently, you connected two departments' 10Base2 networks with a repeater. Now workers on both networks complain that, since the connection, the network is too slow. You run a Windows NT network using NetBEUI and TCP/IP. Users need access to the file servers on both LANs.

   Develop a plan to ease traffic on the network, including any additional hardware requirements. Make a drawing of your plan.

3. Your company is considering connecting your mainframe to the PC network. The mainframe currently only connects to terminals, but management would like to be able to access it from the desktop. You run a token ring network. The mainframe manufacturer supports Ethernet, but not token ring. Develop an outline of possible solutions for making this connection, including hardware options and possible reconfiguration of the mainframe.

4. Your company decided to permit employees to telecommute from home one or two days a week. All employees live in areas that offer CATV service, but some live in neighborhoods that are six miles from the nearest central office. What kind of connectivity solution makes the most sense if you want to use the same technology for all users? What is a possible downside of making such a choice?

5. XYZ Corporation wants to implement an affordable way to establish remote connections for its sales force, who log in from customer sites all over the country, and for its three branch offices. The company's headquarters is in Washington, D.C., and its branch offices are in Santa Monica, CA, Des Moines, IA, and New York, NY. Explain what kind of connections the sales force and the branch offices should use and what kinds of services should be installed on the headquarters network to keep communications costs to a minimum.

12

WIDE AREA AND LARGE-SCALE NETWORKS

After reading this chapter and completing the exercises, you will be able to:

♦ Describe the basic concepts associated with wide area networks (WANs)

♦ Identify the uses, benefits, and drawbacks of advanced WAN technologies such as ATM, FDDI, SONET, and SMDS

♦ Understand how to use the Internet for a private connection using VPNs

This chapter introduces the basic concepts and terminology of WAN transmission, connections, and components. After finishing this chapter, you will be able to identify the features and benefits of each of the major WAN technologies.

WIDE AREA NETWORK (WAN) TRANSMISSION TECHNOLOGIES

A WAN is simply a network that spans a large geographical area. In other words, a WAN is organized to allow each segment or section of a network to be situated in a different building, city, state, or even country. The distances involved in WANs pose intriguing problems for maintaining, administering, and troubleshooting networks.

As far as individual users are concerned, a WAN looks and operates in the same way as a local area network (LAN). Users can access network resources located on their LAN or across the country or globe over the WAN. The interface and access methods remain the same. One distinction is the time delay as electronic signals traverse the globe, which can in some cases be quite substantial, depending on the quality of the network connection.

WANs are often constructed by linking individual LANs to improve or increase the level of communications. These connections are established using special communication devices such as switches and routers, along with communication lines from an Internet Service Provider (ISP) or **telco** (telephone company or service provider). Some of the special communication links employed to construct WANs include:

- Packet-switching networks
- Fiber-optic cable
- Microwave transmitters
- Satellite links
- Cable television coax systems

Because these link types are expensive and complex, most organizations lease their WAN links from a service provider rather than purchasing, installing, and deploying their own long-distance cable or wireless connections. Another benefit of leasing a communications link is that because such transactions often include unlimited use of the link, organizations don't have to pay per-minute charges. Consider how large the phone bill would be to maintain a 24-hour, seven-day telephone link between the United States and Kenya, and then multiply that amount by 10, 100, or even 1000 to get a general idea of WAN link per-minute charges.

Although there are a number of WAN technologies available, as we are about to discuss, it is important to understand that each technology has its own strengths and weaknesses. Organizations or institutions will choose the appropriate technology for their particular needs, based on speed, reliability, cost, and availability. You should also know that the largest WAN in the world, the Internet, uses a combination of these technologies. Therefore, a WAN can consist of one, two, or all of these technologies tied together by routers and gateways.

Three primary technologies are used to transmit communications between LANs across WAN links:

- Analog
- Digital
- Packet switching

The following sections discuss each of these communications technologies.

Analog Connectivity

Your LAN can use the same telecommunications network you use to speak with friends, relatives, and co-workers (in the next cubicle or across the planet) to establish a WAN link to remote computers and networks. This network is often referred to as PSTN, which stands for Public Switched Telephone Network, or **POTS**, which stands for **plain old telephone system**. Figure 12-1 shows a simple PSTN connection. As Chapter 11 described, PSTN uses analog phone lines and requires modems to convert signals to and from the digital formats computers use.

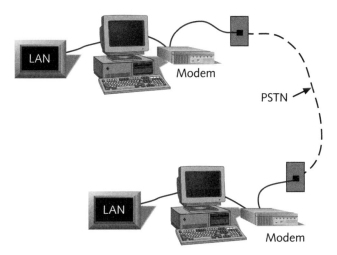

Figure 12-1 Simple PSTN network connection

Unfortunately, the quality of PSTN varies substantially from location to location, depending on the age of the system and the level or quality of installed media. This, and the fact that the PSTN was originally designed to support voice-only communication, makes the PSTN a low-quality but economical choice for most WAN links.

Because PSTN lines require modems to transmit digital computer data over the analog telephone network, the speed of data transmission is extremely slow. Also, because PSTN is a circuit-switched network, the quality of a connection is highly inconsistent; thus, any given link is only as reliable and fast as the circuits linked together to establish the pathway. The greater the distance a connection covers, the more likely a poor or unusable connection.

Recently, telcos upgraded some of their PSTN lines (and are installing fiber-optic cable to support the increasing demand for high bandwidth data communications) to support data transmission more reliably. Table 12-1 lists current PSTN line types and the quality and service capabilities of each type.

Table 12-1   PSTN line types

Line Type	Quality/Service capability
1	Voice only
2	Voice with minimal quality control
3	Voice and radio with tone conditioning
4	Less than 1200 bps data applications
5	Basic data
6	Voice and data over trunk circuits
7	Voice and data over private lines
8	Voice and data over trunks between computers
9	Voice and video
10	Application relays, quality data

One way to improve the quality of a PSTN connection is to lease a dedicated line or circuit instead of relying on the random circuits supplied when you dial in to the PSTN to establish a connection (called dial-on-demand). A dedicated line is more expensive than a dial-on-demand connection, but usually guarantees a reliable connection over the circuits and offers higher-quality, more consistent data transmissions. **Line conditioning**, an additional feature available for most dedicated circuits, requires extensive testing and line upgrades to permit the connection to sustain a consistent transmission rate. This improves overall signal quality and reduces interference and noise. Letters and numbers, such as C1 through C8 and D, define the various types of conditioning. You need to consult individual telco providers to determine what types of conditioning they offer and what benefits such services provide.

When deciding between a dial-up or a dedicated PSTN connection, you need to consider a number of factors, including:

- Length of connection time required (daily, weekly, monthly)
- Cost of service and usage levels
- Availability of dedicated circuits, conditioning, or other quality improvements
- Assessment of need for a 24-hour, seven-day connection

If you need infrequent or limited-duration connections, then a dial-up line is the most cost-effective solution. However, if you need constant access, then a PSTN line might not offer the speed necessary to support your network activities adequately.

Digital Connectivity

Digital Data Service (DDS) lines are direct or point-to-point synchronous communication links with 2.4-, 4.8-, 9.6-, or 56-Kbps transmission rates. DDS links provide dedicated digital circuits between both end points and guarantee a specified quality and data transmission rate. The most significant benefit of digital links is a nearly 99% error-free transmission of data. A typical PSTN connection can experience an error rate of up to 40%. Some DDS line types discussed in this chapter are ISDN, T1, T3, and switched 56K.

DDS does not use modems to establish connections because such communications are purely digital. Instead, DDS uses a special communications device called a **Channel Service Unit/Data Service Unit (CSU/DSU)**. A network uses a CSU/DSU to accept data from a bridge or router. That CSU/DSU then sends the data over the digital network to a receiving CSU/DSU, which hands it to a bridge or router that delivers the data to the remote network. Figure 12-2 illustrates this process.

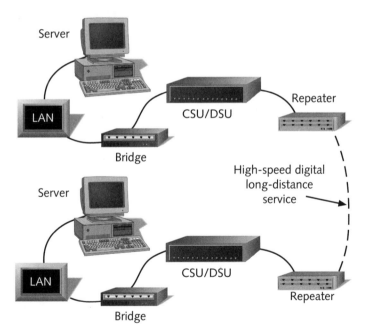

Figure 12-2   Simple DDS network connection using CSU/DSU devices

T1

One of the most widely used, high-speed, digital lines is the **T1**, a DDS technology that employs two 2-wire pairs to transmit full-duplex data signals at a maximum rate of 1.544 Mbps. One pair of wires transmits, and the other pair receives. T1 can adequately support data, voice, and narrow-band video for a moderate number of senders and receivers.

T1 is a fairly expensive digital link that organizations usually purchase or lease if they cannot sustain productive WAN network activity over a lower-quality line. Because a T1 line consists of 24 individual channels, each with a data rate of 64 Kbps, it is possible to subscribe to one or more individual channels instead of an entire T1, in a service called **fractional T1**.

In some countries (mostly European, but also many in the Pacific Rim), a different digital carrier technology—E1—is used. An E1 line supports a signal rate of 2.048 Mbps. Table 12-2 lists the various E class characteristics and data rates.

Table 12-2 E channels/data rates

Voice Channels	Carrier	E1s	Data Rate (Mbps)
30	E1	1	2.048
120	E2	4	8.448
480	E3	16	34.368

Multiplexing

Multiplexing, or **muxing**, enables several communication streams to travel simultaneously over the same cable segment. Bell Labs developed this technology years ago to allow a single telephone line to carry a number of concurrent conversations. Through the use of multiplexing, Bell Labs established a T-Carrier network that greatly expanded its capabilities to support simultaneous communication links over the same set of cables. T1 uses multiplexing to combine data transmissions from several sources and deliver them over a single cable. Once received, a transmission is decoded back into its original form before being sent to its final destination.

Channel Divisions

As mentioned previously, a T1 link comprises 24 separate channels. Each channel supports 64 Kbps of data transmission. Each channel takes a data sample 8000 times per second, and each data sample consists of 8 bits, which produces the per-channel data rate of 64 Kbps. This rate of data transmission is known as DS-0. The rate of a full T1 using all 24 channels is known as a DS-1. The **DS** specifications categorize DDS lines. Table 12-3 lists DS rate levels, their corresponding T designations, and their specifications.

Table 12-3   DS channels/data rates

DS Level	Carrier	T1s	Channels	Data Rate (Mbps)
DS-0	N/A	N/A	1	.064
DS-1	T1	1	24	1.544
DS-1C	T1C	2	48	3.152
DS-2	T2	4	96	6.312
DS-3	T3	28	672	44.736
DS-4	T4	168	4032	274.760

Multiplexing can increase DS-1 rates up to DS-4 speeds. Standard copper wires can support transmission rates of T1 and T2 lines, but T3 and T4 lines require microwave or fiber-optic technologies.

T3

A **T3** line has 28 T1s or 672 channels and supports a data rate of 44.736 Mbps. Many large service providers offer both T3 and fractional T3 leased lines with transmission rates of 6 Mbps and up. A single T3 commonly replaces several T1 lines.

Switched 56K

Switched 56K leased lines are an older digital point-to-point communication link offered by local and long-distance telcos. Before recent advances in fiber-optic and multiplexing technologies, the 56K digital network offered the best alternative to PSTN connections, particularly given its on-demand structure. A circuit was not dedicated to a single customer; rather, each time a customer required a connection, a pathway was established. When the transmission ceased, so did the link. Thus, lease terms were based on per-minute usage charges and not on 24-hour, seven-day dedicated circuit allocation. Today, with ready availability of cable modems and DSL in many locations, switched 56K service is used only when multiple 56 Kbps channels are aggregated for frame relay services or other specialized dedicated digital leased lines are needed (and where bandwidth requirements exceed T1).

Integrated Services Digital Network (ISDN)

Integrated Services Digital Network (ISDN) is a digital communications technology developed in 1984 to replace the analog telephone system. Not as widely deployed as expected, it is available in many metropolitan areas of the United States, as well as in most of Western Europe.

The ISDN specification defines single-channel links of 64 Kbps. With the 10-Mbps LANs of the 1980s, this was more than sufficient, but with today's 100-Mbps or more networks, ISDN offers no significant benefits. If not for private and SOHO (small office/home office) use to establish Internet connections, ISDN might never have been deployed.

One application for which ISDN still enjoys some popularity in corporate WANs is as a backup line. Because ISDN charges are often based upon connect time, a company can use ISDN in standby mode, such that the WAN connection will be established only if the primary connection fails.

ISDN offers speeds two to four times those of the standard POTS modem—not an overwhelming increase in speed, but a vast improvement for SOHO users when faster technologies like DSL or cable modem are not available. The cost of ISDN is reasonable.

ISDN is available in two formats or rates:

- *Basic Rate Interface (BRI).* Consists of two B-channels (64 Kbps) and a D-channel (16 Kbps). Each B-channel can transmit and receive voice or data independently of the other or bonded together for a speed of 128 Kbps. The D-channel is used for call setup and control.

- *Primary Rate Interface (PRI).* Consists of 23 B-channels and a D-channel. Each of the B-channels can be used independently or aggregated. A PRI offers the same bandwidth as a T1 line but uses different equipment at the endpoints and also employs vastly different signaling techniques. As with BRI, the B-channels in a PRI are 64 Kbps channels, but the D-channel in a PRI is also 64 Kbps, compared to only 16 Kbps in the BRI.

Packet-switching networks

Packet-switching networks are often used to communicate data over both short and long distances. Such networks provide fast, efficient, and highly reliable technology. The first part of its name comes from the way it breaks data into small packages, referred to as packets. Switching refers to the delivery and transmission methods used to move these packets over various pathways to a single destination. (Figure 12-3 illustrates the process.) The Internet is a prime example of a packet-switching network.

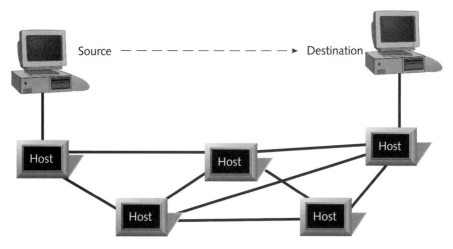

Figure 12-3   Simple packet-switching network

A packet-switching network handles data in the following manner:

1. The original data is segmented into packets.

2. Each packet is labeled with a sequence order and a destination address (a.k.a. the header).

3. Each packet is individually sent on the network toward the destination.

4. As a host receives the packet, it reads its header. If the host is the packet's destination, the host keeps the packet. If the host is not the destination, the host attempts to send the packet to the destination by the fastest, shortest, or most logical route available at the moment of transmission.

5. After the destination machine receives all packets, it uses the sequence information in the packets' headers to reconstruct the original data. It also requests retransmission of any missing or damaged packets.

A key benefit of a packet-switching network is that data delivery does not depend on any single pathway between the origin and the destination. In fact, no two packets are required to take the same route to reach the destination. The sequential information included in each packet header is, therefore, important because packets commonly arrive out of order, and the destination computer must rearrange them before extracting the original data.

The packets are small. If any packet fails to arrive at its destination, the resulting retransmission request can be serviced with minimal time loss. The packets' small size also reduces the time required by each switch or host to receive, analyze, and retransmit them.

12

Virtual Circuits

Many packet-switching networks employ **virtual circuits** to provide temporarily "dedicated" pathways between two points. No real cable exists between the two endpoints; rather, a virtual circuit consists of a logical sequence of connections with bandwidth allocated for a specific transmission pathway. This pathway between sender and receiver is created after both computers agree on bandwidth requirements and request a pathway. To improve the quality of transmission and to ensure successful communications, virtual circuits incorporate communication parameters that govern receipt acknowledgments, flow control, and error control.

There are two types of virtual circuits: switched and permanent. **Switched virtual circuits (SVCs)** are established when needed and then terminated when transmission completes. In other words, the path between the two communication points is only maintained as long as it is in active use. **Permanent virtual circuits (PVCs)** are similar to leased lines in that the pathway between two communication points is established as a permanent logical connection; thus, the pathway exists even when not in use.

X.25

Developed in the mid-1970s, the X.25 specification provided an interface between public packet-switching networks and their customers. Used most often to connect remote terminals with centralized mainframes, the X.25 specification defines how devices communicate over an internetwork. X.25 networks are SVC networks, meaning that they create the best available pathway for transmission *upon* transmission.

Early X.25 networks employed standard telephone lines as communication links, which resulted in numerous errors and lost data. Adding error checking and retransmission schemes improved the success of X.25 transmissions, but severely dampened speed. With its extensive level of error control, X.25 could only deliver 64-Kbps transmission rates. A 1992 specification revision improved the maximum throughput of X.25 to 2 Mbps per connection, but this new version was not widely deployed.

X.25 is usually associated with **public data networks (PDNs)** instead of public or private networks. AT&T, General Electric, Tymnet, and other large commercial service providers offer PDN service. X.25 is also popular outside North America, where the availability of digital communications from service providers is much lower and more expensive than in the United States and Canada.

Using **data terminal equipment (DTE)** and **data communications equipment (DCE)**, connecting to an X.25 network can be accomplished through one of three different methods:

- An X.25 network interface card (NIC) in a computer
- A **packet assembler/disassembler (PAD)** that supports X.25 communications for low-speed, character-based terminals
- A LAN/WAN X.25 gateway

Even though X.25 networks offer reliable and error-free communications, use of the X.25 technology is declining because of its speed limitations and the development and deployment of other, higher-speed technologies such as frame relay and ATM.

Frame Relay

Frame relay is a point-to-point permanent virtual circuit (PVC) technology that offers WAN communications over a fast, reliable, digital packet-switching network. It was developed from X.25 and ISDN technology. Because frame relay does not use error checking, overall throughput is improved. Error checking is not required on the digital fiber-optic links that most frame relay connections use. Instead, the devices on each end of the communication accomplish error checking. Frame relay also uses variable-length packets or frames for data transmission at the Data Link layer of the OSI model.

Frame relay uses a PVC between communication points; thus the same pathway carries all communications, which ensures proper delivery and higher bandwidth rates. A PVC is similar to a dedicated line in that communication devices are not concerned with route management and error checking. Instead, all of the resources of the devices are dedicated to moving data. This is why frame relay technology can maintain transmission rates of 56 Kbps to 1.544 Mbps (T1 speed); T1 multiples are also available.

Frame relay services are quickly growing in popularity. They are inexpensive (when compared to other solutions, such as ATM) and allow the customer to specify the bandwidth needed. Charges for use of frame relay depend on the PVC's bandwidth allocation, also known as its **Committed Information Rate (CIR)**. CIR is a guaranteed minimum transmission rate offered by the service provider.

Customers can purchase frame relay services in 64-Kbps CIR increments. Because customers can pay for a customized bandwidth solution, frame relay is sometimes used in preference to T1, because it is generally a less-expensive solution.

A frame relay connection is established using a pair of CSU/DSUs—just as with T1 lines—with a router or a bridge at each end to direct traffic on and off the WAN link. An important difference between a frame relay connection and a T1 connection is that T1 is a point-to-point link, which means a T1 customer gets full-time bandwidth to the destination (usually an ISP). However, frame relay connections are virtual circuits that go through a switch. This arrangement permits multiple destinations using a single frame relay connection. Thus, a corporate customer can, for example, have a frame relay link to each of its several branch offices, as well as a frame relay link to the Internet while only requiring a single frame relay connection. A simplified depiction of this arrangement is shown in Figure 12-4.

12

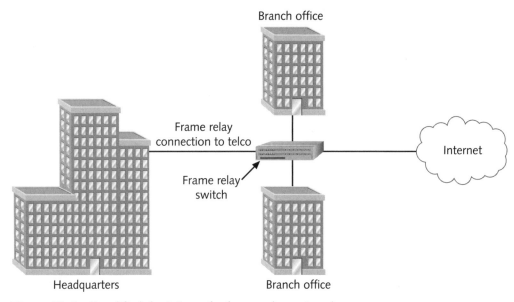

Figure 12-4   Simplified depiction of a frame relay network

Advanced WAN Technologies

Communication over WAN links grows steadily as it becomes increasingly critical for many businesses to exchange data among locations across the globe. Thus, technologies used to establish and maintain long-distance communication pathways are in high demand, pushing the limits of speed and reliability. The next sections look at several WAN technologies.

Asynchronous Transfer Mode (ATM)

Asynchronous Transfer Mode (ATM) is another high-speed, packet-switching technology. Using 53-byte, fixed-length packets and one out of every five bits at the Data Link layer for error checking, ATM offers transmission rates of up to 622 Mbps (and beyond, in extraordinary cases). ATM supports the full range of data-communication types, including voice, data, fax, real-time video, CD-quality audio, imaging, and multi-megabit data transmission.

An ATM protocol data unit (PDU) is called a cell. Its 53-byte length is divided into 48 data bytes and five header bytes. Each cell's fixed length enables the network equipment to move traffic quickly and efficiently. Digital lines are used to support ATM. The resulting noise- and error-free communication enables ATM to deliver its amazing transmission rates. Unlike frame relay, ATM can use either SVCs or PVCs between communication points.

ATM uses hardware-switching devices to transmit at the Data Link layer of the OSI model. ATM switching works as follows: At each switch, the five header bytes just mentioned identify a virtual circuit to the destination computer. The information is transmitted across that virtual circuit. ATM switching can be employed as long as the hardware in use supports ATM's (theoretical) 1-Gbps transmission rate.

The typical speeds of ATM networks are 155 Mbps or 622 Mbps: 155 Mbps is the transmission speed of a high-definition television signal; 622 Mbps is the speed required for transmitting four such signals simultaneously. (The communications rates described in Chapter 7, Table 7-16, for SONET also apply to ATM.)

ATM technology is not limited to ATM-based networks. It can interface and interoperate with various media and transmission types, including coax, twisted-pair, and fiber-optic media; T3, FDDI, and SONET systems; as well as frame relay and X.25 networks.

The ATM specification defines a theoretical maximum throughput of 2.4 Gbps. However, 622 Mbps is the maximum limit for most fiber-optic cable in use today. Many long-haul providers are now switching to higher-grade cable capable of higher data transmission rates. It won't be long before technology is developed to gain higher bandwidth from cables currently limited to 622 Mbps.

Fiber Distributed Data Interface (FDDI)

Technically, FDDI is not a WAN technology; it is simply a method of connecting LANs with high-speed ring networks. FDDI operates at 100 Mbps using fiber-optic media. The real benefit of an FDDI ring network is that more than one computer can transmit data (or a token) at a time—that is, multiple tokens can be used. An FDDI network is made up of two concentric rings, as shown in Figure 12-5. The primary ring carries traffic in one direction and is the primary communication segment, whereas the secondary ring transmits in the opposite direction and provides redundancy in case the primary ring fails or produces errors.

12

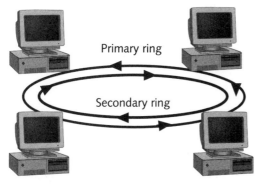

Figure 12-5 FDDI network

The most interesting limitation of FDDI is not speed but distance. FDDI's fiber-optic cables allow a maximum distance of 100 kilometers (62 miles) for any given ring. Still, FDDI is an excellent technology to interconnect relatively close LANs, from campus environments to metropolitan areas (where FDDI is sometimes used to create MANs, or metropolitan area networks).

FDDI is also appearing in some computer facilities, where it interconnects groups of network servers, all usually situated in the same room. Such groups of servers, called **server clusters** or **clustered servers**, function as a single logical server as far as users are concerned. Future developments of server clusters probably will use higher-bandwidth technologies, however, simply because FDDI's 100-Mbps maximum throughput is easily overburdened when two or more servers must exchange large amounts of data on an ongoing basis.

Synchronous Optical Network (SONET)

After the 1984 breakup of AT&T, many local telephone companies faced the problem of connecting with the long-distance carriers. Each carrier used a different interfacing technology, thus making reliable and consistent connections difficult. Bell Communications Research developed **Synchronous Optical Network (SONET)** to eliminate the differences between the interface types. SONET is a WAN technology that uses fiber-optic media to transmit voice, data, and video at speeds in multiples of 51.84 Mbps. SONET enables near-faultless communications between the various long-distance carriers of the United States, Europe, and Japan.

SONET has unified the various interface types of the long-distance carriers. This relatively new system defines the available data rates in **optical carrier (OC)** levels. The first or basic OC level is OC-1, which corresponds to a rate of 51.84 Mbps. The most common OC level is OC-3, three times OC-1, or 155.52 Mbps. Most current physical transmission media limit SONET to OC-24 at 622 Mbps, but the specification defines up to OC-255 or 13.271 Gbps (usually achieved by aggregated multiple individual fiber-optic links).

Switched Multimegabit Data Service (SMDS)

Switched Multimegabit Data Service (SMDS) is a WAN switching technology developed by Bellcore in 1991. It offers inexpensive, high-speed, network communications of 1.544 to 45 Mbps. Like ATM, it uses a 53-byte fixed-length cell and provides no error checking.

VIRTUAL PRIVATE NETWORKS

Virtual private networks (VPNs) represent temporary or permanent connections across a public network—such as the Internet—that use special encryption technology to transmit and receive data. The VPNs are meant to make the packets secure as they are transmitted across the public network. Thus, the connection between sender and receiver acts as if it were completely private, even though it uses a link across a public network to carry information. In fact, this ability to use public resources privately on demand gives a VPN its name (that is, it makes something public behave as though it were private).

VPNs in Windows Environments

Windows .NET Server, Windows XP, Windows 2000, Windows NT 4.0, Windows Millennium, and Windows 98 support a special TCP/IP protocol called the **Point-to-Point Tunneling Protocol (PPTP)**. It lets a user running one of these Windows operating systems dial in to a Windows NT Server running the Remote Access Service (RAS) or a Windows 2000/.NET Server running the Routing and Remote Access Service (RRAS). It supports the equivalent of a private, encrypted dial-up session across the Internet. Similarly, a VPN could be established permanently across the Internet by leasing dedicated lines to an ISP at each end of a two-way link, and maintaining ongoing PPTP-based communications across that dedicated link.

Starting with Windows 2000, Windows also supports a newer, more secure VPN protocol called the **Layer 2 Tunneling Protocol (L2TP)**. Working in tandem with the new IP Secure (IPSec) protocol, these Windows operating systems can use either PPTP or L2TP to create safe, secure VPN connections, either through a private carrier or across the Internet. L2TP supports advanced authentication and encryption technologies; however, it requires Windows machines on both sides of any remote connection.

VPNs in Other Operating System Environments

Windows operating systems are not the only operating systems supporting VPNs. Linux operating systems also support VPN client and VPN server applications. Linux implementations of VPNs typically use PPTP or IPSec and are not compatible with the Windows L2TP. Building VPN connections with Linux is not as straightforward as it is with Windows operating systems, and it often requires a patch to the kernel to be successful.

The most popular method of creating a VPN connection with Linux is by using a process called VPN masquerade. Masquerading is a network arrangement in which one or more computers connect to the Internet using a Linux computer as a gateway. This process enables multiple computers to connect to the Internet while only the Linux computer has a valid IP address.

 There are quite a few configuration details involved in implementing VPNs on Linux systems, and these details are beyond the scope of this book. If you want to learn more, point your Web browser to *www.tldp.org/HOWTO/ VPN-Masquerade-HOWTO.html*.

Novell NetWare (along with BorderManager, which is the Novell firewall) provides VPN server connections into corporate networks for VPN clients. In addition, corporate LANs can be tied together over VPN connections through the Internet to form a VPN WAN.

Mac OS version 9 and above supports VPN client connections to Windows servers using PPTP or IPSec. None of the Mac OS versions support a VPN server service as of this writing.

VPN Operation and Benefits

VPNs work by adding a virtual networking interface to the collection of elements through which outgoing network traffic must pass for remote access. The interface also directs incoming traffic through a virtual private link. Essentially, this allows the virtual adapter to encrypt and encapsulate outgoing traffic through a VPN to reach a remote network. It also allows incoming traffic from a remote network to be decrypted and unencapsulated before it's delivered to the network interface driver, just as if a real network were involved.

The implementation of a virtual interface helps separate the privacy and encryption functions from other networking operations. Yet, it makes those functions fit into the same architecture and data flows that normal non-virtual, non-private networks use. Therefore, VPNs are entirely transparent to most users, who may not even know that they are using a VPN.

VPNs enable organizations to use the Internet as a private dial-up service for users with machines running one of the Windows operating systems. Organizations can also interconnect multiple LANs across the Internet—one pair of networks at a time.

Dial-up use has two clear advantages:

- It is not necessary to install several modems on a RAS server so that users can dial directly into the server machine; instead, they can dial into any ISP. As long as the server has an Internet connection, a private connection can be established. This saves money on hardware and systems management.

- Remote users can usually access the RAS server by making only a local phone call, no matter where they might be, as long as they can access a local ISP. Distance from the RAS server no longer matters; this saves money on long-distance telephone charges.

The VPN is not limited to dial-up connections. Anywhere a user has a connection to the Internet, whether through dial-up, cable modem, or a corporate LAN, a VPN can be utilized.

Cost savings notwithstanding, the greatest benefit of a VPN—whether it uses PPTP, L2TP, or another equivalent protocol—is that it extends the reach of private networks across public ones, both easily and transparently. Used more today for on-demand, dial-up connections, dedicated PPTP or L2TP connections are also increasingly used to connect LANs across the Internet.

CHAPTER SUMMARY

❑ This chapter presents several WAN technologies and related concepts. Linking remote networks and computers creates a WAN across significant distances. From a user's perspective, a WAN and a LAN are the same, with the only possible difference being response time. WANs can employ several technologies to establish long-distance connections, including packet-switching networks, fiber-optic cable, microwave transmitters, satellite links, and cable television coax systems.

❑ Analog WAN connections use conventional PSTN phone lines and offer little reliability or speed. Digital WAN connections offer high-speed connections and much more reliable communications. Digital links range from 56 Kbps to 274 Mbps. A CSU/DSU is required to connect to higher-bandwidth digital media, such as for frame relay, T1, T3, and so forth.

❑ Low-cost, medium-bandwidth technologies such as DSL and cable modem are taking over for SOHO connections, where users always connect from the same location and seek better price and bandwidth than analog modems or ISDN can provide. The users also avoid paying the additional costs for CSU/DSU equipment and bandwidth that frame relay, T1, T3, and so on require.

❑ T1 and similar lines are not single cables but, rather, collections of pairs of cables. Thus, fractions of these links can be leased. Multiplexing is the process of combining and delivering several transmissions on a single cable segment.

❑ Packet-switching networks are fast, efficient, and reliable WAN connection technologies. Packet switching is the process of segmenting data into packets and adding a header containing destination and sequence details. Each packet takes a unique route to its destination, where it is reassembled into its original form.

❑ A virtual circuit is a logical pathway between two communication points. An SVC is a temporary circuit that only exists while in use. A PVC is a permanent pathway that exists even when the circuit is not in use.

❑ X.25 is a WAN technology that offers 64-Kbps network connections and uses error checking. ISDN is a WAN technology that offers increments of 64-Kbps connections, most often for SOHO users.

❑ Frame relay is a WAN technology that offers transmission rates of 56 Kbps to 1.544 Mbps and no error checking. Frame relay uses a switched connection, unlike other high-speed technologies such as T1. This switched connection permits multiple destinations from a single frame relay connection.

❑ ATM, a WAN technology, uses fiber-optic media to support up to 622-Mbps transmission rates. ATM uses no error checking and has a 53-byte fixed-length cell. FDDI is a limited-distance linking technology that uses fiber-optic rings to provide 100-Mbps fault-tolerant transmission rates. SONET is a WAN technology used to interface with dissimilar long-distance networks. SONET offers transmission speeds in multiples of 51.84 Mbps using fiber-optic media. SMDS is a WAN technology similar to ATM in that it has a 53-byte, fixed-length cell and no error checking. SMDS offers transmission rates of 1.544 Mbps to 45 Mbps.

❐ A VPN permits public networks such as the Internet to carry dial-up or ongoing encrypted communications between remote users and private networks, or between private LANs, without fear of exposure to any parties who might attempt to intercept such traffic on the public network. VPNs are supported by most operating systems today, including Windows, Linux, and Mac OSs.

KEY TERMS

Asynchronous Transfer Mode (ATM) — A WAN technology that uses fiber-optic media to support up to 622-Mbps transmission rates. ATM uses no error checking and has a 53-byte, fixed-length cell.

Basic Rate Interface (BRI) — An ISDN service format that consists of two B-channels (64 Kbps) and a D-channel (16 Kbps).

Channel Service Unit/Data Service Unit (CSU/DSU) — A device that links a computer or network to a DDS communications link.

clustered server — A network server, which is a member of a group of two or more servers. All machines in the group employ a combination of special operating system software and a dedicated high-speed link. This permits all machines in the group to behave as one super-powered network server, rather than single, independent, individual servers.

Committed Information Rate (CIR) — A performance measurement of guaranteed throughput rates.

data communications equipment (DCE) — Any type of device, such as a modem, that connects a DTE to a communications line.

data terminal equipment (DTE) — Any device that transmits digital information over a communications line.

Digital Data Service (DDS) — A type of point-to-point synchronous communication link offering 2.4-, 4.8-, 9.6-, or 56-Kbps transmission rates.

DS — A specification level for DDS lines. A T1 is a DS-1 or 1.544 Mbps; a single channel fractional T1 is a DS-0 or 64 Kbps.

fractional T1 — A segmented T1 line where a customer uses or leases one to 23 channels of a T1 to achieve transmission rates in increments of 64 Kbps.

frame relay — A WAN technology that offers transmission rates of 56 Kbps to 1.544 Mbps. Frame relay uses no error checking.

Layer 2 Tunneling Protocol (L2TP) — A Windows technology used in VPNs and which supports advanced authentication and encryption.

line conditioning — Sustaining a consistent transmission rate, improving overall quality, and reducing interference noise levels.

multiplexing — The networking technology that combines several communications on a single cable segment.

muxing — *See* multiplexing.

optical carrier (OC) — A speed level of fiber-optic cable that conforms to the SONET standard.

packet assembler/disassembler (PAD) — A component of an X.25 network that supports low-speed, character-based terminals.

permanent virtual circuit (PVC) — A permanent path defined even when not in use.

plain old telephone system (POTS) — Also known as PSTN, the normal telephone communications system.

Point-to-Point Tunneling Protocol (PPTP) — A special TCP/IP-based transport protocol that encrypts all traffic before transmission across a network link and decrypts all incoming traffic from a network link. PPTP permits the Internet (and other public IP-based networks) to function as part of a VPN.

Primary Rate Interface (PRI) — An ISDN service format that consists of 23 B-Channels and a D-Channel.

public data network (PDN) — A wide area network service, usually provided by private companies, for the purpose of enabling WAN technologies such as X.25.

server cluster — *See* clustered server.

Switched 56K — Digital point-to-point leased communication links offered by local and long-distance telcos. Lease terms are based on per-minute use charges, not on 24-hour, seven-day dedicated circuits.

Switched Multimegabit Data Service (SMDS) — A WAN technology similar to ATM that has a 53-byte, fixed-length cell and no error checking. SMDS offers transmission rates of 1.544 Mbps to 45 Mbps.

switched virtual circuit (SVC) — A temporary path across a switched network that is defined only as long as it is in use.

Synchronous Optical Network (SONET) — A WAN technology used to interface with dissimilar long-distance networks. SONET offers transmission speeds in multiples of 51.84 Mbps using fiber-optic media.

T1 — A type of high-speed digital link offering a 1.544-Mbps transmission rate.

T3 — A communications line comprising 28 T1s or 672 channels and which supports a data rate of 44.736 Mbps.

telco — A telephone company or telephone service provider.

virtual circuit — A term used to describe the pathways created in a packet-switching network to transmit data between connection points.

virtual private network (VPN) — A network link that incorporates connections across a public network, such as the Internet, with protocols such as PPTP to impose encryption techniques that permit the use of public network links for reliable, secure delivery of private communications.

12

REVIEW QUESTIONS

1. Optical carrier (OC) levels define the transmission rates of which WAN technology?

   a. ISDN

   b. SMDS

   c. ATM

   d. SONET

2. WAN connections differ so significantly from LAN connections that users are fully aware of the difference between accessing WAN resources as opposed to LAN resources. True or false?

3. Which WAN technology uses PADs?

   a. frame relay

   b. SMDS

   c. X.25

   d. ATM

4. What types of communication links can you use to create a WAN? (Choose all that apply.)

   a. packet-switching networks

   b. fiber-optic cable

   c. microwave transmitters

   d. satellite links

   e. cable television coax systems

5. Which of the following statements best describes frame relay?

   a. It transmits fixed-length packets at the Physical layer through the most cost-effective path.

   b. It transmits variable-length packets at the Data Link layer through the most cost-effective path.

   c. It transmits variable-length packets at the Physical layer through the most cost-effective path.

   d. It transmits fixed-length packets at the Data Link layer through the most cost-effective path.

6. Which of the following supports analog WAN connections?

   a. ISDN

   b. ATM

   c. SONET

   d. PSTN

7. Which WAN technology is capable of transmission speeds in excess of 100 Mbps?
   a. T1
   b. Switched 56K
   c. ATM
   d. FDDI

8. WANs are created to broaden the resources of the LAN and to improve the communications of an organization. True or false?

9. Which WAN technology was designed specifically to replace the analog telephone system?
   a. ATM
   b. ISDN
   c. frame relay
   d. SONET

10. Why is a non-dedicated PSTN line such a poor choice for WAN connections? (Choose all that apply.)
    a. limited bandwidth
    b. inconsistent quality of equipment
    c. too expensive
    d. originally designed for voice-only communications

11. Which are important considerations when planning to deploy a PSTN link? (Choose all that apply.)
    a. length of connection time required (daily, weekly, monthly)
    b. cost of the service and use level
    c. availability of dedicated circuits, conditioning, or other quality improvements
    d. assessment of need for a 24/7 connection

12. Of the listed WAN technology high-speed links, which is the most widely used?
    a. Switched 56K
    b. T1
    c. SMDS
    d. ATM

13. A DDS line offers point-to-point synchronous communication links with what transmission rates? (Choose all that apply.)
    a. 2.4 Kbps
    b. 4.8 Kbps
    c. 9.6 Kbps
    d. 56 Kbps
    e. 64 Kbps

12

14. Digital lines offer what level of error-free transmission?

    a. 10%

    b. 60%

    c. 99%

    d. 100%

15. What type of device is required to connect to a dedicated digital communications line?

    a. modem

    b. NIC

    c. CSU/DSU

    d. digital recorder

16. Which are characteristics of a T1 line? (Choose all that apply.)

    a. 1.544-Mbps transmission rate

    b. full-duplex communications

    c. supports data, voice, and video

    d. consists of 24 channels

17. Which statement best describes multiplexing technology?

    a. It combines multiple communications lines in a single aggregated pipeline.

    b. It gives users multiple phone numbers.

    c. It enables multiple communications to travel simultaneously over the same cable segment.

18. How many channels are in a full T1?

    a. 2

    b. 24

    c. 48

    d. 64

19. How many T1s does a DS-1C comprise?

    a. 1

    b. 2

    c. 4

    d. 48

20. Which WAN technologies are limited by the transmission rates of fiber-optic cable? (Choose all that apply.)

    a. ATM

    b. ISDN

    c. SONET

    d. SMDS

21. The Internet is an example of what type of network?

    a. analog

    b. digital

    c. packet-switching

    d. frame relay

22. Packet switching segments the original data into little chunks before transmitting it. True or false?

23. Which of the following WAN technologies uses PVCs? (Choose all that apply.)

    a. X.25

    b. frame relay

    c. ATM

    d. ISDN

24. What is the limitation of FDDI?

    a. 100-kilometers transmission limit

    b. analog connections

    c. 64-Kbps transmission rates

    d. single-computer transmission

25. What is the basic transmission rate for an E1 connection?

    a 1.544 Mbps

    b. 2.048 Mbps

    c. 8.448 Mbps

    d. 34.368 Mbps

26. Which WAN technology supports the highest maximum bandwidth?

    a. X.25

    b. frame relay

    c. FDDI

    d. ATM

12

27. Which of these benefits apply to an Internet-based VPN, assuming that remote users dial into an ISP with a local telephone call, no matter where they're located? (Choose all that apply.)

    a. keeps telecommunications costs down

    b. provides easy access for any user with an ISP connection

    c. offers higher bandwidth than a normal dial-up connection

    d. requires no special software for access to remote services

28. Which of these protocols is most secure for VPN access?

    a. SLIP

    b. PPP

    c. PPTP

    d. L2TP

29. Out of the box, only Windows 2000 machines can use L2TP and IPSec for VPN access. True or false?

HANDS-ON PROJECTS

The following Hands-on Projects assume you have access to a computer with TCP/IP installed and a connection to the Internet or an intranet. Projects 12-1 and 12-2 require Windows 98, Windows 2000, or Windows XP Professional. Project 12-3 requires Windows 2000 or Windows XP Professional.

Project 12-1

This project assumes you can reach a network host. If the hosts listed in the project are not present or your computer cannot reach them, use a different known host name or IP address.

To trace a packet-switching route using the TRACERT utility:

1. Log on.

2. Click **Start**, **Programs**, **Accessories**, **Command Prompt** in Windows 2000; **Start**, **All Programs**, **Command Prompt** in Windows XP; or **Start**, **Programs**, **MS-DOS Prompt** in Windows 98 to open the Command Prompt window.

3. Type **tracert www.microsoft.com** on the command line, and press **Enter**.

4. Watch as the routes taken by packets between your computer and the host are timed and identified.

5. Repeat this activity for other hosts, such as **www.course.com**, **www.lanw.com**, and **www.nytimes.com**.

Project 12-2

This project assumes that you have network access and have accessed other hosts while completing the previous projects.

To inspect the current routing table using the ROUTE PRINT utility:

1. Log on.

2. Click **Start**, **Programs**, **Accessories**, **Command Prompt** in Windows 2000; **Start**, **All Programs**, **Command Prompt** in Windows XP; or **Start**, **Programs**, **MS-DOS Prompt** in Windows 98 to open the Command Prompt window.

3. Type **route print** on the command line, and press **Enter**.

4. Inspect the table of data that appears in your command window. It should resemble Figure 12-6.

```
Microsoft Windows 2000 [Version 5.00.2195]
(C) Copyright 1985-2000 Microsoft Corp.

D:\>route print
===========================================================================
Interface List
0x1 ........................... MS TCP Loopback interface
0x1000003 ...00 60 97 1b 7b 01 ...... ELNK3 Ethernet Adapter
===========================================================================
===========================================================================
Active Routes:
Network Destination        Netmask          Gateway       Interface  Metric
          127.0.0.0        255.0.0.0        127.0.0.1       127.0.0.1      1
       172.16.1.0    255.255.255.0      172.16.1.21     172.16.1.21      1
      172.16.1.21  255.255.255.255        127.0.0.1       127.0.0.1      1
  172.16.255.255  255.255.255.255      172.16.1.21     172.16.1.21      1
        224.0.0.0        224.0.0.0      172.16.1.21     172.16.1.21      1
  255.255.255.255  255.255.255.255      172.16.1.21     172.16.1.21      1
===========================================================================
Persistent Routes:
  None

D:\>_
```

Ping uses Icmp

TTL -1

Figure 12-6   Route print command

5. Here's how to interpret the information that appears, starting with the headings:

   ◻ Network Destination (or Network Address)—A network that the current network can reach

   ◻ Netmask—The IP subnet mask that applies to that network

   ◻ Gateway (or Gateway Address)—The IP address of the router that connects to that network

   ◻ Interface—The IP address of the interface that connects to that network

6. Here's how to interpret the information that appears in the columns (the IP address information on your screen will be different):

   ◻ 127.0.0.0—The Class A network address for loopback and testing purposes; it uses a Class A netmask of 255.0.0.0 and the only valid loopback address, 127.0.0.1, for the gateway and interface addresses (which are virtual in this case, not actual).

12

❏ 172.16.1.0—The Private Class B IP network address for the machine where ROUTE PRINT executes, given that the Class C default subnet mask 255.255.255.0 is defined for this subnet.

❏ 172.16.1.21—Under the Gateway and Interface columns, the address of this local machine, and hence, it shows up as both gateway and interface address.

❏ 172.16.1.21—Under the Network Destination column, the address for the local node masked by the "trick" subnet mask of 255.255.255.255 (no host address bits); used to map between the loopback address 127.0.0.1; used for both the gateway and the interface to the loopback network, by convention.

❏ 172.16.255.255—The default subnet mask for the Class B Private IP address 172.16.1.21 and the broadcast address for the 172.16.0.0 network; in this case, this entry is what allows all broadcasts to the 172.16.0.0 network to reach this machine.

❏ 224.0.0.0—The default network address for multicasting RIPv2 router table updates to IP router, based on the RFC that governs RIPv2; if this computer were acting as a dynamic RIPv2 router, it would have to listen on this network address to obtain router table updates.

❏ 255.255.255.255—The general broadcast address for all IP network addresses; included in the routing table to permit all general broadcasts to reach this machine.

7. Type **exit** on the command line, and press **Enter** to close the command-line window.

Project 12-3

This project walks you through the process of creating a VPN client connection in Windows 2000 or Windows XP. If you do not have a VPN server to connect to, you can still go through the steps, but you will not be able to connect to another computer or network.

To create a VPN client connection for Windows 2000:

1. Log on.

2. Go to **Start**, **Settings**, **Network and Dial-Up Connections**.

3. Select **Make New Connection** to start the Network Connection Wizard. Click **Next**. Note that there may be a prompt for the area code and then a confirmation of user location before the wizard can begin. If this prompt appears, your instructor will provide you with the appropriate information to enter.

4. Click the **Connect to a private network through the Internet** option button, and then click **Next**.

5. Under Host name or IP address, type the name or address of the computer you wish to connect to. Click **Next**.

6. Click the **For all users to make this connection available to anyone who logs in to your computer** option button. Click **Next**.

7. Give the connection a name, or you can leave it at the default of Virtual Private Connection. Click **Finish**.

8. You will see a login dialog box. If you have an actual server to connect to, enter your username and password and click **Connect**. If not, click **Cancel**.

9. From now on, you can connect to your VPN by going to **Start**, **Settings**, **Network and Dial-Up Connections** and clicking the VPN connection you named in Step 7.

To create a VPN client connection in Windows XP:

1. Log on.

2. Click **Start**, and then click **Control Panel**.

3. Click **Network and Internet Connections**.

4. Click **Network Connections**.

5. Click **Create a New Connection**. The New Connection Wizard will start.

6. Click **Next**.

7. Click **Connect to the Network at My Workplace**, and click **Next**.

8. Click **Virtual Private Network Connection**, and click **Next**.

9. Enter a company name at the prompt—you may use your name for this. Click **Next**.

10. Under Host name or IP address, type the name or address of the computer to which you want to connect. Click **Next**.

11. Click the **For all users** option button. Then click **Next**.

12. Click **Finish**.

Project 12-4

Frame relay is a commonly used digital communications technology based on leased lines, primarily for higher-bandwidth business use. This project gives you a chance to examine more information and discussion on this technology. This project requires access to the Internet and a computer with an installed Web browser such as Internet Explorer.

To learn more about frame relay:

1. Open a Web browser by selecting **Start**, **Programs**, **Internet Explorer**, or whatever sequence of steps your instructor tells you to follow.

2. Type **www.techfest.com** in the Address text box in your Web browser, and then press the **Enter** key.

3. Type **frame relay** in the Search TechFest text box on the left side of the page, then click the **Go!** button.

4. Select the hyperlink to the first article titled Frame Relay Overview that appears in response to your search. Read the article that appears next. Name three important characteristics of frame relay, including at what OSI reference model layer frame relay operates, how frame relay maximizes transfer speed, and how frame relay treats incorrect or invalid data.

5. Unless you plan to proceed directly to the next Hands-on Project, close the Web browser by clicking the upper-right corner of your browser window.

Project 12-5

Because they offer the ability to use public network connections—especially the Internet—for private purposes, VPNs are becoming increasingly important for remote access and for site-to-site communications. VPNs add an extra layer of encryption and security to communications that occur across public links, and are also easy to use and install, so users may not even know that this extra layer of privacy and security is in place.

To learn more about VPNs:

1. Open a Web browser by selecting **Start**, **Programs**, **Internet Explorer**, or whatever sequence of steps your instructor asks you to follow.

2. Type **http://www.webopedia.com** in the Address text box in your Web browser, and then press the **Enter** key.

3. Type **VPN** in the Search By keyword text box, and then click the **Go!** button.

4. Read the brief description of virtual private networks that appears in response, and then scroll down to the Links section and investigate the articles included in the list. Why is tunneling important to VPN services? How does security figure into the VPN equation?

5. Close the Web browser by clicking the upper-right corner of your browser window to conclude this project.

CASE PROJECTS

1. When choosing a particular kind of WAN link, trading off between bandwidth and expense is often necessary. That is, the higher the bandwidth of a WAN link, the more it costs; this rule applies equally to equipment, installation, and operation costs. Your manager at XYZ Corporation gives you a list of costs and requirements. This list governs your selection of a link between the company's San Jose and San Francisco offices (approximately 70 miles apart):

   ❑ Bandwidth requirements average 128 Kbps but sometimes peak at 256 Kbps. (Peak usage never occurs more than 20% of the time.)

❑ The company cannot afford to spend more than $1000 per month on WAN communications.

❑ Dedicated ISDN lines cost $700 per month; dial-up ISDN lines cost $150 per month.

❑ Frame relay of 256 Kbps costs $1100 per month, in $275 increments for each 64-Kbps channel.

❑ A fractional 256-Kbps T1 costs $1000 per month.

Based on the list's requirements, of the following combinations of WAN links, which fits the company's requirements best? Why?

a. Set up a dedicated ISDN line and a dial-up ISDN line between the two offices. The company incurs costs of only $850 a month, and the lines provide the required bandwidth (128 Kbps) and on-demand access to the additional necessary bandwidth (256 Kbps).

b. Purchase a frame relay link, with equipment for up to four 64-Kbps channels. Because the company only pays for the third and fourth channels when they're being used—only 20% of the time—monthly charges average around $660. This provides the necessary bandwidth much more cheaply.

c. Purchase the fractional T1 line: It meets the bandwidth requirements and stays within budget. It's also the only solution that provides instant access to the full 256 Kbps necessary whenever that speed is needed.

2. Another factor plays a powerful role in selecting WAN links: associated equipment and installation costs. To the requirements listed in Case 1, add the following characteristics and requirements:

12

❑ ISDN equipment costs $1400; ISDN installation costs $1100.

❑ Frame relay equipment costs $2400; frame relay installation costs $1600.

❑ T1 equipment costs $3000; T1 installation costs $3200.

❑ The company cannot afford more than $5000 for installation and equipment costs.

Given these additional requirements, which of the following options now makes the most sense? Why?

a. Set up a dedicated ISDN line and a dial-up ISDN line between the two offices. The company incurs the lowest installation and equipment costs, and the lines deliver the necessary bandwidth.

b. Purchase a frame relay link, with equipment for up to four 64-Kbps channels. Although the frame relay link costs $1500 more than the ISDN, its bandwidth eliminates the "busy signal" that an attempt to dial into an ISP sometimes produces. Because the bandwidth for peak usage is essential, only frame relay provides the necessary guarantee that it's there when needed. This option's costs are within the budget requirements.

    c. Purchase the fractional T1 line anyway; you should be able to convince management to spend the extra $1200 because only the fractional T1 line provides instant access to the additional 128 Kbps needed for peak demands.

3. Executives of ABC Inc. return from a networking trade show, where they saw a real-time video teleconferencing system demonstrated. They ask you to determine the budget and feasibility of putting such a system in place. They expect to realize ongoing savings of $1 million a year on travel, even after paying the expenses of linking all four sites in San Francisco, Seattle, Boston, and New York. Read the following matrix of costs and requirements, and discuss each possible alternative outlined thereafter, in terms of suitability and costs. Assume that all equipment and installation costs will be amortized over three years at no interest.

Costs and Requirements:

❏ Equipment costs per site connection will be $250,000, including conference room facilities, improvements, and associated computers, cameras, microphones, and so forth. Table 12-4 lists equipment and installation costs for the digital lines.

❏ Bandwidth requirements are 6.312 Mbps per connection.

❏ Up to three simultaneous connections might be required from time to time.

❏ Only the New York office must install the equipment necessary to support three simultaneous links; all other sites have to support only one link at a time.

❏ Per link monthly costs are $3000 for each T1; $12,000 for each T2; and $24,000 for each T3.

Table 12-4 shows equipment and installation costs for each type of connection.

Table 12-4   Per-connection equipment and installation costs for T1, T2, and T3 lines

Type	Installation	Equipment
T1	$1500	$1600
T2	$6000	$4800
T3	$30,000	$25,000

For each of the following approaches, determine total up-front and monthly costs involved, and then calculate the total budget over three years. Use this information to discuss each option's suitability to the stated requirements.

    a. For NYC, use three T2s per site, and use one T2 for each of the other sites.

    b. Use one T3 for NYC, and one T2 for each of the other sites.

    c. For NYC, use one T3, and four T1s for each of the other sites.

4. The sales force of XYZ Corporation decided to use remote access services to access the company's headquarters network using dial-up connections across the Internet. What additional networking technology should these staff members employ to protect their privacy and improve the security for remote access traffic? What built-in facilities in Windows NT Server or Windows 2000 Server might they use as part of the solution?

5. ABC Inc. wants to select a medium-bandwidth WAN technology to connect its branch office to headquarters and decided to either:

   ❑ Use two basic-rate ISDN interfaces per office to connect to headquarters through an existing PRI, or

   ❑ Purchase five 56K-committed rate frame relay connections (or 280-Kbps aggregate bandwidth per connection) for each office to connect to headquarters through an existing T1 interface.

Which approach is likely to be cheaper? Which approach is likely to be faster? Which approach provides service with a bandwidth that is easier to increase?

12

13

SOLVING NETWORK PROBLEMS

After reading this chapter and completing the exercises, you will be able to:

♦ Discuss the benefits of network management and planning

♦ Understand the necessity for networking standards, policies and procedures, and documentation

♦ Troubleshoot your network following a structured approach

♦ Discuss the types of specialized equipment and other resources available for troubleshooting

---

The role of a network manager encompasses many areas of responsibility. Typical activities include server configuration, user connectivity and management, data protection, and network planning and monitoring. Preceding chapters covered various aspects of server and client management; this chapter covers two of the most important aspects of network-management—preventing problems and dealing with those that do occur.

This chapter describes how to prevent problems through proper planning and documentation. You also learn how to back up network data, as well as how to monitor your network. This chapter also outlines a methodology for troubleshooting networks, describes related tools and resources, and concludes with a survey of common network problems and ideas on how to troubleshoot them.

PREVENTING PROBLEMS WITH NETWORK-MANAGEMENT AND PLANNING

In a perfect world, networks would always work smoothly and users would be blissfully unaware of network administration. In the real world, however, problems can and do occur. Typically, you resolve network problems in one of two ways: 1) by preventing problems through planning and management (called **pre-emptive troubleshooting** or **trouble avoidance**); or 2) by repair and control of damage that already exists (called **troubleshooting**). This section covers prevention through planning and management. Later sections in the chapter discuss damage control.

Network management and troubleshooting should combine to form an overall network plan. As a network administrator, you need to realize this plan in a comprehensive document that evolves with a network. A network plan, an extension of the network diagram discussed in Chapter 2, should include cable diagrams, cable layouts, network capacity information, a list of all protocols and network standards in use, and documentation on computer and network device configurations, software, and important files.

You should establish the policies and procedures that apply to your network during its planning stages and continue throughout the network's life. Such policies should include back-up methods, security, hardware and software standards, upgrade guidelines, and documentation. Through careful planning, you can minimize the damage that results from most predictable events and control and manage their impact on your organization.

Backing Up Network Data

As discussed in Chapter 10, a comprehensive back-up program can prevent significant data loss. Any back-up plan is an important part of a network plan and should be revised as your needs—and your data and applications—evolve.

To formulate any back-up plan, consider the following topics and issues:

- Determine what data should be backed up as well as how often. Some files, such as program executables and configuration files, seldom change and may require backup only weekly or monthly.

- Develop a schedule for backing up your data that includes the type of backup to be performed, how often, and at what time of day. Table 13-1 outlines several back-up methods.

- Identify the person(s) responsible for performing backups.

- Test your back-up system regularly. The person responsible for backups should perform such tests, which include backing up data and restoring it as well. After a back-up system is in place, perform periodic tests to ensure data integrity.

- Maintain a backup log listing what data was backed up, when the backup took place, who performed the backup, and which tapes were involved. The automatic log created by most tape-backup systems can often augment this backup log.

- Develop a plan for storing data once it has been backed up to tape (or whatever backup medium you use). This plan should include on-site storage, perhaps in a fireproof safe, and off-site storage in the event of a catastrophe. For both on-site and off-site storage, ensure that only authorized personnel have access to the tapes.

Table 13-1   Backup methods

Method	Description
Full backup	Backs up all selected files and marks them as backed up, whether or not they have changed since they were last backed up
Copy	Backs up all selected files without marking them as backed up
Incremental	Backs up all selected files and marks them as backed up, but only if they have changed since they were last backed up
Daily copy	Backs up only files modified that day and does not mark them as backed up
Differential	Backs up selected files only if they have changed since they were last backed up but does not mark them as backed up

Setting Security Policies

All security policies outlined in a network plan should be detailed and followed closely. Your security policies depend on many things, including the value and sensitivity of the data, network size, and your company's security standards. A security plan must include not only data security, but hardware security as well. If file servers are in a common area that anyone can access, security can be compromised quite easily.

You can enhance network data security in several different ways. First and foremost are user name and password requirements. When developing standards for user security, carefully consider the following items:

- Establish minimum and maximum password lengths for user accounts.

- Determine how often users should change their passwords.

- Decide whether users can reuse the same passwords or if users must create unique passwords each time they make changes.

- Know the character restrictions related to passwords, and share them with your users.

13

- Determine if more than one set of standards applies to user passwords. For example, should executive staff be required to change passwords more often than engineers?
- Decide how to define and document exceptions.

You should also establish guidelines for resource access. Generally, it's best to grant access only to those users who specifically require it, and even then, grant only the minimum levels of acceptable access. Granting new access to users is always easier than taking it away when you learn it is not needed.

For dial-in users, special security requirements may be necessary. For example, should all users who dial in to your network be able to use their own logins, or should each be required to use a special dial-in account? If a dial-in account is created, what kind of access does that entail? If users dial in strictly for e-mail access, a limited account that grants access only to that program may be sufficient. It is possible to limit dial-in access only to the machine being dialed in to, rather than permitting dial-in clients to act as remote network clients. This restriction is well worth imposing when dial-in users have no pressing need to act as network clients.

Finally, keep to a minimum the number of users with permission to perform network administration tasks. The more people who have access to administrative functions, the more likely security problems will occur.

Setting Hardware and Software Standards

As an administrator, you are at least partially responsible for supporting the network, so you should also be involved in deciding what hardware and software components to use on that network.

To make hardware and software easier to manage, all network components should follow established standards. When you define standards for desktop computers, establish configurations for several levels of users. For example, a user in the accounting department may need a more powerful system than an administrative assistant in manufacturing. Such standards should cover hardware (for example, processor, NIC, memory, and monitor) and software configurations (for example, operating systems and applications).

You also must establish standards for networking devices, including supported hardware manufacturers and operating systems (and versions), and indicate which networking protocols and services may be used.

You also must define standards for server configurations and document current server configurations, as well as establish guidelines for new server installations. Often, servers are installed haphazardly—as desktop computers sometimes are. An official standard can eliminate the problems a "catch-as-catch-can" server policy can create and make purchasing new servers less arduous.

When establishing hardware and software standards, bear in mind the pace of industry change. To keep up, you must evaluate standards often—ideally, once per quarter. Regular evaluations help ensure that your network does not become outdated, even if you do not make purchases every time standards are updated. This may seem unduly time-consuming, but a solid set of standards makes this review process both simple and painless.

Establishing Upgrade Guidelines

As an extension of hardware and software standards, you also must establish guidelines for upgrades. Vendors often upgrade products and introduce new ones. If you establish guidelines in advance, you can handle upgrades more easily.

To help ease the upgrade process, always give your users advance notice so that they know changes will take place and can respond to them. In addition, disruptive upgrades should not be performed during normal working hours.

It is also a good idea to "pilot" new upgrades with a small group of technically astute network users. This allows you to work through the problems that typically arise without necessarily affecting all network users.

When performing upgrades, always formulate a plan to undo the installation if necessary. Sometimes, it's best to cut your losses and return the system or network to its pre-upgrade state. If this happens, it may be wise to re-evaluate the upgrade and perform more testing.

Upgrades are a fact of life in any network environment. Better computers, peripherals, and software are constantly being developed; likewise, any organization's (or user's) needs may change. Through careful planning and testing, you can make the upgrade process relatively painless.

Maintaining Documentation

As mentioned earlier in this chapter and in Chapter 2, complete, up-to-date network documentation provides an invaluable reference when training or troubleshooting. When a problem occurs, concise network documentation provides valuable information about the network's configuration and the location of remedial resources. This documentation should not be limited to local area network (LAN) information and configuration, but must include wide area connections as well.

If you work in a networking environment that encompasses multiple LANs, each LAN should have its own set of documentation, and each must be documented with the same level of detail. The following list outlines a set of documents that you should include in any network plan:

- *Address list.* This list is especially useful in a network with protocols that use arbitrary addresses, such as TCP/IP. However, you should create a complete list that defines all addresses on a network, including the hardware addresses for specific computers. For example, an ideal list includes the MAC address of each computer's NIC, its IP address, its physical location, and the identity of its primary user.

13

- *Cable map.* This gives a more detailed outline of the cable installation for your network. For example, a cable map for a twisted-pair network includes cable type (for example, Category 3 or 5 UTP), wall-jack numbers and office locations, and the corresponding ports on the patch panel or concentrator. It also includes the cable's maximum speed and the speed at which it is used, if the two differ.

- *Contact list.* Sometimes called an escalation procedure, this should include contacts to be informed in the event of a network problem or failure. The list encompasses not only network administrators, but also vendor contacts, phone numbers, and information such as circuit numbers for wide area network (WAN) links.

- *Equipment list.* This list must include the date the equipment was purchased, its serial numbers, vendor information, and warranty information. In many cases, network administrators keep separate lists for computers and for other equipment.

- *Network history.* This single, comprehensive document outlines all upgrades applied to the network, including what problems have occurred, along with their symptoms, solutions, dates, contacts, procedures, and results.

- *Network map.* A comprehensive network map includes hardware locations and cabling.

- *Networking hardware configuration.* Configuration information includes a hard copy of each server's, router's, or other networking device's configuration files, as well as protocol information.

- *Policies and procedures.* Here you document all tasks performed by a network administrator. Established policies for user and group configuration and naming conventions are prime examples. Also include procedures that outline the steps necessary to set up or delete network users, perform backups, or restore files. Update this information as necessary. These documentation tasks may seem time-consuming, but they pay off quickly by easing the training process when new people join the network. Should the network administrator be unavailable, an accurate set of procedures also ensures that your company's productivity isn't affected.

- *Server configuration.* This should be a separate document for each server and should list the hardware configuration of the software installed (including version number), the type of data stored (file server, database server, e-mail server, and so on), and the schedule and location of backups.

- *Software configuration.* This configuration document defines the software installed on each node on the network as well as its configuration data. This includes the type of drivers installed, the settings within configuration files (for example, use the Print Report feature in MSD.EXE, which is available in all Windows environments, even Windows 2000, or capture the contents of important files like WIN.INI, CONFIG.SYS, and AUTOEXEC.BAT), and exceptions to standard configurations.

- *Software licensing.* This document lists each software product in use on your network, as well as licensing information for those products, including the number of user licenses and the license numbers. This document, once created, *must* be kept up to date.

- *User administration.* This document outlines the types of users defined on the network, the naming conventions used, and network resource assignment for users (for example, which drives are mapped at logon and so on).

Keep documentation in hard copy and electronic form so that it's readily accessible. Complete, accurate, up-to-date documentation helps you troubleshoot your network, train new employees, and plan for growth.

Performing Pre-Emptive Troubleshooting

Although pre-emptive troubleshooting may seem costly in the short term, it saves time when problems do arise, prevents equipment problems, and ensures data security. In addition, a pre-emptive approach can prevent additional expense and ease frustration when trying to identify the causes of failures.

The International Organization for Standardization (ISO) identified five pre-emptive troubleshooting network-management categories:

- *Accounting management.* Used to record and report usage of network resources

- *Configuration management.* Used to define and control network component configurations and parameters

- *Fault management.* Used to detect and isolate network problems

- *Performance management.* Used to monitor, analyze, and control network data production

- *Security management.* Used to monitor and control access to network resources

Do your best to cover all these categories by gathering related information for each type of management before problems occur. You'll be far better equipped to handle trouble in any area if and when it does occur.

Practicing Good Customer-Relation Skills

Technical training programs often place too little emphasis on customer relations. As a network administrator, help desk operator, or network technician, all of the network users are your customers, and your customers are your best source of information when something goes wrong with your network—after all, users are the reason you have a job.

13

Build a relationship with your users so that they trust you and are more likely to provide you with pertinent information when there is a problem. Establish a special relationship with key users throughout the organization who are more technically adept than the average user. These key users will be a source of excellent troubleshooting information, and they can often help you with minor user issues.

All information technology departments should have guidelines that instruct personnel how to interact with users. These guidelines should include appropriate questions to ask users, how to respond to irate users, how to respond to user questions (even if the questions seem dumb), and general user communication etiquette. You will find that users who have experienced proper communication have infinitely greater patience when network or computer problems arise than those users who do not receive such communication.

Using Network-Monitoring Utilities

Today, many programs are available to assist with network management. These programs can help identify conditions that may lead to problems, prevent network failures, and troubleshoot problems when they occur.

Network-management utilities are long-term troubleshooting tools. As a network administrator, you must learn which statistics to monitor. In addition, you must collect data over a period of time to develop an idea of typical network performance. Once you establish a baseline for network performance, you can monitor the network for changes that could indicate potential problems. In other words, you must establish what's "normal" for your network in order to recognize "abnormal" conditions when they occur. Advanced operating systems such as Windows NT Server or Windows 2000 Server include many network-management utilities. Likewise, many third-party products are available to perform such functions or to augment monitors included with these operating systems and other common server operating systems such as UNIX or Linux.

Network-monitoring programs gather the following information:

- *Events.* These include errors, resource access, security settings changes, and other significant occurrences such as the failure of a particular program to load or failure of a service to start.

- *System usage statistics.* These indicate who accesses resources and how they use those resources.

- *System performance statistics.* These indicate processor and memory usage, server throughput, and other indicators of system activity and behavior.

The information gathered by these network monitors enables network administrators to take a proactive role when making network decisions. This information can help:

- Identify those network devices that create bottlenecks.

- Provide information when forecasting growth and planning capacity requirements.

- Develop plans to improve network performance.

- Monitor events that arise from software or hardware changes.

- Monitor trends in network traffic and utilization.

As discussed in Chapter 10, the Performance Monitor utility included with Windows NT and Windows 2000 monitors and tracks many different areas of server performance. As Figure 13-1 shows, it is a graphical tool that can monitor many events concurrently. Using the Performance Monitor, you can analyze network operations, identify trends and bottlenecks, determine system capacity, notify administrators when thresholds are exceeded, track performance of individual devices, and monitor both local and remote computers.

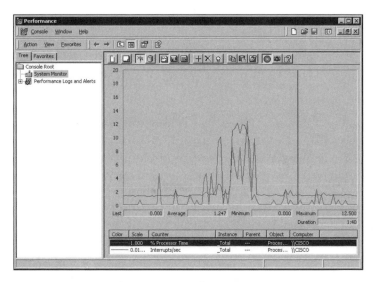

Figure 13-1   Windows 2000 Performance Monitor

Creating a Network Baseline

To use network monitoring effectively as a pre-emptive troubleshooting tool, you must establish a baseline for network performance. A **baseline** defines a point of reference against which you can measure network performance and behavior when problems occur.

You must establish a baseline for network performance over a period when no problems are evident on the network. Once you create a baseline, you can then compare all network performance to that baseline as part of your ongoing network-management and troubleshooting activities.

13

A baseline is exceptionally helpful to identify daily network utilization patterns, possible network bottlenecks, heavy usage patterns, and protocol traffic patterns. Using Performance Monitor and a network performance baseline, you can often avoid potential network problems. A baseline can indicate whether a network needs partitioning, more file servers, or the increased speed that upgraded NICs and networking equipment can provide.

For instance, if a conventional Ethernet network routinely experiences utilization levels of 60% or greater, it's time to either segment the network to distribute the load or move to a higher-speed technology (perhaps some form of 100 Mbps Ethernet). Observing utilization levels over time with Performance Monitor helps you determine if high utilization is an occasional condition (usually remedied by partitioning the network and dividing the load) or a chronic circumstance (best resolved by increasing the bandwidth by upgrading to switched Ethernet or some form of 100 Mbps Ethernet).

A baseline is not a "do it once and forget it" process. Baselines must be taken periodically so that you can recognize trends as they occur, for example, steadily increasing bandwidth usage or an increase in the number of error packets. In addition, baselines must be established whenever significant changes—such as additional segments, servers, or equipment—occur in your network.

Monitoring with SNMP

The Simple Network Management Protocol (SNMP) is part of the TCP/IP protocol suite used for network-management. SNMP is an industry-standard protocol that most networking equipment manufacturers, including Microsoft, support. By default, SNMP management does not load automatically as part of the Windows NT or Windows 2000/XP runtime environment, but you can easily add it through the Network applet in the Control Panel (Windows NT) or the Add/Remove Programs applet in the Control Panel (Windows 2000/XP).

A network environment like the one pictured in Figure 13-2 has **software agents** loaded on each network device that SNMP manages. Each agent monitors network traffic and device status and stores information in a **management information base (MIB)**.

To use the information gathered by the software agents, a computer with an SNMP management program must be present on the network. This management station communicates with software agents and collects data stored in the MIBs on the network devices. Then it combines information from all networking devices and generates statistics or charts that detail current network conditions. With most SNMP managers, you can set thresholds upon which alert messages are generated for network administrators when those thresholds are exceeded.

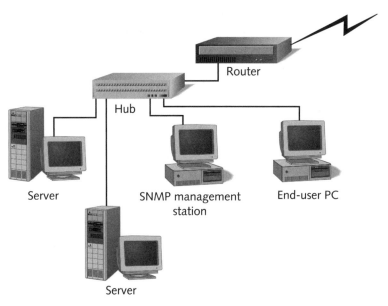

Figure 13-2   SNMP network monitoring and managing

In addition, you can manage many network components using SNMP. Through their software agents, you can configure networking devices and, in some cases, reset them from the management station. SNMP can manage network devices such as bridges and routers and important network resources such as servers. An SNMP management program can interrogate these devices and even make configuration changes remotely to help managers control their networks from a single application.

Using Remote Monitoring (RMON) for Advanced Monitoring

Remote Monitoring (RMON) is an advanced networking monitoring protocol that extends the capabilities of SNMP. RMON comes in two versions, RMON1 and RMON2. Whereas SNMP defines a single MIB type to collect network data, RMON1 defines nine additional MIB types, called RMON groups, to provide a more comprehensive set of data about network usage. RMON-capable devices, such as hubs, routers, and switches, contain software agents, called probes, that collect data and communicate with a management station using SNMP.

RMON1 is designed to capture data and collect statistics at the Data Link and Physical layers. RMON2, on the other hand, can collect and analyze traffic at the Network layer and higher layers, providing the capability for detailed analysis of enterprise-wide network and application software operation.

RMON-capable devices do not come cheaply, but the ability for a network manager to monitor the network and resolve network or application issues before they become serious problems is well worth the expense, considering the increased productivity the organization can enjoy. For more information, an excellent paper on RMON and RMON2 can be read at *www.cisco.com/warp/public/cc/pd/wr2k/cpbn/tech/rmon2_wp.pdf.*

13

SNMP has some inherent security issues of which an administrator must be aware. Refer to *www.comsoc.org/livepubs/surveys/public/4q98issue/stallings.html* for a more complete listing of SNMP and which versions need to be installed.

NETWORK TROUBLESHOOTING

Sometimes, despite all planning, monitoring, and other pre-emptive techniques, problems do occur. When this happens, you must be ready to troubleshoot your network and to diagnose and fix underlying problems.

Troubleshooting Methodology

Troubleshooting skill is not so much taught as it is learned. Through years of working with networks and computers as an administrator, you will develop your own troubleshooting methods. It's most important to stay calm. If you can keep a clear head when errors occur, you are more able to accurately assess your problems and more equipped to solve them.

You can solve most network problems by verifying the status of the affected computers or networking components (or at least, by verifying whether they're working and online). The following set of steps helps you troubleshoot most common networking problems:

1. Eliminate any potential user errors. Politely ask users what they were doing when they discovered the problem. Often, you determine that a user made a mistake or attempted to do something your network does not support. With this as your first step, you may not have to leave your desk to solve many of your "network problems."

2. Verify that physical connections are indeed working. You could spend hours working to solve a problem, only to find a disconnected network cable. Make sure that everything is plugged in and powered on to prevent needless waste of time.

3. Verify the status of any suspect NICs. Most NICs use LEDs to indicate card and connection status. For example, the LED on some 10BaseT NICs indicates the status of their physical connections to a hub. If this LED is off (or red), that's not only a strong indicator that a problem exists, but it points directly to the NIC-cable-hub nexus.

4. Restart the computer. This can solve a surprising variety of problems. Because network computing involves so many system components and software products, system aberrations can accumulate over time. Restarting a computer eliminates these cumulative effects. This solution more commonly works for personal or desktop operating systems like Windows 98 than for Windows 2000/XP or Linux, but it's not a bad strategy to try when all else fails.

If these four basic troubleshooting steps do not solve your problem, it is time to take a more detailed look.

Structured Approach

When tackling complex network problems, many experts (including the folks at Microsoft) recommend a five-step **structured troubleshooting approach**:

1. Set the problem's priority.

2. Collect information about the problem.

3. Develop a list of possible causes.

4. Test each hypothesis to isolate the actual cause.

5. For each potential cause, attempt at least one solution.

Consider each of these steps in turn. Each is a vital part of the structured troubleshooting method that Microsoft recommends.

Prioritize   First, identify the severity of the problem by asking questions such as: "Is the entire department down or just one computer?" "Are the engineers having trouble playing Doom?" "Is the president unable to print his speech to the shareholders?" Once you establish the scope of the problem, you can assign it a priority. If multiple problems manifest themselves simultaneously, tackle them in decreasing order of severity, starting with the most severe problem.

Collect Information   The next step is to collect information about the problem. In most cases, users make general complaints about network operations or behavior. Statements such as "The network's running slow," or "I can't get to the server" are common. By asking specific questions and eliciting additional details, you should be able to determine the cause of the problem more easily and formulate possible solutions.

13

To obtain those additional details, ask the questions in the following list:

- What, exactly, is the problem users are experiencing? Is the network slow? Have certain devices, such as a server, dropped off the network? Is an application unavailable or not functioning predictably?

- How recently did the problem start? Did users just notice the problem, or has it been happening for a while? Is the problem continuous or sporadic?

- What has changed? Has a new piece of network equipment been added recently? Did a user load a new application on his or her computer? Has the user tried to fix the problem unaided? If so, what repairs have been attempted?

Collecting information involves not only soliciting user information but also requires that you scan the network for obvious problems or failures. Such scans should include a quick review of prior network problems; if the problem is recurrent, look at prior solutions.

The last step in gathering information is to determine the scope of the problem. This process begins with dividing the network into many small parts and checking each part individually. Often, a network administrator can perform this task mentally by thinking through the network to determine the extent of the problem. For some administrators, this mental review is second nature. However, a troubleshooting checklist, including the following questions, can make this task more manageable:

- How many users does the problem affect? Is it limited to one computer? Are all malfunctioning computers on one segment? Is the entire network affected?

- Can the affected computer function as a standalone machine, but not on the network?

- What does the network-monitoring software indicate? Is the amount of network traffic larger than normal? Are error rates above normal? If so, what kinds of errors are occurring?

Once you create a comprehensive list of symptoms, you are ready to proceed to the next step to try to establish possible causes.

Establish Possible Causes   Once you have all the pertinent data, you can assemble the information and try to determine the most likely cause of the problem. From your experience with this and other networks, create a list of possible causes. Once you compile this list, rank these causes in order of likelihood, beginning with the most likely cause.

Isolate the Problem   Once you list possible causes, begin your testing with the most likely cause of the problem. For example, if you determine that the most likely cause is the cable that links the computer to the hub, try replacing that cable. If you believe that the NIC in the computer is malfunctioning, replace the NIC and see if the problem persists.

During this troubleshooting stage, it is important to make only one change at a time and to test that change by itself (as described in the next section, Test Results). That way, you can be certain which change corrects, or further isolates, the problem. Also, be sure that whatever changes you make do not introduce new problems. For example, if you replace the cable that links a computer to a hub, be *absolutely sure* to use a good-quality replacement cable.

Carefully document any and all hardware, software, or configuration changes you make. This helps identify an exact solution to the problem and provides a record that indicates what change you must reverse to eliminate any cause of additional problems.

Test Results   After each change, test its results to determine if the change fixes the problem and if the change introduces any new problems. If the change solves the problem and introduces no adverse side effects, document the steps you took to implement the solution. Include this information in your network documentation. If the change does not solve the problem, move to the next possible cause on your list, and continue testing.

Sometimes, a change you apply fixes your apparent problem, but reveals another, deeper problem. In that case, you must begin the troubleshooting approach anew, go back to setting priorities, and continue from there. Although this doesn't happen often, it's wise to prepare for the occasion when a simple apparent problem on a network masks a deeper, more difficult one. For instance, an inability to send and receive e-mail from a group of workstations might look like a problem with a local e-mail server but may instead be related to the imposition of a new set of router filters that blocks e-mail messages. Until you eliminate any malfunction at the e-mail server, you probably won't need to turn to the router for further analysis and testing.

 A simple method to use when approaching some network problems is to divide and conquer. This means that all you really must do is isolate the problem computer, or segment(s) of the network where the problem is located, and work on that one area. This allows for testing and troubleshooting without out disrupting the entire network.

Using Special Tools

Besides using their instincts and experiences, network administrators also can use special troubleshooting tools to help diagnose problems. Many networking problems occur at lower layers of the OSI model, where they are often difficult to troubleshoot. Fortunately, there are tools for diagnosing these problems. The next sections discuss some of the most common tools and their possible uses on a network.

Digital Voltmeter (DVM)

A **digital voltmeter (DVM)**, also called a **volt–ohm meter (VOM)**, is the most basic electrical measuring device. In network troubleshooting, it can measure a cable's resistance and determine if a cable break occurred.

When you connect the test leads for a DVM to either end of the cable and send a small current through it, the DVM measures the resistance. If it finds none, or finds resistance within the cable's rated tolerance, current is flowing properly and the cable is intact. However, if the DVM shows infinite resistance, there may be a break in the cable that does not let the current flow; similarly, higher than normal resistance may indicate an overly long or overloaded cable.

Another application for a DVM in a thinnet or thicknet environment is to connect one lead to the central core of a cable and one lead to the shielding. In this case, if there is no resistance, the shielding is in contact with the core at some point, most often at some connector. Called a **short** (or short circuit), this condition prevents network traffic from traversing the cable and requires repair or replacement of that cable.

When reading the resistance of a terminator for coaxial cables such as 10Base2 and 10Base5, the readings obtained should match the impedance of the cable type in use (50 ohms for both types, because that's where signals stop on an Ethernet segment).

13

However, the readings for T- or barrel connectors should be zero (0) ohms because these components are designed to interconnect cables (and equipment with T-connectors) without adding any resistance of their own.

Time-Domain Reflectometer (TDR)

You can use a **time-domain reflectometer (TDR)** like a DVM to determine if there is a break or short in a cable. Unlike a DVM, however, a TDR can pinpoint how far from the device the break is located by sending an electrical pulse down the cable that reflects back when it encounters a break or short. The TDR measures the time it takes for the signal to return and, based on the type of cable tested, estimates how far down the cable the fault is located. A high-quality TDR can determine the location of a break within a few inches. TDRs are available for fiber-optic as well as electrical cables.

Although cable installers use them most often, TDRs can be invaluable diagnostic tools for network administrators as well. When installing any new cables, ask your cable installer to use a TDR to document actual lengths of all cables. Rent a TDR (or hire someone who owns one) to measure any cables on your network whose lengths are not documented already.

Basic Cable Testers

Basic cable testers can be purchased for less than $100. These testers typically only test correct termination of a twisted-pair cable or the continuity of a 10Base2 cable. These are excellent tools for checking patch cables and for correct termination of a cable at the patch panel and jack. However, these testers can only verify that the cable wires are terminated in the correct order or that there are no breaks in the cable. These low-priced testers cannot check the cable for attenuation, noise, or other performance problems that might exist in your cable run.

Advanced Cable Testers

More expensive than DVMs or TDRs, advanced **cable testers** measure not only where a break is located in a cable, but also can gather other information, including a cable's impedance, resistance, and attenuation characteristics. These testers function at both the Physical layer and the Data Link layer of the OSI model. With this information, such cable testers can measure message frame counts, collisions, congestion errors, and beaconing information or broadcast storms. Thus, they combine the characteristics of a DVM, a TDR, and a protocol analyzer.

Oscilloscopes

Oscilloscopes are advanced pieces of electronic equipment that measure signal voltage over time. When used in conjunction with a TDR, an oscilloscope can help to identify shorts, sharp bends or crimps in a cable, cable breaks, and attenuation problems.

Network Monitors

Network monitors are software packages that can track all or part of the network traffic. By examining the packets sent across the network, the network monitor can track information such as packet type, errors, and traffic to and from each computer. These network monitors can collect this data and generate reports and graphs. Windows NT 4.0, Windows XP, and Windows 2000 all include a scaled-down version of a full-blown network monitor that can monitor network traffic coming into and going out of the machine on which it is installed. Microsoft also produces a network monitor that can measure traffic on the entire network segment, but this product ships only with Microsoft Systems Management Server.

Other common network monitors for Windows networks include WildPacket's EtherPeek, Network Instruments' Analyst/Probe, and Information Solutions Inc.'s PerfMan. Many of these programs also capture and decode network traffic, which allows them to qualify as software-only protocol analyzers.

Protocol Analyzers

Perhaps the most advanced network troubleshooting device available, a **protocol analyzer** (also called a network analyzer), evaluates the overall health of the network by monitoring all traffic. This tool not only monitors the traffic in real time but also can capture traffic and decode packets received.

Protocol analyzers can look inside the packets received to determine the cause of the problem. Because they can generate statistics based on network traffic, they provide a good indication of the network cabling, software, file server operations, workstation operations, and NICs.

The most advanced protocol analyzers combine hardware and software in a self-contained unit. These analyzers sometimes include a built-in TDR to help them determine the status of the network. Some examples of protocol analyzers include:

- *Sniffer Technologies' Sniffer.* Sniffer is one of a family of protocol analyzers from Sniffer Technologies, a subsidiary of Network Associates, that decode and interpret frames from more than 14 protocols, including AppleTalk, Windows NetBIOS and NetBEUI, NetWare, SNA, TCP/IP, Vines, and X.25. For more information, visit the Sniffer Technologies Web site at *www.sniffer.com*.

- *WildPacket's EtherPeek.* Etherpeek is an outstanding software-only protocol analyzer that handles all the major Ethernet protocols, including AppleTalk, ARP/RARP, Banyan VINES, DECnet, IPv4 and IPv6, NetBEUI/NetBIOS, OSI, SNA, and XNS, among others. For more information, visit WildPacket's Web pages at *www.wildpackets.com*.

- *Fluke Network's Protocol Inspector.* Protocol Inspector is another software-based protocol analyzer that handles AppleTalk, TCP/IP, IPX/SPX, SMB, and application-layer protocols for a wide range of applications. You can use

13

Protocol Inspector in a distributed fashion by loading remote agents on computers throughout your network. These agents then forward the captured data to a computer running the console software that decodes and displays the data. For more information, visit Fluke's Web pages at *www.flukenetworks.com*.

Most experienced network administrators rely on protocol analyzers to establish baselines for network performance and to troubleshoot their networks, especially when they suspect software problems, or when network (Layer 3) devices appear to be responsible for network problems.

NETWORK SUPPORT RESOURCES

Many resources are available to help you troubleshoot your network. They come in a variety of formats, including software products, online services, subscription services, and printed material. The following sections discuss some of the better ones, which have won accolades from many different sources.

Microsoft TechNet

The **Microsoft Technical Information Network (TechNet)** is a subscription information service for supporting all aspects of networking, with a special emphasis on Microsoft products. As a TechNet subscriber, each month you receive a set of CD-ROMs, which contains product information, technical support updates, software drivers, and online tutorials. TechNet's easy-to-use interface, shown in Figure 13-3, allows you to access the database of technical information to assist in troubleshooting network problems.

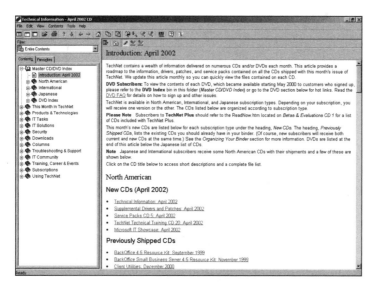

Figure 13-3 Microsoft TechNet interface

TechNet is a valuable tool for gathering information and diagnosing network problems and is well worth its cost. You can subscribe to TechNet through the Microsoft Web site (*www.microsoft.com/technet/*) or by calling 1-800-344-2121, but the online version is available free to the public. The site is often slow and sometimes difficult to search and navigate!

Microsoft Knowledge Base

The **Microsoft Knowledge Base** provides information that's gleaned from its technical support staff's interaction with customers at all support levels. The KB—as it's often called—is free to anyone with Web access, but the TechNet subscription also includes a snapshot of the KB on CD. Figure 13-4 shows the first page of the Microsoft support site, located at *http://support.microsoft.com*, which has a search dialog box for Knowledge Base.

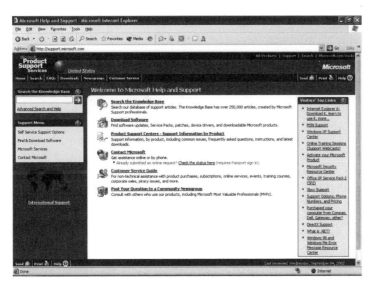

Figure 13-4   The Microsoft support site and Knowledge Base

Linux Information Resources

Just as with Microsoft resources, the burgeoning popularity of Linux as a server and desktop operating system ensures that it too receives copious coverage online. Some of our favorite Linux resources include:

- *www.linux.com* is a great starting place for any Linux-related investigation. The site includes a great search engine, plus a wonderful collection of useful Linux information, downloads, pointers, and documentation. For example, when we looked for sources of Linux distributions, we soon determined that accessing those distributions through *www.linux.com* was easier than visiting each vendor or organization, one site at a time.

- *Everything Linux* includes good troubleshooting information as well. It's available at *www.eunuchs.org.* You'll find this a useful resource for all kinds of Linux-related tips, tricks, and troubleshooting techniques.

- *www.linuxcare.com* is a great source of training, technical information, and for-a-fee Linux technical support. If you're really in a jam and willing to pay to get out of it, this is the right place to ask for help.

Novell NetWare Information Sources

Novell, like Microsoft, has a searchable knowledge base that provides articles and notices about known problems, bug fixes, workarounds, and patches. You can also search for files to download that contain driver updates and operating system service packs. The Novell knowledge base can be accessed from *http://support.novell.com.*

Online Support Services and Newsgroups

Many online support services are dedicated to technical subjects such as networking. These services allow you to tap into the knowledge of experienced networking professionals by posting questions.

The **Microsoft Developer's Network (MSDN)** is a Web site dedicated to Microsoft product support. MSDN is not only a great place to research development topics and issues, but a location where you can also download the latest APIs and other pertinent software. Visit MSDN at *http://msdn.microsoft.com* (add */downloads* to get to the downloads page). MSDN offers more content (and a wider range of information services) to network members, but some free content is available to the public.

Microsoft also operates its own newsgroup hierarchy on a news server named *msnews.microsoft.com.* This is a great place to look for troubleshooting information of all kinds. You should find the following newsgroups especially informative:

- *microsoft.public.win2000.* (This news hierarchy includes nearly 30 elements that cover topics from Active Directory to Terminal Services and several others.)

- *microsoft.public.windowsnt.* (This news hierarchy includes nearly 40 elements that cover everything from applications to Terminal Server and numerous other topics.)

- *microsoft.public.win98.networking*

- *microsoft.public.win98.setup*

- *microsoft.public.win16.programmer.networks*

- *microsoft.public.win32.programmer.networks*

We've also found the Windows Mailing list at Sunbelt Software (go to *www.sunbelt-software.com* to sign up) a worthwhile online resource for information about Windows Server tools, utilities, and troubleshooting tips.

All Linux Web sites mentioned in the previous section also include pointers to mailing lists and newsgroups that cover a variety of Linux topics, including general troubleshooting and information about installation, configuration, and maintenance problems.

Periodicals

Given rapid industry change, periodicals that deal specifically with computers and networking can be the best sources of information on new products, trends, and techniques. Many periodicals are available over the Internet, and some offer free subscriptions to networking professionals. Some of the most popular networking journals include *LAN Magazine, LAN Times, Communications Week, InfoWorld, eWeek, PC Magazine* (Network Edition), and *Network Computing.* There also are several publications that focus on Windows, for example, *Windows & .Net Magazine (www.win2000mag.com)*, and there are Linux magazines such as the *Linux Gazette (www.linuxgazette.com)*, the *Linux Journal (www.linuxjournal.com)*, and *Linux World (www.linuxworld.com)*.

COMMON TROUBLESHOOTING SITUATIONS

Using the structured approach to network troubleshooting described earlier, you can eventually solve your networking problems. To help get you started with this sometimes arduous exercise, this section outlines some of the more common network problems and some possible solutions.

13

Cabling and Related Components

As mentioned earlier, the majority of networking problems occur at the Physical layer of the OSI model and include problems with cables, connectors, and NICs.

The first step in troubleshooting such problems is to determine whether the problem lies with the cable or the computer. One easy way to do this is to connect another computer—ideally, a portable PC—to the cable. If the portable functions normally, you can conclude that the problem lies within the disconnected computer that was replaced by the portable. If the portable exhibits the same symptoms, first check the cable, and then check the hub or whatever device it connects to, and so forth.

Once you determine that the cable is the likeliest culprit, check that it is connected to the computer correctly, and verify that it is the correct type of cable for the connection. Make sure you use the same type of UTP cable throughout the network. Double-check cable lengths to ensure you do not exceed the maximum length limitation for that particular type of medium. By using a TDR or DVM, you can quickly identify and correct these types of problems.

If you suspect a faulty or misconfigured NIC, check the back of the card. As discussed earlier, the NIC may have LEDs to indicate whether it is functioning and if its network connection is active. If the NIC lacks such valuable indicators, you must replace the suspect NIC with a known working NIC—in much the same way you replace a suspect computer with a known working one to determine if the network or the computer is the cause of the problem.

If the NIC seems functional and you are using TCP/IP, try using the PING utility to check connectivity to other computers. (Hands-on Project 13-5 or 12-2 shows how to use the PING utility.) If the NIC works, but the computer still cannot access the network, deeper hardware problems (for example, a faulty bus slot) may be involved, or NIC configuration settings may be invalid. Either way, you must conduct further troubleshooting.

Power Fluctuations

Power fluctuations in a building—due to an electrical storm or power failure, for example—can adversely affect computers. First, verify that the servers are up and functioning. When possible, remind users that after a power outage it takes a few minutes for servers to come back online.

One way to eliminate the effects of power fluctuations, especially on servers, is to connect them to Uninterruptible Power Supplies (UPSs). UPS systems provide battery power to computers so that they can be brought down gracefully—that is, without data loss. Some available packages perform shutdowns automatically, thereby eliminating the need for human intervention whenever power failures or severe power fluctuations occur.

Upgrades

Because networking technology constantly changes, it is necessary to upgrade equipment and software frequently. For example, the operating systems on the network file servers must be upgraded periodically. During these upgrades, it is common for some equipment to run on an old operating system and some to run on a new one. Whenever you perform network upgrades, remember three important things:

- Ignoring upgrades to new software releases and new hardware can lead to a situation in which a complete overhaul of the network may be necessary. This is because many upgrades build on top of others. If the administrator does not keep current, he or she might need to do an overwhelming amount of research and endure a lack of technical support for the older software/hardware. Keep current and do one upgrade at a time to make your life easier.

- Test any upgrade before deploying it on your production network. Ideally, use a test laboratory where you can try all upgrades and work out any kinks. If a test lab is not an option, select a small part of your network—one department or a few users—and perform the upgrade. This gives you an opportunity to work through any issues that might arise before imposing changes (and the problems that sometimes go with them) on the entire network.

- Don't forget to tell users about upgrades: A well-informed user is an understanding user. Everyone who might be affected by an upgrade must be informed when it will occur, what is involved, and what to expect.

Poor Network Performance

If all goes well, the network monitoring and planning you do ensures that the network always performs optimally. However, you may notice that your network slows over time. This may occur quickly, in a matter of minutes, or its pace may deteriorate slowly. Whether performance problems manifest themselves slowly or suddenly and acutely, answering the following questions should help pinpoint the causes:

- What has changed since the last time the network functioned normally?
- Has new equipment been added to the network?
- Have new applications been added to the computers on the network?
- Is someone playing electronic games across the network? (You would be surprised at the amount of traffic networked games can generate.)
- Are there new users on the network? How many?
- Could any other new equipment, such as a generator, cause interference near the network?

If new users, added equipment, or newly introduced applications seem to degrade network performance, it might be time to consider expanding your network and adding equipment to limit or contain network traffic. Higher-speed backbones, network partitions, additional servers, bridges, and routers are all alternatives worth considering when you must increase capacity to accommodate usage levels that have grown beyond your network's current capabilities.

13

CHAPTER SUMMARY

Network-management, planning, and monitoring are critical parts of a network administrator's job. Through proper network-management, you can avoid or minimize many potential problems. In all cases, avoiding potential problems is preferable to solving actual problems. Pre-emptive troubleshooting is therefore the best troubleshooting since it's an avoidance technique rather than a reaction to an existing problem. The key to pre-emptive troubleshooting is to understand and apply the OSI network-management model, which consists of accounting management, configuration management, fault management (the area most commonly associated with troubleshooting), performance management, and security management.

❏ A key part of the network-management process is planning, which includes setting back-up schedules and guidelines, security guidelines, hardware and software standards, and upgrade guidelines. Be sure to create written plans, policies, and procedures to cover these topics.

❏ In addition to network standards and guidelines, you should maintain a complete set of network documentation. This documentation should include a network map, a cable map, an equipment list, a server configuration document, a software configuration document, an address list, a user administration document, a software licensing document, a contact list, a networking hardware configuration document, a network history, and a comprehensive list of policies and procedures.

❏ Many programs are available to assist with network-management and monitoring. Using such tools to monitor your network, you can establish a network-performance baseline against which to identify anomalies. The Performance Monitor included with Windows NT 4.0 and Windows 2000 is a valuable network-monitoring tool that can help you establish a baseline and track network performance. SNMP is a specialized TCP/IP protocol used for network monitoring and management. With an SNMP manager program, you can manage and monitor most network devices.

❏ RMON software probes can provide detailed network and application information to a network manager. RMON1 works at the Data Link and Physical layers, whereas RMON2 can analyze data from the Network layer to the Application layer.

❏ When an error occurs, a structured, methodical approach to troubleshooting eases tension and ensures that all possible solutions are covered. First, don't panic. Then, eliminate user errors and check the most likely causes; this alone fixes many problems. However, at times problems may be harder to pin down. By using a structured approach to troubleshooting, you are certain to cover all possibilities, in order of likelihood.

❏ Many tools and resources are available to help you troubleshoot your network. In addition to hardware specially designed for network troubleshooting, software and Internet resources are available, including Microsoft TechNet, the Microsoft Knowledge Base, the Novell knowledge base and Linuxcare.com. Such resources let you tap into a vast amount of knowledge amassed by networking professionals.

❏ In most cases, troubleshooting solutions fall into one of the basic categories of solutions. These common network troubleshooting scenarios pinpoint many problems. However, when a difficult or intractable problem arises, you should always fall back on the structured network troubleshooting approach.

❏ Change is the most common cause of network problems. Whenever problems occur, always try to identify what's changed recently to help you decide if the change might be causing the problem. Common sources of problem-causing changes include adding new equipment or software, upgrading existing software or equipment, and workload or workplace behavior that manifests in increased network traffic or utilization.

KEY TERMS

baseline — A measurement of network performance over time, against which current performance can be measured.

cable tester — A network troubleshooting device that can test for cable defects, monitor network collisions, and monitor network congestion.

digital voltmeter (DVM) — A network troubleshooting tool that measures voltage, amperage, and resistance on a cable or other conductive element.

management information base (MIB) — A set of objects that contains information about a networking device, and which is used by SNMP to manage that networking device.

Microsoft Developer's Network (MSDN) — A Web site on which Microsoft offers product support, in addition to drivers and patches.

Microsoft Knowledge Base — An online reference for Microsoft and networking information.

Microsoft Technical Information Network (TechNet) — A monthly subscription service from Microsoft that supplies CD-ROMs containing technical information on networking and topics specific to Microsoft. It is also available online.

network monitor — Software that monitors network traffic and gathers information about packet types, errors, and packet traffic to and from each computer.

oscilloscope — A network troubleshooting device that measures the signal voltage per amount of time. When used with a TDR, it can help define cable problems.

pre-emptive troubleshooting — A method of forestalling network problems by planning in advance and performing regular network maintenance.

protocol analyzer — Software, or a combination of hardware and software, that can capture network traffic and create reports and graphs from the data collected.

Remote Monitoring (RMON) — Specialized software that gathers network data and provides statistics to a network-management console.

short — A condition that occurs when conductors that are normally insulated from one another establish a connection. In a coaxial cable, if the shield and the internal conductor become connected, the cable stops functioning because the short blocks all network traffic; the same condition can occur in twisted-pair cable should two or more of the paired wires become connected.

software agent — Part of the SNMP structure that is loaded onto each device to be monitored.

structured troubleshooting approach — A Microsoft-recommended five-step approach to network troubleshooting.

time-domain reflectometer (TDR) — A network troubleshooting device that can determine whether there is a break or short in the cable and, if so, approximately how far down the cable the break or short is located.

trouble avoidance — *See* pre-emptive troubleshooting.

13

troubleshooting — The techniques involved in detecting problems, identifying causes or contributing factors, and applying necessary workarounds or repairs to eliminate their effects.

volt-ohm meter (VOM) — *See* digital voltmeter (DVM).

REVIEW QUESTIONS

1. Which of these services is available from Microsoft for free on the Web? (Choose all that apply.)

   a. TechNet

   b. Microsoft Knowledge Base

   c. Microsoft Developer's Network

   d. none of the above

2. A(n) _____ is able to not only determine whether a cable break or short exists, but also approximately how far down the cable it is located.

   a. oscilloscope

   b. volt-ohm meter

   c. time-domain reflectometer

   d. protocol analyzer

3. At what level of the OSI model do most networking problems occur?

   a. Physical

   b. Network

   c. Transport

   d. Session

4. A(n) _____ is a simple network troubleshooting device that measures voltage, resistance, and current flow on a cable.

   a. oscilloscope

   b. volt-ohm meter

   c. time-domain reflectometer

   d. protocol analyzer

5. What categories of network-management does ISO define? (Choose all that apply.)

   a. accounting management

   b. configuration management

   c. application management

   d. performance management

   e. user management

f. security management

g. fault management

6. Which of the following options represents the easiest way to correct a problem with a computer?

   a. rebooting the computer

   b. reinstalling the operating system

   c. reconfiguring hardware settings

   d. setting up a new hardware profile

7. What is the first thing to remember in network troubleshooting?

   a. Stay calm.

   b. Eliminate user error.

   c. Check physical connections.

   d. all of the above

8. The structured approach is the five-step troubleshooting method recommended by Microsoft. True or false?

9. Which network troubleshooting tool is a software-based solution?

   a. LANalyzer

   b. Network Sniffer

   c. Network Monitor

   d. System Monitor

10. _____ is the best way to prevent network problems.

11. _____ provides CD-ROMs on a monthly basis to assist in troubleshooting.

   a. Knowledge Base

   b. TechNet

   c. Resource Kit

   d. MS-CD

12. Which tool discussed in this chapter gives you the most detailed information about network traffic and trends?

   a. cable analyzer

   b. network analyzer

   c. protocol analyzer

   d. system analyzer

13

13. What are the five steps in the network troubleshooting approach described in this chapter?

    a. Test to isolate the cause.

    b. Study the test results to identify a solution.

    c. Check the system baseline.

    d. Run a protocol analyzer.

    e. Collect information about the problem.

    f. Set the problem's priority.

    g. Develop a list of possible causes.

14. What is the most common network problem you're likely to encounter?

    a. application problems

    b. system problems

    c. cabling problems

15. A _____ can be used to prevent data loss in the event of a power fluctuation or failure.

    a. TDR

    b. UPS

    c. DVM

    d. VOM

16. What is the second troubleshooting step you should always take?

    a. Eliminate user error.

    b. Reinstall the operating system.

    c. Reconfigure hardware settings.

    d. Verify the physical connections.

17. An SNMP network manager program reads the _____ in each networking device to determine its status.

    a. PIFs

    b. MIBs

    c. CIFs

    d. process log

18. When measuring network performance, you need a baseline as a point of reference. True or false?

19. _____ is the TCP/IP protocol used to configure and watch network resources.

    a. ICMP

    b. SNMP

    c. DHCP

    d. SMTP

20. The MSDN service provides software updates by modem. True or false?

21. What condition occurred if the resistance between the shielding and the conductive core of coaxial cable reads zero (0)?

    a. open circuit

    b. cable break

    c. short circuit

    d. None, this condition is normal.

22. What condition occurred if the resistance between the conductor on one end of a cable and the other end of the same cable reads infinite?

    a. open circuit

    b. cable break

    c. short circuit

    d. None, this condition is normal.

23. What condition occurred if the resistance measured for a terminator for 10Base2 or 10Base5 cable reads infinite?

    a. open circuit

    b. cable break

    c. failed terminator

    d. None, this condition is normal.

24. What combination of diagnostic tools can detect a crimp in a coaxial cable? (Choose all that apply.)

    a. DVM or VOM

    b. cable tester

    c. oscilloscope

    d. TDR

25. What is an advanced network-monitoring protocol that has greater capabilities than SNMP?

    a. SNMP-2

    b. RMON

    c. TDR

    d. DVM

13

26. For which of the following network conditions must you use a protocol analyzer or network monitor for further diagnosis? (Choose all that apply.)

    a. cable break

    b. cable short

    c. slow network performance

    d. high rate of transmission errors

27. At what layer of the OSI model does a DVM or VOM operate?

    a. Layer 1, Physical

    b. Layer 2, Data Link

    c. Layer 3, Network

    d. Layer 4, Transport

28. At what layer of the OSI model does a TDR or oscilloscope operate?

    a. Layer 1, Physical

    b. Layer 2, Data Link

    c. Layer 3, Network

    d. Layer 4, Transport

29. At what layers of the OSI model does a protocol analyzer operate?

    a. Layer 1, Physical

    b. Layer 2, Data Link

    c. Layer 3, Network

    d. Layer 4, Transport

    e. Layers 2 through 7, given sufficient protocol decodes

30. Pre-emptive troubleshooting is preferable to actual troubleshooting. True or false?

HANDS-ON PROJECTS

In these Hands-on Projects, you outline and describe the current status of your documentation and use the Network Monitor included with Windows NT Server and Windows 2000 Server to check network functions. You also install SNMP in Windows NT or Windows 2000 and troubleshoot IP network access from Windows 98, Windows NT, or Windows 2000.

Project 13-1

To document your current network configuration:

1. On a blank page, outline the documentation you know currently exists for your network.

2. List the diagrams, standards, policies, and procedures that you must still develop.

3. Create a rough sample for one of the missing standards.

Project 13-2

In this project, you learn how to install the Network Monitor on Windows NT Server and Windows 2000 Server.

We assume that you have access to a computer with Windows NT 4.0 Server or Windows 2000 Server with TCP/IP installed and a connection to the Internet or a local TCP/IP-based network.

Network Monitor consists of two components: the monitor interface tools and a monitoring agent. You can install either the agent only or tools and agent both. If you choose to install the agent only, you cannot configure or view data captures unless you use Network Monitor tools from SMS, which also include remote monitoring capabilities. By installing tools and agent both, you can configure and view data captures locally.

To install Network Monitor on Windows NT Server:

1. Open the Network applet from the Control Panel. (Click **Start**, **Settings**, **Control Panel**, and then double-click the **Network** icon.)

2. Select the **Services** tab, and click the **Add** button.

3. Locate and select **Network Monitor Tools and Agent**, as shown in Figure 13-5. Click the **OK** button.

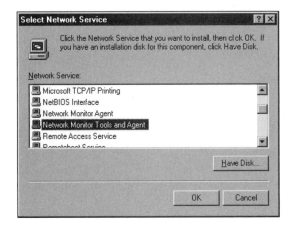

Figure 13-5   Adding Network Monitor Tools and Agent

4. When prompted, direct setup to the proper location of the distribution files—whether on CD-ROM or on hard drive—then click the **Continue** button.

5. Once installation completes, click the **Close** button to exit the Network applet.

6. Reboot your computer.

To install Network Monitor on Windows 2000 Server:

1. Open the Network and Dial-up Connections utility. (Click **Start**, **Settings**, and then click **Network and Dial-up Connections**.)

2. Click the **Advanced** menu, and then click **Optional Networking Components**. The Windows Optional Networking Components Wizard dialog box opens.

3. Select the **Management and Monitoring Tools** item shown in Figure 13-6.

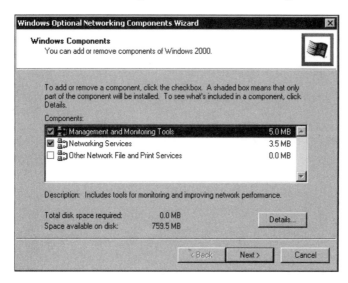

Figure 13-6   Selecting Management and Monitoring Tools

4. Click the **Details** button. The Management and Monitoring Tools dialog box opens.

5. Click the **Network Monitor Tools** check box shown in Figure 13-7.

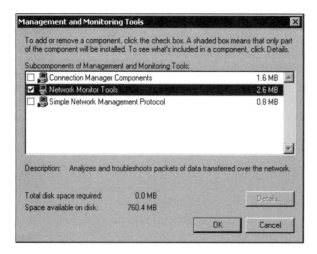

Figure 13-7   Adding Network Monitor Tools

6. Click **OK**.

7. Click **Next**.

8. If prompted, direct setup to the proper location of the distribution files, and then click the **OK** button.

9. When completed, close the Network and Dial-up Connections dialog box by clicking the **File** menu and then clicking **Close**.

Project 13-3

In this project, you learn to use Network Monitor on Windows NT Server or Windows 2000 Server.

We assume that you have access to a computer with Windows NT Server 4.0 or Windows 2000 Server with TCP/IP installed and a connection to the Internet or a local TCP/IP-based network with Network Monitor installed. This project also assumes that you can reach a network host. If the hosts listed in the laboratory are not present, or you cannot reach them from your computer, ask your instructor to supply a different host name or IP address.

To use Network Monitor on Windows NT Server or Windows 2000 Server:

1. Start Network Monitor (**Start**, **Programs**, **Administrative Tools (Common)**, **Network Monitor**). The Network Monitor application appears. See Figure 13-8.

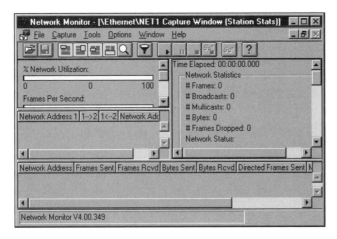

Figure 13-8   Network Monitor

2. From the menu bar, select **Capture**, **Start**. This instructs Network Monitor to begin capturing information. In the next steps, you cause some network activity.

3. Minimize the Network Monitor to reveal the desktop. Next, open **My Network Places**. In Windows NT, the icon is called Network Neighborhood. Traverse the browser listing across a few levels to locate a computer that is not the computer you are currently using.

4. Close all Network Neighborhood windows, and restore the **Network Monitor** from the taskbar.

5. From the menu bar of Network Monitor, select **Capture, Stop**.

6. From the menu bar, select **Capture, Display Captured Data**.

7. Double-click any listed frame to see further details about that frame. An example of such a listing appears in Figure 13-9. When you finish reviewing the details, close the Capture window.

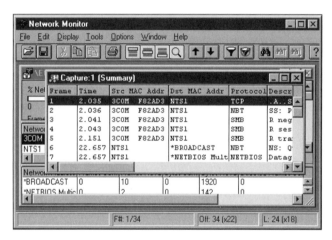

Figure 13-9   Captured data display

8. From the menu bar, select **Capture, Addresses**. The Address Database dialog box displays all network names and addresses stored in the current database. When you finish, click the **Close** button to close this window.

9. From the menu bar, select **Capture, Filter**. If a Capture Filter warning window appears, click **OK**. The Capture Filter dialog box displays a capture filter decision tree. You can edit and manipulate this tree using the Add, Edit, and Delete controls. This activity produces results like those shown in Figure 13-10. When you finish examining this information, close the Capture Filter window.

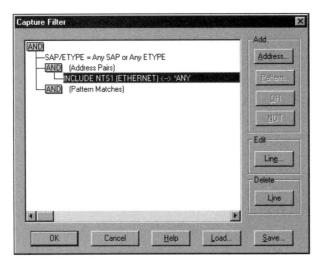

Figure 13-10 Network Monitor's Capture Filter window

10. From the menu bar, select **Capture, Trigger.** The Capture Trigger dialog box controls the triggers used to initiate an action, while Network Monitor is running, that halts data capture if detected. The Capture Trigger window opens. Examine the window, and then close the Capture Trigger window.

11. Close Network Monitor.

Project 13-4

To install SNMP support on Windows NT 4.0:

13

1. Go to the Services tab in the Network applet (**Start, Settings, Control Panel**), double-click the **Network** icon, and select the **Services** tab.

2. Click the **Add** button to display a list of installable network services.

3. In the Select Network Service window, scroll down the list until you see the entry named **SNMP Service.** Highlight that entry, and then click the **OK** button.

 You must have access to the Windows NT CD-ROM (Workstation or Server), or be able to point to a copy of the installation files somewhere on the network, for the install program to access and copy the necessary installation files.

4. A Microsoft SNMP Properties window appears with the Agent tab visible, as shown in Figure 13-11. Type your name on the Contact line and your current city and state on the Location line. You can leave the check boxes in their current default state.

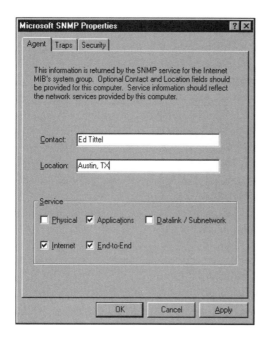

Figure 13-11 Microsoft SNMP Properties window

5. Click the **Traps** tab in the Microsoft SNMP Properties window to bring up the display shown in Figure 13-12. This is where you would enter the names of any SNMP communities (groups of devices managed by a single management application) and the kinds of events or activities for which you want to issue alerts (which is what traps do).

6. Click the **Security** tab in the Microsoft SNMP Properties window to bring up the security display. This is where you would enter the names of those SNMP communities from which your computer is willing to accept trap reports and with which it will be permitted to exchange data. This information helps administrators maintain control over what kinds of information their SNMP application accepts and which computers can send it that information. This limits how much data the system must manage and lets administrators pay attention to only those systems and resources under their purview.

7. Click the **Cancel** button at the bottom of the Microsoft SNMP Properties window to void all this information. (You have been exploring this utility, and the settings may not agree with local network conditions.)

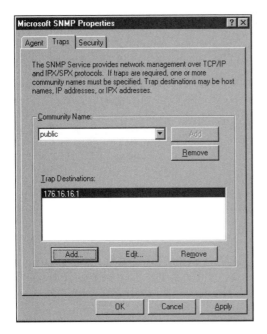

Figure 13-12   Traps tab specifies what events to report and where to report them

To install SNMP support on Windows 2000:

1. Open the Network and Dial-up Connections utility. (Click **Start**, **Settings**, and then click **Network and Dial-up Connections**.)

2. Click the **Advanced** menu, and then click **Optional Networking Components**. The Windows Optional Networking Components Wizard dialog box opens.

3. Select the **Management and Monitoring Tools** item.

4. Click the **Details** button. The Management and Monitor Tools dialog box opens.

5. Mark the check box beside **Simple Network Management Protocol**.

6. Click **OK**.

7. Click **Next**.

8. If prompted, direct setup to the proper location of the distribution files. Then click the **OK** button.

9. When completed, close the Network and Dial-up Connections dialog box by clicking the **File** menu and then clicking **Close**.

SNMP configuration takes place through the Services applet. This applet is found in both the Control Panel and the Computer Management tool. SNMP is configured through the properties of both the SNMP Service and the SNMP Trap Service.

13

Project 13-5

When working in an IP environment, users occasionally report difficulties in accessing specific remote hosts. Sometimes, they may even report problems accessing any remote networks at all. This project steps you through some handy IP-based troubleshooting maneuvers, which you can perform quickly from a command-line interface, to pinpoint where difficulties may be occurring.

We assume you are working on a computer with TCP/IP installed, an available IP gateway, and Internet or other remote access.

To troubleshoot IP network access:

1. Start a command-line window on your computer. For Windows 98, use this menu sequence: **Start, Programs, MS-DOS Prompt**; for Windows NT, use **Start, Programs, Command Prompt**; for Windows 2000, use **Start, Programs, Accessories, Command Prompt**.

2. Document your machine's current IP configuration. Type **ipconfig** on the command line, and record the values for IP Address and Default Gateway in the resulting output. (If this doesn't work for your version of Windows 98, type **winipcfg** instead; older versions of Windows 98 may not recognize ipconfig as a valid command.)

3. Use the PING command to check connectivity. (Explanatory comments are in parentheses; type only the boldface text.)

   PING localhost

   PING <*IP Address*> (Substitute the value you recorded for IP address.)

   PING <*gateway*> (Substitute the value you recorded for the default gateway.)

   PING <*remote host*> (Substitute either **ftp.microsoft.com** or the name your instructor supplies for remote host.)

   You are checking connectivity from the IP stack (localhost) to the local workstation (<IP Address>), to the default gateway, to a remote host. The first two PINGs make sure the local machine is networking properly, the third PING checks the gateway to all remote networks, and the fourth PING makes sure a well-known remote host is accessible (that is, that the gateway is working properly to reach external networks).

4. Next, type **tracert ftp.microsoft.com**, and record the resulting data. (If a printer is available in your lab, you can print the results by typing **tracert ftp.microsoft.com >> traces.txt**, then typing **print traces.txt**; you might also want to delete this file after you finish by typing **del traces.txt**.)

   Now you can systematically PING all the intermediate routers in the path from your machine to the remote machine. This is how you could investigate performance problems (long round-trip times or timeouts) or reachability issues (host unreachable errors) when troubleshooting access problems outside your own network.

5. Type **exit** on the command line, and then press the **Enter** key to close your command window and complete this project.

CASE PROJECTS

1. A user calls to report that she's unable to log on to e-mail. You respond with a couple of quick questions. Because you know that no one else is using the network right now, you cannot determine if the problem is unique to her machine or if the problem affects the entire network. Probing further, you also learn that she's unable to print. You decide this problem is probably easier to troubleshoot from the user's computer.

   Using the structured troubleshooting method covered in this chapter, outline the things you must check and the questions you must ask when you arrive at the user's office. Based on the possible responses to your questions, describe the actions you will take to correct the potential causes.

2. Your network consists of computers on all three floors in each of two buildings. Thicknet connects the buildings, and each floor is wired with thinnet. Your SNMP manager notifies you that in one of the buildings no networking components are responding. In addition to an SNMP manager, you have a Network General Sniffer and a cable tester at your disposal.

   Describe the procedures and equipment you use to determine where the problem exists. In addition, outline the steps you take to alleviate the problem.

3. There is an intermittent problem with one thinnet segment in your building. You try everything to fix the problem, from swapping NICs in the computers to replacing most of the cable. You are at the end of your rope and have exhausted your local resources.

   Describe some steps you could take to use other resources available to you.

4. During the process of testing thinnet network cables and components prior to deployment, you discover the following conditions:

   ❐ A network terminator reads zero (0) ohms.

   ❐ Two T-connectors read 50 ohms; eight others read 0 ohms.

   ❐ Checked center conductor to center conductor, one cable reads infinite resistance; checked center conductor to shield, it reads zero (0) ohms.

   ❐ Two terminators read 50 ohms, two others read 0 ohms.

   Which components listed above are suspect, and what should you do about them?

5. Which of the following tools can help to troubleshoot fiber-optic networks, given the right physical interfaces and ancillary equipment?

   a. VOM or DVM

   b. oscilloscope

   c. TDR

   d. protocol analyzer

   Explain why unsuitable tools do not work with fiber-optic networks, and what roles suitable tools can play on fiber-optic networks.

13

UNDERSTANDING AND USING INTERNET RESOURCES

After reading this chapter and completing the exercises, you will be able to:

♦ Discuss the Internet and its available services

♦ Access resources on the Internet and understand its addressing methods

♦ Discuss ways to establish an Internet connection

The Internet is an ever-expanding, ubiquitous aspect of modern life. You can read a newspaper online, find recipes, chat with friends, listen to your favorite tunes, watch the news, browse through museums, or read entire libraries—all in the comfort of your favorite chair or in your office.

The Internet evolved from the U.S. Department of Defense's Advanced Research Projects Agency Network (ARPANET). For data transport, this network used TCP/IP, which remains the data communication protocol suite used to this day. In its initial implementation, the ARPANET was used primarily to share information among an original group of universities and research labs. Today, however, the primary focus of the Internet has shifted from research and development to commerce and communication.

As a network administrator, you can use the Internet to obtain information about computers and networking, as well as for general reference. The Internet can inform you about products and services, act as your primary source for technical assistance and information, and even supply a convenient venue to look for and download software upgrades, patches, and fixes.

In fact, it seems as if no end is in sight for the growth that the Internet is experiencing, both in the range and variety of its contents and in the business and recreational activities it can support. Because it can be such an important part of business and personal life, you should be familiar and comfortable with the Internet and aware of its many services and capabilities. This chapter provides an overview of the Internet's capabilities and considers its underpinnings as well.

WHAT'S ON THE INTERNET?

The Internet's many different services evolved as technology developed, and its reach expanded to encompass most aspects of everyday life. In many ways, the Internet's evolution parallels that of the PC, in that as PCs became more widely available and vastly more powerful, the Internet's reach extended and its interface became more graphical and user friendly.

Some of the most popular Internet services include:

- *Chat and instant messaging*: As more and more people spend more time online, applications that permit people to interact with each other by typing words on the keyboard proliferate as well. A bewildering array of "chat rooms" are available online—on subjects from networking to needlepoint—at any hour, any day. Likewise, applications like Internet Relay Chat (IRC) and ICQ (a wordplay on "I seek you") make it possible for individuals to chat outside the confines of established chat rooms.

- *Electronic mail (e-mail):* Although e-mail remains primarily character-oriented, its ability to permit individuals to exchange information and files easily makes it the most popular networked application of any kind, whether on or off the Internet. Early e-mail applications permitted only text messages to be sent from user to user. But with today's fast Internet connections and the ability of e-mail applications to handle just about any kind of data, users are taking full advantage of these enhancements by sending photos, HTML-enhanced documents, audio messages, and even video messages to enhance their communication experience.

- *File Transfer Protocol (FTP):* FTP makes moving files across the Internet possible and handles some details involved in moving text and other forms of data between different types of computers (which might represent such data using different formats). Although not a highly graphical application, FTP remains an important tool for individuals and organizations that must exchange files containing data or documents.

- *Newsgroups*: Based on a TCP/IP service known as USENET, **newsgroups** provide a way for individuals to exchange information on specific, identifiable topics or areas of interest. This technology lets users read information on a variety of subtopics that are pertinent to a newsgroup's focus. Here, sequences of messages sent by other users, called message threads, are arranged in order of arrival for posting to the newsgroup. This lets readers follow the interchange of information on a subtopic and post their own messages as they wish. For technical matters, this is an especially useful way to exchange opinions and information on a broad range of topics.

- *Telnet*: One of the oldest Internet applications, Telnet permits a user on one computer to establish a session on another computer elsewhere on the Internet, as if his or her machine were a terminal attached to that remote computer. Given the proper access to remote machines, this program lets users achieve many tasks remotely (from around the world, given the Internet's global reach) that they might ordinarily only be able to accomplish locally. Because it remains character-oriented and command-line driven, Telnet is rather "old-fashioned" as applications go. But its reach and general-purpose capability ensure its ongoing survival—in fact, Telnet is an application of choice for configuring all kinds of networking equipment, especially routers and hubs.

- *World Wide Web (WWW)*: Today, the Web is the premier application for most Internet users. Partly because modern Web clients (Web browsers) integrate e-mail and newsreaders (giving Web users e-mail and newsgroup access), and partly because the Web supports an increasingly interactive, visual, and even animated interface, the Web is the focus of a great deal of serious system development, as well as a popular tool for information browsing and access.

The next sections cover these important Internet services in further detail.

Chat and Instant Messaging

The ability to interact with others in real time, even if only by typing words on a keyboard, has enormous appeal for applications ranging from virtual classrooms to support groups. Many online teaching environments offer scheduled chat sessions with instructors as an online equivalent to classroom interaction or office hours with instructors. Likewise, many Web sites attract users by focusing on specific topics and offering scheduled chats with technical experts, authors, and celebrities.

The authors of this book have participated in many such events, and their frequency only seems to increase. At one point, participating in chats required special-purpose applications or environments (like the CompuServe or AOL software client); today, the tendency is to embed the necessary client software in the form of executable objects on Web pages. This lets users run client-side software provided by the Web site without necessarily even knowing that's what they're doing.

Instant messaging applications permit two users to open a window on their desktops and interact with each other privately, in much the same way that chat rooms permit groups of users to interact with each other publicly. AOL's Instant Messenger application is currently believed to be one of its premier business assets, which helps explain

14

why AOL tries to protect its user base as other vendors such as Microsoft tout their own equivalent software packages. Other popular graphical clients for such applications include ICQ and IRC, both widely available online and non-proprietary. You can obtain a copy of ICQ software from *www.icq.com*; IRC clients of many kinds are available through *http://shareware.cnet.com*.

E-Mail

E-mail, used both across the Internet and within organizations, has become the preferred method of communication for individuals and organizations. It allows easy communication with anyone anywhere in the world who is connected to the Internet. For many beginning Internet users, obtaining e-mail access is the impetus behind connecting to the Internet or joining an online service. Through e-mail, you can send a message to your grandmother without paying for a long-distance call; at work, you can guarantee that every person in a group receives notification of an important meeting.

As with regular mail, you must know the address of anyone with whom you wish to exchange e-mail. When e-mail is addressed for transport across the Internet, the address starts with the recipient's e-mail name, followed by an @ sign, and then a recognizable name for the server where the recipient picks up e-mail messages.

For example, one of the author's e-mail addresses is *etittel@lanw.com*. The first four characters in the string to the right of the @ sign form an abbreviation for his company's name (that is, "lanw" is an abbreviation for LANWrights). The last three letters in the mail server's name indicate the kind of domain involved (that is, "com" indicates a commercial operation) and are discussed in detail later in this chapter. The characters to the left of the @ sign identify a specific account where the message is to be delivered. Such names don't always correspond to specific individuals—for instance, most domains commonly accept mail addressed to *postmaster@att.com* or *support@jump.net*. Here, the first address identifies the individual who runs the mail server at the site, whereas the second identifies the technical support group for an **Internet Service Provider (ISP)**, jump.net.

As a network administrator, you occasionally might need to contact people using e-mail across the Internet. For example, sending a message to a technical support group is often easier than telephoning an organization and waiting until someone answers. Although getting an answer to a question might take longer using e-mail, you can do other things while you wait for the answer.

On the Internet, the most important upper-layer protocol that supports e-mail is called the Simple Mail Transfer Protocol (SMTP). SMTP supports a variety of delivery options, including a way to attach one or more files to messages. The corresponding standard governing such attachments is called MIME (Multipurpose Internet Mail Extensions). It is interesting to note that MIME also is a way to identify the kinds of files or documents that a Web server can accept from or deliver to its users.

File Transfer Protocol Servers

The File Transfer Protocol (FTP) can be used across the Internet, but it also works in any LAN or WAN environment that supports TCP/IP. The FTP service uses a high-level protocol also named the File Transfer Protocol; as mentioned earlier, FTP's primary application is to access files or deposit files on remote servers that run a special-purpose piece of software called an FTP server. Today, an increasingly popular way to use FTP on the Internet is to provide users with software drivers or updates. For example, a virus-protection software vendor might maintain an FTP server to make its most up-to-date virus-definition files available to the public, ensuring that all its users remain protected from all known (and even very new) viruses.

FTP client software is readily available for most types of computers. Figure 14-1 shows a graphical FTP utility called WS_FTP Pro. This particular FTP client is one of many such graphical programs available at low or no cost on the Internet. It is a great deal easier to use than text-based FTP programs such as those included with Windows 98, Windows NT, and Windows 2000, especially when transferring groups of files.

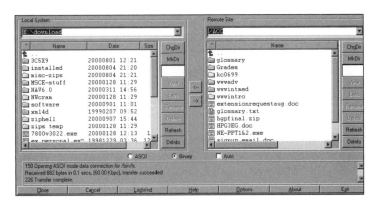

Figure 14-1 WS_FTP Pro

14

However, many **Internet browsers**, such as Microsoft Internet Explorer and Netscape Navigator, also support FTP file transfers. These programs allow you to browse a list of files available on a particular server and to transfer such files to your local drive. Figure 14-2 shows the root directory of the Microsoft FTP site accessed with Internet Explorer. In addition to these browsers, numerous third-party and shareware FTP clients are available, and most Internet browsers support FTP-based file downloads as well.

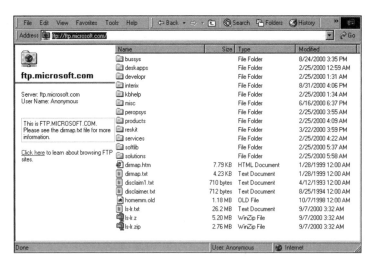

Figure 14-2   Root directory of the Microsoft FTP site

Newsgroups

The **Network News Transfer Protocol (NNTP)** is the Internet protocol that handles distribution, inquiry, retrieval, and posting of news articles. NNTP is used to access any of over 80,000 newsgroups publicly available on the Internet. Network news (also known as USENET) is NNTP's most popular application. USENET supports a staggering variety of chat rooms, bulletin boards, and newsgroups. Thousands of newsgroups are active 24 hours a day, 365 days a year.

To access a newsgroup, you must have NNTP client software on your computer. However, most current Internet browsers also support NNTP, as do many e-mail clients (including Microsoft Outlook). To access any particular newsgroup, you must "subscribe" to that newsgroup. Then, using software that closely resembles most e-mail programs, you can read messages from and "post" messages to that newsgroup.

As you might imagine, USENET hosts newsgroups that cover almost any conceivable discussion topic, from travel, to cooking, to missing children, to drug abuse. No single person nor group of people manages many of these newsgroups; such newsgroups are called unmoderated. Sometimes institutionalized chaos and complete lack of censorship or control result in unfiltered, inaccurate, or downright misleading content.

On the other hand, many newsgroups are explicitly monitored; such groups do not allow inappropriate or inaccurate postings to appear among their message threads. Whether moderated or not, all newsgroups maintain postings for only a short period of time, generally a week or less. The time that any message persists in such a group is called the **scroll rate**; the busier a newsgroup, the faster the scroll rate.

Network administrators find many newsgroups extremely helpful. By discussing your networking problems with other people with similar interests or experience, you can gain a new perspective on your situation. You also can find newsgroups that are invaluable sources of late-breaking news about viruses, system bugs, new software and tools, as well as good places for "peer-level" technical support.

Newsgroups are organized in a hierarchical structure, alphabetically by category. For example, newsgroups that begin with *comp* deal with computers, whereas newsgroups that begin with *microsoft* deal specifically with Microsoft products. Another popular category for newsgroups is *alt*, which contains just about everything else. One humorous example of a newsgroup is *alt.elvis*; you can find anything from Elvis memorabilia auctions to Elvis sightings within its message threads!

To find those newsgroups most helpful to you as a network administrator, you must review them yourself. As of this writing, over 1,000,000 newsgroups are on the Internet. You can obtain a current list of all available newsgroups from any NNTP-compatible newsreader connected to an ISP's news server. You also can visit the Web site at *groups.google.com* to browse and search a listing of all available Internet newsgroups; in fact, this site permits you to search the entire body of known newsgroup postings for information related to whatever search string you might use.

Microsoft maintains its own public news server, which you may visit at *news://msnews.microsoft.com*. Here is a list of some networking-related newsgroups to get you started in your search for networking-related news and information:

- *comp.dcom*
- *comp.os.ms-windows.networking*
- *comp.os.ms-win2000.cmdprompt.admin*
- *microsoft.public.win2000.networking*
- *microsoft.public.win2000.setup*

14

Telnet

Some people think Telnet is an abbreviation for "terminal emulation across the network." This might not be the correct etymology, but Telnet clearly remains an incredibly popular, and useful, Internet service. Primarily, Telnet permits users (including network administrators) to run programs, execute commands, and interact with remote systems elsewhere on the Internet or on any other TCP/IP-based network. Because of its popularity for device management and remote systems access, Telnet is the oldest and most venerable of all TCP/IP-based services.

All Unix- and Linux-based operating systems, along with Windows 2000 and Windows XP, include a Telnet server—sometimes known in UNIX terminology as a **Telnet daemon** or telnetd. (In UNIX terminology, a **daemon** is a component of any server program that "listens" to incoming requests for a specific service across the network.) For Windows NT, you must rely on a third-party vendor to offer Telnet access to your NT server.

Nearly every network-capable Microsoft product includes a Telnet client, which permits computers to access Telnet servers elsewhere on the Internet or on any other TCP/IP-based network. Supported platforms include Windows for Workgroups, Windows 95, Windows 98, Windows NT, and Windows 2000.

World Wide Web

Many people consider the World Wide Web (WWW) and the Internet synonymous, even though the WWW is actually the newest of all the Internet services covered in this chapter. The Web actually consists of untold millions of documents written in the **Hypertext Markup Language (HTML)**.

Using HTML, authors can present text, images, sound, animation, and video in the form of document collections that you can browse by using links between pages within each collection, and using links to elements outside each collection. The primary protocol for documents on the WWW is known as the **Hypertext Transfer Protocol (HTTP)**. Figure 14-3 shows the front page of the Course Technology Web site found at *www.course.com*. (Note that the page contains rotating pieces of information, your screen may look different.) In Web parlance, such a lead-in document is called the **home page**.

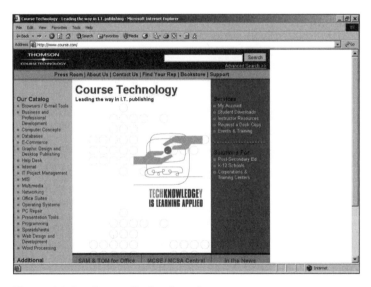

Figure 14-3   Course Technology home page

Many Web sites contain information valuable to network administrators. This section lists some of these sites. To find Web sites that contain specific information, start with sites that perform Internet searches, using special-purpose software called a **search engine**, such as Yahoo! (*www.yahoo.com*) or Google (*www.google.com*).

Most hardware and software vendors publish Web sites. On these sites, you can often find product information, updated documentation, and, sometimes, new drivers and other product-related software. Table 14-1 names a few hardware vendors and suppliers and their Web addresses.

Table 14-1   Sample Web addresses for hardware manufacturers

Manufacturer	Web Address
3Com	*www.3com.com*
Hewlett-Packard	*www.hp.com/rnd/*
Intel	*www.intel.com*

Generally, the Web is an incredibly rich and useful resource, whether you're looking for consulting help, trying to select new hardware or software for your network, or simply trying to learn more about new networking tools and technologies. For the authors of this book, life as we know it would be impossible without access to the Web.

LOCATING INTERNET RESOURCES

To enable users to navigate the Internet, each resource must have an Internet address, just as each computer on a LAN also must have an address. These addresses are generally represented as resource names, with corresponding TCP/IP numeric addresses.

Internet Resource Names

Any Web-based Internet resource has an associated address called its **Uniform Resource Locator (URL)**. The URL for a resource specifies which server to access, as well as which protocol to use to access its named location.

All Web addresses given in this chapter, and elsewhere in this book, are URLs. For example, the Microsoft Web site uses this URL: *http://www.microsoft.com*. This address contains two basic sections: the protocol used to access the resource and its address, which takes the form of an Internet domain name.

The protocol (in this case, HTTP, or the HyperText Transfer Protocol) is the first section of the URL and is followed by a colon. The address begins with two forward-facing slashes (//). It is very important not to confuse these with the backslash (\) used in some computers' directory structures. As another example, consider the addresses for two other Microsoft servers, FTP: *ftp://ftp.microsoft.com* and NNTP news: *news://msnews.microsoft.com*. All three URLs use the same underlying domain name (*microsoft.com*), but each calls the protocol that represents its related service and references a different server name.

14

Domain Name System (DNS)

The DNS protocol is used on a network to resolve symbolic names to their corresponding IP addresses. This works the same way on the Internet but on a much larger scale. For the URLs in the previous section, a DNS server resolves the domain names *www.microsoft.com* and *ftp.microsoft.com* to particular IP addresses on the Internet, such as 207.68.156.61 and 198.105.232.1, respectively.

On the Internet, URLs refer to the domain names for a computer or a group of computers. These domains are separated into categories denoted by the last element in the domain name. (That is, the characters to the right of the right-most period in the domain name; for the Microsoft examples you saw earlier, this is the string "com".) Some common domain types in the United States follow:

.com	Commercial organizations or businesses	.mil	Military organizations
.edu	Educational institutions	.net	Network service providers
.gov	Government organizations (except the military)	.org	Other organizations, usually nonprofit

Internationally, other domain types most often indicate the country of origin for a particular Internet site. For example, the following are country-specific strings:

.au	Australia
.fr	France
.uk	United Kingdom

For a complete, geographically organized list of country top-level domain names and a pointer to domain name registration authorities worldwide, visit the Web site *www.norid.no/domenenavnbaser/domreg.html*.

GETTING A DOMAIN NAME

The process for a company or an individual to register a domain name is extremely simple, and the price is quite affordable. The cost for owning your very own domain name is $35/year or less, depending on the registrar and top-level domain chosen. There are a number of Web sites that you can access that will register your domain name for you. These sites include www.verisign.com and www.register.com. From these Web sites, you choose the domain name you would like, along with the top-level domain. For example, one of the authors of this book has his last name (Tomsho) registered as tomsho.com.

The top-level names you can choose from include .com, .net, .org, .us, .biz, .info, .tv, .ws, and .cc. In addition, a new top-level domain, .name, is reserved for individuals who wish to register their personal name for a personal Web site and/or e-mail address. For example, the author "Greg Tomsho" could register his full name as Greg.Tomsho.name and have an e-mail address as Greg@Tomsho.name or a Web site at www.Greg.Tomsho.name.

After you decide on a domain name, you'll need to verify that the name is not already registered. If the name is not registered, you can own it for the $35/year fee.

 The $35/year fee applies to .com, .net, and .org top-level domains. Other top-level domains cost less—for example, a .name domain costs only $28.95/year.

MAKING AN INTERNET CONNECTION

To access the resources available on the Internet, you must connect your computer to the dynamic collection of information and services the Internet has become. For most users today, this means going through an ISP. ISPs maintain dial-up and dedicated links of all kinds for users and permit them to piggyback on their own, direct, dedicated links to the Internet, primarily as a for-a-fee service.

There are many ways to connect to an ISP. The two most common types of connections for general users are dial-up lines using modems and Integrated Services Digital Network (ISDN), cable modem, or digital subscriber line (DSL) connections. Of course, a great many other kinds of connections are possible, but most are beyond the means of most individuals; some of the largest bandwidth connections (for example, DS-3 or ATM OC-96) are beyond the means of all organizations except communications providers and the largest companies and governmental bodies.

Dial-Up Connections

14

The dial-up protocol you use for an Internet connection depends on your ISP's requirements and capabilities. The three dial-up protocols most prevalent for Internet connections are Point-to-Point Protocol (PPP), the Serial Line Internet Protocol (SLIP), and a compressed version of SLIP called CSLIP. PPP, the newest of these protocols, is the dial-up protocol of choice for ISPs today. This is because PPP supports compression, error checking, and dynamic IP address assignment. The IP address assignment feature makes PPP preferable to most ISPs because using PPP means they need not manage each user's address individually, but can instead assign a block of IP addresses that everyone who connects to the Internet through their service can share.

Digital Connection Types

ISDN connections provide digital lines for voice or data transmission. Using an ISDN connection to reach the Internet, you can achieve much higher speeds than with standard dial-up links, up to 128 Kbps (not including compression).

ISDN's greatest limitations are cost and availability. The monthly service cost for ISDN is generally much higher than for a regular phone line, and ISDN is not available in all areas. Some experts also claim that ISDN represents a case of "too little, too late."

Certainly, new modem technologies have encroached on a single ISDN 64-Kbps channel's capabilities on the low end. In fact, newer connection technologies such as cable modems and DSL offer higher bandwidth than ISDN at lower costs in many major metropolitan areas in Europe and North America. It's not atypical to pay about $40 to $50 per month in the United States for cable modem service, with bandwidth that ranges from 150 to 900 Kbps. DSL tends to cost a bit more—$60 to $75 per month in the United States—but delivers guaranteed bandwidth at 384 Kbps and higher. (Higher rates do cost more, though.)

Connection Considerations

Either dial-up or digital connections can support single- or multiple-user accounts. As a general rule, dial-up connections are more cost-effective and easier to implement for single-user accounts, whereas digital connections are preferable for multiple users because they are faster and offer more bandwidth for multiple users to share. One thing is certain: the greater the number of users who must share a link to the Internet, the more important it becomes to endow that link with as much bandwidth as possible. Larger organizations typically look beyond ISDN and cable modem, and move directly to technologies such as full-bandwidth DSL, multichannel frame relay, full or fractional T1 links, or even more commodious connections such as T3 or DS-3.

Security also must be an important consideration when connecting to the Internet. If you or your organization have a network connected to the Internet—either directly or through an ISP—be aware that just as your users can access computers on the Internet easily and quickly, users on the Internet also can access your network. As you might imagine, this poses a security threat and represents serious exposure to damage and liability from hackers, crackers, and other Internet-based malefactors.

Because of the possible security risks involved, many companies with direct Internet connections use a special software program, called a **proxy server**, to act as a gateway between their network and the Internet. Normally, a proxy server runs on a special boundary device called a **firewall** that sits between the external Internet and the in-house internal networks. The proxy server software filters requests that attempt to traverse the boundary. They can block insiders' access to certain resources on the Internet and also stop unauthorized users' attempts to access—and possibly damage—their network resources. A proxy server gets its name from its ability to store copies of already-requested Internet data locally, so that users who revisit Internet resources need not return to the original site every time they request a particular file or Web document.

Above and beyond playing host to proxy server software, a firewall provides all kinds of address filtering and access controls. For any organization that permits its networked users to access the Internet through a network link of some kind, a firewall/proxy server combination provides an effective security blanket for its network that no savvy administrator should omit when planning his or her network configuration.

 An expanded use of the Internet is its ability to be used as part of a company's infrastructure through a VPN connection. This expanding technology is allowing remote offices and remote individual users to safely access their company's intranet through the Internet—as if they were physically connected to the LAN. One of this book's authors uses the Internet and VPNs, along with Windows 2000 Terminal Services, to allow remote administration of a Web server. Through a VPN connection, a Terminal Services client connects to the Windows 2000 server for the purposes of adding users and creating groups.

CHAPTER SUMMARY

- ❑ The Internet has become an everyday part of life. Network administrators can use its vast resources to retrieve drivers and software updates, get technical support, read periodicals, and discuss problems and ideas through newsgroups.

- ❑ The domain names and URLs associated with particular resources enable users to locate information on the Internet. Setting up a connection to the Internet is simple, but it's important to understand your organization's bandwidth and security requirements and ensure that they are satisfied before establishing any such link.

- ❑ Key services on the Internet include FTP for file transfer, HTTP for Web access, Telnet for remote access, SMTP for transferring e-mail messages, NNTP for access to newsgroups, ICQ and IRC for instant messaging and chat access, among many others. Savvy network administrators know how to make the most of these services to find the technical information, software, and updates that they so often need to do their jobs properly.

- ❑ Users normally connect to the Internet using a modem or low-end digital subscriber connection such as ISDN, cable modem, or partial-bandwidth DSL; businesses often require more bandwidth and use technologies such as frame relay, full-bandwidth DSL, or full or fractional T1 lines to connect to the Internet.

- ❑ Maintaining security is important when exposing information resources on the Internet; for that reason most organizations use firewall/proxy server combinations to isolate their internal networks from the external Internet (or other public networks).

14

KEY TERMS

daemon — A UNIX term for a component of any server program that "listens" to incoming requests for a specific service across the network; for example, a Telnet server might include a Telnet daemon, a program that always runs, ready to serve Telnet requests; the same component of an FTP server is called an FTP daemon, and so forth.

firewall — A special Internet server that sits between an Internet link and a private network, and which filters both incoming and outgoing network traffic, limits the Internet resources that in-house users may access, and severely or completely limits incoming requests for access to the firewall's private network side.

home page — On a Web site, the official "entry page" or the default document associated with the site's base URL (for example, *www.microsoft.com*) is called the home page.

Hypertext Markup Language (HTML) — The language used to create documents for the WWW.

Hypertext Transfer Protocol (HTTP) — The protocol used by the WWW to transfer files.

Internet browser — A graphical tool designed to read HTML documents and access the WWW, such as Microsoft Internet Explorer or Netscape Navigator.

Internet Service Provider (ISP) — A company that connects its clients to the Internet.

network news — Also known as USENET, this is the collection of discussion groups maintained on the Internet.

Network News Transfer Protocol (NNTP) — The protocol used for distributing, retrieving, inquiring, and posting network news articles.

newsgroup — A discussion group in which people share information through USENET.

proxy server — A special Internet server that sits between an Internet link and a private network. It stores local copies of remote Web pages and files that users request (by proxy, as it were, so that it answers subsequent access requests nearly immediately). It also filters outgoing requests by domain name or IP address and severely or completely limits incoming requests to access the proxy server's private network side.

scroll rate — In a USENET or other NNTP-based newsgroup, the amount of time a new message remains resident on a server before newer messages arrive and "push" it out.

search engine — A special-purpose program that solicits strings of text from users and searches a large, indexed collection of files and documents, looking for exact or near matches for that string, in an attempt to help users find resources related to the string.

Telnet daemon — Also known as telnetd, this is the server program that responds to client requests for the Internet-based Telnet remote terminal emulation service; it permits remote users to run commands and programs on other computers across any IP-based network, including the Internet.

Uniform Resource Locator (URL) — The specific address for a Web-based Internet or other IP network resource.

REVIEW QUESTIONS

1. A(n) _____ connection to the Internet provides speeds up to 128 Kbps.

   a. modem

   b. ISDN

   c. T1

   d. T3

2. A(n) _____ connection to the Internet provides variable speeds that typically range from 150 to 900 Kbps.

   a. modem

   b. cable modem

   c. ISDN

   d. DSL

3. _____ is a widely used Internet messaging service that sends individual messages, not news items.

   a. WWW

   b. FTP

   c. News

   d. E-mail

4. _____ is a widely used Internet file transfer service.

   a. WWW

   b. FTP

   c. News

   d. E-mail

5. _____ is the language used to create files for use in the WWW.

   a. URL

   b. NNTP

   c. HTML

   d. HTTP

6. An Internet browser is a graphical interface that allows users to view sites on the WWW. True or false?

14

7. The domain indicator often used by nonprofit groups in the United States is:

    a. .edu

    b. .com

    c. .org

    d. .gov

8. The domain indicator used by for-profit businesses in the United States is:

    a. .edu

    b. .com

    c. .org

    d. .gov

9. The WWW uses the _____ protocol to transfer files.

    a. NNTP

    b. HTTP

    c. SNMP

    d. FTP

10. Which dial-up protocol is used most often by companies that provide Internet connections?

    a. SLIP

    b. CSLIP

    c. PPP

    d. FTP

11. Newsgroup servers use _____ to transfer news messages.

    a. NNTP

    b. HTTP

    c. SNMP

    d. FTP

12. A(n) _____ is a Web site whose purpose is to search for other Web sites.

13. What unique character is used to address e-mail?

    a. %

    b. @

    c. &

    d. #

14. A(n) _____ connection to the Internet is generally most cost effective for single–user accounts.

   a. ISDN

   b. modem

   c. T1

   d. T3

15. The Internet of today began as a network for _____.

   a. the European Economic Community (EEC)

   b. the computer companies known as "the seven dwarves"

   c. IBM

   d. the U.S. Department of Defense

16. What is the acronym for a company that allows you to connect to the Internet through its connection?

   a. PVC

   b. ISC

   c. ISP

   d. ISB

17. A URL is the specific address of a Web-based Internet resource. True or false?

18. Which TCP/IP service is used to resolve domain names to addresses in the Internet?

   a. DHCP

   b. SNMP

   c. DNS

   d. WINS

19. A proxy server is a special-purpose boundary device that separates "inside" from "outside" on a network. True or false?

20. Which of the following functions can a proxy server provide?

   a. prevent internal users from accessing external resources

   b. prevent external users from accessing internal resources

   c. act on behalf of internal users to obtain external resources

   d. act on behalf of external users to obtain internal resources

   e. all of the above

14

HANDS-ON PROJECTS

The Internet provides many great resources for network administrators. For these projects, you access the WWW, FTP, and news sites. Keep in mind that these projects do not provide a comprehensive lesson on using your browser; rather, they are to familiarize you with Internet navigation. For simplicity, these projects assume that you use Microsoft Internet Explorer or Netscape Communicator and you work on a machine with a live Internet connection.

Project 14-1

To perform this project, your PC computer must have Internet Explorer, and an e-mail client with newsreader capability; for example, you must also connect to the Internet.

To access alternate services through a Web browser:

1. Start your Web browser.

2. Type **news://msnews.microsoft.com** in the Address bar in your browser window, and then press **Enter**. A newsreader program should pop up, as Outlook Express does in Figure 14-4, with a message that indicates you currently subscribe to no newsgroups.

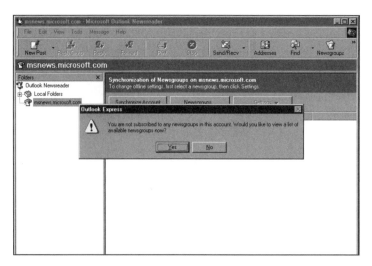

Figure 14-4   Outlook Express newsgroups confirmation box

3. Click **Yes** to view a list of available newsgroups. Be prepared to wait a bit before the entire list downloads. A Newsgroup Subscriptions window appears, with a search text box labeled "Display newsgroups which contain," as shown in Figure 14-5.

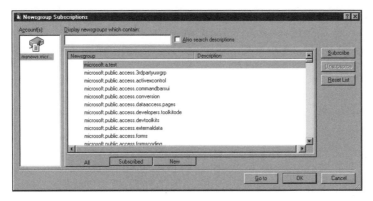

Figure 14-5   Newsgroups Subscriptions window

4. Type the string **public.win2000** in the text box, then press the **Enter** key. This displays a list of all the newsgroups related to Windows 2000.

5. Highlight the newsgroup **microsoft.public.win2000.general**, click the **Subscribe** button to the right of the list display area, and then click the **Go to** button to view the news items for that group, as shown in Figure 14-6.

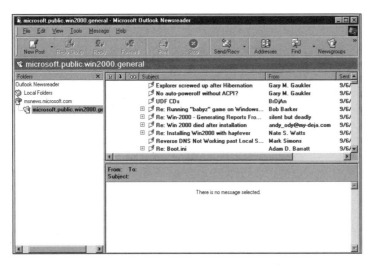

Figure 14-6   News items for microsoft.public.win2000.general

6. Browse through the news items in the upper-right pane. As you highlight them, their text appears in the lower-right pane. Read two or three messages to get a sense of what the traffic is like in this newsgroup.

7. Close the newsreader window. If you do not plan to continue to the next project, close the browser window as well.

Project 14-2

To access the FTP service:

1. In the Address box in your browser, enter **ftp://ftp.microsoft.com**, and then press the **Enter** key.

2. Selecting any Directory entry takes you to that directory. Double-click the **bussys** directory, the **winnt** directory, the **winnt-public** directory, the **reskit** directory, the **nt40** directory, and then the **i386** directory. You arrive at the PC (intel 386) Resource Kit utilities directory for Windows NT 4.0. Double-clicking any file in this directory downloads it to your local machine. In general, this explains how to navigate and grab FTP files through your Web browser.

3. On the toolbar, click the **Up One Level** button. (The icon is a folder with an upward-pointing arrow inside it.) You return to the previous directory. Double-click the **i386** directory to return it.

4. Double-clicking a file on an FTP site either displays the file on your screen (if the file is a .txt, .doc, or image file) or transfers the file to your local drive. Double-click a file with an .exe extension. After the program downloads the file header, you are prompted to choose a directory for the file. Ask your instructor where to place this file, or put it in the root directory of your primary drive (usually C:).

5. Once the transfer completes, the download window closes. Click **Start**, **Programs**, **Windows Explorer**, and delete the file you just downloaded. Then you can proceed to the next Hands-on Project or close the browser, if Project 14-3 is not assigned.

Project 14-3

For nearly every kind of networking software, technology, tool, or utility, there's an associated community of interest. Often one or more e-mail newsletters may serve larger communities of interest, delivering product update information, related news items, and tips and tricks for full-time IT professionals. For Windows operating systems, you can choose from many such newsletters. Sunbelt Software, Inc., a Windows-focused software, services, and training reseller based in Clearwater, Florida, distributes one of the best known and most useful newsletters of this type. In this project, you visit the Sunbelt Web site and learn about its newsletter offerings.

To sign up for a Windows Administrator's newsletter:

1. In the Address box in your browser, enter **www.sunbelt-software.com**, and then press the **Enter** key. This is the home page for the Sunbelt Software, Inc. Web site.

2. Click the **W2KNews** tab at the top of the page. This takes you to the sign-up page for the company's Sunbelt W2KNews Electronic Newsletter. Read the blurb at the top of the page.

3. Type **registry** in the Search W2KNews text box, and then click the **Search** button.

4. Highlight the first entry in the resulting messages found list, then click the **View Message** button to view its contents. This gives you a good idea about the coverage and tone of this newsletter.

5. Once you examine the newsletter, click the **Back** button three times to return to the W2KNews sign-up page. If you wanted to sign up for this newsletter, you'd click the **Subscribe** button and provide an e-mail address for delivery.

6. If and when you do get settled into a network or systems administration job, you will find such newsletters useful and interesting sources of information and news that help you keep up to date on security scares, software updates, and so forth. When you're ready to sign up for this kind of service, you can use an Internet search engine such as Yahoo!, Excite, or AltaVista to locate items of interest by typing search strings like **"Windows 2000" near newsletter** or **Linux near newsletter**. (Use quotation marks around groups of words whenever you want to locate specific phrases.) The keyword *near* means that the word *newsletter* should occur close to the other search term (*Windows 2000* in the first search, *Linux* in the second search), but that it doesn't have to be next to the other term. This technique helps improve the odds of finding something interesting.

7. Close the Web browser unless you plan to proceed immediately to the next project.

Project 14-4

Internet connection technologies most likely to suit small office or home office (SOHO) use include the following:

❏ Conventional analog modems, which top out at 56 Kbps (or lower, depending on line quality)

❏ ISDN, which provides two 64-Kbps channels that may be bonded together to provide a single 128-Kbps connection

❏ Cable modem, which provides up to 1.5 Mbps of bandwidth for any given cable segment, but all active users on that segment share bandwidth

❏ DSL, which provides up to 1.5 Mbps of dedicated bandwidth per connection, but where higher amounts of dedicated bandwidth lead to higher monthly costs

To research Internet bandwidth issues:

In this Hands-on Project, you collaborate with fellow students or investigate only one type of SOHO access device by yourself. The objectives for each type of device are as follows:

1. Determine if the underlying service is available in your neighborhood. Where applicable (analog modem and DSL), also find out what kinds of bandwidth are supported or available.

2. Locate one or more service providers who permit Internet access using that device. Find out what kind of access plans they offer and how much they cost.

3. Based on your ability to use this device and an Internet service, would you actually make this kind of connection for your home or office? Why or why not?

If you can compare results with other students, rank the various device types and access services against each other. How would you decide which one to choose for your own use?

14

To complete this project, you need to use Internet search engines, rely on your own knowledge about local cable and telephone companies, as well as ISPs, and try to determine if some class of service (especially ISDN, cable modem, or DSL) is available in your neighborhood and can be used on your premises. Answering these questions may require making numerous phone calls, searching various Web sites, and so forth. But it equips you with skills you'll put to work many times as you seek to establish Internet access wherever you're living or working.

Project 14-5

The Internet has become valuable to network administrators and support personnel. The ease by which one can retrieve troubleshooting information and updated drivers and software can solve problems in minutes rather than the several days it took in the past.

This project walks you through the process of solving a problem by using a knowledge base. Your problem is that you receive an error when you try to use an HP ScanJet 5100C. The error message is: Stop: 0x0000000a.

To resolve this problem, follow these steps:

1. Open your browser, and type **support.microsoft.com** in the Address bar.

2. On the left side, under Search the Knowledge Base, type **Stop: 0x0000000a**.

3. Click the arrow to start the search.

4. You will see a number of articles matching your search criteria. Because it is time-consuming to read all the returned articles, let's be more specific in the search. Click the **Back** button on your browser to return to the search page.

5. Under Search the Knowledge Base, type **Stop: 0x0000000a ScanJet** and click the arrow to start the search again.

6. This time, only a few articles are returned. Read the articles related to this problem and Windows XP, and then write a synopsis of what is needed to resolve the problem.

7. Exit the site and close your browser.

CASE PROJECTS

1. As a network administrator, you are experiencing a puzzling problem with your token ring network. Your network includes both NetWare and Windows NT servers, and clients running Windows 95, Windows 98, and Windows NT. Outline some Internet resources you might use to isolate and remedy this problem.

2. Assume you're a network administrator who uses 3Com NICs on your networked computers. Visit the 3Com Web site at *www.3com.com*. Notice the "Jump to Driver Downloads" selection at the top of the page. Follow this link, and examine what kinds of NICs 3Com makes. Choose an Ethernet NIC and download the driver. What does this tell you about finding software updates and drivers on the Internet?

3. Visit the Microsoft Web site to look for Service Packs for Windows NT. Given that Service Pack 6, version a, for Windows NT 4.0 is called SP6a, how might you locate this software on their complex Web site? (*Hint*: Use the Search button that appears in the button bar at the top of every page.) Try navigating the Web site's structure from the home page to locate this same information. What does this tell you about the importance of search engines on Web sites, especially large and complex ones?

4. Because your home office is in a neighborhood with no CATV service and is too far from the nearest DSL access multiplexer (DSLAM) for DSL service, you must choose between adding an analog phone line or an ISDN line. For the phone line, you could use a $90, 56-Kbps V.90 modem, with associated costs of $57 per month ($27 for the phone line, $30 for unlimited dial-up Internet access). For the ISDN line, you must purchase an access device for $199, with associated costs of $115 per month ($70 for local ISDN service, $45 for unlimited dial-up Internet access). What kinds of requirements for access would justify the more expensive option? What factors should you consider when deciding whether the extra bandwidth offsets the extra cost?

5. When establishing an Internet connection using a cable modem, the computer attached to the cable behaves much like a machine attached to an Ethernet network—that is, it's just another machine on a shared bus network (except, of course, it's a broadband bus with separate channels to send and receive data). This means that anybody on the same cable segment can view and possibly even access resources on your machine. Explain why this may or may not be desirable, and what kinds of software you might want to install on your machine to prevent snoopers from accessing its contents.

14

A

COMMON NETWORKING STANDARDS AND SPECIFICATIONS

As demonstrated by the discussions and examples in this book and your own experiences in assembling new networks or working with existing ones, a network is built of many parts. These components include the networking media (cabled or wireless), network interfaces and supporting equipment, computers, connections, and many types of hardware. Other parts of a network include software drivers, networking protocols, networking services, application interfaces, and network-related programs. Given the complexity usually involved in assembling a network, it may seem miraculous that networks work at all.

The secret harmony is a result of the presence of networking standards. At every level of the OSI reference model, network standards operate to permit NIC developers to build NICs that attach to standard cables using standard connectors. They also permit e-mail vendors to count on basic delivery services built on the TCP/IP-based Simple Mail Transfer Protocol (SMTP) and to obtain support for attachments of many kinds from the Multipart Internet Mail Extensions (MIME).

If not for standards, networks couldn't work together effectively because pairs or sets of vendors would have to work out the details of managing communications at many levels each time they try to solve a networking problem. Standards let vendors make a great number of simplifying assumptions about the way things behave, connect, and communicate on networks. This appendix examines the major networking standards, from the Physical all the way up to the Applications layer, and gives further pointers to additional information.

STANDARDS-MAKING PROCESS

Committees create most standards because making standards involves numerous groups, each with its own special interests and agendas. Therefore, standards invariably involve compromises and multiple alternatives that exceed practicality and technology.

Nevertheless, it's possible to describe the general standards-making process. The following paragraphs explain this process.

Most standards setting occurs within the framework of specific standards-setting bodies, industry associations, trade groups, or other organizations that consist primarily of unpaid volunteers, with a small core of paid professionals who represent the named organization under whose umbrella the volunteers contribute their efforts.

As the general members propose "hot topics" or specific networking needs germane to the umbrella group, or if ideas come from any of a variety of possible channels, special interest groups (called SIGs) form. Such SIGs include representatives from governments, the vendor community, academia, the consulting community, and user groups (especially large and well-funded ones that can afford staff to participate in this kind of endeavor). Sometimes, zealots representing particular factions also play pivotal roles in such groups.

Within a SIG, working groups coalesce around particular topics. Each group selects a chairperson and appoints members of the working group who address the problems related to that working group's focus area and discuss ideas related to the topic.

Within the working group, constituencies usually propose ideas, which invariably start out based on proprietary technologies or idiosyncratic viewpoints. As a proposal takes shape, it broadens as members of different constituencies work to ensure that their viewpoints are addressed.

Over time, such groups work hard to achieve consensus. Such consensus emerges from a long and heavily commented series of rough draft proposals that are amended until the SIG is ready to submit a rough draft for outside review. This process can—and sometimes does—take years, but three to nine months is a typical time frame for the efforts of many standards-setting bodies. Even so, many rough drafts never go beyond this step, either because the groups cannot reach consensus or because newer technologies emerge and supplant their proposals.

The rough draft is submitted to the SIG for further discussion and approval. Another series of drafts and rewrites occurs. Perhaps the entire SIG reaches consensus that the proposal is worthy of draft status; otherwise, the proposal is abandoned. Again, three to nine months is a normal transit time for this process.

The SIG then submits the draft to its parent group or to the body of the entire organization, depending on the particular organization involved, for more discussion and another approval process, which results in acceptance or rejection. This takes another three to six months.

A

If the entire membership accepts a proposal, it is published as an official standard for that group, when designated members of the working group submit it in a final, approved form for publication. This can take anywhere from several weeks to several months, depending on the size of the proposal document and the remaining work it requires.

Official standards must be reviewed on a regular cycle and amended as needed. Champions or key proponents from the original working group usually take stewardship of such standards and perform the necessary tasks to maintain their currency and accuracy. Reviews typically occur on a yearly or twice-yearly basis (if the membership does not issue a call for earlier review) and can take anywhere from one or two months to half a year to complete.

A standard becomes obsolete when the organization designates it as such. This usually means the organization approved a newer standard to take its place, or a subsequent revision involves so much change that the preceding version becomes obsolete, and its replacement is designated as the new official standard.

Clearly, this is a convoluted, labor-intensive process. The built-in delay inherent in any consensual mechanism explains why proprietary technologies and approaches to networking (among other fields of endeavor) continue to play an important role in business and industry. New and improved proprietary technologies keep the pressure on the standards makers to deliver usable results as quickly as possible and provide a never-ending stream of alternatives.

Among the hundreds of industry consortia, trade groups, professional associations and societies, and SIGs in the networking community, only a small number of such organizations manages those standards that exert the greatest influence on networking hardware and software. The following sections describe the most serious standards makers.

IMPORTANT STANDARDS BODIES

Standards come from many sources, some far more influential and compelling than others. Most of the standards bodies included here exert considerable influence around the world, well beyond the boundaries of their own countries of origin. Some focus more on hardware and signaling issues; others concern themselves more or less exclusively with software. Be aware that many more standards bodies exist than appear on this list. Familiarize yourself, at a minimum, with the main groups and their networking standards, technologies, and related information. For an outstanding general online reference on all kinds of networking standards, visit *www.cmpcmm.com/cc/standards.html*.

Here's the list of the most important standards-setting bodies, each with its own acronym:

- American National Standards Institute (ANSI)
- Comité Consultatif International Téléphonique et Télégraphique (CCITT)

- Electronic Industries Alliance (EIA)
- Internet Architecture Board (IAB)
- Institute of Electrical and Electronics Engineers, Inc. (IEEE)
- International Organization for Standardization (ISO)
- Object Management Group (OMG)
- The Open Group (TOG)
- World Wide Web Consortium (W3C)

The sections that follow cover each of these organizations and their most important standards, and provide contact information for further research.

American National Standards Institute (ANSI)

ANSI creates and publishes standards for programming languages, communications methods and techniques, and networking technologies. ANSI is also the U.S. representative to ISO, the preeminent international standards-setting body for networking and wireless communications, as well as to the CCITT, the preeminent international standards-setting body for telephony and long-haul digital communications.

ANSI programming languages include C, COBOL, and FORTRAN, as well as a dialect of the Structured Query Language (SQL) commonly used in database access and programming. ANSI standards also cover the Small Computer Systems Interface (SCSI) used for high-speed, high-capacity disk drives and other microcomputer peripheral devices. A standard PC device driver, ANSI.SYS, used to drive character-mode screen displays in DOS (and DOS emulation modes), is a file commonly found on PCs.

The following are among the most significant ANSI specifications:

- *ANSI 802.1-1985/IEEE 802.5*: Token ring access, protocols, wiring, and interfaces
- *ANSI/IEEE 802.3*: Coaxial cable standards, CSMA/CD definition for Ethernet
- *ANSI X3.135*: SQL database query methods for client/server database access
- *ANSI X3.92*: Privacy/security encryption algorithm for networked use
- *ANSI X3T9.5*: FDDI specification for voice and data transmission
- *SONET*: Fiber-optic specification for transmitting computer and time-sensitive data (such as real-time video) across a global network

For more information about ANSI standards, visit ANSI's Web site at *www.ansi.org*.

Comité Consultatif International Téléphonique et Télégraphique (CCITT)

CCITT (whose English name is the Consultative Committee for International Telegraphy and Telephony) is a permanent subcommittee of the International Telecommunications Union (ITU), an organization that operates under the auspices of the United Nations. This committee's parent body includes representatives from 160 countries, primarily from national Postal, Telephone, and Telegraph (PTT) services.

The CCITT is responsible for many standards that apply to communications, telecommunications, and networking, including X.25 packet-switched networks, X.400 electronic messaging systems, X.500 directory services, encryption and security, the V.*nn* standards for modems, and the I.*nnn* standards for ISDN. (In these generic standards designators, *nn* and *nnn* stand for sequences of two and three digits, respectively.)

The CCITT works closely with ISO, so many standards carry designations from both groups. CCITT recommendations appear once every four years, most recently in 2000. In March 1993, the CCITT was officially renamed the International Telecommunication Standardization Sector (ITU-T, sometimes called ITU-TS or ITU-TSS), but nearly all resources still refer to this organization by its historical (and apparently more popular) original name.

The CCITT includes a set of 15 named study groups, along with a V and X series of standards. The CCITT study groups are as follows:

- *A, B*: Working terms, definitions, and procedures
- *D, E*: Tariffs
- *F*: Telegraph, telemetric, and mobile services
- *G, H*: Transmissions
- *I*: ISDN
- *J*: Television transmission
- *K, L*: Facilities protection
- *M, N*: Maintenance
- *P*: Telephone transmission
- *R–U*: Terminal and telegraph services
- *V*: Telephone-based data communications
- *X*: Data communication networks

The V Series modem and Teledata Communication standards are as follows:

- *V.22*: 1200-bps full-duplex modem
- *V.22bis*: 2400-bps full-duplex modem

- *V.27*: Fax/modem communications

- *V.28*: RS-232 interface circuits

- *V.32*: Asynchronous and synchronous 4800/9600 bps

- *V.32bis*: Asynchronous and synchronous up to 14.4 Kbps

- *V.35*: High data-rate communications across combined circuits

- *V.42*: Error checking

- *V.42bis*: Lempel-Ziv data compression for modems

- *V.90*: Modem standard for 56 Kbps downstream, 33.6 Kbps upstream

The X Series, which overlaps with OSI standards, includes the following:

- *X.200 (ISO 7498)*: OSI reference model

- *X.25 (ISO 7776)*: Packet-switching network interface

- *X.400 (ISO 10021)*: Message handling

- *X.500 (ISO 9594)*: Directory services, security, and encryption

- *X.700 (ISO 9595)*: Common Management Information Protocol (CMIP)

For more information about CCITT standards, see the Web site *www.itu.ch*.

Electronic Industries Alliance (EIA)

The EIA is an industry trade organization founded in the 1920s and populated by U.S. manufacturers of electronic components, parts, and equipment. The EIA supports a large library of technical documents (many of which are available online), including standards for interfaces between computers and communications equipment of all kinds. The EIA also works closely with other standards organizations, including ANSI and CCITT. Many EIA standards have CCITT counterparts, so that EIA RS-232 is the same as CCITT V.24.

The EIA's best-known standards are those for serial interface connections, particularly for connections between computers and modems, including the following standards designations:

- *RS-232*: The standard for serial connections for modems, including DB-9 and DB-25 connectors

- *RS-422*: Defines a balanced multipoint interface, commonly used for data acquisition

- *RS-423*: Defines an unbalanced digital interface, also used for data acquisition

- *RS-449*: A serial data interface with DB-37 connectors that defines RS-422 and RS-423 as subsets of its capabilities

For more information about EIA standards, visit its Web site at *www.eia.org*.

Internet Architecture Board (IAB)

A

The IAB is the board governing the Internet and is the parent body for the many other boards that govern Internet protocols, technologies, research, and development. IAB can be considered the primary controlling authority over Internet standards, but no single body controls the Internet. For its own part, the IAB is part of the Internet Society, a general membership organization for people interested in Internet technologies and related social issues. (Visit *www.isoc.org* for information on joining.)

The following are some important IAB constituent bodies:

- *Internet Engineering Task Force (IETF)*: The group under the IAB that develops, approves, and maintains the standards documents that define valid Internet protocols, services, and related information. The IETF manages a collection of documents called Requests for Comments (RFCs) that together contain the definitions of draft, experimental, proposed, historical, and official Internet standards. Their Web site is at *www.ietf.org*.

- *Internet Network Information Center (InterNIC)*: Responsible for providing information regarding the Internet domain registration services. InterNIC currently contracts this function to numerous third parties worldwide. The InterNIC Web site, located at *www.internic.net*, includes a database you can check to see if another party already has the name you want to register, a form to report a problem with a registrar, and an FAQ that answers a number of questions regarding domain registration.

- *Internet Assigned Numbers Authority (IANA)*: Responsible for managing the Internet's IP address space as well as related domains and domain names. It is also responsible for doling out IP addresses—typically to ISPs, who then allocate them to their customers. IANA's Web site is located at *www.iana.org*.

- *Internet Engineering Steering Group (IESG)*: Executive group that guides the activities of the IETF's many constituent elements.

- *Internet Research Task Force (IRTF)*: Works on long-term research proposals, new technologies, privacy and security issues, and other aspects of proposed Internet technologies or capabilities with social, as well as technical, implications.

The number and nature of Internet standards is too vast a subject for this appendix. At any one time, one of the RFCs provides a map to all the other current, valid RFCs. At this writing, that RFC is RFC 2500. Titled "Internet Official Protocol Standards," it summarizes all of the current official Internet standards. A Web-based version of this document is available at *www.cis.ohio-state.edu/rfc/rfc2500.txt*. You also can search for the most recent version of this document at any time using the RFC-Full Text Search engine located at *www.faqs.org*. If you search for the RFC number of this version (2500), you should be able to find any older versions, because the new RFCs always list the obsolete versions of the RFCs they replaced.

Institute of Electrical and Electronics Engineers, Inc. (IEEE)

The IEEE is a United States-based professional society that publishes many technical standards, including networking-related standards. The IEEE's 802 Committee, discussed in Chapter 7, developed some of the most important local area network standards in use today. Once the IEEE finishes its work, it usually shares that work with ANSI, which may then forward it to the ISO. This helps to explain why several elements of the IEEE 802 standards family are ANSI and ISO standards as well.

A number of working committees were formed as part of the 802 project at the IEEE, because no single group was judged capable of handling all the many topics involved in this mammoth undertaking. These committees were created to cover the full range of topics that fell beneath the 802 project, as follows:

- *802.1*: Internetworking
- *802.2*: Logical Link Control (LLC)
- *802.3*: CSMA/CD network (Ethernet)
- *802.4*: Token bus network
- *802.5*: Token ring network
- *802.6*: Metropolitan area network (MAN)
- *802.7*: Broadband Technical Advisory Group
- *802.8*: Fiber-optic Technical Advisory Group
- *802.9*: Integrated Voice and Video networks
- *802.10*: Network Security
- *802.11*: Wireless Networks
- *802.12*: Demand Priority Access networks (100 Mbps Voice Grade-AnyLAN)
- *802.13*: This standard number was never used.
- *802.14*: This is a defunct working group. They were involved in specifying data transports over cable television.
- *802.15*: Wireless PAN—Covers the emerging standards for wireless personal area networks
- *802.16*: Wireless MAN—Covers Wireless Metropolitan Area Networks (MAN)
- *802.17*: Resilient Packet Ring—Covers emerging standards for very high-speed, ring-based LANs and MANs
- *802.18*: Wireless Advisory Group—This is a technical advisory group to monitor radio-based wireless standards.

For more information about IEEE standards, visit its Web site at *www.ieee.org*.

International Organization for Standardization (ISO)

The Paris-based ISO, sometimes referred to as the International Standards Organization, focuses on defining global-level standards. Member countries are represented by either government bodies or their premier standards-setting bodies (for example, the ANSI represents the United States, and the British Standards Institute represents Great Britain). The ISO also includes representatives from businesses, educational institutions, research and development organizations, and other international standards bodies such as the CCITT. ISO's overall charter is broad—namely, it serves to establish international standards for all services and manufactured goods and products.

Where computing is concerned, ISO seeks to establish global standards for data communications and information exchange. Such standards intend to promote interoperability across networking environments worldwide and to allow mixing and matching of vendor systems and products without regard to system type or country of origin. The ISO's primary efforts in this area are directed at an initiative known as the Open Systems Interconnection (known variously as OSI, or ISO/OSI). You can find an outstanding overview of important OSI standards at *www.iso.org*.

Object Management Group (OMG)

The OMG represents a federation of over 700 member organizations, from business, industry, government, and academia, all involved in devising a set of tools to permit system vendors to create applications that are platform- and operating-system neutral. The OMG's efforts extend to programming and scripting languages, application and data-conversion interfaces, and protocols. For a fee, the OMG offers certification services to indicate that products conform to standards and specifications agreed upon by OMG member organizations.

The cornerstone of the OMG's efforts is its Object Management Architecture (OMA), which defines a common model for object-oriented applications and runtime environments. A key element of the OMG's efforts focuses on the Common Object Request Broker Architecture (CORBA), a set of standard interfaces and access methods that permit interchange of objects and data across a wide variety of platforms and operating systems. In addition, The Open Group (described in the next section) incorporates the OMG's architecture in its Distributed Computing Environment (DCE) and Distributed Management Environment (DME).

You can visit the OMG's Web site at *www.omg.org*.

The Open Group (TOG)

The Open Group formed in February 1996 by the consolidation of the two leading open systems consortia—the X/Open Company Limited (X/Open) and the Open Software Foundation (OSF). Under The Open Group umbrella, OSF and X/Open work together to deliver technology innovations and promote wide-scale adoption of open systems specifications. Founded in 1988, the OSF hosts industry-wide, collaborative, software research and development for the distributed computing environment. Founded in 1984, X/Open's brand mark is recognized worldwide as a guarantee of compliance to open systems specifications and now includes ownership of the UNIX trade name.

TOG is devoted to defining and elaborating vendor-neutral computing and development environments, with a special emphasis on user interfaces. TOG's legacy from the OSF includes the following significant elements:

- The Distributed Computing Environment (DCE) simplifies development of software for use in heterogeneous networked environments.

- The Distributed Management Environment (DME) defines tools to manage systems in distributed, heterogeneous computing environments.

- The Single UNIX Specification defines a common reference model for an advanced UNIX implementation, with support for SMP, enhanced security, and dynamic configuration.

- The X Window System specification provides a well-recognized industry standard model for a platform-neutral graphical user interface (GUI).

- The Motif Toolkit API is a well-recognized industry standard for a common user interface definition that recognizes IBM's Common User Access (CUA) model.

- Network File System (NFS) specifications define a well-accepted standard model for a UPD/IP-based distributed file system.

- The Common Desktop Environment (CDE) offers a set of tools for building client-side application front ends. Its current release integrates the Motif 2.0 GUI, the X Window System, and a set of common application interfaces that help to standardize application presentations across distributed multiplatform environments.

- Baseline Security Services (XBSS) and Secure Communication Services (GSS-API). XBSS defines a base set of security-related functionality to be provided by open systems with recommended default settings for security-related parameters; GSS-API is an application programming interface that provides applications with secure communications when interacting with peer applications across a network.

- SQL Definitions and Services defines application access to relational databases using the Structured Query Language (SQL) embedded in C and/or COBOL. TOG's XPG4 SQL includes dynamic SQL, which corresponds to ISO/IEC 9075:1992. XPG4 SQL also includes specifications, developed in conjunction with the SQL Access Group, that allow portability of applications to distributed environments.

Visit The Open Group Web site at *www.opengroup.org*.

The World Wide Web Consortium (W3C)

Founded in the early 1990s in the wake of CERN's decision to release its work on HTML and HTTP to the world at large, the W3C is the standards-setting body for Web-related markup languages, specifications, accessibility guidelines, and much more. Organizations such as the Massachusetts Institute of Technology (MIT) in the United States and INRIA (Institut National de Recherché en Informatique et en Automatique, the French National Institute for Research in Computer Science and Control) are deeply involved in staffing and housing this organization.

At first blush, a Web-oriented standards group might not seem to have much, if anything, to do with networking. But we cannot overstate how many trips we made to the Web for the networking information in this book, nor the importance of Web-based services to in-house networks (sometimes called intranets) and to the public Internet. Thus, any savvy network administrator knows how to use the Web; many savvy network administrators must also provide homes for Web servers on the network servers that they manage.

Key W3C standards include:

- *HTML:* The Hypertext Markup Language used to create most Web pages today, and XHTML

- *XML:* The Extensible Markup Language that serves as the basis for XHTML and numerous other XML-based applications

- *HTTP:* The Hypertext Transfer Protocol, which transports Web page requests from clients to servers and related responses from servers to clients

- *Accessibility guidelines:* Guidelines that explain how to make the Web equally available to all users, irrespective of visual or reading disabilities

- *CSS:* Cascading Style Sheets, which provide detailed instructions on how to present content from HTML and XML documents

- *XML-based applications:* Over 30 additional XML-based applications for everything from mathematical notation to wireless telephone access to Web data

For more information on these and a wealth of other standards, tools, and best practices, visit the W3C's Web site at *www.w3.org*.

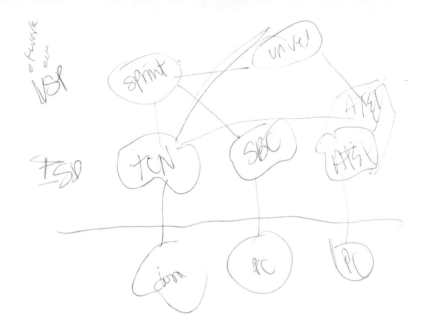

B

PLANNING AND IMPLEMENTING NETWORKS

This appendix provides a "virtual blueprint" to help you plan, install, and implement a network. Most experts divide the network-planning process into the following phases, which are also reflected in the titles of the major sections that follow:

- Assessing and justifying needs
- Creating a network plan
- Implementing the network plan
- Planning for network extensions or expansions
- Obtaining post-sales technical support and information

NEEDS ASSESSMENT AND JUSTIFICATION

Before you plan a network, you must obtain management support both in terms of resources and backing. Resources must include funding, personnel, and sufficient time to do the job; these resources can be difficult to obtain and require working within the budgetary restrictions and funding requirements of any particular organization. More intangible and therefore perhaps more difficult to assess, backing should include at least an enthusiastic endorsement from some member of an organization's executive staff, if not an outright champion for the process. In most organizations, beginning a network plan without both forms of support is pointless.

Establish the Need for a Network

After analyzing your organization's information processing and communication needs, you may realize that a network is not necessary. Especially in small organizations, the added cost and complexity of a network sometimes negate its benefits. When seeking funding—a key ingredient for any network installation—the only way to justify a network is to prove that its benefits outweigh its costs. The best way to do that is to demonstrate that the return on investment (ROI) is greater than the initial and ongoing costs of the network.

Many organizations use formal methods to measure ROI. Before you can tackle this issue, therefore, you need to investigate how your organization calculates the return on its investments. However, determining ROI fundamentally involves only two activities:

- Establish a budget for the planned network that includes all potential sources of cost. In addition to the costs of cabling, equipment, and installation, don't forget to assess costs for employee time (include costs for time spent on design, installation, configuration, and management for IS staff, as well as costs for time spent training employees), consultants, and periods of lost productivity, which often occur when systems change from an old approach to a new one.

- Assign dollar values to the benefits of the network, once it is in place. This often requires estimating productivity increases and then using that figure as a multiplier of current employee productivity to in turn estimate increases in the organization's revenue or employee output.

The good news is that the numbers seldom lie. If you can make a case that productivity benefits will repay the costs of the network, support for its planning and deployment are seldom disputed beyond some reality checks to make sure the assumptions behind the numbers are valid.

One of the best techniques to help justify a network within your organization and to help quantify its potential ROI is to document its potential uses and then try to assign each a dollar value. For most new networks, at least some of the following features apply:

- Improved communications
- Automated information sharing

- Improved information delivery

- Easier sharing of work assignments

- Improved sharing of data across multiple types of computers

- Access to legacy systems and applications (mainframes and minicomputers)

- Improved systems management

- Ability to back up all systems

- Improved security and access controls for sensitive data

- Departments or other organization units take custody of their own data resources

Be sure to examine these possibilities and consider other potential benefits when assessing the basis for your network's possible ROI. Once you obtain the necessary backing for your project, it's time to proceed to the next step—planning your network's design and deployment.

NETWORK PLAN

Planning a network involves more than simply mapping the cable layout, planning equipment purchases, and selecting the necessary software tools. Because adding a network to any organization involves changing the way people work, considering those people is especially important. Among other things, this means any network plan must include the following elements:

- Training administrators and users to work (and think) in new ways.

- Documenting the system and providing key information such as administrator accounts and passwords, and contact information for vendor and technical support

- Procedures for management and maintenance

- A transition scheme to help users switch from their former way of doing things to the networked way of doing things. Among other things, this may mean calling on extra temporary technical support during the transition.

Working with Consultants

For all but the smallest of networks, unless you're an experienced networker, it might be wise to consider enlisting the services of a qualified network consultant in planning and implementing your network. The only caveat is that consultants deliver what you ask for; the more specific and detailed your requests, the better the results.

You may be tempted to turn your network over to a consultant for design and implementation and devote yourself to other activities in the interim. However, you should schedule regular meetings and ask for explanations for each step on the way to network deployment, including at least a detailed plan, a schedule of activities, a list of purchases, and a phased implementation of the network's hardware and software components. Not only does this ensure that you understand what's happening at each step along the way, it also provides important opportunities for feedback in both directions to make sure the network that gets built meets your organization's needs.

An important step you must complete before engaging a consultant is to create an initial statement of requirements for your network and to assess your organization's information-processing and networking needs. This information helps you tell the consultant what you want and also ensures that your organization's networking needs are fully met.

Many networking consultants, or network equipment vendors, provide planning questionnaires that you complete to determine your hardware, software, installation, training, and support needs. Always inquire about such tools, and use them if they're available. You can also find pointers to planning aids on a Web page titled "County Government Sources of Information" *(www.lapeer.lib.mi.us./Tutorial/County.html)*. This page points to network planning aids developed for county governments in the state of Michigan, and includes some useful questionnaires and planning guides that are beneficial when used by private industry.

Identify and Involve Network Staff

Whenever you build a network, it likely will include the efforts of multiple individuals. Depending on your organization's structure, this may involve members of a centralized MIS group as well as MIS specialists from particular departments or other organizational units. The key to a successful network plan—and its deployment—is to identify and involve these people in the planning process as soon as possible. For larger networks, you probably need the additional help anyway. It is worthwhile to appoint a project leader who can then delegate individual planning tasks to team members as needed.

Know Your Organization

As mentioned several times, the human impact of adding a network to an organization is often the most difficult aspect to manage, despite the many hardware and software elements involved in constructing a network. It's essential to analyze and understand a network's potential impact on an organization and to do the best possible job of matching the network to the organization it must serve. This means you need to understand the following components of "organizational culture" to create a network plan that employees embrace and welcome, rather than fear.

- How well does your organization deal with change? Some organizations thrive on it; others seldom deal with it and require extra support. For change-oriented organizations, adapting to a network probably seems like an adventure; for change-resistant organizations, it's wise to plan for extra support during initial deployment phases.

- How quickly does your organization grow? Some companies plan for growth rates in excess of 100% yearly, whereas others grow at much more modest rates, if at all. It's essential that whatever type of network you deploy can accommodate and keep pace with organizational growth; otherwise, the organization may quickly perceive the network as a bottleneck rather than a boon.

- What kind of technical resources and support are available? Organizations with well-defined IT groups and support mechanisms can add networks to their mix of tools and technologies more quickly and easily than those organizations that lack such assets. Either way, access to technical resources and support must be made available.

In the final analysis, successful network deployment is more likely if you work within existing policies and procedures and fit your network to the prevailing mindset within your organization.

Start Planning

Planning for a network is like planning for any other kind of complex system. It requires that you assess your needs against available technologies and pick the solutions that best fit your needs. It also requires that you weigh these solution options against the monetary and staff resources available, so that the solution you pick fits within these all-important constraints. Such an effort can require a significant investment in time and energy and can ultimately be quite expensive. If undertaken in a vacuum, there's also no guarantee that this process can deliver the best of all possible networks.

That's why most networking experts usually start their planning efforts from a set of well-known, standard network blueprints, rather than from scratch. Drawing on the collective wisdom and experience of the networking industry makes it possible to shortcut a complete and total analysis of all the possibilities and, instead, helps you concentrate on a relatively small number of possibilities. Of course, these standard blueprints must be customized to meet any particular organization's requirements, but they can certainly accelerate the development of a network plan if used as a point of departure.

Table B-1 documents the most typical LAN configuration in use today. It works well for networks with up to 50 users; the next step up appears in the third column.

Table B-1 Typical LAN configuration

Element	Implementation	Step Up To
Topology	Switched	Switched high-speed backbone
Cable	Category 5/5E UTP	Fiber-optic for backbone
NICs	Ethernet 10/100BaseT	Ethernet 10/100BaseT for workstations, 1000BaseT for servers
Hubs	Ethernet 10/100BaseT switches	Gigabit Ethernet for servers
Resource sharing	Servers + peer-to-peer	Pure server-based
Printer sharing	Server/workstation-attached printers	Network-attached printers
Other services	Fax, e-mail, dial-in, DBMS	VPN, Groupware

This configuration is an excellent place to start planning just about any network because it addresses needs at a local level quite effectively. Thus, even extremely large networks can include this kind of configuration for local use, no matter what kind of backbone or wide-area links they must also entail. Because technology changes quickly, this recommendation may become dated sooner than you think. That's why all networking professionals should keep abreast of current technology so they can adjust these recommendations to incorporate whatever version of this configuration may make sense in coming years.

Numerous factors may cause you to adjust this basic LAN configuration and to make changes in wiring layouts, equipment, network interfaces, and planned network uses. Typically, these include the following issues:

- *Bandwidth requirements:* For real-time video, high-speed data transfers, or intensely interactive applications (like 3-D modeling or VRML), 10 Mbps Ethernet does not suffice. Be prepared to step up to 100- or 1000-Mbps Ethernet or even faster technologies as they become available.

- *Security:* For extremely sensitive data or high-security operations, fiber-optic cable may make sense because it is nearly impossible to tap without detection. Tight security also dictates pure client/server environments, with beefed-up authentication and encryption software.

- *Size/scale:* As networks grow larger and more complex, they may need more infrastructure. This can involve such things as WAN links, routers, backbones, so-called server farms, and several other bells and whistles. Be prepared for more complexity, higher-speed requirements, and more equipment as networks scale and grow to serve hundreds to thousands of users, and more.

- *Specialized software requirements:* Certain mission-critical applications require specialized hardware or networking attachments; as such systems become more prevalent, complexity and integration issues often become extremely important.

B

A Map Is a Plan, and a Plan Is a Map

As you make hardware selections, decide on cable types and ancillary equipment, you should adjust the basic network model we suggested to meet your particular circumstances, and draw a map of your network. The best way to begin constructing such a map is to obtain a set of architectural plans for the space where the network is to be laid out. Next, incorporate whatever information you can obtain about existing electrical wiring, HVAC, firewalls, and other site improvements that you must contend with when laying cable or situating equipment. If you take this approach to designing your layout and keep it up to date during installation, you create a permanent record of your network's wiring and layout. It will be an invaluable aid whenever you must troubleshoot the wiring or whenever you must extend the network to accommodate growth.

Network Questionnaire

Your instructor can furnish an electronic version of a questionnaire we prepared to help you understand your organization's needs and to pick the various network elements that can help to satisfy those needs. You must answer a sizable battery of questions on general topics, including:

- Network type (peer-to-peer, client/server, or combination)
- Network technology (size, speed, and scale requirements)
- Network cabling
- Network interfaces
- Network protocols
- Printer requirements
- E-mail requirements
- Data and network security requirements
- Network performance requirements
- Compatibility requirements

The questionnaire gives you the opportunity to weigh the answers to over 100 questions. Your answers should help you make most of the hard decisions about a network. Not coincidentally, these answers should also lead you through the selection process for the hardware and software necessary to construct a viable network for your organization.

IMPLEMENTATION PLAN

When you decide what network components go where, and how to run the cable, it's time to get ready to put your plans to work. In the process of building your network map, you should have mapped your wiring layout and the location of your equipment.

You can now address the other factors involved in delivering a working network to your colleagues and co-workers:

- Planning the order of installation and the steps required to connect users to the network

- Observing the daily routine in the workplace to figure out how to minimize the disruptions that a network installation can cause

- Considering the advantages and disadvantages of installing the network over a three-day weekend

- Testing along the way to make sure all parts work correctly

- Arranging a fallback plan, should any part of the network installation fail or be subject to delay

- Learning how to locate and arrange for technical support in a crisis

- Preparing for things to go wrong (for example, failed installations, incompatibilities, and user errors)

No matter how small or simple a network installation may appear, the chances of encountering obstacles on the path to completion are better than 50%, especially for first-timers. Even experienced networking professionals take time to plan carefully, simply because it forces them to consider things thoroughly before the real work starts. An installation plan provides a vital road map through the process, and if you're about to tackle the great unknown, a map can be invaluable.

Good Plans Produce the Best Results

A well-run network is staged like a museum or a theme park in that the users only notice the network's capabilities and services; they don't notice all the underpinnings that make it work. Staging means deciding what must occur for the network to be installed and then determining the order in which events must occur to install the network most efficiently.

Staging is as important to a successful network installation as the initial process of selection that produced the necessary list of elements, items, and tasks required to create the network. As you become more familiar with networking, you quickly learn to appreciate the benefits of obscurity—primarily because networks tend to be noticed most when they're not working properly! Good staging helps to keep your efforts unobtrusive and well-coordinated so you needn't attract any more notoriety than absolutely necessary.

A normal order of implementation for installing a network usually proceeds as follows:

1. Lay out the entire network on paper, including cabling, network equipment, servers, connections, and whatever else you need to put it all together. You usually record this information on a network map.

2. Consult building plans, electrical plans, and other wiring plans (for example, telephone, cable TV, and so forth) to check the planned layout.

B

3. Perform a site inspection to double-check these plans and to investigate traditional problem areas, such as elevator shafts, firewalls, and potential sources of interference.

4. Revise the network layout to reflect what you learned during the inspection process.

5. Calculate cable run lengths, and determine overall wiring requirements, including the exact types of cable to be used. You must check these against applicable building codes and revise if necessary. Then determine the type and number of spools, establish connector types and counts, and establish and order any special needs for ancillary equipment (for example, punchdown blocks for TP wiring).

6. Specify equipment needs in detail, including network gear such as switches, hubs, and routers and network servers. Configuration requirements are particularly important for servers, which can contain several internal and external peripherals and add-ons.

7. Draft a bid list, or request for proposal (RFP). Such documents specify everything you documented to this point to give vendors a chance to compete for your business. Be sure to ask for installation charges if you seek a third party to do this work or to issue a separate bid request or RFP for this aspect of the installation, if necessary.

8. Do-it-yourselfers should order any special-purpose tools they might need at this point. This could include cable construction tools and rental or purchase of test equipment to check newly installed cabling.

9. Evaluate responses to the bid lists or RFPs—and choose one or more vendors to provide the equipment and perhaps undertake the installation work as well.

10. Do-it-yourselfers must construct an installation plan for wiring that includes the order of installation of cables and equipment and establish labeling conventions for cables (and purchase necessary labels or tags).

11. Install, label, test, and measure wiring or cables. (Update your network map.)

12. Install and test equipment. (Update your network map.)

13. Test the network as individual cable segments and ancillary equipment come online. This is also the point to install and test client software, so users can access the network. Until this point, you have tested only individual components; this stage represents the first test of the network's ability to permit multiple devices to communicate.

14. Advertise the network to its users, and begin training.

15. The network can finally be regularly used.

As the composition of this list of activities indicates, you must do a great deal of preparatory work before any of the real installation work begins. A great deal more effort is then necessary before anything that resembles a network becomes available to the users. The installation plan is nothing more than a document that records all the steps just outlined, with all the essential details recorded. Experience indicates that the better the plan, the higher the odds of a successful installation.

Working Around the Users

No matter how good an installation plan you create, it leads to nothing but trouble unless you also grasp the fundamental necessity of working around your users. You earn only ill will if you insist on crawling in the ceiling over their desks or try to install conduit or equipment brackets when they're trying to do their jobs.

This leads to a sad but necessary fact of life for network administrators: because your job is to help other people do their jobs, you often find yourself working when nobody else is around. Nevertheless, you still must be available while they work because you are an important link in the chain to resolution of any network problems.

The best way to work around colleagues and co-workers is to work around their schedules, which means that you should schedule the most disruptive activities for evenings or weekends, when other workers are far less likely to be present and bothered by what's happening. If you hire a third-party installation crew, this means paying overtime and pleading for special treatment. If you can't afford this, or the vendor can't oblige your request for off-hours service, schedule installation during a company holiday, an off-site meeting, or at a slow time of the year (for example, between Christmas and New Year's) to minimize the impact on employee productivity.

A bad experience during installation can sour employees on the network before they ever have a chance to use it. If you schedule your activities so they disrupt things as little as possible, you're far less likely to create a bad impression before the network becomes a part of the workaday world. This, too, improves the chances of a successful network deployment.

Importance of Fallbacks

No matter how carefully you plan an installation and how thoroughly and carefully you perform the work, it's always possible that something can go wrong during the installation process. An incorrect measurement, an unforeseen obstacle, late delivery of critical materials, or a key technician's illness can impose serious delays.

How does this conventional wisdom apply to network installation? Here are some ways you can put this uncertainty to work for you:

- Order 20% more materials than you need for installation, in case something is defective or to compensate for minor mistakes when estimating quantity. It's almost always better to have too much and not need it than not to have enough to complete the job. This is especially important if you plan to build your own cables.

B

- Make sure your supplier has additional stock on hand or can obtain additional stock on short notice. This should cover you if you discover serious material defects or if your estimates are seriously short.

- Test all equipment as it's unpacked from the box. If it doesn't appear to work, don't try to use it; call the vendor and arrange for an immediate replacement. If you have to return equipment by mail or overnight service, ask the vendor for a return merchandise authorization (RMA) number or a return code. Also, ask the vendor to "cross-ship" the replacement, which means they ship the replacement the same day you ship the defective part. Other alternatives are to purchase a pool of spares or to ask your vendor to stock spares for you, should any problems occur with the delivered units. The larger your order, the more helpful and supportive your vendor should be.

- Set up a test installation of the network in a test lab, or a single room, to test network software for servers and clients. (You should have one of each type of client and server you plan to use on the production network.) Build short cables to hook everything together, and then use this environment to became familiar with all the software and hardware you'll use on the production network.

- Build an "installation notebook" as you work with cables, equipment, and software. Record all the details and workarounds you discover as you learn how to make this collection of components work, especially whatever information the installation guides do not include. When you repeat a task, use the notebook to help you shortcut the installation process as much as possible.

If you're ready to deal with shortages, failures, or missing elements, you also are prepared to solve most installation problems you might encounter.

Access to Emergency Expertise

Occasionally, you may find yourself completely stumped by something that crops up during installation. That's when it's a good idea to bring in a professional. If you're determined to build your own cables, do yourself a favor, and first locate a cable installer in the Yellow Pages. Call the installer to learn their hours and rates before you begin; ask how to reach a technician in an emergency. If things get out of control, you have some place to turn for help.

The same principle holds true for network equipment and software installation. Whether you work with your local user group, a network reseller, or a networking consultant, establish a contact list of experienced networkers in your vicinity. You can get free advice before you start, no matter who your colleagues are. In fact, it's usually worth the money to pay a consultant to review your network installation plan and your network map before you start installing. He or she may be able to point out some potential problems you overlooked or even find some outright mistakes. The same expert who can bail you out of a jam charges a lot less to steer you clear of it. Regardless, make sure you have a list of names and numbers of potential sources of expert assistance before you install anything yourself.

Transitioning Users onto the Network

Planning a network deployment also means planning to bring the users on board and to equip them with the knowledge and skills they need to take advantage of the network's capabilities. When planning a transition, your contact with users should include one or more of the following elements:

- *Orientation sessions:* Show the users what they have and how to use it, and answer any questions that come up.

- *Training sessions:* Users often require detailed coverage of new software, tools, and techniques. You may want to schedule some outright classroom training, with equipment, exercises, and opportunities to interact with instructors already expert in what the employees must learn.

- *Job aids:* Quick reference cards, manuals, keyboard shortcuts, and anything else you can give employees to help them learn and make them more productive usually is greatly appreciated. Sanity-check any materials on a group of power users before inflicting them on the general population; share only worthwhile materials with the entire user base.

- *Technical support information:* Even when orientation and training ends (and especially if it's minimal or not offered), users need access to sources of help and information. Make sure each user receives a list of Web pages, online documents, and phone numbers for technical support.

The better you prepare your users to deal with the networked environment, the less work you will have. A little knowledge may be a dangerous thing for all parties, so try to make sure to equip the users with the right amount of knowledge to handle their most routine tasks and with the resources to extend their knowledge bases as their needs and interest levels dictate.

PLANNING FOR NETWORK EXTENSIONS OR EXPANSIONS

To some degree, expanding a network beyond purely local confines means incorporating WAN technologies and WAN links. To that end, we defined a set of extension questionnaires that you can complete to assess your needs in this area. The set is available in electronic form from your instructor, and it can help you deal with issues like the following. (Feel free to skip those parts of the questionnaire that do not apply to your situation.)

- Dial-in/dial-out connectivity

- Needs assessment for ancillary network equipment (repeaters, bridges, routers, gateways, and so forth)

- WAN link requirements, bandwidth assessment, and link selection

The questionnaires should help you to determine what kinds and levels of services you need and to select the corresponding equipment or service arrangements to fulfill them. Remember to research and incorporate cost information, as well as technical requirements—especially for higher-bandwidth WAN services. Costs can rise out of sight faster than you might believe.

OBTAINING POST-SALES SUPPORT AND INFORMATION

To get help with your network or the software that runs on it, you must take the right steps. Getting whatever support vendors supply shouldn't be too difficult, provided you know how to ask for and get the answers you need.

Here, we explain how best to interact with technical support organizations. You can work most effectively with these groups if you prepare to meet their needs and know how to work with them so they can answer your questions. It also helps if you understand what kind of, and how much, help you can expect from vendor technical support groups.

Build a List and Check It Twice!

If you followed the outlined recommendations, you maintained a complete list of network equipment and configuration information during network construction and maintenance. You also should have an up-to-date map that indicates the location of cables and networking components. It's important to have a complete picture of what's on your network, no matter how you get it. You can compile a list of your network assets using any of a variety of network inventory packages, but paper and pencil also work. Compiling a network inventory is boring and repetitive, but important. Without a network inventory, you might find yourself in a situation similar to trying to collect insurance after your house burns down, with no list of what was inside.

Record each of the NICs on your LAN, what type of file server(s) you use, information about each workstation, and which applications each user runs. The following list names the kinds of equipment and software to inventory:

- Cable plant (type, length, location, end-labels)
- Disk storage
- File servers
- Software running on each workstation
- Tape-backup units
- Workstations

Be Familiar with the Assets Under Your Control

You must record each file server's vital statistics: how much RAM, how much disk space, the type of NICs and disk controllers, and the kind of display it uses. Save the information so you can find it when you need it. Next, record the same kind of information for each workstation on the LAN. While you're at it, add to the list the contents of the workstation's configuration files.

After you finish these lists, you should document the software configuration of the LAN. You should record your server's services configuration and build an Emergency Repair Disk (ERD) for your Windows NT Server machines or capture necessary repair and configuration information for Windows 2000, NetWare, or Linux servers. List each of the following items:

- User names on the LAN and their network addresses

- Groups on the LAN

- File and directory attributes and rights for each user and group

- Application structure

- Server directory structure

- Drive assignments for workstations

When you encounter a problem, write down what happened before the problem appeared. List any changes made to files or hardware immediately before the problem occurred, and record any error messages that appear. Recount what application was running or what task was being performed when the problem occurred. When you call a technical support line, you need to provide all this information, so you might as well have it ready.

Ready for Action

Once you record this information, when something goes wrong, you are fully prepared to work with any vendor's technical support staff. When you place a call, have your information ready. Don't expect immediate gratification; instead, prepare for any of these possible outcomes:

- You sit on hold, waiting for what seems like forever for a response. When you do get through, you can only leave voice mail and hope that someone calls back before the end of the year.

- You are told that it is an *operator error,* a term technical support people use when someone makes a mistake. However, the term also seems to come up when they don't want to deal with a question, or when they don't know the answer.

- You may be told "no one in anyone's lifetime has ever done anything this dumb." Even if someone is a pioneer in new realms of the unlikely, the technical support person should still help you.

- The person you contact may not have the answers but will have someone else who can solve the problem get back to you.

- A polite and knowledgeable person helps you solve the problem.

Before you call, gather your information. Better yet, get close to the PC or network device experiencing problems, so that you can step the tech support person through whatever error messages show up (for example, when trying to duplicate the problem).

Escalation

If it seems your technical support representative doesn't want to help you, take the same steps you follow whenever you contest a bill. Ask for a supervisor (in tech support terms, this is called escalating a call). After all, you paid for the product and you deserve help—especially if, as is so often the case with technical support these days, you're also paying extra for the help you're not getting.

The same rule applies to people who don't call back in a reasonable amount of time—one full working day after a call is as long as you should wait. Call again; leave a message. Record the day and time of each technical support call. Record how long it takes for a callback; keep good records. This is another time documentation comes in handy.

Some vendors offer technical support 24 hours a day, seven days a week. When you buy products, find out about the vendor's technical support line. It may be worth paying more initially for access to good support later. Some vendors charge extra for access to telephone support (and may even have a variety of yearly contract options); the more important the network component, the more willing you and your organization should be to pay for such support.

Twenty-four-hour support is critical for network hardware. No reasonable network administrator takes down a network during normal working hours to insert a new NIC in the server. That's why it's important that support be available when you're supposed to be working on your systems—during non-peak working hours—so that such things don't interrupt your users.

C

NETWORK TROUBLESHOOTING GUIDE

This appendix introduces basic questions that you can use to approach a large selection of network problems. Guidelines for troubleshooting specific areas of networking technology also are included.

GENERAL QUESTIONS

When it comes to troubleshooting, the initial question you should ask is, "Has this piece of equipment or procedure ever worked correctly before?" If, in fact, it did work once, your next question should be, "Since then, what has changed?"

The following is a list of useful questions:

- Was only one user affected, or were many users affected?
- Were users affected randomly or all at once?
- Is only one computer down, or is the whole network down?
- Does this problem happen all the time, or does it only happen during specific times?
- Does this problem affect only one application, more than one, or all applications?
- Does this problem resemble any past problems?
- Have you added any users to the network?
- Have you added any new equipment to the network?
- Did you install a new application program just before the problems occurred?
- Have you moved any equipment recently?
- Are any vendor products involved in this problem? If yes, who are the vendors?
- Does this problem occur among components such as disk drives, hubs, application software, cards, or network operating software?
- Has anyone else attempted to remedy this problem?
- Can the computer having the problem function as a standalone computer if it is not functioning on the network?
- If the computer cannot function on the network, have you checked the computer's network adapter card? Is it working?
- Is the amount of traffic on the network normal?

CABLING PROBLEMS

If you suspect a problem with cabling, check the following items:

- Missing or loose connections
- Frayed or broken sections

- Correct length

- Correct resistance (ohms)

- Network adapter card specifications

- Crimped or bent cables

- Location of the cable routing near a transformer, large electric motor, or air conditioner

- Correct termination on bus topologies

PROBLEMS WITH ADAPTER CARDS

Here are some things to check in relation to adapter cards (NICs):

- Do the settings of your adapter card(s) match the network operating system software settings?

- Are there any I/O address conflicts?

- Are there any interrupt conflicts?

- Are there any memory conflicts?

- Are you using the right interface (AUI, RJ-45, or BNC)?

- Is the network speed setting correct?

- Are you using the right kind of network card for the network (Ethernet card in a token ring network)?

- Are there any setting conflicts if you have more than one network adapter card in a computer?

- Are the type and signaling speed correctly set?

DRIVER PROBLEMS

Check the following to isolate driver problems:

- How old is the equipment?

- Have any changes been made to the equipment since it was working properly?

- Has anyone moved any hardware?

- Has software been installed recently?

- Are old drivers being used with the new equipment?

PROBLEMS WITH NETWORK OPERATIONS

Here is a checklist to follow for network operations problems.

1. Inspect the hardware in your server and make sure that:

   ■ It is on the Microsoft Hardware Compatibility List (HCL), or it appears in a similar NetWare or Linux compatibility list (as appropriate).

   ■ It has the correct, most current drivers installed.

   ■ It contains sufficient memory for the network operations you currently perform.

   ■ It has adequate hard drive space for the amount of information you store on it.

   ■ It has plenty of processing power to support your network.

2. Check all your network bindings to make sure that they are correct. Also make sure the most-used bindings are listed first.

3. Double-check your client computers to verify they have the right client software (redirectors) installed.

4. Ensure that your frame types match—that is, the Ethernet frame type of the computer being added to the network must be the same as the frame type used by existing computers on the network.

5. Check that the protocol installed matches the protocol already in use on the network.

PROBLEMS WITH NETWORK PRINTING AND FAX SERVICES

Check the following if there is a problem with network printing or faxing:

■ Is the shared fax's or printer's power on?

■ Is the selected shared printer or fax machine the correct one for the client computer's driver?

■ Are the permissions correct for the shared printer or fax being used by the users and printer/fax managers?

■ Are the cables used by the shared printer or fax in good condition and properly connected?

PROBLEMS WITH NETWORK APPLICATIONS

Check the following for problems with network applications:

- Is the configuration of all the users' scheduling programs and e-mail appropriate?

- Are all of the messaging gateways correctly configured and working properly?

PROBLEMS IN A MULTIVENDOR ENVIRONMENT

Answer the following questions to isolate problems with products from multiple vendors in a single networking environment:

- Have redirectors for every type of server operating system needed by the client computer been configured?

- Are all of the shells or redirectors configured correctly and in working order?

- Are the network services needed by clients configured correctly and working on the servers?

- Are the gateway computers that permit access between environments properly configured and working?

PROBLEMS WITH CLIENT/SERVER COMPUTING

Check the following for problems with clients or servers in a client/server relationship:

- Is the client front end properly configured and working?

- Is the server software properly configured and working?

- Is the network application doing what it is supposed to?

- Does the server running the particular network application have enough RAM, space on its shared disk, and processing power?

- Have the users received proper training in the use of the network application, and are they using the correct methods to get the most out of the application?

Problems with Network Accounts

Here are some things to check if the user cannot log on using a certain account:

- Is the person entering the correct user name?
- Does the correct location of the user account appear in the From box?
- Is the user typing the correct password? Remember that passwords are case sensitive.
- Has the user account been disabled?

Problems with Data Security

Use the following checklist if you suspect problems with data security:

1. If a user can access a resource that should be unavailable or cannot access a resource that should be available, check the following:
   - Does the particular user have the correct rights to the resource?
   - Does the user belong to a group that has the correct access to the resource?
   - Do any trustee assignments to the resource conflict (that is, check share-level permissions versus user-level permissions)?
2. Check if the user belongs to any group assigned the No Access permission.
3. If the user can access previously secured data, or there is a problem with data theft, alteration, or contamination, check the following:
   - Who has access to the server if it is in a locked room?
   - Are any computers being left on, logged on, and then left unattended?
   - Are any passwords written on paper and left in obvious places, such as on the monitor, in a desk drawer, or under the keyboard?
   - Are any users using obvious passwords such as names of children, pets, or spouses?
   - Are any users using the same password with a revision number (that is, Dawn1, Dawn2, Dawn3, and so on)?
   - Do any users have a regular logon name equivalent to a super-user (administrator)?
   - Are any users storing confidential data on their local hard drives?
   - Do any users have their operating system configured to log them on automatically, bypassing the user name and password process?

PROBLEMS WITH LARGE NETWORK COMMUNICATIONS

To start, you troubleshoot a WAN in the same way you do a LAN. However, some considerations are specific to WANs. These types of problems usually require the assistance of vendors or service providers. Here is a set of questions relevant to WAN troubleshooting:

1. Did any vendor replace, add, or remove anything from the WAN?

2. Is the power to the following components turned on, and are the components themselves turned on?

   - Bridge
   - Router
   - Repeater
   - Gateway
   - Modem
   - CSU/DSU

3. For the same components, check the following:

   - Are all cables properly connected and in good condition?
   - Is the component compatible with the communications medium and the communications device at the other end of the link?
   - Is the software properly configured, and does it match the configuration of the connected communications equipment?

NETWORK TROUBLESHOOTING TOOLS

The information you gather about a network problem frequently leads you to a solution, but this is not always the case. There are many times when the information gathered from users or from your own inspections leads you to another, more-serious level of troubleshooting.

This appendix section discusses some popular troubleshooting tools. Some are available free within most operating systems; others must be built into your networking budget.

Ping and Trace Route

Available in all operating systems that support TCP/IP, the Ping and Trace Route utilities are among the most commonly used troubleshooting tools. Ping can be used to test simple connectivity between two hosts, and it can be used to verify correct TCP/IP configuration on a newly installed host.

Note that the Ping utility can also be used to do performance and stress testing on your network. Because the utility displays statistics on the number of packets sent and received as well as the round trip time for the ping echo and ping reply, this utility can be used for a simple check on the responsiveness of a host or network.

Using the available options, you can stress test your network by creating significant amounts of traffic. For instance, you can instruct the utility to send large numbers of packets of varying sizes, thereby testing your network under differing conditions. For a list of possible Ping options in Windows, type ping -? from a command prompt.

Trace Route has similarities to Ping in that you can test connectivity from host to host. Note that Trace Route provides a road map of sorts, showing the user what path the packet takes from source to destination.

Trace Route is useful only in an internetwork that includes routers because the purpose of Trace Route is to display the address of each router a packet encounters from the source to the destination host. In addition to the router IP address, Trace Route will also display the amount of time it took each router to respond and the hostname of the router, if available.

Using Trace Route, an administrator can determine which path packets take throughout the internetwork, as well as potential bottlenecks between the source and the destination. To use Trace Route and view the available options in a Windows environment, type tracert -? from a command prompt.

Cable Testers

For ferreting out cable problems, there is no substitute for a good cable tester. The most basic of cable analyzers simply check the wiremap of the cable termination, verifying that each wire in a twisted-pair cable is connected to the appropriate pin at both ends. This type of tester is inexpensive, typically less than $50.

Intermediate cable testers check for wiremap, length, shorts, and split pairs. An intermediate tester runs from $200 to over $800.

To certify a cable for operation at a particular performance level such as Category 5 or Category 5E, a cable analyzer is required. Cable analyzers check for problems such as excessive crosstalk, attenuation, and noise. These testers inject a signal at one end of the cable and read the results at the other end, comparing the signal read to the signal injected. A tester capable of performing these types of performance tests is costly, ranging from around $2000 to $5000 and more.

Which kind of tester do you need? To check for correct plug installation on a patch cable, a basic tester is usually sufficient. For quick checks on the accuracy of a cable run termination, an intermediate tester is probably required. However, if you want to certify a cable plant for a particular performance level and you want no argument as to whether the cable is working correctly, you need a cable analyzer. If you were running 10Mbps Ethernet today but wanted the cable to handle Gigabit Ethernet down the road, there is no question that each cable should be tested with a cable analyzer capable of testing for Gigabit performance.

Network Monitors

Although the network monitor available with Windows 2000, Windows XP, and Windows NT is a capable program, it is limited to monitoring data coming from and going to the computer on which it is installed. To get an accurate picture of what is happening on your network, you need a monitor that can keep statistics on all packets on all of your network segments. This type of comprehensive monitoring usually involves two software components: a console that allows you to configure and display monitoring information and an agent that you install on various network segments to capture data that is sent to the console program. These agents may be SNMP or RMON agents or proprietary. The most common and most flexible agents are based upon the SNMP and RMON standards.

Network monitors can also come in the form of a hardware device that you plug directly into the network. This type of device has an advantage over software monitors because they are specifically designed to capture and monitor network traffic; plus, because they are portable, they can be taken to the network or part of the network that requires monitoring.

Network monitors typically gather and display statistics on bandwidth utilization, error rates, the number and types of protocols being used, broadcast rates, and the top sending and receiving stations. Some monitors will also inform you of configuration errors such as duplicate IP addresses. Some monitors will also periodically query your network to verify that critical network devices are up and running. You can often set up the monitor to send a message when a device is unresponsive or when traffic patterns exceed configured thresholds. Whatever type of monitor you use, it is important to monitor the network during times when the network is in good working order (referred to as a baseline) so that when there is a problem, you have something to which to compare results.

Protocol Analyzers

A protocol analyzer takes network monitoring one step further. While network monitors capture data for the purpose of displaying statistics, protocol analyzers capture live data and display individual frames and packets. The frames are decoded in a user-friendly fashion displaying all of the layer headers so that you can easily see the data in the Data Link, Network, Transport, and Application layers.

Protocol analysis requires considerable expertise on the part of the network administrator. For example, if the network administrator is trying to debug a login problem, he or she must know what a working login looks like so that he or she can see what is different in a problematic login.

A network administrator typically does not use a protocol analyzer every day or even every week, but when the problem calls for one, there is no substitute. Because protocol analyzers require considerable expertise, those individuals who can use one well are sought-after network technicians. To try your hand at protocol analysis, you can download a free protocol analyzer called Ethereal at *www.ethereal.com*.

D

NETWORKING RESOURCES, ONLINE AND OFFLINE

Numerous resources are available to help you find information you need to implement a network successfully. This appendix identifies many valuable resources in the networking arena. In addition to the resources listed here, you can locate good networking information on the Internet through one of the many search engines available by typing keywords that describe the topic about which you need additional information. You also can visit one or more of the Web sites mentioned in the "Online/Electronic Materials" section later in this appendix.

PRINTED MATERIAL

Feibel, Werner: *Encyclopedia of Networking (Network Press)*. Sybex Books, Alameda, CA, 2000. ISBN: 0-7821-2255-8.

Green, James Harry: *The Irwin Handbook of Telecommunications*, 4th edition. McGraw-Hill, Englewood Cliffs, NJ, 2000. ISBN 0-07-135554-5.

Ibe, Oliver Chukwudi: *Essentials of ATM Networks and Services*. Addison-Wesley, Reading, MA, 1997. ISBN 0-201-18461-3.

McClure, Stuart, Joel Scambray, and George Kurtz: *Hacking Exposed: Network Security Secrets & Solutions, Third Edition*. Osborne/McGraw-Hill, Berkeley, CA, 2001. ISBN 0072193816.

Palmer, Michael: *MCSE Guide to Microsoft Windows 2000 Server*. Course Technology, Boston, MA, 2000. ISBN 0-619-01517-9.

Palmer, Michael: *MCSE Guide to Microsoft Windows NT Server 4.0*. Course Technology, Boston, MA, 1998. ISBN 0-7600-5875-X.

Palmer, Michael, Bruce Sinclair: *Guide to Designing and Implementing Local and Wide Area Networks, Second Edition*. Course Technology, Boston, MA, 2002. ISBN 0-7600-1093-5.

Sheldon, Sheldon: *McGraw-Hill's Encyclopedia of Networking and Telecommunications*. McGraw-Hill, Englewood Cliffs, NJ, 2001. ISBN: 0072120053.

Sheldon, Tom: *LAN Times Encyclopedia of Networking*, second edition. Osborne/McGraw-Hill, Berkeley, CA, 2001. ISBN 0-07-212005-3.

Tittel, Ed, Michael Stewart: *MCSE Guide to Microsoft Windows 2000 Professional*. Course Technology, Boston, MA, 2000. ISBN 0-619-01513-6.

Wells, Nick: *Guide to Linux Installation and Administration*. Course Technology, Boston, MA, 2000. ISBN 0-619-00097-X.

Tomsho, Greg: *Guide to Network Support and Troubleshooting*. Course Technology, Boston, MA, 2002. ISBN 0-619-03551-X.

ONLINE/ELECTRONIC MATERIALS

Acronym Finder
www.acronymfinder.com

ATM Forum
www.atmforum.com

Dan Kegel's repository of ISDN pointers and information
www.alumni.caltech.edu/~dank/isdn/

DSL Life: The consumer's guide to xDSL technology
www.dsllife.com

FDDI Consortium
www.iol.unh.edu/training/fddi/htmls/index.html

The Gigabit Ethernet Alliance Home Page: Everything you wanted to know about gigabit Ethernet and more
www.10gea.org/

How Stuff Works: A great Web site to find out how just about anything works, from networks to yo-yos
www.howstuffworks.com

IEEE Local and Metropolitan Area Network Standards: the place to find information regarding all of the IEEE networking standards, as well as purchase the standards. A PDF format version of the 802 standard is available for free download.
http://standards.ieee.org/catalog/olis/lanman.html

Internet Access Tutorial
www.iec.org/tutorials/int_acc/

Overview of Cable Modem Technology and Services
www.cabledatacomnews.com/cmic/cmic1.html

Protocols.com: Great reference for reviewing packet structure and header fields of all networking protocols
www.protocols.com

TechFest Networking tutorials
www.techfest.com

TechNet online version (also available monthly on CD from Microsoft by subscription, starting at $299.95 per year)
www.microsoft.com/technet

TechWeb Online Encyclopedia (good definitions, great coverage)
www.techweb.com/encyclopedia

Webopedia (great definitions plus pointers to more detailed resources)
www.webopedia.com

Wi-Fi News: A Web site dedicated to the 802.11b wireless networking standard.
http://80211b.weblogger.com/about

Glossary

10Base2 — A designation for 802.3 Ethernet thin coaxial cable (also called thinnet, thinwire, or cheapernet). The 10 indicates bandwidth of 10 Mbps, the Base indicates it's a baseband transmission technology, and the 2 indicates a maximum segment length of 185 meters for this cable type.

10Base5 — A designation for 802.3 Ethernet thick coaxial cable (also called thicknet or thickwire). The 10 indicates bandwidth of 10 Mbps, the Base indicates it's a baseband transmission technology, and the 5 indicates a maximum segment length of 500 meters for this cable type.

10BaseT — A designation for 802.3 Ethernet twisted-pair cable. The 10 indicates bandwidth of 10 Mbps, the Base indicates it's a baseband transmission technology, and the T indicates that the medium is twisted-pair. (Maximum segment length is around 100 meters, or 328 feet, but the precise measurement depends on the manufacturer's testing results for the particular cable.)

5-4-3 rule — Applies to Ethernet running over coaxial cable. The rule states that a network can have a maximum of five cable segments with four repeaters, with three of those segments being populated. It is an "end-to-end" rule, which means that it governs the number of segments, devices, and so forth between any two nodes on a network. It is not a "total population" rule: you can have more than five cable segments, four repeaters, and three populated segments on an Ethernet network, but no more than those numbers between any two possible senders and receivers on that network.

802.1 — The IEEE specification within Project 802 for the OSI reference model and for internetworking and routing behavior at the Data Link layer (where logical addresses must be translated into their physical counterparts, and vice versa).

802.2 — The IEEE specification within Project 802 for the Logical Link Control (LLC) sublayer within the Data Link layer of the OSI reference model.

802.3 — The IEEE specification within Project 802 for Collision Sense Multiple Access/Collision Detection (CSMA/CD) networks. Ethernet users can attempt to access the medium any time it's perceived as "quiet," but they must back off and try to transmit again if they detect any collisions once transmission begins. More commonly called Ethernet.

802.4 — The IEEE specification within Project 802 for token bus LANs, which use a straight-line bus topology for the networking medium, yet circulate a token to control access to the medium.

802.5 — The IEEE specification within Project 802 for token ring LANs, which map a circulating ring structure onto a physical star and circulate a token to control access to the medium.

802.6 — The IEEE specification within Project 802 for metropolitan area networks (MANs).

802.7 — The IEEE specification within Project 802 for the Broadband Technical Advisory Group's findings and recommendations for broadband networking technologies, media, interfaces, and equipment.

802.8 — The IEEE specification within Project 802 for the Fiber-Optic Technical Advisory Group's findings and recommendations for fiber-optic networking technologies, media, interfaces, and equipment.

802.9 — The IEEE specification within Project 802 that addresses hybrid networks, which combine voice and data traffic within the same networking environment.

802.10 — The IEEE specification within Project 802 for network security.

802.11 Wireless Networking Standard — An IEEE standard for wireless networking. A version of the 802.11 standard appeared late in 1997.

802.12 — The IEEE specification within Project 802 for high-speed networks, including Demand Priority and 100VG-AnyLAN technologies.

802.13 — This standard number was never used.

802.14 — This defunct working group was involved in specifying data transports over cable TV.

802.15 — Covers the emerging standards for wireless personal area networks (PANs).

802.16 — Covers wireless metropolitan area networks (MAN).

802.17 — Resilient Packet Ring; covers emerging standards for very high-speed, ring-based LANs and MANs.

802.18 — Wireless Advisory Group; a technical advisory group to monitor radio-based, wireless standards.

Accelerated Graphics Port (AGP) — A special-purpose bus used solely to interconnect PCs with a graphics adapter and one or more display devices. AGP is a high-speed, 64-bit-wide bus capable of bandwidth from 0.25 to 1.0 Gbps.

access control — A method to impose controls that permit or deny users access to network resources, usually based on a user's account or some group to which the user belongs.

access point device — The device that bridges wireless networking components and a wired network. It forwards traffic from the wired side to the wireless side and from the wireless side to the wired side as needed.

account — The collection of information known about a user, including an account name, an associated password, and a set of access permissions for network resources.

account lockout — The process of automatically disabling a user account based on certain criteria (for example, too many failed logon attempts).

account name — A string of letters, numbers, or other characters that identifies a particular user's account on a network.

Active Directory — The directory service environment for Microsoft Windows 2000 servers. Active Directory includes enough information about users, groups, organizational units, and other kinds of management domains and administrative information about a network to represent a complete digital model of the network.

active hub — A network device that regenerates received signals and sends them along the network.

active monitor — A computer in a token ring network responsible for guaranteeing the network's status.

active topology — A network topology in which the computers themselves are responsible for sending the data along the network.

adapter slot — The sockets built into a PC motherboard that are designed to seat adapter cards.

address registries — Any of a number of IP address registry organizations worldwide. (Some are governmental, especially outside the United States and Europe; many are private, for-profit companies.) These organizations dole out IP addresses, manage IP address ranges, and handle DNS domain name registration.

Address Resolution Protocol (ARP) — A protocol in the TCP/IP suite used to associate logical addresses to physical addresses.

American National Standards Institute (ANSI) — The U.S. representative in the International Standardization Organization (ISO), a worldwide standards-making body. ANSI creates and publishes standards for networking, communications, and programming languages.

American Wire Gauge (AWG) — A numeric classification and naming scheme for copper wiring: the higher the gauge, the narrower the diameter of the wiring.

amplifier — A hardware device that increases the power of electrical signals to maintain their original strength when transmitted across a large network.

analog — The method of signal transmission used on broadband networks. Creating analog waveforms from computer-based digital data requires a special device called a digital-to-analog (d-to-a) converter; reversing the conversion requires another device called an analog-to-digital (a-to-d) converter. Broadband networking equipment must include both kinds of devices to work.

antenna — A tuned electromagnetic device that can send and receive broadcast signals at particular frequencies. In wireless networking devices, an antenna is an important part of the devices' sending and receiving circuitry.

AppleTalk — The protocol suite/stack native to the Macintosh operating system.

AppleTalk File Protocol (AFP) — Apple's remote file-management protocol.

AppleTalk Transaction Protocol (ATP) — AppleTalk's session protocol.

Application layer — Layer 7 in the OSI reference model. The Application layer provides interfaces to permit applications to request and receive network services.

application protocol — A type of protocol that works in the upper layers of the OSI model to provide application-to-application interaction.

application server — A specialized network server whose job is to provide access to a client/server application, and, sometimes, the data that belongs to that application as well.

ARCnet (attached resource computing network) — A 2.5 Mbps LAN technology created by DataPoint Corporation in the early 1980s. ARCnet uses token-based networking technology and runs over several kinds of coaxial cable, twisted-pair, and fiber-optic cable.

ARCnet Plus — The successor to ARCnet. It supports transmission up to 20 Mbps.

asymmetric communication — Communication in which data travels in the download direction at a speed different than the upload direction.

Asymmetric Digital Subscriber Line (ADSL) — A digital telecommunications technology that uses different speeds for downloading and uploading data.

asynchronous — A communication method that sends data in a stream with start and stop bits indicating where data begins and ends.

Asynchronous Transfer Mode (ATM) — A WAN technology that uses fiber-optic media to support up to 622-Mbps transmission rates. ATM uses no error checking and has a 53-byte, fixed-length cell.

Attached Resource Computer Network (ARCnet) — An inexpensive and flexible network architecture created by Datapoint Corporation in 1977. It uses the token-passing channel access method.

attachment unit interface (AUI) — A standard Ethernet connector, also called a DIX connector.

attenuation — The degradation or distortion of an electronic signal as it travels from its origin.

auditing — Recording selected events or actions for later review. Audits can help establish patterns and note changes in those patterns that might signal trouble.

back end — A server in a client/server networking environment.

backbone — A single cable segment used in a bus topology to connect computers in a straight line.

bandwidth — The range of frequencies that a communications medium can carry. For baseband networking media, the bandwidth also indicates the theoretical maximum amount of data that the medium can transfer. For broadband networking media, the bandwidth is measured by the variations that any single carrier frequency can carry, minus the analog-to-digital conversion overhead.

barrel connector — Used in Ethernet 10Base2 (thinnet) networks to connect two cable segments.

base I/O port — The memory address where the CPU and an adapter check for messages that they leave for each other.

base memory address — The memory address at which the transfer area between the computer's main memory and a NIC's buffers begin, bounded by the size of its extent, which is the size of an area that describes the upper limit of a memory region on a PC named by a base address that indicates the starting point (upper bound = base address + extent).

baseband transmission — A technology that uses digital signals sent over a cable without modulation. It sends binary values (0s and 1s) as pulses of different voltage levels.

baseline — A measurement of network performance over time, against which current performance can be measured.

Basic Rate Interface (BRI) — An ISDN implementation that provides two 64-Kbps B-channels and one 16-Kbps D-channel. Generally used for remote connections.

baud — A measurement of modem speed that describes the number of state transitions that occur in a second on an analog phone line.

beaconing — The signal transmitted on a token ring network to inform networked computers that token passing has stopped due to an error.

bend radius — For network cabling, the bend radius describes the maximum arc that a segment of cable may be bent over some unit length (typically, one foot or one meter) without incurring damage.

Binary Synchronous (bisync) communications — A synchronous communications protocol.

binding — The OS-level association of NICs, protocols, and services to maximize performance through the correlation of related components.

bis — A French term for *second*, which describes the second version of an ITU standard.

BNC — Bayonet nut connector or British Naval Connector (preferred Microsoft usage); also known as bayonet navy connector or bayonet Neill-Concelman connector. This is a matching pair of coaxial cable connectors, male and female. The female connector consists of a ferrule around a hollow pin with a pair of guideposts on the outside. The male connector consists of a rotating, locking wire nut, with an inner sleeve with two channels that match the female connector's guideposts. A pin projects from the center of the male connector and connects with the hollow pin in the center of the female connector, while the guideposts and locking wire nut ensure a tight, well-seated connection.

Boot PROM — A special programmable chip that includes enough software to permit a computer to boot sufficiently and access the network. From there, it can download an operating system to finish the boot process. This is also known as PXE compliant.

boot up — The process a computer goes through when starting, also called booting.

braiding — A woven mesh of metallic wires, usually either copper or steel, wrapped around the outside of one or more conductive cables. It provides shielding against EMI, RFI, and crosstalk from other cables.

bridge — A networking device that works at the Data Link layer of the OSI model. It filters traffic according to the packet's hardware destination address.

bridging table — A reference table created by a bridge to track hardware addresses and to track on which network segment each address is located.

broadband optical telepoint network — An implementation of infrared wireless networking that supports broadband services equal to those provided by a cabled network.

broadband transmission — An analog transmission technique which may use multiple communication channels simultaneously. Each data channel is represented by modulation on a particular frequency band, for which sending or receiving equipment must be tuned.

broadcast packet — A packet type whose destination address specifies all computers on a network or network segment.

broadcast signal — A technique that uses a transmitter to send signals, such as network data, through a communications medium. For wireless networks, this involves sending signals through the atmosphere, rather than over a cable.

broadcast storm — Phenomenon that occurs when a network device malfunctions and floods the network with broadcast packets.

brouter — A networking device that combines the best functionality of a bridge and a router. It routes packets that include Network layer information and bridges all other packets.

buffer — A temporary storage area that a device uses to contain incoming data before it can be processed for input or to contain outgoing data before it can be sent as output.

bus — A network topology in which computers connect to a backbone cable segment to form a logical straight line. Also, an architecture consisting of parallel lines used in a computer to transfer data between the CPU and peripheral devices or from one peripheral device to another.

bus mastering — The quality of an adapter card's circuitry that allows it to take possession of a computer's bus and coordinate data transfers without requiring any service from the computer's CPU.

bus width — The number of parallel lines that make up a particular kind of computer bus. For example, ISA supports 8- and 16-bit bus widths, EISA and MCA support 16- and 32-bit bus widths, and PCI supports 32- and 64-bit bus widths.

cable modem — A networking device that permits a computer to send and receive networking signals, primarily for Internet access, by using two data channels on a broadband CATV network.

cable tester — A network troubleshooting device that can test for cable defects, monitor network collisions, and monitor network congestion.

Carrier Sense Multiple Access with Collision Avoidance (CSMA/CA) — A contention-based channel access method in which computers avoid collisions by broadcasting their intent to send data.

Carrier Sense Multiple Access with Collision Detection (CSMA/CD) — A contention-based channel access method in which computers avoid collisions by listening to the network before sending data. If a computer senses data on the network, it waits and tries to send its data later.

Category 1–5E — The EIA/TIA designations for unshielded twisted-pair cable, described in terms of categories, labeled Category 1, Category 2, and so on. Often, these are abbreviated as Cat 1, Cat 2, and so on.

Cellular Digital Packet Data (CDPD) — A cellular communications technology that sends packets of digital data over unused cellular voice channels at a rate of 19.2 Kbps. CDPD is one member of an emerging family of mobile computing technologies.

cellular packet radio — A communications technology that sends packets of data over different radio frequencies than those used for cellular telephones; a generic term for an emerging family of mobile computing technologies.

central office (CO) — A phone company's or communications provider's local facility where copper local telephone cables (sometimes called the subscriber loop or the "last mile" of cable in the telecommunications infrastructure) link to long-haul, all-digital, fiber-optic communications lines.

central processing unit (CPU) — The collection of circuitry (a single chip on most PCs) that supplies the "brains" for most computers.

centralized computing — A computing environment in which all processing takes place on a mainframe or central computer.

channel access method — The rules used to determine which computer can send data across the network, thereby preventing data loss due to collisions.

Channel Service Unit/Data Service Unit (CSU/DSU) — A device that links a computer or network to a DDS communications link.

cheapernet — A synonym for 10Base2, also known as thinnet or thinwire Ethernet.

chip — A fixed-sized element of data broadcast over a single frequency using the spread-spectrum radio networking technology called direct-sequence modulation.

cladding — A nontransparent layer of plastic or glass material inside fiber-optic cable; cladding surrounds the inner core of glass or plastic fibers. Cladding provides rigidity, strength, and a manageable outer diameter for fiber-optic cables.

Classless Inter-Domain Routing (CIDR) — A more efficient way to assign IP addresses than using IP address "classes."

client — A computer on a network that requests resources or services from some other computer.

client network software — A type of software designed for workstation computers, and that enables the use of network resources.

client-based multivendor solution — When multiple redirectors are loaded on a client, the client can communicate with servers from different vendors.

client/server — A model for computing in which some computers (clients) request services and others (servers) respond to such requests for services.

client/server computing — A computing environment in which the processing is divided between the client and the server.

client/server relationship — Applications may sometimes be divided across the network, so that a client-side component runs on the user's machine and supplies request and display services, while a server-side component runs on an application server and handles data processing or other intensive computation services on the user's behalf.

clustered server — A network server, which is a member of a group of two or more servers. All machines in the group employ a combination of special operating system software and a dedicated high-speed link. This permits all machines in the group to behave as one super-powered network server, rather than single, independent, individual servers.

coaxial cable — A type of cable that uses a center conductor, wrapped by an insulating layer, surrounded by a braided wire mesh and an outer jacket or sheath, to carry high-bandwidth signals such as network traffic or broadcast television frequencies. The word "coax" is often used as a shortened form of "coaxial cable."

collision — Occurs when two computers put data on the cable at the same time. This corrupts the electronic signals in the packet and causes data loss.

combination network — *See* hybrid network.

Committed Information Rate (CIR) — A performance measurement of guaranteed throughput rates.

communication server — A specialized network server that provides access to resources on the network for users not directly attached to the network or that permits network users to access external resources not directly attached to the network.

communications carrier — A company that provides communications services for other organizations, such as your local phone company and the long-distance telephone carriers. Most mobile computing technologies rely on the services of a communications carrier to handle the wireless traffic from mobile units to a centralized wired network of some kind.

concentrator — Used in an FDDI network to connect computers at a central point. Most concentrators connect to both available rings.

conduit — Plastic or metal pipe laid specifically to provide a protected enclosure for cabling of any kind.

congestion control — A technique for monitoring network utilization and manipulating transmission or forwarding rates for data frames to keep traffic levels from overwhelming the network medium; gets its name because it avoids "network traffic jams."

connection-oriented — A type of protocol that establishes a formal connection between two computers, guaranteeing that the data will reach its destination.

connectionless — A type of protocol that sends the data across the network to its destination without guaranteeing receipt.

contention — A channel access method in which computers vie for time on the network.

cooperative multitasking — A form of multitasking in which each individual process controls the length of time it maintains exclusive control over the CPU.

copy backup — Copies all selected files without resetting the archive bit.

counter — A certain part of an object. For example, the Processor object has counters such as % Processor Time and % Interrupt Time per second.

crosstalk — A phenomenon that occurs when two wires lay against each other in parallel. Signals traveling down one wire can interfere with signals traveling down the other, and vice versa.

cut-through switching — The fastest switching method, in which the switch reads only enough of the incoming frame to determine where to forward the frame.

Cyclical Redundancy Check (CRC) — A mathematical recipe that generates a specific value, called a checksum, based on the contents of a data frame. The CRC is calculated before transmission of a data frame and then included with the frame; on receipt, the CRC is recalculated and compared to the sent value. If the two agree, it is assumed that the data frame was delivered intact; if they disagree, the data frame must be retransmitted.

daemon — A UNIX term for a component of any server program that "listens" to incoming requests for a specific service across the network; for example, a Telnet server might include a Telnet daemon, which is a program that always runs, ready to serve Telnet requests; the same component of an FTP server is called an FTP daemon, and so forth.

daily backup — Copies all files modified on the day of the backup.

data channel — The cables and infrastructure of a network.

data communications equipment (DCE) — Any type of device, such as a modem, that connects a DTE to a communications line.

data frame — The basic package of bits that represents the PDU sent from one computer to another across a networking medium. In addition to its contents (payload), a data frame includes the sender's and receiver's network addresses as well as some control information at the head and a CRC at the tail.

Data Link Control (DLC) — A network protocol used mainly by Hewlett-Packard printers and IBM mainframes attached to a network.

Data Link layer — Layer 2 in the OSI reference model. This layer is responsible for managing access to the networking medium and for ensuring error-free delivery of data frames from sender to receiver.

data section — The actual data being sent across a network. The size of this section can vary from 512 bytes to 16 kilobytes, depending on the network type.

data terminal equipment (DTE) — Any device that transmits digital information over a communications line.

database management system (DBMS) — A client/server computing environment that uses SQL to retrieve data from the server.

datagrade — A designation for cabling of any kind; datagrade indicates that cabling is suitable for transporting digital data. When applied to twisted-pair cabling, datagrade indicates that the cable is suitable for either voice or data traffic.

datagram — The term used in some protocols to define a packet.

DECNet — Protocol suite of a company known at the time as Digital Equipment Corporation.

dedicated circuit — An ongoing (but possibly transient) link between two end systems.

dedicated server — A network server that acts only as a server and is not intended for regular use as a client machine.

Delivery Datagram Protocol (DDP) — Data transport protocol for AppleTalk.

demand priority — A high-speed channel access method used by 100VG-AnyLAN in a star hub topology.

demand signal — A signal sent by a computer in a demand priority network that informs the controlling hub it has data to send.

designator — Associated with drive mappings. Working in coordination with a redirector, it exchanges the locally mapped drive letter with the correct network address of a directory share inside a resource request.

desktop software — Sometimes called client software or productivity applications, this type of software is what users run on their computers (which are usually on a desktop).

device driver — A software program that mediates communication between an operating system and a specific device for the purpose of sending and/or receiving input and output from that device. These drivers are operating-system dependent. They also need to be kept up to date per the information on the manufacturer's Web site.

device sharing — A primary purpose for networking: permitting users to share access to devices of all kinds, including servers and peripherals such as printers or plotters.

diagnostic software — Specialized programs that can probe and monitor a system (or a specific system component) to determine if it works properly and, if not, to try to establish the cause of the problem.

diagram — A term used to describe a network's design.

Dial-Up Networking (DUN) — The program included with Windows 95, Windows 98, Windows Millennium, Windows NT, and Windows 2000 that allows connectivity to servers running RAS or RRAS.

dictionary attack — A method of attempting to determine an account's password by attempting to log on using every word in the dictionary for a password.

differential backup — Copies all files modified since the last full backup.

Digital Data Service (DDS) — A type of point-to-point synchronous communication link offering 2.4-, 4.8-, 9.6-, or 56-Kbps transmission rates.

digital modem — A hardware device used to transmit digital signals across an ISDN link.

Digital Subscriber Line (DSL) — A digital technology that uses specially tuned telephone lines to deliver network and Internet access at bandwidths from 384 Kbps to 1.5 Mbps.

digital voltmeter (DVM) — A network troubleshooting tool that measures voltage, amperage, and resistance on a cable or other conductive element.

Direct Memory Access (DMA) — A technique for addressing memory on some other device as if it were local memory directly available to the device accessing that memory. This technique lets a CPU gain immediate access to the buffers on any NIC that supports DMA.

direct-sequence modulation — The form of spread-spectrum data transmission that breaks data into constant length segments called chips and transmits the data on multiple frequencies.

directory server — A specialized server whose job is to respond to requests for specific resources, services, users, groups, and so on. This kind of server is more commonly called a domain controller in Windows NT Server and Windows 2000 networking environments.

directory service — A comprehensive network service that manages information about network services, resources, users, groups, and other objects, so that users may access resources and services by browsing for them, or asking for them by type, along with maintaining and enforcing access control information for directory objects.

discovery — The process by which dynamic routers learn the routes available to them.

disk duplexing — A fault-tolerant disk configuration in which data is written to two hard drives, each with its own disk controller, so that if one disk or controller fails, the data remains accessible.

disk mirroring — A fault-tolerant disk configuration in which data is written to two hard drives, rather than one, so that if one disk fails, the data remains accessible.

disk striping with parity — A fault-tolerant disk configuration in which parts of several physical disks link together in an array, and data and parity information is written to all disks in this array. If one disk fails, the data may be reconstructed from the parity information written on the others.

diskless workstations — Network computers that require a special type of ROM because they have no built-in hard or floppy drives.

distance-vector algorithm — One method of determining the best route available for a packet. Distance-vector protocols count the number of routers (hops) between the source and destination. The best path has the least number of hops.

DIX (Digital, Intel, Xerox) — The group that introduced the first Ethernet connector.

domain — A uniquely named collection of user accounts and resources that share a common security database.

domain controller — On networks based on Windows NT Server or a Windows 2000 Server, a directory server that also provides access controls over users, accounts, groups, computers, and other network resources.

domain model — A network based on Windows NT Server or Windows 2000 Server whose security and access controls reside in a domain controller.

Domain Name System (DNS) — A TCP/IP protocol used to associate a computer's IP address with a name.

drive mapping — The convention of associating a local drive letter with a network directory share to simplify access to the remote resource.

driver — An abbreviation for "device driver," a small program that mediates between an operating system and the hardware device it knows how to access.

DS — A specification level for DDS lines. A T1 is a DS-1 or 1.544 Mbps; a single channel fractional T1 is a DS-0 or 64 Kbps.

Dual Attachment Stations (DAS) — Computers or concentrators connected to both rings in an FDDI network.

dual-cable broadband — A broadband technique in which two cables are used; one is for transmitting, and one is for receiving.

Dynamic Host Configuration Protocol (DHCP) — A TCP/IP protocol that allows automatic IP address and subnet mask assignment.

dynamic routing — The process by which routers dynamically learn from each other the available paths.

electromagnetic interference (EMI) — A form of electrical interference caused by emissions from external devices, such as transformers or electrical motors, that can disrupt network transmissions over an electrical medium.

electronic eavesdropping — The ability to "listen" to signals passing through some communications medium by detecting its emissions. Eavesdropping on many wireless networking technologies is especially easy, because they broadcast their data into the atmosphere.

Electronic Industries Alliance (EIA) — An industry trade group of electronics and networking manufacturers that collaborates on standards for wiring, connectors, and other common components.

electronic mail (e-mail) — An abbreviation for electronic mail, a networked application that permits users to send text messages, with or without attachments of many kinds, to individual or multiple users, or to named groups of users.

encoding — The representation of zeros and ones as a physical signal, such as electrical voltage or a light pulse.

enterprise network — A large-scale network usually connecting many LANs.

Ethernet — A networking technology developed in the early 1970s and governed by the IEEE 802.3 specification. Ethernet remains the most popular type of networking technology in use today.

Ethernet 802.2 — Ethernet frame type used by IPX/SPX on Novell NetWare 3.12 and 4.x networks.

Ethernet 802.3 — Ethernet frame type generally used by IPX/SPX on Novell NetWare 2.x and 3.x networks.

Ethernet II — Ethernet frame type used by TCP/IP.

Ethernet raw — Ethernet frame type, also called Ethernet 802.3.

Ethernet SNAP (SubNetwork Address Protocol) — Ethernet frame type used in Apple's EtherTalk environment.

EtherTalk — The standard for sending AppleTalk over Ethernet cabling.

Event Viewer — A Windows NT and Windows 2000 tool that records events in three logs based on type of event: security, system, and application.

Exchange Server — A BackOffice component from Microsoft that acts as a sophisticated e-mail server.

Extended Industry Standard Architecture (EISA) — A 32-bit PC bus architecture that is backward compatible with the older, slower 16-bit ISA bus architecture.

extended LAN — The result of certain wireless bridges' ability to expand the span of a LAN up to 25 miles. Microsoft calls the resulting networks "extended LANs."

fast Ethernet — The 100 Mbps implementation of standard Ethernet.

fault tolerance — A feature that allows a system to continue working after an unexpected hardware or software failure.

fault-tolerant disk configuration — An arrangement of physical or logical disks such that if one disk fails, the data remains accessible without requiring restoration from backups.

fax server — A specialized network server that can send and receive faxes on behalf of the user community that it supports.

Federal Communications Commission (FCC) — Among other responsibilities, the FCC regulates access to broadcast frequencies throughout the electromagnetic spectrum, including those used for mobile computing and microwave transmissions. Where these signals cover any distance (more than half a mile) and require exclusive use of a particular frequency, FCC requires a broadcast license. Many wireless networking technologies make use of so-called unregulated frequencies set aside by the FCC. These frequencies do not require such licensing, but they must be shared with others.

Fiber Distributed Data Interface (FDDI) — A high-speed LAN technology that uses dual counter-rotating rings.

fiber-optic — A cabling technology that uses pulses of light sent along a light-conducting fiber at the heart of the cable to transfer information from sender to receiver. Fiber-optic cable can send data in only one direction, so two cables are required to permit any two network devices to exchange data in both directions.

file and print server — The most common type of network server (not considered a specialized server). It provides file storage and retrieval services across the network and handles print jobs on behalf of its user community.

File Transfer Protocol (FTP) — A TCP/IP protocol and application used for file transfer and file manipulation over a network or the Internet.

firewall — A special Internet server that sits between an Internet link and a private network, and which filters both incoming and outgoing network traffic, limits the Internet resources that in-house users may access, and severely or completely limits incoming requests for access to the firewall's private network side.

FireWire — A high-speed, external serial bus that supports bandwidths up to 400 Mbps and that can connect up to 63 devices. Also known as IEEE 1394. FireWire is used for streaming video and multimedia, networking, and to attach video devices to computers.

flow control — An action designed to regulate the transfer of information between a sender and a receiver. Flow control is often necessary when a speed differential exists between sender and receiver.

fractional T1 — A segmented T1 line where a customer uses or leases one to 23 channels of a T1 to achieve transmission rates in increments of 64 Kbps.

fragment-free switching — A switching method in which the switch reads in enough of the frame to guarantee that the frame is not less than the minimum frame size allowed for the network type.

fragmentation — The process of breaking a long PDU from a higher layer into a sequence of shorter PDUs for a lower layer, ultimately for transmission as a sequence of data frames across the networking medium.

frame — The unit of data with which bridges and switches work. Frames contain physical address information and are defined at Layer 2 of the OSI model.

frame fragment — A frame error that occurs because the frame is less than the allowable size for the network type. A frame fragment usually occurs due to a collision or a device malfunction.

frame relay — A WAN technology that offers transmission rates of 56 Kbps to 1.544 Mbps. Frame relay uses no error checking.

frame type — One of four standards that defines the structure of an Ethernet packet: Ethernet 802.3, Ethernet 802.2, Ethernet SNAP, or Ethernet II.

frequency-hopping — The type of spread-spectrum data transmission that switches data across a range of frequencies over time. Frequency-hopping transmitters and receivers must be synchronized to hop at the same time, to the same frequencies.

front end — A client in a client/server networking environment.

full backup — A copy of data that resets the archive bit on all copied files.

gateway — A networking device that translates information between protocols or between completely different networks, such as from TCP/IP to SNA.

geosynchronous — An orbital position relative to Earth where a satellite orbits at the same speed as Earth rotates. This permits such satellites to maintain a constant, fixed position relative to Earth stations and represents the positioning technique used for microwave satellites.

Gigabit Ethernet — An IEEE standard (802.3z) that allows for 1000-Mbps transmission using CSMA/CD and Ethernet frames.

global group — A group meant to be used in more than one domain.

group — A named collection of user accounts, usually created for some specific purpose. For example, the Accounting group might be the only named entity permitted to use a bookkeeping application.

groupware — A type of network application in which multiple users can simultaneously interact with each other and with data files.

hard page fault — An exception that occurs when data needed by a program must be called back into memory from its storage space on the hard drive. Hard page faults are relatively time-consuming to resolve.

Hardware Compatibility List (HCL) — A list of hardware devices compatible with a particular Microsoft operating system. This list is maintained by Microsoft and is found at their Web site.

Hayes-compatible — The modem standard based on the Hayes Smartmodem.

Hertz (Hz) — A measure of broadcast frequencies, in cycles per second; named after Heinrich Hertz, one of the inventors of radio communications.

hexadecimal — A mathematical notation for representing numbers in base 16. The numbers 10 through 15 are expressed as A through F; 10h or 0x10 (both notations indicate the number is hexadecimal) equals 16.

High-level Data Link Control (HDLC) — A synchronous communication protocol.

home page — On a Web site, the official "entry page" or the default document associated with the site's base URL (for example, *www.microsoft.com*) is called the home page.

hot-swappable — Components such as power supplies or disk drives that can be removed and replaced without shutting off power to the computer, thus eliminating down time.

hub — The central concentration point of a star network.

hybrid hub — A device used to interconnect different types of cables and to maximize network efficiency.

hybrid network — A network that includes both wired and wireless components. Also, a network that incorporates both peer-to-peer and server-based capabilities.

Hypertext Markup Language (HTML) — The language used to create documents for the WWW.

Hypertext Transfer Protocol (HTTP) — The protocol used by the WWW to transfer files.

IBM cabling system — Numeric cable designations (Type 1 through Type 9) representing the grades of cabling recognized by IBM's Cabling System. Types 2 and 9 are the most commonly used networking cables; Type 3 is voicegrade only, which is unsuitable for networking use.

impedance — The resistance of a cable to the transmission of signals. Impedance accounts for attenuation in a cable.

incremental backup — Copies all files modified since the last full or incremental backup.

Industry Standard Architecture (ISA) — Originally an 8-bit PC bus architecture, but upgraded to 16-bit with the introduction of the IBM PC/AT in 1984.

infrared — That portion of the electromagnetic spectrum immediately below visible light. Infrared frequencies are popular for short- to medium-range (tens of meters to 40 km) point-to-point network connections.

insertion loss — The weakening of signals that occurs on a cable segment each time a network device is attached. Necessary restrictions on the maximum number of devices keep the signals that traverse the network clean and strong enough to remain intelligible to all devices.

Institute of Electrical and Electronics Engineers (IEEE) — An engineering organization that issues standards for electrical and electronic devices, including network interfaces, cabling, and connectors.

Integrated Services Digital Network (ISDN) — A WAN technology that offers increments of 64-Kbps connections, most often used by SOHO (small office/home office) users.

Intellimirror — A Windows 2000 client/server application that creates a "smart back-up copy" of a Windows 2000 system on a Windows 2000 server. All the files, applications, and customization resident on users' home desktops can be accessed by them on any other Windows 2000 machine that can establish a working connection to the Intellimirror server where their home desktop images reside.

International Organization for Standardization (ISO) — The international standards-setting body, based in Geneva, Switzerland, that sets worldwide technology standards.

International Telecommunications Union (ITU) — The standards body that developed the V-series modem standards.

Internet — The global collection of networked computers that began with technology and equipment funded by the U.S. Department of Defense in the 1970s. Today it links millions of computers worldwide.

Internet browser — A graphical tool designed to read HTML documents and access the WWW, such as Microsoft Internet Explorer or Netscape Navigator.

Internet Control Message Protocol (ICMP) — A TCP/IP protocol used to send information and error messages.

Internet Information Server (IIS) — A Microsoft BackOffice component that acts as a Web server in the Windows NT Server environment.

Internet Information Services (IIS) — The Windows 2000 version of Internet Information Server.

Internet Message Access Protocol (IMAP) — An Internet e-mail standard that may someday replace POP3 because of its advanced message controls and fault-tolerance features. The appeal of IMAP (a more modern client message transfer protocol) is that it permits clients to read and manage messages locally, while leaving them stored on the server.

Internet Protocol (IP) — TCP/IP's primary network protocol, which provides addressing and routing information.

Internet Service Provider (ISP) — A company that connects its clients to the Internet.

internetwork — A complex network created when two or more independent networks are connected using routers.

Internetwork Packet Exchange (IPX) — IPX is a Transport and Network layer protocol that handles all addressing and routing on a network. IPX is a connectionless protocol that provides fast, but unreliable, services.

Internetwork Packet Exchange/Sequenced Packet Exchange (IPX/SPX) — The protocol stack Novell developed for use with its NetWare networking operating system software.

Interrupt Request Line (IRQ) — Any of 16 unique signal lines between the CPU and the bus slots on a PC. IRQs define the mechanism whereby a peripheral device of any kind, including a network adapter, can stake a claim on the PC's attention. Such a claim is called an "interrupt," which gives the name to the lines that carry this information.

intranet — An in-house TCP/IP-based network, for use within a company.

IPSec (IP Security) — An Internet security protocol that's gaining acceptance as a way to protect network traffic from unwanted snooping.

IPX Routing Information Protocol (IPX RIP) — IPX RIP is a distance-vector protocol that uses the number of hops between points to determine the best path for a packet to take from sender to receiver.

IPX/SPX — An abbreviation for Internetwork Packet Exchange/Sequenced Packet Exchange, the set of protocols developed by Novell. Most commonly associated with NetWare, but Microsoft and other vendors' networks also support it.

IrDA — A device that is compliant with the Infrared Device Association's specifications for infrared components and devices.

jack coupler — The female receptacle into which a modular TP cable plugs.

jacket — The outermost layer of a cable.

knowledgebase — A searchable database that contains problems and errors, along with their solutions, related to a manufacturer's product.

latency — The amount of time a signal takes to travel from one end of a cable to the other.

Layer 2 Tunneling Protocol (L2TP) — A Windows technology used in VPNs that supports advanced authentication and encryption.

layers — The functional subdivisions of the OSI reference model. The model defines each layer in terms of the services and data it handles on behalf of the layer directly above it, and the services and data it needs from the layer directly below it.

layout — A term used to describe a network's design.

learning bridge — Another term for a transparent bridge that learns the hardware addresses of the computers connected to each network segment.

light-emitting diode (LED) — A lower-powered alternative for emitting data at optical frequencies. LEDs are sometimes used for wireless LANs and for short-haul, fiber-optic-based data transmissions.

line conditioning — Sustaining a consistent transmission rate, improving overall quality, and reducing interference noise levels.

line of sight — A term which describes the requirement that narrow-band, tight-beam transmitters and receivers have an unobstructed path between them. If you can see from sender to receiver, they can also exchange data with one another.

line-of-sight networks — Networks that require an unobstructed view, or clear line of sight, between the transmitter and receiver.

link-state algorithm — A method used by routers to determine a packet's best path. In addition to the number of routers involved, routers using link-state algorithms take network traffic and link speed into account to determine the best path.

local area network (LAN) — A collection of computers and other networked devices that fit within the scope of a single physical network and provide the building blocks for internetworks and WANs.

local group — A group meant to be used in a single domain.

localhost — A special DNS host name that refers to whatever IP address is assigned to the machine where this name is referenced. (Think of this as a special way to access your current IP address on any computer.)

locally attached — Describes a device that's attached directly to a single computer, rather than a device that's available only over the network (which may be called network-attached or server-attached, depending on whether it has a built-in network interface or must be attached directly to a server).

LocalTalk — The cabling system used by Macintosh computers. Support for LocalTalk is built into every Macintosh.

Logical Link Control (LLC) — The upper sub-layer of the IEEE Project 802 networking model for the Data Link layer (Layer 2) of the OSI reference model. It handles error-free delivery and controls the flow of data frames between sender and receiver across a network.

loopback — A special DNS host name that refers to the reserved Class A address 127.0.0.1, used to confirm that a computer's IP configuration works.

MAC address — The number that identifies the physical address of a computer on a network. This address is hard wired into the computer's NIC.

mail server — A networked server that manages the flow of e-mail messages for network users.

management information base (MIB) — A set of objects that contains information about a networking device and that is used by SNMP to manage that networking device.

map — A diagram of a network's layout, including the locations of servers, workstations, computers, jacks, hubs, switches, and so forth, and the type of cabling along segments.

maximum segment length — The longest legal segment of cable permitted by a particular networking technology. This limitation helps network designers and installers make sure that the entire network can send and receive signals properly.

Media Access Control (MAC) — A level of data communications where the network interface can directly address the networking media. Also, the unique address programmed into network adapters to identify them on a network. Also, the lower sublayer of the IEEE project 802 networking model for the Data Link layer.

medium interface connector (MIC) — One of a number of fiber-optic cable connector types. MIC connectors feature a separate physical connector for each cable in a typical fiber-optic cable pair.

member server — Any server on a Windows NT or Windows 2000 network that is not responsible for user authentication.

mesh — A hybrid network topology used for fault tolerance, and one in which all computers connect to each other.

Message Handling System (MHS) — A Novell-developed standard that is similar to X.400.

metropolitan area network (MAN) — Uses WAN technologies to interconnect LANs within a specific geographic region, such as a county or a city. In most cases, however, a municipality or a communications carrier operates a MAN; individual organizations must sign up for service and establish connections to use a MAN.

Micro Channel Architecture (MCA) — IBM's proprietary 16- and 32-bit computer buses. Originally developed for its PS/2 PCs, MCA is now popular on its midrange RISC/6000 computers.

Microsoft Developer's Network (MSDN) — A Web site on which Microsoft offers product support, in addition to drivers and patches.

Microsoft Knowledge Base — An online reference for Microsoft and networking information.

Microsoft Technical Information Network (TechNet) — A monthly subscription service from Microsoft that supplies CD-ROMs containing technical information on networking and topics specific to Microsoft. It is also available online.

mid-split broadband — A broadband technique in which two channels on different frequencies are used to transmit and receive signals using a single cable.

mixed mode — A domain configuration in which a Windows NT Server functions as a domain controller with Windows 2000 Active Directory Servers.

mobile computing — A form of wireless networking that uses common carrier frequencies to permit networked devices to be moved freely within the broadcast coverage area yet remain connected to the network.

modem (MOdulator/DEModulator) — Used by computers to convert digital signals to analog signals for transmission over telephone lines. The receiving computer then converts the analog signals to digital signals.

mount point — Terminology that describes a portion of a file system published for access through NFS to users who are authorized to add that file system portion to their local file systems. NFS originated in the UNIX world and is still common on UNIX and Linux hosts.

MT-RJ — A fiber-optic connector that provides a high-density connection utilizing two fiber-optic cables.

multicast packet — A packet that uses a special network address to make itself readable to any receiving computer that wants to read its payload. Multicast packets usually transport streaming broadcast data, such as video programs, teleconferences, or live audio broadcasts, where many receivers want to access data from the same sender.

multiplexing — The networking technology that combines several communications on a single cable segment.

Multistation Access Unit (MAU or MSAU) — An active hub in a token ring network.

multitasking — A mode of CPU operation where a computer processes more than one task at a time. In most instances, multitasking is an illusion created through the use of time slicing.

muxing — *See* multiplexing.

Name Binding Protocol (NBP) — AppleTalk's data transport protocol.

naming convention — A predetermined schema for naming objects within network space. It simplifies the location and identification of objects.

narrow-band radio — A type of broadcast-based networking technology that uses a single, specific radio frequency to send and receive data. Low-powered, narrow-band implementations do not usually require FCC approval, but are limited to a 250-foot or so range; high-powered, narrow-band

implementations do require FCC approval and licensing.

narrow-band sockets — An emerging programming interface designed to facilitate communication between cellular data networks and the Internet.

native mode — A domain configuration in Windows 2000 that supports nesting of groups within groups; no Windows NT Servers may act as domain controllers in that domain.

Nearest Active Downstream Neighbor (NADN) — Used in a token ring environment to describe the computer to which a computer sends the token.

Nearest Active Upstream Neighbor (NAUN) — Used in a token ring environment to describe the computer from which a computer receives the token.

NetBEUI — A network protocol developed by IBM and Microsoft specifically to provide transport services for Network Basic Input/Output System (NetBIOS).

NetBIOS Enhanced User Interface (NetBEUI) — An enhanced set of network and transport protocols that carry NetBIOS information. Built in the late 1980s, when earlier implementations became too limiting for continued use, NetBEUI remains popular on many IBM and Microsoft networks.

NetWare Core Protocol (NCP) — Novell's upper-layer protocol, which provides all client/server functions.

network adapter — A synonym for network interface card (NIC). It refers to the hardware device that mediates communication between a computer and one or more types of networking media. *See also* network interface card (NIC).

network adapter — *See* network interface card (NIC).

Network Address Translation (NAT) — A process by which an organization may assign private IP addresses to workstations; those addresses are translated to public IP addresses when access to the Internet occurs.

network administrator — An individual responsible for installing, configuring, and maintaining a network, usually a server-based network such as Windows 2000 Server or Novell NetWare.

network applications — Enhanced software programs made possible through the communication system of a network. Examples include e-mail, scheduling, and groupware.

Network Basic Input/Output System (NetBIOS) — A connection-oriented protocol used by Windows 98, Windows NT, Windows 2000, and LAN Manager; closely related to NetBEUI.

network card — Synonym for network interface card (NIC).

Network Device Interface Specification (NDIS) — A standard for providing an interface between a network interface card and the network medium that enables a NIC to use multiple protocols.

Network File System (NFS) — A distributed file system originally developed at Sun Microsystems. It supports network-based file and printer sharing using TCP/IP-based network protocols.

network interface card (NIC) — The hardware device that mediates communication between a computer and one or more types of networking media.

Network layer — Layer 3 of the OSI reference model. The Network layer handles addressing and routing of PDUs across internetworks in which multiple networks must be traversed between sender and receiver.

network medium — Usually refers to the cable (metallic or fiber-optic) that links computers on a network. Because wireless networking is possible, it can also describe the type of wireless communications used to permit computers to exchange data via some wireless transmission frequency.

Network Monitor — A Windows NT and Windows 2000 network service that you can use to capture network frames based on user-specified criteria, such as a software protocol analyzer.

network monitor — Software that monitors network traffic and gathers information about packet types, errors, and packet traffic to and from each computer.

network news — Also known as USENET, this is the collection of discussion groups maintained on the Internet.

Network News Transfer Protocol (NNTP) — The protocol used for distributing, retrieving, inquiring, and posting network news articles.

network operating system (NOS) — A type of software that controls both the local hardware activities of a computer and that serves as a manager for applications and the user interface to a computer.

network protocol — A set of rules for communicating across a network. To communicate successfully across a network, two computers must share a common protocol.

network resource — Any kind of device, information, or service available across a network. A network resource could be a set of files, an application or service of some kind, or a network-accessible peripheral device.

network services — Those resources offered by a network, and not normally found in a standalone OS.

network termination (NT) — Part of the network connection device in an ISDN network.

newsgroup — A discussion group in which people share information through USENET.

NFS volume — An NFS mount point that functions as a standalone local drive on a user's desktop; it may also sometimes refer to an NFS mount point situated at the root of a drive on the machine where the mount point is exported.

nonroutable protocol — A network protocol that does not contain Network layer information, but instead relies only on Data Link layer addressing. A nonroutable protocol cannot be routed in an internetwork.

Novell Directory Services (NDS) — The centralized database of user, group, and resource information that permits one or more NetWare servers to handle network logins and resource access requests, and to manage resource information for an entire network.

Novell IPX ODI Protocol — The name that Windows 98, Release2, gives to the Microsoft implementation of the IPX/SPX protocol suite for that operating system.

NWLink — An abbreviation for NetWare Link, a set of Microsoft-developed protocols that behaves exactly like Novell's IPX/SPX (but is named differently to avoid trade name infringement).

object — A portion of software that works with other portions to provide services. Each component in Windows NT and Windows 2000 is considered an object.

on-board co-processor — A special- or general-purpose microprocessor that appears on an adapter card, usually to offload data from a computer's CPU. NICs with on-board co-processors usually employ the special-purpose variety.

Open Data-link Interface (ODI) — A specification developed by Apple Computer and Novell that simplified driver development and enabled the use of multiple protocols from a single NIC.

Open Shortest Path First (OSPF) — TCP/IP's link-state routing protocol used to determine a packet's best path through an internetwork.

open source — Software that's always available at no charge, even after modifications to its source code.

Open Systems Interconnection (OSI) — The family of ISO standards developed in the 1970s and 1980s and designed to facilitate high-level, high-function networking services among dissimilar computers on a global scale. The OSI initiative was unsuccessful, owing to a fatal combination of an all-inclusive standards-setting effort and a failure to develop standard protocol interfaces to help developers implement its many requirements.

optical carrier (OC) — A speed level of fiber-optic cable that conforms to the SONET standard.

oscilloscope — A network troubleshooting device that measures the signal voltage per amount of time. When used with a TDR, it can help define cable problems.

OSI reference model — ISO Standard 7498. It defines a frame of reference for understanding and implementing networks by breaking down the process across seven layers. By far, the OSI reference model remains the OSI initiative's most enduring legacy.

packet — The data unit associated with the Network layer of the OSI reference model.

packet assembler/disassembler (PAD) — A component of an X.25 network that supports low-speed, character-based terminals.

packet data unit (PDU) — A data unit associated with processing at any layer in the OSI reference model; sometimes identified by the particular layer, as in "a Session or Layer 5 PDU."

packet header — Information added to the beginning of the data being sent, which contains, among other things, addressing and sequencing information.

packet switching — A transmission method that sends packets across a networking medium that supports multiple pathways between sender and receiver. Transmissions may follow any available path, and multiple packets may travel simultaneously across the network. Thus, packets may arrive in an order that differs from that in which they were sent. X.25 is a common type of packet-switched network.

packet trailer — Information added to the end of the data being sent, which generally contains error-checking information such as the CRC.

Palo Alto Research Center (PARC) — A Xerox research center where Robert Metcalf and David

Boggs developed an early version of Ethernet in 1972.

parallel transmission — The technique of spreading individual bits of data across multiple, parallel data lines to transmit them simultaneously, rather than according to an ordinal and temporal sequence.

parent hub — The central controlling hub in a 100VG-AnyLAN network to which child hubs are connected.

partition — A logical separation of disk space that is viewed as a separate logical drive.

passive hub — A central connection point through which signals pass without regeneration.

passive topology — A network topology in which the computers listen to the data signals being sent but do not participate in network communications.

password — A string of letters, numbers, and other characters intended to be kept private and used to identify a particular user or controls access to protected resources.

patch panel — An element of a wiring center where individual cable runs are brought together. By making connections between any two points on the patch panel, the physical path of individual wires can be controlled and the sequence of individual wires managed. The so-called data path is particularly important in token ring networks, where patch panels are frequently found.

payload — The data content within a PDU.

payload data unit (PDU) — The combination of the data content plus the header and trailer information that make up an entire PDU.

PC cards — Credit-card size expansion cards used to add functionality to laptop computers.

PCMCIA cards — *See* PC cards.

peer-to-peer — A type of networking in which each computer can be a client to other computers and also act as a server.

Performance Monitor — A Windows NT and Windows 2000 tool used for graphing trends, based on performance counters for system objects.

Peripheral Component Interface (PCI) — The 32- and 64-bit PC bus architecture that currently prevails as the best and fastest of all available bus types, operating at 33 and 66 MHz. PCI-X supports 64-bits at 133 MHz for 1 GB/s data transfers.

peripheral device — Any hardware component on a computer that's not the CPU. In a networking context, it usually refers to some kind of device, such as a printer or a plotter, that users can share across the network.

permanent virtual circuit (PVC) — A permanent path defined even when not in use.

personal area network (PAN) — A short-range networking technology that uses the body for transmitting signals used to connect handheld or wearable computing devices.

personal digital assistant (PDA) — A handheld computer used to perform personal organization tasks such as appointment and address book management.

Physical layer — Layer 1, the bottom layer of the OSI reference model. The Physical layer transmits and receives signals, and specifies the physical details of cables, adapter cards, connectors, and hardware behavior.

plain old telephone system (POTS) — Also known as PSTN, the normal telephone communications system.

plenum — The area between a false ceiling and the true one in most commercial buildings. Used to circulate heating and cooling air; it's sometimes called the plenum space. Many types of cable, including networking cable, also run through this space.

plenum-rated — Cable that has been burn-tested to make sure it does not emit toxic fumes or large amounts of smoke when incinerated. Most building and fire codes require this designation for any cable to be run in plenum space.

Plug and Play — The Microsoft requirements for PC motherboards, buses, adapter cards, and operating systems which let a PC automatically detect and configure hardware on a system. For Plug and Play to work properly, all system components must conform rigorously to its specifications; currently, only Windows 95, Windows 98, and Windows 2000 support this architecture.

Point-to-Point Protocol (PPP) — A remote access protocol that supports many protocols, including TCP/IP, NetBEUI, and IPX/SPX.

Point-to-Point Tunneling Protocol (PPTP) — A special TCP/IP-based transport protocol that encrypts all traffic before transmission across a network link and decrypts all incoming traffic from a network link. PPTP permits the Internet (and other public IP-based networks) to function as part of a VPN.

polling — A channel access method in which a primary device asks secondary devices in sequence whether they have data to send.

Post Office Protocol version 3 (POP3) — An Internet message transfer protocol that e-mail clients use to copy messages from an e-mail server to a client machine to be read and managed on the local desktop.

power conditioning — A method of balancing the power input and reducing any spikes caused by noise on the power line, thus providing better power for delicate components such as computers.

power-on self-test (POST) — The set of internal diagnostic and status-checking routines a PC and its peripheral devices perform each time the computer is powered on.

preemptive troubleshooting — A method of forestalling network problems by planning in advance and performing regular network maintenance.

preemptive multitasking — A form of multitasking where the NOS or OS retains control over the length of time each process can maintain exclusive use of the CPU.

Presentation layer — Layer 6 of the OSI reference model. Here data may be encrypted and/or compressed to facilitate delivery. Platform-specific application formats are translated into generic data formats for transmission, or from generic data formats into platform-specific application formats for delivery to the Application layer.

primary device — Used in a polling network to manage data transmission. The primary device asks each secondary device if it has data to send and controls the data transmission.

Primary Rate Interface (PRI) — An ISDN implementation that provides twenty-three 64-Kbps B-channels and one 64-Kbps D-channel.

primary ring — The FDDI ring around which data is transmitted.

Project 802 — The IEEE networking initiative that produced the 802.x networking specifications and standards.

propagation delay — Signal delay created when a number of repeaters connect in a line. To prevent this, many network architectures limit the number of repeaters on a network.

protocol — The rules and procedures for communicating.

protocol analyzer — Software, or a combination of hardware and software, that can capture network traffic and create reports and graphs from the data collected.

protocol data unit (PDU) — A packet structure as formulated by a specific networking protocol. Such a structure usually includes specific header and trailer information in addition to its data payload.

protocol stack — An ordered collection of networking protocols that, taken together, provide end-to-end network communications between a sender and a receiver.

protocol suite — A family of related protocols in which higher-layer protocols provide application services and request handling facilities, while lower-layer protocols manage the intricacies of Layers 1 through 4 from the OSI reference model.

protocol type field — Field used in the Ethernet SNAP and Ethernet II frames to indicate the network protocol being used.

proxy server — A special Internet server that sits between an Internet link and a private network. It stores local copies of remote Web pages and files that users request (by proxy, as it were, so that it answers subsequent access requests nearly immediately). It also filters outgoing requests by domain name or IP address and severely or completely limits incoming requests to access the proxy server's private network side.

public data network (PDN) — A wide area network service, usually provided by private companies, for the purpose of enabling WAN technologies such as X.25.

public switched telephone network (PSTN) — Another term for the public telephone system.

pulse code modulation (PCM) — A technique for digitizing analog signals. PCM introduces less noise into the signal than traditional modulation/demodulation techniques, therefore boosting the total number of bits per second.

punchdown block — A wiring center used for telephone and network TP cable, where bare wire ends are inserted (punched down) into specific connectors to manage wiring layout and the data path. In effect, a punchdown block is the equivalent of a patch panel.

Quality of Service (QoS) — A networking term that specifies a guaranteed level of service when applied to applications that require high bandwidth.

queued commands — Commands awaiting execution but not yet completed.

radio frequency interference (RFI) — Any interference caused by signals operating in the radio frequency range. This term has become generic for interference caused by broadcast signals of any kind.

Radio Government (RG) — The coaxial cable designation that reflects coaxial cable's original use as a conveyance for radio frequency data and signals. The cable designation for thinnet is RG-58; for CATV, RG-59; for ARCnet, RG-62; and for thickwire, either RG-8 or RG-11.

RAM buffering — A memory-access technique that permits an adapter to use a computer's main memory as if it were local buffer space.

Random Acess Memory (RAM) — The memory cards or chips on a PC that provide working space for the CPU to use when running applications, providing network services, and so on. Where RAM on a server is concerned, more is usually better.

raw data — Data streams unbroken by header information.

reassembles (reassembly) — Reconstructing a larger, upper-layer PDU from a collection of smaller, lower-layer PDUs. Resequencing and recombining may be required to reassemble the original PDU.

receiver — A data communications device designed to capture and interpret signals broadcast at one or more frequencies in the electromagnetic spectrum. Receivers are necessary for both cable- and wireless-based transmissions.

redirector — A software component that intercepts requests for service from a computer and redirects requests that cannot be satisfied locally across the network to whichever networked resource can handle the request.

Redundant Arrays of Inexpensive Disks (RAID) — Two or more drives on a network server that provide fault tolerance (via disk mirroring or disk striping with parity). Also known as Redundant Array of Independent Disks.

reflective wireless network — An infrared wireless networking technology that uses a central optical transceiver to relay signals between end stations. All network devices must have an unobstructed view of this central transceiver, which explains why they're usually mounted on the ceiling.

registered jack (RJ) — Used for modular telephone and network TP jacks.

Remote Access Service (RAS) — Service available in Windows NT to allow dial-in connections to the network.

Remote Monitoring (RMON) — Specialized software that gathers network data and provides statistics to a network-management console.

Remote Routing and Access Server (RRAS) — A software component bundled in Windows 2000 that combines RAS and Multi-Protocol Routing, in addition to packet filtering, demand dial routing, and support for Open Shortest Path First (OSPF).

repeater — A network device used to strengthen signals to accomodate longer media distances or more computers.

request-response — A description of how the client/server relationship works by referring to how a request from a client leads to some kind of response from a server. (Usually, the response is the service or data requested, but sometimes it's an error message or a denial of service based on security.)

requester — The term used by Novell for a redirector.

rights — Actions that the user of a particular account has permission to perform.

ring — Topology consisting of computers connected in a circle, forming a closed ring.

RJ-11 — The four-wire modular jack commonly used for home telephone handsets. *See* registered jack (RJ).

RJ-45 — The eight-wire modular jack used for TP networking cables and also for PBX-based telephone systems. (Take care which connector you plug into an RJ-45 coupler.) *See* registered jack (RJ).

root hub — *See* parent hub.

routable — A protocol that includes network layer information and can be forwarded by a router.

routable protocol — A network protocol that contains Layer 3 (Network layer) addressing information, which permits packets to be routed throughout an internetwork.

router — A networking device that operates at the Network layer of the OSI model. A router connects networks with different physical media and also translates between different network architectures, such as token ring and Ethernet.

routing — A Network-layer service that moves data across multiple networks via routers.

Routing Information Protocol (RIP) — Used by TCP/IP and IPX/SPX; a distance-vector routing protocol used to determine a packet's best path through an internetwork.

routing table — A reference table that includes network information and the next router in line for a particular path.

Samba — An open source software suite that makes Linux servers look and act like Windows Servers. It permits DOS or Windows clients to access Linux- or UNIX-based file systems and services without special software on the client end.

satellite microwave — A microwave transmission system that uses geosynchronous satellites to send and relay signals between sender and receiver. Most companies that use satellite microwave lease access to the satellites for a fee.

scatter infrared network — An infrared LAN technology that uses flat reflective surfaces such as walls and ceilings to bounce wireless transmissions between sender and receiver. Because bouncing introduces delays and attenuation, this variety of wireless LAN is the slowest and supports the narrowest bandwidth of any of the infrared technologies.

scheduling — A type of network application in which multiple users share a single appointment book, address book, and calendar.

scroll rate — In a USENET or other NNTP-based newsgroup, the amount of time a new message remains resident on a server before newer messages arrive and "push" it out.

search engine — A special-purpose program that solicits strings of text from users and searches a large, indexed collection of files and documents, looking for exact or near matches for that string, in an attempt to help users find resources related to the string.

secondary device — A device, such as a computer, in a polling network where the primary device controls communications.

secondary ring — An FDDI ring used for the sole purpose of handling traffic in the event of a cable failure.

security — For networking, security generically is the set of access controls and permissions in place that determine if a server can grant a request for a service or resource from a client.

Security Accounts Manager (SAM) — Part of the Windows NT Executive Services that maintains user and group account information.

security feature — In terms of NICs, a feature that allows the card to handle security-related protocols, including encryption services.

segmentation — Decomposing a larger, upper-layer PDU into a collection of smaller, lower-layer PDUs. It includes sequencing and reassembling information to permit restoration of the original upper-layer PDU on receipt of all the smaller, lower-layer PDUs.

segmenting — The insertion of a bridge or router between two cable segments to direct traffic more efficiently to its destination and reduce traffic on each part of the network.

Sequenced Packet Exchange (SPX) — Novell's connection-oriented protocol that supplements IPX by providing reliable transport.

Serial Line Internet Protocol (SLIP) — The dial-up protocol originally used to connect PCs directly to the Internet.

serial transmission — A technique for transmitting data signals, which set each bit's worth of data (or its analog equivalent) one at a time, one after another, in sequence.

server — A computer whose job is to respond to requests for services or resources from clients elsewhere on a network.

server cluster — *See* clustered server.

Server Message Block (SMB) — A block of data comprising client/server requests or responses. All areas of Microsoft network communications use SMBs.

server network software — A type of software designed for a server computer; this software enables the hosting of resources for clients to access.

server session — Connection between a network server and another node.

server-based — A type or model of networking that requires the presence of a server, to provide services and resources and also to manage and control access to those services and resources.

server-based multivendor solution — A server, such as one running Windows 2000 Server, that can readily communicate with clients from multiple vendors.

Service Access Points (SAPs) — Logical interface points used to transfer information from the LLC sublayer to the upper OSI layers.

Service Advertising Protocol (SAP) — Used by file and print servers on Novell networks to inform computers of the services available.

Service Lookup Protocol (SLP) — SLP is a new IP-based NetWare protocol that applies when clients want to look up the services available on an IP-only network.

Session layer — Layer 5 of the OSI reference model. The Session layer is responsible for setting up, maintaining, and ending ongoing sequences of communications (called sessions) across a network.

share — A network resource made available for remote access by clients.

share-oriented security — Security information based on the object being shared.

shared adapter memory — A technique for a computer's CPU to address memory on an adapter as if it were the computer's own main memory.

shared system memory — A technique for an adapter to address a computer's main memory as if it were resident on the adapter itself.

sharing — One of the fundamental justifications for networking. In Microsoft's lexicon, this term refers to the way in which resources are made available to the network.

sheath — The outer layer of coating on a cable; sometimes also called the jacket.

shell — The command-line interpreter on a UNIX or Linux system. The shell also includes built-in redirector functions.

shielded twisted-pair (STP) — A variety of TP cable, wherein a foil wrap encloses each of one or more pairs of wires for additional shielding, and where a wire braid or an additional layer of foil may enclose the entire cable for further shielding.

shielding — Any layer of material included in cable to mitigate the effects of interference on the signal-carrying cables it encloses.

short — A condition that occurs when conductors that are normally insulated from one another establish a connection. In a coaxial cable, if the shield and the internal conductor become connected, the cable stops functioning because the short blocks all network traffic; the same condition can occur in twisted-pair cable should two or more of the paired wires become connected.

sideband link — A special-purpose network connection used only to ferry data for a specific purpose (usually, a separate high-speed network that interlinks storage-area network components), not to ferry general-purpose client/server network traffic. This terminology reflects such a link's use of a separate network that operates "off to the side," apart from regular network connections and traffic.

signal bounce — A phenomenon that occurs when a bus is not terminated and signals continue to traverse the network.

Simple Mail Transport Protocol (SMTP) — A TCP/IP protocol used to send mail messages across a network. SMTP is the basis for e-mail on the Internet.

Simple Network Management Protocol (SNMP) — A TCP/IP protocol used to monitor and manage network devices.

Single Attachment Stations (SAS) — Computers or concentrators in an FDDI network that are connected only to the primary ring.

single-frequency radio — A form of wireless networking technology that passes data using only a single broadcast frequency, as opposed to spread-spectrum, which uses two or more frequencies.

Smart Multistation Access Unit (SMAU) — An active hub in a token ring network.

sneakernet — A metaphorical description of a non-networked data exchange method: someone, presumably wearing sneakers, copies files onto a floppy disk on one computer and then hand-carries the disk to another computer.

soft page fault — An exception that occurs when data must be called back into a program's working set from another location in physical memory. Soft page faults take comparatively little time to resolve.

software agent — Part of the SNMP structure that is loaded onto each device to be monitored.

source-routing bridge — A type of bridge used in IBM token ring networks that learns its bridging information from information included in the packet's structure.

specialized server — Any of a number of special-function servers—an application server, a communications server, a directory server or domain controller, a fax server, an e-mail server, or a Web server, among others.

spread-spectrum radio — A form of wireless networking technology that passes data using multiple frequencies simultaneously.

SQL Server — A Microsoft BackOffice component that provides a standard database management system (DBMS) for the Windows NT Server and Windows 2000 Server environments. SQL Server may be used as a standalone database server but is also required to support other BackOffice components, most notably Systems Management Server (SMS).

standalone computer — A computer that's not attached to a network.

standby monitor — A computer in a token ring network that monitors the network status and waits for the signal from the active monitor.

star — Major topology in which the computers connect via a central connecting point, usually a hub.

star bus — A network topology that combines the star and bus topologies.

star ring — A network topology wired like a star, which handles traffic like a ring.

start frame delimiter (SFD) — A field in the Ethernet 802.3 frame that defines the beginning of the packet.

static routing — A type of routing in which the router is configured manually with all possible routes.

station identifier (SID) — The hardware address for a computer in an ARCnet network.

storage-area network (SAN) — A specialized networking system that centralizes disk storage in a high-speed, high-capacity, high-reliability storage cluster. It uses high-speed sideband network connections so that users perceive no difference between a SAN and disk subsystems attached directly to a server.

store-and-forward switching — A switching method in which the switch reads the entire frame to check for errors before forwarding the frame.

straight connection (SC) — A type of one-piece fiber-optic connector that is pushed on, yet makes a strong and solid contact with emitters and sensors.

straight tip (ST) — The most common type of fiber-optic connector used in Ethernet networks with fiber backbones. These connectors come in pairs, one for each fiber-optic cable.

Structured Query Language (SQL) — Standard database query language designed by IBM.

structured troubleshooting approach — A Microsoft-recommended five-step approach to network troubleshooting.

sublayers — The two components of Layer 2, the Data Link layer (DLL), of the OSI reference model. Elaborated upon by the IEEE 802 project, they are the Logical Link Control (LLC) sublayer and the Media Access Control (MAC) sublayer.

subminiature type A (SMA) — Yet another fiber-optic connector, this connector twists on and also comes in pairs.

subnet — A portion of an IP address that identifies the network portion of that address.

subnet mask — The "all ones" bit pattern that masks the network portion of an IP address. For a Class A address, the default subnet mask is 255.0.0.0; for Class B, 255.255.0.0; for Class C, 255.255.255.0.

supernetting — The operation of "stealing" bits from the network portion of an IP address to extend the host address space for a group of contiguous IP addresses. For supernetting to work properly, the group of IP addresses must be contiguous and consist of a binary number made entirely of ones (11 or 3; 111 or 7; 1111 or 15; and so on).

surge protection — Power protection that evens out spikes or sags in the main current and prevents them from affecting the computer.

switch — A special networking device that manages networked connections between a pair of starwired devices on a network. Also, a hardware device that opens and closes electrical circuits.

Switched 56K — Digital point-to-point leased communication links offered by local and long-distance telcos. Lease terms are based on per-minute use charges, not on 24-hour, seven-day dedicated circuits.

Switched Multimegabit Data Service (SMDS) — A WAN technology similar to ATM that has a 53-byte, fixed-length cell and no error checking. SMDS offers transmission rates of 1.544 Mbps to 45 Mbps.

switched virtual circuit (SVC) — A temporary path across a switched network that is defined only as long as it is in use.

switching — Using a network switch to manage media or channel access. It helps increase overall bandwidth, provides greater bandwidth to senders and receivers, and can emulate other access methods based on the switch's built-in capabilities.

Symmetric Digital Subscriber Line (SDSL) — Uses equivalent speeds for downloading and uploading data.

synchronous — Communications type in which computers rely on exact timing and sync bits to maintain data synchronization.

Synchronous Data Link Control (SDLC) — A synchronous communication protocol.

Synchronous Optical Network (SONET) — A WAN technology used to interface with dissimilar long-distance networks. SONET offers transmission speeds in multiples of 51.84 Mbps using fiber-optic media.

Systems Network Architecture (SNA) — IBM's native protocol suite for its mainframes and older minicomputers. SNA is still one of the most widely used protocol suites in the world.

T1 — A type of high-speed digital link offering a 1.544-Mbps transmission rate.

T3 — A communications line comprising 28 T1s or 672 channels and which supports a data rate of 44.736 Mbps.

TCP/IP — An abbreviation for Transmission Control Protocol/Internet Protocol.

telco — A telephone company or telephone service provider.

Telecommunications Industries Association (TIA) — An industry consortium of telephone equipment, cabling, and communications companies, that together formulate hardware standards for equipment, cabling, and connectors used in phone systems and on networks.

Telnet — A TCP/IP protocol that provides remote terminal emulation.

Telnet daemon — Also known as telnetd, this is the server program that responds to client requests for the Internet-based Telnet remote terminal emulation service; it permits remote users to run commands and programs on other computers across any IP-based network, including the Internet.

ter — A French term for *third*, which describes the third version of an ITU standard.

terminal adapter (TA) — Part of the ISDN network interface. Sometimes called a digital modem.

Terminal Services — A software subsystem for Windows NT and Windows 2000 Server that permits clients to run large or complex applications on computers with minimal processing power by transferring the burden of client processing to the server.

terminator — Used to absorb signals as they reach the end of a bus, thus freeing the network for new communications.

terrestrial microwave — A wireless microwave networking technology that uses line-of-sight communications between pairs of Earth-based transmitters and receivers to relay information. The large distances the signals must extend requires that microwave transmitters and receivers be positioned well above ground level, on towers, on mountaintops, or atop tall buildings. Such equipment is usually expensive.

thicknet — A form of coaxial Ethernet that uses a rigid cable about 0.4" in diameter. Because of its common jacket color and its rigidity, this cable is sometimes called "frozen yellow garden hose." Also known as thickwire and 10Base5.

thickwire — A synonym for thicknet and 10Base5.

thin client — A networked computer with keyboard, pointing device (mouse), display, network interface, and sufficient processing power to access terminal services or a mainframe, where the real application processing occurs.

thinnet — A form of coaxial Ethernet that uses a thin, flexible cable about 0.2" in diameter. Also known as thinwire, 10Base2, and cheapernet.

thinwire — A synonym for 10Base2 and thinnet.

time slicing — A method of granting different processes CPU cycles by limiting the amount of time each process has exclusive use of the CPU.

time-domain reflectometer (TDR) — A network troubleshooting device that can determine whether there is a break or short in the cable and, if so, approximately how far down the cable the break or short is located.

token — Used in some ring topology networks to ensure fair communications between all computers.

token passing — A channel access method used mostly in ring topology networks. It ensures equal access to all computers on a network through the use of a special packet called the token.

token ring — A network architecture developed by IBM, and which is physically wired as a star but uses token passing in a logical ring topology.

TokenTalk — The standard for sending AppleTalk over token ring cabling.

topology — The basic physical layout of a network.

traffic management — In terms of NICs, features that improve network accessibility for remote users, especially those using applications that require higher bandwidth, such as streaming video or multimedia.

transceiver — A device that transmits and receives network information.

translation bridge — A bridge that can translate between network architectures.

Transmission Control Protocol (TCP) — The core of the TCP/IP suite. TCP is a connection-oriented protocol responsible for reformatting data into packets and reliably delivering those packets.

Transmission Control Protocol/Internet Protocol (TCP/IP) — A protocol suite that supports communication between heterogeneous systems. TCP/IP has become the standard communications protocol for the Internet.

transmitter — An electronic device capable of emitting signals for delivery through a particular networking medium.

transparent bridge — Generally used in Ethernet networks, these bridges build their bridging tables automatically as they receive packets.

Transport layer — Layer 4 of the OSI reference model. The Transport layer is responsible for fragmenting large PDUs from the Session layer for delivery across the network, and for inserting sufficient integrity controls and managing delivery mechanisms to allow for their error-free reassembly on the receiving end of a network transmission.

transport protocol — A protocol type responsible for providing reliable communication sessions between two computers.

trouble avoidance — *See* pre-emptive troubleshooting.

troubleshooting — The techniques involved in detecting problems, identifying causes or contributing factors, and applying necessary workarounds or repairs to eliminate their effects.

trust relationship — An arrangement in which a domain permits members of another domain to access its resources.

twisted-pair (TP) — A type of cabling where two copper wires, each enclosed in some kind of sheath, are wrapped around each other. The twisting permits narrow-gauge wire, otherwise extraordinarily sensitive to crosstalk and interference, to carry higher-bandwidth signals over longer distances than would traditionally be possible with straight wires. TP cabling is used for voice telephone circuits as well as for networking.

Uniform Resource Locator (URL) — The specific address for a Web-based Internet or other IP network resource.

uninterruptible power supply (UPS) — Power protection device that includes a battery backup to take over if the main current fails. Usually incorporates power conditioning and surge protection.

universal group — A group available in Active Directory native mode that adds another option for administrators to manage cross-domain resources.

Universal Naming Convention (UNC) — A standard method for naming network resources; it takes the form *servername**sharename*.

Universal Serial Bus (USB) 1.0 — A hot-pluggable Plug and Play serial interface that operates at a maximum data transfer rate of 12 Mbps. USB ports support peripheral devices such as mice, keyboards, and other pointing devices, in addition to some printers, scanners, telephony equipment, and monitors. USB 2.0 supports up to 480 Mbps.

unshielded twisted-pair (UTP) — A form of TP cable that includes no additional shielding material in the cable composition. This cable encloses one or more pairs of twisted wires inside an outer jacket.

user — An individual who uses a computer, either as a standalone or to access a network.

user account — Collection of information known about the user; usually includes an account name, an associated password, and a set of access permissions for network resources.

User Datagram Protocol (UDP) — A connectionless TCP/IP protocol that provides fast data transport.

user-oriented security — Security information based on the account of the user accessing an object.

V-series — The ITU-T standards that specify how data communications can take place over the telephone network.

vampire tap — A two-piece apparatus with a set screw on the upper half that permits the pointed end of the screw to penetrate thickwire coax to a precise depth, where it taps into the center conductor without breaking it. This permits a transceiver to connect to the cable, thereby enabling devices to attach to the thickwire segment. The set screw that penetrates the cable is called, in keeping with the name of the tap, the "fang."

virtual circuit — A term used to describe the pathways created in a packet-switching network to transmit data between connection points.

virtual docking — One of numerous point-to-point wireless infrared technologies that permit laptops to exchange data with desktop machines or permit data exchange between a computer and a handheld device or a printer. Because this capability replaces a cable between the two devices, this technology is sometimes called "virtual docking."

virtual local area network (VLAN) — A feature of switches that allows network administrators to logically group users and resources, irrespective of the physical location of the user or resource.

virtual private network (VPN) — A network link that incorporates connections across a public network, such as the Internet, with protocols such as PPTP to impose encryption techniques that permit the use of public network links for reliable, secure delivery of private communications.

voicegrade — A designation for cable (usually TP) that indicates it's rated only to carry telephone traffic. Voicegrade cable is not recommended for network use.

volt-ohm meter (VOM) — *See* digital volt-meter (DVM).

wall plate — A module that includes couplers for telephone (RJ-11) and network (RJ-45, BNC, or other female connector) jacks.

Web browser — The client-side software that's used to display content from the World Wide Web; also called a browser.

Web server — The combination of hardware and software that stores information that is accessible over the Internet via the World Wide Web (WWW).

wide area network (WAN) — An internetwork that connects multiple sites, where a third-party communications carrier, such as a public or private telephone company, carries network traffic from one location to another. Because WAN links can be expensive with charges based on bandwidth, few WAN links support the same bandwidth as that available on most LANs.

Win32 Driver Model (WDM) — A unified driver architecture that allows a single driver to be written for both Windows 98 and Windows 2000/XP.

wireless — Indicates that a network connection depends on transmission at some kind of electromagnetic frequency through the atmosphere to carry data transmissions from one networked device to another.

wireless access point (WAP) — The central device, or hub, through which signals pass in a wireless network.

wireless bridge — A pair of devices, typically narrow-band and tight beam, that relay network traffic from one location to another. Wireless bridges that use spread-spectrum radio, infrared, and laser technologies are available and can span distances from hundreds of meters up to 25 miles.

wiring center — A set of racks with associated equipment that generally includes hubs, punch-down blocks or patch panels, backbone access units, and other network-management equip-ment, which brings TP-wired network cables together for routing, management, and control.

workgroup model — The Windows NT and Windows 2000 name for a peer-to-peer network that includes one or more Windows NT-based computers.

working set — Data that a program actively uses at any given time. The working set is only a small subset of the total amount of data that the program *could* use.

World Wide Web (WWW) — The TCP/IP-based collection of all Web servers on the Internet, which in the words of one of its originators, Tim Berners-Lee, comes as close to containing "the sum of human knowledge" as anything available on any network anywhere.

X.25 — An international standard for wide-area packet-switched communications. X.25 offers 64-Kbps network connections and error checking for users.

X.400 — A hardware- and software-independent message-handling protocol.

X.500 — An improved message-handling protocol from CCITT. Able to communicate across networks and maintain a global database of addresses.

Xerox Network Systems (XNS) — A protocol suite developed by Xerox for its Ethernet LANs. The basis for Novell's IPX/SPX.

Index